JOY OF THE BIRDS

A Novel By
Gale Cooper

GELCOUR BOOKS

COPYRIGHT © 2022 Gale Cooper
All Rights Reserved
*Reproductions, excerpts, or transmittals
of the author's original text or cover art in this book
are prohibited in any form whatsoever
without written permission of the author.
Infringers will be prosecuted
to the fullest extent of the law.*

**THIRD EDITION EDITION © 2022
ISBN: 978-1-949626-36-0 HARDCOVER
ISBN: 978-1-949626-37-7 PAPERBACK
LIBRARY OF CONGRESS CONTROL NUMBER:
2022905928**

SECOND EDITION © 2012
ISBN: 978-0-9845054-5-6 HARDCOVER
ISBN: 978-0-9845054-6-3 PAPERBACK

FIRST EDITION © 2008
ISBN: 978-1-4343-8218-4 HARDCOVER
ISBN: 978-1-4343-8216-0 PAPERBACK

GELCOUR BOOKS
Albuquerque, New Mexico

ORDERING THIS BOOK:
Amazon.com, BarnesandNoble.com, bookstores

**COVER AND BOOK DESIGN
BY GALE COOPER**

Printed in the United States of America
on acid free paper

For William H. Bonney

"Who are the dancers and who the dance?"
The Dancing Wu Li Masters
by Gary Zukov

CONTENTS

PREFACE

ix

FIRST CYCLE

1

SECOND CYCLE

211

THIRD CYCLE

363

PREFACE

The author of this here book undoubably asked me to write this here piece cause I'm an old-timer who's lived all my life right in Lincoln town, Lincoln County, New Mexico, good old U.S. of A.

Us old-timers, like me, with families going back to Billy Bonney's day, know the facts. So I can fill in where this here book leaves off in July of 1881 when Billy was killed. When you've got you a town - like Lincoln - just a mile long, there ain't secrets; but you keep them local or you don't make it to old-timer - if you get my drift.

Anyways, I growed up hearing family stories about Billy Bonney - only his enemies called him Billy the Kid. He'd visit my mother's grandmother, Gram Barton, when he come to Lincoln town; and my mother told me Gram's stories. Gram Barton said Billy had a big appetite and wrote a fine hand. And he was always in a happy state of mind; and he was basically a good boy.

My mother had a tintype with Gram Barton and him and Gram's dog, Buster. But it's lost, cause my mother lent it to some fella writing a book on Billy. Then her memory went and she forgot his name.

Gram Barton also met Pat Garrett and John William Poe. Garrett wasn't re-elected as sheriff of Lincoln County cause of him killing Billy; Poe was instead. People blamed Poe less. Gram Barton couldn't abide neither. Not that she showed it outside the family, cause it was plumb dangerous taking Billy's side with him being framed as the worst outlaw in the country, and then getting his ambush bullet.

Anyways, my family knew Gram wouldn't have shed no tears about Pat Garrett's murder in 1908, by that Wayne Brazel, who shot him down right when he'd gotten out of his buggy and was taking a leak. Then Brazel and the buggy driver left him dead on the road. Then the jury let Brazel off. Seems Garrett wasn't a popular sort.

Well, my mother willed me a brown cardigan sweater she said was Billy's. Gram Barton got it from old man Gottfried Gauss, who supposably found it in the courthouse-jail here in Lincoln after Billy escaped from it just before his hanging day and beat the odds. Collectors after anything of Billy's have told me cowboys didn't wear no cardigans. But I went to the museum here in Lincoln, when they still had that tintype of Billy standing with his guns and all, and, I tell you what, there was that sweater. My wife was alive then. She agreed. So I've kept it. It might be worth a lot; specially since some billionaire guy recently shelled out $2.3 million to get that tintype for hisself. And my cardigan's in better condition.

Now I should mention that, even in these parts, soon after Billy's day, people gossiped that Billy and Paulita Maxwell had been sweethearts. Her family owned the whole town of Fort Sumner back then. So with Paulita being the richest heiress in New Mexico Territory, and young and pretty, and Billy being a homeless drifter, that was downright remarkable: a regalar Romeo and Juliet tragedy - specially after Garrett plugged Billy right in her family mansion.

After my granddaughter visited Billy's grave in Fort Sumner, she told me Paulita's buried just forty strides from Billy under the name Jaramillo: that fella, José, people say Paulita married quick to protect Billy's kid she was carrying when he was killed. She divorced quick too. Never remarried. Died in 1929. Tell me what you think.

And since I'm chewing the rag about love, I might as well mention Deluvina, this Navajo woman Paulita's family kept as a slave. She laid wildflowers on Billy's grave every year on his murder day for forty years. Billy had that kind of effect on good people.

I do agree with this here book that New Mexico politicians back then were varmints; but they'se the same today. In Billy's day, they was called the Santa Fe Ring. You know what a Ring is? It's a bunch of cronies so crooked they screw on their sox. They're government guys, sheriffs, judges, lawyers, and rich fellas in cahoots to line their own pockets. And if you're a little guy trying to fight them, every whichaway you turn, you're blocked by one protecting the other; and even the newspapers hide their dirt under the rug. So beating them's about as possible as scratching your ear with your elbow.

That Ring come up with the fake legend of Billy the outlaw kid to frame him and hide their own outlaw shenanigans that Billy and his side was fighting. That Ring's other fake legend is that the Ring never existed. Truth is, it existed back then and still exists; but now its called "the good ol' boys;" though some are good ol' gals. And people still feel vunreble cause getting on the Ring's bad side is like being bare-assed in a nest of rattlers; same as when Billy was alive - which is why he was put to bed with a pick and shovel at twenty-one.

Here's another dirty secret: another cover-up six feet under. It's about them that died on Billy's side in that July, 1878 freedom fight against that Santa Fe Ring that happened here in Lincoln town, making it called the Lincoln County War. All them heroes, that Billy would have looked up to, is still right here in town, but in unmarked graves. How's that for the Ring burying the truth?

So here's the facts. Just east of John Tunstall's original store, we got us Englishman, John Tunstall himself; Attorney Alexander McSween; law intern, Harvey Morris; cattle detective, Frank MacNab; and Attorney Huston Chapman. They is under some old shed in a regalar house's backyard. And there's nary a marker for a clue.

But for tourists, the tourism folks put up a few fake crosses behind John Tunstall's store, where, in Billy's day, it was just a corral with horse manure. Maybe cause I'm long in the tooth and close to that Big Divide myself, I take that kind of tomfoolery personal.

Also, other things in Lincoln town hasn't changed much from Billy's day. In my life, they only patched up the old buildings and paved our one street. They never even rebuilt the big house of Alexander McSween that was burned down by the Ring in the Lincoln County War. And that war wasn't no World War II.

Something else. The author of this here book told me, with a funny look, that there's more then meets the eye in Lincoln County - like some battle of Good and Evil. Wasn't news to me. They don't call New Mexico the "Land of Enchantment" for nothing. Some say Lincoln town's got a curse cause of Billy being murdered by Lincoln County's Sheriff: Pat Garrett. I even heard that somebody, in my own day, once saw the Devil running down its one street, except it was only legs - hairy with hooves. And those legs was taller then a man.

Seems I should mention that recently I was walking down that same street and I got chill bumps. It hit me that this here book's finally setting the record straight. And, right quick, what come out of my mouth surprised the heck out of me. It was: "Dadgumit" - excuse the French - "Billy's finally gonna finish what he started." Some want him to get that governor's pardon that he was promised back then. Course I want that too. But more, I want like a second Lincoln County War where the good guys finally win by blasting that Santa Fe Ring cover-up sky high.

I tell you what: democracy comes with a price that ain't for the lily-livered. And if you figer today's fights are just against foreign enemies, you're plumb wrong. Who'd give much for an apple that's rotten on the inside - if you get my drift?

So I'll leave you with a warning. When you read this here book, you become a part of it. What I'm meaning is that after you know about the path in life that the author called "joy of the birds," you'll have to face Billy Bonney's question yourself: would I risk all them things that you gotta risk to stand up to corruption so's democracy is protected? Like the author told me, ain't many like Billy willing to follow that path to the end.

Vern Blanton Johnson, Jr.
Lincoln, Lincoln County, New Mexico
July 14, 2017

FIRST CYCLE

APRIL 20, 1874   4:08 PM   MONDAY

They were dancing. They were laughing, twirling around the dining-table in their log cabin, a small, knobby-jointed, adolescent boy with honey blond hair flying; and a gaunt woman of forty-five.

She was breathless, but laughing, saying, "Billy. Oh, Billy. Faster! Come now. Faster!" The red clay of their New Mexico Territory floor could not hold them; high stepping, they were airborne dancers.

Suddenly coughing, the handsome woman halted, panting. Dance gesturing, she flourished from her sleeve a handkerchief, coughing onto its white a shocking ruby clot, set in blood. Defiantly she said, eyes glittering with fever, "Sing, Billy. Sing 'Turkey in the Straw.'"

His lovely voice whirled them with frothing petticoats of her girlish tartan dress and flickering shoes.

He sang, "I came to the river and I couldn't get across, / So I paid five dollars for an old blind horse. / Well he wouldn't go ahead, and he wouldn't stand still, / So he went up and down like an old saw mill. / Turkey in the straw, haw, haw, haw. / Turkey in the hay, hay, hay, hay, / Roll 'em up and twist 'em up/ a high tuck-e-haw, / And hit 'em up a tune called / Turkey in the Straw."

Finally, the woman sank into the wingback chair at the fireplace while he still danced; shouting, "Silver City!" in motion's ecstasy.

In vague delirium, she saw Billy at five, in their Indianapolis cottage, sitting on her lap. "Precious," she was saying, "sun's in yer hair; sky's in yer eyes, all fer luv o' you." Snuggling into her nightgowned chest, saying the sun loved her too with her hair all gold; he was slipping, laughing, tickled in her knowing-fingered attack, onto the floor; until, scrambling up, so thin, he kissed her kissing lips.

Forced back to Silver City, back to Billy asking if she was sick, her trilling brogue lied, "Only tirrred. But a glass o' water t'would be nice. Josie didn't fill the keg. Soon seventeen, but he's morrre child than you." Billy went to get it, relishing triumph over his only sibling.

Her daydreaming resumed: November 23, 1859; it was Billy's birth. Only remembered was bliss and a New York tenement room.

A midwife splayed her legs into a weightless crouch as, abandoned to passion, her perspiration-wet hair snaked and her eyes rolled up in ecstasy. "Is there no shame in this woman?" the midwife thought, watching her kneading milk-distended breasts, frustrated by their covering smock; as sliding boy parts and stiff cord pressed her, and brilliant light glory filled her skull. Away slipped the infant into that stranger's hands. Behind spasmed orgasmic thighs.

"Tis a Devil's birth," thought the midwife. "Of pleasure, not pain as the good Lord ordained." But she said, "Catherine Bonney, yuv got a fine son. What's t' be his name?"

From rapture came "William Henry ... McCarty. McCarty's his father's name."

The midwife thought, "Tis a lie of a name without God's union;" brushing back dull hair, hands damp from washing him, now back with his mother. "Damnation from birth," she thought; but said, "He knows what t' do; that's fer sure, dearie."

His sucking gushed thick pleasure. "Billy," Catherine whispered. He stared upward. "Oh, my Billy," she said, drenched with insatiable passion for the beloved.

At the same time, eight hundred ninety-nine miles southwest of that city, in Claiborne Parish, Louisiana, a nine and a half year old, long-legged boy, with blowing slick black hair, had loped in his family's cotton plantation, calling imperiously to his playmate, while swinging a rifle. The other shouted, "I can't hear you, Pat Garrett."

"Let's shoot squirrels!" he yelled back, gray eyes bright with predatory zeal.

In the Silver City cabin, Billy's return broke his mother's reverie. Catherine said, "That bucket's heavy, Precious. And you so small." Not small, he countered, just waiting to grow, and flashed the playful, blue-eyed, sidelong glance she adored.

Concealing terrible fatigue, she asked him to make dinner. Concealed even from herself was its truth. Behind a defensive barrier of three years, stood Dr. Walsh in Wichita, Kansas. Consumption, he had said. Her response had belied her fine intelligence: "So I have a minor lung condition." Only her comment lingered.

Now, to Billy, she said, "A minor lung condition can't bring down us Scotch-Irish." As he went to the kitchen, she called, "Did y'hear about the barefoot girl from Arkansas?" The stove lid clanked. Wood thumped into the firebox. "She was by a campfire. Her grandma said, 'Sally yer foot's on a coal.' Says Sally, 'Which foot, granny?'"

Laughing boisterously, Billy emerged. "I'm the same," she said. "Tough." He laughed more. "And, Precious, make extra in case yer father's back from the mines."

"Stepfather," he growled, face flaming.

"Billy," she scolded, ambiguously criticizing yet encouraging that rivalry, "tis nigh on nine years yuv known Antrim; and with us married over a year." Billy's wide-spaced eyes slitted. He said he'd left soon as she got sick.

"I'm not sick. And he's seekin' a silver strike." Hostilely Billy eyed the front door. She said, "My little rebel."

"Don't make fun of me, Ma." Bellicosity edged mature threat.

"I'm not. You and me have the same spirit. Like Cú Chulainn's."

Billy was too angry to hear. Catherine said, "A wild goose never raised a tame gosling;" and thought, "Tis in me. Me father, too. That Bonney rage."

It was a conflagration, white heat more irresistible than lust: ferocious culmination of four hundred generations of rampage and rape in territorial strivings of Stone Age aborigines arriving in future Scotland; followed by Iron Age Picts; then by Celtic invaders; soon also mingling in brutality or desire with Vikings, Romans, and Teutonic Angles and Saxons; until descendants in the early 17th century, now Protestant, were lured across the channel to northern Ireland by English king, James I, to gain land in his Ulster Plantation and become a fierce buffer against encroaching Catholics. Then Scotch-Irish, their motto was: "No one attacks me with impunity."

In the Silver City cabin, Catherine's fever-driven thoughts drifted irrationally. Would Billy kill for her? Die for her? She said to him, "I'd die fer you, Precious. Fer luv;" and thought, "Well, Bonneys may have killed. But only fer the right."

That word "right" linked, in her mind, to her first crisis: a lover's betrayal. Then, still so young, in Ulster, virginity just lost, she had declared, aware of prudish malice in her mother's eyes, "I'd a right t' luv;" while thinking, "She's spiritless. 'No Bonney,' like Father says."

Now she was free; she had escaped Ulster.

She thought, "In writing, I'm McCarty": an Irish Protestant girl concealed by an Irish Catholic name; an exiled princess, royal nonetheless. "Precious" her father called her, and "me clever girlie;" educating her himself, as she had Billy.

Billy broke Catherine's rumination by saying, "All Antrim cares about is money. Buying land with money *you* make. You said the mining here's bad for your lung condition. Let's you and me go someplace better."

"He's a good man, Precious. Twixt us two we got that land in Indianapolis, then in Wichita; and, all along, that let me make my laundry business the success we needed fer this good life."

Billy's pouty bowed lips, with indented corners misleadingly simulating a smile, showed clenched teeth. He said, "You didn't need Antrim. You were the only woman on Wichita's Founding Council."

Her brogue cooed, "But I luuuv him." Scowling, Billy left.

She had met Antrim in August of eighteen sixty-five in the Marion County, Indiana, land office by asking the clerk if he knew a handyman for her cottage. He pointed. There stood Antrim: slim, hair red-gold like precious metal, and twenty-three. She was thirty-five. He was clean-shaven. In Silver City he grew that full beard to withdraw from her. Back then, he said, "I live northeast of here in Huntsville; and his wandering eyes showed appreciation.

"Maybe you could come by my place, Mister ..."

"Antrim. Go by 'Billy.' Name's William Henry Harrison Antrim."

"How strrrange. One of my sons is William Henry, after me father. I call *him* Billy. My other one, Josie, he's eight. My Billy's five and a half." Interest waning, Antrim said she looked young for those sons. "I'm widowed," she lied and said, "I've got me a cottage on Lot eighty-three near the White River in Indianapolis Township Section sixteen. And was thinkin' now t' buy me Lot eighty-four too."

Unnoticed covetousness ignited Antrim's brown eyes. He said, "This afternoon, I could be out your way." That was the start.

Billy's return with two laden plates brought Catherine back to the cabin. He said, "Josie's probably still gambling at the Orleans Saloon. The boarder won't be back till next Wednesday - if he's back at all."

She rose, chattering to distract from frailty. "D'ye remember our boarder last year: Ash Upson? That out-of-work newspaperman? One day, says he, 'Yuv got an unusually intelligent son. The world will hear of him.' What d'ye make o' that?"

"He was real interesting, but loco. Said he'd remember me 'cause our birthdays are the same."

As Billy ate heartily, she picked anorecticly at her portion.

When again in the wingback chair, she still wanted Billy close, and said, "D'ye remember when we left New York fer Indianapolis - when our travelin' began?" Billy added wood to the fire, becoming lost, with her, in brief attraction to its dangerous surge.

She said, "Billy, brrring me yer Father's cardigan from my trunk at the foot o' the bed. I'm feelin' chilled t' the bone."

While she wrapped herself in its heavy brownness, he left for more wood with gliding feline grace.

To her shock, replacing Billy's image, was his father's. Her heart contracted with yearning. When that man's trajectory first converged with hers on April 20,1851, she had been unaware of his epiphany a half hour earlier. That secret would destroy all their lives. Michael McCarty, she never admitted, was insane.

In 1851, a laborer, lithe and handsome, after the potato famine, he had traveled to Belfast for his passage to America. Smooth-strided as a dancer, on that April 20th day, Michael McCarty had descended the gangplank at New York City, and, at first bare earth, had dropped bizarrely to his knees amidst the drab parting sea of other immigrants; and murmured Heavenward, "I - less than a speck of dust in the universe - accept it." Westward stretched a country of 2,992,747 square miles. He believed it was now his personal possession.

From opalescent sheeting clouds, he heard God's confirming voice intone, "As I promised." That voice, since his adolescence, had vied for his soul with demon-jabbering, hallucinatory, mental cacophony.

Prostrating in his America, Michael McCarty answered, "Oh Lord, fer this land, I will give you the fruit of my loins; like Abraham, who gave you Isaac." Wind, his deity's affirmation, stroked his thick chestnut hair as his arched lips smiled in mad transcendence.

When he stood, a sunlight shaft pierced clouds to strike yellow hair of a distant girl: God's obvious presentation to him. Michael McCarty pushed through the crowd, calling, "I'm here fer you."

As Billy returned with fireplace logs, Catherine said, "You look so like yer father."

Startled, he asked, "You remember my *real* father?"

She laughed, having concealed Michael McCarty for good reason, but now in need of enlivening stimulation. She said, "You ne'er ferget a trueluv. I'd just come off that boat from Ireland. There came this handsome Michael McCarty. Says he, 'I'm here fer you.' "

Billy asked if it was love at first sight. She teased, exaggerating purring r's. "And how d'ye know about that, me laddie? Yerr dime novels arrrre about Wild Bill Hickok and Kit Carrrson."

Anticipating a story, Billy sat on the floor beside her chair. Her loving fingers buried caresses in his wavy curls, rippling familiar sweet tingling down his neck. She said, "Never did I understand him. But Michael McCarty was the luuve of me life." A smile was in her voice. "Along with you." Billy noticed Antrim's exclusion. He said, "Josie told me you weren't married."

"We considered ourselves ..." Coughing, she gasped, "Water. And a handkerchief. Better ... take blue dishrag ... cut squares ... fer extras."

Returning with a full glass, the fabric, and her sewing shears, Billy sat again at her chair with his task. She continued. "Yer eyes are the blue of Michael McCarty's. And yerrr nose - so straight from yer brow. And yer square jaw. And yer lips." He smiled at this paternal identification.

She sighed. "Michael showed me signs and wonders. Losing him twas like losing sight. Ah, and how he sang. T'would melt yer heart. "But when'ere he drank, he was changed."

Then she had feared him, feared his incomprehensible ranting about the land needing its sacrifice of blood, as he obsessively sharpened his butcher knife until its belly became concave.

She said to Billy, "So you and me never did live with Michael. Josie did though," she added placatingly; as if Billy was his father to whom she had selfishly yielded that less-loved son for her freedom. "Promise me this, Billy: never drrink."

Feigning sincerity, and amused by protective effort in his utterly unsupervised and secretive life, Billy said, "Sure. But, Ma, you asked if I remembered when we first moved. Did Michael McCarty do something about the moon?"

For Billy, only that trace remained of August 24,1864's terror. It began with Josie, two years and five months older, but almost twice his size, pulling him distractedly into the path of a carriage clattering on the cobblestone street. The swerving driver's curse of "lousy Street Arabs" was lost in the populous din near their tenement in New York City's lower east side.

Josie said, "The voices are talking, Billy. They say, 'Kill Da' ": the Old Country identifier Michael McCarthy used. Billy's alarmed eyes widened. "He done bad things to me," Josie said with crudity reflecting his deprived life among street urchins.

Josie led Billy into an alley between eight-story buildings, and ordered, "Lie on them bundles." Agilely Billy perched on the rag pickers' sacks, asking if it was a game.

"Yeah. Da's. On your back." Above, in the blue rooftop-framed corridor, Billy saw an almost-full, white, day moon.

From his shirt, Josie pulled a rope. It passed behind Billy's back to bind his arms. Next, with newspaper wrap fluttering away, was revealed Michael McCarty's butcher knife, whose handle was riveted to ten inches of steel, whose hollowed honed blade belly gave the wider tip a spoon shape.

In the voice of their father, Josie hissed, "This is my sacrifice to God." The raised knife silhouetted black against the skeletal moon.

Screaming, Billy leapt off the ragbag, running and slipping upward his bond.

Josie easily caught him; while yelling to his inherited, psychotic, commanding voices, "I'll do it!"

Billy, wailing, rolled into a ball. Identifying with that panic, Josie dropped the knife. "They's saying to stop ... Billy? Wanna go to Ma?" Billy was fixated on an afterimage of the strange, vicious blade.

Josie said, "Da done that to me. But the voices said if you was the sacrifice I wouldn't be. And he said you're too evil."

"Too evil," echoed in Billy's mind, melting the present into a year before; when, stripped naked and petrified, also lying flat, but where, but gloaming, he was sprayed by close cruel lips and alcohol odor. "Ye bit blood from the hand of yer Da, who had the right - like Abraham - t' sacrifice ye t' God." The face - dark shadow eyes in silvery skin - pressed closer, until it was a giant circle beside that same, strange, upheld, butcher knife blade. "Yer too evil t' see me ere again."

That night, looking out the tenement window of home, Billy again saw the searching cavernous eyes in the glowing orb. Hysterically, he screamed to his mother, "God's looking at me. He's going to kill me;" as, dismayed, Catherine assured that it was only the moon.

By the time Josie led Billy from the alley, all that remained in the child's traumatized memory was the moon circle. The current and past experiences were as lost to him as if in another's mind. Forgotten also, the sacrificial knife lay in that alley of binding and sacrifice, freed to enter the world.

In the Silver City cabin, Catherine spoke. "We left New York in August of sixty-four. Josie was having fits with his voices. But I understood that something bad happened because o' Michael - surely 'twas drink. So we had t' leave."

Billy, impressed by that romantic drama, asked, "Even though you loved him?"

"Yes." A secret slipped out. She said, "When we were in Indianapolis, there came a letter from Michael. "He'd fought fer freedom in the Civil War. He'd been wounded. When I got it, he was dead." She guessed Billy would connect death to that wound. A lie was unnecessary.

Billy gasped, first craving for a father making splendid that death for freedom.

She continued, "Yer father died bravely on April twenty-eighth of sixty-five, two weeks after President Lincoln was assassinated."

She visualized Michael McCarty's bold artistic script and his actual death. He had written, "*Abandoned by YOU I am left only with my pistol.*" It ended, "*I leave it to GOD to complete the DESTINY for my sons that I began in HIS name.*"

That letter had been sent to her by an attorney who had learned her whereabouts from a tenement neighbor, and had enclosed an explanation that the Greater New York Consolidated Life Insurance Company had no exclusionary clause for suicide. There had been a bank note for a substantial sum.

To Billy, she said, "Yer father had a fine life insurance policy t' protect us. Its money bought us our firrrst property, then the second; after I met yer ..." Coughing, she managed, "On the washstand ... medicine. Laudanum."

Billy rushed back to her with a little brown bottle. She panted, "Ten drops in glass o' water."

Soon, with fear dissolving in opiate haze, she led Billy into the bedroom shared with Antrim. The fourth, and last, was for boarders; and sometimes for Josie.

Billy joked about the oversized cardigan. She said, "Tis from Irrreland. Worn by farmers who fight fer freedom. A rebel's sweater."

Getting in bed, she propped pillows. "Sit beside me, Precious. I'll sing ye a song. When y'were a baby, I'd sing ye t' sleep with it.

"D'ye remember this? 'I bear orders from the captain, / Get you ready quick and soon, / Forrr our pikes must be together / By the rising of the moon. / Death to everrry foe and traitor, / Forward on the marching tune, / And a million pikes were shining / By the rising of the moon.' " While Billy thrilled to the martial arousal, she finally slumbered.

Back in the parlor-dining-room, Billy unrolled his pallet, and stretched out to relaxing dreams mirroring her denial. But for him remained only 149 days holding mother, shelter, and certainties.

Also asleep, and also unaware of approaching doom, another child, Paulita Maxwell, in a New Mexico Territory mansion, two hundred sixty miles to Silver City's northeast, born that day ten years before, wore a skin-warmed gift strand of pearls whose cost could have purchased his town. In 461 days, death would leave her, like Billy, fate's seeming cursed or chosen.

APRIL 26, 1874   10:36 AM   SUNDAY

With misleading remissions, tuberculosis bacilli festered in Catherine Antrim's lungs, though she only looked more spare. But she no longer danced.

Billy, holding a dime novel, and contentedly inhaling pie aroma from the cabin's kitchen, straddled the wingback chair, legs close to hot hearth flames, while merging with the paper cover's pistol-brandishing hero, galloping his horse under his name: *Rollo the Boy Ranger*. Billy read: "In addition to the rifle slung over his shoulder and the silver-mounted revolvers he wore in his belt, he carried a saber."

Shaking his shoulder, his mother said, "Tis easier t' wake the dead when yer reading."

"Ma, listen. There *is* romance in my books: 'Town Farnesworth felt a thrill of joy, and his arm stole softly about the slender waist of the maiden.' "

Catherine's kiss smeared saliva on his lips. Billy blushed. "Y'read beautifully, Precious. Yer so smart. Twas easy fer me t' teach you."

Billy diverted her effusions. "My teacher, Doctor Webster, said in class that I stole his arithmetic key."

"Ye don't do stealing d'ye? I never did tell you, but Sheriff Whitehill came by in February when the butcher, Richard Knight, had thirty-five dollars stolen from his cash box. And last month he was back when the Book Exchange Saloon was robbed."

Not guilty of those crimes, but of others, cautiously Billy asked what she had said. "That he'd best question his *own* sons, Henry and Wayne; orrr his nephew, Charlie Stevens. What about that stolen key t' the school, Precious?"

"I didn't say *that*, Ma. Anyway, if I took a key to the first school ever in Silver City, I'd be the only kid wanting to break in, instead of out." They both laughed.

"Here's what happened. Doctor Webster was asking arithmetic problems. I called out the answers. A key's the teacher's answers. Anyway, he looked for the key under my slate, 'cause I was right. Then he made me stand in front and read me more problems. I answered each one. Then all the kids laughed at him."

She said Doctor Webster was a terrible man. Billy smiled. "You're always on my side. I'm Rollo the Boy Ranger and you're my partner."

Catherine laughed. "Help me hang laundry, partner." He hinted that the pies smelled good. She said, "Later I'll make ye one.

"These are fer the Truesdells. They just bought the old Star Hotel on Spring and Hudson. Intendin' t' rename it the Exchange."

Behind the cabin, at her laundry tubs, instead of her usual working, Catherine sat listlessly on a barrel and watched Billy labor. "D'ye remember staying at that fine Exchange Hotel in Santa Fe? Taking that name's wishful thinking fer Clara Truesdell, I'd say."

"Sure I remember. It was *just* last March that you married Antrim."

She sighed and said, "March first. The First Presbyterian Church of Santa Fe, with that serrrious Reverend David McFarland and his serrious daughter Katie and his serrious wife fer witnesses."

Aggressively, Billy wrung a soggy sheet, fantasizing dripping water as blood of mortal combat, and asked why they'd stayed so long. "Fer marriage, ye must reside in Santa Fe a month. Yer father wanted t' live in style. D'ye remember that y'bought me sugar-candy hearts?"

"From a peddler in front of the Palace of the Governors. Ma, d'you remember that the jail was close? Rollo the Boy Ranger could break prisoners out." Wind flapped the heavily hanging sheet. He dodged agilely. "Rollo rescues people from injustice."

She laughed. "Billy Antrim, you and me always fight with glaary."

He flushed and included his lost father with that glorious rebellion. And the enemy was William Henry Antrim.

APRIL 27, 1874   4:18 PM   MONDAY

In gold letters, the cover of a book on the cabin's dining-table said *Consumption Cured*. Billy picked it up. His mother said, "Tis from Mary and Henry Hudson fer their Hudson Hot Springs Hotel. They say its mineral waters cure consumption; so, thought I, they'll surely cure my minor lung condition." Catherine resisted the next words. "So I decided t' stay a few weeks."

Cajolingly, Billy asked to go too. "You have school, Precious."

"No I don't. The semester ended March twenty-eighth with our play at the theater." Billy teased, "How could you forget me as Puck?" He gesticulated dramatically, saying, " 'Lord what fools these mortals be.' May eighteenth we get a new school and a new teacher."

Billy sat at the table, flipped the consumption book's pages, and said, "No wonder it's a rib *cage*. Their picture looks just like one.

Listen to this. 'The heart is situated between the lungs and under the breast-bone, inclining a little to the left side.' So *that's* how Wild Bill gets his man! He knows where the heart is!"

Catherine stroked his thick hair and said she'd take some locks with her. "Take me. With the whole head."

She smiled. "You imp. If the boarder returns, ye'd have t' cook."

Billy sighed, turning pages. "Ma, listen. 'The womb is situated between the bladder and back passage.' What does that mean?

"Found it. The womb's right above a towel they wrapped around the lady they cut in half."

"Death," she thought, but said she just needed a water cure.

Billy sprang up exclaiming, "You've got something better: my love." Bear-hugging her waist, he tried to lift her.

Laughing, gasping, she said, "Come, let's make supper ..." as the door opened, revealing William Henry Antrim.

Golden-bearded, Antrim hesitated, eighty feet of Main Street's red earth behind him. "Hello, Catherine," he said in his deep emotionless voice, and entered, leaning into weight of his canvas satchel, across which lay his miner's pick. The boy disappeared into the kitchen.

Delighted, Catherine embraced Antrim, happy that she had washed her hair that day, and yellow curls hung down her back. "I'm dirty from the mine," he said, backing, eyes cold. "You don't look well."

His marriage now seemed to him a mistake, proceeded by years of cohabitation and dependence on her hearty sexuality. But six months before it, he had read pamphlets and became obsessed with mineral wealth, "the big strike;" which to him meant self-worth. Marriage had felt necessary for this move to Silver City, where she could support him by the laundry business; and any property they acquired would legally become his: a reservoir, if needed, to continue digging. But all these schemes depended on her health.

Catherine said, "Oh, William, y'do worry so." Suppressed anger at his restraint made his arced miner's pick, with pointed ends, remind her of a Celtic weapon in an Ulster display. She half-taunted, "Cú Chulainn returns with the horns of the Mighty Bull."

From the kitchen doorway, Billy asked who Cú Chulainn was. She'd said it before. "A famous, glarious, cattle raider in ancient Ireland; a hero who stole a giant red bull fer a queen. When terrribly wounded in a battle, he had his men tie him t' a rock so he could fight t' the death."

Antrim's eyes hardened. "You're putting defiance in the boy."

She laughed merrily and said, "Ye'rrre in time fer dinner." Walking to the kitchen, she called back, "A wild goose never raised a tame gosling."

"Trouble will come of it, Catherine," he retorted, as Billy sat on the wingback chair with a chunky green book: *Kit Carson's Life and Adventure's by His Comrade and Friend Dewitt C. Peters*.

Antrim told him to get up. He needed the warmth after his wagon ride from the Silver Flat mine.

Sullenly Billy went to the table. To himself, he read: "Kit, feeling that salvation of the entire party rested upon his courage, made up his mind that boldness was the wisest policy."

Antrim interrupted. "Henry, I was thinking: you're small; but you could work with me." Billy glared, saying he just hadn't started growing yet. And he didn't like the name Henry.

"We decided on using your middle name years ago, boy. I'm Billy Antrim. You're Henry Antrim." Billy said his Ma called him Billy.

Antrim smiled, saying no one could tell her what to do, culinary fragrances assuaging his doubts. He called, "Catherine, this lot here's doubled in value. Just one big strike and we'll be rich!"

Billy said, still in the thrall of Kit Carson's heroics, "Wild Bill Hickok, the quickest draw in the world, is the marshal in Abilene, Kansas. He's not afraid of anything."

Antrim responded, "Yesterday, I heard that George Kitt struck a silver vein assayed at one hundred dollars a ton. Think of it, boy. Sometimes gold's mixed in! Silver's a dollar an ounce. Gold's twenty."

Billy asked why he smelled so bad. Antrim sniffed his jacket. "Black powder: exploding sulphur to find my own Legal Tender Mine. Bullard's going to make hundreds of thousands from that."

Billy said, "Smells like the guts of a dead cat," and stalked to the kitchen to help his mother.

When they were all at the table, Billy lifted his fork. "Grace," objected Antrim, and said, "Thank you God for this food. Preserve us in prosperity. Amen." Mother and son were silent, sharing her aversion to organized religion.

Catherine moved bowls solicitously to her husband, while Billy reached competitively to take extra for himself.

Antrim finally said to Billy, "I'll tell you more about mining." His dirt-stained hands were corded and powerful.

Catherine cleared the table and brought back an apple pie. "That looks fine," Antrim said, desire flickering. She smiled coyly at him.

He continued, "Precious metals mix with rock." Billy countered with gold nuggets. "That's so. But with silver, you crush its rock. The greasers here learned from Spaniards to crush it with an arrastra."

"Mexicans," Billy interrupted.

"William, he has Mexican friends. He doesn't use 'greasers.' "

Antrim asked, "Are you going to Chihuahua Hill to those Mexican shacks, Henry? We didn't get a house on Main and Broadway for you to go up there." Catherine offered more pie. Her diversion worked.

Antrim resumed. "These arrastras are just a turnstile with a horse pulling a grindstone. Too slow for us Whites. We've got stamp mills. Drop a thousand pound iron block on the rocks. Mix their powder with water and mercury, and the silver - and sometimes even gold - join together with it ..." Billy asked how they join. "I don't know, boy. But it makes a paste." Antrim smiled, tentatively paternal. Billy did not smile back. Antrim felt the intended rebuff, but said, "You squeeze the paste in a canvas bag to get rid of the water. You're left with silver and gold." Billy asked about the mercury. Antrim said, "You've got a smart son, Missus. Remembers things." She smiled adoringly at Billy. "Mercury's expensive. So you put the mix in this thing like a whiskey-still to catch it to reuse. Then you melt the ore in a smelting furnace to make silver ingots for the assay office."

Antrim felt happy, marriage fears gone, just as Catherine's coughing flight out of the room shattered peace and hope.

Billy took his Kit Carson book to the wingback chair. Antrim asked, "What do you say, boy?"

"Smells like the guts of a dead cat," Billy answered scornfully.

Enraged, Antrim lunged, chair clattering backwards. Catherine rushed in and saw his blow hurl Billy to the gaping blazing fireplace.

Twisting, wrenching, Billy lurched out, face contorted with hatred, yelling in fury, and astounding his listeners with accentless fluent Spanish. Then he screamed in English, "You smell like filth. All your silver and gold is dirt."

William Henry Harrison Antrim, shaken, faced his immobilized wife and said, "He drove me to it. You put defiance in him. Your other son's a worthless gambler. I cannot - will not - stay under this roof."

He lifted his satchel and miner's pick. Billy stared savagely at the weapon-like tool, visualizing combat. He was Cú Chulainn.

Antrim vacillated. "Catherine, what do you say?"

"Tis apologizing t' *ourrr* son that y'must do." Antrim refused.

Contracting muscles of Billy's arms and back responded to his fantasy. The pick completed an arc, penetrating Antrim's skull, which exploded like a watermelon, shattering pulpy red.

Catherine said, "Then I want *one thing*, William."

The man and boy waited, as if for a verdict to decide their fates. "Leave yer gun. Fer protection."

Apprehensively, Antrim glanced at the glowering boy with thick split lip, but took out a worn holster sheathing an almost-new, Colt .45 revolver, its original seven and a half inch barrel shortened for portability. Firelight glinted in the boy's eyes as the weapon passed to his mother's hands.

Catherine asked, "D'ye want some clothes?"

"Only my cardigan."

Then the front door swung open to Main Street. Wind whipped fireplace flames. The door closed behind Antrim. Mother and son stood silent. But Billy, in altered reality, pointed that gun, defending them both against William Henry Harrison Antrim, attacking with his pick. A log broke, hissing through the grate. Then Billy was shooting, shooting, shooting.

MAY 26, 1874   12:10 PM   TUESDAY

William Henry Harrison Antrim's departure coincided with almost continuous rain; whose dampness left Catherine bedridden, but claiming recuperative rest. To Billy, at their open front door, she called, asking if Clara Truesdell, nursing her to earn extra money for the planned hotel, was there yet.

To check, Billy stepped out into crazily dancing porch shadows of newly-leafing sapling elm to the north and older cottonwood to its south. Ahead, San Vincente Creek - once a little arroyo, a gully down Main Street's center - tore five feet deep and red, fed by unimpeded runoff from the Piños Altos Mountains, ravaged of timber by the miners. Wind carried stamp mill drumming and blasting from the west, where smoke marked smelting furnaces. Donkey-drawn carreta carts, with primitive wood-disk wheels skreaking on wooden axles, passed him with goods from Mexico.

Southward, across Broadway, at Clara Truesdell's house on the corner, her ten year old, round-faced, son, Chauncey, waved at him from the doorway and shouted, "Wana play horse racing?" Chauncey called back inside, "Mom, Henry's waiting."

Clara Truesdell said to tell him that their architect couldn't be rushed. Pudgy and auburn-haired, she smiled ingratiatingly across her dining table at the dapper, mustached, pretentious man, who said, "Like I told your husband, Gideon, with the fine red brick made right here in Silver City, nothing stops me and my brother making 'palatial properties' - like we say in our *Mining Life* advertisement."

"Just money, Mister Black," she answered, extremely stingy.

"Vision, I'd say. This town can be a San Francisco - with its hilly landscape. Just needs settlers like you and your husband."

"Why thank you. And getting rid of eyesores like on Chihuahua Hill. The view from there's lovely." Condescendingly, the builder said he'd never been there.

Back inside the cabin, Billy carried bowls of stew to his mother's bed, to eat beside her. Antrim's absence had brought relief. Billy basked in her exclusive love. She eluded conjugal exertions.

Concealing excitement, he asked, "Ma, remember you once said you liked blue turquoise better than diamonds?" She coughed. He said, "Hudson Hot Springs didn't help." She was silent.

"Well, there's a necklace in the Derbyshire Furniture Store and News Depot with *blue* Persian turquoise. You said it reminded you of," he looked flirtatiously sidelong, "my eyes."

His fantasy spilled out. "The necklace is being raffled. I'm going to win it. You'll wear it to a dance at McGary's Hall, 'cause you'll be well." Next was the obstacle. "The raffle tickets are twenty-five cents."

"We're a wee bit short, Precious." She changed that frightening subject. "Why arrren't you in school? Didn't it start on the eighteenth in that fixed-up building?"

"Did." His mouth was full. "But the roof leaks. So the new teacher, Miss Pratt, keeps calling class off. The raffles are from a Mexican circus in town. Every time I go ..."

She asked how he got money. "Uh," he awkwardly lied: "I think I hear Missus Truesdell at the door."

When Billy returned alone, to his disappointment, his mother persisted. So he lied again. "Harry and Wayne Whitehill, and their cousin, Charley Stevens, *took me*."

"Tis unlikely Harvey Whitehill and Isaac Stevens would give their sons money fer that."

Billy asked, "Can you keep a secret?" She smiled, enjoying their collusions. "Remember the robberies from the Book Exchange Saloon and Richard Knight's cash box? You thought it was them. It *was*. So *they* had money."

And, do tell, she asked, how he knew facts of their crime. "Like Rollo the Boy Ranger would say, 'It weighed heavy on their consciences.'"

She laughed. "Yer an imp, Billy. An incorrigible imp." Coughing, she groped for a blue cloth. "Precious," she whispered. "I need more Laudanum from Doctor Bailey's today. It's our little secret." She was embarrassed by the craving; he, titillated by conspiring.

Walking on Main Street, Billy tossed twigs into the red creek, to watch them catapult southward: his direction. He waved to Clara Truesdell, picking across mud with heal prints of her heavy tread. She called, "Be home before nightfall, Henry," resenting financial necessity that forced connecting with a family subject to town gossip.

Billy passed Broadway's intersection, the town's commercial heart, when Chauncey ran out to join him. To their right, was the stuccoed adobe of Dr. G.W. Bailey with his sign: APOTHECARY AND POST OFFICE. Billy said, "I'm getting Ma something." Together they crossed the creek on bridging boards.

Inside the store, Billy looked ingenuously over the counter at side-whiskered Dr. Bailey, who asked, "More Laudanum *already*?" He probed salaciously: "Heard your father stayed at the mines ..."

"Ma, says put it on her account." Billy spilled marbles from an old tomato tin onto his palm. The largest was opalescent, with shadowy swirls: a moon. It remained in the skin pouch at his thumb when the others clinked back in the tin.

As he and Chauncey exited, Billy looked across the creek-split street and said, "I need to check Derbyshire's." The child demanded horse racing. "After," Billy said in his soft blurred voice, "and you'll have the grand champion."

He leapt, spanning the gorge. Chauncey clomped across its planks.

Matt Derbyshire's brick building had fancy, high-arched, display windows. In one, below the sign, *CIRCUS RAFFLE*, was a black velvet-covered board with a silver necklace suspending fused flying swallows with blue turquoise eyes. The center bird dangled a big heart with a flawless cabochon, also so blue.

Billy gazed covetously at the jewelry as Harry and Wayne Whitehill and Charley Stevens approached with tagalong, tubby, eight year old Louie Abraham.

Chauncey Truesdell boasted, "Henry's going to win this raffle. He's my racehorse. We bet against you, Harry. What's the prize?"

Billy held up the moon marble, transformed by sunlight into a thing of wonder.

"I say how the race goes," said broad-featured big-nosed Harry Whitehill, at sixteen the oldest, and emulating his father's nasty authoritarian style. "We start at Henry's. Then run 'long the creek to the next street, at the corner of Main and Spring."

Competitively, Harry tightened his cap. "And, if Henry wins, I give twenty-five cents," he mocked, "for the raffle."

Chauncey patted mud for hoof tonic on Billy's high-laced shoes. All walked northward, each in a shirt with vest over suspenders pulling up woolen pants.

Billy stopped with the creek to his right. Wayne called the count. Immediately, Harry careened sidewards, maliciously knocking Billy to the torrent; and kept running.

Billy swung around desperately - again thrown, first to fire, now to water - right foot splashing down, but left leg bent with foot at the earth edge. Springing up, howling fury, he sprinted after the large boy, slamming him full force into the water.

Harry thrashing, red silt streaming, screamed, "I can't swim! Help me! Help!"

Billy stared, face inhuman, lip contracted in a snarl, as Antrim bobbed - not Harry - in red, in bullet-riddled red rushing blood.

A passing laborer hauled gasping Harry out, as a foppish man, in derby hat, rushed panting to the scene, saying, "Owen Scott, here. New owner. *Mining Life*. What happened?" The soaked rescuer, in Spanish, backing anxiously, denied fault, and hurried away.

Billy reported that Harry had pushed him into the creek. Harry, avoiding Billy's eyes, said *he'd* tried to drown *him*. With disgust, Owen Scott said to Billy, "Look at the evidence, boy. Who's wet? I've got my story. Anyways, Harvey Whitehill's son wouldn't lie."

Billy glared viciously at the man's plaid-suited back, departing north to the next cross street, Yankie, and his *Mining Life* building.

Louie Abraham, catching up, piped, "You pushed first, Harry."

Harry Whitehill said, "Shut up or I'll throw you in too."

The little boy retreated, trudging on Broadway, one block over to Bullard, where his family lived above their dry goods store.

To Billy, Harry jeered, "Your father left your mother;" and shouted, "Bastard!" as he and his brother ran away.

Chauncey asked who got the marble. "Nobody," said Billy, again preoccupied with the raffle. "I've got to talk to Charley."

After Chauncey left, Billy said, "Let's go to the Bedrock." That saloon was at the east corner of Main's intersection with Spring Street.

He and Charley sat on its porch bench. Billy said, "It's about stealing the circus jewelry."

The red-headed boy smiled broadly. "Figers you'd figer it was me an' Harry an' Wayne wha' pinched the money from Knight an' the Book Eschange." The indented corners of Billy's lips turned up more. "Bu' Wayne almos' snitched t' 'is Dad. So Harry askt, 'Wha' happins t' boys who rob?' An' 'is Dad sez t' 'im, 'They puts 'em in jail.'"

Billy questioned how long, not having considered consequences. "Till Districk Court; an' tha's jus' twice a year."

Convinced only that an accomplice was needed, Billy withdrew a rolled pamphlet and said, "Listen to this, Charley. It's a Munro Novel: the *Rover of the Forest*. About brave men." He ended brief reading with, "'You shall feel my vengeance;'" and added, "Nothing scared the Rover. He'd use the alley behind Derbyshire's."

Almost converted, Charley confided, "Chauncey tol' me 'bout a fella callt Sombrero Jack. Buys stuff offa kids when 'e passes through. Gave Chauncey a penny for doin' somethin'."

Billy said, "I don't need selling, just you standing guard;" and declared, "Rover to Rover oath." Charley gave his hand. Billy, just like the Rover, said, "At night-time's nine, tomorrow we'll do the deed."

A trumpet blared. Cymbals crashed.

Billy sprang up, wild with joy, and raced toward that day's Mexican circus parade which was climbing Broadway's hill and trailing a throng of Silver City boys. Hindmost of the performers were two, gold-braided sombreroed, singing men, pulling a wheeled cage. Through its flat iron bars, a small black bear peered, goaded by another costumed man to its display irritable teeth.

Billy ran past; past jugglers singing; past the pretty trapeze lady singing on a white horse led by a dark tightrope walker, singing; and past a fat lady with a black beard, hauled by the strongman and seated on a platform in androgynous immensity, both singing. Finally, Billy came to the musicians, bright-sashed, silver flashing conchos down pants' sides, also singing the happy song, while playing guitar, tambourine, and cymbals; as the trumpeter exploded sunlit air with brassy wild blasts.

Then Billy was in front, prancing and singing and shouting their circus song; leading their circus parade to clapping and laughter of everyone, now all his audience for his jubilant audacity.

MAY 27, 1874   6:10 PM   WEDNESDAY

Leaving for the day, Clara Truesdell asked Billy snidely, "Where's your brother Josie? I heard they got some new women at the Orleans. One even walked this street wearing *diamonds*!" Billy looked so perplexed that she asked his age. Fourteen-and-a-half, he said. She daubed her eyes. "Mine too ... when my mother died."

Approaching the bedroom, Billy saw his nightgowned mother frantically rummaging through the trunk at the foot of the bed. She asked where her Laudanum was. He took the bottle from his vest, as she watched voraciously and said, "Precious, put twelve drops in water." He objected that the bottle said eight. She hesitated. "Fer a small glass. Ours are big."

After sipping, Catherine said, "Tis fer this touch o' pain;" pointing to a suggested breast's nipple, which made Billy's eyes flee. Deterioration, to Catherine, had become unrelated tribulations, all assuaged by narcotic's gay oblivion.

Billy noticed, for the first time, a blue cloth's red violation. She saw and said, "Tis nothing, Precious." Fleetingly, he doubted, feeling fear.

While he made dinner, she called, "More! More! More Laudanum to celebrate spring!"

When the food tray was on her night-table, she greedily gulped the refilled glass, then, so quickly, pulled him to her, drunkenly wetly nuzzling his neck. Then she bit. Shocked, Billy jerked back, with confused red-faced anger.

Oblivious, she hummed, beautiful haunting humming, and said, "I was rememberin' an old Irrrish ballad." More humming slaked Billy's tumescent irritability, while its melody swelled unnamable hot longings.

"Tis 'bout a boy with yourrr name and a girrrl named Barbara Allen." She sang, slurring: " 'Sweet William died fer me fer love, / And I will die fer him fer sorrrow.' / They buried her in the lone church yard / Sweet William lay a nigh herrr. / An' from his grave grew a red, red rose, / And ou' o' 'ers a briar." Then she slept.

Seduced now, intoxicated now by contagion, her Sweet William, her brave Billy - who would risk death; who would kill for love or glory - with surging bravado, whispered, "When you wake up, Ma, there'll be something so beautiful, you'll get well."

The mantle clock said eight fifty-two when Billy strode onto silver-skyed silvered Main Street, sliced by wheel-rut shadows from the full moon. Turning left at Broadway, he scanned perpendicular Hudson, from which an alley led to the Derbyshire Furniture Store and News Depot's rear. But a buggy approached.

Billy dawdled innocently. The Polish merchant, David Abraham, with curly black beard, reined in his well-groomed horse and asked about the creek incident. Billy said, "It was nothing. Harry Whitehill slipped. Louie's a good boy, Mister Abraham."

"Dank Gud. Ve know. Zo I zay guud night." Reins slapped. The vehicle trailed scent of fresh wax from its black-lacquered wood.

At Hudson, Billy checked north and south. Far to his left, on its southeast corner with Yankie, the next cross street, a light still burned at Richard Knight's Butcher Shop. The vaquero, Juan Mejilla, with family on Chihuahua Hill, was butchering calves. Billy whistled "Turkey in the Straw" as he turned right.

Meanwhile, in the dark Derbyshire alley, Charley Stevens, beside his father, gazed up at Roman-nosed Harvey Whitehill and said, "Henry Antrim h-had me hypnitized till I sez I'd rob the jewry." Charley turned to overweight Matt Derbyshire. "I'd never steal nothin', Sir."

His father, Isaac Stevens, said, "We know, Charley. You did good te tell me."

The three men and the boy stood in savored comradery. "I figure it this way," Harvey Whitehall said. "We're family. Hell, Isaac, with my sister married to you, it's like we're brothers. And with your sister Mary married to Richard Hudson, all of us are connected family-wise and business-wise. Just got to get you hitched, Matt."

All laughed except Charley, who said, "Mister Whitehill, please don' say I squealed. H-Henry'd kill me. Like he tried Harry."

Whitehill's angrily working jaw was invisible; but Charley could see the three men silhouetted, massive and protective like the black Mimbres Mountains behind them, before they left him to hide for the ambush in the unlit store.

Charley was fantasizing the Rover's revenge when Billy approached. Charley whispered, "Les not do it. I changt my min'."

"Got to," said Billy. "We made an oath."

Standing on a crate, he pulled outward the framed side-hinged window, and climbed into blackness.

Instantly, lantern light whipped shadows over storeroom stock and walls. Billy was thrown down and held to floorboards. Manure stank on boots at his face. A voice said, "Say you won't run." He did and stood, seeing Isaac Stevens exit.

"Kid," Harvey Whitehill said, "we know you're here to rob." Isaac Stevens returned with Charley. Whitehill said, "A drunk at the Bedrock heard you boys planning."

"Which drunk?" Billy asked insolently, convinced of Charlie's betrayal, but attributing it to cowardice in accomplices that even the Rover had to endure.

"Quiet, kid," said Whitehill. "A boy like you's only trouble." Charley coughed. "Boys like you," Whitehill corrected.

Billy said, "I haven't done anything." But he had a sudden and grand recognition: they all feared him.

A shot reverberated. "From the Bedrock!" shouted Harvey Whitehill, throwing open the door.

So Billy ran out.

Rushing to the saloon with Matt Derbyshire and Isaac Stevens, Harvey Whitehill realized that he detested the boy.

Billy ran cannily, not back to the cabin, but in its opposite direction - northward on Hudson - then between Richard Knight's Butcher Shop and the J.B. Bennett Store.

Suddenly the ground became tractionless splashing slime. Only Billy's extraordinary coordination saved him from a fall. It was blood from Knight's slaughterhouse spillway.

A dog barked as Billy ran northward onto Yankie Street. Then he ran west.

South on Main Street, glared the Orleans Saloon. In front, stood its owner, Joe Dyer, with handlebar mustache and satin brocade vest. He asked, "Lookin' fer yer brother, kid?" Billy lied affirmation.

Joe Dyer called into haze, raucous laughter, and cursing, "Hey, Antreem. A high roller te see ye."

Josie, angular, large-featured, clean-shaven, and intoxicated, appeared, inviting Billy in. But Billy wanted to go home.

Walking with him and sobering, Josie said, "You smell funny." Told it was blood, Josie asked, "Killed somebody?" Billy responded with exasperation that he had cut through Knight's.

Repeatedly and senselessly checking his jacket pockets, Josie finally focused on Billy and said, "I got my own gambling table now. Rent it from Dyer. You can help me."

In the dark cabin, Billy checked their sleeping mother as Josie lit the oil lamp over the dining table while muttering to his voices: "My brother wouldn't go against me. Shut up."

When Billy returned, Josie said, "I need you to tell me what's in players' hands in draw poker." Billy said he wanted to stay in school. "After. Watch."

Josie dealt. A flying card curled momentarily upward. Billy identified it. "Good. And some decks now got indexes: the number and suite on corners. Makes this easier. Here's the hard part. They'd kill us if you told me. We need signals."

Billy's pupils dilated in anticipation of crafty powers. He said, "Tell me. I'll remember."

JUNE 30, 1874   8:10 AM   TUESDAY

The too tall, pox-scarred teacher from St. Louis, Miss Pratt, late and miserable, resigning to spinsterhood, but stooping hopefully, hurried in powdery dust southward on Main Street toward the schoolhouse, thinking that after so much rain it was now so dry your lips cracked. Twenty-one of her twenty-eight students waited restlessly.

Twenty-one sets of eyes watched her struggle futilely with key and lock. Then Harry Whitehill's seven year old sister held out a black-eyed Susan. To the apple-cheeked girl, whose family delighted in her soft necklessness, Miss Pratt said with annoyance, "Thank you, Olive," and stuffed the flower into her purse.

"Ollie," the little girl piped. "It 'ill die there, teacher."

Ignoring her, Miss Pratt called to a slovenly man weaving from the Orleans Saloon, on the northeast corner of the block. He easily unfastened the door. As the children filed in, she realized he was staring at her flat chest: her greatest embarrassment. She handed a quarter; he reversed in return to the saloon.

The doorway framed one room with whiff of mold. Rainwater, pooling on that old adobe's flat mud roof, seeped through to its ceiling of tree trunk beams, the vigas, and rotted cross-slating branches.

Miss Pratt entering the noisy chaos, where long tables with benches arranged her class, by age, into five rows, almost collided with Charley Stevens, running to hit his cousin, Wayne Whitehill.

Blond, freckled Susie Brown, her skinny body incongruously breast-heavy, called from the fourth table that Harry Whitehill had pulled her hair. Billy in row three, wiping his wood-framed rawhide-bound slate with a handkerchief, added to the din by shouting, "I need chalk!"

Miss Pratt sat behind her desk and, in a brittle voice, began roll call, using her painstakingly drawn, month's grid. A check meant present, an X, absent. "Anthony Connor?" At "Susan Brown," boys in row five snickered. At "Miguel Hernandez," Roscoe Gill jumped up, urgently waving. To change his X to a check would be unsightly. She left it. Harry Whitehill called out that after two months she should know names. Flushing, she stood. "I'll have no impudence. You, you, come to the front."

Seated again, she queried, "Harry Whitehill?" Little Ollie Whitehill pointed. Her brother waved mincingly from behind Miss Pratt. An angry check flooded his box and dribbled ruinously.

She said, "Now that we're done …" Al Rosenkranz taunted that it was time to leave. Everyone laughed. Sternly, she said, "You go to the front too." Almost seventeen, the big boy sauntered insolently.

"Who wants pen, ink, and paper for the English lesson?" Everyone raised their hands. "Only the older children." Miss Pratt splayed *Harvey's Elementary Grammar and Composition*. "We will do the conjugation of the verb 'to love.' " At the slate, which Mr. Black had installed as civic charity, she chalked, "*PRESENT TENSE, PRESENT PERFECT TENSE, PAST TENSE.*"

Unmonitored, her students tore paper corners to chew for missiles. Charley Stevens scribbled a humorous cartoon.

She turned and read, "To love. Present Tense Singular. I love. You love ..." There was a thud. The roof's falling! cried Louie Abraham. Miss Pratt realized her neck muscles were a sheet of pain. Mud had fallen through again. She noticed Billy writing assiduously.

"Scorpion!" shrieked Susie Brown.

Approaching Miss Pratt, with implacable eight-leggedness, was the venomous arachnid, departing dropped debris and seeking refuge in an overhanging shadow. She screamed, comprehending his plan, and lifted skirt and petticoats. Billy watched skittering ankle-high shoes and surprisingly lovely calves, stockinged naked white. His ears blazed. An older boy clapped. "Oh, help," wailed Miss Pratt. Harry Whitehall crushed the animal. Billy stared at his teacher's lowered hemline, while pleasure rippled down his back.

To Harry Whitehill and Al Rosenkranz, Miss Pratt said tartly, "You may return to your seats. We will continue." There were groans. "We shall love. You will love. They ..."

Billy again wrote urgently. Someone passed him a paper, which he passed to Wayne Whitehill, who giggled. Miss Pratt saw, and advanced in brisk fury, grabbing both boys' sheets.

Back at her desk, Miss Pratt felt sick and ended class, but kept Billy and Wayne. She said, "I'll tell you both first: I'm leaving at the end of this term. It's impossible to teach here."

When alone, she checked their papers. First was Charley Stevens's sketch, with dotted face and chest as two straight lines. On the skirt was a Y shape with "to love" and a pointing arrow. Tears filled her eyes. On the other, with spatters, was Billy's "*CONCHEWGASHUN OF LOVE*," and his attempted transcription of her lesson.

Outside, Billy jogged up the southward ascent of Arizona Street, his rhythmically lifting legs renewing the white-stockinged pleasure. Passing buildings first imitated urban Victoriana, but as roadway rose toward sky, the rigid grid of Silver City, arrogantly and irrationally cutting over ridges and waterways, disappeared and habitations became earth's redness. These dwellings of Chihuahua Hill blended with the land. Billy waved to recognized people; and mutual greetings were in Spanish.

Almost at the crest, Billy stopped, looking down at Silver City, sprawling like a melted cross with Main Street its long axis and Broadway its central transection. Due north were the blue-green Piños Altos Mountains, and east, the Mimbres. To the west, stretched mines and mine towns, Silver Flat and Chloride Flat; and farther westward was another Territory, Arizona, with its border mining town of Clifton. Beyond was California, where they were rich with a quarter century of gold.

Proceeding, Billy paused to play marbles with children, who admired his moon marble, already a famous shooter in the town below.

Finally, he arrived at the adobe that Juan Mejilla, the vaquero, had built for his injured brother and grandmother. "Beelly, come in," the stout, golden skinned woman with silver hair said warmly in Spanish, which, for him, melded welcome and belonging.

A swarthy youth, sprouting first black mustache, was on a cot. The old woman said, "I will give you food. Sit with Fernando."

Billy pulled up a straw-seated chair as the young man unwound bandages from what was left of his legs, while saying, "You never saw them before. The worst is the memory. The explosion. I do not remember pain. Just no feet. They said I cried, 'My feet, my feet.' "

Billy handed Fernando a ten dollar gold piece, his overt reason for the visit; and said, "I earned this gambling with my brother. For you to see the doctor again."

Fernando waved it high. The woman said, "Please, Beelly, stay away from the saloon." She placed, on the table, tortillas and lamb stew, red with ground chilies. Billy ate ravenously, Clara Truesdell having made no provision for his meals. At Porter's General Store, told his mother's credit had expired, he had been refused food. So he ate from the cabin's dwindling dried and canned supplies.

Fernando maneuvered with crutches to the other bench, saying, "Anglos are fools." The woman scolded that, from them, the boy could learn hatred. "That is not hatred, just the way the world is," said Fernando. "Listen. They say we Mexicans know nothing about mining. Then tell me how Lorenzo and Juan Carrasco - who made the first silver smelters in Chloride Flat - have processed three thousand tons with arrastras and have gotten two hundred thousand dollars? But the greedy Anglos blast and blow off my legs."

When Billy's plate was empty, his eyes closed in satiation. Head on folded arms, he slept. The woman whispered, "Fernando, do you realize what his life will be when his mother dies? Señora Santana - who cleans for Señora Truesdell - has told me that the stepfather already is trying to sell their house. And she heard Señora Truesdell say to Señora Hudson that there are no plans for the boy."

She made a sour expression. "Tell me what dying mother makes no plans for her child?"

"So he will have injustice. Like us. He has enough spirit."

Billy awoke to Fernando's guitar strumming. Late sun slanted through the wide-open door, casting a bright rectangle over furniture. Billy stretched and said, "I was dreaming about love and freedom." Fernando laughed that those were his songs.

Billy followed the old woman out into sunlight. A flock of bandtail pigeons circled. Wanting to give him strength for his hard life to come, she pointed to them and said, "I will teach you the joy of the birds. They fly with joy, and without fear, because they know there are millions of moments to be alive, only one moment of death, and then you have forever. You were listening?"

Music poured from inside. "Let's dance," Billy said. "Dance the joy of the birds."

Fernando called for him to carry out his chair and guitar. To a slow tune, Billy and the old woman stepped. When the tempo increased, Billy danced alone as the birds circled.

Dancing, he became aware of stamp mills pounding, of explosions, of pulverized rocks and flesh, of a Main Street that becomes a red river, of a small black bear in a cage, of blood-stained blue cloths, of a thousand pikes shining in a moon of rebellion, of a hero tied to a rock so he could stand, of boots that smelled like manure, of a blow hurling one to fire-singed hair, of a miner's pick sharp at both ends, of a revolver passing from a man's hand to a woman's. And his face contorted in sorrow and rage.

But as intoxicatingly fragrant piñon wood smoke swirled from the chimney, he was liberated; and he danced on the hill that was in the sky, and found the joy of the birds in the space between the touchings of his feet to the ground. And he was not imaging flying, but was flying; then singing, "To fly, to fly, to fly;" as the youth with no feet played faster, to join the dance and to fly.

SEPTEMBER 15, 1874   7:33 AM   TUESDAY

Billy and his mother danced, but the room was unfamiliar; and she was mechanically repeating, "faster, faster, faster," when heavy tread woke him, still sitting at the cabin's dining-table.

Clara Truesdell asked, "Did you get these yesterday from that new teacher, Mary Richards?" Up most of the night, Billy yawned and nodded. Around him were horizontally-elongated copy books, steel-nibbed pen, and ink jar. One open book had pre-printed words above columns of his improving emulations.

The woman said, "I heard she's a real beauty and a fancy Englishwoman. She's met famous British writers. Maybe the Queen."

"Queen Victoria? Ma once told me Queen Victoria loved her husband, Albert, as much as a woman could love a man. Then he died. So she just wears black." He added, "Ma had a sound in her chest. But she was sleeping good."

"It's in the Almighty's hands," Clara Truesdell said reflexively. "I need you back after school, Henry. Gideon and me are meeting with our architect, Mister Black." She hesitated. "We've been talking. You could work at our new hotel. In exchange for board, I mean."

"Board? I live here." His obtuseness was irritating. The idea had been hers. Ostensibly charitable, it got free labor.

Billy said, "I practiced a signature." Over and over on the back page of his copybook was *Mary Richards.*

Clara Truesdell laughed. "Another conquest!"

Soon, from the kitchen, she called, "How'd you get all those books? Don't steal, Henry." Never, he said.

When approaching the school, Billy concealed the pilfered pile of copybooks inside his vest, under his compressing right arm.

Entering to rose scent, he saw their profusion in a vase on the teacher's desk. Mary Richards smiled and said, "You are my first student today, Henry Antrim."

Billy realized her large eyes were neither green nor brown: a color he had never seen. Brunette hair, center-parted and shimmering, dipped back to coils he had studied the day before. Her long neck left space for a ribbon band above the fitted collar of her blue-green bodice, from which little buttons continued onto her skirt. His eyes were following them to mysterious regions when he heard her lovely accent: "Would you wipe down the slates?"

Of necessity, Billy used his left hand. Mary Richards asked, "Are you ambidextrous?" Delightedly, he said he'd thought his Ma had made up the word, because they both were. She said, "And I am too." Billy's breath caught.

"Please watch the room whilst I get more water for the flowers. Mister Scott, from *Mining Life*, gave them to me from his garden."

As soon as she was gone, Billy rushed to his desk area to deposit the hidden copy books, as students entered.

When Mary Richards returned, she greeted them warmly. "Let us begin our second day together." Ollie Whitehill walked to her and took her hand. "Why don't we both start the class, Ollie?"

The child's eldest brother called out, asking *his* name. Smiling, Mary Richards gave it. He retorted, still testing, that she was the prettiest teacher in Silver City.

Without embarrassment, she said, "Thank you, Mister Whitehill. But I am the *only* teacher; so that could make me superlative in *everything* - good or bad." The children laughed, none understanding the word, but believing she liked them.

She returned Ollie to her seat. "Who remembers the name of the penmanship we shall learn today?"

Chauncey tried to read from an older student's copybook: "Speceriam."

"Very good. It's 'Spencerian,' the name of its inventor. Could someone tell me what they learned about him in quiet reading period yesterday?" There was no response. "You, there, Henry Antrim." Dreamily, he had been staring at her. "Please stand."

Billy stayed mute. About to rescue him, Mary Richards thought, "Their primitive educations may have left them irreparably slow."

Billy began. "Platt Rogers Spencer was born in New York State, like me; but not in New York City, like me. He was born in eighteen hundred, exactly. He always wanted to write good, even when he was little. Then he moved to Ohio. I was about his age when we moved to Kansas. In Ohio, he liked the looks of round pebbles on the shore of Lake Erie. So he drew lines around them. I guess he used sticks. When he was twelve, he wanted a piece of paper. So I'd imagine he was real poor. But he finally got one. He figured out that the best way to write's to make lines like Nature makes. Like water moving 'round rocks. And like vines. I guess by then he was older. Then he decided that writing's a rhythm. He must have liked to dance. He said you had to use your whole arm and finger muscles. And, to practice, he gave everyone as many copy books as they wanted." There was silence of astonishment.

"My goodness," said Mary Richards, "no school boy in England could have recited better."

Al Rosenkranz called, "A cheer for the Silver City hero!" Billy bowed, laughing and gesticulating.

At the end of class, Billy lingered. "I've got a question, Miss Richards. You and me are ambidextrous. Maybe we're relatives?" She had heard his mother was dying, smiled compassionately, and said they probably would know. He smiled blandly back, concealing that his real triumph of the day was masking disappointment at a hope dashed.

Back in silent cabin of his sleeping mother, Billy found a sack of dried pinto beans left by Clara Truesdell, who had basted a rodent-gnawed hole, after deciding that food was unfit for her family. He put some on to boil with the last dried chilies.

Sitting on the bed with his mother in her medicated stupor, Billy talked with animation. She had previously malingered that these one-sided conversations made her feel better. After Billy finished his rendition of the school day, he said, "I'll sleep here in case you need something."

On his mattress, unrolled on her floor, visualizing rafter-graining as Spencerian letters, and aware of insulated privacy so like his secret inner world, Billy suddenly was seized by an urge. Bedstand and chest of drawers were searched, then the trunk. Breathing rapidly, adrenalin outpouring, at last, he clutched Antrim's Colt .45, now wrapped in red calico. Stripped naked, it joined him.

Lying on his back, he was the Rover. Stealthily he looked up to check his sleeping mother, while cradling the blued steel frame and barrel. Hinging open the rounded loading gate, to the right and behind the drum-like cylinder, he exposed golden backs of two cartridges, while gazing from a bloody fantasy. Closing the gate, he grasped the varnished walnut-gripped butt, inserting index finger through the arced guard onto the trigger. Using all muscles, like in the Spencerian System, he extended his arm. The two and a half pound weight balanced and conjured power.

Billy sat. Once a customer in the Orleans Saloon had explained to him how a Samuel Colt had invented the bored-out cylinder, creating name and concept: the revolver. That rotating mechanism enabled six shots, or rounds, to be fired before reloading. And just a year before, the model he held had become available. That man had shown him the parts of the cartridge, whose gunpowder-filled shell was golden, and whose silver tip was the lead bullet.

His eyes flicked to his mother. He was her champion. Through her gapping door was the parlor-dining-room, into which could enter "the adversary." The revolver pointed; single action, it awaited his next intent. His thumb cocked its spur-like hammer. Billy knew, concealed by the grips, a steel spring now bowed lethally. If he pressed the trigger - he pressed enough to feel its resistance - the released hammer would strike a cartridge back, initiating the killing explosion.

The Rover restrained the hammer while retracting the trigger to uncock the mechanism. But he throbbed mysteriously. Hand under shirt, and on corrugating ribs, Billy located his pounding heart.

Again he pointed the bobbing weapon, now vibrating to excited pulse of realization: to penetrate the heart, one aimed at the right side of the chest of "the adversary" facing you.

Billy's lip contracted to a cruel sneer before he returned the gun to the trunk. But their first intercourse had consummated a fusion of insatiable incestuous passion and insatiable aggression.

SEPTEMBER 16, 1874   11:21 AM   WEDNESDAY

Clara Truesdell knew that death was imminent for Catherine Antrim; but she thought, "I refuse to waste my time today. To no profit. To her or me." She watched Billy - sitting on the bed and staring at his mother so intensely - having asked him to stay home from school. She thought, "Poor child, so skinny. Maybe the good Lord will take him too. Surely no one wants him."

The sleeping woman's cachecticly hollow cheeks ridged on teeth. Her unaware hands, bones fanning from each wrist, rested on the neatly flapped quilt with underlying blanket. The nightstand held an untouched bowl of corn mash and a glass of water.

Clara Truesdell tapped Billy's shoulder and said, "Make sure she eats. I won't be back till night. Don't you be leaving her." Walking out, she added, "If she needs the chamber pot, help her." Billy blushed at the outrageous suggestion.

Catherine coughed weakly. Eyes opened, sunken in sockets. Billy smiled. "Mornin', Ma. Hungry?" He fed mush. Moving jawbones hinged visibly. Then she choked, spraying cereal and blood. With a blue cloth, he wiped her gasping face, asking what to do.

Water, she whispered. To her lips, he tipped the glass, but the liquid ran out. Kneeling on the bed, he spooned it. She made little thirsty swallows. He said, "You'll get better now. Want me to sing?"

"Merry," she gasped. "Never ... apart."

He sang "Barbara Allen" until her eyes closed. Instantly, he felt hunger. The porridge was hers. He was not to leave her.

He urinated in the chamber pot. From a little bookshelf, he took his Kit Carson book and read, "We must stand our ground together, and if we have to die, let us take with us each his warrior." He remained in that brave world until daylight faded in the open window and Catherine stirred.

Her eyes opened, terrified and rolling, blind to him. Febrile convulsions then flung her in agonized unconscious abandon, as outside, strangers passed unaware.

Her flesh burned Billy's hand. That abnormality he blamed. For cooling, he soaked her blanket in the ceramic wash basin, and lay it on her thrashing body. She quieted, but every breath rasped. He took her hand, felt fingers tighten, and said, "I won't leave."

Curling against her, he put his head on her clammy covered chest with hard moving bones. "I love you," he said with all his heart. "When you're well again ..." He stopped because a single breath was so deep. Its exhalation rattled. No breath followed.

"Ma," he urged, "wake up. It's *me*: Billy." She was not there. He shook her. Her head flopped crazily.

He realigned it and pealed off the blanket, hanging it over the washstand rail, his back to her. Expecting life, he turned.

Against the pillow was a waxen creature, dun-colored hair disheveled, red trickling from its lax mouth. Her wet nightgown stuck to hip bones, like two mountain ranges paralleling a valley. Hesitantly he approached and drew up the quilt.

Then he lay. First there were small sobs. Then his mouth gaped like hers, wailing for them both. Eyes flowed; nose flowed; fluid choked him. Then he was oblivious; though it was not sleep.

The oil lamp glared. Clara Truesdell asked, "When did she die?"

"Die?"

Anxiety lurched, but Clara Truesdell touched Billy's shoulder.

He recoiled violently, as, for an instant, he became aware of betrayal and abandonment before they coalesced into murderous rage. He snarled, "Don't come near us;" and balled up, knees to chest, facing her with furious eyes, guarding his mother.

Terrified, Clara Truesdell thought, "He's gone mad;" and escaped.

SEPTEMBER 17, 1874   10:48 AM   THURSDAY

For Catherine Antrim's funeral, in misty drizzle, David Abraham and his wife arrived in his coffin-bearing buckboard at the cabin; along with his hired men, Porfirio Ponce and Emilio Augustine, from Chihuahua Hill.

The night before, Clara Truesdell, brimming with gossip, had chattered to the Abrahams about death and madness. Earlier that morning, she and his wife had persuaded Billy, with difficulty, to let them wash and dress the corpse.

"Pleaz, take in de coffin," Abraham said to the men, while warily eyeing Billy standing at the doorway; and speaking to him loudly, as if insanity was akin to deafness. "Ve vant to put your mudder ..." Billy interrupted that he knew Porfirio and Emilio, and asked where Missus Truesdell was. "She and her huzband are cominck vif de Vhitehillz, de Ztevenz, de Knightz, and de Hudsonz. Den ve all go to de zemetery."

"Cemetery?" Billy asked, dazed.

Amelia Abraham said to Billy, "I have food for the people. Where is your brother?" Billy did not answer.

He followed the workers carrying, into the bedroom, two chairs. They became coffin rests. "Amelia," her husband called. "Be vif us ven ve move her." Catherine's emaciation and translucent skin made her look like newly-hatched birds Billy sometimes found dead, fallen to the ground in early spring. When they all left the bedroom, Billy stayed in the pine scent of fresh boards.

Abraham gave the men a plot diagram for digging the grave. His wife said, "Her husband did nothing. If you hadn't offered to buy the plot and make a service, they would have had nothing."

"It iz vamilies like dis dat make you count your blessinks," said David Abraham.

When David Abraham's buckboard, with Billy beside the coffin, rolled through wet fog from the cabin, followed by buggies of the others, San Vincente Creek prevented crossing to Main Street's left side, necessitating detour eastward on Broadway before turning northward onto Hudson. Passed were streets 6th to 9th, until the thoroughfare dipped to lowland, where 10th, 12th, Santa Rita, and West Streets bordered the cemetery.

There, Josie, with Isaac Stevens, was laughing loudly. He was drunk. "Got Ma?" he shouted to Billy.

Billy did not answer.

He followed Porfirio and Emilio with the coffin. Into yawning redness, slung ropes lowered it, so vulnerably pale.

David Abraham, at grave's foot, spoke somberly to the gathered mourners. "Catrine Antrim and me vere immigrants. Ve vanted, vor our children, a bedder life."

From his overcoat, he took a small metal-edged book, opening it opposite the familiar manner. "I vill read vrom my prayer book vrom Poland. 'Against dy vill vast dou born; and against dy vill dost dow live; and against dy vill dost dow die; and against dy vill must dow receive judgment in de prezence of de zupreme King of Kings, de holy Gud, blezzed iz He.'"

Rain droplets struck the page, swelling little circles. Future reminders, Abraham thought, that he, a merchant and a Jew, had once conducted a funeral.

"Vould you boys like to zay zomethink bevore ve vinish?"

"Can I look in again?" asked Billy.

"No. You can shovel virst."

Billy seemed confused. Josie grabbed the shovel. Billy watched thudding red clods.

David Abraham announced, "Porifiro and Emilio vill vinish," after he returned from his wagon carrying a long white board lettered: "MRS. KATHERINE ANTRIM 1829-1874."

Billy said, "It's C, not K. Her real name's McCarty. Before that Bonney."

Amelia Abraham asked, "Do you want to ride back with us?" Billy said he'd walk home. She whispered to her husband, as they watched him depart, "Home. What home?"

After nightfall, Billy returned to the grave-marker, glowing in quarter moon light, and spoke to his mother's presence, as real to him as in her times of oblivion. "Mister Abraham's nice, but he said things like 'against thy will.' But you and me are free. And I know about the joy of the birds. That means there's nothing to fear. I'll bring you roses from Mister Scott's garden. I'd bring you a briar too, but maybe they're just from Ireland. And I won't drink." Following his moon shadow out of the cemetery, he felt a strange mixture of chaos and calm.

Chaos and calm also formed the mood of a handsome, black-mustached, twenty-four year old, six hundred and eighty miles due east of Silver City, in Denison, Texas.

After a modest poker win from a saloon stranger, he confided with boozy self-pity, "My family had a big Louisiana plantation. Lost everything. Yankees stole us blind. Then carpetbaggers and scalawags put the nails in my Papa's coffin. He shot one. The bastard lived. Nobody pressed charges. All that killed him anyway by sixty-eight. Then this bastard, Larkin Rudolph Lay - a brothel owner, who sweet-talked my sister into marrying him - used the courts to sell off our land. For her, I didn't kill him.

"Now I'm a dirt farmer. Couldn't get cowboy work. At six feet four, they figure you'll ruin the horses. My Papa didn't raise Patrick Floyd Garrett to be a dirt farmer."

He teased, "Remember that name: Pat Garrett." Concealed was humiliation and certainty that he deserved its revenge.

APRIL 20, 1875   10:19 AM   TUESDAY

The rotating Earth and its circling moon had completed one revolution around the spinning sun since Billy had last danced with his mother. And in the flooding lowlands of Silver City cemetery, her thin-walled box and her flesh and bones, dissolving, were being freed to become dancing concentrations of vibratory energy more numerous than all suns and planets in the material dimension.

Her son, now a wanderer, precociously self-sufficient, by forgiving her mortality, had retained her enveloping aether of love, and had tempered his violent nature by pity.

His unhealable wound was paternal. Even William Antrim, who had plundered everything - stolen back the gun, its potency now entangled with him - was craved as a father; while Michael McCarty dazzled in war's magnificence, but left a genetic legacy of madness and passion. That was why, though still small, Billy seemed ominous and older than his 15½ years, but also radiated brash wild charm.

Sitting at a table in Josie's room in the Orleans Saloon's warehouse, and breathing familiar stink of unbathed body and alcohol, Billy listened to his brother, who was drinking heavily. "They woulda run me out of town, if you hadn't said it was you that used that Barlow knife."

"Why'd you kill that kitten?" Billy asked.

"It was the Devil." Josie raked back greasy auburn hair. "Want whiskey?" Billy shook his head. "Was Antrim hard on you?"

"Well, I was surprised he gave me that Barlow folding knife - day after we buried Ma. Like he wanted to be a father ..."

"Guilt. He knew he was throwing us out on the street. You were lucky the Hudsons took you in."

Billy sighed, clinging to that paternal fantasy. "That day, Antrim told me about mining in Clifton, Arizona; how I could visit him when he moved there. Then, two days later, he finds the knife in that flour sack with the kitten. The kitten was Ollie Whitehill's. Real expensive, with fluffy gray hair."

"Gray as Hell-fire smoke. Came to our place on purpose. The knife was on the table."

Billy said, "It made my reputation with Ollie's father worse; especially this week, when he caught me with stolen butter. Here's what happened. Remember, after the Hudsons, I lived with the butcher, Richard Knight, and his family? Now I'm working at the Truesdell's hotel. I take their buckboard to buy supplies. And add extras to sell for myself. They don't pay me. So, at Martin Amador's grocery store, I took a big crock of butter from this farmer named Abel Webb. Big mistake. It had blue letters saying WEBB. And Harvey Whitehill was just elected sheriff. *Mining Life* said the last one, Charles McIntosh, never made an arrest; and *he* stole three thousand dollars of county funds. So Whitehill promised to be hard on crooks. So he showed me the jail. Said I'd probably end up there."

Josie had paid no attention and continued, "I decided to tell you something important." Too upsetting, it was immediately repressed. Instead, he said, "I got me opium. Stops the damn voices. A Chinamen sells it at Charlie Sun and Sam Chung's laundry on Ballard."

Another memory came. Josie said, "Watch out for an Anglo from Mesilla: Sombrero Jack. He wears one."

Billy said, "I heard about him before Ma died. Charley Stevens told me he buys from kids. That he'd given Chauncey Truesdell money. But that's strange. Chauncey doesn't steal."

Josie asked, "Have you had a woman?" Billy evaded, embarrassed by circumstantial virginity. "If Jack touches you, I'll kill him."

"I can take care of myself. Does he pay much?"

"Haven't heard complaints. Sorry 'bout not using you more for the gambling. Dyer got suspicious. I been thinking 'bout Globe - in Arizona Territory. Its got gambling and saloons. How else 'ill you get money 'sides stealing?"

"I don't know. But I go to Miss Richards' classes when I can. Sometimes she schools me before class." Billy unfolded a paper. "Listen. This is from *McGuffey's Reader*. Called 'Works of the Coral Insect.' *'It is by the persevering efforts of creatures so insignificant, working in myriads and through ages, that enormous structures are erected, at length overtopping the ocean, which are destined to form new habitations for man to extend his dominion.'* Isn't that interesting?"

Josie wanted to know who wrote it. "I'd say McGuffey. The first page said eighteen thirty-seven. That's thirty-eight years ago. By now, coral insects must have made islands."

Josie said he meant the writing was beautiful. Billy was delighted. "That's me! It's Spencerian. But I changed it. It was curly - like vines. I like big trees with wind blowing through branches better."

"Good. Here's something for getting money. Heard of Three Card Monte?"

"Yes. Once, you'd left the Orleans; a stranger came in from Las Vegas. It seemed easy: guess which of three cards was the ace. But I couldn't. I lost everything you'd just paid me."

"That's it. Watch."

From a deck, Josie took the ace of spades and two red queens. These were laid face-down in a row, then rearranged.

"Show me the ace." Billy pointed. It was the queen of hearts. "Take these three," Josie said. "To 'member me when I'm gone." His eyes fled love in Billy's.

Josie replaced those cards with a red ace and the remaining two black queens; and said, "Watch." He showed each, before placing it face down. The ace was to the right, the two queens leftward. Deftly, his right hand plucked up the central card: index finger at top, thumb at the bottom. It was laid on the ace, then both lifted. In a blur, left hand took the remaining card; hands crossed; and left hand dropped its card. Finally, the right hand dropped its two cards one at a time.

Billy pointed to the left-most card. Surprisingly, it was the queen of clubs. Josie showed the ace - in the center - and said, "Here's the trick, kid," eyes again fleeing his brother, now smiling at paternal-sounding "kid." Josie showed that the crossing left hand was a purposeful distraction for the right-handed maneuver below it. That right hand - too fast to see - let its top-most card, the queen, slide off sideways, between its widely pinching fingers. So the queen dropped first; but it looked like the bottom ace was landing.

Josie said, "That's how they lose the ace. After that, they're just following the wrong card. But let 'em win once to get 'em going." Billy grinned and stood.

Departure cracked Josie's mental block. He said, "Wait. I 'membered what I wanted to say. If I go, I'm not sure when I'll tell you. 'Bout our inheritance. Da told me. God gave him Americer. He's dead. So it's ours, right?" Billy sat again and teased about voices saying it, not Father. Josie responded with the concrete humorlessness of schizophrenia. "It *was* Da."

Repetitively sliding queen over ace, Billy finally said, "I'll tell you something. When I'm riding - like toward the Burro Mountains ..." Josie interrupted that he had no horse. "I 'borrow' one. All I need's a halter and a rope. But when I'm galloping ... it's not exactly mine, but I know I'm where I'm supposed to be. I belong."

Josie continued, "Here's the thing. Da said he promised you to God in that land deal. Said he was like this fella Abraham who God told to kill his son Isaac. But you bit him." Billy laughed. "You were little. Da said it proved God 'id take care of it Himself."

Josie became agitated. "Making me 'member. Something 'bout a knife." He pulled at his stubble-covered face. "But Da kept it up with me. Calling me Billy."

Billy asked who Abraham and Isaac were. "Bible people. Da scared me bad."

"He's dead. It's over."

"I hope so," said Josie.

After Billy left, walking south on Hudson, he was approached by a long-nosed man, almost as small as himself and wearing a conical-crowned sombrero.

The man asked, "Do you work at the Star - where pay is only board?" Exchange, Billy answered coldly. The man tipped his big hat saying, "I'm Sombrero Jack ... Henry Antrim. A friend of boys in need. Mind if I follow along?"

Billy said coldly, "Anyone's free to walk the streets;" and crossed a southwest diagonal to the rear of Porter's Store, which fronted on Main Street. "My brother told me to keep away from you."

The little man said, "Nevertheless, your delectable friend, Chauncey - with that tightwad mother - has appreciated my ... pennies. But to you I turn for other talents, for an endeavor which could pay you half a hundred dollars. The rest can remain my unfulfilled curiosity and your missed opportunity."

Billy glanced side-long, saying he had a way with words. Sombrero Jack said, "I've heard you like to read. Maybe my poetry will find a way to your ... heart."

"You're lucky. Josie could 'ave killed you. Somebody else probably will."

"Death is but pleasure's goad. As to stealing, may I advise? Taking food marks an amateur. Possibly we could discuss my higher-class endeavor? When do you finish work?"

"Eight thirty."

As Billy turned to Porter's Store's rear entrance, Sombrero Jack heard whistled "Turkey in the Straw," exuberant with returning excitement of William Henry Harrison Antrim's dangerous revolver.

At the same moment, two men, a mile apart, in prairie two hundred and fifty-eight miles northeast of Silver City, checked their holstered revolvers, as they approached each other on a road paralleling the forested east bank of the Pecos River: the only dramatic feature in land meeting circumference of horizon.

Through high grass, wind blew in eastward waves over forty thousand square miles of the great Staked Plains, the Llano Estacado, the high desert of northeastern New Mexico Territory and western Texas. On Earth there was no flatter land.

The southbound horse, a rare, black, Andalusian stallion, with cresting neck and mane tossing to his shoulders, bore, on a silver-encrusted saddle, a handsome, middle aged rider, with morbid parlor. Once a mountain man, his bronze hair still curled below hat brim and jacket collar. Between himself and the high horn, was mounted his diminutive young daughter. Two miles behind them lay the town of Fort Sumner, which, in its entirety, was his.

The brown eyes of the other rider, a broad-chested bony-faced man with handlebar mustache, squinted in leathery splays from under an old Stetson. Along the Pecos River's other side, for a hundred and fifty miles of its length, and westward for forty miles, grazed his eighty thousand, long horned cattle: the largest herd ever amassed by one man.

"Papa," demanded the child, "make Centauro run faster than the wind." Impetuously she kicked her custom-made boots against embellished saddle skirting.

Her father laughed softly, sky-blue eyes beaming, as he relished her impetuosity, and watched her long auburn hair sparking red. "And when we beat the wind, where will we go, my birthday daughter?" Just to run, she said.

He teased, "Fire in your hair and fire in your spirit;" but that was what he loved. And land and sky blurred liquidly past them.

She turned, shouting over the pounding hooves, huge dark eyes bright with reckless excitement, "I know. Back to Cimarron! To our white castle!"

Slowing, he said, "It wasn't a castle, Paulita. It was just a very big house." She persisted, excitedly desiring again the tallest building in the world: the stone one. He stroked wild fullness of her hair. "That was just our three story grist mill."

Her mind raced toward this new goal: finally a focus to nameless longing. "Let's go back Cimarron, Papa! Don't *you* want to go back?" Through blurring tears, he said more than she could imagine. "Look!" she cried, sharp-eyed. "Mister Chisum! We've found him."

Finally joining, the prancing black stallion contrasted that man's coarse red-roan gelding, striding tractably. "Good boy, Ol' Steady," Chisum said, and patted the powerful shoulder of his cow horse.

The child's father asked, "Where're your men, John? I thought you traveled with protection now."

"Catron: the bast ..." Chisum stopped for the girl, and continued with his drawling irony. "I rode ahead. No purpis worryin' like a long-tailed cat uner a rockin' chair. Rumor's that yer sick, Lucien."

Lucien Maxwell responded with forced jocularity, "Rumors kill a man," concealing the illness, which he alone knew would be fatal; and the lesion to his soul, which made him long for release at last.

"An' tha' daughter o' yers is gettin' more beautiful; even if ye do dress 'er like a son." Chisum referred to her trousers and shirt.

"I can wear whatever I want. Papa said so." Briefly, both men were distracted by her exquisite beauty: like finding a diamond in wasteland; startling and foreshadowing future men's bewitchment.

"Paulita's eleven today," Maxwell said proudly, his hand on her belly drawing her closer. "And Luz has a feast prepared for you. "How's that new ranch of yours at South Spring River?"

"Oly moved in two mons 'go. Like the Square House well 'nough. Patterson built i' like a fortress with those parapets when he had i'. Might come in handy now," Chisum hinted intentionally. "Bu' I'm keepin' my Bosque Grande Ranch longer. Brings back memries o' sixty-seven, an' my firs' big drive from Texas. Finly adaptin' t' our ol' plains, afta leavin' yer two million acres?"

"It's not easy," said Lucien Maxwell. "Adam survived leaving his Garden; but I don't know how."

"Prolly by bein' angrier 'en a new-made steer." John Chisum's canny eyes - which could pick out one problem cow from hundreds - glanced to monitor Maxwell's reaction.

Maxwell sighed deeply. "I can't complain. Luz is the best wife I can imagine. And this daughter's the joy of my life."

Chisum asked about his son. Paulita flashed her huge dark eyes and said, "Papa hates Pete. He won't let him come in *our* house. Not one of *our* twenty rooms. I hate Pete too. He's mean. He makes roosters fight till one kills the other. Deluvina told me."

Lucien Maxwell said, "That's her nurse, John. A Navajo slave I bought in Cimarron years ago."

"I love Deluvina. She knows everything about the world," Paulita said.

"Maybe yer Papa kin ask 'er wha' t' do 'bout tha' Leviathan: Thomas Benton Catron. If we don' do somethin', 'e'll swalla us all. How much 're ye gonna put up with, Lucian? 'E got yer two million acres; 'im an' 'is Santa Fe Ring."

"I got back a great deal of money," Maxwell said, avoiding debilitating resentments and missing attempted manipulation.

" 'Cept fer wha' 'e got resellin' i' right off. Face i': Catron's destroyin' our lives. Makes me bilious. Those small ranchers down at Seven Rivers may be rustlin' my cattle, fas' as they can burn a brand; bu' when I heard that Catron's goin' inte the cattle business too, I said, 'Time t' git my money ou', 'fore real rustlin' ensues.' I'm sellin' my entire herd t' tha' beef concession ou' o' Sant Louis: Hunter an' Evans. Reckon i'll take me years t' finish delivery over this Terretory, Arezona, an' Texas.

"Bu', Lucien, we gotta do somethin' bout Catron's Santa Fe Ring 'fore we're all grazed out by 'im. These 're fightin' times, not time t' preetend dung's wil' honey."

Maxwell responded listlessly, "Nobody's beaten the Devil yet."

"Bu' 'e' keeps us prayin'." True bitterness broke through the cattle king's habitually feigned affability. "An' right now, I'm prayin' fer war."

SEPTEMBER 5, 1875   8:00 AM   SUNDAY

In her boarding house, Mrs. Sarah Brown, blond braid banding her crown, seeking distraction while anticipating a guest, knocked at Billy's room. She fingered prematurely loose, neck skin and smoothed her silk dress, her best one, thinking, at least, she hadn't gone to fat. So much depended on her body. She opened the door.

For a moment, the boy, twisting to her, stomach-down on the bed, reading his usual dime novel, betrayed disappointment; expecting someone else. She noticed that the lid of his overfilled trunk bulged up. He smiled engagingly. To say something, she asked him to remind her how long he had been at her place. "I left the Truesdell's July thirtieth. So it's thirty-seven days today."

"Too bad you had to leave 'cause of Chauncey's troubles." Ingenuously, Billy said he knew nothing.

"Well, *I* had concerns about *you*." Sarah Brown sat on the single chair. "Then you went and saved Charles Bottom. What with you working like some Mexican at his butcher shop. And Knight's too."

"I just rode his racing mare to get him some cherry bark medicine."

"Risking your life in Apache land. Covering twenty-eight miles in record time. Nobody 'ill forget that."

She saw, against a wall, dime novels and newspapers. "You sure do read. Not like your brother." Billy sat at the bed's edge facing her. She said, "Josie, *he* gave me concern also." She sighed. "But with my husband, Robert, a gambler too, I can't throw the first rock.

" But Sheriff Whitehill did come by. Said you steal." Billy called it a misunderstanding. "I hope so. I run a high-class establishment."

Billy looked beyond her. Sombrero Jack stood at his open door. She smiled. "Why, George Schaefer, here you are my border, and I never do see you. Have you two met?"

Sombrero Jack responded, "I do so admire the young. Like your daughter, Susie. Hovering like a fairy at the cusp of womanhood."

Sarah Brown stood. "Henry, I came by to say I'm getting a special guest today. So don't look for me. I don't need your work today."

Sombrero Jack said, "Then he may have the luxury of time to direct me to *local sights*."

He entered and closed the door. Billy pointed truculently to the chair. "As you wish, dear child. I come purely to heap praise concerning our mutual escapade of last evening. Though the sight of you with your delectable little bottom slipping through that tiny window in Charley Sun's and Sam Chung's house almost brought me to my knees. And your brilliant discovery of those two revolvers and fine California blankets left me merely a humbled pilferer of laundry off the lines."

Billy said he wanted to keep a gun. "No, my dear. Weapon sales increase our credibility. But your profit can achieve that."

"It's hard for a kid to buy one. When do I get my fifty dollars?"

"Where did you hide the booty?" Billy pointed to the trunk. "Excellent. The rest is in an abandoned stamp mill ten miles from here - in Georgetown.

"At this moment, I have but three silver dollars for you. This evening, the remaining forty-seven will receive my full attention. But now, bereft of your intimacies, I must seek others."

As the door swung open, Billy asked if word was out about the robbery. "As imagined, Charlie Sun and Sam Chung are aroused. Sheriff Whitehill is swearing retribution. I predict that Owen Scott must be so tired of saloon clientele murdering each other, that a creative crime like ours will get front page in *Mining Life*.

"But, dear boy, 'robbery' sounds trite. It's redistribution." He winked. "Equalizing." Sombrero Jack left.

Again Billy read. Again knocking interrupted. He opened to small, freckled, full-chested Susie Brown, blond hair in long dangling braids. Now almost sixteen, she sashayed to his bed, picked up his dime novel, and asked if it was interesting. "Very. It's about Wild Bill Hickok: my favorite." Billy closed the door; hoping for opportunity, hampered by ignorance. "Uh, want t'hear 'bout him?"

"Maybe. Later. What would you give me if we played together?"

"Depends on how good a time I had, I guess."

"You be polite. I'm a lady." Hand on hip, saucily she jutted out the elbow.

Billy abandoned caution for enticement, saying he had real pretty clothes. From the trunk came a calico skirt.

Out wafted clean sharp traces of lye soap and starch, recalling his mother; but not that the laundry theft, almost at her burial anniversary, had felt like snatching her back from the grave.

Susie smiled, revealing big square teeth. "That's good enough. We can go for a walk. First I'll get something." Returning with a bundled checkered cloth, she led him, heart pounding, out into cool fog.

"Mama says they'll be building a bridge 'cross the creek at Main and Broadway. I forgot something. I'll be right back."

Billy waited in mist holding male voices from saloons southward along Hudson. Mrs. Brown's boarding house was on the block's northeast corner with Kelly Street. South, across Market, and on the same side, stood the dilapidated courthouse and jail. A riding stranger approached, calling drunkenly, "Kid, where's whores?"

" 'Round here," Billy said. The man continued, hooves slapping sodden; while Billy felt happy kinship.

Susie returned with a floppy homemade doll. "Mama's got a special visitor: Mister Larson. If she's nice, he gives her money."

Sunlit trails streaked the moist air. Walking, immersed in fantasy, Susie said, "Mama and Pa are taking air with their little girl."

Billy asked, "Wana race?" Her glance of feminine disdain was sufficient denial. They continued south on Hudson.

"Uh, what else do Mama and Pa do?"

"They eat. Mama cooked special. I took us some muffins."

His mouth watered. "Call me Billy. What my Ma called me. My real name."

They walked westward on Kelly, crossing boards fording San Vincente Creek on Main Street; and passed Bullard, Texas, Arizona, and Piños Altos. On an eminence, Susie stopped. "See them hills? We live there, Pa." After descending past Bayard, Cooper, and six more streets, they came to the last: E Street. Beyond, a small stream raced through steaming lowland.

"Ford the river, Pa." Gentlemanly, bearing parcel and doll, Billy leapt. Following, Susie slipped. He steadied her, saying she had real pretty, yellow hair. "You can unbraid it. Later."

She took back her doll, but left him blushing as she tromped up an overgrown path. At rock debris tumbled from a gaping hole, she said, "This was Crazy Old Sam's mine. He never found no ore. But he died. We're almost home, Pa."

Ahead was dead Sam's little cabin, boards black-brown, and shingled roof mossy; morning sunlight making glossy the wet wood. Billy cupped hands at a dirt-hazed widow, and made out a bare cot below it, a potbellied stove, and a table with two stools. He handed Susie the bundle. She went in. He did not.

Cautiously, he circled the building, as would the Rover, Rollo the Boy Ranger, or somebody a sheriff might be seeking for a theft. If one had to escape, the window was large enough.

Through it, he saw, on the table, the checkered cloth and muffins. Susie was using her skirt to wipe a tin plate. Freckled legs were bare.

He entered. The doll lay atop a quilt on the cot. "Where'd the cover come from, Susie?"

"Say Mama. I keep it in a tarpaulin Crazy Old Sam left." She fetched her doll. After they ate in silence, she asked, "Are my freckles ugly? They're all over." Missing her innuendo, Billy said they made her unique. "What does 'unique' mean?" she asked hopefully. When he said no one could look like her, she smiled broadly, showing her square teeth. "Like I said, they're all over."

Finally he understood. His eyes moved to her chest. She sat the doll on the table and said, "Her name's Susie. She knows about playing wiggler." Billy hesitated, unwilling to reveal ignorance.

Susie went to the cot. There, she removed shoes, and sat where a pillow should have been; pipestem ankles and little white feet protruding from her skirt. Billy mimicked, glancing sidelong. She said, "Your eyes are beautiful."

Impatiently, aggressively, he said, "I know. My Ma told me. I want to see the freckles." It was too cold, she complained. His eyes narrowed dangerously, and muscles tightened, but split logs caught his attention. "I'll make you a fire," he said; but sighed. "No matches."

"They're on the shelf, Pa. Where you left 'em when we came on the wagon train." Hurriedly Billy worked, saying it was fun to play Mama and Pa. "You're fun to play with too. The other boys just want to play wiggler."

"Other boys?"

"Harry Whitehill. Al Rosenkranz. Anthony Connor. If they give me something nice. But who taught me wiggler is a secret."

Hunkered down, flame tongues lapping hot from the stove, he felt the restlessness which woke him in the night.

She said, "But I'll tell you *part*. Once I looked for Mama. The bedroom door was a teeny bit open; so I peeked. Mister Larson and Mamma were playing wiggler. Then they fell asleep." Billy sighed at the inadequate information. She added, "They were naked."

Billy managed to ask if they could play like that. "Yes," Susie said. "It's warm now." He watched unhesitating removal of dress, corset - which her mother had forced since she was eight - chemise, and drawers. Back in bed, she waited, quilt pulled to waist. "Come on, Pa," she said.

With burning face, Billy hesitated, inhibited by secret throbbing in long-underwear bottoms. Turning around, he declared, "I'll get the other Susie;" and stripped while backing.

The bare mattress felt gritty. Bashfully, he looked sidelong, as he handed the toy. "Dear little Susie," she said, kissing it and erupting his arousal into tickling and tussling; his leg crossing her bony hip, his chest pressing speckled soft firmness he dared not touch.

But she sat, pulling back and asking, "Are the freckles ugly, Billy?"

"Uh, uh." His mind whirled. He said, "Most beautiful freckles in the world." She slid down - immobile, numb.

He poked futilely. Finally defeated, flopping back, swollen aching, he stared at window-lit dust motes in frenzied oscillations.

She said, "I *will* tell you the secret. Mister Larson played wiggler with me *first*. He did this." She spit on her palm. "To get in. He gave me a whole silver dollar."

Again, Billy was over her, penetrating blindly, eyes dazzled by sunlight. Then he was thrusting in a dance of pleasure, sweet as mouthfuls of honey. Far away, he heard his voice calling, "Susie, Susie ... silver and gold;" and there was a shuddering in which honey became melting fire.

Someone was talking. "Do I get the skirt, Billy?"

"Two skirts," he murmured. "Or three."

SEPTEMBER 23, 1875   6:46 AM   THURSDAY

Only in retrospect do events gain inevitability, which may have been real: history's web over eons, but hidden. On that day, there was an approaching storm.

Alone in her classroom with Billy, before her class, Mary Richards felt uneasy, as, seated behind the first row table, he was answering her question with characteristic precision, but was somehow different. He said, "When you came on September fourteenth last year, I'd been in real school eight months and nine days. And it's been another year and nine days to today. So my schooling - except from my Ma - has been for one year, eight months, and eighteen days."

"Your mind is a pleasure, Henry Antrim." Her emotion, Mary Richards realized, was shyness. Recently, his gaze was disconcertingly penetrating. Gambling and darker activities were rumored. She ventured, "I have been meaning to ask: How do you get money?"

Mischievously, he held up palms. "Blood." His eyes gleamed with the sexuality she had resisted. "Bottom's City Meat. Just before here. And I still work at Richard Knight's slaughter house."

She sighed, and addressed him as the innocent child she preferred. "I brought you a surprise today."

Approaching him with a small, crimson, leather bound-book, she did not notice his small nostrils dilating sensuously for her violet perfume. She laid it open.

Written on the first page was, *To Mary Richards. Alfred Lord Tennyson.*" She turned pages. "This is real literature, Henry. It is the 'Charge of the Light Brigade.'"

She read, " 'Forward the Light Brigade! / Charge for the guns!' he said. / Into the valley of Death / Rode the six hundred." Finishing, she impulsively gifted him the book.

As she returned to her desk, he said, "Miss Richards, before we stop, I want to ask a Bible question. What happened to Isaac after his father said he'd kill him?" She answered that God accepted the sacrifice of a ram instead. Billy asked, "Why'd God do all that?"

She said, "To test faith. Isaac lay willingly on the altar. He believed - like his father, Abraham - that we can trust the ways of God; though they can be frightening and mysterious."

"So Isaac didn't die?" Not then, she said.

Later, when Billy was passing the Orleans Saloon, Joe Dyer angrily motioned him in. "Yer gaddamn brother hasn' paid fer 'is table in months." Flapping aside his left jacket panel, he revealed a shoulder holster with butt-forward revolver over his satin brocade vest. "Tell 'im, if he don' bring the money right now, I'll kill 'im."

In the warehouse, Billy knocked on his brother's door, and heard, from within, a disgruntled female voice. Then, naked before him, was his bleary-eyed brother. Explaining the threat, Billy entered to an important odor of rut. On the bed was a fat naked woman, glowing in gloom. Josie mumbled, "I go' bizess, Emma;" and said to Billy, " 'Member thiz: never mix opium an' alchol."

Josie stumbled back to Emma, kneeling between her massive legs, her huge breasts lolling to her armpits. Josie slurred to Billy, "Insi' my travelin' bag's my money belt. Take a tweny to Dyer."

Billy found the coin, then watched transfixed.

The woman said, "You ain't worth a damn, Antrim." Attempting to remedy himself, Josie shouted Billy out.

Billy found the owner, and said, "Josie will pay the rest tomorrow and apologizes for the inconvenience. How much is Emma?" Joe Dyer was amused. Dollar, he said.

When Billy returned, his brother, in pants, said to him, "I'm leavin'. Takin' the stage te Globe. Pass's Clifton. Mi' vist tha' basard, Anrim, there." Billy helped Josie finish dressing. The back door led to an alley. They would never see each other again.

To Emma, Billy said, "I'm Josie's brother." With tangled hair and a missing tooth, she chuckled and said, "Still in the family;" as he put one of his three silver dollars on the table and hurriedly undressed. She said, "You're shur little." Reflexively came self-promotion: "Don' matter what you've had afore; you ain't never had Big Emma."

Into her flaccid bulk arm thighed embrace, he nestled on velvet flesh, and mounded her breasts to tentative sucking. She whispered, "Still a boy, Darlin';" stroking his back's lordotic curve, molding his urgency into her plenty.

Starving, discovering starvation, he became a bow suspended from sustenance to receptive depths. He heard, within sweat-drenched desperation, "Yes, you want Emma." He heard, "Yes, boy. All for you, boy," and was freed to ferocious newly-born desire, within pleasure everywhere, before disappearing hot oblivion.

Pillowed on her, Billy opened his eyes. Gap-toothed, she smiled. "You was good, boy. You with your blue eyes. Many a gal 'ill soon 'nough 'member you. Hey, now! Ready for more? Get on, now!" She was laughing. "Never gonna forget Big Emma, 're you?"

The Orlean Saloon's front door opened into last bright light before the storm. Half the sky was dark. Against it, rose Chihuahua Hill, illuminated like an enchanted kingdom.

At the Derbyshire Furniture Store and News Depot, Billy fingered his vest pocket with the two remaining silver dollars, and went to the dime novels. Matt Derbyshire called, "Got in stuff from Mesilla, from the late sixties." *DeWitt's Ten Cent Romance* announced, "Wild Bill's First Trail. As He Told It, by Colonel Christopher Forrest."

Lost reading it, Billy heard his name spoken loudly. Looming was Sheriff Harvey Whitehill.

A warrant was shown. "You're under arrest for the September fourth theft from Charlie Sun and Sam Chung." The store's door opened in brief promise of freedom, terminated by a bruising grip on his shoulder, as fat Matt Derbyshire rushed out.

Harvey Whitehill said, "We're heading to jail. Give me trouble, and I'll shoot you. You're the goddamn bad seed in this town."

Derbyshire's excited running resounded over bridging creek boards to Bailey's Apothecary and Post Office. "Doc," he puffed, "Whitehill just arrested the Antrim kid. The little one. For that Sun and Chung laundry stealing." Customers listened eagerly. Bailey told his messenger boy to get the *Mining Life* newspaperman.

On Main Street, Billy assessing the flowing ditch for vaulting, was directed away, rightward onto Broadway, to arrive at Hudson; then led northward. The curious and familiar waited, watching at the brick, cast-iron trimmed, J. B. Bennett Mercantile Store.

Sheriff Harvey Whitehill said, "You deserve this disgrace, Henry." A procession of two, they diverted wagon and horse traffic. Ignoring Whitehill, Billy, head high, strode in swelling exultation of outlawry and injustice; or of a prince walking crimson carpet to his coronation.

They passed Richard Knight's Butcher Shop on the southeast corner of Hudson and Yankie, as mounted Owen Scott bounced to them at a trot. He leaned over, saddle leather creaking, warming the sheriff to attention of penciled notes.

Whitehill said, "Here's how I nabbed him. He gave stolen property to Missus Brown's daughter. So Missus Brown searched his room. Found more in his trunk. Said she was upholding her reputation." Scott commented that she needed more props than that.

"Look, Owen, you're new. This here's a mining town. I was elected 'cause I know citizens' priorities. Back to this kid. There was a second thief: an unemployed stone mason with alias Sombrero Jack. He got away with the other half of the goods. But this one will be cooling his heels in jail till his Grand Jury trial."

Owen Scott nervously checked the ominous sky, and asked when the Grand Jury met, and what was the maximum sentence. Whitehill said, "District Court's December thirteenth. With robbery and burglary - and with my testimony about his past offences - he'll probably get the maximum: ten years hard labor; and thirty-nine stripes to his bare back." The newspaperman questioned exceptions for kids. Billy listened.

"Tried as an adult. We've got the Kearny Code in this Territory, from forty-eight when General Stephen Kearny captured Santa Fe in our Mexican War. Ten years - *if* he survives the whipping."

Arriving at Hudson Street's old jail, Billy assessed it with frantic care. Cracked old mud-stucco exposed its adobe bricks. From its flat roof, protruded a brick chimney, whose big, cinder-guard, top tile, elevated by vertical bricks, was broken. Only half remained.

First drops struck. The storm had arrived.

Billy and Sheriff Harvey Whitehill entered a room with a barred, high window. To their right, was a rounded adobe fireplace. Billy heard tiny beating, like a miniature heart, and realized rain was falling through the chimney. A table and chair stood on packed earth.

Whitehill said, "Orville Ainsworth's the jailer. Should be here soon. Head there." He pointed to a doorway.

Through it, the space was transected by a barrier of flat vertical bars making a cell. Windowless, it cramped only a cot and chamber pot. When inside, Billy asked about food. "Orville takes care of that. Damn. Forgot to search you."

Whitehill found the small red book. "Says 'To Mary Richards.' You're the worst, Henry. I'll give it back to her. Know what the law's for? Crushing troublemakers."

Outside the bars, Harvey Whitehill lit a cigarette, then looked in, expecting fear. Instead, the boy's lip was raised in a snarl. And his eyes glared with such inhuman savagery that Whitehill turned away, hairs rising at the back of his neck as rain pounded.

They heard the outside door open. An elderly man, in dripping hat and tarpaulin coat, limped in. Whitehill said, "He's all yours, Orville." Ainsworth responded that the prisoner was just a child. Whitehill said, "Know about the kitten?" The oldster shook his head. "Just as well," Whitehill said, and walked out.

Ainsworth said, "Mighty col' in here, boy. Wan' me to light a fire?"

"No. Feels just fine," said Billy. He already had an escape plan.

SEPTEMBER 25, 1875   4:09 PM   SATURDAY

Waiting at the cage-like wall, Billy heard two talking men, and readied himself. "Another murder at the Bedrock Saloon." Approaching, Harvey Whitehill called back, "We'll get supper there, Orville. I've got to finish my report with the owner: Milby."

Billy, contritely mimicking reform, asked the sheriff for the time; then announced pathetically, "That's almost fifty hours without exercise. Couldn't I walk around inside?"

"Okay. But we'll be back in an hour. Enough time for exercise."

Billy pointed to the chamber pot, taking small revenge. "Hell. Orville didn't do that? Hand it over. Public never knows what a man stoops to for a public office."

When they were gone, Billy thrust the front room's chair below the window, and, standing on it, pulled its immobile bars.

Next, he ran to the fireplace, kneeling and peering in. Far above, was a blue radiant triangle: sky constricted by the broken tile. Grimed mud-cementing oozed sharp-toothed between bricks.

Removing the grate, Billy crawled in. Shoulders made upward passage impossible. Out again, he scanned the room futilely. The only possibility was the chimney. Hurriedly, to conceal activity, he left jacket and grate under his cot.

Inside the fireplace again, he lifted his arms. Shoulders became even wider. Then began desperate transformation. It was the moment of the fox, the wolf, the coyote, the badger; when the steel trap that holds the leg leaves only one possibility for freedom; and that possibility is accepted. It is the moment when it becomes necessary to tear off, to chew through, to crack apart your flesh. And one can do this, because freedom is more important than a limb, and more important than the possibility of death.

The creature now knew that the arms must be crossed over the chest so tightly that the bent elbows overlapped and the hands reached to opposite sides. The young animal scuttled so that its spine pressed deep into one angle of bricks.

A rhythm began as feet and hands synchronized, extruding upward the body oblivious to tearing by the cruel canal. In darkness, erupted ejaculations of strain, urgency, growling rage, and coughing from noxious inhalation.

Vague outlines of bricks appeared, dripping mortar in downward shadows, while above was pure light. One hand slammed off the broken cinder-guard tile; and light blew against wetness of hair and face of a panting boy, streaked with soot.

Then, extruded was the body, whose feet found chimney edges. Crouching, the boy assessed the wind. Then he stood.

Arms in tattered bloodied sleeves, extended like wings, with palms catching last sun heat; and honey hair danced in the wind.

High over him circled band-tail pigeons. Billy shouted, "Joy of the birds! Joy! Joy! Joy!" - before leaping onto the flat roof, and into cold shadows and remembrance of danger.

He peered down to the rear alley. The jail's viga beams protruded. From one he hung, then dropped. Escape. But where?

A sombreroed, seraped peddler led a firewood-laden donkey. A filthy boy called to him in Spanish: he wanted to buy his clothes. The peddler said irately, "You are loco!" Billy held out a silver dollar, noticing his bleeding strips instead of nails. Grinning, the man said, "Now I am sure you are loco." Billy added a bundle of wood to the bargain, and to his disguise.

A woman at the back door of the Exchange Hotel rebuffed a Mexican boy trying to sell Clara Truesdell firewood. To her unresponsive scorn, the boy added urgently that he also carried a message from someone important. She hastily left for the woman.

At Clara Truesdell's heavy step, Billy put down the firewood and hung the sombrero. First declaring innocence, he casually mentioned his escape.

Reflexively, the woman asked if there was a reward; then felt shame. Pleading child-eyes stared at her from blackened face. He said, "You're my only hope, Missus Truesdell. Like you helped Ma."

"Well, take off that filthy blanket. It probably has lice. Gracious, your clothes are ruined. What to do? Gideon's in Chloride Flat. He can't admit mining's not for him. Not like your step-father."

Billy said he was in Clifton. "Then that's where you've got to go till Harvey Whitehill realizes his mistake. The stage to there and Globe stops right here. Eight in the morning. Tonight you can sleep with Chauncey."

Leading Billy to the family rooms, she called, "Chauncey!" and said, "Play with Chauncey while I make you a bath."

Chauncey entered, slumping in a chair, apathetically depressed. Billy hunkered down. From his ripped vest, he held up the opalescent shooter marble. "Magic moon," he said, like a grown-up. "It's yours now;" and watched it lessen distress he alone understood.

To Clara Truesdell's call, Billy entered a room with steaming metal tub. As he bathed unashamed, she washed his pants in a sink, and said, "I simply have none to fit you. These will dry fast on the stove's towel rack. The oven's still hot."

Meaningfully, Billy asked if supper was over. "Oh, yes," she said obliviously. "How did your clothes get so torn up? They didn't torture you like a criminal, did they?" He shook his head. The water was pink from his burning cuts. "Let's see. There's that shirt that's too big for Chauncey. And his old cap. You'll have to make do with a vest and jacket of Gideon's. Moth holes shouldn't matter."

After Billy dressed, he located her in the bedroom. "I sure appreciate all this," he said. "Especially the vest. For my money." He displayed his last coin.

"Oh, how your mother would weep," Clara Truesdell said. "A fugitive orphan with only one dollar to his name."

"No. Ma'd be laughing. I'm free."

"Henry, you are the strangest boy. But I'll give you this." From a bureau, she took a coin purse. "All I can spare is coach fare."

Maintaining wide-eyed innocence, Billy asked if her husband had an old deck of cards. She clumped out and returned.

He wanted only three.

Clara Truesdell said, "Finally, I understand you, Henry. You're a sentimental boy." His eyes slit with that irony as he pocketed two queens and an ace of spades.

SEPTEMBER 26, 1875   7:52 AM   SUNDAY

In chaotic delirium, Billy, fully clothed in bed, and prepared for escape either to stagecoach or from Harvey Whitehill, had spent the night beside sleeping moaning Chauncey, still fisting the moon marble. Images of "the adversary," now Whitehill, coalesced from bedroom shadows: in his jail, shot, falling; on Hudson Street, shot, falling; at the bedroom door, shot, falling. In transitory dreaming, Sombrero Jack winked and said "Equalizing;" or Josie repeated "God gave us Americer," amidst Big Emma's sweet surfeit; while he and William Antrim, laughing together, both fired revolvers at nebulous attackers, until the moon marble rose gigantic and lit the room.

Billy lurched upright into daylight and distant sounds of the stagecoach. The running out - the most dangerous moment - and the leaving of Silver City with ghosts of the familiar - each implicit with fear or sadness - caused neither. There was only urgency. He raced, in full view, as the vehicle approached.

The driver opened its red lacquered door, like an exotically chitinous beetle wing, to three rows of tufted leather benches. Billy slid onto the middle backless option, avoiding the windowed sides; and faced two men in the rear, the front seat being cluttered with boxes. The boot and top rack were likewise filled.

Swaying, the carriage started, its four horse team soon trotting; its ox hide slings absorbing jolting, yellow, iron-clad wheels pounding jubilantly: "Escape! Escape! Escape!"

One passenger, portly and rubicund, in velvet-collared frock coat, balanced a shoeless foot on a pillow. "Gout, son," he said to Billy's curious gaze. "Miner's son? Heading to Globe?"

"Clifton," said Billy.

Nervously, the other man - thin, with limp-crotched plaid trousers - said, "I worry about highwaymen. I wonder if we have a payroll strongbox for Arizona Territory? That huge Hooker cattle ranch is in the Sulphur Springs Valley." Billy noted those places.

The fat man said jovially, "And *I* was wondering about those meat pies." Soon, skinny fingers and greedy sausage-like ones unwrapped fragrance of spices and meat.

Billy's stomach gurgled hungrily, empty since the day before in the jail. His eyes closed in escaping dream. Clara Truesdell, carrying his mother's sickroom tray heaped with meat pies, was saying, "You'll need this." But as he followed, ahead was the circus cage with the little black bear. Billy reached, but out through bars, himself inside with his back wedged into a corner. Into wakefulness he escaped.

Outside was freedom. The town had disappeared. The heavy man was saying, "That's 'the Frontier.' When were you born, son?" Billy answered. "Well, at eighteen fifty-nine, yours will be the 'Frontier Generation.' Sounds good for marketing or politics: my bailiwicks."

Pedantically, the thin man said, wire spectacle-supports pressing greenish hair, "I myself am a naturalist from Harvard College, here to collect that Frontier's specimens - as curiosities - since their extinction as less fit creatures is inevitable with man's superior advances. They're in these boxes."

"Impressive," the fat man said insincerely. "Me, I'm here to get land for the Atchison, Topeka, and Santa Fe Railroad. In Santa Fe, I met with an old Missouri compatriot for that: Thomas Benton Catron. He's the big boss in New Mexico. He went into a law partnership, in sixty-six, with another Missourian: Stephen B. Elkins.

"That B is for 'Benton' also. We Missourians honor our native son: Senator Thomas Hart Benton. He kept up the Frontier business started in eighteen-o-three by Jefferson's Louisiana Purchase of our land from the Mississippi River to the Rockies."

Billy looked, from the man's jiggling adipose-stuffed jowls, outside to racing clouds. Pungent sagebrush scent penetrated the coach, along with shrill sentry cries of prairie dogs challenging, from miles of their mounds, the coach's noisy alien atrocity. A roadrunner, mostly tail, flashed through red-barked mesquite bushes, which penetrated downward hundred foot, thirsty roots. High cholla cactuses snaked acres of thorn-bristling thin trunks; some, dead and fleshless like honey-combed woodwind instruments. Occasional yuccas - huge, lethally spiked rosettes - still supported summer's single stalk, tall as a sapling; and grew in soil whose microorganisms, in one shovelful, were more numerous than the one billion humans on the planet.

"Yes," said the fat man. "Thomas Hart Benton. Our Senator in the forties. Heard that call for what that newspaperman, John O'Sullivan, called our Manifest Destiny: getting our continent. When Benton's daughter married that trapper, John C. Frémont, Benton got him government funding for exploring. His guide was Kit Carson." That name caught Billy's interest.

"Of course, it was really reconnaissance on all that Mexican land. Remember, Mexico'd gotten independence from Spain by twenty-one; and their Republic included Texas and what's now *our* Territories of New Mexico, Arizona, and Colorado; as well as California, Utah, and Nevada. Those Mexicans did us a favor by fighting Spain for it. We just had to fight that fool Santa Anna in the Mexican War to get what was rightfully ours.

"What a deal! In forty-eight, with that Treaty of Guadalupe Hidalgo, we got half their country and fixing the boundary of Texas.

For fifteen million dollars and cancellation of debts, we got five hundred twenty-five thousand square miles!

"One problem: that damn Treaty let the Mexicans, already here, keep their land. Some of it was huge tracts: prior land grants from Spain, then Mexico. Listen to how smart Tom Catron and Steve Elkins are. Tom explained it to me.

"They set up their law practice to get that grant land *themselves*. They do it by representing the Mexican owners. The owners have to prove title to the U.S. government. After that, Catron and Elkins buy it from the fools, at a pittance, and resell at massive profit.

"Biggest money comes from railroad investments. Like I let Tom Catron know, our Atchison, Topeka, and Santa Fe has its eye on the Old Santa Fe Trail going over the Raton Pass at the northern border of this Territory. That land's part of the two million acre Maxwell Land Grant. Catron and Elkins already got control of it from its fool owner.

"Fact is," the fat man chuckled, "Tom Catron and Steve Elkins made so much money on that deal, that it started their control of New Mexico Territory. Tom joked that they're called the Santa Fe Ring. So I say the Frontier's just one big piece of real estate."

The fat man adjusted his pillowed foot, swollen with gluttony. "Son, as the new generation, what's the Frontier to you?"

"Freedom, Sir."

"Way station stop!" called out the driver.

The three passengers stepped out into dense silence. Billy walked toward a distant couple with pack donkey and cook fire. "Watch out, son," called the fat man. "Mexicans can be rough." Billy ignored him.

At the young couple with an infant, in Spanish, Billy asked to pay for food. The woman also offered goat milk. Billy smiled. "Of all food, I hate only milk. Is this Arizona Territory?" The man nodded. Billy asked, gathering information, "You are from this area?" Pueblo Viejo, the man said. More to the west and farther south. On the Gila River. Billy asked about the Hooker Ranch, and learned that it was the biggest. It was southwest of Bonita, a town just south of the big fort, Fort Grant, at the foothills of the Pinaleño Mountains.

Back in the coach, the fat man called Billy lucky. They had a day's ride to Globe; he was only an hour and a half from Clifton.

Exaggerating bashfulness, Billy responded, "I've got a little game for spending time: guessing one of three cards." The Harvard man said statistically that was no challenge. Billy answered, "Must be why people make bets: to make it more fun."

"Clifton!" the driver finally shouted. The fat man said, "I did find that ace once. That fun *was* worth my ten dollars." Not worth his twenty, the other said acidly.

In twilight silhouetting towering monolithic rocks and ridged terrain, Billy stepped onto the primary street of Clifton's make-shift town; built for silver, hope of gold, and recent discovery of copper.

A miner, eyes haunted by quest, directed Billy to William Antrim's place. Climbing a winding path and irrationally excited about seeing his step-father, Billy saw the unlit shack. He knocked.

"Open it yerself," he heard. In near darkness, a stringy-haired man smoked at a table. Getting permission to wait, Billy sat.

The man went to his disheveled pallet. Across the room was another, neatly made. Lifting a miner's pick and a file, the man said, "Damn points break off;" returning to rasp the metal. His cigarette smoke swirled with the swinging opening door.

"Hello, Cappy," said William Antrim, not noticing Billy.

As Antrim lit an oil lamp, Billy stood, removing cap, saying hello, and smiling, tentatively filial. His bearded stepfather stared ambiguously.

Cappy said, "Picks ain' worth a piss in a pot." Antrim answered that he should buy another. "Buy this, buy tha', ye say. Ye'd think we'd foun' the Comstock Load. 'Cept ye wan' me te do the buyin'. I'm goin' te Millbrook's. 'E's got 'im extrees."

Antrim said, "He's down at Gordon's Saloon. I just saw him."

After the door closed, Antrim took newsprint from a pocket, and read aloud: "**Henry Antrim, a Silver City resident, who was arrested on Thursday and committed to jail to await the action of the Grand Jury upon the charge of stealing clothes, blankets, and revolvers from Chinamen Charlie Sun and Sam Chung, escaped from prison yesterday through the chimney. His accomplice was 'Sombrero Jack,' whose whereabouts are unknown.**"

Antrim said, "Somebody left today's copy of *Mining Life* at Gordon's. When I get back, I want you out of Clifton." At the door, Antrim said, "Next, I want to read that you're hanged."

Billy, utterly alone in the world, and staring blankly at a spider spinning her web at a window frame, suddenly shuddered at slippage in his fractured psyche. Enraged, he sprang up. *His* gun was somewhere. The ransacked dresser yielded it.

Thrust fiercely leftward into his waistband, it mimicked Joe Dyer's butt-forward pistol. That was not enough. Grief was seeping through, bringing lost mother wrapped, on that last dancing day, in comforting wool. The Irish cardigan sweater was located. Billy put it on.

Descending, he saw Gordon's Saloon below, washing light onto its hitching post. Close water-flow, he guessed to be the Gila River, on which was distant Pueblo Viejo. At cottonwoods, whose autumnal leaves flapped like pale moths in cold night wind, Billy lurked as a man rode up. To Stanley Gordon, welcoming him as he entered, the man said, "Picking up assay samples. Glad they gave me this fast horse. Need him to make good time back to Mesilla."

Briefly, that horse's shadow thickened, then glided along the ground at the windowless side wall of the saloon. A distant coyote howled. Another joined. A night song began. Billy shortened the stirrups and mounted. Soon, galloping, he worried that the gun might jar loose, and pulled open its gate as a hook.

Hours passed as Billy ignorantly stopped repeatedly to water and rest the horse. At the little town of Pueblo Viejo, outside an adobe, he tied the animal at a hitching post. A man exited. Powerful-looking, he crossed his arms, pressing his jacket against the chill. A black mustache bristled to his wide jaw. In Spanish, Billy asked for food.

The man responded, "Someone came earlier. Riding rapidly to catch a horse thief." Billy sidled toward his knotted reins. There was a grim laugh. "You think Ramón Gómez is a fool? You escape as slowly as you ride."

Two youths emerged from behind a shed. One said, "Ramón, shoot him already, and take the horse. Like the cursed gringos just did to Juan Mejilla."

Billy exclaimed with anguish, "Not Juan Mejilla from Chihuahua Hill?"

The other youth said bitterly, "A gringo stole a cow. But its owner killed Juan."

"The Mejillas are our cousins," Gómez said. "Juan talked of a gringo boy who speaks perfect Spanish. Carlos, Joaquín, peace. We will give him another horse."

One that would not go lame, Billy said. Ramón Gómez smiled at the audacity. "Horses have no guarantee. But your horse has one: hanging." Billy asked what he would do with him.

"There is a Jessie Evans - not a friend, but necessary for my business. From Nuevo Mehico. He makes horses disappear." Billy asked if Evans worked only in that Territory. Again, Gómez was amused. "Yes," he said.

After the youths left, Gómez said to Billy, "Watch. It seems you will require this in the future." He retied the reins in a slip knot. Billy replicated it at first try. The man's teeth showed in a smile.

On the way to the corral, Billy asked Ramón Gómez how far it was to Bonita, and then to Hooker's Ranch. "Over forty miles. A trail follows south along the San Simon River, then joins a military road that circles the Pinaleño Mountains at their eastern side, and goes west to the town. Then, across the Sulphur Spring Valley, the ranch is maybe eight miles."

Billy asked about Globe and saloons. "Eighty miles. But for saloons you need only Bonita. You need drink?" Billy said someone he knew might be there. The catch in his voice went unnoticed.

They looked at the dark horse forms. Ramón Gómez asked, "Will it matter if that brown gelding bucks?" Billy shook his head. "His name is Delgado. Slim like you." Saddling the barely-tame mustang, Gómez said, "I think we both did well tonight."

"I agree. You got the better horse. I got rid of him." The man laughed.

An hour later, at the San Simon riverbank, under cottonwoods filtering crescent moonglow, with a blanket from Ramón Gómez, and propped against the saddle, in the alluring outlaw aura of Jessie Evans, who was part of his rescue, Billy camped; escape now real.

Total aloneness must be freedom, not orphaning; sniffling tears must be joy, not sadness. He remembered the gun.

With the avidness of a lover reunited with his beloved, Billy withdrew from his waistband the Colt, all weight and dull gleaming. He caressed. Under its barrel ran the ejector tube, tense with a spring-loaded rod. Half-cocking the hammer to free the cylinder for spin, Billy opened its gate.

And, with a lover's possessive confidence, he repeatedly pulled back the flat head of the ejector rod to poke out each cartridge. William Antrim had loaded five, with customary caution of leaving empty the chamber at the hammer.

Closing the gate, Billy fully cocked the hammer, to touch its sharp firing pin. When it struck a tiny cap at a cartridge's base, a flare would burst to the interior through a pin-hole, igniting the black gunpowder, whose tremendous pressure in the casing would shoot out the bullet. Billy pressed the trigger. Hammer struck only air; but he had fired his gun for the first time.

Finally, Billy lay back, pushing gunbarrel under waistband. But wanting more, he slipped the hard shaft against belly skin. Through branches, stars became far-away explosions into sleep as filled with latent violence as was the weapon and himself.

SEPTEMBER 27, 1875   7:25 AM   MONDAY

Waking to bird calls and river slappings, Billy had found himself hilariously covered by orange-gold cottonwood leaves. With almost forgotten playfulness, he had kicked his blanket, releasing them to wind-blown freedom like his own.

Now he and Delgado were tracing the map of Jessie Evans's associate, Ramón Gómez, under a sky dome where gray clouds curtained diaphanous rain, too far away to arrive. Into the two thousand square mile Sulfur Springs basin, Billy and his horse descended, horizon purple-fringed by the Dos Cabezas and the Dragoon Mountains to the south and the northward Galiuros range. Wind rippled grama grass: cattle food rich with protein-laden seed heads, sinuous as calligraphic flourishes. Rounding the eastern end of the Pinaleño range, they progressed westward.

When the sun was overhead, distant congregated shapes, separated by his road, were man's. Soon, happily, Billy joined traffic of civilians and soldiers. To his right, the Pinaleño Mountains made a wall behind distant Fort Grant. Left, across the road, was the town of Bonita.

Bugling, signaling time and duty, and human calls, and wagon sounds were absorbed and muffled by that flat land, scudded by cloud shadows. Forty million year old Mount Graham, the highest peak embedded in the Pinaleños, brooded like a primeval god; possibly lamenting passing trumpet notes and lives, possibly mocking events not paced to lifetimes of stars.

Billy explored Bonita, turning onto its first side street. To his left, was a long adobe with false high-fronted façade, poignantly artificial in side view; but lettered as ELLIOT'S SALOON. Across was an unmarked adobe. That was all, as street disappeared into scrub.

From the main road, the next intersection was Fort Grant's right-angled thoroughfare, where a lone small building, a quarter mile up the chalky length to its distant entrance, was the only structure. A little sign with pointing arrow indicated HOTEL DE LUNA. Next, fronting his road to the left, was Bonita's general store, whose sign said McDOWELL'S. Beyond it, Billy turned left onto a lane with an adobe named ATKIN'S CANTINA. It faced a frame blacksmith shop with CAHILL painted on its side in blood-red.

Billy stopped at cookhouse aroma of Atkin's Cantina.

Inside, the bar was just a big long crate. Three men sat at a round table. One, bull-necked, huge armed, and with drooping black mustache, held forth in drunken loudness: "So I said, 'John Chisum, if you'd a used "Windy" Cahill's services ...' " He glanced at Billy, ordering food. "Chisum says, Windy, I could use a blacksmith like you on my big ol' ranch on the Pecos.' " Cahill appraised Billy, taking a seat; but shouted at the greasy-skinned proprietor, approaching him with a bottle, "Tom Varley, where you been so long?"

Cahill's tablemate corrected: "Wasn' Chisum, Windy. Was his trail boss, George Teague, on that drive."

Enraged, the big man leapt up bellowing, "You calling me a liar, Frank Simmons?" Finally placated, he deflected belligerence to Billy and asked, "New here?" Passing through, Billy said. Cahill responded, "Make it quick. I don't want no runts here."

"Windy," said the other man, "Frank an' me better get back to Hooker's. Oly so long ye kin be gettin' supplies."

Cahill laughed uproariously. "Frank Simmons an' Jack Coleman, you dogs. Getting supplies 'cross the street at Hog Ranch! Ask Windy to give the gals a breather first.

"Supplies!" he called after them, as he walked to Billy's table and said, "Remember this: I'm not crazy;" before leaving also.

Greasy-skinned Varley asked, from behind the bar, "Where you heading, kid?" Billy said Hooker Ranch. "Sorry 'bout Windy; we've learned to live with him. His name's Frank Cahill. Called Windy 'cause of his tall tales."

Billy next went to McDowell's. "Need help, boy?" quavered the old man behind the counter, finger joints like walnuts. Billy asked for twelve boxes of forty-five caliber cartridges. "My hearing ain't good. Two?" Billy repeated twelve loudly. "We ain't having no war," the old man joked. "That's six hundred rounds. Know that?" Billy said he did. "What?" the old man asked; but shuffled arthritically to his task, penetrating his penumbra of pain.

The onerous weight of each box gave his crippled retrieving fingers slow ritualistic ceremony. They stacked, rectangular tops having a yellow label, wood-blocked with a revolver picture, "CENTRAL FIRE METALLIC CARTRIDGES," ".45 cal.," "50," and "MANUFACTURED BY UNITED STATES CARTRIDGE COMPANY."

The old man squeezed his finger joints and said, "Jacob in the Bible, he had to wrastle an angel to prove something. Got some reeward. I got to wrastle this damn rheumeetism every day, and I get nothing." Distractedly staring at the bounty, Billy asked if Jacob was any relation to Isaac. "His kid," was the answer.

The man put pencil to receipt. Biting his lip for counterpain, he made jagged words and numerals, as if tiny lines were easier. He concluded, "Twelve dollars and eighty cents. Got that much?"

Billy handed the Harvard naturalist's twenty dollar gold piece. The old man raised his eyebrows, but began slow retrieval of change.

"Wait," Billy said. "I remembered: Gun oil - sperm oil if you have it - and a cleaning tool for a Colt forty-five. And something to unscrew its screws."

"Sure, kid. Colt makes a little L-shaped thing for screws. Where'd I last see it?"

"And a few days supply of jerky." Noticing a tall jar, Billy said, "Also, a stick of peppermint candy." He paused. "Make that two."

By late afternoon, Billy approached Hooker Ranch buildings. Cowboys, striding with equine grace, wore broad-brimmed hats, jackets, and pants stuffed into high boots. Some had red bandanas, flashing scarlet insolently against nature's implacable brown and green. One pointed Billy to the house of the foreman, William Whelan, who hired for the owner, Henry Clay Hooker.

Rangy William Whelan opened the door while appraising him. Billy's oversized cardigan sweater was over a shapeless plaid jacket; pants revealed his chimney-scraped high-laced shoes. From under a flat cap, hung unwashed hair. Billy said, "I'm looking for work. I can do anything."

In a wistful voice, Whelan answered, "Well, I'm needing hay baling. Seems to me you're not big enough. Still, I'll give you a try. You can bunk with the boys in that east building. Wages 're fifty cents a day. How old 're you?" Eighteen, Billy said; and Whelan suppressed a smile. "Ask for Frank Simmons. He'll show you where to go in the morning. He was in Bonita. Should be back by now." Billy thanked Whelan, confident he would succeed.

SEPTEMBER 30, 1875   6:27 AM   THURSDAY

Dejectedly, Billy ate beside Frank Simmons in the Hooker Ranch bunkhouse. The man said, "Don' take bein' fired hard, kid. The others hired was twice yer size. An' I 'preesated yer sayin' nothin' 'bout me an' Hog Ranch. Try other spreads fer daywork. Bu' not dresst like some country jake." There was no recognition. "Hayseed."

That afternoon, Billy reentered McDowell's store. The old man teased, "Need more amminition for your war, boy?" Billy grinned, saying he'd come for used clothes.

Soon his selections were on the countertop. "Let's see now," said the old man. "We got us boots, felt hat, wool pants, courdry jacket. Leave here what you got on, it'll be fifty cents credit." Billy asked about keeping the sweater. "Same. No call for 'em." Red bandanas were out of stock. Billy took a blue one, and was directed to a room to change.

Soon, visualizing Henry Clay Hooker's long-legged men, Billy walked out on sounding boot heels, into restless wind.

Turbulent wind also rattled windows two hundred eighty-two miles northeast of Bonita, in New Mexico Territory, in a large adobe ranch house where a small, weeping, middle-aged woman in black mourning sat with her friend on a serpentine-backed sofa. Nearby was the grieving woman's gristmill; and surrounding her ranch house was grazing land she controlled through water rights along the Hondo River. The comforter, resting a work-reddened hand on her shoulder, said, "My heart breaks for you, Ellen. If only I could ease the pain of Robert's death."

Ellen Casey, pinched face ashen with grief, answered, "Murder, Barbara, not death. Murder." A big comb unattractively protruded atop her head, anchoring a skimpy bun.

Ellen Casey's companion, of the same age, was lovely, with limpid, brown, compassion-filled eyes. Black hair, also fastened upward, was softened by a spray of forehead curls. She said, "I don't know what I'd do if Heiskel died. But I just can't believe Jimmy Dolan was behind it." Ellen Casey's thin lips tightened. "Though I know you do. I'm just trying to ease your suffering."

"I know, Barbara. You're everybody's dear 'Ma'am Jones': nurse to all our ills. But Robert told me there'd be risk. He spoke out against Murphy and Dolan that noon, August second. And, just two hours later, he was shot there in Lincoln; right after James Dolan's partner Lawrence Murphy lost the election. And you expect me to believe James Dolan wasn't behind it? And to believe that tramp, Willie Wilson, killed Robert for eight dollars owed in back wages?"

Barbara Jones persisted, "But how could Jimmy Dolan - who's helping us small ranchers at Seven Rivers - do something so bad? Why, he's even taking our side against that greedy John Chisum. And I've heard that him and Lawrence Murphy and a John Riley have got an important political connection in Santa Fe - a man named Catron. Murphy lost by a lot. Wouldn't that take more than a speech?"

"I tell you, it was revenge, Barbara. Robert said that Murphy and Dolan are part of something evil called the Santa Fe Ring." Ellen Casey pressed her handkerchief to her eyes. "Can you believe that monster, Wilson, ate at the Wortley Hotel with Robert, knowing he was going to kill him? Then, when Robert walked to a house east of it - someone told me it was the Mills's - Willie Wilson was hiding behind it. He shot Robert in the hip." She paused. "Since girlhood I've lived with this crippled hip. If only that was all. But Barbara," her voice rose, "then he shot Robert in the face - his dear, dear face. People took Robert to Steve Stanley's house and got a Fort Stanton doctor. By then I'd arrived. He died the next afternoon."

She almost screamed, "And, Barbara, no one at all tried to stop a man hunting down another man in Lincoln town."

Ma'am Jones was silent, going to the kitchen, saying she'd make food before she left. "You're a god-send," Ellen Casey said and sighed. "Dick Brewer - one of those homestead farmers near the Ruidoso River - is here grinding his corn. Please make extra for him."

Becoming embarrassed, she called, "No. I'm indulging in self pity. I got a message from Juan Patrón: that fine Mexican man from Lincoln. He might drop by. I have to provide for my guests."

She limped to a window. "Oh my, here's Juan's buggy." In the kitchen she said, "You do know that John Riley - Murphy's and Dolan's friend - shot Juan in the back three weeks ago. I'm positive they wanted to kill him for taking Robert's side. The jury called it self-defense only because they were scared of James Dolan."

Barbara Jones said, "To think that Juan would leave his sick-bed for a condolence call."

"Oh, Barbara, you refuse to see bad."

"I'm just saying that people want peace."

Outside, blond Dick Brewer, good-looking and with big awkward hands, helped Juan Patrón, limping with a cane and in a ready-made suit with cheap celluloid collar.

After they ate, Barbara Jones and Dick Brewer left, leaving Juan Patrón sipping coffee with Ellen Casey, again on the sofa. Suddenly she asked him, "Who was behind your shooting?"

With dark melancholy eyes, Juan Patrón gazed at her, mustache precisely rimming upper lip. "As you know, it was John Riley. Right now, that is all to say. The Lord spared me."

"Forgive me. You all did a miracle in the election. Robert died knowing it. That's my only comfort." Her sharp features became ugly. "But I want revenge." She hissed, "I pray for war against them all."

Superstitiously, Juan Patrón heard that as a curse, wanted to cross himself, but instead soon left.

Ellen Casey did not hear the outside door close. Abruptly, as if drawn by hatred's miasma, a short even-featured man, with wavy raven hair, barged in. He stopped so close to her that his extravagance of black, tailored frock coat and pants, and linen shirt with starched collar precisely splaying a thin black tie, totally filled her vision. Shocked, she sprang up. "How in God's name did *you* get in?"

"Juan Patrón kindly directed me," his courtly resonant voice droned hypnotically. From chalk-white face, sapphire-blue eyes, accentuated by black brows, stared penetratingly. "To pay my respects after that tragedy, that tragedy befalling Robert."

Struggling with rage and terror, she stammered, "If-if there's a God in Heaven, James Dolan, you'll get the punishment you deserve."

"I have heard rumors, Ellen - of course, I have heard rumors - that you blame me." He sighed histrionically. "I ask only to explain."

As if drained of will, she sank to the sofa. He drew a chair close. Again there was only his image. He said, "I want you to realize how often *I* think about God." His dark lips curled in a subtle smile. "And I admit to envy. Wishing that I could be ..." She anticipated "like," but heard only "Him." Dolan sighed. "And I swear before God, I had nothing, nothing to do with Willie Wilson."

"You are the Devil himself," she said.

The odd smile returned. Coaxingly, hypnotically, Dolan said, "You really do believe that, Ellen. Really believe ..." She felt faint, as if falling, while "in me, in me" seemed to echo before she roused; hearing: "I want you to know that I and my partner, Lawrence Murphy, will be there at Willie Wilson's gallows. And John Riley will stand right beside the executioner."

Dolan rose. She startled. Revealed, leaning against a wall, was a man with a gunbelt. Dolan turned. "Ellen and I were so absorbed, so absorbed, that we did not hear your entry. I must introduce you."

The young man, clean-shaven like Dolan, launched himself forward by his booted foot, which, raised, had been pressed against the wall; and enjoyed Ellen Casey's obvious fear. Jutting orbital ridges made his narrow eyes recede into expressionless shadow. He held a Stetson of finest beaver felting, his short-cropped hair making a pelt like an animal's. With muscular arms hanging away from his sides, his jacketed chest swung shoulder right, shoulder left, while he walked, full-crotched, with legs astraddle. He stopped at Dolan's side. "This is Jessie Evans," Dolan said and smiled pleasantly. "I hope to convince him to remain in Lincoln County."

When they were back in his buggy, James Dolan said, "Jessie, I sense your impatience. But rest assured, your day will come."

Jessie Evans listened with adulation that a vicious dog gives its master: aware of its own power, but accepting one higher.

And in the brilliant and insatiably restless mind of Dolan was such an unceasing fiery storm of rage and craving, it was as if he was cursed to contain all the lusts and depravities of humanity, without the balm of insanity's oblivion.

JUNE 4, 1876   8:00 AM   SUNDAY

Pots and a frying pan released appetizing aromas to fit and neat Miles Wood, savoring release from their responsibility, while watching busily efficient Henry Antrim cooking at the massive cast iron stove in the kitchen of his Hotel de Luna.

Wood said, "That stove's the most expensive thing I ever bought. Figured if the military let me be the only civilian on their road, it should be a show-place. What brought you to these parts, Henry?"

"A brother in Globe. But he'd moved on. I stayed."

A pompadour and luxuriant mustache compensated Miles Wood for the ugly squint in his left eye, which pulled inward, and was habitually concealed by a brush of his hand. Wood said, "I'm glad I hired you. It's hard to find trustworthy help - what with horse rustling from here to Globe becoming a problem this year. It's a temptation - what with forts from east to west: military horses.

"Know what I'd like some day? Sure, I like just being made Justice of the Peace. But what I'd really like is owning one of those big gambling hotels - like in Las Vegas, New Mexico Territory. Like Moore's Hotsprings Hotel there. Reminds me: I heard you've been seen gambling way up at Cedar Springs."

Billy glanced ingenuously. "That's a boy who looks like me: *Austin Antrim*." Wood tried to stare skeptically, diverting from his bad eye by asking about a book on a chair.

Billy said, "From McDowell's. *Ivanhoe*. Someone from England told me about Sir Walter Scott. She said he was good."

"She?" Wood asked slyly. "Speaking of gals, kid, I've heard you're the talk of the señoritas. Go to all their baile dances. Is that *you* or that other Antrim?"

Billy laughed. "Me."

Someone entered the dining-room, ending Miles Wood's risky interrogation. "Mornin'," Billy heard Wood say.

The man returned. "Ex-soldier out there. Kicked out of the Sixth Cavalry a few years ago - a shooting incident. After I serve him, I'm leaving. Take the night off. Go see that English gal!"

When alone and in charge, with coffee pot, Billy entered the dining-room to a pleasantly strong-featured man. He had a purple-red birthmark, spilling down his left temple into a short curly beard; and was dressed like a shabby cowboy.

As Billy poured coffee, brown eyes watched him merrily. The man said, "I'm in the market for a horse. In the corral, one caught my eye: a bay gelding with a white snip line across his muzzle and a hind white sock. Know who owns him?" Billy said it was his. "Well, seems we've got *identical* taste. Name's Mackie. John Mackie. I almost got myself an *identical* one at Fort San Carlos." Billy said he was for sale. "*That one* cost nothing. I know. They said *I* stole him. How 'bout us meeting at Elliott's at three? To talk about my business."

Billy blushed, need pricked by that warm familial intimacy. He laughed and said, "I'll be there. Call me Billy."

When Billy entered Elliott's false-fronted saloon, he was greeted by its fat big-nosed owner, Lou Elliott. John Mackie was not there.

At a table, Frank Simmons and Jack Coleman were with a third cowboy. Simmons called to Billy, "Wan' ye te meet our new man: "Gus Gildea." That youth, with black curls, boastfully fingered his red silk bandana. "Gus's quit John Chisum's outfit."

Windy Cahill entered, hitching up his pants. "Lou, you got some nice new neighbors," he said. " 'Specially that Mattie. I'll be back for

Mattie." Seeing Billy, he taunted, "Runts should be drowned. You keep crawling back. You ..."

Frank Simmons diverted, asking Cahill about his soldiering days. Passing Billy, the blacksmith purposely bumped him. "I've got good memories of Fort Crittenden," Cahill said. "Liked shooting Injuns."

From outside, a female voice called, Frank! Frank Cahill! He chuckled. "Mattie." Leaving, he repeated his assault, but Billy side-stepped; and Cahill stumbled against the bar, rattling contents. Cahill growled, "You're lucky today. Won't always be."

Still John Mackie still did not arrive. Billy went outside to check just as he approached at a hectic trot. Tying his mount, Mackie said contritely, "You probably gave up on me."

"Figured you'd come. Nice horse. That's your business? Horses?"

Mackie was relieved at the complacency. Lateness was high in his litany of self-deprecation. He said, "Right now, it's just saddles and blankets. Be interested?" Again he was relieved by immediate acceptance.

That evening, Billy rode toward the sinking sun, wary of witnesses, and with eyes darting excitedly. Cricket chirring began as he turned north onto Pinaleño Mountain foothills. There, mesquite concealed a cave. Near its plateau entrance, with hidden fire pit, he tethered his gelding, and gave him a nosebag of dried corn. Hand on satin-brushed shoulder, Billy savored preoccupied herbivorous grinding, before entering the cave's darkness.

An oil lamp lit. Re-emerging, Billy carried pre-cut firewood, and had the radiant expression of an acolyte entering ecstatic mysteries. He was there to create ammunition.

A grill covered fire pit flames. A tarpaulin was spread for a spilled bagful of cartridge cases; saved from clandestine target practice, rinsed of black powder residue, and rid of spent primer caps - pried out with a pick on his Winchester reloading tool. Then came a lit lantern, a sack, three boards, and a pot holding a coiled, half-inch wide, lead ribbon, which was put on the fire to melt.

From the sack, Billy took a brass bullet mold; a pliers-like, big-headed, Winchester reloading tool - gold-painted cast iron with duck-billed handles - and a one pound, square, keg of black gunpowder: potassium nitrate, charcoal, and sulphur.

A smaller bag yielded a stolen Hotel de Luna soup spoon, crimped for pouring, with handle insulated with wood; and two previously-modified cartridge cases. One, wire handled, was a tiny scoop; the second, a punch, its lip filed razor-sharp. Also there were pasteboard scraps; gauntleted gloves, forgotten by a Hotel customer; a broomstick sawed to a short dowel; and a little, round, brass canister whose red label said: "PRIMERS," "250", and "Winchester Repeating Arms."

At last, Billy could enter his real life: the world of the gun. His other was merely for survival. This, of obsessive passion, was a hero journey for himself alone.

Hunkered down, firelight in eyes, he spread open the reloading implement with its multi-task head. From one of its cavities, the unneeded depriming pick was removed. Into another of its holes, Billy slipped one shell after another, backside-up, to receive a primer cap, embedded in the center by a squeeze of the jaws.

Entirely absorbed, using the scoop, he next filled each primed shell with black powder. Then, twisting the punch, he cut pasteboard circles, pressing them on top of that gunpowder to make a protective wad for the bullet to be added.

From the cave, Billy brought out two pans of previously-molded lead bullets, standing on end in solidified bees' wax and sperm oil: a filling for those bullets' double circumferential grooves, called cannelures. When the bullets flew hot through the gun barrel, this embedded waxy mix would melt and flush out residues, enabling more shots before necessary cleaning.

These bullets from the pan were inserted into the gunpowder-filled casings for finishing by the reloading tool. Into its hollow nipple-like extension, each future cartridge was slipped nose first. Squeezing crimped each gold brass casing to its silver lead bullet.

After four hours, the completed ammunition, lifted as tenderly as wren's eggs, was gathered into a canvas bag.

Bullet-making for future use followed. Into the pot of now-melted lead, Billy added, for fluxing, two thumbnail-sized chunks of the wax-oil mixture; which burst into flame. The wood-handled spoon stirred and skimmed impurities off that moonlit surface circle.

The brass bullet mold had skinny, scissored handles and a head consisting of two blocks, each with half of a hollow bullet-form. When closed, a hole in one half-block received molten lead; and had a lid-like sprue cutter to slice off residue. Held with the gloves and heated in the fire, that bullet mold received spoon-ladled lead. Rapping with the dowel released each bullet from the mold for placement in the new tray of wax mixture.

When everything was re-hidden in the cave, manufacturing was complete. Deep in its bowels, scraped-away rubble revealed a board over a hole in which was a crate. Reverentially, a canvas-wrapped cartridge belt with thirty-five loops and an attached holster was withdrawn. Then came Antrim's meticulously cleaned and wrapped revolver. When cartridge-filled and holstered on that also cartridge-filled belt, the thrillingly heavy armament was strapped on.

On his bedroll, inside that lantern-lit cave, Billy slid out his Colt .45 to mark the ceiling with shadows violent, heroic, sexual, and secret, while singing: "The moon was shining brightly / Upon the battle plain; / The gentle breeze fann'd lightly / The features of the slain; / The guns had hushed their thunder, / The drum in silence lay, / When came the señorita, / The maid of Monterey."

JUNE 5, 1876   5:16 AM   MONDAY

Into lead-silver dawn, shot after shot rang out. With cartridge-filled pockets and full cartridge belt, Billy fired when crouching, fired when running, fired flopping belly down, fired dodging behind rocks, fired whirling, and fired with each hand; but always aiming at a target - some aerial, tossed upward; some waiting high or low. Then he was galloping and shooting, or hanging off his horse's side and shooting. And the mountains echoed with his shooting: practice for an unknown goal.

That same, explosive, impatient drive was in a naked man sitting moodily at a bed's edge, in a rooming house in Tarrant County, Texas, seven hundred and thirty-six miles southeast of the Pinaleño foothills.

A woman, also naked, in her own opinion not pretty, still in bed, cajoled, "You're sooo handsome." His black straight hair was sleek as his mustache. "Stay, Pat. Amy knows it's her Daddy's birthday." He said she was only two. "Old enough to celebrate," she teased.

"Patrick Floyd Garrett, when the Creator made you, he worked extra - like some high-priced sculptor." She crawled behind, lifting his unresponsive left hand, and cooed, "Wouldn't a gold band look pretty!"

He yawned. "I don't need some paper to say what we're doing anyway, Clarissa."

"*I* do. My friend, Katie, says I've got 'head tilt love.' One look up at the height of you, and there I am: head over heels in love."

"Seems you could love *me*, not my body - like some whore."

She lost control of anger. "You're mean. Like a little snapping poodle. You're the meanest man I've ever known."

"How many *have* you known?"

Tears made her look appealingly vulnerable. He lied, "I love you;" his gray eyes finally stimulated by his sado-masochistic game.

She reached. "Birthday surprise! I'll rub you."

It was too late. He knew he could not function. He said, "The word's 'caress.' You're being crude to keep me away." Sighing, she retreated. "Bitch," he rationalized, "trying to force me."

Both were unaware how fragile was his self-esteem; how easily he plummeted into depression; how even adoration leaked away, necessitating another sexual conquest or flaunting of his plantation origins. Bearing his father's entitlement and disordered biochemistry, he blamed others, not only for his pain - barely controlled by his alcoholism - but also for his acts. Worse, his perception of other people's emotions was impaired; he could mistake fear for rage. That was why he was dangerous. Unwittingly, he could attack in service of his malignant narcissism. And he had already killed.

He now blamed Clarissa for his crushing sense of failure. He said, "I'm twenty-six today and I can't enjoy it with you." In the next room, their baby wailed. Clarissa was unsuspecting that he had already made plans; not just for that day, but for the future.

Pat Garrett entered Mouton's Saloon, aware of customers' glances at his impressive height; and only slightly late for his birthday gathering, arranged by his new business partners: Willis Skelton Glenn, a Georgian three years older then himself; and Luther Duke, a thirty-two year old Kentuckian. Duke called to him, "The South regroups fohr attack."

Garrett smiled. They respected him. And they were ugly skimpy men. "Seen Briscoe?" Garrett asked. Skelton Glenn groused about taking him along. Proud of the boy's adulation, Garrett said, "Joe's followed me around Texas. He'll fit in fine."

That gawky, pasty, flat-nosed youth of nineteen soon rushed to them, piping girlishly, only to Garrett, "Sorry I'm late. I went to Mass;" and sat down next to him.

Garrett draped his arm over the boy's chairback and said, "Joe's a real practicing papist. Sister in a convent. Cross around his neck. Want a drink, kid?" Briscoe accepted ambivalently.

Willis Skelton Glenn said he'd finished the preliminaries. By October, they'd be off to Fort Griffin and the buffalo range. Garrett smiled. "Like any man, the sport that appeals to me. Damn big animals. And they're saying: 'Kill the buffalo, kill the Indians.'"

"Pat," asked Joe Briscoe, "did you fight in the Civil War?"

Garrett laughed. "How old do you think I am? It ended when I was turning fifteen. But listen to this, you all. I was born rich in Alabama. When my granddad, Patrick Floyd Jarvis, died in fifty-two, he even willed me a slave. By the time I was three, we had a big plantation in Louisiana. But the War lost us everything. The reason I ended up here in sixty-nine."

Luther Duke said he'd heard he'd killed a niggah. Evasively, Garrett answered, "Plenty uppity ones were wandering around after the War. Advantage to killing buffalos is: no Indian lovers."

All laughed except Joe Briscoe, who said, "I worry 'bout Injuns dying before they're saved."

Garrett sighed humorously. "Sounds worse than he is. He leaves me alone; and I'm an atheist."

"But did you kill a nigger, Pat?" Joe Briscoe asked.

"Some in Bowie County thought so last year when they arrested me. But it couldn't be proved." Garrett felt justified. A Negro, who should have been a slave, had demanded wages. Killing was revenge - revenge like his own father's shooting of that carpetbagger - revenge for the War's losses; revenge for what that nigger brought on himself. That was not murder.

Pat Garrett slapped Joe Briscoe's back, raising his shot glass to the bartender. He was happy. Four months to be rid of that woman and child forever; four months till hunting. A mosquito landed on the boy. Solicitously, Garrett killed it.

Near mosquito-infested Blackbear Creek, two hundred forty miles due north of Tarrant County, on a new reservation in Oklahoma Indian Territory scrubland, a gray-braided infirm Pawnee, draped with a military-issue blanket, despairingly heard their pestilential buzzing, as he walked, seeking a correct place, with his eight year old grandson.

He was recalling his native Nebraska and its beautiful wide river, called by Whites the Platt, and defiled - before his tribe was forcibly relocated to this place - by their trains along its north bank, snaking filthy black smoke, and carrying men shooting buffalo as sport from windows. And, over all that Pawnee land, they also killed the buffalo.

To the boy, he said, "In our homeland, I wore the scalp lock, stiff with buffalo fat. Its power went through my body."

"And me, Grandfather, will I have the scalp lock?"

"No. Those days are passed." Finally, he stopped at bare ground, exposing Mother Earth's body. On Her, he lay his long medicine bundle, and said, "Because my remaining days are few, I must teach you now; though the knowledge must enter your heart before age gives you its understanding."

The boy watched swollen-veined hands unknot buffalo hair rope and unroll wooly buffalo hide to reveal sacred contents.

As instructed, the child touched those gifts of the Great Spirit, Tirawa: lightening struck wood, colorful bird skins, a grizzly bear claw, pouches of tobacco, and smooth stones.

His grandfather spoke. "Sad times have come to our people. I prayed to my Spirit, the Grizzly, to understand why. He came to me in dream - tall as a tree, shining golden - and said, 'The battle of Darkness against Light will soon begin. A boy will be its Messenger.'

"Then I awoke, believing the boy is you. 'But what is this battle?' I wondered. I prayed to Tirawa to understand. And I understood. I will now teach you.

"Our people know that, before the Beginning, all beings slept deep in Mother Earth, in Darkness, until Buffalo Woman herself awoke. She saw Light through an open flap - like the flap on the earth lodges of our homeland. And she walked to the Light.

"As she passed sleeping people and sleeping animals, they too awoke. And they followed her. First to wake and to follow her were the buffalo. And she led all out from the dark underground into the light of our homeland. There, she promised the people and the buffalo that they would be always be together."

The boy interrupted that no buffalo were at this reservation.

"I understood that as the sign of the battle to come. I understood that Darkness also followed Buffalo Woman out, hoping to bring all beings back to himself. But Darkness had no power until the white men became his ally by beginning their hunt with the buffalo."

The child said that meant white men were bad. "Not bad. Blind. They cannot see the Light that awoke Buffalo Woman. The Light is knowledge that all is aware; all is sacred. Can you blame a blind man if he walks on his new corn and crushes the seedlings? He will starve himself. The white man was tricked by Darkness, because he was blind.

"And he is deaf. The white man cannot hear the frightened voices of the rivers, the trees, and all living beings. Can you blame a deaf man if he cannot hear his children screaming when his train will run over them? He will grieve when they are dead; but it will be too late. The white man was tricked by Darkness, because he was deaf.

"But who will win: Light or Darkness?" asked the child.

"If the hunger of his starving spirit comes to him, if the guilt of his killings comes to him, the white man will fight the Darkness. Then Light will win.

"As the Messenger, you will speak for the buffalos, who are the sacred sign of Light and life. At your birth, did I not dream that your Spirit and the Spirit of the Great Buffalo were one - so if one died, so would the other?"

The child said he was afraid, surprising his grandfather by comprehension, because death's possibility for the Messenger, who would fight that war with Darkness, had been hardest for him to utter and to accept. The old man said, "We are Pawnee. We have courage when we need it.

"Now, I will show you how to wrap the sacred bundle. Soon it will be yours." The old man heard distant notes of white man's music, but decided it was imagination.

Billy rode into melancholy harmonica notes filling hot dry air, eight hundred and eleven miles southwest of the Pawnee reservation, and spilling from John Mackie's Pinaleño foothill shack. Hitching his horse, Billy sang along, "Oh, who but Lady Greensleeves?"

Inside, John Mackie bemoaned missing Fort Grant's 6th Cavalry, missing bugling. He had played in their band.

Billy asked about the shooting Miles Wood had mentioned. Mackie, sighing, said, "Another injustice." The harmonica notes had entangled lost love with the name "Hartman."

Billy noticed a wooden saddle frame, and asked why he had stolen it. Mackie smiled. "An early Collins Brothers' saddle. I'm studying it. Before I enlisted, I almost apprenticed with a saddle maker: Sam Stagg. A genius. I didn't do it. So now I'm just a saddle stealer."

"Mackie, why don't you take the horse too?"

The port-wine stain engorged as he stammered about hanging, about being afraid to die. With adolescent admiration, Billy said, "You're real brave, Mackie."

The man re-directed that praise, saying, "Knowledge helps you steal better. Take this saddle tree: perfect. A saddle's not just for the rider. It has to keep weight off the horse's backbone, shoulder blades, and withers. Here's how you check the fit."

Billy said, "I enjoy learning this learning. If you're on the run, your saddle's as important as your Colt ... uh, *if* you had one. Are the cinch rings where you attach a Winchester carbine scabbard?"

"Yes. You really think a lot about guns." The boy's dark brows rose innocently.

By nightfall, having ridden into Bonita bareback, Billy and John Mackie were outside Hog Ranch. Soon they departed fully saddled, and, when out of earshot, laughing.

AUGUST 4, 1876   9:10 AM   FRIDAY

At his shack, John Mackie said to Billy, "When you quit the Hotel de Luna last month, it got me daydreaming about having a big operation like Jessie Evans has in New Mexico Territory." Billy said he'd heard that name; rustling. "Yes. Evans started on the dodge from Kansas for counterfeiting. So, if I expanded to horses - 'course, by now you probably changed your mind - would you be interested?" Billy agreed with such infectious enthusiasm that Mackie finally overcame trepidation and actually made up his mind.

Just then, seven hundred ninety-seven miles northwest of Arizona's Pinaleño Mountain foothills, in California, a British citizen, John Henry Tunstall, excited about new plans, adjusted, with long sensitive fingers, linen cuffs extending from his wide-lapeled tweed jacket. With tourist's gratification, he looked out the window of his room in the Cosmopolitan Hotel at San Francisco's urban panorama, before addressing an envelope: "*John Partridge Tunstall, Esq. and Family, 7 Belsize Terrace, London, England.*"

The neat handwriting of John Tunstall's completed letter was idiosyncratic only in its signature. A huge happy "J" was underscored by a swirling vortex, into which darted a line, like a child's retreat against his mother's enveloping skirt.

The tender communication stated: "*My Dearest Parents and Three Sisters (My Trinity). It is unbelievable that I have not seen your beloved faces since August of 1872. It seems only yesterday that I was boarding the Calabria with her billowing sails for this great adventure across the ocean. Though you have made us wealthy, dear Father, I feel that I as an only son am your emissary, sent to build on the family's fortune.*

"*And how could our plans fail being grounded on a foundation of love? In fact, there is probably no family in England or these United States that (tarnashion as they say here) loves each other more than we do.*

"*How you have provided for me. The grand tour when I was sixteen with Paris, Berlin, Vienna, and Switzerland left in my heart an indelible love for our European heritage. What a pity that the United States is not still a part of England. With its endless resources, I assure you that Americans have the land of the future. How I wish I could let you see what I have, though of course it would be from my good eye only. (But I do fancy the blind right one as a bit eagle-like in its appeal.)*

"*I am now even more certain I made the right decision to leave our Turner, Beeton, and Tunstall mercantile 'empire' in British Colombia. Since I arrived here in February, I have heard that the future is in New Mexico Territory where one can cheaply acquire land for livestock. And what thief can carry off acres?*

"*And, my dear Father, I feel secure knowing you will invest in whatever venture I finally choose. And, dearest Mother, cease your worrying. I avoid places and practices that put one at risk.*

"*And my dear sisters, my pets, Minnie, Punch, and Jack, as to your suggestion that I keep a journal for publication as a traveling Englishman in the wild American West, I am amused rather than inclined. Let anyone invest a penny in the 'London Journal' to find adventures far more exciting than will ever befall me.*

"*But with my knack for presentiment, this Adventurer feels New Mexico Territory is where his destiny awaits.*"

As Tunstall folded his missive, with crisp friction of an ivory paper knife, thinking how unlike his family was to those tainted with animosity, one thousand one hundred forty-five miles southeast of San Francisco, in New Mexico Territory, a brother and a sister, in a magnificent Fort Sumner mansion, shouted viciously at each other in a spacious room which had been their father's office. Incongruously present, was now a bed, redeemed by its high headboard and footboard, as baroquely carved as were the original patriarchal desk and fireplace seating.

The plump man shrieked, "Paulita, you shame our Maxwell name. You're already thirteen, but still a ruffian." A decade and a half her elder, he poked a threatening nail-bitten finger.

With huge dark eyes blazing, and long auburn hair falling wildly over her shoulders, she yelled, "Nobody - especially you, Pete - tells me what to do." She stamped her satin slipper. "If Papa was alive, he'd take me back to Cimarron. And leave you."

Peter Maxwell ran his hand over wavy reddish hair and mustache, slow-wittedly seeking a retaliatory insult. From her porcelain-doll beauty, which he jealously despised as claiming their father's love, came an obscenity. "Then take a little bag of sand like an Apache girl."

Naïve about chastity protection, but not to be outdone, Paulita countered spitefully: "And I'll give you a little sign for your door" - she pointed to the one which led to the outside - "that says 'Patrón.' Otherwise nobody would know."

The interior door to that room swung inward. Their mother, Luz Beaubien Maxwell, in black mourning, entered; dark, silvered hair coiffured by one of her maids into an ample chignon. "Stop immediately, Peter," she said with weary self-absorbed grieving. "You have taken your father's room, not his place. He would protect her from your cruelty."

"Pro-tect her!" Maxwell fumed. "Lucien Bonaparte Maxwell's dead. *I'm* the one protecting our family honor now. And I won't let my sister to run wild like any child of the hired help. How can you let her wear pants and ride alone who knows where?"

"That's a lie! You're lying!" Paulita yelled; trying to decide how he knew her secret.

Luz Maxwell became imperiously vehement. "You have no right to criticize, Peter. You brought misery to your father."

Paulita shouted, "And you look like a frog!" She ran out.

He poured whiskey from a decanter on the desk. "I hope you're satisfied, Mother. Making me look the fool. And us the richest family in the Territory..."

"Richest. Rich in what?" Luz Maxwell said.

At the same time, with John Mackie at their campsite, Billy became restless, and said he needed to head out for a few days. Mackie asked, "To be with Mexicans again? You talk Mexican just like a greaser. It's for señoritas, isn't it?"

The boy scowled ominously.

The port wine stain flared with alarm. "Sorry, kid." Mackie ventured, "I've never seen a temper like yours. Like you shooting at me last week." Sullenly, Billy said he hadn't aimed. "Thanks. I didn't even know you had a gun."

Antrim's Colt .45 had joined Billy after Mackie's rustling decision: a homage to fantasized Jessie Evans, and concealed in his waistband.

With secret breached, without inhibition, Billy now lay that revolver on his bedroll, along with his cleaning kit. Immediately, his concentration was complete. His L-shaped tool removed the screw in front of the frame to release the base pin, allowing the cylinder to be expelled and checked. Held to the sky were its six, chambered circles in its fluted metal skeleton. With a wet rag on a wire, Billy plunged them and the barrel. Lubrication followed.

Then, as Mackie watched fascinated, the gun was rotated to reflect sun into the boy's captivated eyes.

AUGUST 15, 1876   3:16 PM   TUESDAY

"Wild Bill Hickok's dead," Billy announced to John Mackie as they rode in the Pinaleño foothills.

"Said so in the *Globe Herald*. Shot thirteen days ago. In sixty-seven, Wild Bill Hickok hit David Tutt perfectly in the heart at a hundred yards. And Tutt was shooting at him."

Mackie asked, "Who got a gunman that good? Wait! Where'd you get a *Globe Herald*?"

"Privy paper. It was an ambush. In Deadwood, South Dakota. Wild Bill had just gotten married. He was playing poker with his friends, Carl Mann, Captain Frank Massey, and Charlie Rich, in Mann's Number Ten Saloon. This coward, Jack McCall, shot him in the back of his head. First time Hickok didn't sit with his back to the wall. They said Hickok's cards were two black aces, two black eights, and the jack of diamonds. That 'ill be called the 'dead man's hand' forever."

"*Forever?*" Mackie smiled. "Means there's room at the top, kid."

"It's no joke. Wild Bill Hickok was my favorite."

Re-opened was pain of his lost Silver City life and mother, with a new recognition that none were immune to death.

OCTOBER 28, 1876   8:19 AM   SUNDAY

Willis Skelton Glenn had driven the two horse buckboard the one hundred eleven miles westward from Fort Worth; Luther Duke beside him. Pat Garrett and Joe Briscoe rode in the wagon bed.

"Fort's up ahead," said Skelton Glenn. "On that hill: Government Hill. We go to the Flats below - to Hidetown. Some soldier back at Fort Worth said Fort Griffin was built in sixty-seven to keep the Comanches and Kiowas down."

Joe Briscoe, crouching in the swaying vehicle, said he could smell the place already. "Might as well get used to it, kid," said Garrett. "Like on those train platforms in Fort Worth."

The boy answered, "Those hide piles were big as buildings. And that mountain of skulls!"

Fiddle music and shouts mingled with occasional feminine shrillness in the town's crowded dirt road, fronted by frame buildings: supply stores, blacksmith shops, and many saloons. Luther Duke gave a rebel yell. "Ah want me a drink! Then a wooman!"

Some Fort Griffin soldiers walked by, with a few Indians in long shirts, dark vests, buckskin pants, and knee-high moccasins; and carrying brass tack-ornamented rifles. "Indian scouts," said Willis Skelton Glenn. "Track down other Indians. Don't know they're next."

Scurrying to their halting vehicle, a little, wiry, bearded man, in filthy clothes and with rat-like pointy features, said, "Looks like yer startin' ou' as runners. Back when I started, in seveny, we ran 'longside buffs like Injuns. Hell, alls ye do now is te set an' shoot." He laughed mechanically, "Ha, ha, ha," and slapped his thigh as part of a comical audition for potential employers.

Joe Briscoe asked how he knew they were starting out. "Ye ain' scratchin'." Rotting teeth grinned. "Nick Buck. I'm a skinner. An' I workt fer the bes'," he lied. "Heerd o' Frank Mayer er the Mooar Brothers er John William Poe?" No one responded. "Well, I got everythin': knives an' grinstone. Bufflo Bill Cody namt 'is rifle Lucretia Borgia. I namt my skinnin' knife, Sally.

"In seveny-four, Charlie Mayer sez to me, 'Buck, we's in fer a harvest wha' could make a man sixy thousan' a year.' Back then, was sixy million buffs from Caneeda te Colarada. Recenly, they came down te Texas. Ifen ye'se wan' te hear more, thay's a good place te set."

"Sure," said Skelton Glenn to the garrulous man, who hesitated. "And we'll buy the drinks."

"They got a church here?" asked Briscoe. "It's Sunday."

" 'Pends on wha' ye prays te. Mos' 'ere, prays te the dolla. An' we got soiled doves, who'll answer mos' prayers fer a price." The men laughed. "Ye shur 're a tall un," Nick Buck said to Garrett. "Ye'd need a soiled swan."

The skinner led them to the Bee Hive Saloon, whose sign, with a breast and insect swarm, was lettered: "In this hive we're all alive, / Good whiskey makes us funny. / If you are dry, step in and try / The flavor of our honey."

While they ordered drinks and food, Pat Garrett noticed a saloon girl beside a man, but eyeing him. He smiled back in mutual denigration of their companions. "Ureen," Buck was saying. "Many a runner, who's been shootin' eight rouns a minute, cools down tha' hot barreel wit piss - ifen he ain' got snow - so's the bullet won' waver.

"Buffs is so easy te kill, tha' Frank Mayer says we'se killin' the goose wha' lays gold eggs."

Briscoe asked why buffalos were easy to kill. Nick Buck said, "Stoopid, boy. Ifen somebody was tryin' te kill ye, wha'd ye do?" Briscoe said he wasn't sure. All laughed. "Hate te say, bu' they's the same. I'll 'splain. They travels in bunches; like 'bout sixty."

As Buck continued his prater with chewing cheeks pouched, he rubbed his left, index finger stump, amputated by Sally. Garrett noted the deformity with repugnance. "When ye fin' a herd, ye hides near 'em. Rifles like the Sharps Big Fifty shoots easy at six hunred yards. Whiles they'se eatin', ye figer who's the leader - kin be a bull er cow - te shoot firs'. They'll stampeede oly ifen the leader runs.

"So ye shoot the lights - the lungs - an' 'e dies slow. Tha' way ye kin kill all o' them yerself. Oly problem is, even wit a prop, yer shootin' arm gits tired. Ha. Ha. Ha."

"They don't attack?" asked Briscoe.

"They'se too stoopid. Bu' they kin be trouble. Frien' o' mine was cuttin' ou' the tongue ... Mos' takes oly hides. Some, like 'im, takes the tongue and hump fer smokin'. So, wit my frien', turns ou' this bull wasn' deed. Throws 'isself on 'is fee' afore 'nother runner shoots 'im agin.

"Real danger's Injuns. They hates runners, cause we'se killin' their livelihood. Lookahere." Nick Buck separated slipped-together cartridges. Out fell a blown-glass tube with white powder. "Cynide. Ifen yer cornered by Injuns, bite 'i an' die right.

"Lissen te this. Dave Dudley's pard foun' 'im wit a stake trough 'is belly. Scalpt. 'Is privates tied in 'is hand.

"Now, 'bout skinnin'. Ye rolls buffs on the back. Then cuts wit a ripper knife - not Sally. Like takin off a union suit by unbuttonin' the fron', then cuttin' 'long the arm an' leg. Then Sally cuts the hide loose. Then ye pulls." He grasped Briscoe's collar like a scruff. "Ties i' te a wagon. Whups the team. Teers i' off. Course, ye lose un in four."

Then they died for nothing, Briscoe said. "We all die for nothing," said Garrett.

Nick Buck continued, "In camp, arsnic kills lice on the pegged an' scrapt hides. Then ye sells 'em an' gits rich. How's 'bout hirin' me?"

Laughingly they agreed. "An' I got a cook throwed in. Frien' by the name o' Grundy Burns. Place fer outfittin' yerselfs is Frank Conrad's." After more shotglasses, Buck slurred, "Conrad's covers four acres on Govemen' Hill. Got thiry tons lead, five tons gunpower."

When his new employers left, Buck scratched his beard and drank down Briscoe's glass. Then he sang to himself: "Our meat's the bufflo hump, / Our staff's the sore-thumb bread. / An' all we 'av te sleep upon's / The bufflo hide fer a bed." Drunkenness dulled memory of angry past hunters, trapped on the range with his incompetence.

OCTOBER 29, 1876   12:34 PM   SUNDAY

Riding northwest from Bonita to Cedar Springs with Billy, paternal affection made John Mackie say, "Sometimes I think about having a family." Billy said he'd never heard him say that. "In my head." Concerned, Billy asked if he heard voices. Mackie responded, "You've got no words in your head?"

"'Course not. Except for what I hear. You're teasin', right?"

Surprised but protective, Mackie said, "Sure," and returned to his didactic intent. "For our horse business, we can use what I learned in the cavalry. Bad movement's key. Feels bad, and the horse breaks down. Looking tells a lot. The hocks shouldn't point to each other - called cow-hocked. And the chest should be broad; so the front legs don't cross and cause tripping."

In Cedar Springs, they strolled to a hitched bay mare. Mackie continued, "Overall, alert and healthy. Eyes big and kind-looking. Large nostrils to get wind. Her shoulder has a backward slant for a comfortable ride. And those powerful hindquarters for running. Last - which we can't do - is run your hands for pain or swelling. Also check if she's head shy." He flapped his hat. She stood calmly. "What do you think?"

"Let's take her," said Billy. Mackie laughed.

Laughing to himself in Santa Fe, three hundred twenty-nine miles northeast of Cedar Springs, a man was considering vagaries of fate. He stood behind the reception counter of Herlow's Hotel, on San Francisco Street and facing perpendicular Burro Alley, which was clogged with those creatures of poverty. At the hotel's rear, its corral fronted on Water Street and the even more unsavory neighborhood of courthouse and jail.

Awaiting his daily amusement of fate's events, the man twirled his waxed, ginger mustache to reinforce startling upward crescents. Not tall, he was prodigiously muscled by obsessive exercise with dumbbells. Each night, in his second floor room, he smugly admired his shaved nude body. Each morning, he also shaved his hairline to enhance what he called "the high-domed forehead of the Teutonic race."

Waddling to him, was a fat, agitated, derby-hatted guest asking, "You're the owner, Paul Herlow, right?" Herlow nodded. "Well, I'm Room Ten. I've got a complaint. Where were you at midnight?" Asleep, Herlow said. "Well, right outside this place, *I* was almost killed. I heard this dragging skirt. I turned. This lady with a Bowie knife was about to stab me. I caught her wrist. Says she thought I was somebody else and walks off. I'm from Eureka, Kansas. That would never happen there. This Territory's not civilized."

Herlow said, "Hopefully the rest of your stay will be more peaceful."

"I'm leaving." His bill was efficiently processed. Watching him depart, the owner said, "Thank you for staying at Herlow's Hotel."

Because his hotel was neither the lowest bunk-style rooms, nor the pinnacle, the Exchange Hotel - blocks to its east on the good part of San Francisco Street - Paul Herlow saw "his people" as either on upward or downward trajectories. And he believed he was intrinsic to their fates. Like billiard balls, struck and rebounding, they would never be as before meeting him.

From Room Three, tweed-suited John Henry Tunstall approached, calling out an affable greeting of "Herr Herlow! Mein host!" with infantile innocence which Herlow had already noted; recalling to him a saint or an idiot.

Tunstall's luxuriant light-brown hair was brushed backward from the upright forehead of his long face, where hazel trusting eyes gazed limpidly; though the right was darker. Fair wispy mustache and silky jawline fringe, in the least light, made a radiant glow.

With his usual good-natured sweetness, Tunstall said, "It was most kind of you to make me this business contact. Is this Alexander McSween punctual?"

"It depends," said Herlow. "He is the only lawyer in a hundred and fifty mile radius of his office in the town of Lincoln."

Tunstall mentioned possible rain. Herlow asked, "Does gloom affect you? I am curious because I study character. And, when people come together, I can find affinities."

"I rather like precipitation. But how do you locate affinities?" Tunstall asked with a dilatant's eclectic inquisitiveness.

"With Phrenology. Ah, here comes the good lawyer, McSween."

Entering briskly, the urbane man said insincerely, "My apologies for being late." John Tunstall extended his hand as they exchanged names. His grip was firm; Alexander McSween's flaccid and moist.

Paul Herlow noted trim McSween's brief wheezing, while deciding that most noteworthy was his nose. Tight-skinned like a burn victim's, it was a nubbin with forward-facing nostrils. Yet his face's elegant severity, with contrasting dark-auburn hair and mustache arcing profusely to his jawbones, was pleasantly intriguing. Posture was the deficit: repeatedly straightening from a slouch, as if thwarting deflation or cowering.

Herlow said, "You have both usurped my introducing. So I now offer food." Tunstall demurred with reservations for six at the Exchange Hotel. "Then there is time," persisted Herlow.

Soon, Herlow, with a thick book, joined them in the dining room.

Tunstall already had brandy; McSween was sipping coffee. Herlow asked, "Alexander, I have known you how long?"

"Since seventy-five. My wife and I arrived in Lincoln from Saint Lewis on March fifth."

"Ya, well, and today you may learn what is fated." Herlow patted the tome. "This is my bible." McSween's eyebrows rose. "There will be no blasphemy. I will tell you, Mister Tunstall, that Alexander almost became a minister. The calling comes easily back."

Herlow showed the spine: *New Physiognomy or Signs of Character*. He said, "Phrenology: the teaching that each function of the brain has a location. The bigger the area, the more developed that faculty. So one's nature is pre-determined."

He opened to a profile with bald cranium divided into thirty-seven labeled sections. "You see," he said, "at the lower regions are animal natures, like Greed and Destructiveness. In the back, are social functions like Love and Friendship. In front are moral qualities like Benevolence and Spirituality. The forehead" - he swept his hand over his own - "shows Intellectual and Perceptive abilities."

Alexander McSween's labored breathing returned. Herlow asked, "Is the asthma troubling you?"

McSween lied, "No. My health is perfect." To him asthma represented shameful failure of will, akin to sinfulness.

"May I check your head?" Herlow asked Tunstall.

"If peculiarity will not dismay your other guests," he answered genially, leaning forward.

Herlow sighed. "It is no secret what I am." His fingers pressed. "Enough Acquisitiveness for a businessman. And much Adhesiveness showing that you easily make friends of associates - though it interferes with your seeing their evils." With gullible admiration, John Tunstall confirmed the test.

McSween checked his pocket watch, but failed to deter Herlow, who said, "Ach, you are no extrovert like out great local attorney, Thomas Benton Catron. I will be rapid." Herlow had to circle the table to him. "Well, I warn you, Alexander, Acquisitiveness is very prominent: a temptation to attain worldly goods at any cost."

McSween frowned, saying it wasn't the best advertisement. "To the contrary. It enables you to better advise clients or friends."

"You avoided my legal censure," McSween said, attempting humor. "And now, we really must go." Herlow asked if he was correct. McSween glanced with haughty intelligence and residual resentment and said, "You'd make a good attorney." They stood.

Following doggedly, Herlow said, "My conclusions: Alexander, you can warn of evils. Mister Tunstall's optimism can make them seem surmountable. McSween and Tunstall, your affinities are ideal for business." He gestured open-palmed outward. "Your fates await."

John Tunstall and Alexander McSween turned right, strolling eastward along the south side of San Francisco Street.

Tunstall said, looking toward the intersection with Shelby Street, at whose east corner the lavish adobe Exchange sprawled amidst waiting rich carriages, "It appears the Hotel is doing cracking business."

After the waiter brought their orders, Tunstall said, "Thanks to Herr Herlow, I consider our beginning provident."

McSween made a tight-lipped smile, distracted by a legal case necessitating his travel to the States the following day; and still irritated by Herlow's imposition of a fruitless social exercise.

He obsessively adjusted the back of his starched linen, detachable collar. That annoying necessity of checking whether it had ridden up from his shirt came from his refusal to buy a more expensive version with back as well as front stud.

To pass time, he asked, "Have you seen local sites? The First Presbyterian Church - my denomination - is the first Protestant one in this Territory. And the Palace of the Governors is the oldest public building in this country, built between sixteen ten and twelve."

Tunstall said, "I did peruse the latter; with fantasy of presenting to Queen Victoria a big mud-brick building as a palace." He smiled.

McSween continued by rote, "Nevertheless, it's housed the governors through Spanish and Mexican rulers. Now, our Territorial governor, Samuel Beach Axtell, is there.

"The original Spanish conqueror, Juan de Oñate, came in fifteen ninety-eight. To subdue the local Pueblo Indians, he captured all their males and cut off their right foot."

"A barbaric founding," said Tunstall. "Fortunately civilization has advanced." The lawyer expressed skepticism. Tunstall said, "Come now. Ours is an enlightened age.

"But speaking of buildings, noteworthy is the one forming the east side of the Plaza: that two-story with bric-a-brac porchway ..."

McSween interrupted, "That's the Johnson Block. Where that attorney Paul Herlow mentioned - Thomas Benton Catron, the U.S. Attorney - has his office. Catron's made a *questionable* fortune, I might add."

Missing that hint, Tunstall asked if it too was an official building. "No. Though in this Territory private gain often mixes with government positions."

Tunstall countered that the unscrupulous were everywhere; adding that the Church of Saint Francis, with its two crenellated towers, did look advanced. McSween said, "It's got this Territory's first Archbishop - named Lamy. He built it."

"Being a Londoner does jade one," said Tunstall. "But I feel opportunity in all this newness. In fact, I have convinced my father that if he gives me seven thousand pounds, I should soon make a handsome return on his investment."

Startled, McSween cleared his suddenly dry throat. "Seven thousand pounds! That's about thirty-eight thousand dollars, isn't it?"

"Yes," Tunstall said. "And far more is available. My family owns an extensive mercantile and shipping business."

"Mister Tunstall ... may I call you 'John?' " He smiled assent. "You may be the man I've prayed for. There's a line in the Bible you may know: 'The ungodly are like the chaff which the wind driveth away.' "

"No, but an interesting sentiment. My creed has more to do with moral quality. And, at the end, I would hope my life was both usefully and blamelessly spent."

"Just don't forget the glory beyond. But to get back: thirty-eight thousand dollars cash! Do you realize that in Lincoln County - where I live - that would be a fortune? There's *no cash at all*. Everything's based on credit. A man with cash could take it over. And I'm talking about twenty-seven thousand square miles: the largest county in this country."

John Tunstall said, "I fear you've not touched your food. My wild turkey was roasted to perfection."

Not listening, Alexander McSween was abruptly flooded with obsessive anxiety, as he thought, "What if I have an asthma attack. He'd lose confidence."

Attempting to eat, he stopped with another fear, and cautiously asked, "By the way, have you heard about *the* Ring?" Tunstall was blithely unaware. "Santa Fe Ring. Thomas Benton Catron is its head. They control a lot of the politics here." Tunstall asked if that was good. McSween said, "It depends on your relationship to it."

"If it is an advantage, why not make one's own Ring?"

For the first time, McSween smiled genuinely, and said, "Now *that* would change things!" He leaned closer. "I'm privy to Ring secrets. When I first came to Lincoln, my biggest clients were a Lawrence Murphy and a James Dolan: Ring men.

"Listen to this unbridled arrogance. Campaigning for election recently, Murphy said to a man, 'You can stop the waves of the ocean with a fork easier than stopping us.' With their big store and other enterprises, they control Lincoln County. But *they've got no cash!* Any man with cash, setting up competition, can eliminate them!"

McSween straightened his back. "I'd propose this. Build a competing store in Lincoln. By purchase and by the Homestead Act, get ranchland along Lincoln County rivers like the Feliz and the Peñasco. Build a grain mill to get the Post Trader contracts to sell the beef and flour to the local Indian Reservation, the Mescalero, and the local post, Fort Stanton. Murphy and Dolan have the traderships now. But they sell both places stolen cattle, and the Indians mealy flour.

"Also, I'd introduce you to my client, John Chisum, a major cattleman. He cleverly uses government land along the Pecos River for free, by calling it 'right of discovery.' In fact," McSween whispered, "Murphy and Dolan steal their cattle from him."

"By Jove, what an astounding opportunity! To get a monopoly with a mere seven thousand pounds, and, at the same time, to do good. What more could a man want?"

Tunstall beckoned for a waiter. "What would you suggest, Alexander? Bread pudding or chocolate torte?"

"Yes," said McSween euphorically. "Same as yours."

"Then, my good man," Tunstall said to the arriving server, "we shall both sample your chocolate torte. Do you recommend it?" The waiter said he'd take the pudding. It tasted like his mother's. "Then bread pudding is fated. That and our coffee, please. And an after-dinner liqueur."

McSween, with lungs cramping, asked, "Might you be interested?"

"I am a man of action. And I say, 'Onward! To Lincoln!' "

The waiter set down the order. Noticing the alcoholic beverage, McSween announced self-righteously, "I'm a teetotaler." Tunstall affably called sobriety another plus.

Alexander McSween continued, while Tunstall ate bread pudding. "I came here with Juan Patrón, Lincoln's leading Mexican. I'm leaving to the States on business; but he's driving his buggy back to Lincoln this Friday. I'm sure he'd take you."

But McSween's anxiety flared as he thought, "Maybe he's not convinced. Try harder." He said, "Things are worse for Murphy and Dolan than they realize. I'll tell you about this probate matter I'm handling - the reason I'm traveling - one that can help put them out of business. And you'll see my shrewd strategy.

"The case goes back to June twenty-fourth of seventy-four when Murphy's first partner died - an Emil Fritz. For final farewells, Fritz returned to family in Stuttgart, Germany. But on the way, in New York City, he took out a ten thousand dollar policy with Merchants' Life Insurance Company. The beneficiaries were listed only as Fritz's 'heirs.' There were relatives in this Territory: a brother and sister: a Charles Fritz and Emilie Fritz Scholand. They became the will's administrators, and eventually retained me to represent the estate, because they were having problems collecting the ten thousand. First, Merchants' Life fraudulently claimed Fritz died of consumption - which was exclusionary. It was alcoholism. He was a dissolute. Then the company suspiciously claimed bankruptcy. That's why I'm going to New York. To confront Merchants' Life.

"But back to that ten thousand. Murphy and Dolan want it. They claimed Emil Fritz had no will - though they probably destroyed it - and that he owed everything to *them* for company debts.

"Here's the rub. Without that cash, *they might go bankrupt.*" Fanatically, McSween added, "I won't let that money get into the Devil's coffers. Even if it's my last act." He stopped, afraid that he had become alarming; and glanced apprehensively.

John Tunstall laughed. "Mark my words - and I have a certain knack of presentiment - Lincoln County will never be the same after Tunstall and McSween."

"Like a lamb to slaughter" sprang into Alexander McSween's mind, then discomfort at hoodwinking. As a release, he interlaced fingers and cracked outward. He thought, "We'll be able to afford that big house Susan wanted. It's God's will." He obsessive-compulsively checked his collar.

NOVEMBER 8, 1876   11:59 AM   WEDNESDAY

In Elliott's Saloon, John Mackie, with birthmark brightly scalding, said to Billy, "These horse jobs really rattle me. At least, Hog Ranch's owner, George McKittrick's, has a grudge against Louis Hartman." Billy looked questioningly. "A soldier at the Fort." Mackie drank his second shotglass. "Can you handle it?"

"Check me. Major Compton made Hog Ranch off limits to soldiers 'cause they were loosing horses. Didn't stop 'em from coming!" Billy doubled over with glee. "And that rope plan to trick us! Picture them with the girls - but holding onto a rope!" Mackie was quiet. Billy said, "Don't worry. You're just there with McKittrick and step out: my signal it's off." Billy looked through the open door. "Here they come!"

Billy watched Mackie's broad muscular body cross the street to Hog Ranch, then studied his quarry. Alongside the buckskin he and Mackie had ridden in together, Privates O'Connor and Burns tied their horses. Then, each knotted a rope to his halter. Laughing, uncoiling their ropes, they entered the brothel.

Billy felt delicious fun. Cutting the ropes with a folding knife, he tied them to the hitching post. Mounting Burns's horse, he led O'Connor's by its reins. Soon Billy galloped, laughing to thundering hooves, a fantasized member of Jessie Evans's "big operation."

Also fantasizing a transformation, but of the town he was in, John Henry Tunstall, two hundred seventy-six miles almost due east of Bonita, Arizona, was writing a letter in a humble adobe.

"*To my Beloved Parents, and Dearest Trinity (Minnie, Punch, and Jack). As you can see from my address, your Columbus has finally arrived in his New World, in this case the New Mexico Territory town named Lincoln. I feel happy as a big sunflower. As to my journey to my fate, I departed Santa Fe for my Lincoln fact finding mission with Alexander McSween's friend, Juan Patron, who has extended the hospitality of his house.*

"*Poor Patron. Last year a fellow Lincolnite shot him in the back so he uses a cane and drags his left leg. I think I have found (in local parlance) the toughest spot in America.*

"*But this little town of Lincoln is most charming. In 1869 its mostly Mexican residents voted to change its name from La Placita del Rio Bonito (most sensible since it was absurdly long) to Lincoln in patriotic homage to that assassinated president. The day after I arrived were local elections. The citizens were proud that no one had gotten shot! One gets used to this. In Santa Fe, most were armed with a great six shooter on their hip.*

"*I also stopped by the existing large store (given the moniker The House) and met a man Alexander McSween considers an adversary, James Dolan. Nevertheless I found him charming and friendly. In fact he offered to assist me in finding land, etc.*

"*Today I visited McSween's wife, Susan. They live in a modest mud brick house on a large piece of property they own on the north side of the main street (actually the only street) in Lincoln. With much domestic talent, Mrs. McSween, a city woman from St. Louis, Missouri, has furnished it most charmingly. True to Scotsman's frugality, McSween's contribution is horsehair upholstery, since it never needs replacement.*

"His better half was dressed in the latest fashion of la belle France with slim silhouette of long cuirasse bodice nipped in courageously at the waist with shorter overskirt and form-fitting underskirt. The full rear's dragging peacock's tail effect implies a lady of leisure, though her choices of frills, flounces, and fringes, and accumulation of patterns might appear garish to your eyes. But she would be excellent advertisement for local dry goods.

"She also makes every effort at etiquette and said that the standard to which she and her husband espouse evokes jealousy. She even showed me her silver-plated dinnerware with twelve kinds of forks and fifteen of spoons, and confided that some here still vulgarly eat everything with a knife, including peas. She is also given to exclaiming 'sacre bleu' with fine accent but amusing unawareness of its hint of bawdiness.

"Juan Patron has recommended my meeting some small farm holders close to Lincoln who are named Richard Brewer, Frank and George Coe, Charles Bowdre, and Josiah Scurlock.

"About sixty miles to the east, is the north to south Pecos River along which graze a rich John Chisum's thousands of cattle. He, as Alexander McSween's friend, would be mine also.

"Fortunes are to be made here. I heard of one Mexican Land Grant of two million acres sold by a certain Maxwell family now moved to Fort Sumner on the Pecos River (they own the whole darn town as they say here) which netted them a huge figure when it was sold.

"And Dearest Minnie, I will wear till death that ring you hid in the Christmas pudding you sent me in 1872. It is on the third finger of my right hand as our sacred family bond. And I am convinced that our future will be made in this little town of Lincoln."

NOVEMBER 28, 1876   7:23 AM   TUESDAY

Into oppressive cloud cover manifesting his depression, Pat Garrett emerged from the buffalo hide tent he shared with Joe Briscoe, blanketed together for warmth, but with limbs touching and sexual tension. A few hides stretched on frames and in a small pile, represented the paltry sum of all their hunting.

Scrawny, bearded Grundy Burns, their cook, was spilling buffalo chip kindling into the fire pit, dug when they made this campsite in the grasslands of the Double Mountains region, a hundred miles northwest of Fort Griffin. "Slep' late," Burns said to him.

Offended, Garrett responded, "Isn't a cattle drive." As the cook chopped wood, Garrett called into the tent, "What the hell 're you doing, Joe?"

Grundy Burns added the wood to the fire and said, "Pleasurin' hisself. Somebody oughta feel good."

"What?" Garrett asked. Grundy Burns ignored him and bit a tobacco plug. Garrett asked, "Where's Nick Buck? Sleeping off a drunk? He can't skin. We're loosing everything."

Grundy Burns lifted a short log. His ax split it violently. He said, "Nick's good 'nough for this outfit."

"What?" Garrett asked, but again did not persist. He said, "Shouldn't have gotten a Winchester. Skelton and Luther are doing better with Sharps." Burns laid a grill for the coffee pot, and left the ax beside the pit.

Garrett asked, "When will Skelton and Luther be back from Fort Reynolds?"

Burns said, "Gettin' Skelton's gun reepaired. Should be today."

Joe Briscoe emerged, holding long underwear and dragging off his bandana. Catching his chain, it pulled out the cross. Garrett said provocatively, "That's like girl's jewelry. And it doesn't bring luck. We haven't seen buffalo in more than a week."

"It's not for luck. It's the symbol of our Savior. I'm gonna do washing. Even if the water doesn't kill these buffalo lice, at least they'll be clean."

"The lice?" Garrett mocked. The boy looked stupidly confused. Garrett said, "Bites are mortification of the flesh, Joe. Get you to Heaven."

Briscoe laughed his high-pitched girlish sound. "I've got it. Your wet, buffalo hide, leg wraps 're getting to you. You'd make a bad wife. You can't sew." Calling Garrett a woman, just when feared failure and feared sexuality had combined, was disastrous.

Dimly recognizing the man's anger, the boy said, "Going now," adding cheerfully, "Whosoever strike thee on they right cheek, turn to him the other also."

Garrett stared coldly; then asked Burns, "When's food ready?"

"No law 'gainst the hunter helpin' the cook." Grundy Burns spit tobacco saliva onto a rock at the fire edge and watched it sizzling. "Get whiskey from the wagon. Warm you."

Garrett did take a few swigs and then decided to clean his Winchester rifle, taking it back to the fire and sitting on a piece of hide to avoid puddling mud.

Both men noticed the boy returning from the gully. Garrett called, "Only someone dumb would call it washing when he was making his clothes dirtier than he started;" and laughed at his own joke.

Briscoe said to lay off, and hunkered down, draping his dripping bandana on a stick over the flames.

Uneasily glancing, Burns poured their coffee. Garrett glumly watched the boy's flaccid fabric in the smoke and said, "You're gonna smell like buffalo chips. And I've got to sleep next to you." Briscoe glowered, but was silent.

Garrett irritably decided Briscoe's broad nose and fleshy lips looked like a white nigger's. Provocatively, he pushed the boy's shoulder. Clumsy Briscoe sprawled in slippery mud.

When he sat, he saw his bandana burning, and grimaced.

Garrett misread the expression and growled, "Stop laughing at me." Angrily he banged down his cup beside the rifle, and pushed the boy hard. Briscoe fell backward, hand slamming scalding rock. He screamed, groping for anything to right himself.

Garrett saw the moving ax and grabbed his rifle. "Stop!" Briscoe shouted; lurching to his feet with the randomly clutched tool.

Garrett fired point blank.

Briscoe fell backward, head and neck banging on the grate. Suddenly, bizarrely, his hair ignited like a halo. Then Burns was dragging him by the feet. The cross, having dangled into flames, had sprung from the grill. Hideous on the right cheek was its red brand.

Pat Garrett said, "He was going to kill me. You saw the ax." They both looked. The handle was gripped backwards.

In panic, Garrett ran with mental chaos of shot uppity nigger, shot white nigger, and hanging for murder.

Grundy Burns heard his galloping horse. He knelt and said, "Kid, you shoulda stayed with your mama;" and squeezed tearing eyes.

When Willis Skelton Glenn, Luther Duke, and Nick Buck returned, Grundy Burns pointed to a blanket-covered form. Glenn lifted an edge and asked what happened. The cook said, "Garrett called it self-deefenz. Boy's got an ax. I didn' change nothin'."

Luther Duke turned to Glenn. "Think what ye want, Skelton, Ah'm quittin' soon. That goddamn cross on his cheek. How the hell did that happen?"

"When the kid wuz shot, he fell onto the fire," Grundy Burns said; and hoped they would let him report murder.

NOVEMBER 29, 1876   6:34 AM   WEDNESDAY

Tensely, the men in camp watched Pat Garrett ride in, long legs dwarfing his horse. Skelton Glenn said, "Burns 'ill testify to self-defense. Better head to Fort Griffin and surrender to the authorities."

Garrett said, "I've been suffering. That kid made me do it."

His listeners were unmoved by his self-pity, but were unwilling to risk their enterprise.

FEBRUARY 16, 1877   9:28 AM   FRIDAY

With grim purpose, against oppressive backdrop of eleven thousand foot Mount Graham - inhabited, Indians knew, by restive spirits - three soldiers rode southward down their chalky arrow-straight road from Fort Grant. The commander, big-thighed Major Charles Compton, yellowish face enraged, intoned, "To save a horse or any military possession is as important to me as saving a man."

Compton had served as a Union Lieutenant Colonel in the Civil War; and, at thirty, had mustered out in March of 1866, reenlisting four months later. But he detested this isolated outpost and many of his men, who entered as criminals and departed as deserters.

His companions, First Sergeant Louis Hartman and Private Charles Smith, were startled by his vehemence. Lean Hartman thought, "That smooth-talking bastard Antrim. Steals my Black Eagle; and I stupidly let him off when I catch him."

Now on the purloined animal, he decided that its praiseworthy recovery by him was actually justification for his promotion to non-commissioned officer: his only achievement in a life of brawling. Only luck had saved him a Court Martial after his shooting incident with John Mackie, whose dismissal had made the rank available.

When fit and neat Miles Wood opened his door to the three in visored caps, dark blue jackets, and light-blue pants tucked into black mid-calf boots, Major Compton demanded to see the Justice of the Peace. Hand passing apprehensively over bad eye, Wood identified himself, realizing the man's rank by his jacket chest adorned with fancy, black, quatrefoil braiding.

In his dining-room, with relief, Miles Wood decided from the commander's punctilious rendition, that the officer was performing a procedural requirement. Compton continued, "Our posts have been targeted by horse thieves since approximately February of last year; and certainly by March nineteenth, when Private Smith's mount was stolen when he was at Fort Goodwin. And on November eighth, two more were stolen at McDowell's Store. Nine days later, First Sergeant Hartman's was taken from the same location - though it was recovered. And last month, two more: those of Privates Burns and O'Connor, from McDowell's Store."

Wood joked that Hog Ranch wasn't exactly McDowell's. Compton's shout was unexpected: "Hog Ranch! Sir, you've failed your job!"

"One of the thieves was even your past employee: Henry Antrim. Last November twenty-fifth, First Lieutenant Hartman and Private Smith trailed him to the mining camp of his father near Fort McMillen. Hartman's horse was there."

Miles Wood offered, "Then John Mackie must be involved."

Responses were immediate in Louis Hartman and Charles Compton. The First Lieutenant's rage returned. And the commander accused Wood of concealing information.

Wood's nervous hand brushed his bad eye. He said, "Major, this problem's been military. For civilian warrants, I'd need a complaint."

Lois Hartman volunteered, purposefully combining revenge against John Mackie and deflection of Compton's anger. He said, "Mackie's dangerous. Remember, he shot me in seventy-four."

He wrote for Wood: *"This here is a Complaint against John Mackie and Henry Antrim for stealing horses Top Scout and Brave Boy, property of U.S. Government, Sixth Calvary, Fort Grant, on January 17, 1877."*

After they left, Miles Wood called into the kitchen, "Hey Caleb, did you hear *that*?" His new cook, son of McDowell's arthritic shopkeeper, entered in a grease-stained apron, protruding upper teeth fanning through lips and mumbling yeah. Wood said, "I'm making you my constable. There's no town money for a reward. I'll have to pay. Can't afford trouble with the soldiers."

Caleb passively watched Wood printing: *"WANTED FOR HORSE THIEVING. JOHN MACKIE AND HENRY ANTRIM. REWARD $20 FOR CAPTURE. MILES WOOD, JUSTICE OF THE PEACE."*

Wood said, "Post copies 'round Grant County and Pinal County - where Henry Antrim's father is."

Riding back, with the fort two and a half miles ahead, Major Compton, face mottled, screamed at Hartman; as Smith pretended not to hear. "Hog Ranch! Hog Ranch was off limits! You violated my order! Punishment for insubordination is Court Martial! For disobedience to orders, it's being reduced to the ranks, confinement to the guardhouse ..." As the diatribe continued, Louis Hartman was mentally repeating that he would kill Mackie, kill goddamn Mackie.

As if inundated by impending danger, the Messenger, the Pawnee boy, hallucinating in smallpox fever, within a military-issue tent in his reservation, seven hundred fifty-three miles northeast of Fort Grant, cried out. Instead of his scab-faced mother, just recovering from the disease, he saw a horrific four-eyed spider and heard, "They will not let us build earth lodges. So cold ... So many dying."

Then the spider said in the sweet voice of his mother, "Fight the fever, my child." She pressed closer his deceased grandfather's medicine bundle, and prayed for its power to save him from the epidemic.

FEBRUARY 23, 1877   8:17 AM   FRIDAY

In obstinate denial of repeated rejections, Billy was at William Antrim's camp north of Globe, asking for a loan. Billy said, "You got Ma's money;" eyes welling. "Seems you'd want to act like a father."

"I regret even 'stepfather.' Get out now, I say."

As Billy mounted his horse, two rough-looking strangers galloped into the clearing. One shouted, "Stop! We're after a Henry Antrim for horse thievin'."

Antrim pointed. Billy said to his betraying face, "That's not my name. It's my stepfather's."

"Don' matter. You're arrested." The man located and took Billy's concealed Colt .45. Antrim decided not to mention it was his.

Proceeding down the path with the bounty hunters, suddenly Billy crouched and raced ahead into a low-branched thicket. The men dared not follow; as Billy inhaled intoxicating scent of freedom.

That scent of freedom was also in icy wind whipping over the Llano Estacado, five hundred seventy-three miles due east of that mining district. An old bull buffalo, roaring into it, flared nostrils of his naked nose patch. For twenty-five years, he had followed that sweet current, and had led his herd southward, finally to Texas; comprehending, like other survivors, that the smell of men, and the smell of his kind's rotting flesh on their trails thousands of years old, were linked, and must be avoided. But like his progenitor, the ancient, east Asian bison, which had crossed the Bering strait land bridge to that continent lacking predators, he had no inherited fear.

John William Poe had seen that stand of sixty-three the day before. Now he was positioned downwind, wearing drab camouflage. His fifty caliber Sharps rifle rested on its Y-shaped branch support. Cartridges two-and-a-half inches long and a half-inch wide, each with a four hundred seventy-three grain lead projectile backed by a hundred grains of gunpowder, lay in meticulous rows on grass he had flattened on the snow-covered ground.

In the Indian reservation, three hundred eighty-five miles northeast of that Texas flatland, the Pawnee boy's mother was listening to his delirious words. Suddenly he exclaimed, "The Spirit! The Buffalo!" He struggled to rise, but recoiled as if struck.

The huge bull shuddered, but stood still. Thunder had clapped. John William Poe calculated, "Makes almost seven thousand this year." The old bull coughed. On the snow he saw blood's redness. He must run. He took a skittering step, tail raised. Poe smiled at comical mimicry of play before death. An old cow approached. She had borne that bull eight calves. As he dropped, she gave a guttural cry. Others drifted toward her. "Next leader," thought Poe. He fired, penetrating her heart. The old bull was aware of his fallen mate, knowing her scent. Then all that was left was the blowing wind.

In the reservation, the Pawnee boy whispered, "The battle has begun," and sighed so deeply. His mother wept, recognizing death, and wondering at his mysterious message.

At the same time, Billy's two bounty hunters stopped for the night at a town near Fort San Carlos, to drown failure in drink.

FEBRUARY 24, 1877   8:42 AM   SATURDAY

Billy made no attempt to elude the two surprised bounty hunters when he rode into town.

Five hours later, as they all neared Cedar Springs, the taller man said, "Still sixteen miles to Bonita." Billy slowed, then veered away. The two men chased briefly, firing a few rounds. None came close.

Billy's captures made so little impression on him, that he forgot to tell John Mackie; though the man would have recognized that they were now in tremendous peril.

MARCH 25, 1877   7:35 AM   SUNDAY

In the Hotel de Luna, Caleb the cook whined, "I did try to find 'em, Miles. Anyways, they gave back them horses to the soldiers." Teeth splayed on pouting lower lip.

Wood said, "But I'm still left with those damn warrants."

Five miles to the northwest, camping with Billy, John Mackie shivered in bitter wind and said, "We've gotten so few horses that you must think I even failed as a rustler." Billy teased that he was the only man he'd met who could beat himself single-handedly. Mackie smiled sheepishly and asked, "Think anyone still wants to arrest us?"

"Why? And I'd sure like real breakfast at the Hotel de Luna."

Later, Caleb, looking out a window, said, "Miles, I just done my constable duty."

Barely breathing, Wood took Billy's and Mackie's order. Waiting, Billy played with the salt shaker, dexterously unscrewing and re-screwing its cap. Wood returned, sliding his laden tray onto their table, and revealing his pointed Colt .45 under it. Billy's hand closed over the shaker. Wood said, "You're both under arrest." He called, "Caleb, we're taking them to the fort." Billy volunteered that the Major had said it was settled. Wood said, "This is a *civil* arrest."

"Couldn't us *civilians* make a deal?" John Mackie asked. "Commander Compton might feel dictated to."

Wood hesitated, confused. Just then, a man and a woman entered. Representing the civilian population he served, they tipped his decision. "Folks," he said, directing them to the table's food, "help yourselves. We're heading out on an errand."

Entering biting wind, gusting across the cold, empty, flat land, Billy, Mackie, Wood, and Caleb walked the straight road toward brooding Mount Graham and the fort. Wood spoke blown words to Mackie. "You were a fool with Hartman. Mess with his girl. Then shoot him. Then steal his horse."

Billy asked Mackie about the girl. Mackie said, "I was in the Sixth Cavalry. She worked at Hog Ranch." Billy sidled closer, eyeing escape opportunities. "She meant something to me. Hartman got rough with her. I called him on it. He's violent. Shot at me. My bullet hit his arm. So I got a Dishonorable Discharge. Gave her all my money. Told her to get out of the county. She deserved better than me."

They passed the fort entrance. Billy studied its buildings, arranged around a square parade ground. A soldier approached. Miles Wood said, "Tell First Sergeant Hartman I'm bringing in prisoners." Unnoticed was the quizzical expression at the rank.

When Louis Hartman approached with Charles Smith, he too was in private's uniform, and pale after three weeks in the guardhouse.

Taking Mackie aside, Hartman snarled, "You're going down;" and savagely kicked dirt. Stepping back, he said, "Private Smith 'ill take them to the guardhouse."

Peak-roofed, the guardhouse's twelve foot, windowless walls were vertical boards. Sole light came from a ventilation opening, extending along opposing wall tops. A long bench was at either side. The door closed behind the prisoners.

Mackie said in voice flattened by concealed fear, "It's not luxury; but it's home." Billy laughed, testing wall boards for looseness; while Mackie sat enervated on a bench. In the gloom, Mackie saw that Billy took the salt shaker from his jacket and emptied it into a pocket.

Banging on the door, Billy called, "Guard! Privy! Quick!"

It was Smith. As they walked, Billy noticed that the private's holster flap was unfastened, exposing the front-facing Colt .45 butt.

At the privy door, Billy whirled, hand flying from pocket with salt spray. Smith clutched burning blinded eyes as his revolver was wrenched away. Billy ran.

"Escapee!" Billy heard, rounding a building; and, almost colliding with a soldier. He was tackled.

Smith ran up, eyes streaming, yelling, "Bastard." In frenzy, Billy was pulled up; pinioned. Jacket roughly searched. Gun snatched back. Punched hard in belly. Dropped writhing. Kicked. Kicked. Dragged up, semi-conscious. Slapped, blood dripping from mouth. Smith's voice: "Take him back before I kill him."

A shove sent Billy onto the guardhouse floor. The door slammed. Billy managed, "Failed 'scape attem'." Mackie carried him to a bench and used his jacket as a pillow. Almost immediately, Billy fell asleep. Beside him, Mackie sat shivering.

Several hours later, Private Charles Smith ordered Billy out. To the boy's surprise, Windy Cahill stood grinning, holding leg shackles. Billy watched the kneeling blacksmith's mammoth back. Each clawlike ankle cuff was a hollow tube penetrated by a circular ratcheted end; screwed tight by an internal rod, turned with a big cylindrical key. Before the door closed behind him, Billy heard Smith say to Cahill, "Enlisted men's shindig tonight."

That evening, in the unlit guardhouse, Billy made a salt slurry in his tin cup for his swollen-lipped mouth. He examined his side. "None broken." Unable to free his legs, he finally said, "Anyway, chains don't stop you getting 'round."

Wretchedly, John Mackie thought, "Getting around? We're trapped." Billy fell asleep on a bench as inrushing air vibrated mournfully under the high roof. Mackie visualized Hartman's vicious boot kicking an earthen grave and sobbed about his own death.

Distantly, the military band tuned. Billy awoke, stretching, saying, "My escape song." Mackie was incredulous. "That roof space up there. I just need a hand."

Standing on the bench, Mackie made a stirrup, lifted, and said, "Bye, kid. I ... I won't see you again." He would, Billy answered. Wood made a mistake. Mackie thought, "You'll be the only one to remember my name." Huskily, he said, "Look for Jessie Evans."

Billy, laughing, presuming a joke, grasped the top beam, swung a leg onto it, then extended lengthwise, peering out. No guard. Lizard-flat, sliding out, roof shingles scraping his back, he emerged; clutching the beam. He hung, then dropped into music.

The illuminated building across the parade ground had hitched horses, but his leg chain prevented mounting. He ran, holding it.

At the cook-shed of Atkin's Cantina, Billy found the surprised greasy-skinned owner and asked, "Got a file? Windy gave me a gift."

Tom Varley said it seemed his face got others; but it would not be the first time he had removed Windy's handiwork. And he should leave Grant County. Billy said, "Can't. I'm waiting for Mackie."

MARCH 28, 1877   1:16 PM   WEDNESDAY

Back at Atkin's cookshed, Billy asked a worker if Mackie was out yet. Wordlessly, the uncomfortable man, looking down, handed him a copy of the *Grant County Herald*.

Billy read: "The death of John Mackie, a horse thief with a reward on his head, happened March 13th when he was attempting escape from the guard house at Fort Grant. According to Private Louis Hartman, who did the shooting, Mackie grabbed the gun of Private Charles Smith. The Coroner's Jury concluded that the shooting was self-defense and bruising was from an earlier escape attempt. Commander Charles Compton said, 'The action of Private Hartman is commendable. This warns horse thieves to stay out of Grant County.'"

"Sorry, kid," the worker said.

"Thanks for showing me this," said Billy, masking horror and disbelief.

AUGUST 1, 1877   10:08 AM   WEDNESDAY

Four, aimlessly violent, target-shooting months had buried Billy's pain by secret shooting and rage in the Pinaleño Mountain foothills; as new insatiable hunger had fed his changing body.

Now, in Atkins Cantina, a lanky youth, with jutting shoulders of adolescent angularity, called out from a table, "Hey Gus! Gus Gildea!" to an entering young man, who responded uncertainly. Billy smiled, reminding him of June a year before: at Elliott's Saloon with Frank Simmons and Jack Coleman.

"Hell, you've put on size!" exclaimed mustached Gildea, sitting. Henry Clay Hooker's employee was now flamboyant. A cartridge belt crossed his chest, in addition to the holstered one at his waist. Gildea said, "Just got me tintypes made by a traveling photographer set up at McDowell's. I'm doing *special* work for Hooker now."

Unaware of the hint, Billy said he was looking for cow work too. "Maybe I can help," said Gus Gildea, privy to a rumor that created attractive commonality.

Gildea said, "Mackie's dying was a damn shame." Billy's jaw tightened. "Isn't there a warrant on you too?" Billy teased that they'd returned the *missing* horses.

Gus Gildea smiled, but said, "And Windy's got something against you. He's crazy. He'll kill somebody someday."

Billy took a deck from his vest and meditatively shuffled, saying everything was a gamble. "That's the point," said Gildea. "Your odds in Bonita, with that warrant and Cahill, are bad."

Billy dealt Gildea a card, then himself. He showed his: the ace of spades. He reshuffled and dealt again. Gildea got a different card. Billy's was still the ace. Billy said, "Give yourself the best odds. The game's about freedom. One I'll never lose." Billy's face had changed. Gildea had seen that expression on men capable of anything.

"Well," Gus Gildea said, "stay away from New Mexico Territory. I heard that its cattle king, John Chisum, had a war there four months ago against small ranchers rustling his cattle. But he's got herds arriving here now. I'll take you to his cow camp to meet the boss, Sorghum Smith, for work. Smith owes me a favor from when I was with their outfit. Her name was Jane. So you need money for a new gun?"

Surprised, Billy asked why he had said that. "Even if it's hidden, you can tell: still a man with a gun." Gildea revealed what made Billy appealing. "I heard 'bout your shooting. Frank Simmons once snuck up on you practicing. Fact is, that's my job for Hooker. A gunman's worth a lot." Billy absorbed only the paternal solicitude reminiscent of John Mackie's.

Later, from a high ridge, Billy and Gus Gildea watched the Chisum herd: a ribbon of cattle and occasional horsemen from horizon to horizon, emerging from opaque dust raised by hooves.

Gildea said, "Cattle boom's just starting. There're thousands of miles of trails: in New Mexico Territory; over Texas, Colorado, Kansas, and Missouri, up to Saint Louis; and north to Nebraska; and through the Territories of the Dakotas, Wyoming, and Montana."

They descended. Gildea said, "Look at that steer! Easily seven foot horns." The stream of life flowed past. There were blacks, reds, browns; pale ones with dark stripes down their backs; blue-grays and pintos. Gildea laughed. "Doing cow-herding, I liked the food best. Prairie oysters. Come spring branding, you cut 'em, and drop the suckers in the branding fire."

They rode alongside. The immensity, individual and collective, was awesome. On cloven hooves the size of a man's head, the huge creatures, with slabed chests tucking high to belly, walked with antelope grace; ponderous wedged heads laden with curving horns. High-humped withers rippled muscle, as sheeted skin flapped from neck to chest. But it was their eyes, bulging from bony sockets, which captured Billy's attention. They were eyes of acceptance, eyes approaching the final vision of slaughter.

In Lincoln, two hundred ninety-three miles northeast of Chisum's herd, full from a meal of beef stew, two cousins, Frank and George Coe, were in the just completed, double-winged adobe of Alexander McSween and his wife, having been hired from their Ruidoso farm, twelve miles away, to fiddle for its house-warming, combined with celebrating the opening of Tunstall's store. In the parlor, they tuned their instruments. Fair-complected good-natured men, they shared slope-shouldered wiry build, light eyes embedded in rubbery lids, large straight noses, and fingers agile with musical talent.

A McSween employee, George Washington, joined them with his fiddle. "Miss the soldierin' in Texas?" asked Frank, as the man pulled up a chair.

"Had my fill of white officers for colored regiments. Wasn't our hair that got us the name buffalo soldiers; it was toughness. We helped win that War." Bitterness flickered across the muscular man's dark clean-shaven face.

"Guests will be arriving soon," said George Coe, wanting to retain his happy mood. "Tunstall and McSween worked damn fast: finishing that store and this house in two months."

Washington said, "George Peppin - after building just about everything in this town - knows what he's doing. He's just about finished with that underground pit jail here. Did you hear he's been deputized by Sheriff Brady? Soon, there'll be so many jobs, we'll all have a few."

"Well," said George Coe, "Tunstall's taking on enough himself, what with that cattle ranch on the Feliz and his store. And I heard McSween's brought in his brother-in-law for a law partner - him and his family. Is it true Tunstall's putting in a bank in his store?"

"Yes," said Washington. "Lincoln County Bank. John Chisum's president."

"When Murphy an' Dolan come to the dance tonight," said Frank Coe, his light-brown beard, like his younger cousin's, extending to his chest in an inverted V, "they'll probly beat their usal whiskey barrel in the mornin' an' whiskey barrel at night, jus' to keep poolite with all this compeetition."

His cousin said, "Tunstall's made our neighbor on the next farm - that Dick Brewer - his foreman."

"Tunstall's hiring guns too," said George Washington. "Met John Middleton, Fred Waite, Jim French, or Henry Brown?"

"Yup. Come to a dance at our farm," said Frank. "Middleton shur looked rough. Waite's a half-breed, ain' he?"

"Yes," said Washington, disliking racist innuendo. "Protection's smart. Nobody's forgotten Robert Casey; or John Riley shooting Juan Patrón."

George Coe, laying his fiddle on a chair to straighten his suspenders, said, "But now we've got a celebration. Us three are fiddling in a new day in Lincoln town." For warm-up, they chose "Turkey in the Straw."

At the same time, Gus Gildea, enjoying Billy's attentiveness, was showing off knowledge, as they followed Chisum's herd toward the camp. He said, "With John Chisum's problems, you might get a job like mine." The boy just laughed. "Then there's a job that makes twice the trail boss's: cook. Hundred a month. Cowboy gets thirty. But after a three or six month drive, the boys feel pretty flush.

"You know, these longhorns started out as fighting cattle brought by conquistadors. Still fight. Can jab a horn, and tear out your horse's guts. Anyways, in spring roundup, you sort 'em out: some for market; and you brand the calves. You got stamping irons with a welded-on brand, or running irons - just a loop you run. That's how Chisum does his Long Rail: one line from shoulder to hip."

Gus Gildea laughed. "And his rustlers run cinch rings on green sticks. Chisum tried to outdo them by inventing the split ear: makes a hanging flap called the 'jinglebob.' Can't change that.

"Hardest is starting a drive. Cattle hate leaving home range. So you move 'em fast - not the usual fifteen miles a day. Nights, you stop at the bedding ground; and herd-riders circle to keep 'em calm with singing. Here's something strange. Near midnight, the cattle stand up and sigh."

Billy said, "Maybe remembering they're far from home."

Entering camp, Gus Gildea led the way toward the spoke-wheeled chuck wagon, once a Civil War ambulance, canvas still covering its square frame; and converted for cooking. The inspiration was by an early cattleman, Charles Goodnight, who added a high rear cupboard, the chuck box; and a drop-hinged, back-board, work surface.

The cook stood there. Smoke skimmed from his long fire-pits, where iron rods held up big black pots on hooks; and brushwood fuel had been piled by cowboys hoping for extra pie.

"Cookie's alone," said Gildea. "Horse wrangler's supposed to help; but he's being fired. Bad for Will Arden's rattlesnake temper. But if he likes you, you could be the new wrangler. Cookie!" Gildea called.

The sinewy man tipped up his battered Stetson with a knuckle. Beside his dough-lined pie tins, was a whiskey bottle rolling pin. "Hell, Gus," he shouted, "don't bring in no goddamn grit."

Gildea and Billy circled downwind and tied their horses. "Bringing me a helper, Gus?" The aproned man's leathered face had lips like a tear in hide. At a round Dutch oven, embedded in one trench, Will Arden lifted its flat charcoal-laden lid with a gonch hook rod; and his forearm looked hard as a horse's foreleg. Billy said he'd cooked, but not chuck wagon. "Ain't no comparson," said the man.

Gus Gildea left them, noticing a past acquaintance. Billy waited, buffeted by wind, and said, "Blowing 'ill fan the coals one-sided at your oven. Make a hot spot." Arden responded that he wasn't dumb; and told him to add water to the beans, handing a pot, cocking his head toward the wagon's water barrel. Billy said, "If I don't heat it first, they'll end up tough. Ruin your reputation."

The man laughed. "Hell, boy, you're nickel plated! Boss'll probly hire you. So I'll show you something. 'Cept for me, it's the most important item here." In a chuck box cubicle, rested a five gallon crock. "My starter. Reason my sourdough biscuits are famous. And when I give 'em to my boys, with frijole beans and salt pork, steak covered in flour and fried in tallow, till it's so tender that they can cut it with a fork - with pan gravy a'top – and finish with my fruit pie, with a pouring of tallow and molasses lick, and all the coffee they want, you couldn't find happier people on this earth. And when we stop, I always face my wagon tongue north. I give 'em all they need - even die-rection."

That night, Billy sat on the ground with Gus Gildea and the Chisum cowboys, in cookfire glow chiseling faces under hat brims and jaggedly tracking angular bodies. He listened to drawling anecdotes of stampedes - a fallen man crushed so that only his face was recognizably human - near-misses of lightening bolts, and stretches of land so dry that cattle went blind before they died; all told with soldierly jocularity that invigorates danger and makes hardship belonging's badge.

Gildea asked one cowboy, "What do you think of Chisum, Lee? Henry got hired." The man said Chisum was tight, but a good boss; as all looked at Billy with new and friendly interest.

Later, Billy, on his bedroll, remained awake amidst sleeping men on their big tarpaulins folded in summer's warmth, but also potential rainshields and wrapping for blankets and possessions. Breeze carried night riders' songs: "... bye old Paint, I'm a leavin' Cheyenne ... foot in the stirrup, my ..." and the smell of sweat, tobacco, and leather. Sprawled sinued limbs, in long-john sheathing, were relaxed in latent potency of unashamed crotches heavy with maleness. One man rose, stallion white, with muscle-rippling walking, then arced moon-lit liquid before returning. On those men's bodies would hang metal of spurs, metal of guns, metal of cartridges, pounds of metal in maleness; while now they lay amidst their leather of belts, of holsters, of boots, of saddles: their cattle transformed into their maleness.

The bull, horns thick as a man's arms, and spreading longer than a man's body, was defeated by their maleness, which consumed his flesh and the flesh of his females and children, and which braided their skins into riata ropes to snake forty feet and capture and throw them down to burning hide branding, without pity and with eager excitement of maleness.

Trampled tails were six months long in maleness; latent also in the huge sleeping cattle whose insane murderous stampede torrent could not be resisted by any living thing.

And Billy fell asleep absorbing potency within that sleeping maleness, absorbing belonging, peaceful in the warmth and the moonlight, peaceful in the regenerative hope of youth; and not expecting that this new haven, like all his others, would soon be lost.

AUGUST 17, 1877   10:53 AM   FRIDAY

A Chisum man, though the youngest, Billy, with newly purchased revolver secreted in waistband, entered Lou Elliott's Saloon for the first time since Mackie's death. Immediately, the fat big-nosed man mentioned everything. Blocking returned grief, finishing his coffee, Billy left into burning heat.

Across the dirt strip road, in the shade of Hog Ranch's porch, a lithe woman stood and boldly called, "That you, Henry Antrim?" while squinting into brightness and smoothing damp strands of pinned-up blond hair.

Billy stepped off the planking. A dust devil, a miniature tornado, swirled sixty yards away, before dissipating into a powdery wind.

He asked how she knew his name. "I'm Mattie. I came when you were with Mackie. You sher have grown." Her pale skin looked like a candle's melting rim. "You sher look hot. I got me a tub o' cool water. I'd wash yer back." She walked in. Billy followed.

Paunchy George McKittrick was on a dilapidated cushioned chair reading the *Arizona Citizen* newspaper. Mattie said, "Showin' him 'round." Billy followed her past closed doors.

The last opened to a small room, with window bisected by the Pinaleños and webbed by a lace curtain. Its light, through rose silk folding screen panels, was sunrise tint on the tin tub's water. Her ornate iron bed had chipped paint. Beside a hat rack, was a chair.

Mattie said wistfully, "Once I had a kid. I was thinkin' he might look like you." Billy hung his hat. She said, "His father took him. That felt bad. But the way Mackie died was bad 'nough. He didn' deserve that. Girls here told me 'bout Cathy. In my o-pinion she shouldn'a left without him. It ain' easy to find love."

She went to her dresser. Yellow hair, yellow as his mother's, fell wavy from its pins. "I wanted to get to know you. I seen how you're always lookin' 'round so careful like. Like me. You an' me don' fit into the bunch." Gently Billy answered that there was nothing to fit into - just living. "Maybe," she said, and understood that he had said no.

Without resentment, she drew back the need for her lost son or for rescue like Cathy. Behind the screen, she became a fuchsia silhouette, while he disrobed, hiding the Colt .45 under his clothes on the chair.

Mattie emerged in a sashed silk robe; open enough for a skin path and a golden tuft. Billy asked if she would still wash his back. "What I promised. Figured you weren' here to steal horses." Laughing, he glanced sidelong, blue flashing.

Into wet coolness, he submerged, knees sharp-angled to fit the tin tub. Behind, she dipped soap and held his shoulder to stabilize scrubbing. His knees were mountain islands encircled by liquid silver ripples. Underwater, pearly legs, feet, forearms, and hands were a disconnected puzzle of surface reflections through which something unrecognized, but present, miraculously flowed out, leaving buoyancy and yearning. He had been running so long just to reach this water-filled place.

She shifted alongside, robe open. He stood, but impulsively crouched, dunking his head into artificial current, and with liquid forelock, took an offered towel; telling her his real name was Billy.

"You sher do look good, Billy," she said and directed him behind her screen. A standing mirror was full length. His ears rimmed red at first sight of his entire body. She said, "You're half boy an' half man. It 'ill never be like this again."

On the desert-hot bed, with sheets warm as living flesh, with her all ivory and caressing, he heard her say, "My boy, my man." Boy-man associations, entangling with just suppressed Mackie pain, returned rage. Suddenly, there was only hard thrusting: thrusting of gun barrel and thrusting of gunpowder-engorged lethal-headed casings; thrusting death, death, death. He hurtled through. He lay panting and wet against her, as she murmured pleasure; and he reveled in new power.

When he was dressing, she called from behind the screen, "You got money, Billy Antrim?" He said no. "How 'ill you pay me?" He'd come back, he said. Barefoot, laughing, she emerged in chemise and corset and said, "You do just that, Billy Antrim." He embraced her, hand on her buttocks, hand on her back, pressing her close. "Thank you, Mattie," he said, put on his hat, and walked out.

In heat making far flatland waver in watery mirages, Billy rode to Atkin's Cantina singing "Old Dan Tucker," drifting his exuberant tenor into silence of Mount Graham's ambiguous vigil. "Now old Dan Tucker is a fine old man / Washed his face in a fryin' pan / Combed his hair with a wagon wheel / Died with a toothache in his heel."

When Billy entered the busy saloon, greasy-faced Tom Varley followed him to an empty table, talking low. "I heard Major Compton got in trouble for not telling Miles Wood to drop those charges. So Mackie died for nothing." Rage tore through Billy, as Varley greeted an incoming man. "Hey, John Murphy! Congratulations on that race."

The gentrified man laughed. "Thanks, Tom. Cashaw's the best in Grant County all right. Keep an eye on him, will you? I got some business at Norton and Stewart's store at the fort. Heading there with Norton on his buckboard."

After he left, Varley said to Billy, "You look upset. Take a look at Cashaw. He'll take your mind off anything." There, in sunlight, gleamed the big bay. Reflexively, Billy scanned Mackie's checklist.

When Billy returned, his fried steak had been left. He sliced aggressively, aware that it had been alive and killed. Distracted, biting a chunk, he heard, "So you're back."

Windy Cahill, smiling broadly, took a chair. "Somebody just told me you ain't no runt no more. Figured we'd celebrate." Cahill looked contrite. "I know 'bout that dropped warrant." His big hairy hand, with wrist almost as wide as its base, pressed the tabletop to turn. Over his shoulder, he called, "Tom, we need a bottle."

Then amber liquid streams poured like twisted ropes into two glasses. Cahill drank. "Bottoms up," he said encouragingly.

Billy could smell the close alcohol: odor so familiar, odor of men. He was aware of Cahill's closeness, Cahill's smiling; Cahill wanting to initiate him, welcome him, no longer a runt. Billy smiled back tentatively, and lifted weightlessness. Windy Cahill gulped another, as if showing how.

Billy threw back his head, relaxing tongue to welcome the alcohol. Burning seared. He gasped. As if connection to his body had been severed, he could not breathe. Choking, flushed, he shyly met the man's eyes; a moment before unseen and crafty, now attentive, his initiator. Cahill said, "Seems you don't drink much." Old promise, Billy managed to say. Cahill drank again. Billy watched more liquor swirl with pleasant drifting lethargy into his own glass.

This time, Billy drank wanting its coursing heat promising sun's power, as fluid fire seared outward, eliminating skin; and leaving him boundaryless and omnipotent in a wildly exciting room of clinking glass, voice fragments, and darting light. His hands, at table-edge, discovered no parallel to the floor. The room had abandoned horizontal and vertical arbitrariness, and melted into a marvelous kaleidoscopic dream.

His arm was being roughly shaken. Fetid drunken words were close. "I seen Mattie. Said *you* were with her. She's *my* whore. I gave her a lesson. She got mad. Says *you're* too good to pay.

"So I says to myself, 'I's all clear. That bisnes with Mackie was no bisnes with horse stealin'. Was pimpin'.' I want to fight."

Billy's unresponsive tongue struggled, saying he had no reason to fight. "Hell you don'. I was *there* when Mackie died. Know tha' big red mark? He had one somewheres else." White heat shot across Billy's brain. He heard, "And they killed him like Injuns' kill - so he could watch. Somebody had to hold him."

Billy lunged snarling. Varley rushed, ordering them out. Dragged through the door by Cahill, Billy was yelling, "You son of a bitch."

On the porch, Billy wrenched free, punching concussively. Blood streaming from his nose, Windy Cahill bellowed, throwing the boy onto the roadway, his hat flying off.

People collected to watch the dramatic mismatch. Cahill grabbed Billy's hair, shouting, "Bastard pimp;" beating his head against dirt as Billy kicked into a constricting funnel of darkness.

Then there was silence. Possibly he was dead. But he realized he had been released. Straddling him on knees, the man lifted, intending to smash him backward and crush his skull. But too drunk, Cahill lost balance, falling on him. Then the big belly rose just enough. Instantly, Billy's hand darted across his waistband for his gun.

Its muzzle stabbed the belly's bulk. Billy pulled the trigger. In the shell, compressed was an explosion with 15,000 pounds of pressure per square inch, bursting out a bullet at 830 feet per second in sulphurous smoke.

Squealing, Windy Cahill, pouring blood, flopped down his imprisoning weight; but his writhing agony freed Billy to stand, as horrified witnesses watched.

Cashaw. To Tom Varley at the doorway, Billy shouted, "Tell John Murphy he'll be back."

The big bay had to maneuver around a flailing supine man and silent people. Then he galloped, snorting aggressively. It was east.

Into their dust, Billy looked back. No one followed. His gory hand stuck to the reins. Switching, he spit, and rubbed the hand on his thigh. In the setting sun behind, clouds were scarlet wounds. Abdomen heaving, retching, Billy leaned to vomit.

Finally, the moon's sliver illuminated sheep in a valley. Herd dog barking alarmed their shepherd, who grabbed his old muzzle-loading rifle. Aroused sheep rose awkwardly, with straightened hind quarters and struggling bent forelegs.

The man called, "Beelly?" The shirt of the walking boy had dark stains. The shepherd said, "I ask no questions."

Billy asked if Ramón Gómez had any horses. "Only one left. A paint. Cowboys want no paints. Only Indians. And I will give you a shirt. And a hat with a red band for an Indian peace sign. There is an Apache uprising. With it, you will ride safer."

Soon Billy led a bony black-and-white mustang to the spring where he had left Cashaw. "You're going home," he said numbly to the big bay. Released, slapped on the rump, again Cashaw ran.

The paint moved willingly, but with rough short strides much in contrast to his predecessor.

Hours later, no demarcation indicated New Mexico Territory; but Billy's arms lifted as if becoming wings. Stars scintillated through tears. Into the night he called, "Home! Home! Home!"

One hundred eighty-seven miles northeast of that borderland, in Lincoln, darkness crouched in clouds' opaque destruction of stars and moon. Illumination along the town's single street was only at the Wortley Hotel, across from the two-story Murphy-Dolan store.

Sam Wortley, its portly bald proprietor, stood behind the bar, briskly drying glasses and listening. On his chin, a big hairy mole clung like a beetle. Two men occupied a table. Wortley made out: "We've accomplished so much ... But Susan says we'll rue competing with Dolan." Alexander McSween immediately regretted that exposure, and compulsively adjusted his shirt collar.

"On the contrary," said John Tunstall, sipping brandy and smiling sweetly, "competition stimulates business. With two big stores here, we shall draw more customers for all."

McSween bowed interlaced fingers with cracking hyperextension, and laughed at himself. "You're right. Susan thinks me, you, and her are the only civilized people here."

The door opened. Tunstall rose, warmly greeting a rustically dressed man as: Mister Matthews!

The newcomer said, glancing meaningfully at Sam Wortley, "Didn't expect *you'd* be here this late." His small head drew back with distaste, its expansive forehead and insignificant features, accented only by a mustache, having blankness of a slab.

McSween asked where he'd be investing his seven hundred dollars from his land sale to Tunstall. Matthews said, uncomfortably lying, "Still thinking."

Leaving, Tunstall and McSween passed James Dolan, entering and feigning graciousness.

From darkness near the Wortley Hotel's long path to the street, a figure said to them, "Night, Englishman. I'm Jessie Evans."

Tunstall reached to a painful grip, and exclaimed lightheartedly, "You certainly are strong, Mister Evans. Would you like my given name?"

Insolently, Jessie recited, John Henry Tunstall. "Ah, yes. The local style of monikers. If you are interested, I am currently hiring."

A short laugh sounded. "I'm workin' now, Englishman."

Proceeding eastward on the street, McSween said that Jessie Evans was a tough. Tunstall laughed. "Tough-fibered loyalists would be rather jolly." Disapprovingly, McSween cited Chisum's gunmen, not having met those already hired. "Actually," Tunstall said, "I was fancying King Arthur's knights."

As they continued along the road's north side, McSween regained enthusiasm, and said, "I'm sure Dolan's gnashing his teeth since we transferred our mail to that new post office in Roswell. When he was made postmaster in April, I surmised he'd spy on our plans. And the Roswell postmaster seems intelligent: that eccentric journalist from Silver City, Ash Upson."

Tunstall replied, "Hopefully, Mister Upson's intemperate use of alcohol does not bring him the seeming fate of James Dolan's partner Lawrence Murphy - following on the sorry heels of your deceased Emil Fritz."

McSween said, "By the way, I'm winning that Fritz case. When I was in New York last November, I hired a law firm - Donnell, Lawson, and Company - to go after that crooked Merchants' Life Insurance Company. On July nineteenth, Donnell and Lawson recovered the ten thousand; though - after deducting their fees and expenses - only seven thousand one hundred forty-eight dollars and forty-nine cents was left. I put that in my Saint Louis account.

"Emil Fritz's two siblings want it, but there's a delay: heirs in Germany. I represent the estate, not them."

Tunstall asked about Dolan's claim. "Irrelevant," said McSween. "He hasn't even proved in Probate Court that Fritz was indebted to their business. The law - meaning the truth - always wins."

At their adjoining structures, McSween opened the gate in a picket fence. Tunstall continued on to his store, which held his spacious apartment.

Dolan had joined Matthews after Sam Wortley's deferential greeting. Sipping whiskey, Dolan said unctuously, "Jacob Basil Matthews ... a man learning business." Bootsteps sounded. Without turning, Dolan said, "Do join us, Jessie. Share this bottle with me and Billy. I recall you prefer 'Billy.' Seven hundred dollars cash has made Billy a silent partner in the House."

Matthews's mustache pressed his shotglass's rim. Dolan said, "Tunstall and McSween never realized that you had no title to that land, did they, Billy?" There was a startled jerk. "One hundred percent profit ... *if* no one claimed fraud."

Matthews looked terrified. "Ain't no way they'd find out."

"*I* did." Fearfully, Matthews asked what he wanted. "Just to realize that, as a partner, you are now our friend."

AUGUST 18, 1877   5:48 AM   SATURDAY

Escape seemed certain to Billy, as ahead, fiery dawn stained mesas and road red; and white sky saturated azure. Suddenly, behind, hoofbeats pounded. He braced, prepared to fight.

"Howdy," a test greeting, was soon shouted. The ruddy-faced young rider slowed, looked relieved, and said, "Your hat ... Some Injuns wear a red band to trick you. Run into that Apache Victorio, you're dead." The glances were too curious. Testing for a bounty hunter, Billy complimented a scabbarded carbine. "Thanks," said the youth. "I'm doing the mail run from Ralston in Arizona Territory."

"Wait a minute! You're little Henry Antrim! 'Cept not little! I'm Anthony Connor. You were smartest in class." Billy laughed, relaxing, recognizing. "I work for Richard Knight. Now he's got a stage stop up ahead: Knight's Station. And he's got the Grant County mail contract." Connor grinned. "You sure made a fool of Sheriff Whitehill. The chimney!"

"Innocent till proven guilty," Billy teased, but felt a battle-tried soldier's impassable gulf.

Anthony Connor exclaimed, "You didn't wait, Henry!" Both laughed. Connor said, "I heard there was a shooting in Bonita. But that Territory's tame compared to here. People 're saying there'll be a war in Lincoln County. And that cattle king, John Chisum, already had one near Seven Rivers on the Pecos. But he wants another."

When Anthony Connor galloped ahead, Billy retained Seven Rivers as a destination. He said aloud, "War," with a thrill immediately contaminated by nausea at Cahill's blood.

Nausea also contracted Pat Garrett's stomach as he stood in Hidetown's oppressively hot humidity, five hundred fifty-six miles due east of Billy's road, swatting flies and watching their black swarms clouding mountainous stinking stacks of buffalo skins.

When he entered the noisy Bee Hive Saloon, the proprietor said. "Heard 'bout yer troubles, Pat: Luther Duke pullin' out. Injun raids. Anyways, here's some luck. See them two sittin' there? This winter they got eight thousan' hides. Them's the best." One was fair and big, with a handlebar mustache; the other, dark, raw-boned, and short.

At their table, Garrett said, "Heard you all are hide men like me. Pat Garrett. Mind if I sit?"

"Not at all," said the big man sociably. "Name's John William Poe. This here's John Jacobs: my pard. Two Johns. I go by John, him by John Jay." Garrett sat. Poe continued, "Only thing I like more then talking about buffs is ..." Shooting buffs, bearded Jacobs interrupted. Poe chuckled. "We've been together so long he finishes my sentences. Our only difference is him wanting a golden-haired gal to settle down with. I'm still on my original rails."

Garrett said, "I'm with you. Heard your outfit's the best."

"Ain't easy nowadays," said Jacobs, "what with fifteen hundred men sharing our range." Poe smiled. With large head, heavy jaw, and broad nose, he exuded satisfaction in his unassuming plainness.

Feigning success, Garrett said a man could still find nice-sized stands. Poe's eyes strayed in possible boredom. So Garrett, trying to be ingratiating, asked how he'd started out.

Poe said, "I was raised on my paternal granddad's, Kentucky, tobacco farm. When I wanted to go West, he said, 'You'll go to the dogs.' So far, I've proved him wrong. When I came here, I heard about another Kentucky boy, who was raising corn - John Jay here - and joined him. We'd already counted our future money when a black cloud came." Grasshoppers, John Jacobs said. Ate everything. Poe continued, "Best thing for us. Back then, in seventy-three, everybody said there was fabulous profit on the range. So we got Joe McCombs for a skinner. He kept us laughing."

Poe's small eyes teared as he stifled laughter and said to his partner, "Remember in seventy-five, when you were in town looking for a bride - so to speak - and Indians stole everything at camp? And me and McCombs had to sleep in green hides?" Sniggering, John Jacobs finished that *his* was lose; *McCombs's* was tight. Poe said, "So, by morning, McCombs was a frozen-solid cocoon. Me, I was up making coffee. Finally, McCombs says, 'Goddamnit, roll me over there and melt me out.' " Both men roared.

"Bad loss from Indians?" Garrett interrupted, jealous of the excluding hilarity. "We had that. This past February that Comanche: Nigger Horse. Again this May, that white man turned Indian: Herman Lehmin. My partner, Skelton Glenn, is buying me out. So I'm looking for opportunities." That was as far as he could beg.

Poe said they were already set up for the coming winter.

Garrett felt rejected, and responded with self-aggrandizement. "I'm also considering relocating to this big town in New Mexico Territory on the Pecos River: Fort Sumner. One rich family owns it: the Martells." Maxwell, Poe corrected. And he'd heard it was pretty desolate there.

As if challenged, Garrett abruptly decided. "That's the place for me." His mood rose. He joked, "Like Fort *Sumter* and the start of the Civil War. I'll make history."

John William Poe asked if he knew *its* history. Garrett feigned interest. Poe said, "Well, if the Mescalero Apaches and Navajos believed in Hell, they'd call it Sumner. In sixty-two, the government made a reservation there for them: Bosque Redondo.

"Fort Sumner was built on the east bank of the Pecos River to contain them. After the Confederates lost in New Mexico Territory, Union Brigadier General James Carleton used his troops and Colonel Kit Carson to round up Apaches - then Navajos - for it. By sixty-three, Kit Carson had four hundred Apaches. The next year, he got nine thousand Navajos to surrender in what they called their homeland. Made 'em walk the three hundred miles to it. They called it 'The Long Walk'. They knew Carleton's Indian policy: 'Kill all the men, and maybe the squaws and children too.' A long walk was better than no walk." Poe smiled at his humor: a bracing conviction of his own goodness.

"But nobody'd considered that Navajos and Apaches were enemies, not exactly like putting two pups in a basket. Also, they didn't cotton to being civilized Christian farmers - even if you leave out the Christian part. Thousands died of starvation. And the Apaches escaped. In sixty-eight, the government sent the Navajos home. Should be called 'Two Long Walks.'" Poe chuckled.

"In seventy-two, Apaches were put in another reservation: the Mescalero. So Fort Sumner was vacant till Lucien Bonaparte Maxwell bought it in seventy."

Garrett had paid no attention, and continued from where he had left off. "My life seems heading northwest: Alabama, where I was born. Louisiana, where I grew. Texas. Fort Sumner next. I feel something big is waiting for me."

Poe listened with interest. "Me," he said, "I'm considering law enforcement. Hidetown's been an all-night hurrah town long enough. The U.S. Marshal here, Flemming, has been wanting me as a deputy. You'd make some lawman yourself with all that height."

Immensely flattered, Garrett smiled. All stood. Garrett leaned to shake John Jacobs's hand, then faced John William Poe eye-to-eye, savoring their handshake and the placid confidence he longed for in himself; while fending off plummeting depression by focusing on Fort Sumner, the Pecos River, and the future.

SEPTEMBER 3, 1877   10:17 AM   MONDAY

After working only four days at the farm of "Hog" Davis, near Knight's Station, Billy had urgency strong as a migratory drive, Now, that bandy-legged man squatted with a twig to scratch, in red dirt, Billy's desired directions to Seven Rivers and the Pecos River.

That red dirt held two hundred eighty million years of mineral memory, of ancient rivers' labors in reducing granite, feldspar, mica, and quartz to sand; which accumulated during flooding in tidal flats, estuaries, and stream valleys as sediments so deep that they compressed to rock; which, in turn, became soil in weathering eons of Earth's single early continent: Pangea. Remembered everywhere was iron, because the desert preserves it in dryness; and transforms it, by oxidation, to rust redness. Without water to leach it away, iron's red stain stretched to the horizon; stretched ahead on Billy's route, like the mark of blood.

Hog Davis said, "First you head to Mesilla." He paused. "Why not Silver City? They got minin' there." Billy said he wanted cattle work. "Welll," Davis said, making an X, "yer here, by a main road. North it heads to Silver City. Southeast to Mesilla, in 'bout two days." Mesilla was the next X. Far to the right, was scratched a long north-to-south line. "Pecos River." An X for Seven Rivers was on its west bank, due east of Mesilla. Billy said that looked easy.

"Ain't. "Cause o' Injuns, ye head north first." Northeast of his Mesilla X, Davis incised a north-to-south zigzag. "Organ Mountains. Look like church pipe organs. Ye cross 'em at the San Augustin Pass. Jus' so ye know," he extended their zigzag, "they meet the San Andres Mountains." His twig traveled the route from Mesilla across the San Augustin Pass, and continued northeast until stopping at a new vertical zigzag. "Sacramento Mountains," said Davis. Billy repeated that due east looked easier.

Hog Davis said, "Lookahere, boy," making a north-to-south zigzag west of Seven Rivers and cutting across that straight route. "You'd need te cross these here Guadalupe Mountains. Full o' Apaches. Heard o' Victorio?"

"What's between the Organs and the Sacramentos?"

"Tularosa Valley. Got cattle work there too. Right after you cross the San Augustin Pass is Shedd's Ranch." Billy repeated his Pecos destination. "Okay, boy. Welll, fer sights," he made an upright oval northeast of the San Augustin Pass, "ye'll pass the east side o' this big white desert: White Sands. From there, it's 'bout three days to the Sacramento Mountains.

" Ye follows the Tularosa River through 'em, an' through the Mescalero Reservation." That was a large vertical rectangle. "In it's a way station: Blazer's Mill. Then yer road heads toward Fort Stanton, an' turns southeast, followin' the Bonito River. Passes through a town called Lincoln. There you got supply stores." He drew Lincoln's X. The scratched-in Bonito then joined a due east river. "Hondo," Davis said. "Road follers it to Roswell, near the Pecos." He made its X. "Then you head south 'long the Pecos to Seven Rivers." Billy said that due east seemed faster.

With exasperation, Hog Davis said, "Yer damn hard-headed. Go east an' ye'll end up in Heaven or Hell - dependin' on your sins - but not Seven Rivers." Billy could barely wait to saddle the paint.

Impatiently, in Fort Sumner, two hundred ninety-seven miles northeast of Hog Davis's ranch, Paulita Maxwell, in boy's shirt and pants, fidgeted on a stool at her bedroom's dressing table, while watching her mirrored reflection of lush, long, auburn hair being brushed by familiar hands. She said, "Deluvina, I've got to go. Centauro's waiting. There's a wonderful wind."

"Sit quietly, child," the short fat woman, in a shapeless, yoked, cotton dress, said; her own iron-gray hair braided and in a bun. "This hair needs care." Her Navajo accent blunted "th" and drew out vowels. A subtle stop inflated each word, as if with extra meaning.

Petulantly, the girl said they should cut it off. "And break your mother's heart?" asked Deluvina.

Paulita signed. "And Papa's - if he was alive. Why did you say I had to grow up just because of some blood. Maybe it was a scratch?"

"Because a girl's body shows her the blood of life, so she will hold sacred the path of becoming a woman."

Paulita sprang up, hugging soft pendulousness of breasts, which hung almost to the belly. "I won't stop wearing pants," she said. "Victorio's sister Lozen is a great warrior, and *she* wears pants." Deluvina asked how she had heard of them. "Pete was talking to his new foreman, Barney Mason. Victorio's an Apache chief. Nobody can catch either of them.

"And I hate Barney Mason as the new foreman. Papa's Jesús Silva was better. Make one long braid."

Sitting again, Paulita said, "If I was a slave, I'd run away."

"It has been many years. And I would miss you. I love you." Paulita said freedom was better than love. The woman laughed. "The things you say. I would choose love. But I wish both for you. And it is your nature to love."

"But I'll never marry. Only Papa let me be free. Tell me again how he bought you."

Without rancor, Deluvina repeated her oft-told story. Emancipation, the post-war law of the land, had occurred neither to the Maxwells nor to her. "I was of the Navajo people - the Diné - and lived in happiness. I was nine years old. I lived with my father and my mother - who knew hidden meanings - and my fifteen year old sister and my three brothers. Then, in Canyon de Chelly Country - the land of my people - my father said one day, 'Let us gather piñon nuts.' But Indians who were enemies of my people captured us."

Paulita said she was ready for the bad part. "My mother threw her body over me." The girl wept quietly. "I saw a man leading away my father and my brothers. There were four shots. Then there was one shot. My mother fell on me. Me and my sister were spared. I was taken to Cimarron, to the town belonging to your father and mother."

"Then Papa bought you for ten dollars; and you were happy; but you never saw your sister again." Deluvina finished the braid. "Don't tell Mama or Pete that I've gone."

"Have I ever told one of your secrets?" The girl, disguised in the clothes Deluvina provided, said never; and earnestly kissed her nurse's firm cheek.

SEPTEMBER 5, 1877   8:16 AM   THURSDAY

Jingling Three Card Monte profit from the previous night, Billy explored Mesilla, crossing its plaza and turning at its southeast corner. There, a large dreary adobe extended to a complex of similar ones, and proclaimed importance by oversized, double doors.

Billy crossed its dirt street to a more hospitable, white-washed stuccoed adobe with blue-framed windows and a sign saying CORN EXCHANGE HOTEL, just as a scruffy red-headed adolescent furtively grabbed something at the threshold of the big double doors. Billy, guessing a fellow drifter, hailed him, asking, "New to these parts?"

"Wh-wh-why you askin'?" the youth responded warily, face distorting with his speech impediment. Billy said he was passing through. The boy lit a match to his find: a cigar stub. "Let's g-go. This is the c-courthouse. Next's the-the jail."

As they walked along the plaza, Billy asked if he was in trouble. There was an ambiguous sound. Billy asked his name. "T-T-T-Tom O'Keffe." Billy gave his as Henry Antrim. The boy said, "I'm fixin' to head to the Pe-Pe-Pecos valley. For c-c-cattle work."

"How about company?" Tom O'Keffe agreed. "I heard a good place is Seven Rivers," Billy said.

After they bought beef jerky for the trip, on the way to the livery, Billy said, "Damn, I forgot to buy sox. My last pair wore out." Barefoot in his boots, he decided to go back, but first entered a privy.

Inside, on the newspaper pile, was a front-page banner: "**ARIZONA CITIZEN, August 25, 1877.**" Immediately, he saw the headline, "**CORONERS JURY DECIDES ON CAHILL KILLING.**" He read: "The murdered man, Frank Cahill, lived long enough to make a final statement: 'I, Frank Cahill, say that yesterday, August 17th, Henry Antrim shot me.' The Coroner's Jury found the killing to be unjustifiable murder of an unarmed man and Henry Antrim was found guilty. He has not been taken into custody yet." Page crumpled, it disappeared into the privy hole.

Outside, O'Keffe was tossing away the cigar fragment. He asked, "You s-s-smoke, Henry?"

"No. Don't like the taste. Hey, Tom, call me Billy. Sounds better. And we should leave immediately."

Billy led Tom O'Keffe along Hog Davis's twig path. To their right, were the jagged Organ Mountains. Enthusiastically, O'Keffe's saliva sprayed. "O-o-on the other side, I want to see them Wh-White Sands. Li-like sugar o-o-of rich people."

Atop the San Augustin Pass, they viewed the great Tularosa Valley containing that white desert, legacy of the land's cataclysmic birth and an ocean's demise. That primordial water, 400 to 250 million years earlier, had waxed and waned over Pangea, itself fragmenting into modern continents 200 million years before Billy's and O'Keffe's presence. Twenty million years past, the southwestern portion of the North American continent, erstwhile sea-floor, was stretched by geologic tensions; until splitting fault edges were heaved skyward into mountains from which land sloped eastward for hundreds of miles.

Rainwater, coursing down that young San Andres range, had carried the ancient ocean's minerals, including gypsum; and a later ice age lake accumulated those sediments. After that lake also dried away, those minerals were pulverized by wind. And the granulated gypsum crystals remained as the desert of White Sands.

After descent into the Tularosa Valley, Billy and O'Keffe turned northward, first on red earth, then on bleaching innocence of white waves amidst grasses; as if confirming rebirth, confirming cleansing, even from Cahill's blood, still dried in the killing Colt's crevices.

Kicked-up dust from their horses carried gypsum's sweetness to their lips, as sky finally met only white dreamscape and soaring white dunes of White Sands. There, Billy dismounted, first tentatively stepping in yielding white; then clambering up a thirty foot white crest, shouting joyfully, all directions only white, until whiteness entered him and he expanded into it, and was silent.

Hearing, "Billy?" he laughed. From reverie had come the new name: his real name.

He leapt. With great sliding strides he descended, eyes wild with driving intensity, and said, "Tom, I've got a new plan. Last night an old-timer told me more about the Guadalupe Mountains - due east. First there's a climb, but then they slope down forty miles to the Pecos River. Only drawback I've heard about is Apaches." The unconcern convinced O'Keffe.

On their new course, Billy sang merrily, "Get busy on a day that is fair and bright, / Then pitch the old roof till it's good and tight.' / But the old man kept on a-playing at his reel, / And tapped the ground with his leathery heel. / 'Get along,' said he, for you give me a pain; / My cabin never leaks when it doesn't rain.' "

Like all the nonsense songs Billy loved, "Arkansas Traveler" sounded lighthearted, but spurned danger. Danger could not stop his headlong rush to his new life: his real life.

SEPTEMBER 7, 1877   5:28 AM   FRIDAY

Billy excitedly woke to a cloudless cold morning at the foothills of the Guadalupe Mountains. He said to Tom O'Keffe, "We'll be at Seven Rivers by nightfall."

Soon their horses climbed upward past water-polished gray limestone, like giant bones strewn on the declivity of the Guadalupe Mountain's entry point: Russell Gap.

Their steep upward trail was still the primordial sea's floor: once a barrier reef where calcium carbonate-laden organisms, dying over millions of years, had lithified in layers thousands of feet deep. Geologic upheaval had lifted them seven thousand feet as these mountains; baring those ancient sediments to wedge fissuring of ice, scouring by wind, and carving by carbonic acid from carbon dioxide dissolved in rainwater.

Attaining the top of Russell Gap, Billy and Tom O'Keffe saw, with surprise, that, rather than mountainous roughness, before them stretched seemingly endless, flat expanse; the range's prominences being far away and continuing southward into Texas. But the old sea, in its death's revenge, had left potash, repellant to life; now stunting infrequent cactus and mesquite on bare gray scrabble.

Tom O'Keffe said, "Hu-hungry."

"We'll stop later," Billy said. "Let's make good time. This looks easy."

To replenish their water, Billy led to distant vegetation, marking an arroyo. Down thirty feet, its canyon bottom was dissected by meandering tributaries joining at an eastward turn.

Billy gave O'Keffe the paint's reins, and crossed the webbed cotton slings of their canvas-covered, tin, lenticular-shaped canteens bandolier-style for the precipitous descent. But one bumped against his concealed revolver.

He left it in his saddlebag and said, "Tom, ride ahead with my horse. If you see Indians, get to safety; then come back for me."

"I-Injuns? I th-th-th-thought we d-d-didn' have to worry."

"We don't."

The gully's base was rimmed with mesquite bushes. Crouching in their water-fed profusion, Billy cupped coolness, splashing his face in baptism. When both canteens were full, he heard a rifle crack, and plunged into the vegetation. Then there was a scream.

Motionless for hours, Billy cautiously rose. Ravens flew fearlessly low with flapping whine, indicating no close humans. Retrieving the canteens, he saw mesquite thorn scratches webbing his hands.

Then he climbed out.

Tracks revealed milling of horses, but no other clues in flatland leaving him totally visible. To his right, and across the arroyo's continuation, he saw a low rise with horizontal cave mouths. Darkness was his only hope. Billy felt implacable calm of single focus: survival.

Entering one of the caves, he attained the relief of nocturnal beings, and pulled his boots from bare feet. His life would depend on that leather and that flesh for the forty miles to Seven Rivers. He removed his hat and slept.

When Billy awoke, the cave entrance was ultramarine. He slapped his inverted boots for scorpions or centipedes, sipped from one of the 2½ pint canteens, and walked out into the first night; into new moon's pitch darkness, punctuated by distant Indian campfires. Wind from behind impelled with attainable freedom that drew him eastward without requiring Polaris, the north star, for orientation.

SEPTEMBER 8, 1877   5:18 AM   SATURDAY

As pre-dawn lit the flat horizon, Billy pocketed sharp rocks as missiles for a rabbit; though he saw none. Inside another cave for daytime, thirsty and hungry, he drank too much. When he removed his boots, there were sore places. To go were twenty-four miles.

Night of the second day began with gnawing hunger. Only strenuous massage allowed his boots to slip on swollen feet. One mouthful emptied the canteen; but Billy kept it with the full one. Cave mouth framed star-filled sky. Wind beckoned, washing watery, like phantom waves of the lost ocean.

SEPTEMBER 9, 1877   5:49 AM   SATURDAY

By early dawn's walking, no sign of water had been seen, all running under inclined layers, not to surface until the Pecos River.

Inside another morning's cave, Billy dared not remove the boots. Sleep was assailed by dreams of animals savagely biting his feet.

Awaking to darkness, he finished the last of his water. Absentmindedly licking salty perspiration beading his upper lip, he crawled out, dragging one canteen, forgetting the other.

He stood, but dropped in pain. His mouth's dry membranes were tight as his face's skin; but water was unnecessary. Deliriously, he slipped off and dropped the last canteen. Collecting himself, he listened to strident chitinous cacophony of crickets and sighing wind, and stumbled into the third night; each step on the hard scrabble forcing mindfulness of its importance by its pain.

SEPTEMBER 10, 1877   3:07 AM   MONDAY

Far ahead, in darkness, appeared a tiny stretch of lights: a line of stars on the ground, proving his direction was correct. Billy was a moth, so light drew him. Beside the building, whose windows were the stars, was a thicket. Moths hide. He was within branches when a voice with command and fear said, "Come out. I've got a gun on you." A woman held a rifle.

His arm was slung over her back. He was in her kitchen on a wingback chair beside a hearth. There she had been sitting vigil for her fifteen year old son who, that afternoon, had fallen onto bottle glass, severing his left upper eyelid. With his head pressed to her lap, she had stitched it back. To her pride, he yelled but did not move.

She was asking questions. His name? Billy. His full name? Billy. "I've gotten those boots off. Stuck on with blood and such, Billy. The soles were worn through. You were as good as barefoot."

He was shivering, naked, covered by a blanket, washed, feet soaking in a bucket. She was offering warm milk. Through cracked lips, he said, "I won't drink ... milk."

"You've got to start easy." His blue eyes hardened obstinately. "Billy, I've raised eight sons and one daughter. And another son just arrived. They all drank milk." His lips tightened. "The spunk of him," she thought. Half dead, but he'll fight. She said, "I'll hold your nose and pour it like caster oil." He grimaced, gulped, and fell asleep.

She managed to dress him in a pair of her eldest son's, long-john bottoms; then maneuvered him to a room with several beds, one of which had a sleeping form.

Billy's eyes opened to daylight; a soft bed; and, beside him, a waking boy, with an eye like a plum. He had to escape. He sat at the edge. The room spun. He looked down at feet with blue-black toes puffed together.

"Mornin'," said his companion. "You musta' came in late;" and gingerly touched his injured eye. "What's your name?"

"Billy. I got to leave. Know where my clothes 'id be?"

"My name's Sammie. What's your last name?"

Henry Antrim was wanted for the murder of Frank Cahill. A father, unremembered, was McCarty. There had been a mother with joy, with dancing, with freedom. He said, "My name's Billy Bonney." He lay back. "Where am I?"

"Seven Rivers." Billy sighed with relief. "You look sick," said Sammie. "I'm getting Ma'am." He climbed over Billy, again asleep.

There was a gentle voice. A lovely woman, with large kind eyes and black hair piled high, was looking down. "Everyone calls me

Ma'am. Ma'am Jones." Billy pulled himself up, saying he had to get outside real quick. "Here's a chamber pot. I've nursed men older than you. There's no shame of bodily needs in my house."

On a bedside table, she had placed a tray with a bowl of thick soup. She examined his feet, announcing no infection, while he swallowed starving saliva. She set the tray on his lap. Daintily he spooned. She said, "If it stays down, we'll try solid. Now I've got to check Sammie."

As soon as the door closed, Billy raised the bowl; slurping, dribbling soup down naked chest, fingers scraping up scraps.

When Ma'am Jones came back, he said, "Real good. I'm ready for that solid food." He smiled gratefully, certain that his history and tendencies were concealed.

SEPTEMBER 15, 1877   10:31 AM   SATURDAY

Billy wanted to laugh out loud. With the new name was a new life, a new belonging. He had escaped.

Unseen at the doorway, Ma'am Jones listened to him, sitting on the floor barefoot and reading, with humorous animation, to her younger children. Four boys ranged from Sammie to a four year old. The only girl was Minnie, fourteen, and dark. Ma'am called her "black Dutch" like herself, the boys all "red Irish" like their father. The infant slept in a cradle.

Billy said, "So the boys gave Tom Sawyer a kite, an apple, and a dead rat on a string, so he'd let them paint the fence." Given Sawyer's manipulative genius, that seemed paltry. He added, "Then Tom said, 'I've got a game with three cards. Winner gets a penny.'"

Startling him, Ma'am Jones exclaimed, "I'm astonished. Card playing. The man who sold that to Heiskell said it was a Christian book."

She sat on a bed, gazing lovingly at her brood, and said, "All my twigs." Added up they were unbreakable, Minnie told Billy, repeating her mother's motto; as John, the eldest, entered.

Dusty and dressed like a cowboy, the round-shouldered, twenty-three year old smiled shyly at his mother. Narrow-faced like the others, he had a silky red mustache and goatee. At her request, he got Billy a pair of his boots. Ma'am Jones said to Billy, "I hope you learned your lesson: always wear sox."

Later, Billy rode north with John Jones, who talked with the friendly open style of his family. "We're headin' to the Beckwith's, across the Pecos. Ol' Hugh Beckwith was the first settler here. Came in forty-nine.

I want you to meet his sons, Bob an' John. I told them - an' others too - 'bout how good you shoot." Uneasily, Billy said they'd just done target practice.

Turning eastward, Jones said, "Grass here's belly deep to a horse in spring. Man can make a life here raisin' cattle." Ahead, a green swath exuded river wetness. They followed it north.

Through multi-trunked cottonwoods, was visible the wide torrent, blood-red and opaque. Jones said, "This here Pecos flows almos' the length o' the Territory. Joins the Rio Grande in Texas. Carries 'gyp' water, heavy in alkali. Everything here's 'bout water. Irrigation ditches 're called acequias. Ol' Beckwith he's got one from the Pecos to his ranch. A few feet deep, that acequia's life."

John Jones noticed circling vultures. "People 're sayin' war's comin' to Lincoln County. Us small ranchers already fought this big cattleman, John Chisum. He got his start drivin' cattle here from Denton, Texas, in sixty-seven; after Goodnight an' Loving got rich sellin' beef to Fort Sumner for the Bosque Redondo Resavation. Chisum made him a ranch called Bosque Grande, twelve miles south o' Sumner. Then it come to him that there were four million acres o' free government range. 'Tween seventy-two an' seventy-five, the greedy bastard drove in herds.

"Now he's got almost a hundred thousan' head. An' he's moved closer to our range. Made him South Spring River Ranch at this big spring he's claimed near Roswell; where my Dad an' me an' my brothers, Jim and Bill, made us a store. A family friend's started up a post office aside it: Ash Upson."

Billy hid shock at their past Silver City boarder's name.

Having crossed the Pecos River at shallows, they could see distant buildings. "Beckwith's place," John Jones said. "Chisum 'cuses us o' rustlin'. But unbranded calves can be anybody's. That caused our Pecos War. Bastard called it 'The Rustlers War.' April twentieth. He brought his cowboys - he's got eighty - an' surrounded this here ranch. Blocked its water for a siege. But it ended quick, 'cause our shootin' made his boys ride off. He never pays 'em right."

John Jones and Billy approached the main house. Jones said, "Old man Hugh Beckwith, he's a real proud Virginian. Jus' recently, a brother o' one of his hired men, Wallace Olinger, arrived: Bob Olinger. A gunman. Beckwith's ready for the next war."

They stopped at a hitching post as two youths approached. "The Beckwith boys," said John Jones.

As if telling a secret, he added rapidly, "My family just moved from Texas this year 'cause I killed a man there. Burks by name. Over ownership o' a calf." Billy glanced, but Jones kept his face in profile. "I can kill too." He called out, "Hey, John! Hey Bob!"

A half mile to the south, Jessie Evans advanced toward them. His fine dark-bay gelding loped through clicking and whirring of hundreds of grasshoppers launching themselves in terror. Squinting alertly, he swigged whiskey from a silver flask, while observing a lone figure, then a wind-caught skirt. Vegetation near her indicated a spring. Behind mesquite, Jessie dismounted. "Greaser," he thought, "day workers;" trying to determine her age. She put down her bucket. Shadowed breasts were on her blouse.

Popping of grasshoppers alerted her; but Jessie was close enough to grab, laughing, trying to kiss. She kicked; only a sandal, but it was resistance. Enraged, he threw her down. Soundlessly, she was praying, "Mother of God protect me. Mother of God protect me."

The coarse skirt was pulled up; drawers made from a flour sack were torn off. Jessie's hand sliced between rigid thin thighs. "Goddamn," he growled, thumbnail ramming fibrous obstacle and slashing inner flesh. Screeching, she reared up, instinctively clawing for eyes, but raking cheeks. Furiously throttling, Jessie paused when aware of her limp weight; and culminated with a few bestial thrusts.

He stood, but saw her blood dripping from him. Irascibly, he wiped with her underpants, then stretched in sexual satisfaction.

At the bunkhouse, stocky Wallace Olinger said to Billy, "Sorry my brother Bob's not here to meet you. Heard you can shoot. My brother, Bob, he can shoot."

John Jones said, "Why'd Bob buy an ol' Whitney shotgun?" Wallace answered that it was cheap.

Gaunt John Beckwith, like his brother with long mouth and meager mustache, said," 'Cause it ain't worth nothing. Eli Whitney's son shoulda stuck with cotton gins."

As they talked, a broad-torsoed young man, Stetson tipped ruffian's right, galloped up on a funnel-nostriled dark-bay gelding. "Runnin' from somethin'?" joked John Jones. Ignoring him, he dismounted, as they waited with servile expectancy. Jones asked, "What happened to your face?" He responded that it was nothing.

John Jones said to Billy, "This here's Jessie Evans."

Ignoring Billy, Jessie snarled, "I was a' Dolan's cow camp. Wha' the hell's slowin' yer work? 'E was 'spectin' more Chisum cattle."

Jessie slid his Winchester carbine from its scabbard. Swishing, it pointed at Billy. He did not flinch. Jessie said, "John says ye can shoot. Les see."

"Sure, Mister Evans."

As they walked from the group, Jessie said, "Poolite, ain' ye?" Suddenly, carbine butt raised to his shoulder. He fired. In flight, a meadowlark exploded into yellow, black, and brown feathers.

"See tha' tree? I'll put a hunred dollar bill there. Hit i' an' i's yers."

Billy said he had no gun. Jessie handed his Colt .44 from its holster; not seeing the boy's muscles, from trigger finger to thumb base, bulging anticipation.

Billy spun the cylinder, commenting on no empty chamber. Jessie said, "I likes six, when I wan' six."

A bill peeled from a big wad was anchored in bark. Billy asked him where to hit. "Anywheres." Billy hesitated. "Col' feet?"

"I've got a question. Are you *the* Jessie Evans?"

"Ain' no other."

"Well, I heard *a* Jessie Evans manufactured bills." Menacingly, Jessie flipped down his carbine's finger lever to lift a new cartridge into firing position. Billy continued, "So if I hit, I'd take a fifty dollar gold piece instead."

Jessie glanced with new interest. "Hit Abe Lincoln's head. Tha's where."

Billy fired. At the tree, Jessie glanced at the presidential portrait in a medallion to the upper left. Returning with narrowing of his deep-set eyes, he wrapped the targeted one outermost on his roll.

As Billy pocketed the coin, Jessie exclaimed, "Goddamn! You swiped three cartridges! Kid, ye earnt this." He handed the revolver butt first, its left side on his palm.

As Billy reached, the gun flipped upright and spun on Jessie's index finger in its trigger guard. Muzzle pointed. Three hammer clicks taunted. Jessie said, "Road agent spin. Ye got lots te learn, kid."

Billy smiled, eyes laughing. Jessie realized they were blue, lighter blue than Dolan's. He gave the revolver again. Billy said, "Thanks, Mister Evans," slipping it into his waistband.

"Jessie'd be 'nough," he said gruffly, concealing admiration. "I got a job in three days. Kin ye herd hosses?" Billy nodded. "Englishman named Tunstall's got some - an' some mules - tha' 're too good fer 'im. Keeps 'em at a ranch o' a man named Dick Brewer. Got a hoss?"

"Lent by John Jones. To go to James Dolan's cow camp to ask the foreman, "Buck" Morton, for a job."

Jessie laughed. "Buck works fer us. I hires. Bu' go meet 'im. I'll git a hoss an' rig t' ye." Billy asked if the horse was to keep or on loan. "Yer one hell o' a kid." Billy waited.

Jessie scowled. " 'Pends on how ye do. An' a good shot could be a risk. I could kill ye ifen I waned." The blurred Colt pointed. The Winchester muzzle, however, touched Billy's chest. Both grinned before they continued side-by-side; Billy feline gliding, and Jessie stiff-chested and tight-buttocked, with his broad-based step.

By late afternoon, approaching Dolan's cow camp, Billy heard fierce male yelling and answering cries in Spanish. Through bushes, could be seen the shouting man's back and a skinny adolescent, protesting that he had stolen no horse.

The man said, "I don't understand greaser talk; but I'm gonna kill you." As Billy dismounted, the boy screamed that then *he* would go to Heaven; but he was going to Hell.

Billy said, startling both, "Mister, he's saying he didn't steal it."

The skinny boy sprinted across the road into underbrush. There he lifted a bony arm; defiantly pumped his fist upward; and yelled, "Pimp for the Devil!" before disappearing.

The slim-hipped handsome man, with pencil mustache, said, "You helped him escape;" and reached for his gun. Billy's was already drawn. More carefully, the man asked, "What brings you to these parts?" Billy said Jessie Evans had sent him to meet Buck Morton for work. "I'm him. I got some say. I don't want you here."

Retracing the road back to the Jones's ranch, Billy saw the skinny boy, and called to him in Spanish, "Amigo, come ride with me;" and was joined behind his saddle. Billy asked where he was going.

"I live north of the Capitan Mountains near Lincoln," he answered, sixteen year old voice cracking. "Las Tablas. Maybe a hundred miles. But I have friends near here." Billy smiled, asking if he needed a horse. "I need nothing. What is your name?"

In response to Billy's, he declared, as if his own last name announced its Spanish aristocracy, "I am Yginio Salazar." The first was a melodious ee-hee-nee-O. "I will never forget that you saved my life. In seventy-three, Anglos murdered my father. He was Town Constable. A brave man."

Billy turned to look into the ardent blue-gray eyes. "They did not think Yginio could run our lumber mill for my mother. But I did. Mexico may have lost this Territory, but we have not lost our souls or our spirit. And we will fight for our land. Anglos are stealing it. My father told me."

Yginio challenged, "Why were you at Dolan's cow camp?"

Looking for work, Billy said. Staying at the Jones place. Yginio Salazar said, "They are good. But when the war comes, they will fight on the wrong side. They do not understand that any who take liberty from one people would take it from all."

They rode in silence until Yginio sang with deep feeling, "¿A donde irá veloz y fatigada / la golondrina que de aquí se va? / O, si en el aire gemirá estraviada, / buscando abrigo y no lo encontrará. [*Wence flies the weary swallow / exiled from her land? / Alas, finding no safe haven, / high above she grieves.*] "

Billy's eyes misted with the song's longing. Yginio said, "That is 'La Golindrina,' the song of an exiled Spanish Moor. You like music?" Billy nodded. "Then come to San Patricio to a baile. It is seven miles southwest of Lincoln. I go there. To dance and dance."

Both laughed as, behind, sky dimmed violet. But they rode to low golden sun, reveling in impulsive bonding of adolescent affection.

SEPTEMBER 16, 1877   9:14 PM   SUNDAY

As Billy absorbed vicarious family at the Jones's over-sized dining-table, Ma'am spoke lovingly to her husband, Heiskell, returned from his buying trip for their Roswell store. Meditatively, he stroked his gray-flecked red beard. Patriarchal dignity was in his aquiline nose and bushy eyebrows, moral rectitude in the horizontal of his flat-brimmed hat. Minnie listened while re-fluffing old wool mattress stuffing.

To Billy, Heiskell Jones said, "We were honored that you shared our Bible service today, son. A person doesn't have to participate to add fellowship."

Ma'am added, "You already feel like one of my own: with your light hair and gentle ways." Billy's eyes flicked, but detected no sarcasm.

Heiskell said, "Minnie, get me writing things. I'll make you a map, son. Help you find the right job. Take my oldest: John. For him, it's cattle. Me, I'm a farmer; like to see things grow."

"Minnie, time for bed," Ma'am said, and kissed her forehead. "I'm going too. Don't you both stay up too late. Billy has a job tomorrow."

"Daywork," Billy said defensively to the diligently writing man.

Heiskell Jones said "damn," as ink spattered: profanity spared Ma'am. "All right. This line from top to bottom's the Pecos. Way up north on it is Fort Sumner, Pete Maxwell's place. Sheep people." Three perpendicular rivers ran to Heiskell's Pecos line. "Most north is the Hondo. Roswell's 'bout five miles inland on it.

" 'Fore he got murdered, a Robert Casey was makin' himself a big cattle spread 'long the Hondo's western part. Widow Casey still lives there."

A sideways V made the Hondo's two westernmost origins. The upper arm, identified as the Bonito River, got a dot. "That's Lincoln. County seat since sixty-nine. Go west on the Bonito, an' you got Fort Stanton. Made the town grow. White settlers felt safe. Englishman named John Tunstall just made him a big store there." Billy asked if Lincoln was where fighting might be. "So you've heard. Hope not."

Heiskell pointed to the lower arm of the V, saying it was the Ruidoso River. "Just west of where it meets the Bonito, you got a

Mexican town: San Patricio." Billy's dark brows rose. "Along the Ruidoso, you also got small farmers. Some of them work part-time at Tunstall's ranches. Like Dick Brewer, farming on its south bank."

Billy asked if Brewer kept horses and mules for Tunstall. "Yep. Till Tunstall sets up his own ranches. Other Ruidoso farms are Charlie Bowdre's, "Buckshot" Roberts's, an' "Doc" Scurlock's. An' the Coe cousins - nice fellas.

"South of the Hondo's the Feliz River. Tunstall's bought a ranch on that one. He's got 'bout four thousand acres along it an' along the river most south - the Peñasco - where he's got 'nother spread. That means he controls grazing land for miles.

"West o' his Peñasco ranch is the small one o' John Meadows. Nice fella. To his west is W.W. Paul's big ranch - somehow connected to James Dolan."

Heiskell drew clustered wavy lines south of the Hondo, Feliz, and Peñasco junctions with the Pecos. "Here's our seven rivers. Farther south on the Pecos is Dolan's cow camp."

Billy looked at the inky web with blots like trapped insects. Heiskell said, "In all Lincoln County there's under a hundred o' us Whites. Rest: Mexicans, an' Indians on the resavation - when *they're* not running off with Victorio."

He pointed past the page top to the left. "Santa Fe: the capital. With the big politicians." He laughed. "*There's* a job for you! Then you don' have to work."

Ma'am returned, a shawl over her nightdress. "I thought of a job, Billy: day work for Ellen Casey. Tell her I sent you. Oh, I almost forgot. A man came from Dolan's cow camp named William McCloskey. He said to tell you that the horse was in our corral and the gear in the shed. And to meet them - whoever he meant - at Paul's Ranch by late tomorrow."

Just then, eighty-three miles northwest of Seven Rivers, in Lincoln, foreboding woke Alexander McSween. Putting on slippers, he padded across his bedroom toward the door that led to his wife's in their partitioned west wing, built without a hallway. Abruptly, his nightshirt collar felt constricting, as his lungs tightened asthmatically. He unbuttoned it, and took his Bible from his nightstand. Again at the dividing door, he queried, "Susan?"

His graceful wife, with small masculine features, opened; rubbing her eyes, and wearing a French nightgown. "Sacre bleu!" she said. "Trouble sleeping again?" and concealed impatience.

Curly bright-red hair hung over her shoulders; bangs, frizzed daily with a hot iron, were disheveled. She yawned, covering her mouth. Two years before, he had said, "You're so lovely, Susan -

except when you yawn. It makes your nose look ..." He had not finished, but she had never exposed herself likewise again.

Sitting on a balloon-back chair, as she returned to her bed matching his, McSween said, "How do you sleep with that open window, and never get sick?" They both knew he admired her health. "I hope you don't mind talking." His eyes looked pleading.

"I don't." In her cold insincere tone he heard the stubborn self-control which bolstered him, while allowing her to enjoy that strength. This equilibrium they called love.

She was turning a gold ring with a two carat ruby on her right ring finger, and recalling her childhood poverty; with competitive satisfaction that, though she and her sister had married lawyers, hers was more successful.

Looking at the black book perched on his lean-thighed lap's taut fabric, she said, "Alexander, you were born with a Bible."

He smiled and said, "People are flocking to Tunstall's store. And I'm inflaming their righteous wrath against the House. I found out that a farmer, named Dick Brewer, had been paying Murphy and Dolan for his land, though they had no title to it.

"And the Mexicans were so controlled by their usurious credit loans that they were like indentured servants. I'm on God's stream of destiny."

"That sounds like old-fashioned Presbyterianism: scaring people by saying everything's preordained; that you're saved or damned at birth."

"But one elected by God knows in his heart that he's saved. Though, for me ..."

"Alexander," she urged, "come to bed. You look chilled." She made room for him.

To painted ceiling muslin, concealing vigas and cross-struts, he said, "Also, I was thinking about our fourth wedding anniversary on the twenty-third. I feel I've failed my ... duties."

She pictured her valuable ruby, and did not care. For her, copulation was menstruation's messy sister. When first married, she thought it would be the price to escape poverty. But he left her free of frigidity's confession. This secret success she never told her sister, though it was galling that Elizabeth, about to have her fifth child, pitied her barrenness; when all she desired were possessions and money to cover poverty's humiliation. There were beautiful clothes, beautiful furniture, the biggest house in town, the growing bank account, and luxury to wish for even more.

But there was a childhood memory of a box turtle in a garden, trying to force its way between two rocks. It would not, possibly could not, back up. Finally, one rock moved. It continued on. She admired but pitied that turtle, sensing its tenacity, but also its sad vulnerability in rigidity; as if, like herself, it was just a shell around emptiness.

When her rhythmic breathing indicated sleep, McSween sighed. He had avoided voicing his actual anxiety: that the divine current was carrying him into difficult rapids. But beyond conscious tolerance lurked Robert Casey's murder two years before: one consequence of opposing James Dolan and the Santa Fe Ring.

SEPTEMBER 18, 1877   2:00 PM   TUESDAY

Riding ahead of a herd of eight stolen horses and two mules, beside Jessie Evans, Billy kept glancing at him, as if at the Rover incarnate. Jessie noticed. Other gang members controlled the animals.

At the sides of the herd were blond Tom Hill and dark Frank Baker. Behind Baker, fat George Davis bounced flab, like breasts. Nicholas Provencio had the rear and the dust.

Jessie said, "Likt the way ye headed inta tha' co-rral with ol' man Gauss shootin', an' got them two dapple grays. Bullets don' make ye nervis?"

Billy laughed. "Not his. He couldn't aim. And, with that dust, I bet he can't even identify us."

"Jimmy 'ill be satisfied. Tha's Dolan. 'E's the boss 'ere; 'im an' 'is parners, Murphy an' Riley." Billy asked if he worked for Dolan.

"I works for Jessie Evans. Bu' Jimmy's somethin'. I tol' 'im 'bout yer shootin'." Jessie took a pull on his silver flask. "Wan' some? Bes' whiskey. Jimmy gives i' t' me." Billy shook his head.

"Wana see Lincoln town?" Billy accepted enthusiastically. Jessie called Tom Hill, whose upturned broad nose and round cheeks were unpleasantly porcine. "Bring 'em t' Shedd's. Give me supplies."

Watching his men galloping southwest, Jessie scowled. "Runnin' 'em too hard. Goddamn fools."

He and Billy continued northward. "Yer oly as good as yer boys. I relys on Hill. Bu' lisen t' this. Murphy an' Dolan was puttin' in a special room in the secon' floor o' their big store in Lincoln - callt the House. Somebody lockt the doors. So Jimmy has Hill climb a ladder t' tha' room. Then, Hill comes down the stairs, opens the door fer Jimmy, heads back upstairs, an' climbs down the ladder!" Billy and Jessie laughed to tears.

Jessie continued. "Frank Baker likes killin', bu' can' aim. George Davis is so lazy 'e'd like somebody t' pull 'is trigger. Provencio's a greaser I kin abide. Bu' ye haven' met Buck Morton." Billy said he had. "Well, Buck he kills good."

At the Ruidoso River, as they watered the horses, Jessie asked, "I gave ye good gear, didn' I?"

"Well ... the horse could be better."

"Sonoabitch! One goddamn job, an' ye wans a better hoss?" Billy was silent. "An' I gave ye tha' Col' forty-four an' the rig."

Billy squinted against the glare. "You got me started here. I'll never forget that."

Jessie recoiled inwardly at the unexpected sincerity and warmth. Abruptly happy, he exclaimed, "Race ye t' tha' rise." Of course, Billy lost. "I'll git ye a better hoss," Jessie said.

By evening, their trail climbed continuous, high, unnamed hills bordering the southern side of the ten mile wide Bonito River valley. North lay a parallel mountain range: the east to west Capitans. Fifteen hundred feet below, lights sprinkled the valley. "Tha's Lincoln," said Jessie.

Their campsite, on the descent, had a rusted firepit grill. Billy started a fire, while whistling "Turkey in the Straw;" then gave the horses nosebags of corn. Jessie poured canteen water and coffee into a can. His blanket stretched opposite Billy's, the flaming pit between them. An owl hooted. "Tha's our call," Jessie said.

As meat pies pleasantly dripped grease on their dry hands, they watched coffee's rising steam. With his bandana, Jessie wrapped the hot tin. They would share. He leaned back against a boulder, motioning Billy beside him. "Like rustlin'?" Billy nodded. "Maybe ye'll like stagecoaches. Sometimes I thinks 'bout banks."

"You've got the name," Billy said smiling. "*Jesse* James. He's in the papers."

Darkness hid Jessie's blush at his illiteracy. He said, "Somebody 'ill git tha' Jesse. Not this un." He laughed. "Unreconstructed Rebel, tha' Jesse. Got un on the Ruidoso. This farmer: Charlie Bowdre. Las' month 'e shot up Lincoln town. Bu' 'e works fer Tunstall."

Billy said, "I wouldn't like banks. Walls block freedom."

Jessie smiled. "Ye say things good."

Billy returned to his blanket, coiled his gunbelt like a snake beside his saddle, and slipped its revolver into his waistband.

Jessie asked, "Could ye kill a man?" Depends, Billy answered, and added firewood; unaware of the conflagration he was creating.

Jessie gulped whiskey from his flask, and said, "I've killt. I got stories." He visualized his revolver butt beating a pulpy head, as agonized screams came from its bloody hole. He felt uneasy. "How come yer gun's on?"

"I got separated from one once. Won't happen again."

This was commonality. Jessie relaxed. Across the flames, Billy's cheeks glowed downy. Jessie stiffened. More beast than man, Jessie had primitive instincts so amorphous, that his emotions were not localized - he could as easily think his feelings were the boy's. So Jessie Evans, sensing danger, was becoming dangerous. He thought, "This kid could cause me trouble." Once, there had been another boy, head blasted, who had awakened him by stroking.

Billy smiled. "What stories have you got?"

"A minute, kid." Jessie drank deeply. Billy's moist bowed lips parted in anticipation. Suddenly, homosexual panic erupted in Jessie, as his longing for affection was mistaken for sex. He sprang up, feeling murderous, and strode to the horses. There, he remembered he had a second flask, and relaxed.

Jessie poured more coffee. Billy joined him, sitting close. It was alright. Jessie scratched his crotch, and said, "I was born in Missouri in fifty-three. Ye was almos' righ' 'bout the countafeitin'. My Ma an' Pa passt bills. We was 'rested in Kansas. I was eighteen. I 'scaped.

"Bu' I'd seen my Pa kill. Men in the business. 'E walkt inta a room shootin'. They was dead afore they could scream. 'E tried t' kill me pleny o' times. When I was 'bout yer age, I was gonna kill 'im. 'E was passt ou' drunk. Ma was passt ou' drunk. I thinks, ' 'E ain' worth a bullet. Ma ain' worth protectin'.'

"I tried cowhand work; bu' I was ust t' more money. An' too hot-headed. I'd kill people jis' t' see 'em kick. There was un, she was offerin' me anythin' not t' be killt ..." Billy interrupted, shocked. Jessie had found a limit. "Mean' 'he.' "

Billy concealed queasiness. "Like huntin', kid?" For food, Billy said. "Well I *really* likes huntin' - 'specially men." Billy stared into the valley's blackness. "You ain' lookin' at me no more," Jessie said suspiciously. Billy turned back pale, but without visible repugnance. Jessie felt relieved, smiled, and rolled a cigarette.

He said, "Name t' 'member's John Kinney. Headquarters near Mesilla. In Doña Ana County. Callt 'King o' the Rustlers.' Even does 'is own butcherin'. Killin's alays memrible with Kinney. On New Years Eve, seveny-five, 'im an' me was at a dance near For' Selden - north o' Mesilla. Soldiers there gave us trouble; so we shot up the place through the windas. Killt some.

"Same year tha' I done a big job fer Jimmy. This Robert Casey was makin' rumors 'round Lincoln. So I got a frien', Willie Wilson, t' plug 'im. Bu' Wilson was so dumb, tha' when they caught 'im, 'e says i' was 'cause Casey owed eight dollars. Tha' ain' a good motive. So people said Jimmy was ahind i'.

"Anyways, Willie Wilson was the firs' man hanged in Lincoln town." Jessie grinned. "Firs' time fer the hangman too. So Wilson sat up in the coffin! Had t' hang 'im twice." Jessie laughed and slapped Billy on the shoulder. "Migh' as well turn in."

But Jessie remained awake, studying the sleeping boy. Misgivings returned. Finally he lay, hat over face.

SEPTEMBER 19, 1877   7:08 AM   WEDNESDAY

Jessie Evans was dreaming. He and Billy were at a stand-off on Lincoln's broad street. Billy drew; but he, frozen, could not take his eyes from the boy's muzzle hole. Billy fired. Jessie could see himself in a coffin. People were singing. A great light shone. With dread, Jessie opened his eyes. His hat had slipped off.

On a ledge overlooking the valley, Billy was singing. Hundreds of feet below him, heavily settled fog in bright sunlight had made a milk-white river, flowing ten miles wide between the parallel ranges, like a purifying tributary from White Sands.

Drowsily, Jessie inhaled coffee aroma, until jolted by alarm. To get coffee, the boy must have come beside him.

His hand jerked to his revolver. It was there. His greeting was answered cheerfully. Jessie realized he felt good.

After they ate, Jessie, basking in glances of hero-worship, said, "I know everythin', 'cause Jimmy Dolan tol' me. Wanna hear?" The boy looked eager.

"Ye could say the House idea begun in the sixties when Emil Fritz, Lawrence Murphy, an' William Brady - 'e's sheriff now - was soldiers at For' Stanton. Brains were Fritz an' Murphy. Injuns was the start. Firs', Injuns was in a resavation 'roun' For' Sumner, on the Pecos. Nex' they put Apaches in a resavation hereabouts callt the Mescalero. An' made For' Stanton t' keep em' in.

"An' Injuns an' soldiers needed beef an' flour. So Fritz an' Murphy' made a sutler's store at Stanton; an' sold t' the Injun Agen' a' the resavation. Jimmy Dolan was jis' a drummer boy from the War workin' at their store.

"In seveny-one, Murphy an' Fritz was billin' the govmen' fer four hunred Injuns, an' two years later fer three thousan'. Got caught. This miltary report said they was lyin'; er Injuns breed like rats. An' tha' they was sellin' whiskey t' 'em. Was true.

"Also, they was sellin' i' t' soldiers in Lincoln, a' Sam Wortley's Hotel. They was makin' i' with a still in a cave near Stanton. Even had a printin' press there fer countafeit bills.

"Anyways, Murphy fixed the problem: said, 'We controls the Injuns.' The soldiers didn' wan' no uprisin'.

"Nex', the business was callt L.G. Murphy an' Compny; 'cause Emil Fritz got 'im a big life insurance polcy an' died.

"Then Murphy made Jimmy 'is parner; so i' was Murphy an' Dolan an' Company.

"Anyways, Jimmy's hot temper changt the business. Some soldier was gripin' 'bout Murphy. So Jimmy shot 'im. Got 'em throwed ou' from Stanton. So they built the House in Lincoln. Jimmy lived there with Murphy - opposit the room where Hill was stupid.

"Bu' Murphy got sick from drink; so Jimmy took over. Now i's J.J. Dolan an' Company. Fer parner, Jimmy took John Riley - rough as 'im. In seveny-five, Riley shot Lincoln's head greaser, Juan Patrón, fer talkin' like Robert Casey. Riley got off on self-defense. Patrón got quiet, an' got a bad leg.

" 'Self-defense' means friens - the judge - an' fear - the jury. Fer zample, Jimmy got off on self defense afta 'e killt a Lincoln greaser. Was a favor fer George Peppin, who'd jis' built the House. Peppin waned the greaser's bride. Jimmy even cut hisself with a knife t' look good." Jessie laughed, oblivious to Billy's discomfort about Mexican victims.

"So Lincoln's Jimmy's town. Bu' friens help 'im hold i'. Big boss ahind New Mex-co poltics is U.S. Attorney Tom Catron. 'E's a frien'. Govnor Sam Axtell gits big loans from Jimmy; so 'e's real frienly. An' Jimmy helpt Sheriff Will Brady buy 'is thousan acre ranch: Walnut Grove. Brady's got eight kids. Gits store goods free. All these friens is callt the Santa Fe Ring.

"Everythin' was goin' good till troublemakers come t' Lincoln: Tunstall an' McSween. Firs' was McSween: a Sant Louis lawyer with a fancy wife. 'E brung in tha' Englishman. Nobody in Lincoln County's got cash. Tunstall's got a rich Pa; so 'e does.

"Jimmy tried t' be friens with Tunstall. Tried sellin' 'im Murphy's ranch. Bu' McSween tol' Tunstall the title was bad. Leas' 'e didn' mess with Billy Matthews sellin' Tunstall 'is ranch on the Peñasco.

"Jimmy says Tunstall an' McSween 're ou' t' ruin 'im. Opent a big store in Lincoln town t' compete. José Montaño an' Isaac Ellis got stores there too; bu' they're nothin'.

An' McSween built a big house aside Tunstall's store, an' brung in his brother-in-law - 'nother goddamn lawyer - fer a parner, an' t' live there. Namt Shield. Shield brung 'is wife - Missus McSween's sister - an' their kids. An' they all live rich. Got the oly piano in town. Showin' off the goddamn money.

"McSween's a crook. Jimmy tol' me 'e even pocketed the money from tha' Fritz life insurance policy, 'cause 'e was the lawyer. Jimmy said Emil Fritz owed 'im tha' money. An' McSween's turnin' Jimmy's customers 'gainst 'im. Nobody was talkin' afta we finisht off Robert Casey. Now they'se talkin' again."

Billy asked how many Mexican's lived in the town. "Good number. An' there's close greaser towns t' the south: San Patricio an' Picacho. An' over the Capitans is Las Tablas.

"Bu' lisen t' this. Tunstall opent a bank too. Chisum's presiden'. So they's got a store, a bank, cattle ranches, an' sonsobitches got cash. Jimmy shoulda' kept 'is press. I tol' 'im. Oly thing good is they's sof' as baby birds. John Chisum's boys is rough; bu' 'e don' pay 'nough fer 'em t' fight.

"Course, Chisum ain' happy with our rustlin'. Bu' now tha' 'e's backin' McSween an' Tunstall, 'e's gonna be more unhappy." Jessie laughed. "Big diffrence 'tween a king o' cows an' a real king like Jimmy."

Jessie walked to look into the valley. He said, "Fog's burnt off. Les pack the gear."

They rode downward until Jessie stopped and handed Billy leather-covered brass field glasses. Through them, Billy saw a farmland grid behind structures hugging both sides of an east to west, red earth road. Parallel to it, and a quarter mile north, flowed the green-banked Bonito River. Jessie pointed to the biggest structure: the first building on the south side of the thoroughfare, the side closest to them, and said, "Tha's the House." Two-story, with peaked roofs, that adobe was a gargantuan bulk of two fused buildings; the eastern higher and more than twice the size of its mate. Its forty acre plot, with perimeter split-rail fencing, had additional frame buildings and a corral surrounding a stable.

Jessie said, "Tunstall's store's east. On the north side o' the street. The un with the big corral." Billy said, "But it's only about a quarter mile from Dolan's. From what I saw higher up, the whole town's just about a mile long. Too small for two big stores."

"Jimmy says i' too. Wortley Hotel - 'cross from the House - is where all us Murphy-Dolan's eats free; For' Stanton soldiers do too. The commander, George Purlington, is in Jimmy's pocket.

"McSween's house is tha' big horseshoe-shapt 'dobe, left o' Tunstall's. Eas' o' Tunstall's, tha' tower's callt the Torreon. Ol' time greasers made i' 'gainst Injuns. Eas' o' i', an' set back, is Saturnino Baca's li'l L-shape 'dobe. 'E's our spy. 'Cross is the li'l Montaño Store. Ike Stockton's got a saloon there. The districk courhouse is 'cross from the Torreon. Roun' the bend in the road is tha' limpin' greaser's house, Juan Patrón. An' 'cross from Patrón's, George Peppin's finishin' the firs' jail. They 'cused Jimmy o' pocketin' the three thousan' it cost. Was true. Easward four miles, is Brady's ranch.

"Then there's 'Squire' Wilson, Justice o' the Peace. 'E's got that li'l adobe almos' 'cross from Tunstall's; bu' set back t' these foothills, with vegetable patches in fron'. We can' figer which side 'e's on. Res' 're greaser houses. Like Cisneros, eas' and 'cross from Tunstall's'. 'Fraid o' Jimmy, like mos' greasers."

The boy still looked through the flared eyepieces. Jessie asked, "Wha' 're ye thinkin'?"

"From up here it looks like a toy town. But those people - no bigger than ants - think it's worth fighting for. Why don't they just move someplace else?"

" 'Cause they's grabbin' everythin' t' git rich. My job's t' make sure our side wins." Jessie decided on a risk. "I'll take ye t' meet Jimmy *now*. Ifen 'e likes ye, i' could be yer job too."

The steep descent down the high hills required alternating diagonals. Once they were on the valley floor, those hills looked like a wall as far as the eye could see. Across the valley was the parallel mountainous barrier of the Capitans. The effect was either sheltering or suffocating; but one was closed off from the outside world.

Jessie Evans, like a dog retrieving to a cruel master, became tense in approach. Defensively bombastic, he said, "All 'em big guys keeps t' the street here. Bu' I knows all the windy trails." He tried to clarify that superiority. "Like findin' a nest o' li'l pink mice when you's walkin'. An' ye wans t' crush 'em uner yer boot. An' ye does. An' they turns inta red jelly in the dirt."

Billy looked at Jessie uncertainly before the town seized his attention. Ahead loomed the rear of the House, its adobe bricks unstuccoed, the larger of its two parts to their right. Its monumental pitched roof multiplied two-story height to three. Its smaller narrower section created a partial courtyard, bounded by the bigger building's west wall. Bloated, the edifice belonged to no known time or place, and was created for intimidation; its architectural presence an act of frozen violence.

A man opened a rear gate and took their horses. Other workers glanced furtively. Jessie pointed to a plank structure and said, "Public ouhouse. Whole town uses i'. Alays somethin' goin' on 'round here. Jimmy likes i' tha' way."

Increasingly apprehensive, he scanned Billy and frowned. "Can' say as I noticet. You looks like a tramp cowboy. Maybe I kin git Jimmy t' give ye somethin' better. My boys ain' tramps. Make ye nervis meetin' a big man like Dolan?"

"No."

From the partial courtyard, they stepped onto a board walkway skirting the larger division of the House. Jessie knocked a patterned staccato on a side door in its west wall. A man opened, saying he'd tell Mister Dolan.

They entered a landing facing a long storage area. Jessie told Billy to wait. Jessie's steps resonated across the wooden plank floor, and disappeared into a door at the far left. Billy followed the landing along the left wall. It ended at a narrow stairway.

When Jessie returned, smiling and smelling of alcohol, he led Billy across the storeroom to another door where he knocked the code, and opened to oil-lit gloom of drawn curtains.

James Dolan sat facing them, face in chalky contrast to black hair and clothing; and, behind his desk's expanse, elevated on an invisible pillow. His small white hands were rotating a gold letter opener: a mock dagger pointing briefly in dangerous trajectory.

He stood, revealing his diminutive height, intersected by the polished surface almost at his waist. In a resonant and gracious voice he said, "I am so pleased to finally meet you, Billy. So pleased." His sapphire eyes were almost warm. Only when he turned to walk around his desk, the expression, no longer exposed or needed, was briefly replaced by reptilian blankness.

Firmly he shook Billy's hand; gestured to a chair; and said, "Jessie, Billy and I will, I believe, do well enough on our own."

Jessie Evans glowered enviously as he exited through a door, which, Billy noted, led outside.

Dolan asked, "Would you like a drink?"

"No thank you, Mister Dolan."

"Please, please. Jimmy. We are all friends here. *I* would, though. From a small table with two chairs, Dolan took a decanter and shotglass. An empty glass remained. Billy assumed it was Jessie's.

Dolan, sipping, again faced Billy across the desk, and observed his unexpected ease. He said, "Jessie sang your praises. So I decided to cancel my appointments this afternoon. To get acquainted." He sipped again. "So excellent. Can you be tempted?"

Billy smiled. "Thanks, Jimmy. But no."

"Jessie said you want work. If it could provide any reward, what would you want?" Billy had no idea. Dolan was again surprised, fancying himself a master of temptation. He said, "You may not realize your talents' potential."

Billy felt delightful contact, but novel, as if a velvet-gloved hand was delicately probing. "Wealth? Power? Do they interest you?" Billy did not respond, immersed only in paternal essence.

Dolan laughed: a light pleasant sound. "I would say you were not listening." The hand was wise. When the correct place was found, the other would seek. Then the hand would reassure that the need was no longer secret, but found by both. And the touch also lulled, numbing conscience while arousing desires until they became insatiable.

"Jessie suggested better garments," Dolan said, again searching. "I can extend our courtesy."

"I wasn't planning to buy new clothes. But thanks, Jimmy."

"No. No. No." Dolan chuckled. "Gifts. And I'll show you our establishment."

From his office, they entered a room with cubby-hole shelves. Dolan said, "The Lincoln Post Office. I am Postmaster *too*." The next door led to the building's front room: a merchandise-filled space soaring two-stories to a raftered ceiling. A carved oak bar at its west wall had a window-like service-opening to the adjoining room, whose door Dolan opened. Billy realized it represented the entire ground floor of the smaller building. Dolan said, "Our billiard room."

That elaborate table joined round ones with chairs. Five men, gambling at one, turned questioningly. Dolan said, "This is also our meeting place. Before introductions, let us go outside." Lightly, he touched the boy's back.

Double doors in the big front room opened to an expansive porch under a white-columned overhang. Billy's eyes flicked up. Dolan said, "My balcony." They descended steps to the street and, looking up, Billy saw that the balcony was surrounded by a balustrade and had second-story double doors mimicking the ones below.

Breathtaking was that the combined structures now presented the House's single monumental façade.

Billy also noticed the lack of balcony stairs, and asked how people got to it. Dolan said, "Only from inside." Studying the boy while pensively squeezing the sides of his lips, he said, "The upstairs is my private area. Where Larry ... Lawrence Murphy and I lived. Where *I live alone* now."

When they turned the building's east corner, Billy again stopped, eyeing a big second-story window facing the town. He commented that from the porch and that window a person could keep an eye on things. Dolan's eyes hardened strangely. At the building's rear, they saw Jessie Evans. Dolan nodded: a sign unnoticed by Billy.

Dolan then led Billy back to the billiard room. At the occupied table, a paunchy, drunk, red-faced man, with walrus mustache, stood up; obsequiously extending a beefy hand, even before they were close. Holstered was a Colt .44 with ostentatious turquoise grips. Dolan said, "William Brady, our sheriff: the law of Lincoln."

Brady, perplexed at lavish efforts for the shabby youth, said with heavy Irish brogue, "And pleased I am to meet you, me boy. As the old cock crrrows, the young cock learns. And Jimmy keeps loyalty in a man's heart by keeping money in his purse." William Brady's companions laughed tensely.

Unperturbed, Dolan introduced George Peppin, with a handlebar mustache and big Adam's apple on his very long neck. "Our master builder and a deputy." Beside Peppin, a fleshy individual shifted old hernias from a bucking horse fall. "George Hindman, another illustrious deputy," said Dolan. Hindman also bore wounds of a bear attack and a past partner's murder attempt. Here he felt safe.

"Jack Long," interjected a raw-boned man, whose keloid-magnified knife scar slashed his cheek and once-split lip. His mustache made no attempt to hide this gruesome deformity.

A slim rustically-dressed fellow with mustache framing weak chin, compliantly set his cards face-down. Under a slab forehead, his tiny close-spaced eyes met Billy's. Dolan said, "Billy Matthews. A new associate, and a friend."

Billy was thrilling to the brotherhood of crime, until smells of cigarette smoke and alcohol brought back Windy Cahill's fetid breath and its day of blood.

Billy felt queasy, as Dolan turned him back to the main room where a servile salesman was given Billy's battered red-banded hat. Dolan selected instead the finest Stetson, in black, saying, "It suits your coloring." When Billy tilted it right, in imitation of Jessie, he missed Dolan's brief smile. New boots were presented as "the best quality - other than custom-made."

Billy put them on, but kept the other boots, saying they were not his. Then he looked hungrily into the sapphire eyes and said, "I'd like another thing, Jimmy." James Dolan's dark lips curled. Finally, the boy was succumbing. Billy said, "That jar has peppermint balls. I'd like one." Dolan's smile strained. He told the salesman to give Billy paper for extras. Billy, sucking his, took three more.

Back in the dim office, at the little table, with their knees close, James Dolan droned, "Like getting to that porch, you must be let in. To get to the top. To the top." Billy felt thick torpor, as his chair's velvet seemed decaying slime. Nausea swept over him. He said he needed the outhouse. Dolan smiled. "Exciting, isn't it? More than a body can stand."

Outside, Billy revived. Circling the outhouse, he noted four doors, before choosing one.

When he returned, Dolan handed him a paper strip with bold writing, and said, "Jessie found you quite intelligent. This might amuse you."

Billy read to himself, *Claudicant Dame Saveloy Frache Fiveate Dollars Drawcansir Gravey and Fowling Drawcansir himself Dame Walloon Gravey Wareful Warily peeress Fowling capitulary Bacchanal Your Niece Acerous.*

Back with Billy at the little table, Dolan said, "I know Jessie told you about our friends. But I want you to feel our power."

Gaping open the back lid of his gold pocket watch, he handed it, saying, "Look closely." Exposed was its golden mechanism, whose balance wheel, ticking time, swung, swung, swung.

"Keep looking." The boy's eyes were caught. Billy heard, "See how it meshes: predetermined, unstoppable. Like us." Dolan leaned close, eyes sadistic with hypnotic dominance. Echoing was "Power ... cannot resist, cannot resist ... me."

In the mechanism were ruby jewels. Or drops of blood. Blood on blue cloths. Blood on lost Colt. Billy snapped shut the lid and returned the watch, saying, "Problem is, watches need winding."

Dolan persisted by logic. "The spring powers the gears. Our spring is Thomas Benton Catron. A brilliant mind. He even taught himself Spanish in his month's travel here from Missouri." With evident interest, Billy asked why. "To read land grants owned by Spaniards and Mexicans when this became a Territory: millions of acres."

Billy listened alertly. It repeated the fat man's words in the stagecoach. It had something to do, Billy sensed, with Yginio Salazar's rage. Dolan said, "But they only had crude maps, and no idea what land was worth. Tom once told me a Mexican sold eighty-one thousand acres to someone for eighteen dollars!

"Tom's business machine meshes like gears. First is the grants themselves. Under U.S. law, owners must present their papers and get a new survey. Tom becomes their attorney. For payment, he takes a percentage of their land. When ownership is approved by the Land Office in Washington, Tom *advises* on its sale. Think of what he and his friends can get!

"For the gear of law, Tom is our U.S. Attorney, the highest Territorial position. For a Washington gear, his partner, Stephen Elkins, is now our Territorial Delegate to Congress. The gear controlling the surveys is Elkin's brother, a surveyor. Then there is the gear of Governor Sam Axtell. And - if anyone dared litigation - there are gears of the Third District judge, Warren Bristol, and the district attorney, William Rynerson.

"Our beautiful machine works perfectly. Tom Catron already owns six million acres - more land than any man in the history of the United States. And he owns banks. Mines. Now he wants Lincoln County. He is buying a cattle ranch in Carrizozo: forty thousand acres thirty miles from here.

"Jessie told you how we keep our watch clean. Dirt that gets in - like Robert Casey; and, now, Tunstall and McSween - is eliminated. And our watch gets lubrication. Voters, jurors, and opposing lawyers are 'helped' to make correct decisions. And connections must enable stock to 'disappear.' "

The black Stetson framed handsome young features focused on him so appealingly that Dolan was tempted to boast.

Sneering, he said, "*I* am the power behind that spring. Catron gets his power from *me*. He must *believe* in me, *rely* on me, to get what he now craves.

"But Tom is brilliant. Look again at that paper. That is his code, used in all our communications. Impossible to understand, isn't it?"

Billy said he hadn't had enough time to study it.

Dolan laughed, took out the watch, and said, "Fifteen minutes to tell me what it says."

Billy said he'd need to write. Dolan pointed to his chair: a place no one had ever dared occupy. Billy sat without hesitation.

Finally Dolan called the time, smiling at the absurd presumption.

Billy said, "Here it is, Jimmy. The trick was figuring out the first word. I got '*claudicant*,' 'cause you said Catron speaks Spanish. And in Spanish 'claudicante' means halting or limping. So I took a guess: a telegraph's got a halting code. So it says, 'Through telegraph I know from someone named Dame something about this Dame knowing or saying that a sum of money - you'd need to know the code to translate 'Fiveate Dollars,' but for Catron it must be thousands - can be paid to a Gravey. Then Dame can draw for himself the sum of 'Fowling' - probably hundreds. Then Dame will do whatever 'walloon' means. Then it seems Gravey's worried about getting his 'fowling.' The last words seem to be a promise."

Dolan sprang up crying, "Impossible! Absolutely impossible!"

With trembling hands he leafed through papers, then read aloud, "*I have telegraphic communication with Dame in which he says one thousand four hundred dollars is due Gravey and five hundred dollars is due himself Dame will wait as long as possible Gravey in want of money Wants you if possible to pay five hundred dollars cash balance Your note will be accepted.*"

Billy whooped. The door burst open to Jessie Evans pointing his Colt .44 aggressively. Dolan said, "It is all right. Billy was just laughing." Jessie scowled and left.

With sadness of the fallen angel, gazing up to Heaven irretrievably lost, James Dolan stared at the boy's radiant face. He said, "This is totally unexpected." He walked to Billy, resting a hand on his shoulder. Billy looked up trustingly.

Dolan said, "I was an orphan, Billy. I left Ireland as a child. When I met Lawrence Murphy, he found in me something he … needed. He created all this for me. I would like to do the same for someone."

The hand pressed, the barrier of fabric expressing the yearning for contact he sensed in the boy, but was in himself.

Billy said, "I hope you find that person, Jimmy."

Pain briefly welled in the sapphire eyes. The hand withdrew. And of all the cravings that at all times preoccupied Dolan, paramount now was to possess the soul of this boy.

He said, "There are those who would kill for what just happened. We will be great friends or great enemies."

"Right now, Jimmy, seems we're just getting acquainted."

From those words, Dolan renewed hope as Billy returned to the original chair facing the desk.

Dolan said, "Jessie mentioned your interest in guns." From a desk drawer he lifted a mahogany box. "This was presented to me. But I will loan it to you for your pleasure." From blue satin lining, Dolan raised a revolver, smaller than a Colt .44, and said, "This is the Lightening. A Colt double action, just out this year." Customized by silver-plating, engraving, and pearl grips, it was thirty-eight caliber. "The hammer cocks automatically when you pull the trigger. Six shots, yet easy to conceal." Beside it, Dolan lay a box of cartridges.

At last, passion ignited the boy's eyes; but now Dolan wanted it for himself. He said, "Jessie and I will talk; then he will meet you."

Going out, Billy picked up John Jones's boots.

Later, at the corral, Jessie said to Billy, "Jimmy likt ye. Why was you in 'is chair?" Billy said he had to write.

"Well, I tol' 'im ye wasn' happy with the hoss. " 'E says, 'Let 'im use my bay mare.' " Jessie paused. "An' 'e wans a favor tha' needs long ridin'."

They both looked at the horse. "So ye'll do i'?"

Billy answered that he had not said what it was. "Ye wan' too much afore yes," Jessie said irritably, rolled a cigarette, dragged on it, then threw it smoking at Billy's feet; and went into the outhouse.

When he returned, Jessie said, "Jimmy tol' me: 'I'm findin' the pas' on this Billy Bonney.' " He looked over his shoulder. "You got a pas'?"

Billy laughed. "You need one to get to the present."

Jessie did not smile. "Don' unerestimate Jimmy is alls I'm sayin'. 'E wans ye t' go t' Fort Sumner an' check ou' hosses. Lucien Maxwell's son has hosses fer racin'. Jimmy wans some."

"How may should I get?"

Jessie laughed. "Firs' I thinks you's gonna be picky. Now I fins you's gonna do the whole job yerself! Jis' bring Jimmy a sample. Sumner's on the eas' side o' the Pecos. Ye cross a' shallows callt Navajo Crossin' - 'bout twenty miles south o' the place."

Jessie punched Billy's arm playfully. "Git the gear from tha' shed. Jimmy sen' word ye'd need i'."

"How'd he know I'd accept?"

"Guess nobody's said no t' 'Jimmy, as yet."

That evening, as the enormous full moon rose, Billy, caressed by wind, rode south out of Lincoln, exploring. Crickets chirped futilely, their decimated autumnal numbers too small for the chorus they sought.

An hour later, the wind brought almost imperceptible singing of unspeakable loveliness, drawing Billy to tiered hills against phosphorescent sky and dwelling-lights flickering like candles on a church altar. As the melody condensed into Spanish words reviving Chihuahua Hill's enchantment, Billy crossed a bridge over the Ruidoso River and leading to a town; and the song condensed into a male singer's voice, coloring moonlight with golden pleasure of sun: "Peña del cerro alto, / Peña la consentida, / Peña la vida mía, / morena hermosa, / no me vayas a olvidar. [*Peña of the hills so high, / My sweetheart Peña, / Peña my life, / You dark lovely, / Don't ever forget me.*] "

Acequia irrigation channels made quicksilver bands through passing fields. At a higher plateau, Billy entered the central street of the town, above which was another rocky surge, but uninhabited.

From a parapeted rooftop, came a hostile, "Stop, Gringo!" A man rose with a rifle. Through a vertical porthole glinted a second gun barrel.

"Where am I, amigo?" Billy asked in Spanish.

"San Patricio. Who sent you?" the man asked. Yginio Salazar, Billy said. "Then you are welcome. I am José Chávez y Chávez, Town Constable."

The other man stood and said, "I am Enrique Montez. Where are you going?" To the singing, Billy answered; and the men laughed. Just then, began "La Golindrina." Billy rode to it, delaying his mission for James Dolan.

SEPTEMBER 20, 1877   2:17 PM   THURSDAY

Saturated with San Patricio's allure, Billy had left his over-night hosts, the family of Enrique Montez, riding east to Roswell, en route to Fort Sumner; while singing newly learned songs, as hilly terrain became flatlands.

At the small town of Roswell, he found John Jones, greeting him from the family store; one of two adobes joined by a frame warehouse. Jones exclaimed, "You got a damn good horse! An' some fine clothes!" Billy said he'd brought back his boots. "Those ol' ones? Yer the damndest. Come to the other side an' meet Ash Upson, Roswell's first postmaster."

The one room post office reeked of alcohol. A man, with his back to them, and almost concealed behind his counter because of stunted humped size, had a wiry bush of brown hair. At his name, his oversized coarse-bearded head turned with intoxicated disorientation. His flattened nose was another part broken in life's assault.

With great dignity, he asked, "What time of day is it, John? Morning, midday, or evening?" Getting the answer, and an introduction to Billy, Upson declared, "You look familiar." Jones said he'd traveled so much that people must start looking the same.

Upson said, "I may be a rolling stone, but I never forget a face. Eventually, I'll remember. The question is: will it be helped by drinking more or less today, my core dilemma: persuading my brain to give me a livelihood, which this miserable body cannot."

"Ash, you always call yourself down," said John Jones. "Fine newspaperman like you."

"Years ago. An unproductive past with an uncertain future." Billy was fully aware of the risk Ash Upson represented to his own.

SEPTEMBER 21, 1877   2:45 PM   FRIDAY

Nearing Fort Sumner in glaring plains, Billy was changing, as if manifesting slow poison: face distorting with cruel glee as Dolan's protégé, and body tightening with Jessie's vicious hubris; when, ahead, he saw a rider turning tight circles to control a skittish black horse, the most beautiful he had ever seen.

Maliciously, Billy approached the diminutive thief, reminiscent of Yginio Salazar, as the stallion, with crested neck, became increasingly wild: pawing while throwing his head high with rolled-up lip and shrill cry, causing Billy's mare to side-step and lay back her ears.

"Want to trade horses?" Billy taunted, planning to push the tike off and keep both, completing his mission for Dolan.

"No!" the boy called and glared, dark brows drawn fiercely.

Billy, assuming a concealed weapon, was ready to murder. "You've got no choice," he shouted, hand flying to Colt.

Screaming rage, the boy exploded into gallop - directly at him. Billy's terrified shying mare stumbled and fell. The black body thundered, leaping over Billy, on the ground, his gun fallen at a distance. He braced for the fatal shot, as the stallion wheeled and returned. Looking up, Billy ventured, "Guess my horse stumbled."

"You were trying to steal mine."

"Yours? Sorry. Real sorry. Thought *you* were a thief. Just doing a good deed. Came looking for work. Tried Lincoln County. Heading to Fort Sumner." Ingenuous blue eyes assessed less angry dark ones.

Billy stood carefully, brushing pants, adjusting hat. "Also, I worried you'd be thrown."

"You're on the ground," the boy said scornfully. "And you're loosing your mare." Uninjured, she was wandering. "I can catch her for you." Billy glanced at his Colt. "And I don't think you'll shoot."

"You're right. You won him fair. I'll ride on him with you."

"I didn't *win* him. He's *mine*. And I don't trust you enough yet." The boy smiled sweetly, and effortlessly turned the stallion, surprising Billy with his mastery.

Finally remounted, Billy had an urge to befriend this feisty mite, reminiscent of himself in Silver City. He followed alongside.

A golden eagle circled. The child announced, "Deluvina would say that's a sign. She's very wise." Billy asked where Deluvina lived. "At my house. You can meet her." Billy asked if he was invited after all that. "Yes. Deluvina says trust your heart. Mine said get to know you."

Impetuously, from his shirt, the little fellow pulled out a long thick braid. A few tosses released it.

"You're ... you're a girl!" Billy stammered, astounded and flustered.

She giggled. "I fooled you *completely*," and galloped ahead, long auburn hair streaming helter skelter; then slowed, looking back, eyes sparkling in reckless game with this unknown youth, who had almost attacked her.

Billy rode up laughing. She said, "You remind me of Papa." It was his roguish blue eyes. "Mama will say so too. But he's dead. I miss him." He asked her name. She said, "Paulita."

"Mine's Billy." They rode north in unremittingly bare, flat land. "Why d'you wear pants?"

"Because I do what I want. Except if my mean brother, Pete, finds out. So I keep secrets from him. Anyway, Lozen, the great Apache chief Victorio's sister, wears pants." Inexplicably included in her confidence, Billy felt giddy and made a crooked little smile. "Deluvina meets me in our peach orchard with a skirt to keep my secret."

He asked her age. "Fourteen and a half. How old are you?"

"Eighteen in two months," he said. Then he was still seventeen, she said. "And you're only fourteen," he teased; but she frowned.

She said, "You're lucky your mare wasn't in season. Centauro was checking." His face flamed. "Pete uses him for breeding. Haven't you watched a stallion cover a mare? It's interesting." He choked, and managed to ask where she lived.

"In the big house. It's beautiful here when the peach trees bloom. And I like galloping as fast as you want, because nothing stops you. And, when you're not listening to the wind, you can listen to the Pecos. And there are huge lightning storms. But Deluvina won't let me go to them. Someday I want to go out when lightning's all around."

"You could get killed," he said, breathlessly anticipating her response.

"But you'd see a lot of lightning first." Billy recognized the recklessness in her eyes.

With heart pounding, he said, "Someday *I'll* show you lightning in a storm. D'you like to dance?"

"I don't know. Pete said I was too young." Someday he'd show her how, Billy said. "Oh, promise soon! Tonight's the full moon. Sometimes I climb out my window and walk in the moonlight. I'd like riding in it too." He asked if she had. "No," she said.

Sweet poignancy inundated him. Without awareness of the words, he sang a song of his mother's: "If you will answer these questions for me, / This very day I'll marry with thee." She blushed, because she had been pretending they were married. She asked his last name, and gave hers.

Paulita Maxwell, he repeated softly. She answered playfully, "Billy Bonney! Billy Bonney! When we get to my hiding place, Jesús Silva will take Centauro to the stable. He was Papa's foreman. Now it's Barney Mason. I hate him. Pete made him foreman. Mama and Pete won't be back from Las Vegas 'till tomorrow.

"Deluvina will give us supper. I'll tell her you saved me from a rustler." But that wasn't the truth, he said, suppressing a smile and soaring exuberance.

She looked into his eyes. He realized hers were huge, as their brows arched innocently. "It's a secret made with words." He laughed loudly. She said, "Don't laugh at me."

"I'm not laughing at you. I'm happy. Happy we met."

A quarter mile from the town, Paulita pointed eastward. Pickets, stained sanguine by late blood-red clouds, enclosed a square half acre. She said, "That's our cemetery. Papa's there. Mama says we'll all be there. Once soldiers from Fort Sumner were there; but Papa made the army take them away."

Their road paralleled the Pecos River on their left and the town's west side to their right. Billy whistled "Turkey in the Straw" as they approached the rear of a dramatically large, two-story, white, frame building to their right. Its first floor was surrounded by a portico with colonnades of white pillars, in allusion to temples of antiquity. The primary roof, peaked and penetrated by dormers and brick chimneys, flared eccentrically past the second floor to meet that of the porch. The property was surrounded by high white pickets matching the cemetery. The building's south façade overlooked a few acres of vegetable gardens, likewise enclosed.

Paulita pointed. "That's my room." It was at the northwest corner. "See its big window? That's how I get out." Incredulously, he asked if it was a house. She laughed. "That's where I live. Where Mama and Deluvina live. Pete lives there now that Papa died. There." She pointed to the southeast corner. "At least he's as far as possible from me." Billy decided it was a boarding establishment.

Passing the town, she said, "There's the peach orchard." To their right were acre upon acre of the fruit trees with leathery foliage, soon to fall; ending brief lives. She lead him into its depths, toward a squat portly woman with a loose brown dress and shawl. A black puffy cap with floppy brim shadowed her broad face. Billy lagged discretely. "Where's Jesús?" he heard the girl call.

"Coming, child. You are late."

"I was rescued from bandits by Billy," Paulita said dismounting. "They were desperados! Billy galloped up, shooting his pistol; and they ran away." As he dismounted also, Paulita smiled at him with disconcerting adulation. Deluvina handed her a bundle, as a man approached; and the girl led the stallion to him.

Expressionless, Deluvina demanded to see Billy's hands. Her thumb pressed their muscles. She said, "They know guns and their temptation. Paulita lies badly. *You* should have told the story."

A smile flickered at the deep corners of his mouth. "Seems she doesn't recognize danger, Missus Maxwell, Ma'am," he said, confused about her relationship to the girl.

"For now, she knows enough. She would like you to eat with us at six-thirty. I am called "Maxwell" because her father gave me that name when he bought me."

Both watched Paulita running back in a ruffled silk skirt with unbuttoned bodice flapping away from the boy's shirt. "Do you like him, Deluvina?" she called excitedly.

"Yes, Paulita. He is good."

When Billy rode alone, in early sunset, from the orchard, shaken by Deluvina's gun comment as if waking, he went southward to explore the town, still with military conception of a square parade ground. Its red earth expanse stimulated, not quite déjà vous, but importance: as if a mariner, long at sea, had found land's signs, anticipating journey's end.

Paulita's residence took up most of the western perimeter. The eastern and southern boundaries were prior adobe barracks, now converted for townspeople. Traffic concentration at the south indicated the main entrance. The northeast perimeter held the old quartermaster's building with the sign: HARGROVE'S SALOON. To its east, were corrals and a fort-sized stable, where waited the man from the orchard, Jesús Silva, with thick gray hair and mustache. He said to Billy, "I was told your horse will be inside."

The animals stood in elegance of adobe-walled stalls topped by polished brass railings. Jesús Silva said, "Beautiful horses, no?" speaking Spanish, as had Billy. "Many are from Centauro: Andalusians crossed with thoroughbreds. Some are a new breed called "quarter horse." The patrón, Señor Peter Maxwell, appreciates racing. Betts, who trained for the father, trains for the son."

Billy said a man in Lincoln named James Dolan had told him that Maxwell had good horses. Jesús Silva spat onto the raked walkway and said, "Dolan is no friend to Mexicans."

Back on the parade ground, on foot, Billy crossed a westward diagonal to Paulita's place, fronted by a perimeter path which he followed to the south side, where it passed a saloon lettered BEAVER SMITH'S. It was adjacent to an empty dancehall, terminating at the entrance corridor, which was lined by attached adobes.

Across from that entrance, were other south-side adobes, aromatic with Mexican cooking. Attracted to the third in the row, Billy stopped before turning back and following a northwest diagonal on the parade ground to the mansion.

Its entry gate, in the picket fence, was south of center. At the baronial front doors, Paulita met Billy with hair neatly drawn back; and exclaiming, "You came!" Behind her stretched a corridor festooned with crystal chandeliers.

As he walked with her, bejeweled with crystals' rainbows, she turned at a back hallway leading to a huge kitchen. Confused, Billy asked if it was a hotel. Paulita laughed and laughed, overwrought with excitement. "It's our *house*! Twenty rooms. Mama and Papa - I mean when he was alive - like guests." Billy barely heard, having noticed curling baby's wisps at her hairline.

At the huge stove, Deluvina turned from her cooking to Billy's smile, refused his offer to help, but assured him that they would eat together. Paulita said, "We always do, except when I have to go to "a," she made a wry expression, "ga-ther-ing."

After they ate, sitting on benches along a plank table, Paulita, disconcertingly close to Billy, said admiringly, "You ate *three* whole pieces of peach pie," as he spooned much rare white sugar into his coffee. Paulita dipped in her spoon, and licked; her pink tongue tip making his ears red. She said, "Toooo sweet."

"Child, it's his coffee. Come for your own."

As Paulita did, she glanced near the stove and exclaimed, "Look, Billy! A gold web. There's the spider. Her food's wrapped. A beetle. It's so much bigger than her."

Deluvina joined them and said, "Life catches each of us the same: one strand at a time." Paulita said she wouldn't be like that beetle. Or the spider. "But she must eat," said Deluvina. "And each must die. The meat we just ate was from a calf born here, who now hangs on the north porch."

Paulita said, "Tell Billy about Spider and Dragonfly."

Deluvina asked him to add wood to the fire; she felt a chill. Paulita objected that the room was hot from the stove. "Then more heat won't matter," said the woman.

They sat, Paulita again beside Billy. She said, "It's a sad story. I'd lean against Papa if I was sad. Can I lean against you?" His breath caught. He nodded.

Deluvina stared into her coffee's darkness, and said it was a Navajo story. "You believe them," said Paulita. "Not just what the Bible says."

"All people have found the truth, only in different words." Deluvina began. "Long ago, the First People became so wicked that the Great Spirit sent a storm to drown them in a flood. But First Woman showed them a hole in the sky. It led to a new world. She said, 'Someone must help you get there.' She wanted to prove to the Great Spirit that all were not selfishly evil.

"Dragonfly said, 'I will.' He called to Spider, 'Spin a rope. Tie one end to my arched body. I will fly up with the rope so all can climb it to safety.'

"Spider said, 'Anyone tied to my rope dies. If you still accept, say 'yes.'

" 'Yes,' said Dragonfly." Paulita sniffled. "And Dragonfly flew up through the storm, and held the edges of the hole with his six strong legs. When all climbed out, Dragonfly died. And the Great Spirit turned his body into stars so people would remember what he did."

Paulita said, "I hate death. The story's so sad."

"What do you think, Billy Bonney?" Deluvina asked with hidden purpose.

"Somebody once told me about the joy of the birds. They know death's just a second; life's millions. So I'd say Dragonfly gave his second for a purpose. And he could fly. That's a happy story."

Hastily, to escape renewed chill, Deluvina stood, "Dragonfly" sounding in her mind as a premonition.

Washing dishes, she listened. Paulita said that Dragonfly was brave. But she hated Spider. She killed him. The boy said Spider hadn't. He chose; he said yes.

"Deluvina," Paulita said, "tell Billy why Navajos won't go near a dead body." Because the spirit stays near, Deluvina said. Paulita asked Billy if he'd ever seen a dead body.

"Enough, Paulita," interrupted Deluvina. "Today, death has no place here." To Billy, she said, with private plan, "Paulita's mother should meet Paulita's rescuer. She returns tomorrow." He asked if she knew Paulita rode Centauro on the plains. "She knows Paulita rides different horses - and that I protect her." He rose, smiling at their subterfuge. Deluvina said, "You can stay in a guest room."

"Thanks. But I like sleeping out." He glanced at Paulita. "When the moon's full."

As that moon rose over a Ruidoso River farm, one hundred six miles southwest of Fort Sumner, four men spoke tensely in an adobe farmhouse, whose big-bodied young owner said, "Mister McSween, I blame myself for letting Mister Tunstall down," as he ran calloused hands through thick blond hair. He spoke with his parents' Vermont accent, though he had grown up in Wisconsin. "He trusted me when he left on that back-East buying trip."

"Mister Brewer," said the lawyer, "you can't be blamed for desperados. Gottfried Gauss, the witness, thought he'd be killed." Dick Brewer repeated that he should have been there.

"An' me an' Doc shoulda beaten the North in the Wahr," mocked hook-nosed Charlie Bowdre, with volatile brows. Cavalier-style, he had a dark drooping mustache and goatee; and his square-crowned hat right tilted enough to show premature balding and defiance. "An' we wouldah been rougher then ol' Gauss." Bowdre swiveled on his stool, his straddled legs shorter than his long torso implied. "Doc, happy yeh left medicine in Alabamah fohr this fun?"

His little, peculiarly pear-shaped friend said, "Not complaining," flashing intelligent eyes through circular spectacles, anchored by thick-rimmed ears, which flapped forward from center-parted sandy hair. His mustache, imitating Bowdre's, exaggerated his boxy chin.

Brewer said, "I can't believe Jessie Evans's cheek. We found the horses and mules at Shedd's Ranch; but he wouldn't give them back."

Charlie Bowdre added, "Evans said, 'Them mules is mah pay.'"

"I'da thot him and taken the conthequences," Scurlock lisped.

"Easy tah say with yaw luck," said Bowdre. "Know why Doc's got no fron' teeth, Mac?" That new nickname was as odious to the lawyer, as were these men; whom he snobbishly scorned, but unconsciously envied, for their raw masculinity.

Bowdre continued, "In a card game, a bad sport shot Doc. Bullet went intah his mouth an' out his neck. Only took those teeth."

Scurlock said, hissing through that gap, "Then I converted him to fertilithzer."

Compensating for his appearance, which locals called "a gun wearing a man," Josiah Scurlock emulated hot-headed Charlie

Bowdre's bravado, and kept secret that squeamishness had ended his medical studies, which granted him the "Doc."

To Brewer, Bowdre said, "Least ye told Evans tah go tah hell. That gumption mighta won ye that Matilda Jane Davis back in Wisconsin, 'stead o' her marryin' yaw cousin."

McSween interrupted, "Like John Tunstall, some men prefer bachelorhood."

"To Manuela Herrera Bowdre's regret," teased Scurlock.

"Not one goddamn bit," answered Bowdre easily. "One damn satisfied wife."

Alexander McSween noisily cracked his knuckles, and said, "Our builder, George Peppin, told me the underground jail will open next week. I predict Jessie Evans and his boys will be its first inhabitants. My editorial for the *Mesilla Valley Independent* may guarantee that."

From his frockcoat, he withdrew the newsprint. "Its owner - an attorney named Albert Jennings Fountain - is taking a stand against outlawry." McSween read: "**On September eighteenth, horses and mules of John H. Tunstall were stolen from a ranch on the Ruidoso River. The stock was valued at over two thousand dollars. The mules were the most handsome team around, and, among the horses, was an exceptional pair of dapple gray thoroughbreds. For recovery a liberal reward will be paid.**"

Just before midnight, after impatiently waiting for lights in the Maxwell mansion to extinguish, Billy walked stealthily to its rear porch, testing the planks, black-banded with moonshadows from its grand columns. Soundlessly, he rounded the north corner to check the walkway along that side. Down its length, as Deluvina had said, hung the side of beef in a canvas shroud.

Billy returned to Paulita's open window, and glanced over his shoulder. No one was on the flatland. Far below the rise on which the town stood, bare cottonwoods webbed the Pecos River. He cupped hands to the glass. Her bed was at the far left corner, its carved headboard flush with the wall.

She slept under a satin cover, in window's moonlight, nacreously violet as oyster shell lining. Headlong passion had brought him; but now he realized her loveliness. Billowing hair framed her heart-shaped face. Lips peaked with infant softness. Impetuosity melted into reverence. "Paulita," he whispered.

Immediately awake, she looked backward to her door, then to her window. She leapt up, running to him, pushing up the frame, and extending her leg. The silk nightgown slipped revealingly back. Flushing, he said, "Easy. Wait a minute." The naked leg reentered.

"You, uh, wanted to ride in the moon." He was looking into dark eyes where the moon was already. "You'd need clothes." He paused, embarrassed by presumption. "I mean, if you'd want to go."

"Oh, yes! Yes!" She threw open her armoire's tall mirrored doors, blocking his view, and returned in boots and a jacket over the nightgown.

His face turned crimson. "Uh. We'll be riding." She giggled, remembering pants, and tucking in the gown. When she was back at the window, he chivalrously reached to assist. She bristled, asking how he thought she'd gotten out before; sat on the sill; but launched herself, without warning, into his surprised arms.

Walking with him down land sloping to the Pecos River, she whispered, "I told you it would be beautiful." Even more beautiful, he murmured. At his mare, he asked dreamily where they should ride. She said, "Along the river. After the peach orchard and cornfields, you go east; and the Llano Estacado goes on forever."

He smiled wistfully and repeated his gallant error by reaching to lift. Her outrage was placated by his mounting first and freeing a stirrup. She climbed behind and demanded, "Push forward more." He looked back, asking about teasing. "Why would I? Why's your face all funny?" Again he was touched by her unpredictable mix of precocity and naïveté, and was quiet as they left the town behind.

But on the llano, on its luminous mirage of ocean bounded by horizon, he threw back his head with coyote yips, and they raced, as she shouted faster, faster, we're on the moon!

Finally, Billy slowed. The mare stretched her wet neck. Then he was shocked. Paulita lifted his jacket to pat his vest. With tenuous control, he asked what she was doing. "Found something," she said. "Papa carried surprises." She held Dolan's packet of peppermints. He said she could have one. "I area'y d'," she answered, mouth full with all. "Wa un?" A sticky ball reached around.

Laughing, he accepted, discovering tingling ambrosia, her arms around his waist, her open legs pressed to him, and heard: "I wonder where Dragonfly's stars are, Billy?" He looked to faraway suns, pulsating and swirling. And each breath mounted ecstasy, until her against him reverberated bliss; and moon, land, and Paulita merged in ravishing wonderment.

She was squeezing his waist playfully. He teased that she was strong for a girl. "Or boy," she said. "Put your hand under my knee." His fingertips slipped gingerly. She crushed. He cried out, not all in jest, and dared not look back.

When they dismounted near a small spring to water the mare, he said, "I'll show you how to dance." Her childlike rejoicing reinforced his new continence. He took her hands. Singing, he turned them in a circle, time marked by the spring's reappearing plants. Faster they turned, his hand now at her waist; until, for Paulita, there were two dances: one in moonlight, one in her body.

Finally they stopped. She declared, "My favorite part of dancing is the moth between your legs. Like when you hold one you catch inside, to carry it outside. Is that your favorite part too?" The pallid light hid his blush. He managed to say he knew what she meant.

When she was back in her room, looking out at him, she asked if he was still coming to meet her mother. "Yes," he said, and forced himself to leave, confused by feelings that filled his eyes with tears and his heart with joy.

SEPTEMBER 22, 1877   1:00 PM   SATURDAY

In wind trying to hurl him away, Billy waited under the Maxwell mansion's prodigious front porch. The door opened to Deluvina. "Big house," he said, following her along the hallway of chandeliers.

"Yes. But many of these would have fit inside theirs in the north. Cimarron," she whispered as they came to a drawing-room.

In its curtained paneled glow, Paulita and a woman, whose back was to them, faced each other on armchairs near a monumental stone fireplace. Deluvina announced, "Mister Bonney to see Doña María de la Luz Beaubien Maxwell."

Billy noticed that, at Paulita's midnight-blue dress's hem, beside empty satin slippers, her little toes busily dug into the Persian rug; and was red-faced just as her mother rose.

Walking serenely with swishing black taffeta of perpetual mourning, Luz Maxwell noted the superlative quality of his hat and boots, and said with haughty graciousness of wealth's generations, "We owe you a tremendous debt, Mister Bonney," in an exotic blend of French, Spanish, and English accents.

Grasping his hand in soft surround of hers, a diamond pinky ring dazzling, she made an emotive sigh. "Risking your life with that gang shooting at you. And to think of Paulita side-saddle on her little Welch pony." The girl giggled. The woman smiled. "Still my little girl." She gestured to a couch, saying, "Paulita told me that you are a newcomer and have also visited Lincoln County. What is your impression of it?"

"Well, Ma'am, your past matters less than how you use a gun."

She laughed heartily for the first time since her husband's death; and thought, Lucien would have said that. "You are young. How young?" she asked. Almost eighteen, he said. "Still, you realized that underneath this Territory's violence is freedom. My deceased husband, Lucien Bonaparte Maxwell, loved that also. Paulita, do get the Cimarron album."

When they were alone, Luz Maxwell said, "You do so remind me Lucien. Would you like to hear about him?" Billy nodded with polite disinterest. Paulita returned.

"Dear, give it to Mister Bonney." Its cover was inset with a decorative mirror. Briefly Billy saw his face framed on their family book.

Paulita said, "I'm going. It makes me miss Papa too much to listen." She ran, calling, "I'll be back before night."

Her mother said, "She has his spirit. Uncontrollable." She sighed. Life stretched ahead of the girl, while, at only forty-eight, she felt hers ended. Self-absorption blunted the fact that her child, just rescued, was running back to the same risks.

Abruptly she asked, "May I see your concealed pistol? When you reached for the album, I saw it and became curious."

"About me?" he asked casually, while checking windows for escape.

"No. The gun. Its odd butt." She received its curved, bird's head profile of pearl-handled grips. Enthusiastically, Billy hunkered down beside her, face dewy young like her daughter's, close enough to touch, with blurred voice saying it was the new Colt Lightning. Double action! Think how fast you can shoot! Her eyes brimmed. "Go on, Bi ... Mister Bonney." He said to call him Billy.

"Oh, Billy. My Paulita said you'd bring back memories." She felt like a girl again, showing off. Lucien had taught her to hunt. Together they had ridden in Cimarron, and had made love in pine forests where the Rio Grande spilled hundreds of feet down golden granite. Now she cherished her grief like she had cherished the man, and took advantage of this boy to relive.

Again on the couch, Billy waited.

"This is how I met Lucien. In the winter of forty-one, Kit Carson brought him to our home in Taos - when it was still the Mexican Republic." She knew Kit Carson, Billy asked with awe. "Oh, quite well. My father was Charles Hipolite Trotier de Beaubien, a French Canadian, who settled in Taos in twenty-three. The Mexican people had just won their independence two years before. He renamed himself Don Carlos.

"My mother, María Paula Lovato, was a daughter of the most prominent Spanish family there. She was a great beauty, my mother, Paulita. You know Paulita's lovely eyes?" He blushed. "Those are hers. When my father died in sixty-four, she followed in just six months. It was a great love.

"But on that evening when I met Lucien, a freezing draft blew from the entry hall. Well, I was raised like a princess. I called, 'What fool left open the door?' In came a young frontiersman, smelling like fresh snow. He said, 'I'm that fool. And I'm making Taos my home. I damn well deserve a good welcome.' And I fell in love right then - if you can believe that."

"I can," Billy said raptly.

"We married in six months. Lucien was from Illinois; his father, Hugh Charles Maxwell, had come from Dublin in seventeen ninety-nine. His mother, Marie Odile Menard, was from a distinguished Illinois family. Her father, Pierre Menard, was in Illinois government when it became a state. Lucien could have stayed and been a success. Instead, he set out to explore the whole Southwest. And I let him." She had been rebellious too, even with her satin slippers and shawls of gold and silver thread.

She went to Billy and sat, enveloping him with lovely perfume; and said, "The land where I was born had been the Utes' and the Jicarilla Apaches' before recorded time. The Spanish had it for almost three hundred years, then the Mexicans for over a quarter century.

"My father loved it. He and Guadalupe Miranda, a full-blooded Mexican, petitioned his friend, Governor Manuel Armijo, the last of the pre-conquest officials, to get a land grant in partnership."

She reached to Billy's lap, opening the album with pages framing documents.

There was the yellowed petition of January eighth of forty-one. There was Armijo's approval in three days. Three years later came the Mexican government's confirmation on April fifteenth. She said, "It was named the Beaubien-Miranda Land Grant."

She returned to her chair, concealing agitation, and continued. "On January eighteenth of forty-seven, a massacre occurred there. The local Mexicans and Indians revolted. Father was away on business, and Lucien was on another expedition with Kit Carson. The attackers mutilated and scalped my brother, Narciso. He was twenty-one, and my father's heir to the Grant."

In her mind, she again fled the house, and hailed a worker, who hid her in his wagon. She had abandoned Narciso. No one knew. If she had stayed, would Narciso have been spared? This life of hers resulted from his death; she had taken his place. Had God cursed her? Had it brought tragedy to the Grant, to Fort Sumner? All because of the curse of Narciso.

She said, "That massacre changed Lucien. He settled down. We had Peter Menard first. Then two daughters who died as babies. Last was dear Paulita: on April twentieth of sixty-three."

"April twentieth," Billy repeated, as if acquiring a treasure.

"My father and Lucien became close. Lucien began to build towns on the Grant: first Rayado, then Cimarron. Then, in fifty-eight, Guadalupe Miranda wanted to sell his half. My father wasn't interested. But Lucien bought it for two thousand seven hundred and forty-five dollars. When my father died in sixty-four, he left his half to my six sisters. By seventy, Lucien had bought their shares. Then, everyone called it the Maxwell Land Grant.

"Lucien built us a beautiful house in Cimarron. This one is its re-creation, though so much smaller; like the ghost of all that is lost." Luz Maxwell sighed. "Cimarron became famous for Lucien's hospitality. He made a race course for the best blooded horses. He had hundreds of acres under cultivation. He would walk barefoot in the acequia irrigation ditches. Just to feel his land.

"And Paulita, how he loved her. Watching them together, I realized he would never grow old. I'll give you an example. It is said that gold was discovered on the Grant in Baldy Mountain in sixty-six. But Lucien knew about it all along. The Indians and trappers had brought him nuggets as large as hen's eggs in trade at his Cimarron store. I'd find him and Paulita playing with them. It's true he made much money, but only because there was such plenty. A newspaper said his Aztec mine was the world's richest."

Now she was mistress of this Fort Sumner wasteland, when once mistress of the biggest land-holding ever privately possessed in America. Now she was left with showing this boy all that she had been, as a diversion from boredom of servants; squabbles of Peter and Paulita; extravagant dressmakers in Las Vegas, with black the only color; the gatherings; and unremitting grieving, as if the land expressed its forlornness through her.

What kept her alive was hatred. Buried was hatred at Lucien for abandoning the Grant, then her. Consciously, it was hatred of Thomas Benton Catron. That hatred drew her to Billy. Would he have killed to protect her Paulita? Could he be stimulated to avenge her?

She said, "Lucien called our land Eden. But a Serpent came into our Garden: a man named Thomas Benton Catron. In sixty-six, Attorney Catron was introduced to us in Cimarron by Lucien's lawyer at that time, Stephen Benton Elkins; right after Catron joined Elkins in his law firm in Santa Fe. How were we to know that Catron's greed would destroy all we loved? He saw that Lucien was staggering under the weight of managing the ranching; the farming; the Indian trade; and the gold mining, with its horrid influx of squatters. So the Serpent offered Lucien the most tempting apple: freedom. Catron convinced him to sell the Grant.

"Attorney Elkins - as corrupt as Catron - had it surveyed. It came to one million, seven hundred fourteen thousand, and seven hundred sixty-four acres. About two million. It took in a good deal of the northern part of this Territory and extended into what became Colorado.

"Catron, through foreign investors, made a bond scheme which finalized on July twenty-third of seventy. Lucien got six hundred thousand dollars. Later we found out that the sale had yielded an additional seven hundred fifty thousand dollars.

"We never knew how much Catron and Elkins kept; but the total sale was really one million three hundred fifty thousand dollars - more than double what Lucien realized. Being defrauded broke his will.

"So instead of turning against Catron, Lucien turned to him. In September of seventy, Catron pursuaded him to invest one hundred fifty thousand dollars to start the First National Bank of Santa Fe. Catron and Elkins made him its president. The next year, they secretly started the rival National Bank of New Mexico, whose competition convinced Lucien to sell them his shares at a loss. Then those villains replaced him at First National with Elkins as its president.

"Lucien had kept his beloved Cimarron, but after that, he wanted to escape all memories, and sold it too. Then Catron had him contribute to founding the Texas Pacific Railroad. When its bonds devalued, Lucien lost two hundred fifty thousand dollars.

"It was Catron who convinced him to buy this Fort Sumner property, left vacant by the military since the late sixties. Also, I'm sure Lucien knew of it through Kit Carson, who - I'm sorry to say - was a part of the tragedy of the Indian people here.

"I have been told that, wherever our workers dig, they find human bones." She sighed. "This is the desolation east of Eden; and Lucien was the man driven from Paradise. That's what he used to say."

Finding herself at the verge of revealing a family secret, she hesitated, but wanting to unburden, rationalized that Billy was no risk. "For five thousand dollars Lucien purchased, from the United States government, all the fort buildings. That did not include its thousands of acres of land. But Lucien was led to believe that title could be easily gotten. Even that was a lie. The case is still pending in Washington.

"But he was still Lucien. He converted officers' quarters to this house, and made the barracks into a town. He planted corn fields and the peach orchard, and ran ten thousand head of cattle and fifty thousand sheep. But he never recovered.

"By July twenty-fifth of seventy-five, he was dead - five years almost to the day of the Grant sale. As if July is cursed: a memorial to evil's power."

Billy said, "Seems you've still got a fight. Is your son doing it?" Her eyes blazed like Paulita's. "Catron may have been the destroyer, but Peter could have saved his father's life by giving him hope.

"Oh yes, we're still making money; and so much of the fortune remains. But we are trapped on this cursed land. I am positive it's cursed."

Luz Maxwell heaved her corseted bosom with morbid self-pity. She could look forward only to a grand match for her daughter. The rich Jaramillos in Las Vegas had been family friends since Cimarron days. They had a son.

She said, "I haven't talked this much since Lucien died. And I enjoyed it." Flattered, Billy glanced sidelong, testing his appeal.

Both standing, Luz Maxwell, with a sweet wave of desire, said, "Paulita mentioned that you like to dance." Billy blushed.

"We have a dance hall. And our town baile dance is in two Saturdays: October sixth. Paulita had pleaded to go. Her brother, Peter, has been protective of her - and I can't disagree with that. But if you came, I'd let her go with Deluvina."

Billy, not noticing the chaperoning condescension, said, "I'll be there sure as the Pecos keeps on flowing."

The woman smiled and asked, "Do you believe in the supernatural? I just got a feeling that our lives will be linked."

"Thank you," Billy answered uncertainly.

Luz Maxwell followed him to the front door, where his gliding strides onto the parade ground filled her with remembered pleasures; though she would have been horrified to know his plans for the intervening time.

OCTOBER 1, 1877   8:49 AM   MONDAY

As if his life was controlled by a pendulum swinging between good and evil, Billy returned to Jessie Evans; and, when giving back the bay mare to James Dolan, provided the excuse that Fort Sumner horses were too well guarded to steal.

Now, to ambush and rob the Butterfield Stage, Billy, wearing double cartridge belts like Jessie and his boys, rode with them toward Cook's Canyon, in the Cook's Mountain Range, west of the San Augustin pass. Their fresh horses, obtained near Mesilla, were from rustler, John Kinney; Jessie's a red roan mare which he had recognized. Billy had received a chestnut gelding.

Jessie called, "We'll stop at a way station." Billy asked if he paid for everybody. Jessie laughed hard and said, "Jessie Evans pays fer nothin'. They's happy they's alive! Kid, you's a mix: rough an' then - I don' know - somethin' else."

Later, when lurking at a blind turn within Cook's Canyon, in gritty wind funneled through its walls, Frank Baker, with angry prognathous jaw, said to Jessie, "With that kid, seems yer fergettin' them who's earned their places."

Jessie said loudly, "Kid. Baker an' Morton got somethin' 'gainst you. Wanna make somethin' o' it?" Billy ignored him, excited by distant hooves.

When the coach rounded the bend, Jessie's Winchester bullet whistled near its two drivers, who braked and climbed down as ordered; while three frightened passengers emerged: two men and a woman.

Billy clambered to his job of searching the top rack. There was no strongbox; luggage had paltry contents: a valise with frayed feminine draws and threadbare petticoats; and a trunk with newspaper-wrapped dishes. But a canvas satchel yielded a pouch of gold coins.

Billy tossed it to Jessie, who said, "Good. Throw down everythin', so's we don' miss nothin'."

Billy objected that the dishes would break. Jessie retorted angrily. Crockery smashed; newspaper and clothing blew.

The woman, with old-fashioned full-skirted style of Billy's mother, ran back crying, "Stop. Oh, stop;" but paused with shame at the underwear, as if stripped herself. At the dishes, she dropped to her knees weeping.

Jessie pulled her up and said something. She swayed, as if swooning, but walked ahead of him back to the group. Billy followed.

There, the smaller male passenger wrung his hands. Over his ear, a greased, hair strip hung absurdly, blown from his bald pate.

The other, broad and with kinky red beard, had a cheap, rabbit fur-trimmed overcoat. Solemnly he said, "We plead for our lives."

He turned to Billy. "I'm Mister Carpenter, boy. From Silver City." Billy had no recognition. "You're Henry Antrim. I once bought a pie from your mother."

Jessie said belligerently, "Don' matter who ye 'members. Bu' Jessie Evans sez ye kin live."

When the gang finally rode past their victims, Billy saw, in their watching eyes, the watching eyes of calves and lambs as he, at Richard Knight's butcher shop, raised a heavy mallet and let it fall. Horror and remorse shuddered through him.

When they slowed, Jessie called to the others, "Go back te Kinney's. I got business with the kid."

Alone with Billy, Jessie said, "So yer name's Henry Antrim," and laughed. "Ye picked good. Billy Bonney's better."

Billy smiled wanly. "Wha's wrong? Tomorra we's doin' cattle." There was no response. "You's definily in a mood."

Billy said it was the people's frightened faces. Jessie chuckled. "Yeah. 'Cep' fer money an' killin', I likes tha' bes'. Like you's God."

Billy felt nausea. "Wan' some jerkey?" Billy refused. Jessie said, "We need a tree an' a big rock."

Billy forced a laugh. "Sounds like a hanging. Next you'll say you like that."

Ain' bad, he answered, missing the sarcasm. "I's fer yer mood."

They dismounted near a run-off channel from the San Andres Mountains, and tied the horses beside sandstone blocks. Jessie gave Billy the canteens to fill, and waited till he was out of sight before pivoting his mare's rear to a rock platform, hobbling her rear legs, and climbing up behind her. She shifted, uneasily imbalanced. He brandished his thonged quirt, growling, "Don' move, bitch." Lasciviously, he eyed her rosey-roaned haunches and reddish tail, shiny like woman's hair, as he readied himself and moved her compliant tailbone, past beatings remembered.

When Billy returned, he saw Jessie pulling back on the cantle. Then he comprehended. Jessie made a final drooling grunt, and lay forward, mumbling, "Makin' shur she was ready." Back down, buttoning pants, he said, "Damn good mare. Now you use 'er."

Eyes wide with astonishment, Billy shook his head. "You's missin' somethin'." Jessie noticed his red cheeks. "Anyways, ye looks better."

Billy said, "After her, a man could be easily satisfied."

Jessie laughed. "I shur like ye. Bu' yer a hard keeper." He hunkered down at the mare's hobbles to avoid the boy's face. "Figer on doin' tomorra's job?" Billy agreed. "Afta tha'?"

"I'm helping the widow Casey on the Hondo." Though that intent had just come to him, he said it decisively. Jessie asked if he was coming back. "Sure," Billy said, and meant it. Jessie smiled.

This time, Billy accepted jerky. Jessie watched him chew, and sighed deeply; releasing tension at threatened loss of the only person he had ever loved.

OCTOBER 6, 1877   3:44 PM   SATURDAY

Coming from Ellen Casey's ranch, approaching Fort Sumner for Luz Maxwell's dance invitation, Billy's eye was caught by a small golden disk in crescendo decrescendo of blowing high grass. It was a plains sunflower, a single sprout from withered, six foot stalks with dead blooms' bristly husks. "Optimist," Billy said smiling, taking it for a boutonniere in his jacket.

In the dancehall, adjoining Beaver Smith's Saloon, was a large, festively clad crowd, mostly Mexican. Through animated bodies, Billy saw a singer and musicians with accordion, fiddle, and guitar. Someone, in broken English, asked him in to take off his gun.

Coyly smiling women, hands masking like fans, received a friendly tip of his hat; as men, in minority, responded to the music with exuberant eees, trilled rrrr's, or drunken cowboy shouts. Paulita was not there.

Billy invited a plain round-cheeked girl, after just missing her more attractive companion. She said shyly, "No dance good." He smiled, reassuring in Spanish that he could lead. Soon she stepped happily. When they stopped, the previous girl joined them.

His partner said, "This is my sister, Apolinaria Gutierrez." Billy asked her name. "Juanita. Juanita Gutierrez."

Then Paulita entered, lovely in green silk, with Deluvina. The band started.

Boldly, Juanita's sister said, "Now *we* dance," seizing his hand, pulling him to a polka-like schottisch.

Finally, Billy freed himself and called to Paulita, who was remonstrating with Deluvina across the room. Paulita saw him, ran, was buffeted by a drunken man, then pulled Billy, blushing at their clasped hands, to Deluvina. Paulita said, "Tell her to let me dance, Billy. She says Mamma won't let me. We'll keep it secret." His exaggerated perusal of the crowd made her and Deluvina laugh.

Eyes flashing playfully, Billy said, "Always stick to the truth, Paulita." The music began: a corrido, a ballad of a hero.

Billy danced before her. First was treading, as music entered him; then toe-heel rhythm. As people stopped to watch, a half moon space was filled by his body, knees high lifting. Then he took Paulita's hands, drawing her into the room.

For her, Billy became the unquenchable forces of freedom: wind, thunder, lightening, vast plains, and promise of Cimarron; until, dance-wet, he removed the sunflower and handed his jacket to the people.

For her, he next danced the miracle of the flower resisting winter: the defiant dance of life itself. While his lithe body moved with brash potency, upheld with thumb and index finger, the flower made a secondary dance of exquisite tenderness: of a fragility hovering and protected. In the flourish of last notes, Billy, bowing, extended to Paulita that blossom. To clapping, they returned to Deluvina.

Breathing rapidly, Billy declared to the woman, "I danced for both of us." He and Paulita looked into each other's rebellious and excited eyes and laughed and laughed.

A hawk-faced man had been watching. After Deluvina escorted Paulita out, he asked, deep-voiced behind Billy, "Want to dance, kid?" Billy turned at an anticipated joke, and saw a mustached man in shirt, vest, and dark pants. Around his left arm was knotted a red bandana.

A youth explained in Spanish, "This is our foreman, Barney Mason. Red means he dances as a woman. We never have enough at our bailes."

Barney Mason gave no expected clownish grin. He had watched enviously; and not just Billy's dance, but his immediate popularity.

Mason knew his detestation by the hirelings; though he rationalized it as transferred from Peter Maxwell. Now he hoped to impress his men.

Mason gave Billy his raptor profile, eyes glinting sidelong, powerfully corded neck displayed. Clasping Billy's hand and underestimating the boy's strength, Mason misstepped, his boot striking with bell-like ringing. Billy saw his flashy Spanish spurs with huge, sharply serrated rowels. From each mounting pin hung tear-shaped clappers named jinglebobs, like Chisum's dangling ear splice. Mason said, "Let's see what you can do."

Neither took the female role. Barney Mason did a stiff cowboy two-step, made dramatic by his hard muscles, seen as legs or buttocks pressed pants; while jinglebobs sounded to slamming feet. Billy, less earth-bound, laughed at the novelty. But feeling ridiculed, Mason added clogging strides. Billy countered with jig-like rhythm.

Men clustered. One shouted, "I bets on the keed." Another said, "Whatever you bet, I double it on Mason." The band, realizing their intrinsic role, extended their repertoire. Soon, the red bandana ends clung to Mason's sweat-soaked sleeve like fierce gashes.

Billy was disappearing into the dance of roosters, of stags, of all beasts that tested and realized masculinity by pitting body to body. It was a contest where glory gushed with blood, so chest swelled and maleness pulled up tight.

"Tired?" Barney Mason called out.

"What?" answered Billy, too absorbed to comprehend words.

Pugnaciously, Mason hooked his left arm into Billy's right. Both spun, joined at the elbows.

Suddenly, Mason slashed his sawblade rowel. It flew ringing past Billy's dodging limb. Men went wild, shouting, "Cockfight! Kill him, kid! Kill him, Barney!" Sensing trouble, the band slowed, but male voices threatened; and the mad dance continued.

Hawk-faced Mason, exhausted and angry, grabbed the boy's hand, pulling him to kicking boot teeth, aimed at his crotch. Instantly, Billy used that rigid arm to thrust Mason to his unsupported side. Mason landed hard.

Sitting, he reached into his vest. A man shouted, "Watch out, kid!"

Aimed were vertical double muzzles of a .41 caliber Remington derringer. In the hush, it was easy to hear Billy's calm voice: "Heck of a time for *the foreman* to remember to leave his gun at the door."

Barney Mason smiled grudgingly and said, "You win." There was laughter, then huddling to settle wagers. Standing, Mason, struggling with humiliation, asked, "What's the secret of your dancing?"

Billy smiled, wiping perspiration. "My Ma - she was a good dancer - always said, 'Only point your toes up in your coffin.' " Mason chuckled stiltedly and exited.

A Spanish-speaking man returned the jacket to Billy, who gave his name, and was answered: "Soon all of Fort Sumner will know that Billy Bonney gave to Señor Mason what he deserved. I am Francisco Lobato." And he identified the young singer as Paco Anaya.

Billy asked about water. "Go next door to Beaver Smith's." Lobato laughed. "He has four ears. Drunk Chisum cowboys split his ears in the jinglebob. It is bad for health to ask about it. But it is worse to make Barney Mason angry." Lobato laughed again. "You are welcome at my camp. I am one of the patrón's sheep herders."

At the saloon's bar, burly red-faced Beaver Smith sported strategically shaggy, muttonchop whiskers. In a gravely voice, he asked, "You the famis kid?" Billy laughingly asked what he was famous for. "Fer winnin' Hilario Gonzales a hunred fifty dollas. Whaever ye wan's on me."

When Billy reentered the dancehall's thick warm air and jocular congratulations, he realized that a buxom young woman, black hair satin in lamplight, was vying for his attention. Sequins sparkled on her fiesta skirt over ruffled scarlet petticoats. Pouting fascinating lips, she said in Spanish, "Poor Celsa. Waiting to meet you. First you dance with my sister Juanita, then my sister Apolinaria. But do you dance with Celsa? No. Poor Celsa Gutierrez is left alone."

In Billy's arms, Celsa molded, not to music, but to him. They sought the excesses permitted by dance: to touch, to press, to smell desire's pungent odor.

The room became her: mounting lust of cascading hair below reach, of black eyes flashing, of breasts fluctuant beneath blouse curtain, of soft sinuous back; as their besotted legs became so yielding that they needed to sink downward, to lie downward, to lie together, pressed in the dance.

Still dancing, Billy heard Celsa laugh. The music had stopped. The lamps were low, the room almost empty. Still he held her, asking if she was leaving with her sisters. They were long gone, she said, and pressed his hand to her voluptuous chest.

Being led out by Celsa, Billy exclaimed, remembering, "My rig!" Then they emerged into darkness of the new moon.

Uncontrollably, Billy kissed lips flagged by blowing hair. Then distant footsteps froze him. Celsa whispered, "Only the patrón." Billy sighed. The oddly-placed front gate opened. The figure disappeared in blackness.

She said, "My house is down this street. The third. You will come?" Billy could barely whisper yes.

"Then meet me at the back door. Go down the town entrance. Then turn left at the first alley."

After Celsa was gone, the west wind, moaning desire, urged him instead through the mansion's vegetable garden and to its northwest corner window. The dark interior revealed nothing. Caressing the sill, Billy knew it was Paulita he wanted. In her impetuosity, in her innocence, she would yield easily - in secret. Now.

Wind communicated subliminally. Big Emma, forgotten only as one forgets one's bones, had returned as Celsa, again offering plenty and his mother's forbidden hungers. Conscience makes ingenious bargains, joining taboos to their punishment: an equilibrium of glory with pain - like Cú Chulainn's binding to his rock. All Billy knew was that Paulita must be protected from himself.

Celsa's back window, with lacy net curtain obscuring an interior lit from an adjoining room, was beside a back door. Opening it barefoot, she whispered, "Did you get lost?" Billy just smiled.

She closed shutters, while he saw that the small room had a rough-hewn bed and simple chair. On the wall was a crucifix beside a tin holder with a candle. To his left, a doorway led to the eating area. Beyond it was another room with a hanging blanket nailed to its lintel. He asked if she lived alone. She said, "Sometimes others stay. The Gutierrez family is hospitable. You want food? Drink?"

"No," he whispered. "I want you."

Celsa lit the candle, and lifted off her loose blouse. At last there were the golden-skinned breasts; then red petticoats falling from her golden ripe body. Billy's hectic kissing embracing was a confusion of his disrobing, then her kneeling to unthoughtof pleasure; but instead, his lifting her to the bed.

In the room with one candle, a single shadow rose up and writhed downward until the wax was consumed. Left with touch, their drenched bodies still sought ravenously. When shutter light slashed their bodies, they knew day had returned.

Celsa lifted her wet hair. "We have been swimming," she said. Swimming in rainbows, he murmured, face pressed to her hair to smell their lovemaking.

Cupping him possessively, she purred, "Next month, I marry. It has been arranged for years. My cousin: Saval Gutierrez, an old man. He supervises the herders. He is away sometimes for weeks."

"I could come back?"

"Yes, Billy. Come back. Come back to Celsa now."

OCTOBER 19, 1877   9:20 AM   FRIDAY

Having ridden a sleet-stormed night, seeking family warmth, Billy was received by Ma'am Jones, who affectionately directed his icy coat sleeve to the kitchen, saying later, when he heard men in the dining room.

While Minnie served him stew, Ma'am asked about Ellen Casey. But Billy wanted to know who was there.

Ma'am sighed. "Something bad's happened. Just when Heiskell, Bill, and Jim are away. My John and Andy Boyle - a local rancher you haven't met - and others are there. First tell me about Ellen."

Eating voraciously, Billy said, "Well, like she told me, she's lonely; what with her husband murdered. So she left yesterday to his family in Texas."

"Left!" Ma'am exclaimed with shock and loss. "Why now?"

" 'Cause Mister Tunstall bought some of her cattle. She sold him two hundred nine, for one thousand three hundred dollars. But he paid that money to merchants she owed credit. Seems that confused her, 'cause she figured they were still hers. So she took 'em along with the rest of her herd. She wanted me to come too." Ma'am asked why he hadn't. " 'Cause I belong here."

He blushed. "Uh. She's *real* lonely." At Ma'am Jones's questioning expression, he said gently, but not truthfully, "Nothing did happen."

For the first time, Ma'am Jones noticed his startlingly blue eyes; sighed; then smiled tenderly, and said, "You filled her back up with life, Billy. I'm not educated, but I trust my inner sense. There's something in you that brings out, I guess, whatever's inside people. Even I feel a little different."

Neither realized that this charisma was a siren song that had already claimed three victims - Frank Cahill, John Mackie, and Tom O'Keffe - stimulating love, hatred, need, hope, courage; all leading to wreckage. So seductive was this prancing leader of the long-ago circus parade - exuberant in youth's glamour; deceptively compliant; audaciously confident in charming, manipulating, shooting, and escaping - that none would be immune to his spell; until the conflagration, begun at Jessie's campfire, would consume them all.

When Billy entered the dining room, talk stopped. At the table's head was Andrew Boyle, rugged and black bearded, with piercing eyes and thick triangular brows. The Beckwith brothers, Bob and John; Wallace Olinger; and a big heavy-set stranger were there; as were John Jones and Sammie, with his left eyelid half-open. As Billy sat, Buck Morton, Billy Matthews, and Nicholas Provencio entered noisily. Sammie asked Billy, "Where you there too?"

Ma'am Jones entered with coffee. "Sammie," she said, "you're too young for this talk." Reluctantly, he followed her out.

John Jones resumed. "So they got Jessie?" Bob Beckwith answered that Jessie had figured the dugout chosa house at their place was a safe hide out.

The big stranger said, "I'd 've blasted those cocksuckers." John Jones introduced him to Billy as Bob Olinger. Fat padded Olinger's face with its long turned-up nose; and made his neck appear goiterous. Jones added for Billy that Andy Boyle was their leader.

Bob Beckwith resumed. "So the bastards arrested Jessie, Baker, Hill, and Davis. Here's how. McSween forced Sheriff Brady to make Dick Brewer a deputy sheriff, saying Brady'd done nothing to get back Tunstall's horses and mules. So Brewer rode out to our place with Brady and Tunstall's boys. They surrounded the chosa before dawn this past Wednesday.

"I heard, when they surrendered, Jessie was yelling at Brewer, 'You don't even know how to take cover! But I kept missing!'" All laughed. "Right now, they're on their way to jail in Lincoln."

Billy asked why Brady couldn't just let them out. Wallace Olinger said, "That's dangerous talk, kid. Only the guard's got the keys. Brady would be accused. Worse, they'll be in leg irons attached to a log. George Peppin told us."

Buck Morton said, "So Jimmy wants *us* to get Jessie out." Billy asked if there was a plan. Morton taunted, "Maybe *you'll* make one."

"Seems like there isn't," Billy retaliated.

He said, "First, Jessie needs files." Bob Olinger guffawed, saying it sounded like he'd had experience. Billy said, "It's obvious." The man flushed angrily. Others laughed. Andrew Boyle objected that there would be locks on the door and pit trap. "Rocks," Billy said. "That jail couldn't have cost three thousand. They'd be easy to smash."

Billy smiled. "When I checked out Lincoln, I figured the jail was of interest. I got the guard, Maximiano de Guerara, to show me around. Over the pit is a one room adobe with two north windows - without bars. A ladder goes to the pit: a miserable place. An acequia's too close; so water's seeping in. Anyway, the guard gets nights off. After the files - I'll do that - you boys can get them out. So it's Jessie and his boys, right?"

Billy Matthews said, "And two greasers: Lucas Gallegos - killed his cousin - and Catarino Romero, who helped. McSween's their lawyer. Says some Anglos framed 'em."

Surprised, Billy asked if McSween defended Mexican people. "You missed the point," Matthews answered, squinting his tiny eyes. "Most of Lincoln County's greasers. Tunstall's giving 'em credit in his store that Dolan can't match. And McSween's representing 'em in court."

"Careful," said pencil-mustached Morton. "He's a greaser-lover."

Andrew Boyle broke the impasse by asking when he would do it. Billy said, "I'll wait this storm out. Then I'll get daywork at one of those Ruidoso homestead farms for cover.

In that ice storm's misery, sixty-three miles northwest of Seven Rivers, on the road paralleling the Hondo River, a laden buckboard was being driven eastward by an exhausted man. Ahead, approaching riders blurred in his good eye, tearing after a night spent stranded, when his horse refused to continue. He clucked to the plodding white pony and said, "Come now, White Mouse. On girl." A single rider came closer. "Dick Brewer!" the man called. "Halloo, Dick!"

Brewer joined alongside the slowly rolling buckboard. "Morning, Mister Tunstall. I'm surprised to see you."

"It has been rather arduous. On Sunday I arrived back in Lincoln and found an order from John Chisum. But Long Tom was lame. Down from sixteen hands of prime horse flesh to this mite for delivery. Alexander then informed me my best livestock had been stolen by rogues."

John Tunstall halted at the unshaven group, recognizing only Doc Scurlock and Charlie Bowdre; and said, "Jolly good hiring, Dick. But why ride about instead of capturing those thieves?"

Frank Baker called, "Don' ye know if we got Brewer; er he got us?"

Jessie rode to the high buckboard seat and taunted, "Englishman, 'member me?"

"Ah, yes, Mister Evans. So *you* are the thief. Are these your accomplices?" Jessie doubled with laughter; and his boys laughed.

Riding forward, came a muscular man with fierce emerald-green eyes, large handlebar mustache, and black shoulder-length hair. In his hatband was a wing feather of a golden eagle. He said, "I'm Fred Tecumseh Waite, Mister Tunstall. We're all your men except for Jessie here, and three of his boys." Waite pointed. "We're taking them to jail."

Porcine Tom Hill called out that they wanted whiskey. Tunstall laughed lightly. "I have only a dram with me; that means 'a bit.' But in spirit of negotiation, I shall come to your goal with enough to soak you all."

Fred Waite's brows drew together at his employer's lax and muddled responses, aware that they represented risk to them all.

OCTOBER 28, 1877   4:04 PM   SUNDAY

The look-alike Coe cousins, on ladderback chairs in their farmhouse, spoke to Billy, looking up at them, in connived boyish innocence, from his bolster-like bedroll on the floor.

Frank said, "Sure's a goldarn coinceedence, kid, way you wandered in jus' when we needed help - what with havin' to help our neighbor, Dick Brewer, since he became Tunstall's foreman." George, puffing on his corn-cob pipe, rocked his chair to its back legs.

Frank said, "An' you sure as hell can work. You an' me's laid up a month's worth of meat this week. George, I didn' tell you 'bout the five snowbirds yestaday. This boy kin shoot. Those ptarmigan grouse turn so white in winter, they're good as snow. An' way they take off fast, maybe I could'a gotten one. He got all five!

"Kid, that leaves me with a question." Billy braced for a failed ruse. He had an escape route planned; but was prepared, if needed, to kill them with the concealed Lightening. "That big ol' mountain ram. You shot wild to scare 'im off. Right?"

"We had enough, Frank. No need to kill more."

"That's real sentimental. Only one I know shoots good as you's Charlie Bowdre's wife's brother: Fernando Herrera. Or Charlie's neighbor, Buckshot Roberts."

Frank added more wood to the potbellied stove and said, "Tearrible weather fer Dick to be chasin' afta them Wida Casey cattle." Billy showed surprise. "She stole 'em from Tunstall. Brewer an' his boys caught up with her at the Texas border, kid."

He added, "Goldarn, I plumb fergot yer name."

"Does 'Kid' suit you?" asked George. Billy nodded.

George continued, "Brewer's hiring for Tunstall: those that can use a gun. You'd like John Tunstall, Kid. He arrived last year. And with this lawyer, Alexander McSween, he got busier then a one armed monkey at a flea festival." Billy smiled.

"No joke. That Murphy-Dolan bunch had loaded us with debt like pitiful packhorses."

Frank said, "But we're buckin' since McSween told Brewer that Dolan didn' even own the farm he was sellin' him for crop credit."

George said, "Mexicans have it worst. 'Specially after Juan Patrón was shot by John Riley right afta they murdered Wida Casey's husband. Riley's Dolan's partner now. Patrón's respected, but the fight went out of him. Not that he doesn't hold public offices: jailer now."

Billy asked if they'd heard of a Salazar family on the north side of the Capitans in Las Tablas. He'd met the son, Yginio. Reluctantly, George said, "Takes after his dead father with crazy ideas 'bout rebellion. Makes people nervous."

Frank interrupted, "Let's make some music." They got their fiddle cases. "Ever heard 'Silver Threads Among the Gold?' "

Billy shook his head. "You'll like it - bein' sentimental."

Both men fiddled, but George, lowering rubbery lids, sang with a nasal twang and bathos: "Darling, I am growing old, / Silver threads among the gold / Shine upon my brow today, / Life is fading fast away. / But, my darling, you will be, will be, / Always young and fair to me."

When they finished, Frank asked, "Liked that, Kid?"

"Yes," Billy answered almost inaudibly, with nostalgic images of his mother, and brief longing to be truly part of their kindhearted world.

At the same time, John Henry Tunstall was feeling compassion as he stood exhaling condensation thirteen miles northeast of the Coe farm, on Lincoln's red street, and in front of the pit jail. Brought out to him had been shackled Jessie Evans, Frank Baker, George Davis, and Tom Hill. From a canvas satchel, Tunstall withdrew a whiskey bottle and said, "For your Captain to dole out."

Tall guard, Maximiano de Guerara, leaning against the jail building, patiently watched. Jessie checked the label before guzzling.

Completing the dregs, Davis scratched his fat sides and said, "Ain' right puttin' a man unerground lest 'e's dead."

"Precisely," said Tunstall to Jessie. "I merely want the return of my animals. Beyond financial value, I have a deep attachment to them."

Jessie grinned wickedly. " 'Tachments t' hosses?" Hill drunkenly said mares.

Tunstall responded, "I too have considered mares. Some say their endurance is better than males. What have you found?"

Jessie laughed to choking. "You's so funny, Englishman. I may 'ave 'eard yer mules was sol' in Ol' Mexico."

Tunstall sighed, saying that was disappointing; but he would, nonetheless, give them the second bottle for later use.

"Hell, later," Jessie said, tossing its cork and drinking greedily before handing it to the others. Stumbling closer to Tunstall, dragging leg chains, Jessie whispered, "Be a frien. Git us ou' now."

"Not without a firm promise." Jessie hissed that he'd kill him. Tunstall wagged a finger. "I fear the beverage goes to your head, Mister Evans. Another day, we shall talk more."

That night, when the Coes were asleep, Billy snuck out. He followed the road to Lincoln, riding his chestnut gelding, received on the Cook's Canyon day, symbolic of gang membership, symbolic of belonging.

Inside the jail, at the barred trap door, Billy called, then dropped down files. From below, Jessie said savagely, "Kill the goddamn guard an' git us ou'."

"Jimmy wants it like this. Reattach the links till the Seven Rivers boys come."

Jessie said, "Goddamn Dolan fer splittin' the three thousan' with Peppin, an' makin' this goddamn pit."

Billy teased that he could say thanks. Jessie said, "Go t' hell," heard Billy laugh while departing; and laughed himself.

"Goddamn crazy kid," he said with admiration at the boy's daring; again secure in their relationship, as was Billy.

NOVEMBER 3, 1877   8:47 AM   SATURDAY

On his way to Fort Sumner, Billy again stayed with the Montez family, feeling welcome, but oblivious to attentions of María, the ungainly overweight daughter. She had followed him out, shyly giving him wrapped tortillas and tamales.

Later, near the town, he had camped in a salt grass-padded hollow.

Now Billy lay against his saddle, Lightning in waistband, enjoying breeze massaging his toes.

Suddenly, beyond the rim, was growled, "Got you, Billy Bonney!"

With his exceptional reflexes, he was airborne, finger pressing the Lightning's trigger at guiltily visualized Coe cousins or Dick Brewer, revenging his trickery.

Long auburn hair blurred. Wrenching, but gun cracking, he fell.

On his back, in silence, Billy numbly looked at sky.

Then Paulita bounded down laughing. He gasped, "I almost ..." She knelt, giggling that he was totally fooled.

Lingering horror, her incomprehension of danger, and joy at seeing her, tangled. He caught under her arms, and swung her, while half singing, half shouting, "You almost missed the chance to fly!"

"More!" she shouted. "More! More!" until he sank down vertiginously close to her huge eyes, filled with unexpected longing. She said, "Billy, I want something from you very very much."

"Yes," he said fervently.

With delight, she embraced him. "You *will* teach me to shoot!"

Face burning, laughing, he threw himself backwards onto grass spongy laughing softness.

When Billy stood, he said they'd leave the horses. Indignantly, Paulita asked if he thought she would shoot them. He said, "A bullet can head unexpectedly. Lets go to those cottonwoods." From his saddlebag, he took a packet.

At the trees, with his folding knife, he cut a small branch and unwrapped tortillas. "Your targets," he said, skewered one, and led her fifteen paces away. "See how my gun's back ..."

"Butt. Hogleg butt. Papa would have let me shoot."

Billy smiled. "Well, the butt's high in my holster, so it slips out easy while I'm cocking the hammer. Cross draw's where you reach across yourself. Watch me." His right hand whipped to the Lightening. Three shots cracked.

Paulita was unfazed, asking what was next. Checking the target, he said. At the tortilla, she declared a single hit. He lifted her. "All *three* pressed together," she said in awe.

As they walked back from a new target, he opened the gate, ejected the three casings, and got replacements from a pocket. She asked, "Why aren't they from the cartridge belt?"

"You noticed," he said with new intimacy, as if she had joined him in his secret, Pinaleño foothill cave. " 'Cause ammunition is different sizes. The Lightning uses thirty-eight caliber, meaning it's barrel's a thirty-eighth of an inch across. The Colt in my holster is wider: forty-four caliber. Its cartridges are called forty-four *forty*, 'cause they have forty grains of gunpowder."

He handed her the Lightning. It drooped. "Use your middle finger to balance behind the trigger guard. Grip the butt with the next two." The gun rose. "Cross the thumb for a tight ring."

"Now can I shoot?"

"First aim. Bend your elbow a little so the muscle braces." He touched her biceps. "Aiming's different depending on the distance. After twenty-five yards you lose range. You need a rifle or carbine.

"Close, like under five yards, you use the front sight on the barrel tip to line up the target. Ours is fifteen. So hold the gun chin level and use the rear sight too: that groove along the top of the frame. Pull the trigger smooth. And don't get scared when the gun jumps."

She glared, saying she never got scared. "You sure have a strong temper," Billy said.

"Unlike you."

He laughed. "And, if somebody was shooting at you, you'd stand sideways to give the least target." She said she'd hide behind something. "Smart girl. Shoot."

After the loud report, she darted, leaping over salt grass clumps. At the tortilla, she fired the remaining rounds to the sky. Near the center was a hole.

He wanted to cry and laugh. "Billy," she asked, "will you be my dance teacher? Mama said you could. Can it be tonight?"

"I will. But not tonight. There's some ... some business I've got to do. Then I ride back to Lincoln County."

"Billy, I want to tell you something: I like you very much. Are we friends?"

"We surely are." There was a lump in his throat.

After they separated, Billy visited Bob Hargrove's saloon for the first time. Later, at Celsa's front door, he grinned sheepishly. "I was passing through. I thought I would say hello."

She hurried him in, complaining, "In an hour, Saval will return." Her black eyes flared. "I waited and waited; but you did not come. But now you have the need, no?"

Seductively he murmured, "So you felt the need too?" and gazed with helpless longing that transformed her fierceness to fierce desire.

In so little time, on the bed where the other man's sheepskin jacket lay, Billy sat straddled by her upright embrace, and upward sought, in bitten pounding, gasping completion.

Celsa fingered his damp curls and said, "Soon, I will give you a haircut. And I will knit you a muffler. It is so cold. You ride so far." Awkwardly, she stepped off.

But dreamily he lay back, pants open. Celsa thought how vulnerable he looked - even blood on his neck; licking her lips for its taste - as triumphant pride stimulated her. "My Billy," she said and believed.

NOVEMBER 6, 1877   8:13 AM   TUESDAY

At his Feliz River ranch property, John Tunstall, with two employees, Fred Waite and John Middleton, waited outside a chosa dugout house, tapered into an embankment. That building, a tack shed, and a lean-to in the corral were his only completed structures. Tunstall said, "Lateness may be another freedom of your countrymen." Waite answered in his slow deep voice that the boy wasn't late yet.

Tunstall pulled his felt hat lower and adjusted his scarf, neatly tucked into his heavy tweed jacket. "Terribly cold, don't you think, Mister Middleton?" The brutish heavy-jowled face grunted. "Pardon me?" He could use whiskey, Middleton repeated.

"Herr Gauss," Tunstall called into the single room structure. The old, but energetic man emerged, clipped gray beard and brushed-back hair enhancing clean tight features. "Mister Middleton feels inclined to partake."

As John Middleton followed the cook inside, Billy appeared, hitching his mount beside a tall bay like Cashaw, with two, expensive, California blankets tied behind his cantle; and regretted that he and Jessie had missed him in the horse and mule theft. Then Billy approached the chosa with a spy's titillation. His dupes waited.

Tunstall introduced himself and Fred Waite, whose emerald scrutinizing eyes made Billy uncomfortable.

From the interior, next introduced, John Middleton raised his glass in mock toast. Tunstall said, "And our much appreciated cook, Herr Gottfried Gauss, from Baden, Germany."

There was Gauss. There were four men around him. Impossible to escape. It was over. Tunstall asked, "I assume you understand the purpose of our meeting?"

"Uh. Checking me out - I mean, for work."

"On the contrary, you *are* hired. The Coes' praise preceded you. Pay is a dollar a day."

"Accept. I accept." It bought time. Where was Gauss?

Tunstall said, "I am so glad this turned out simply. I understand the ideal number of horses for cow work is at least three; but brigands reduced my stock. I can give you only one."

"I accept," Billy said. Where was Gauss? Middleton was in the shadows too. Waite was behind him. Billy stepped clear, walking toward his chestnut, and said, "I've got this horse."

Tunstall glanced disparagingly. "You may have noticed my favorite beside him: Long Tom." Gottfried Gauss came out with coffee, and smiled tentatively: an excellent ruse. Billy visualized the thick dust cloud in the theft corral. Maybe the man was still unsure.

Then Billy was led by Tunstall and Fred Waite to a corral to pick his horse. The animals were of such astonishing quality that Billy forgot himself. "Those? To use, right?"

"To own," said Tunstall. "I believe a horse and a man deserve that bond."

Billy was shaken by this first discovery of empathy: of a desire to foresee and fulfill deepest needs of man or beast. A protective shell cracked, releasing a lifetime's pain of unknown isolation.

Billy was being introduced. The British accent was bringing back Mary Richards. Two men had come from the corral's lean-to. Dick Brewer gripped his hand. The other was a reedy barely-pigmented youth with white-blond hair and mustache. "Hendry Brown," he said thickly through a nose crushed in an old fight. Now there were two more armed men. But Gauss had no chance yet to inform. He had to pick a horse; act normal. "Can I shoot my pistol, Mr. Tunstall?" A smile played over Waite's sensuous lips. Tunstall nodded.

After watching the horses' responses, Billy entered the corral to John Mackie's presence: kind and gentle like John Tunstall. There she was. How Mackie would have enthused. Silver-gray, moon dappled, arching her graceful neck to brush her flexible lip over his palm. Billy slipped on a waiting halter with lead rope.

To Fred Waite, Tunstall said, "By Jove, he picked he best," and called that he could get saddle and bridle in the shed.

Waite opened the gate as Billy mounted bareback. Tunstall said, "If you prefer to ride her there ..." But Billy loped past, then galloped into the flatland. Tunstall sighed to Waite, "Stock retrieval may be our major endeavor." But soon hoofbeats returned.

Billy rode up, flushed. "She's wonderful!"

Tunstall said, "To choose her call name, her pedigree may help. She is a pure-bred Arabian, registered as Sultana's Desert Wind."

"Uh," said Billy, lost in her beauty, "I'll call her Gray Sugar." He blushed. "About papers ... a bill of sale would be good."

After Billy selected his gear, Tunstall said, "An employee meeting will be at my store on Monday the nineteenth." He then agreed to keep Billy's chestnut gelding at the ranch. Nether could have conceived that the gelding would change their lives.

After leaving, still stunned, Billy proceeded northward, in the flat lonely land, over the fifty mile route back to the Coes' farm.

The trail tracked through the north-to-south Nacimiento Mountains, with ancient granite core, 1.6 billion years old, and layering of the primordial ocean's limestone; all upthrust 55 million years before his journey.

Hoofbeats were following. It was Fred Waite. Gauss must have informed. Billy was prepared to kill.

The man looked peaceable, asking only to ride along, saying he was going to Lincoln; adding, "Heard you're quite a shot. What brought you to Lincoln County?"

Billy mumbled about cattle work. "Work here's about driving men, not cows. A war's coming. I like to know my fellow fighters."

"Me, I'm half Chickasaw. Father white. I went to Illinois Industrial University and Mound City Commercial College in Saint Louis. My father has a business in Oklahoma Indian Territory. Wanted me to work for him; but I decided to explore his white world.

"And Lincoln County showed me that Whites are doing worse than Adam. He stuck to apples. They're gobbling everything in their path."

Billy smiled and said, "The Coes told me Tunstall wants to make things better. This horse sure is the best thing I've ever gotten for free."

"You don't know her cost yet. Ol' Chickasaw saying: 'Watch the feet.' See what a man does, not what he says. I'm older than you; so I'm an ol' Chickasaw. My saying." Billy laughed.

"My middle name's Tecumseh. A name to live up to. A great Indian leader, murdered by Whites because he could have united the Indian people. They'll kill Victorio too, because killing the leader kills the fight."

They camped in the Nacimiento foothills. After they ate in silence, Waite spoke, while Billy cleaned his Colt .44, loaded with six cartridges in emulation of Jessie Evans. "George Coe said you could be paid in ammunition." Billy laughed.

Emerald-eyed Waite took off his hat, and meditatively stroked its golden eagle feather, long hair bright in firelight. "Yes, New Mexico Territory: world center of the Seven Deadly Sins. Ol' Chicasaw saying to remember them: 'People Can Learn And Get Every Sin.' That means Pride, Covetousness, Lust, Anger, Gluttony, Envy, Sloth." Billy asked what sloth was. "Not working. Forcing others to work for you."

Billy said they did not seem that bad- like murder. "Ol' Chicasaw saying: 'All the Seven Deadly Sins lead to murder.' What we'll be fighting: deadly sinners.

"It's not obvious as the Civil War. But a man's a slave if someone controls his life. That's what's happened here. Once corrupt big money, politicians, and law enforcement join forces, you've got slavery. Heard of the Santa Fe Ring?" Billy shrugged ambiguously. Waite said, "Well, I'd sacrifice myself to stop them.

"Speaking of sacrifice, some Indian tribes sacrificed people till the thirties. They believed - and maybe I do too - that every rock, plant, creature, even the planet, is conscious. All waiting for man's correct actions to maintain harmony. Sometimes sacrifice was for fertility of crops. Chickasaws' sacrifice was waiting to eat their new corn until they purified everything: a new beginning."

Billy asked, "What was the month? How'd they time the cycle?" "July. Far as I know - always July."

Billy stretched. "Seems religions have sacrifice. Like Abraham with Isaac, or Christ's father, or the Navajo's Dragonfly dying to save the world. And Tecumseh - and maybe Victorio - sacrificing themselves. Why d'you figure people do that?"

"You make a man think. Maybe I was wrong about leaders. Maybe knowing someone cared enough to die for you, proves the rightness of your cause. Like making it sacred."

Abruptly Billy understood. He said, "Then it's a sacrifice to other people. But to you, it's living like you want."

Reawakened were heroic yearnings of childhood. After that, Billy became almost inseparable from the man.

NOVEMBER 16, 1877   2:36 AM   SATURDAY

Yielding to habitual insomnia, John Tunstall got out of bed, right elbow and knees aching, and put on a heavy robe. In the adjoining room of his Lincoln apartment within his store, he set a kettle on a potbellied stove. Yellow, flowered wallpaper covered plastered adobe, and jewel-toned furnishings were grouped for office and sitting. Oriental rugs furthered urbanity's illusion. He prepared his tea, and carried cup and saucer to his desk.

There, he wrote: *"To My Beloved Parents and Trinity. I must first apologize for so few letters. I have not had a moment. But to follow up on that brigand Jessie Evans in the local gaol, I believe my growing friendship with him will protect my livestock.*

"The Sheriff, an Irishmen named Brady, however, is replacing him as a problem. This bit of disturbing news came from Juan Patron, who you may recall was my first host in Lincoln, and who holds the post of Jailer. It appears that he was informed of escape plans by Mexican prisoners, also in the gaol. Evans and his men had received files and were awaiting liberation. Patron of course told Sheriff Brady.

"I cannot leave to your imagination what Sheriff Brady did, since it is beyond conception. First of all, he did not replace the shackles. And two days ago, intoxicated (and one learns to deal with him in terms of degrees of intoxication, but this time to the extreme), he accused myself and Alexander McSween of being in a plot to free the prisoners. When we stoutly denied this, he reached for the basic article of local dress, namely his pistol, and threatened my life as an accomplice to the future crime. Alexander intervened and said it did not behoove a man of the law to behave that way. Nonetheless, departing in a state of high dudgeon, Sheriff Brady did make the unfriendly statement, 'I won't shoot you now, but you haven't long to run.'

"It appears that this whole matter may be one of jealousy. My men have gotten the credit for apprehending the brigands and he may feel it should be his (though heavens knows why).

"Otherwise things are going swimmingly. I arrived here as the Adventurer seeking my fortune, but I have come to feel deeply for these lands and their people."

Less than a quarter mile northeast of the Tunstall building, behind the pit jail, Billy waited on Gray Sugar, silhouetted in moonlit mist, watching thirty approaching riders, Andrew Boyle in the lead: the fruition of his labors. When Billy raced away with those men, he heard someone calling, "Jessie's wantin' the kid."

The galloping group did not slow until flatlands near Blackwater Canyon, on a military trail leading eastward toward the Pecos River. Jessie smiled at Billy, asking, "Where'd ye steal a hoss this good?" Billy denied stealing. "Hell ye didn'. Where'd ye git 'er?" Jessie teased, feeling marvelous.

"Tunstall," said Billy, ambivalently mixing criminal comradery and rebellious insouciance.

Jessie heard betrayal. Murderously jealous, he asked, "Where's the hoss I loaned ye?"

"You never paid me. I figured that chestnut was payment."

"Was a loan," Jessie growled, whipping his mount into an enraged run; followed by his comrades.

Billy did not follow. Without intending a final breech, he turned Gray Sugar back toward Lincoln.

NOVEMBER 19, 1877   9:08 AM   MONDAY

Missing Jessie Evans's toughness, and experiencing John Henry Tunstall's softness with mixed pity and scorn, Billy had, nevertheless, set out from the Coes' farm, on his prancing young mare, to attend Tunstall's meeting, following the noisy rock-strewn Ruidoso River and piñion pines sun-jeweled in night-rain droplets.

On the red earth, main thoroughfare, five miles from Lincoln, he had passed, to his right, a house-sized golden hued boulder, under which, he had heard, was buried a man, identity and reason forgotten, but bequeathing the name: Dead Man's Rock.

At a buckboard's rattling, Billy recognized, holding the reins, hook-nosed goateed Charlie Bowdre, square-crowned hat tilted; and Doc Scurlock, big lenses glaring circles and gap-toothed in friendly grinning, calling to him, "Firtht meeting of uth Tunthtall boys."

They stopped. "Ye'll meet McSween," said Bowdre. "Smahrt lawyer, but preachy. An' Tunstall shur gave us damn good ge-ah." He patted his new Winchester carbine and reached for his flask.

Scurlock lisped, "Charlie, thith is medical advith: thick to coffee. Tunthstall thinks we're gentlemen in dithguise. Don't enlighten him on day one." Passing the House, Bowdre spit tobacco juice at it.

When they came to Tunstall's store, Fred Waite hailed them from the east side of its covered porch, calling that Gauss had coffee and food out back. They followed past the long eastern facade to an adobe wall, attached to it at a right angle to form the front of the split-rail corral. As Billy swung open one of that wall's double gates, Bowdre commented, "We jus' passed the castle o' the English lohrd." Billy realized it was a wing of the front structure, whose rear had an attached a frame warehouse where Gottfried Gauss was serving food to Dick Brewer, Henry Brown, John Middleton, and the Coes.

Again, the old man stared too hard. "Here, boy," he said, giving coffee and cornbread. Soon, Billy flicked a sidelong glance. Gauss was still watching. Real good, Billy said cautiously. Gauss smiled.

Before leading them all to the front entrance, Brewer said to Frank Coe, "All here except for Jim French. He's called 'Frenchie?' "

"Yep," Coe answered. "Jumpiest cuss I've ever seen."

As the group walked the porch, and Gauss, from inside, opened one of the central double doors, from the opposite side came Alexander McSween, in professional dress, accompanied by clean-shaven and muscular George Washington. The loud, plank-trembling, weaponed, male mass halted the lawyer with claustrophobia. "George," he said, "I didn't know *that* was what John was hiring."

Washington said, "This town's rough, Mister McSween. I'd be grateful."

"I'm going around to John's side. Get them my four client chairs from the bank office. Not mine. The rest will have to make do." He patted his pocketed Bible for courage.

The loud-talking men waited inside the large long store, bright with large front windows and brass oil lamps hanging from vigas. It had a giant, wrought iron, coffee grinding machine; and back wall profuse with stocked shelves fronted by a glass display case running their length. Billy noted that the apartment wing included an L-shaped extension of the store, which had another showcase and wall racks displaying long-guns.

While Billy helped George Washington arrange seating with added barrels and crates, and decided on escape routes, in rushed a bony, mustached, young man with greasy hair straggling from his hat. Charlie Bowdre called, "Hey, Frenchie!" He acknowledged with jerky bird-like movements.

From the apartment, McSween and tweed-suited Tunstall emerged. Tunstall said heartily, "Good morning, my fine fellows. Shall we tour our - so to speak - headquarters? Do step into my abode." While the men glanced uneasily at his unmasculine décor, Billy tapped his boot heel, saying the floor sounded hollow. Tunstall said, "Yes, but merely a few feet above the ground."

When Tunstall led them back, Billy slowed at the guns, then stopped. Under glass of the showcase fronting that display, as if reversing time, was the dark-brown cardigan sweater.

Tunstall, distant and at an open door in the west end, was saying, "Here is the Lincoln County Bank office, where Attorney McSween will also practice."

Billy hurried to join the group, and sat on a high narrow barrel, near a front window webbed by frozen condensation. Tunstall said, "Now we shall get to the meat of the meeting: our plans."

McSween went behind the showcase, straightened his slumped back, tapped the back of his collar, and thought how absurd it was of John to insist on making ranch hands privy to plans.

He said, "As most of you know, I carry no weapon but man's strongest." He raised his Bible. "Using its principles, we're going to change Lincoln County. It's not virgin territory ..." French, seated with crossed leg frenetically kicking, tittered salaciously. "It's got people who think they're above man's and God's laws.

"Here's what's already accomplished: this store, the bank, and two ranches. Next will probably be getting the post tradership for Fort Stanton and the Mescalero Reservation.

"And, east of this building, will be a school and a place of worship. The J.J. Dolan Company doesn't stand a chance against all that."

Bowdre interrupted. "Tah kill a rattlesnake, ye don' shoot his tail, Mac. Ye shoot the he-ad. Lhike they shouldah done in the big Wahr." Washington made a hostile sound. "George, Ah'm not bad-mouthin' niggahs."

McSween responded, "We know what we're doing. After all, John Chisum is the bank's president." Drowsing, Middleton roused, saying Chisum was a tightwad. McSween ignored that.

He said, "In fact, next month, Mister Chisum, myself, and my wife are going to Saint Louis to further solidify business relationships."

Distractingly, Jim French went to pace in the back, where the Coe cousins were whispering.

"What's come up is land ownership. Since sixty-three, using the Homestead Act for the Territories, a man could get a hundred and sixty acres free; if he agreed to make improvements on it for three years. Then, for a dollar an acre - one hundred sixty dollars - it was his.

"But this March third, the Desert Land Act was passed. Now six hundred forty acre parcels - a square mile - can be gotten with down payment of twenty-five cents an acre - again a hundred sixty dollars. After three years of improvements, it can be bought for a dollar an acre - six hundred and forty dollars.

"Being a British citizen, John Tunstall doesn't qualify. But he'll explain his ideas about that." McSween had strongly disagreed, but the man had been unswaying.

John Tunstall centered his chair in front and sat. "My good fellows, my goal is to unite us all for mutual profit and community benefit. To commence that goal, I shall purchase parcels of six hundred forty acres beside my Peñasco property for Mister Waite and Mister Bonney - one parcel for each - for a partnership to create a single ranch."

His astounded men glanced at the two surprise recipients. "I do not mean as 'front men,' but as real owners - as eventually will be the rest of you."

Fred Waite stood and said, "I can't accept anybody choosing a partner for me." Tunstall said, as senior employee, the choice was his. Waite walked to Billy, and grasped the smiling boy's hand.

Tunstall felt moved. "The words of Alfred Lord Tennyson - which some of you may know - come to my mind: 'Courage!' he said, and pointed toward the land, 'This mounting wave will roll us shoreward soon.' Thusly will our competition's wrong-doings roll us in our direction."

Billy asked, "What about guns, Mister Tunstall?"

"If you mean violence, I know about the Santa Fe Ring. But its existence relies on secrecy impossible in our age of modern communication. We have newspapers and telegraph. Why, just last year, a device called a telephone was invented, which transmits voice over electrical wires.

"One must simply inform the voting public - as we shall do in our editorials - and that Ring will be defeated by the next election.

"As to our business, a man spends half his income on particulars of living. If your fair dealings are likewise advertised, you will get fifty cents on each of his dollars.

"It is clear as the nose on one's face, that people have free will to choose. And since most people are good, they choose good.

"Though men of science claim that the cosmos is but a machine - like a pocket watch, geared to make future destined by the past - I have a knack for presentiment. And I say that future thinkers will prove that nonsense. The proof is simply that each of us is free to make the world a better place."

Intrigued with that optimistic and utopian view, Billy repeated, "But what about guns?"

Tunstall answered, "Their dangers can be avoided by not frequenting places of intoxication and loose morals." Charlie Bowdre and Doc Scurlock grinned.

"But I am not naïve. An untimely end may befall me. But I know that you cannot kill the truth. I merely stand for fairness and goodness, that are as much a part of each person as their beating heart.

"In fact, I recommend the mottos by which I live: 'To thine own self be true. Do not give up. Do not back down.' Follow these, and any one of you can change the world."

Billy sighed with sheer pleasure at this vision so exceeding his own heroic fantasies. He asked, "So you'd be satisfied if your ideas lived on?"

"Indeed not. I want to enjoy the fruits of my labor. But it would be a satisfaction to know one had an effect."

Bowdre said, "Mister Tunstall, Ah'm on yaw side." There was an assenting murmuring. Billy heard, "Damn right ... Mister Tunstall, that part 'bout land ..." He felt feverish, blood pounding in his ears. The room dissolved into dazzling luminosity. He was falling into it.

A strong hand caught him. Billy looked into Tunstall's kind eyes. He heard, "I do believe that barrel tipped, Mister Bonney. I have made a lucky catch. I have now proven, I fear, that I am a moving speaker." Billy heard friendly laughter.

He listened to the man again addressing the group; no longer hearing words, but drinking him in, trying to memorize every feature, every gesture. Then the nameless feelings erupted into awareness. For this man he would fight. For him he would willingly die.

Later, exiting with Billy, Fred Waite said, running fingers over his golden eagle feather, "He's got less than a year to live." Billy questioned dreamily, without impact on his new passion. "He's like a white deer in the forest. And Lincoln County's got a lot of hunters."

On his way back to the Coes' farm, approaching Dead Man's Rock to his left, Billy noticed Gray Sugar's ears strain forward. A rider emerged from its far side on a bald-faced chestnut, the white extending back past the animal's eyes like exposed skull. Jacob Basil Matthews spoke guardedly. "Dolan wants to meet with you. Said come to his office day after tomorrow. Eight in the morning."

Billy said, "Tell Jimmy I'll be there." The man departed eastward.

Abruptly, Billy wanted to tell Yginio that the people's champion had been found; deeper still, their lost father had been found. In a few more miles, he would be at Capitan Gap, a crossing over the Capitan Mountains to Las Tablas. Cheeks burning with love, Billy rode, feeling so clean, as if bathed in the Bonito River's icy freshness.

NOVEMBER 21, 1877   8:00 AM   WEDNESDAY

Billy entered James Dolan's office. Behind his desk, the man gestured graciously to the facing chair. With pleasure, Dolan said, "How you managed, in under a month, to infiltrate the enemy is beyond my comprehension. As I said before, I can offer the promise of kingdoms. I, like Lawrence Murphy, want an heir." Listlessly, the boy's hand hooked over the chair arm: convincingly receptive.

Dolan said, "Tunstall is such a pale shadow of us. And John Chisum is only using him to hurt your friends: the Seven Rivers ranchers. All Tunstall has are a few farmers and some motley gunslingers. He's dumber than Dummy."

Dolan asked Billy to open the door, and called, "Dummy! Come here!" A disheveled man, who had been sweeping the storage room, hesitated at the threshold, fear on his puffy mongoloid face. Dolan said, "Dummy, you're not the only dummy in town any more."

Dummy cried out, "Don't make Jessie hit me," and cringed.

Dolan ordered the retarded man out, and said to Billy, "Amusing, isn't it? Ours is the winning side." He walked toward Billy, confident and amorous, saying, "Some truths, a man cannot resist." Behind, he sensuously squeezed Billy's shoulders as he continued. "I could not tolerate loosing your potential. It could not be per ..."

His voice broke, as desire to possess the boy hurled him into his inferno of hellish hunger, beyond endurance of the flesh in which he was trapped. Worse, he knew that this conquest, like others in what seemed an eternity, would bring no slaking surfeit or salvation.

Billy looked upward. "You called me a man, Jimmy. A man makes decisions."

Dolan forced a smile, but achieved only a lascivious grimace. He returned to his desk while exerting the force of will that allowed him to emerge from his pit of perdition long enough to savor drawing down another with him. "Billy, Billy, Billy," he croaked, "who knows what we - you and me - can achieve? Your decision will profoundly affect both our lives."

Billy said, "I believe everything you said." Dolan excitedly anticipated the capitulation. "Their cause is near hopeless."

"It *is* hopeless," Dolan corrected.

"That it's *near* hopeless, unless they get help. I'm going to fight for them." It felt like beginning a dance to exquisite unearthly harmonies; whereas all this man's offerings were clumsy discordances.

"You surprise me, Billy." The sapphire eyes concealed fury. Stripped of power to create, Dolan had only impotence's consolation: power to destroy. So he embraced that darkness now, all focused on the boy; all because he had wanted him so much. He stood. "Excuse me. I need a few minutes ... to collect my thoughts." Passing, he made an arc, as if around Billy was an impenetrable force field.

In the billiard room, Dolan got Billy Matthews, and led him up the narrow back stairway to the second floor hallway. Matthews started to cross it to Dolan's apartment at the right, but was directed left through a small room with a fireplace. Dolan unlocked its far door to darkness. He lit a lamp. Matthews gasped.

In the curtained long room, there was an oddly low pulpit facing rows of audience chairs. Framed pictures had pyramid-like signs and men wearing loin-cloths over regular clothes. Matthews exclaimed, "What the hell's t-this?"

"A place to talk, Bi-lly." Dolan's voice caught at the name. "All of us are Masons: Catron, Murphy, Elkins, Brady, Rynerson, Bristol."

"I ain't religious, Jimmy; but but I don't want to stay here."

"Nonsense. Masonry is not a religion. We are a society of friends." Matthews asked if Catron knew about the place. "No. This is not a *real* place, merely one of harmless fantasy. Lawrence Murphy and myself created this in imitation of a true Masonic Lodge - for privacy with friends receiving special tasks. I have such a task for you. I am now meeting with Billy Bonney. In the next hour you will *kill him*."

Matthews stammered, "I-I've never ..."

"But you will *now*, won't you?" Dolan interrupted brutally.

When Dolan re-entered his office, on his desk were the Lightning, cartridge belt with holster, and the Colt .44. Billy said they were his. Dolan resumed his seat and said, "It could have been so simple. You know what happened to Robert Casey. Now would have been the same. One death, two deaths, and it would have been over."

Dolan's voice mounted in violent crescendo. "But if we are opposed, the outcome will still be the same; but a river of blood will flow." Dolan's tone became low and ominous with grandiose and mystical innuendos. "I will tell you something else about myself. I *too* am a fisher of men. And if one is a fisher, all he needs is a hook - so small and insignificant - yet, with it, one can capture prey completely.

"Before you is a choice between life and death. Not many get that." Dolan felt delusory hope, as if partial revelation of both threat and plot could bring the boy back.

Billy said, "A man's got to decide how he wants to live; and, at times, I'd imagine, how he wants to die. Right now, I know how I want to live." He stood. "I appreciate you trying, Jimmy. I do believe you offered me the best you could think of."

"Get out," Dolan shouted.

As Billy rode weaponless toward the gravestone rock, the bald-faced chestnut burst forth. "Dolan sent me," Matthews said grimly, Colt .44 pointed.

A boy's clear voice startled from the boulder's abutting high ridge: "Buenos dias, Señor Matthews. Possibly you want to delay going where you belong?" Yginio Salazar rose with aimed Winchester carbine. Matthews's revolver hit the ground.

Yginio said, "So we are finished. Go back to your master. Say the heavens opened. And you saw an angel!"

Matthews spurred his horse. Yginio was laughing. To Billy he said, "You are invited again for dinner."

"Yginio," Billy said, "that was close."

The skinny boy's black hair blew. "Last night, you said where you were going. When one visits the Devil, one needs watching from above." From his perch, Yginio jumped to the huge rock, then climbed down. "Today I will ride with you only to the Bonito. There I have my own horse." As they rode on Gray Sugar, into a beautiful wide canyon, Yginio said, "Someday I will own this land, and remember here I returned what you gave me: life."

NOVEMBER 23, 1877   5:17 AM   FRIDAY

Excitedly talking most of the night about Tunstall, Billy and Yginio had finally slept until awakened by Isabella Salazar, who was lighting candles on the family altar. Yginio joined his small mother at painted pine, santos figures on that table and wall-hanging effigy of Christ on a contorted cross. He said to Billy, "All were carved by my father. Except that crucifixion. He said it was a miracle. He found it - just a cottonwood root - exactly as you see it. He believed we live in constant miracles. But some are easier to see."

After they fed Gray Sugar and the family horses, Yginio smiled at his palomino gelding, who laid back his ears, rolling eye whites at Billy. Yginio said, "I did not tell you his name is Torcio."

"Twister?" asked Billy, using the English translation.

"Yes. My untamable twister lets only me ride him. Our loyalty and work are only by our choice."

Billy's return to Lincoln was wary; not by Capitan Gap, but, as suggested by Yginio, rarely-used Five Mile Gap to its west. After that, the deep-banked Bonito River provided concealing vegetation until Tunstall's property, where Billy rode up the high tiered incline to the corral.

In the store's east wing, John Tunstall greeted him, unaware that his bashful demeanor was atypical. The secret son had returned to the secret father. Tunstall said, "You are due firearms. There has been quite a run on them. Just yesterday, Mister Matthews purchased a Colt revolver." Tunstall took out a cartridge belt, with brass clip-cornered buckle gleaming in lamplight; and added a holster.

Customers entered. Tunstall said, "I must excuse myself. My new shopkeeper, a Mister Sam Corbett, did not show up." Tunstall called greeting to the people, and quickly added a rectangular pasteboard box, topped with a magenta wood block of a Colt revolver and with side saying ".44 cal." Then laid on the counter was a Winchester '73 carbine with its saddle scabbard and a few boxes of ammunition. "Also I shall leave another cartridge belt to be certain of the fit."

Alone, Billy opened the Colt box. The blued steel revolver with five-and-a-half inch barrel and varnished walnut grip rested in newly-minted perfection. His would be the first touch, other than that of its makers in the Hartford, Connecticut, factory. He checked it before adding cartridges to it and both belts.

To focus on the carbine, Billy wiped euphoric tears, then tested its lever action - which would cock the mechanism, lift a new cartridge to firing position, and eject a spent shell - and cocked and uncocked the hammer: the second firing option for this single action weapon. Then twelve .44-40 cartridges were pressed into its lozenge-shaped loading port slot, filling its magazine: the spring-loaded tube below its twenty inch barrel.

Tunstall, having returned unnoticed, spoke. "As I was asking, Mister Bonney, do you require a leather-punch to adjust what I see constitutes utilization of both belts?"

Billy made a crooked silly smile. "Everything's perfect, Mister Tunstall. In my whole life ..."

"No need to continue. I know you will say you have never seen such efficient service. That leaves only gloves. This way." They had flaring gauntlets and distinctive, double-stitched back ribbing.

And they had been beside the dark-brown cardigan. Billy asked its price. "Strange that you should inquire. Among a certain class in Ireland, it is rather like a second skin; but, since imported, it is costly. Five dollars."

That was prohibitive. Billy requested to see a dime novel, smiling when Tunstall commented that his young boy recipient certainly would enjoy it. On the cover of the thirty-one page booklet was: "*The Deadwood Dick Library. The Double Daggers; or Deadwood Dick's Defiance. 1877.*" Tunstall said, "Do keep it for free."

Billy, regaining composure, asked about extra cartridges. "Hopefully this will do for now." Twenty boxes of fifty were added. Billy said he just didn't know how to thank him enough. "Actually, there is something," Tunstall said.

Inside his private quarters, John Tunstall positioned a chair for Billy beside his desk, where, atop a leather-bound volume, was a nickel- plated stubby revolver with checkered walnut grips.

He asked, "You are interested in my book, Mister Bonney?" Billy flushed, saying it was the pistol. "Oh that. My British Webley Bulldog. Recommended for shopkeepers. But I carry it in my pocket on long rides. If an accident should befall my mount, at least I could spare the poor beast its misery."

They sat. Tunstall patted the book. "Tennyson. Do you like his work?"

Billy said, "Yes. 'Into the valley of Death / Rode the six hundred;' " and smiled, relishing the overlap with Mary Richards. "You sure seem to like bright colors and light," he added.

"In fact, I am color blind. With regard to brightness, I am blind in my right eye, and it assists vision." Billy's own eyes softened with pity.

"Well now, on to this unpleasant task. Fred Waite is unwell, but might be unaware, since my discovery occurred when we spent the night alone at the chosa. Awake with insomnia, I noted his movements during a dream. But no. It was not a dream. Under his blanket was repetitive thrusting of his arm in the groin area."

Billy grinned. "Mister Tunstall, you're the best joker I ever heard."

"Distress is not a joke. He has epilepsy. I leave it to you."

Billy managed, "I'll do my best." Then curiosity took over. "Mister Tunstall, how old 're you?" Thirty-two on the sixth of March. Billy said, "Meeting a woman isn't easy ..."

"Ah, I understand," Tunstall replied, wagging a finger. "You are quite young ..."

"I'm eighteen. Turned eighteen today." Tunstall congratulated, and said it was no wonder that, being so young, he had questions about the fair sex. Billy used that opportunity to probe and asked, "What's the purpose of marriage?" Economic security. "Had he ever seen a naked woman?" Of course. In paintings in art galleries. Billy was perplexed, and went for the bull's-eye. "How does a couple - married, of course - get children?" Tunstall said that a current, rather like electricity, went from the man to the woman during sleep. Thus, it was called sleeping together.

Billy's heart welled tenderly at the startling innocence, though neither recognized its origin in asexuality: total blindness to earthly passion.

Tunstall stood. "For another matter, let us return to the store."

From behind the cabinet in the store's wing, Tunstall said, "I would like you to take over my deliveries to the South Spring River Ranch of John Chisum, and to the Roswell post office. And to a remote town called Fort Sumner, to its owner: a Peter Maxell.

"And one last thing: my birthday gift to you." Billy stared dumbfounded as Tunstall took out the Irish cardigan sweater.

Thanking, with unashamed tears of gratitude, protectiveness, and love, Billy wedged the cardigan against the Winchester scabbard, along with the wrapped extras; all now symbolizing John Tunstall, and all precious to him.

DECEMBER 1, 1877   9:47 AM   SATURDAY

Back in Fort Sumner, Billy went first to the saloon near the stable, going to the bar for coffee and saying, "Mornin', Mister Hargrove" to the gangly brown-haired proprietor.

"I seen you enough. Call me, Bob. Fella over there's staring at you, kid."

In the bar's mirror, approached a sinewy little man in an old sombrero, sheep-skin jacket, and loose pants. He announced, "I am Saval Gutierrez. I hears about you, Beelly Bonney. From my *wife* Celsa."

Billy decided his weapon was concealed, and said evenly that he'd only met her at a baile, didn't know about the marriage, and offered to buy a drink. Gutierrez said, "Coffee only. That I does for the patrón. For me the alcohol ees much strength. Yes. I am married Celsa at end of last month. She tells me you speak Spaneesh perfect." He continued in that language. "I have known her since she was a child. Her father said I could end her wild ways. But I wanted to meet *you*." Billy readied for the challenge. "After that baile, she is - how can I say it - different. I worried I could not satisfy her. But she is content. The world surprises a man."

"It does, Mister Gutierrez."

"Saval, please. You are here for much time?"

"Only today. Señora Maxwell wanted me to give a dance lesson to her daughter." Then he should stay the night as their guest, Saval Gutierrez said. Celsa needed company of young people.

When Billy walked across the parade ground, the intensity of recent experiences reached a critical mass and shifted perceptions. Immensity of sky miniaturized the town. But the never-ending wind returned focus to infinite particularity, animating each dust particle as Billy moved willingly within its current and eagerly to Paulita.

Deluvina led Billy to the drawing-room where Paulita, in fitted top and layered skirt, ran to him and rashly seized his hands, calling "My dancing teacher," to her seated mother with her air of morbid self-pity. Their musician, with guitar, was Paco Anaya, the young singer from the baile. He recognized Billy and smiled.

Billy suggested more light. Luz Maxwell commented that she had not realized how dark the place was since Lucien died, and told Deluvina to open the heavy draperies.

Paulita was impatient. Billy said, "Here's the key to dancing."

"I know. The moth." Paulita giggled. "I mean: a moth got in."

He blushed. "The key's to touch the ground just enough to lift you up - free in the air." Her mother was catching his eye flirtatiously.

He was showing off for her too. "That spring's on the beat; so you stay with the notes. And balance makes you light." In demonstration, he leaned so far that a foot rose. "But you only need a little shift.

"For rhythm, you've got one-two or one-two-three." He named a waltz for Paco Anaya. He and Paulita danced.

Suddenly the music stopped. A pudgy man slouched louchely against the entryway. Billy assumed he was a worker, and said, "Another real important part is the backside."

"Excuse me!" the man interjected. "Did you say 'backside' to my mother and sister?" Billy nodded. The man demanded, "Who are *you*?"

Luz Maxwell said with hauteur, "Mister Bonney is Paulita's dance instructor, Peter. And what he said was: 'get back, side by side.' Deluvina and I are to learn the steps to continue her practice." Triumphantly, flirtatiously, competitively young, she glanced at Billy.

"And, mother, where's the guest with that magnificent gray Arabian at the stable?"

Billy said she was his. Again bested, Maxwell left. Then Paulita, her mother, and even Deluvina, laughed as Billy, included instead of the true son, flashed at them eyes of unforgettable blue, that soon would flash as delightfully into the olive-black ones of Celsa.

DECEMBER 2, 1877   1:59 AM   SUNDAY

Asleep on a cot in the Gutierrez's guest room, Billy heard Celsa's whisper. He shifted to creaking. Quickly she knelt. "Lie still. The wood will betray us. I want ..." Saval, he whispered. "Asleep. Drunk. I am so hungry. Let me." Her thick braid glided like a long rope, following her hand to his long-john bottom. "Say yes," she said.

He moaned loudly with passion. Celsa moved back, passing a silencing finger to his lips. He licked. Its wet trail traced down his throat and became many paths over his chest and belly. "Yes," he murmured, and was held sensuously, while her other hand reached back to scratch long tingling lines. Then he was in wet compressing depth, thighs bared to new raking heat, reveling in inflaming filaments pulling him high to that open center until, wrapped in a fiery sheath, he was liquefying; flowing through those webs converging at one place as yes, yes, urgently yes, his creamy essence passed to the waiting hunger and oblivion.

When Billy's eyes opened, he was alone. Over his body, he realized, were razor-thin pulsations. He discovered welts, all stopping at his moist manhood, all exquisitely horrifying, but without regret, before their burning desire returned him to dreams of Paulita.

JANUARY 14, 1878   7:07 AM   MONDAY

Alexander McSween, suffocating, clawed desperately, buried alive. The voice of the Devil intoned, "For-sa-ken." Hurled gasping from sleep by unabated terror, McSween realized the dream's reality as airways constricted asthmatically.

Panicking, he leapt up, eyes darting, incoherently registering fireplace, chair, shadow on wall. Struggling for each wheezing breath, he paced, repeating in his mind, "Holy, Holy, Holy is the Lord of hosts; the whole earth is full of his glory."

He entered his wife's empty room - empty when he needed her most. In her dressing table mirror, for a horrible dissociated instant, the pale terrified man was unrecognizable. Susan had left a vial of rosewater perfume. He inhaled it, and believed his lungs relaxed.

But he was still trapped, still in the nightmare, as his anxiety attack surged with thought-rupturing claustrophobic waves. Arrested. Ring target. Twenty-seven days had changed everything. Maybe he had been too happy. Going to Saint Louis. Excellent business prospects. Chisum with him and Susan. Gay laughter. Then Dolan had released the dogs of Hell. December 24th, the day before the birth of the Lord, their carriage surrounded by that posse; Susan screaming. He and Chisum dragged out, beaten. The Las Vegas jail. Meeting with Susan in the office of the sheriff named Romero, stinking of onions; until her accusatory animosity made that man leave. He had concealed from Susan his realization that trapped in his body, now held captive, he was also trapped in his fate and utterly alone. He had told her, "This is a legal travesty;" reassuring himself also, and insisting that she proceed to St. Louis on her own. She had answered if there was a fight, she was coming back. He had embraced her, saying her worth was far above rubies. She had teased that - when it was all over - she would like those rubies as earrings to match her ring. Then he was transported to Mesilla for indictment.

McSween was startled by a knock. Through the door, George Washington asked if he was ready. Tunstall's men were arriving. Washington entered. "Good Lord. I'll say you're too sick."

"Must explain to them what happened. Coffee ..." Then was wheezing.

When alone again, McSween knelt at her bed, praying to the muslin-masked ceiling for strength. He lay his head on her bedspread, logically knowing that worry about the legal entanglement was absurd; but his joined hands remained over his neck, as if shielding from a blow. At footsteps, he rushed to her chair.

Washington said, "Here's hot cereal along with the coffee."

As McSween balanced the tray, Washington said, "Think I'll stay. I fought in the War and served in the Ninth Cavalry in Texas. Times come when a man could use the company of other men."

"God bless you, George."

Washington said, "He's trying, but I'm not the most docile of his flock." He sat on the bed, monitoring response at the informality. "Yes," he said, "the Lord he drew out Jonah from the whale. The Lord had Joshua blow his trumpet; and down fell the walls of Jericho. A man of God like you knows the Lord's always with him."

When Alexander McSween, professionally clad, entered the Tunstall store, filled with seated employees, he was accompanied by Washington and a stranger. Square-shouldered, that man had a short dark beard, flat-brimmed hat, plain brown jacket, pants over boots, and a badge. Dick Brewer brought a chair. McSween gave it to the stranger.

John Tunstall, behind the counter, arranging merchandise, announced, "Both Alexander - or Mac as you all apparently now call him - and I want to explain the state of affairs."

McSween straightened his back and spoke. "There've been fake rumors. Unnecessary alarms. We wanted to set things straight." The men's belligerent faces were reassuring. He felt less frightened, less alone.

"First, I want to introduce San Miguel County Deputy Sheriff Adolph Barrier. I'm in his custody. He insisted on that, instead of leaving me at Sheriff Brady's mercy." The stocky man nodded in modest discomfiture. "Good men like Adolph Barrier prove there's hope for this world.

"What *is* true is that I've been indicted for embezzlement. It's a faked charge; but it was a hook." Billy started. Waite glanced perplexed. "James Dolan did it to get at the same money I'm being accused of taking: proceeds of a life insurance policy of the House's deceased senior partner, Emil Fritz: ten thousand dollars. I collected on it as the attorney for the estate. Dolan's been after it for years.

"Back in seventy-four - when no will was found - Dolan and Murphy said Fritz had left that money to them. Truth is, the policy was made out to Fritz's heirs. And Fritz had siblings - Charles Fritz and Emilie Fritz Scholand - in this Territory. As administrators of his estate, in seventy-six, they made me its attorney because of collection problems. By the way, they speak German, and don't understand English. I've had to use interpreters.

"Dolan next cunningly alleged that Emil Fritz had paid for all the House merchandise on *his* credit - to Spiegelberg Brothers supply company - and wanted Fritz's Estate to pay that outstanding bill.

"I told the siblings I'd set up an account for policy proceeds in the First National Bank of Santa Fe. Payment came this July nineteenth; but the net wasn't ten thousand - since subtracted was a collection company fee, my costs, and an actual Spiegelberg bill of about eight hundred dollars. I put that money in my Saint Louis account."

"Why not the First National Bank of Santa Fe," asked Fred Waite. "Like you told the heirs?"

"I had second thoughts. The Santa Fe Ring controls it."

Waite responded, "Then why not give the relatives the money and figures?"

With the stubborn inflexibility and miserly parsimony which were the underpinnings of his character, McSween answered, "As attorney, I'm obligated to the estate to divide the assets among *all* beneficiaries. There are additional heirs to be sought in Germany. Also, the Fritz siblings are gullible - as, sadly, you'll soon see. They'd be conned by Dolan into misappropriating the assets by handing them over to him.

"Anyway, now that I'm indicted, it's beyond that. It's a legal principle now." He pushed down his wayward collar.

"We've been hearing that Chisum was killed," said Waite.

"He's alive, but was arrested too. Here's how the web was spun."

Billy watched a spider descending on her silk strand, and disappearing close to Tunstall.

"Knowing I was going to Saint Louis with my wife and John Chisum for business, James Dolan decided to try again for that money. On December fourth, he convinced Charles Fritz that I'd collected the full ten thousand, and was going to run off with it.

"So, on December seventh, that gullible man petitioned the Lincoln County Probate Court to order me to turn it over. On December tenth, I appeared before Probate Judge Florencio Gonzales. But his sister, Emilie Scholand, didn't come. As the other administrator, she was required by law to be there for any action. So the case was postponed; and James Dolan was foiled again.

"Then we left, going through Las Vegas to get the stagecoach to Pueblo, Colorado, where we'd pick up the Atchison, Topeka and Santa Fe line to Saint Louis.

"But unbeknownst to us, Dolan was desperate for the money. On December twenty-first, in Mesilla, he got Ring loyalist, District Attorney William Rynerson, to prepare an affidavit for Emilie Scholand, saying I'd fraudulently taken money owed her and treated it as my own. That's embezzlement, a felony. She signed it in her home in nearby Las Cruces. Remember, she can't read or understand English. District Attorney Rynerson then telegraphed Thomas Benton Catron, who, as U.S. Attorney, telegraphed San Miguel County Sheriff Desiderio Romero to arrest me.

As harassment, Catron also cited John Chisum with a colonial law called a 'Writ of ne exeat regno,' which means: 'Let him not leave the kingdom.' "

Charlie Bowdre called out America wasn't a kingdom. "Catron's trying to remedy that," Fred Waite said.

"So Sheriff Romero stopped us. But he didn't have warrants; so he couldn't hold us. But when we were back on the road, the warrants arrived; and he apprehended us. I was ordered to Mesilla: the court in the district of my alleged offense against Emilie Scholand. I sent my wife on to Saint Louis, assuring her - as I do all of you - that this foolishness merits no concern.

"And they underestimated John Chisum. They tried to force him to list his assets against faked debts, by threatening eight weeks in the Las Vegas jail. He chose jail. Said he'd use the time to write a book on the Santa Fe Ring.

"Deputy Sheriff Barrier was assigned my transport to Mesilla. He understands what's at stake. So now, I'm just waiting for my Hearing with Judge Bristol on the charge. Obviously he'll dismiss it. Though his recent illness, so far, has forced postponement.

"And seven days ago, Murphy and Dolan finally presented their claim before Probate Court. They alleged that the Emil Fritz debt to the House was the preposterous sum of seventy-seven thousand, eight hundred two dollars and sixty-four cents."

"Are thoth thiblings idioths, Mac?" asked Scurlock, peering through his spectacles. "They turn to Dolan to get ten thouthand; and heth planning to fleethe them for thventy-eight?"

"Sadly, the common man is easily tricked. But not the law." McSween smirked. "On the tenth, Probate Judge Florencio Gonzales dismissed Dolan's claim as unsubstantiated." Bowdre and Scurlock cheered. "Better yet, this past Saturday, Dolan and Riley filed for bankruptcy! That's why Dolan was so desperate for that policy money. They mortgaged everything - the House and their Pecos cow camp - to Catron. He's putting his brother-in-law, Edgar Walz, in charge."

McSween grasped his lapels, confidence regained, earlier panic seeming absurd. He said, "The law always wins. The mills of God grind slow; but they grind exceeding fine."

George Coe said, "All you need, Mac's, to get that Hearing over with; and it's over."

Tunstall spoke. "And our war of words has begun. On January third, Alexander and I wrote an editorial for the Las Cruces newspaper, *Eco del Rio Grande*, stating all that you just heard. Over the next few weeks the papers will literally burn with our revelations. Victory is just over the hill."

As they walked out, handsome mustached Waite said to Billy, "I'm not convinced. One: Chisum's a wily fox. The Las Vegas jail is a nice place to sit out a war. Two: who's replaced Dolan? Catron himself - in the form of a brother-in-law. Three: we haven't been paid. Ol' Chickasaw saying: 'No pay in the beginning, no pay in the end.'"

Billy did not want to believe McSween and Tunstall were wrong, but Dolan's final threat to him at their meeting cast its shadow - a river of blood would flow. He was silent and confused.

JANUARY 26, 1878   7:46 PM   SATURDAY

Around George and Frank Coe, in their farmhouse's main room, were merry townspeople, as they and Washington rested from fiddle playing. "Seems everybody's here to dance on the grave of the House," said George Coe.

He turned to Billy. "I was thinking: when I'm old, I'll wish I could see you again, singing like a bird or going all those gaits."

"Celebrate when you can," said George Washington. "You know Jessie Evans is back?"

"Yep," said Frank. "An' got his comeuppance. I heard last Sataday, when him an' his boys were stealin' horses from a Mexican rancher near Las Cruces, he got shot in the ass. He made it to Shedd's Ranch, where he's bein' cared for by none other than Jimmy Dolan himself."

Washington said, "And Mister McSween left for that Mesilla Hearing on that Fritz money. He told me Dolan would be there too. Celebrate if you want; but I still say things are beginning, not ending."

"What's beginning," said George Coe, ignoring the cynicism, "is victory. I like the way Tunstall called it 'a war of words.'"

"Kid, you probably didn't see his *Mesilla Valley Independent* editorial. Get it, Frank."

Billy then read it to himself: "A TAXPAYER'S COMPLAINT FROM JOHN H. TUNSTALL, January 18, 1878. Delinquency Notice: 'The Sheriff of Lincoln has paid nothing during his present term of office.' This extract is a sad comment on Sheriff Brady. As County records show, he collected over $2,500 in Territorial funds. Of this sum, Alexander McSween paid him $1,500 by cheque. This same cheque was presented for payment by John Riley of J.J. Dolan & Co. to Underwood and Nash for cattle. We wonder where the remainder of the $2,500 is. A delinquent tax payer is bad; a delinquent tax collector is worse. J.H.T."

George Coe smiled. "Evans is shot in the ass with a bullet; Dolan got his with bankruptcy. And that Hearing's about to set things straight. Time to dance, Kid!"

Billy danced alone, and the dancing people watched his one-two beat become the pulsation of the body, which was the pulsation of the heart. And he became the one-two-three-four rhythm: the dance of the horse people, whose remembering bodies lived in pounding meter of hooves. And the room filled with his exuberance of hope.

But then he danced with fierce energy, lip raised in bellicosity. This dance was of war. Some felt fear and contraction of spirit. But Billy danced ever more defiantly, until triumph seemed inevitable.

As all stood murmuring, George Washington rose and sang in his deep reverent voice, "Glory, glory hallelujah! / His truth is marching on;" because he understood, and accepted, and could still give thanks, for the holy mystery of trials and sorrows he was convinced were to come.

JANUARY 29, 1878   7:32 AM   TUESDAY

Billy and Paulita watched Deluvina pat dough balls into perfectly formed tortillas, while saying she was honoring the Spirit of the Corn for giving its body.

Paulita announced, "Mama's got a sick-headache; so I'm taking Billy to Stinking Springs for a picnic - instead of a dancing lesson." Deluvina countered that he had ridden much of the night. "I'm getting another horse so Gray Sugar can rest." She ran out.

Neither spoke until Billy asked, "Deluvina, why d'you let me ride out alone with her?"

"My own blood are all dead, except possibly a sister. Paulita is," black eyes glanced, "almost the only person I love." She added vehemently, "I am a slave. But *I* can give *her* freedom."

As Deluvina wrapped their food, she said, "I have heard a war is coming to Lincoln County. You will fight?" If it came, Billy said. "Then listen. Hear what you can. This is the 'Blessingway' of my people: 'Before me it is blessed, behind me it is blessed, / Below me it is blessed, above me it is blessed, / All my surroundings are blessed as I found it, I found it.' " He thanked her and left. She sighed and whispered, "Dragonfly."

Billy and Paulita rode eastward for two hours toward Stinking Springs. Finally, Paulita pointed south over flatland cut by small arroyos. In one, near the eponymous springs, lay a dead white greyhound. She said, "A shepherd has them for hunting. How sad. To die alone;" and resisted a whim that death now permeated the place. On a nearby rise, was a rectangular structure: their destination.

That long windowless shelter for shepherds was oriented west to east, and, though it had viga roof beams, was constructed of mortarless flat stones. Paulita said, "A man named Alejandro Perea built it for Papa." At its south-facing front, was a doorless opening and a hitching post. She said, "You start the fire. I'll lay the picnic blanket." Inside, wood was stacked near a potbellied stove.

Out again, Billy discovered only the spread blanket at the east side. Walking with concern, calling her name, he noticed a distant eastward channel. Intuitively, he turned south, and gasped in surprise. A precipitous drop-off was so level with its far side, that an intersecting deep wide gorge had been invisible.

Paulita, hiding with hands and knees on its sloping wall, in line with the door, was peeking out. Stealthily Billy crept the side, scrub bushes as cover. When close, he gave war whoops and caught her. Laughing and laughing, she said she'd tricked him.

He said it really was something, and asked if had ever been used for an ambush. A dozen men could hide. "But who'd want to ambush a shepherd?" Paulita asked. Both laughed.

After eating in sheltered warmth of the rock house wall, Billy presented Paulita with the dime novel from Tunstall, its cover having a masked youth with rebelliously tipped hat. She said he looked just like him: handsome. Billy blushed and said, "Uh, he's Deadwood Dick. I brought it to read to you."

Page one announced, "*A Tale of the Regulators and Road-Agents of the Black Hills* by Edward L. Wheeler." Billy said, "Dashing Dave's the leader of the Regulators. And they're after Deadwood Dick. The Regulators strike blows in defense of justice."

As he read, Paulita pulled his arm over her shoulders, snuggling against his side. He glanced down, but said, "So they finally captured Deadwood Dick."

She placed his free hand on hers, and said his was much bigger. "But yours is perfect," he said. "Uh, I mean for someone your size."

Continuing to hold his hand, she listened. "Dashing Dave seemed an upright gentleman, yet was bad." Billy added, "What I like about these stories is you're never sure who's good or bad. So now we have to wonder about Deadwood Dick."

She objected that he was already hanged. Billy turned the page. "The note, pinned to the corpse, said, 'Though life may become extinct from the body, the spirit never dies.' That's a clue, Paulita."

Dramatizing, he continued, " 'Gerald! My dear brother! Is it possible?' 'Ah!' said Deadwood Dick, 'I am not your brother, but be calm, for he is dead.' "

"So they hanged her brother and not him? Anyway, now I'm on Deadwood Dick's side. Billy, when we're together I'm happy and sad: happy you're here and sad you'll leave."

"I get that too," he said softly. "Here's the end. 'This very night I will go to Deadwood for a preacher to join us in wedlock. Is this agreeable, sweetest?' 'It is, Dick, and I am so happy. It seems that there is no power so divinely exquisite as love.'"

Paulita said, "That was a happy ending. All they have to do is move far away."

As they stood, she said, "I had a strange dream. You were riding a red horse, red like ..." - she could not say blood - "... like 'crimson lake' in my watercolors. Up in the sky. I called; but you didn't hear. Promise you'll listen. Even in a dream."

"I promise," he said seriously, and brushed moist eyes. She wanted to know if he dreamed about her. "Sometimes. We're, uh, looking at each other. Would you still remember me if I couldn't come for a while?" She said of course.

Not wanting to dwell on that, or the foreboding she had tried both to describe and conceal in her dream, she shouted for him to catch her. He ran slow strides and watched her looking back with the face that was in his dreams.

At the same time, three hundred seven miles southeast of Stinking Springs, in Hidetown, Texas, Willis Skelton Glenn said to Pat Garrett, "After I bought you out, I thought hiring you would work." Angrily, Garrett said he couldn't make buffalo appear. Glenn said, "I heard Poe got *his* ten thousand. I'm for giving up this outfit."

"Suits me fine," Garrett said defensively. "Goddamn wasting my time here anyway. Pay me the sixty dollars you owe me; and I'm on my road to destiny: Fort Sumner."

FEBRUARY 4, 1878   12:14 PM   MONDAY

Though irritated by the Hearing's interruption to his busy practice, Alexander McSween felt complacent as he ate in Mesilla's Corn Exchange Hotel, across from the courthouse and jail. With him were his brother-in-law, David Shield, for legal representation; John Tunstall; Deputy Sheriff Adolph Barrier; and Lincoln Justice of the Peace John "Squire" Wilson.

Shield, a nervous sensitive man, said, "Too bad they haven't extended the Atchison, Topeka, and Santa Fe line yet. It would have spared us that rigorous trip."

Old Wilson, a fuddy-duddy pig-headedly clinging to the fashion of his youth, had white hair blunt-cut at his earlobes, knee-length frock coat, and high-standing collar into which jowly cheeks of his soft wrinkle-crazed face nestled. He said, "Judge Bristol's sure been sick long. And his house is a heck of a place for a Hearing."

"We're fortunate, Squire," said McSween, "that he's getting it over with. It's just to decide if there's merit to my charge. There's none."

David Shield stroked his full beard. "I should have brought my law intern, Harvey Morris."

Adolph Barrier said, "I just don't like that James Dolan and Charles Fritz will be there. Why?"

McSween smiled superciliously. "Fritz is probably my doing. I contacted him. I figured out a clever probate matter after reviewing old House documents left over from when I worked there. Turns out, when Emil Fritz died, there were uncollected business debts. His share would have been half. So I informed Charles Fritz that I'd present for him a suit against J.J. Dolan and Company for their amount: twenty-three thousand three hundred seventy-six dollars and ten cents. As to paying that sum, Dolan's bankruptcy is irrelevant; Catron assumed all the business debts.

"And how about this to make your hearts sing? I found out that Catron paid Brady's delinquent taxes! *That* will make a pretty editorial in our war of words. As to James Dolan being there, it's irrelevant intimidation."

David Shield said, "I hope Bristol's feeling better. He really made a mess of proper procedure Saturday - even forgetting a court reporter for a transcript.

"And did you hear this about District Attorney Rynerson?" Barrier listened intently as Tunstall placidly ate wild turkey and vegetables. "In sixty-seven, Rynerson fatally shot the Chief Justice of New Mexico, John P. Slough! He only got off because he was represented by Catron's law partner, Steven Elkins."

McSween said, This certainly isn't Saint Louis, David. Murder hardly distinguishes Rynerson."

Shield blurted, "And Warren Bristol is in the Santa Fe Ring." McSween said it was irrelevant. He couldn't get around the law.

"But, Alexander," Shield continued, asymmetric pompadour making his face look unbalanced and vulnerable, "why does Bristol keep asking if you two are partners?"

Tunstall smiled, saying they would be as of May. "But he kept saying you were *now*, said Shield. And you never said '*We're not.*' "

"It's irrelevant, David," said McSween impatiently, regarding him as an intellectual inferior.

"And," the slender man added, "Bristol and Rynerson were so impolite."

"I agree," said Tunstall. "For example, Judge Bristol's saying, with that rather nasty look, 'So, McSween' - a most impolite address - 'do you think you can conceal your property in Tunstall's?' "

Portly Wilson said, "That's why I like growing vegetables. Words just tangle up your head, and leave nothing to eat at the end of the day." They all laughed at the old curmudgeon.

Soon, in Warren Bristol's modest adobe house, they found him, eye sockets deep and fleshless, still propped in bed; along with James Dolan and Charles Fritz seated across the room. Chairs awaited them. Robust brown-maned William Rynerson, standing at the fireplace, glared from under dense brows, long mouth stretched in unprovoked rage within fierceness of mustache and chest-length beard.

All watched the judge's bony hand grasp a water glass on his bedside table. Hair, dry as of one exhumed, fringed his mottled dome and made a spiny beard. He sipped, then spoke in a strong voice, belying his appearance; as if he embodied death rather than mortality. "I'm ready to respond. Firstly, it's my impression, McSween, that you are in a business partnership with John H. Tunstall. Secondly, I find that, with malice aforethought, you violated a contractual agreement by withholding monies rightfully due Charles Fritz and Emilie Scholand.

"Nevertheless, I can't make a final decision, because I'm lacking a crucial witness with regard to the estate: Probate Judge Florencio Gonzales. Therefore, I have to postpone and bind over this civil matter to the next meeting of the Lincoln County District Court in April."

"So we can go now?" David Shield responded.

"Almost. With regard to McSween's proposed claim against J.J. Dolan and Company for alleged monies owing the Emil Fritz estate, this has been rejected by this Court on the basis that the heir, Charles Fritz, here present, refuses to press the matter." McSween interrupted that there were other heirs. "The matter's closed," said Bristol.

"And, although your civil matter has been postponed; the *criminal matter* is not. The Court finds that you, McSween, have fraudulently converted money in your control - but belonging to your employers, Charles Fritz and Emilie Scholand - to your own use; and have refused their demand to turn over said money, being the amount of ten thousand dollars. Therefore, the Court finds that the criminal charge of embezzlement stands. Therefore, probable cause exists both for your arrest and imprisonment.

"Consequently, I set bail for you at eight thousand dollars." Bristol's white-caked tongue flicked. "Set with the specific stipulation that it be approved solely by District Attorney Rynerson.

"And I order Deputy Sheriff Barrier to transport you to Lincoln to the custody of Sheriff Brady."

"I ... I object," stammered Shield. "There exists *no* sum of ten thousand dollars. And Charles Fritz and Emilie Scholand *aren't* his employers; the Emil Fritz estate is. And ..."

McSween interrupted, struggling for calm, and said that he'd take out a note for bail at a local bank. In his deep arrogant voice Rynerson responded, "Refused. I wouldn't believe a word you said."

After they left, Bristol said to Rynerson, "For this Wednesday, we'll need the Charles Fritz affidavit and the document for Brady."

"Charles Fritz? Wovon reden Sie?" the confused mustached man beside Dolan asked. Slowly, Dolan said, papers to sign. For his ten thousand dollars. The man nodded.

To Rynerson, Bristol said, "Use my a lap desk. I'll tell you what to write for my Clerk of Court, John Crouch. Jimmy, make sure you get Emilie Scholand there to sign also. And I want Attorney Albert Jennings Fountain's signature on the documents too in his capacity as Deputy Clerk."

Bristol first dictated an affidavit for the postponed civil case, in which the Fritz siblings would confirm breech of contract for the sum of ten thousand dollars.

Bristol added, "Say that McSween's attempt to leave the Territory to evade payment makes it necessary to attach his property to that amount to protect and satisfy a possible verdict against him in the April session of District Court. That was Tom Catron's bright idea.

"For that, get me a Writ of Attachment form that's in my desk. Underline the part that says, '*You are hereby commanded to attach the goods, chattels, lands, and effects, in whosoever hands they may be found.*' That's the important element."

Rynerson said, "It's genius, Warren. Make it hot as Hell for them; especially since scientists are writing that Hell's not real. Not true. It's here in New Mexico." He laughed sardonically.

To that Writ of Attachment add, continued Bristol, "*And said property of Alexander McSween exists as joint property of the partnership with John H. Tunstall. And said Attachment is ordered to begin immediately upon receipt.*"

Bristol asked Dolan whether the relay horses were ready. They were. Billy Matthews would be making the ride. Bristol turned back to Rynerson. "Telegraph Catron. Tell him: 'It is done.' That is, Jimmy, if you, Brady, and Jessie can't take care of it on your own first. It's a long trip back to Lincoln. They'll need to spend a night at the Shedd's Ranch way station." Dolan said Jessie was waiting there.

Charles Fritz smiled inanely, not understanding the diabolical plan which - if justifiable homicide in "self-defense" failed - consisted of a criminal case requiring $8,000 bail or imprisonment for an allegedly embezzled $10,000, and a writ giving the right to Sheriff Brady to attach property to satisfy that "embezzled" amount; all to bait the hook for the intended victim: John Henry Tunstall.

FEBRUARY 6, 1878   7:18 AM   WEDNESDAY

In return to Lincoln, John Tunstall and his group had camped at Warren Shedd's Ranch after crossing the San Augustin Pass. By then, Alexander McSween had convinced the others, except Adolph Barrier, who kept silent, that the Hearing had represented only harassment by jealous Dolan and his Ring partisans; but was legally irrelevant, merely delaying his vindication to the April Grand Jury.

In his own mind, had been a more dire adaptation. This would all be worth it, he had thought. I'll go down in Lincoln County history as standing up to the Santa Fe Ring. God is testing my resolve. As if sealing off rooms in a big house, however, to endure his fear, McSween also blocked remembrance of Robert Casey's assassination and Juan Patrón's shooting.

Now, David Shield's strained voice addressing someone woke John Tunstall. He focused his good eye and said, "Why, Mister Evans, good morning." Using hands to crawl up bent legs, he said, "Do excuse me. My rheumatism stiffens me. You are recovering, I hope?" Jessie said he couldn't ride yet, but Jimmy was coming for him in a buggy. Tunstall smiled. "I shan't try to match your legal system to our British one. Here it appears that your escape was the equivalent of winning a game."

Jessie laughed and squinted southwest, where he noted the distant dark carriage, as Tunstall led his group to the way station for breakfast.

When they emerged, Adolph Barrier saw armed men leave Warren Shedd's house, and warned of ambush. "Nonsense," said Tunstall. "They must be James Dolan and Charles Fritz. It is only polite to greet them." He walked to that building.

Dolan turned its corner with pointed carbine. "Good morning," said Tunstall. "So sorry to have startled you."

The sapphire eyes glared with feigned rage; and the dark lips retracted to a rabid square exposing upper and lower teeth. "This is cocked for you, Tunstall. That *Mesilla Valley Independent* article was against *me*, not Brady."

Dolan spat repeatedly to the side, and hissed, "I want to fight."

Jessie sauntered out, flipping his Winchester lever. Aware of approaching footsteps, Tunstall turned.

Adolph Barrier said sternly, "Let's settle this peacefully."

Finally comprehending a challenge, Tunstall said, "Mister Dolan, if you feel I have insulted your honor I shall accommodate you. These two men can be our seconds."

"Wha' the hell's 'e sayin', Jimmy?" asked Jessie.

Dolan swung his barrel upward, signaling termination, and concealing anger at failed provocation.

One hundred twelve miles northeast of Shed's Ranch, in their secret cave high on the north face of the Capitan Mountains, Billy was listening to Yginio Salazar say, "Finally the time has come. Some of the viejos, the old ones, have waited a lifetime."

Billy said they could hide his gambling money in the cave - to pay for their help. Yginio laughed derisively. "For this fight, no one will want money." But when Billy said it could be used to pay debts to the House, the skinny boy relaxed his habitual intensity and agreed.

Yginio added, "Tonight, in San Patricio, we will meet at the Montez house with my friend, Martin Chávez, from Picacho. He brings others."

Billy said, "We need men who stay when bullets fly."

"I know," said Yginio. "If people did not fear death, the world would be so different."

FEBRUARY 8, 1878   1:08 PM   FRIDAY

Behind James Dolan's erstwhile desk, sat a newcomer facing six men, including Dolan, who affably introduced him as Edgar Walz.

That short fat man, with gopher-pouched cheeks, squeaked, "Ed, please. Tom - my brother-in-law, you know - told me you boys will be doing the work. I'll be at his Carrizozo ranch. Small price to pay. Marrying into his family was my lucky day." Little hands smoothed silky beard in absentminded grooming.

Dolan continued ingratiatingly, "Ed, this is our sheriff, William Brady. And making all this possible is our messenger here: Billy Matthews." Walz looked blank. "He is the one," Dolan said with forced patience, "who rode in relays to bring us the Writ of Attachment."

Dolan next gestured to a red-headed man. "My current business partner, John Riley. And Deputies Jack Long, George Hindman, and George Peppin. And at," he hesitated to control resentment, "*your* cow camp, there is Buck Morton, who has the Seven Rivers men on alert. I only wish Lawrence Murphy could be here; but he is desperately sick." Walz responded that everybody dies sooner or later.

Billy, fifty two miles to Lincoln's southeast, increasingly certain of fighting, hitched Gray Sugar at the Feliz Ranch chosa. He nodded after barely-pigmented Henry Brown asked, "Bwas id your idea do pud up dese sanbags 'round de frond like dis?"

"Hosses shur look good," said bony, mustached Jim French, turning his head jerkily toward the corral. "Even that chestnut o' yers is lookin' like some 'spensive Tunstall hoss."

"Bud why'd he buy dad big black he calls Colonel?" asked Brown. "He's blind." Protectively, Billy said, "Tunstall told me he followed leads real well ... and the owner was going to kill him."

Billy changed the subject, suggesting they clean guns; and said, "Wouldn't want my last words to be, 'Goddamn, it's jammed.'" Brown and French laughed.

At the same time, in Lincoln, Josephina Baca, reputed to be the most beautiful of her sisters, secretly exited the back door of the house of her father, Saturnino Baca, into drizzle; and covered her head with a rebozo shawl. Striking drops crackled like fire, she thought. She noticed things differently now that she was in love. She planned to sneak, hidden in river's underbrush, past the stone Torreon and the Tunstall corral, through the McSween stable yard, and to the house's west wing. To visit secretly George Washington.

Finally peering into the window of the west wing's terminal room, which had a stove, but was used for storage, she tapped on its door.

"Made it," Washington said smiling, as she lowered her moisture-pearled rebozo from rippling black hair. "Missus Shield and the children are on the other side. Did she see you?" Josephina shook her head. "Maybe that law clerk, Harvey Morris?"

"No. He is with Papá. Papá he is angry. They talks about the rent to Señor McSween."

Washington changed the subject. "So you came to hear my songs?" From behind a trunk, he removed his fiddle case. "If we hear anyone, you scoot mighty fast out this door, you hear?" She promised, and followed through the interconnecting rooms.

In Susan McSween's, he said, "Want to smell something nice?" He pulled a glass wand from a little vial on the dressing table. There was fragrance of roses. "Missus McSween gets this in Saint Louis. I'd let you put some on, but your Papa'd smell it." Josephina pleaded. She would wash it in the river. She held out her hand. He thought how much its color reminded him of his mother's.

She sniffed herself as they passed through McSween's room, and came to the long parlor in the front section.

Washington sat on the piano bench beside the upright mahogany instrument; and she on one of the slippery, horse-hair upholstered chairs cluttering the room, as he tuned his strings. "They're used to my singing. But don't talk loud." Pressing the fiddle to his shoulder, he began. "I'm a rambler, I'm a gambler / I'm a long way from home. / If your people don't like me / Let 'em leave me alone."

Dolan, exiting the House's front with Brady, George Peppin, Jack Long, George Hindman, and Billy Matthews, hissed that Edgar Walz was a fool. Brady said, "Therrre's no mistaking that billy goat's beard for a stallion's tail, as said me dear old father in County Cavan."

Peppin laughed. "Today begins the revenge of the Irish on the English, Will."

Matthews asked nervously, "What if McSween and Tunstall come back?"

"Protect yourselves," said Dolan. This was tacit mandate for murder during the intended ravishment of their properties. "You have the Writ of Attachment, Will?" He nodded.

George Washington asked Josephina if she liked to sing. "Yes. I know much himnos from church."

To the right of the five men striding the red mud street, was the adobe of the Stanley family. To their left was the smaller house of Ham Mills, a past sheriff, who had recently abandoned his Hispanic wife, now living there alone. Ahead, to the left, was the McSween's picket fence.

Washington sang, "Oh he taught me to love him and called me his flow'r ..."

Thwack! The front door was struck.

Josephina sprang up. "Scoot!" Washington said.

Men crowded under the entrance porch. Brady said, "We're here to serve this Writ," fumbling for it through jacket pockets.

Washington read the preprinted form with particulars inked in on dotted lines. On the bottom was handwritten: "*This is an action of Assumpsit by attachment brought by the Plaintiffs against the Defendant to recover Ten thousand dollars for money received by the Defendant for the use of the Plaintiffs.*" He returned it uncertainly. "Attorney McSween will take care of it when he's back," he said.

"Get out of our way, nigger," Brady growled. "You're obstructing the law."

Peppin said uncomfortably, "We're listing McSween's things."

" 'Cause they're no longer his," said Jack Long; his gruesome scar distorting a sneer.

Washington gave way. The five entered the parlor. "Goddamn," said Brady, "that bastard's made himself a palace." Long remarked on the famous piano.

But all hesitated, inhibited by civilization's orderliness.

George Hindman lifted a French porcelain of a courtly lady gesturing miniscule fingers at her courtier, and, misjudging its weight, lost hold. It shattered dismemberment on carpet over plank floor, breaking the spell.

Washington stepped toward it. "Don't move," said Matthews. "And stay with us. I'm not taking no chances."

"Peppin, you got the writing board?" asked Brady. It was under his jacket. "Start writing. Parlor Room: One piano. One sofa. Five paintings. One sofa." Peppin corrected that sofa was said twice. "Then wrrrite it once. Goddamn job. Desk. Two sets window curtains. Some kind of colored carpet." The Persian rug was soon tracked with mud. Instructed to look for anything hidden, Jack Long jerked a curtain so forcefully that its bracket tore away, collapsing fabric.

Washington retrieved the fiddle, saying it was his. "I'll grrrant that," said Brady. "You built any concealed places here, George?"

"No, Will. Just muslin over the vigas - to look more like Saint Louis."

"McSween's never getting back there," Brady laughed as they walked to the other room in the front section: a dining-room with shelves of legal books. "First count 'em, then pull 'em down," said Brady. On the floor, soon lay four hundred thirty-seven volumes, purposefully trampled; one of which was Susan McSween's *Perfect Etiquette* by Albert Cogswell. Brady dictated.

At "sewing machine," Brady asked, "Who the hell sews here, Washington?" It was the teacher, Susan Gates, who had come with the Shields for their children. Brady resumed. "One fancy table clock."

"My Missus 'id like that," said Matthews.

"We'rrre not thieves," said Brady. Going back through the parlor, they entered the west wing. "Bedroom," said Brady. "Looks like McSween's. I heard they don't sleep together." At the next room, he said, "Smells like roses, don't it? No wonder she's called a whore." Washington's clenched fists made nail grooves in his palms. Matthews lingered and slipped the perfume vial into his jacket.

He caught up at that west wing's final room, as Brady was tossing out contents of trunks and boxes, and saying, "I keep seeing McSween in that jail. If you open the acequia sluices, that pit floods." Peppin said he'd told Jimmy they needed a drainage system. "You missed the point, me boy. You don't rescue a drowned man."

Brady sighed. "We still got the east wing." They walked back, mattresses pulled off, rugs heaped, pictures torn down, clothing strewn, inured to their path of destruction.

Shield's wife, in wrapper housedress and with wavy blond hair pulled back in a bun, infant girl in arms, and with her four other children, encountered their noisy group at the dining-room. A girl's voice called, "Do we have company, Elizabeth?"

Startled, and with trepidation, Elizabeth Shield asked, "Where's David?" Then she realized the mayhem. She shrieked, "Get out! Get out!" The baby wailed. A plain-faced girl rushed to her. "Susan," she gasped, "take the children." But the dazed the girl only repeated what's happening, what's happening. The two youngest boys, four and three clutched their mother's skirts. The older girl, twelve, and boy, six, stared. "Get out of my house!" Elizabeth Shield screamed again.

"It's not yours," said Brady. "It's joint property of McSween and Tunstall."

Peppin said, "At the end of the east wing's their kitchen. Put them there, Will."

George Washington, in helpless humiliation, avoided Elizabeth Shield's horror-struck eyes. Numbly, she led the children past Susan Gates.

Matthews said he'd take Gates, grasping her shoulder. Sadistically tumescent, he opportunistically jostled hardness into her shirts when she roused and screamed "Minnie!" as the oldest girl ran back in.

Undersized for twelve, with pinched serious face and short brown hair held behind her ears, Minnie picked Brady and said, "You're a bad man." Stick-like wrists hung calmly at her dress, with its frugally hemmed, growth tucks. Brady threatened that, if she was one of his eight, he'd whip her. "You can't scare me," she said. "God protects good people." She left.

George Peppin said this was making him feel sick. "To hell with you," Brady said. "It's the law."

After completing their damage on the Shield side, they advanced out the front door to premature dusk of storm, and to the Tunstall store. There, middle-aged Sam Corbett was locking its front door for the day. Thunder crashed. Lightning flashed. Rain fell in a sheet. The street became a river running red. "I'm finished for today," said Matthews to the assenting others. He fingered the stolen vial in his pocket, imagining rose fragrance on his wife's naked chest.

FEBRUARY 10, 1878   9:10 AM   SUNDAY

Alexander McSween, having returned from Mesilla to rampage, had secured more doors within his shrinking mental house. Fear and anger were impermissible; he was documenting harassment for some indistinct reckoning by man and God.

Now, with Deputy Sheriff Adolph Barrier, McSween faced Sheriff Brady at the Tunstall store's gaping front doors. Inside were Deputies Jack Long, George Peppin, and George Hindman. All heard a crash. Dummy, brought to carry heavy articles, had tripped against a showcase. McSween said, "You're here illegally. This is John Tunstall's property."

Dummy walked out. "Look at me, Sheriff Brady." In one of Tunstall's tweed jackets, mismatched buttonholes made a shoulder buckle upward. Brady joked that the Englishmen had changed. "I wants it." Mongoloid eyes puffed to sobbing slits. "I'm cold."

"You can keep it," said McSween. "The man who owns it would let you." Wiping dripping mucous on the sleeve, Dummy reentered.

"Sheriff Brady," said McSween, "you must recognize the sin you're committing."

Brady's face darkened. "Make accusations and I swearrr on me mother's grave that this 'ill be your last place on earth."

McSween said, "I've calculated that you've inventoried property worth forty thousand dollars - far in excess of the ten thousand required." Brady taunted that his job was to list, not appraise.

McSween continued, "And I've written out names of men willing to post my bail far in excess of the eight thousand dollars: to the sum of thirty-four thousand five hundred."

Brady said, "It's refused by Rynerson. I might as well take you into custody now."

Barrier possessively grasped McSween's arm, and said, "Sheriff, since you'll have to telegraph Judge Bristol about those bondsmen, let him know I'm continuing my custody." Brady backed away.

FEBRUARY 11, 1878   8:43 AM   MONDAY

During the turmoil, John Tunstall had changed focus to his ranches. In his store's warehouse, he introduced two new employees to Fred Waite, Billy, and John Middleton; as Gottfried Gauss heated coffee on the potbellied stove. Gesturing to a grizzled man with weathered face, Tunstall said, "Mister William McCloskey was selected by Mister Brewer." Perspiring profusely, McCloskey noticed Billy staring at him, both recalling that the past September he had left Billy a horse at the Jones's from Dolan's cow camp.

"And from John Chisum comes Mister Frank MacNab, who has worked for Hunter and Evans as a so-called cattle detective." Without Tunstall's knowledge, MacNab was being embedded by the cattleman for his own purposes. "And there is no doubt that we need stock protection.

"Also, I do apologize about this legal muddle." Tunstall sighed audibly. "I now have the unpleasant task of trying to talk reason into our stubborn Irishman of a sheriff." He asked Billy and Waite to accompany him. "This dispute seems to have made fashionable armed entourages." Billy wore his double cartridge belts and carried his Winchester carbine.

As Billy walked through the corral's adobe wall gate, Waite noticed him cock the carbine's hammer. People on the street, seeing a possible confrontation, dispersed.

"Good morning, all of you," Tunstall said to Long, Peppin, and Hindman on his store's porch. "This is damned high-handed: preventing my conducting business and leaving my establishment a bloody mess."

Hoofbeats made all look eastward. Sheriff William Brady was arriving from his ranch on his big sorrel gelding, whose right shoulder had an indistinct brand, a result of John Kinney's alteration. The flashy horse, Dandy Dick, was a Dolan gift.

At Tunstall's beckoning, Brady reluctantly hitched him. Tunstall said, "Hang it man, the issue - if there is any at all - is with an alleged debt of Alexander McSween's."

"You're partners," said Brady, his meaty hand rubbing his eyes, already bloodshot from alcohol. "I'm just waiting for any excuse to finish this. Next is the Feliz Ranch to attach *McSween's* cattle."

"But he has *none*, my good man. The only cattle there are primarily mine: two hundred and nine purchased from the widow Casey, and three hundred ninety-one from John Chisum - a total of six hundred. The rest, fifty one, belong to my foreman, Richard Brewer." Tunstall sighed. "But I want to assure you that the life of one man is worth more than all I own." Waite glanced at Billy, listening reverentially.

Then Tunstall smiled with sudden hope about the matter most distressing him. He said, "I want to clarify my horses. In my office are bills of sale showing my sole ownership for five of the six currently here in the corral; as well as for those now belonging to my men - except for those of my new employees, Frank MacNab and William McCloskey ..."

"McCloskey?" asked Brady, surprised. Billy's eyes narrowed suspiciously.

At his desk, Tunstall sighed at the attachment's depredations, but located the documents. He added, "I almost did forget: the sixth horse in the corral here: the chestnut gelding." He turned to Billy. "What do you call him?" Billy said just Chestnut. "He belonged to Mister Bonney prior to his employment by me.

"So I can consider them all free of the Attachment?" Not having listened, Brady yawned and said he guessed so. Waite asked Tunstall if he wouldn't want that in writing. With some pique, Tunstall responded, "If one cannot trust a sheriff, whom can one trust?"

When the lawman remounted, his skittish animal turned, revealing Brady's own BB brand on his left hip, before being roughly directed toward the House.

As Tunstall returned through the adobe wall gate with Billy and Waite, he said, "This brings me to a decision. I shall send Misters McCloskey and MacNab to the Feliz Ranch with three of the horses. Later this afternoon, the two of you and Middleton will take there that chestnut gelding of yours, Mister Bonney, and the remaining two."

After Fred Waite left, Billy asked to speak. Tunstall said, "If it is about salary, the answer is that John Chisum has promised to manage that when released from the gaol. You have all the equipment you need?" Billy did; but said they should take the guns and ammunition from the store. And they shouldn't ask Sheriff Brady. Tunstall responded, "That is not above-board."

Billy followed Tunstall toward the warehouse. "Why'd you hire William McCloskey? He worked for Dolan. The last thing we need is a spy." Tunstall called that a serious accusation without foundation. "Also Frank MacNab. He's hated by the Seven Rivers ranchers." Tunstall said that they could not humor that crowd, whose rustling was the bane of Mister Chisum's existence.

"Please. Please hear me. You don't want all those small ranchers against us, do you? In the long run, your fair business tactics," tears welled, "and just, just your good," Billy paused to collect himself, "good nature would bring them around." Tunstall asked why he was so overwrought. He had no intent to lead them into danger. Billy smiled gently. "I know that, Mister Tunstall. Not willingly."

In the adjoining property to the west, in his parlor, Alexander McSween was speaking to his companions as George Washington listened from the dining-room. Smirking, he said, "The Ring men are digging their own graves by the magnitude of legal improprieties. They finally justified my writing a complaint to Secretary of the Interior, Carl Schurz. The Hayes administration isn't corrupt like Grant's." Law student, Harvey Morris, young, fair, fat, and clean-shaven, objected earnestly that it had carry-overs. McSween smiled. "David's doing a good job. Giving you a legal mind. But the Hayes administration will care."

McSween lifted the letter from his desk. "Tell me what you think. He read: "*Sir. I am writing to inform you about the management of the Mescalero Apache Reservation. It looks as though the Indian Agent named Frederick Godfroy is under the control of James J. Dolan and John H. Riley, known here as J.J. Dolan & Co. These men have long held the flour and beef Post Tradership contracts and have delivered produce unfit for use It is also known that they deal in rustled cattle to supply the beef. I suggest that you send a Detective to ferret out this matter. P.S. Government officials in this Territory have interests in these frauds."*

David Shield enthused; but Harvey Morris said, "Sir, I agree that - even with declaring bankruptcy - their corrupt business is still going on. But we're in a crisis."

McSween smiled condescendingly. "Good logic, Harvey. But good lawyers build a case. This letter proves our opponents' lack of credibility. And we have time."

Adolph Barrier and George Washington, without realizing the coincidence, simultaneously sighed.

FEBRUARY 12, 1878   7:19 AM   TUESDAY

James Dolan, again behind his desk, was enraged, addressing Brady; as Billy Matthews and John Riley listened.

"Will, how could you tell McSween that Rynerson refused those bondsmen *before* you even got his list? You still don't realize that this is *not* the Robert Casey situation. We may have to bear outside scrutiny.

"Today you have just two tasks, Will. First to confirm your posse - at this moment arriving at Paul's Ranch. Matthews will be your Chief Deputy. Others are Andrew "Buckshot" Roberts ..." Drunkenly, Brady called Roberts the best goddamn shot with a Winchester.

"John," said Dolan, "write out this list for Will to sign." He dictated the names: "Seven River's boys - put Buck Morton there - then Manuel Segovia 'the Indian,' Pantaleon Gallegos." When he finished, Dolan said, "That should total forty-four including me.

"And add, 'By decree of Lincoln County Sheriff William Brady, no *known outlaw* is permitted on this posse.' That covers for Jessie and his boys.

"The second thing, Will: deliver this telegram to McSween - which did, in fact, arrive today from Rynerson. It denies his bondsmen's sureties. Tell him you will continue to block public access to the store until ranch inventories are completed."

This was continued provocation, but Dolan had a new plan. His research on Billy Bonney was yielding fruit; and he recognized the boy's zeal for Tunstall. An attack on that man, rightly timed, could precipitate the necessary fight and fatalities.

Ideal was the Feliz Ranch. As a guarantee, Dolan would go there himself with Jessie and others.

FEBRUARY 13, 1878   6:43 AM   WEDNESDAY

John Tunstall, with bemusement at the legal absurdities, had ordered his men to round up the cattle for the inventory.

That day, left in the chosa were only Gottfried Gauss and Dick Brewer, with William McCloskey surreptitiously interrogating them for James Dolan. Brewer had told him that, of the eight horses present, six were exempted and two were his.

McCloskey asked, "Don' John Chisum's guns back ye up?" Brewer asked what for. Hoofbeats resounded.

Brewer ran out. Alarmed, big fists opening and closing helplessly, he yelled that there was trouble. Galloping toward them were Jessie Evans, Frank Baker, Tom Hill, and George Davis. At a distance, Dolan, Billy Matthews, and George Hindman halted and waited.

Jessie, Winchester pointed, shouted, "You sonoabitch, Brewer. Puttin' me in tha' hole." He glanced around. "Ain' the Englishman here?" Thwarted, he said, "Food smells good. I'll call Jimmy in."

The sandbags provided the seating as the intruders ate and joked. When Brewer asked if he could join them, Dolan replied archly, "You *are* the foreman here; though your *false* accusations about our land dealings hurt me deeply, Dick. But today we came to do the Attachment." Brewer asked about Jessie and his boys with such simple-minded incredulity that all laughed. Dolan said, "Billy Matthews is Brady's Chief Deputy. Coincidentally, Jessie has business with Billy Bonney."

Conversation froze with the arrival of Billy and the others. "Hello, Jimmy," Billy said casually, diffusing tension. Again Gauss served. Billy said, "Heard you were shot, Jessie."

The gray eyes flicked in sullen fantasy of killing Tunstall. Dolan announced, "Except for Jessie and his associates, of course, we are the sheriff's agents. But the inventory must await John Tunstall. Possibly we will find him in Lincoln." Billy lied that they were heading that way too, more certain of Tunstall's immediate risk. The sapphire eyes darted to William McCloskey, who met them.

By late evening, Billy and Fred Waite were in Tunstall's apartment. When Billy told him that Jessie Evans was riding with the sheriff's men, he responded that it proved the leeway of Territorial law. His pressing concern was for the horses' safety.

Billy interrupted, "What about John Chisum's cowboys for reinforcements?" Tunstall merely smiled at adolescent dramatics. "And did you get the ammunition out of the store?" Waite glanced at Billy with surprise, while Tunstall advised him to struggle against deviousness.

As Billy walked across the moonlit corral with Fred Waite, the man said, "We've got bad odds."

Billy stretched, as if breaking through tremendous tension. Watching, emerald-eyed Waite fantasized a dragonfly in effortless suspension, when, abruptly, a vision dissolved the boy's chest, leaving only moonlight and the eerie impression of immunity to material objects like bullets. And the boy's face was radiant, as if participating in this metamorphosis.

At the warehouse, Billy said he felt like walking. Opening his bedroll, Fred Waite decided that fatigue had magnified his imagination, and was soon asleep.

Billy descended the tiered riverbank behind the property, making hooting signals. Yginio Salazar emerged silhouetted against the rippling Bonito, and said, "They are gathering at Paul's Ranch. Most from Seven Rivers. It is a lost cause."

In English, Billy said, "I'm not backing down." In Spanish, he continued: "Even if Tunstall cannot believe my warnings. We will take the ammunition from the store. To bring to the cave." He stretched luxuriantly, invigorated by certainty of a fight. He asked, "Want to swim?"

When the two boys emerged from the Bonito, the moon claimed their naked bodies with its iridescence. And the droplets in their hair were stars.

FEBRUARY 15, 1878   12:18 PM   FRIDAY

With carbine, Billy sat, taut in frustration, beside Fred Waite on the Tunstall store's porch edge. Danger to John Tunstall was mounting; but he was helpless to prevent it. Still guarding the store, were Billy Matthews, Jack Long, and George Hindman.

Billy watched an approaching stout bald man, and abruptly walked westward to him. Hindman called, "Tell Sam Wortley to rattle his hocks. We're all hungry." They went inside. Waite saw the boy's carbine disappear - pointed. Wortley reversed; and Billy returned.

When the three men came out again, Billy sneered and said, "No food."

"You bastard," growled Matthews. Billy spoke with ominous atonality, "Turn loose, you sons of bitches. I'll give you a game;" just as Dummy rushed out, whining about hunger and innocently shielding. The men hurried back into the store.

Waite asked, "You'd have shot them, Kid?"

"Sure." For the first time, Fred Waite realized how easily the boy could kill.

FEBRUARY 16, 1878   6:27 AM   SATURDAY

In big-lapelled tweed jacket, jodhpurs, and high riding boots, John Tunstall briskly entered the warehouse, greeting Billy and Fred Waite and saying, "I made a decision. I said to myself, Adventurer - I call myself that to my family - why not seek advice of seasoned allies, as Mister Bonney suggested? So I shall ride today to John Chisum's South Spring River Ranch. Both of you go to the Feliz Ranch where I shall return by tomorrow."

Billy said he should get men for their side. Tunstall sighed. "It is a sorry state of affairs to call it 'sides,' is it not? But since it is fifty miles each way, I shall cover all topics."

FEBRUARY 17, 1878   9:28 PM   THURSDAY

Gazing over Paul's Ranch flatlands, lit by the almost-full moon, James Dolan, in an open black greatcoat, stood on a rise. No wind blew, as if the always restlessly alive desert air had disappeared, leaving only stifling vacuum. Before him, campfires burned with upright darting flames, as harsh smoke spread listless pollution. In that hellish wasteland, men waited on shroud-like tarpaulins for his words. Not visible, behind his promontory, were Jessie Evans and his three companions.

Dolan began, resonant voice filled with confidence, warmth, and sincerity. "My fellow oppressed citizens, the time has come for you to say, 'Never. Never again will I be oppressed.' You have come to fight John Chisum, usurper of your river and your land. You have come to fight his ally: John Tunstall. And you have said never to that villain, McSween, who tried to get away with robbery. For what is his embezzlement but robbery of an inheritance - to which any of you could have been victim? Our cause is one cause. You and I are one."

Dolan raised his arms, long coat flaring in black cloaking silhouette. He shouted, "War! War!"

In moonlit silence, ten miles northeast of Paul's Ranch, at the Feliz chosa, John Tunstall was arriving on Long Tom. "The poor creature," he said, handing Jim French the reins.

William McCloskey asked if Chisum was sending men. "No," Tunstall sighed. "I had forgotten that he was still in that gaol. And his brothers, Pitzer and James, merely said he made the decisions."

Tunstall asked Brewer when the sheriff's men would conduct the inventory. He was unsure. Billy asked, in tacit warning, what they would do if they had many men at Paul's Ranch. Tunstall said, "Then many would be wasting time."

As the men prepared for sleep, Billy restlessly exited to stare over the moon-silver land, eager for the encounter. Only its time and circumstances remained uncertain.

FEBRUARY 18, 1878   1:01 AM   MONDAY

Under his thick blankets, John Tunstall, arthritically aching, thought, "Even fingers. Too much riding in too few days." He smiled compassionately at his sleeping men. "So primitive a code that they would fight to the death. Defending what? Honor? Absurd."

He sighed, thinking, "At this moment, I could be in a manor house; but where am I? In a tale so fantastical that, in a London club, men would say, 'Come now, aren't you overstating a bit?' " There was a fire in a stone fireplace. Pleasantly warm. Loud vibrating of a man's soft palate intruded.

Awake again, Tunstall listened. Middleton's snoring had a pattern: upsurge then stop. "Morbid fascination. Would he breathe again? How many times in a life one contemplates death. The figure was astronomical. Yet each continues as if immune.

"Repeat their names. That could bring sleep. Simple sounds, yet, in a room filled with chatter, if you heard your own, it would magnify. Odd. Your uniqueness. John Middleton, Gottfried Gauss, William McCloskey, Henry Brown, Jim French, Frank MacNab, Richard Brewer, Fred Tecumseh Waite, Billy Bonney. Men hardened by adversity. What other would choose such lives?"

He smiled. "John Henry Tunstall, *you* are here too." A thrill passed through him. "I do love it here."

He glanced at Billy. "The Kid. So young, yet so self-sufficient. This Frontier produced that. The word 'kid' is correct. A hard sound. A savage land gives no time for 'lad,' 'young gentleman' - no cloud of irresponsible years.

"On this very site I shall build the main ranch house. John Chisum talked about building a mansion at South Spring River Ranch. And put in his own lake right at the front door. To fish from the porch. A country where you could dream anything. Then do it.

"Alexander McSween." There was a comforting sensation. "Commitment to the law. The goodness which gives victory to civilization. Eventually."

Coyotes were howling, then barking and yipping. "Their chase. Their kill about to come. Joyful probably."

There was no sleepiness. Quietly, Tunstall walked out. "Magnificent landscape." Running his hand over the night-moist sandbags, he thought, "The Kid built a fortress: a Tintagel of the imagination to defend." He sighed. "If not for this blasted legal entanglement, I might have been in England this past Christmas. Now, when will have time to get there? 'The best-laid schemes o' mice an' men / Gang aft agley.' "

Back inside the chosa, he did not notice Billy, with head propped on folded arms to feign sleep after waking to his rising, watching him: the beloved man.

At 3:04 AM, Tunstall was driven from sleep by violent vision of conflict. "Halloo, men!" he called. All stirred. "I have made a decision. I cannot risk bloodshed." Dick Brewer asked, what if they sold the cattle for meat. "Then that is our cost at this stage.

"Mister McCloskey, I should like you to ride to Paul's Ranch ..." Billy interrupted that he would go. Tunstall smiled paternally. "No, Mister Bonney. My decision is to take the horses back to Lincoln for safekeeping. I shall need your skills.

"This is your message, Mister McCloskey: 'No opposition is to be feared.' Nonetheless, my hope is for the cattle to remain here with yourself and Mister 'Dutch' Martin Martz - I know he works at Paul's Ranch - until the April Court makes its decision."

When William McCloskey asked how many men he was leaving at the ranch, Tunstall answered, "Only Herr Gauss. And I want to tell you our route. We shall begin shortly after eight ..."

Billy called out - urgently trying to prevent exposure - that right now he would help McCloskey get ready. "No," Tunstall said. "Stay. We must all be in full understanding. We shall take the back route through the Nacimiento Mountains, past Pajarito Spring for watering the horses; then stop at Dick Brewer's farm, leave his two horses, and proceed to Lincoln to corral the others. Mister Waite will drive the buckboard on the flatland wagon road."

Billy pleaded that, if there was trouble, they'd need every man. "There will be no trouble. The horses are excluded from attachment. And now, let us get needed repose."

As the others fell asleep, Billy eyed fiercely the empty space left by William McCloskey's departure right after the route's disclosure.

At 9:44 AM, of the forty-seven horseman who thundered in two groups into the Feliz Ranch, one was not James Dolan. Leading the larger body were Billy Matthews and George Hindman. The smaller group had Jessie with Frank Baker, Tom Hill, and George Davis.

Gottfried Gauss emerged to the noisy rabble. "Guten mornen, Herr Matthews," he said, remembering Dolan's saying that he was Chief Deputy. "You got many vor to count cattle. But only me iz here." Matthews frowned, asking who was supposed to turn them over. " 'Dutch' Martin Martz von Paul's. Iz dis not vat you know von

McCloskey?" Matthews said McCloskey had stayed with Dolan, and asked when the men had left. Gauss, convinced of danger, responded that he was not sure.

Jessie called to Gauss to start cooking. That they had riding to do. Gauss did not move. Men walked past him into the chosa. Soon he heard, "Catch up with 'em ... They'll pay ... Put up long enough ... Where's Dolan?"

Finally, Dolan's telltale dust-cloud appeared. Remaining mounted, he nodded to Billy Matthews and Buck Morton, who followed him to the corral. Matthews said unhappily that they were gone. Dolan sneered. "I know. McCloskey came through. I can't talk directly to Jessie, but, Buck, tell him the route's the back one to Brewer's farm. They left with eight horses; so they'll be slow. Make sure you, Jessie, and his boys stay far ahead.

"Your job, Matthews, is to keep those posse fools back. Then let them ride in to add legitimacy, or fight - if anyone is left."

Pencil-mustached Morton crowed about finishing them off. Dolan said, "Before celebrating, I want to see scalps, Buck. And Matthews, tell them you're authorizing me to pick the possemen to ride after those lawbreakers trying to evade the Writ by escaping with stock. And make clear that Jessie came only to recover a horse stolen from him by Billy Bonney. And leave the rest to do the inventory."

From a distance, Gauss watched Dolan with his billowing greatcoat and index finger of his chalk-white hand pointing. Those chosen went to their horses as possemen. When Morton galloped past, Gauss heard him shout, "My knife's sharp and I feel like scalping!"

By 5:02 PM, Tunstall and his six men had been in the saddle for almost nine hours. Much earlier, Henry Brown's horse had torn off a shoe; and Tunstall had sent him back to the ranch. Over sunlit land, the rest had ridden, as hawks and turkey buzzards circled, hunting for prey or death. Billy, at his own request, rode in the rear, and frequently checked for pursuers.

In lowering light of winter's short day, they gained elevation on the muddy trail through pines among bare deciduous trees.

The view of their distant destination, Dick Brewer's farm in the Ruidoso valley, was obscured by the winding path.

Billy heard Brewer call excitedly, "Wild turkeys!" Turning a bend, Billy glimpsed him, Frank MacNab, and Jim French galloping leftward. One ungainly bird flew up, bald bluish head and red-wattled neck extended in alarm. A carbine cracked. Erratically imbalanced, it continued. John Middleton's booming voice urged Tunstall to join.

Looking back, Billy saw riders racing toward them: Jessie Evans, Buck Morton, Frank Baker, and Tom Hill - George Davis not yet visible. Yelling, "Attack! Attack!" he spurred Gray Sugar forward, while frantically waving his hat to scatter the herd.

Low light gleamed mahogany on Long Tom. Blind Colonel, in the herd, stumbled and blocked Billy from reaching Tunstall.

Middleton, galloping, shouted run to the man, who exclaimed, "What, John? What?" but did follow their fleeing direction.

Suddenly, all were in a clearing, having covered a quarter mile. They were not pursued. They stopped. To their right was a high bowl of rock-studded hillside. "Where's Tunstall?" Billy asked with anguish.

John Tunstall, though following, first believed his men had irresponsibly ridden ahead after wild turkeys. Then he halted and thought, "No. Billy Bonney was agitated. He must have seen approaching possemen. I must turn back and explain to the sheriff's men that we have only agreed-upon stock."

In dimming light, he now blinked his watering and blurred good eye, realizing that Long Tom had wandered to the right, thirty yards off the trail. He heard hoofbeats. "Halloo!" he called.

A voice answered, "Englishman! I's me: Jessie Evans!"

The shadowed roadway exposed sky silhouetting a rider. Tunstall did not see the others. Pencil-mustached Buck Morton growled, "He's mine," swinging up his carbine.

Its bullet cut light wind at over 1,200 feet per second, shattering Tunstall's right collarbone; piercing his right lung; exiting through his shoulder blade; throwing him off the horse; and grazing a piñon pine, which began to bleed pale juices.

Long Tom affectionately nosed his stunned rider. Tunstall clawed the clammy ground, trying to rise, right shoulder collapsing.

A horse loomed. Jessie dismounted. "Englishman," he said, "good t' see ye."

Struggling up with hope, Tunstall said, "I've been shot. Why would anyone ..."

Jessie heard posse horses, and cursed to himself Matthews's insufficient delay. "Hill," he called. "Come quick!"

Hurriedly, Jessie located Tunstall's pocketed Webley Bulldog revolver and said, "Do some target practice an' catch 'is hoss."

Jessie supported Tunstall's back. The man leaned gratefully. Jessie unholstered his own Colt .44 and said, "Look fer the moon."

Tunstall, perplexed, gazed skyward. Jessie grabbed his thick hair, wrenched head back to the muzzle, and pulled the trigger.

Hot gases sizzled around the flaming hole, from which an explosive fracture, punctuated by the bullet's exit at the left eyebrow, encircled the skull.

Tom Hill's careless double shots from the Webley Bulldog were simultaneous with the posse's arrival. Stupidly, in front of all, porcine Hill returned to hand Jessie the foreign pistol.

Seeing the sprawled prone corpse, all realized it was an execution.

But as big-jawed Frank Baker and flabby George Davis joined them, Jessie, at least, asked, "Did ye git the chesnut hoss Bonney stole from me?" He ordered the crowd, "Head ou'. We'll take back them other stolen hosses." The possemen left with secret knowledge.

Sending Baker and Davis ahead, Jessie said, "Hill, Morton, I ain' finisht." At Jessie's orders, the two draped the body over Long Tom's saddle. Jessie mounted and led them into a hollow beside a small creek. To Hill, he said, "Go back an' git me the bastard's hat."

Jessie spread one of the California blankets. With Long Tom beside it, he flung down Tunstall's body onto its back. Straightening its limbs, he told Morton to hide the saddle for later retrieval.

After Tom Hill and Buck Morton left, Jessie put his Colt to the temple of obediently waiting Long Tom, and fired.

When Hill returned with the hat, Jessie demanded help in rolling over the dead horse. Morton, coming back, exclaimed that they should get the hell out. Jessie said, "Shut up, Buck! Ye failed. The goddamn posse almos' foun' the goddamn bastard walkin' 'round like 'e was a' some shindig."

With the struggling group, Jessie, at last, got the carcass on its back beside the corpse. Jessie set the retrieved hat on the animal's head. "Man an' wife," he said. His companions laughed. "Buck," he said, "head ou'. Hill an' me 'ill catch up."

With savage obsession, Jessie unsheathed his Winchester and smashed its butt into Tunstall's face. Crouching, with his hunting knife, he slit open the jodhpurs and undergarment. Drooling with sexual arousal, he next slashed open Long Tom's sheath and groped. Remembering Hill, while holding the horse's severed member, he mumbled, "Meet ye at the road." Hill grinned with morbid excitement he always felt witnessing Jessie's depravity.

Alone, Jessie aligned the horse's penis to the man's nakedness. The Webley was laid beside the right hand, after Minnie's thin, gold, Christmas pudding ring was stolen from its middle finger.

Unbuttoning his own pants, Jessie splashed urine over the desecration. Finally, he addressed his victim, "Englishman, take a message t' yer sweeheart: Billy Bonney. Tell 'im: 'The good times is over - thanks t' Jessie Evans.'"

When Jessie caught up with Tom Hill, he said, still furiously aroused, "Goddamn Matthews lettin' tha' goddamn posse so goddamn close. The Englishman didn' suffer near 'nough."

Soon their hoofbeats were lost in the hidden place. Cautiously, a meadow mouse emerged from his nest and balanced on spidery toes, tiny hands pressed to white breast. Though a seed eater, he appreciated flesh. His needle nails climbed tweed as he dragged his scrotal sac to mark urine's claim, and leapt onto the mutilated face.

Absorbed in feasting, he was unaware of a silent form swooping from a tree. That form, after observing the evening's events, finally comprehended their meaning. The clawed toes of the owl closed around the squeaking being, and carried him into the night.

Tunstall's waiting men had heard the first shot echoing in their natural amphitheater. Then Billy had noticed movement on its high promontory. Gun was drawn, but it was just the wounded turkey attempting return to forever-lost sky.

A second shot had shattered their silence. Two more followed. Billy said he was going back, ignoring John Middleton's insistence that Tunstall was already dead.

Turning anyway, Billy had been dragged by Middleton from his saddle. Then, pinioned by Middleton, Billy had thrashed, trying to bite. "Kid," Dick Brewer had said, "we're leaving. Don't get killed for nothing."

Now, Billy, on Gray Sugar, wandered the trampled clearing of the killing, bright with the low full moon, a bloated illusion of immensity.

He sat on a rock, unaware that murder's blood-soaked ground was only yards away; and wailed as the moon rose to become a small streaked marble in the star-filled sky.

Billy renewed searching, leading Gray Sugar, as red mud accreted on boots and hooves; while he stumbled and struggled against immensity of life-resisting forces; calling, "Mister Tunstall! Long Tom! Mister Tunstall!"

Only an owl competed, whooing death's omen, as night granted only moonlight, confirming that what Billy sought was gone.

SECOND CYCLE

February 18, 1878   8:13 PM   Monday

Farmer, John Newcomb, hearing his neighbor, Dick Brewer, shouting wildly, opened his door to milling mounts. Brewer panted, "Help me! Tunstall's murdered!" and told the others, "Get the Coes. Charlie. Doc. Meet at McSween's!" Brewer dismounted, large confused hands gesturing as if to grasp air. "Help me get a tracker."

By 10:02 PM, freezing wind lamented through the moonlit valley between the Capitan Mountains and the high hills to their south. In the glaring billiard room of the dark House, George Peppin and Jack Long sat with William Brady and John Riley, both drinking heavily. Long remarked that it must be over, causing Riley to panic and whisper drunkenly that they knew nothing. Brady laughed sarcastically and said, "Lay wi' dogs, you rse wi flss."

Abruptly red-headed Riley stood, mumbling about innocence; and stumbled out the front door. At Alexander McSween's, a cluster of fifty local people watched Riley's weaving approach.

In McSween's parlor, crowded with Tunstall's men, Riley slurred, "I'm in'cent;" and, in confused show of weaponlessness, flung pocket contents onto a small table. McSween said gently that his Creator, not them, would judge. Riley fled back to the House.

More people pressed inside the parlor. Alexander McSween announced, "In the morning, I'm going to Fort Stanton to get help from Commander George Purlington." "Squire" Wilson added that he'd appoint Dick Brewer as a Special Constable after the Coroner's Jury inquest. To make arrests. That is, if they found the body.

Fred Waite pointed below the small table. McSween retrieved John Riley's dropped little ledger, holding a folded paper. He thumbed its pages, and declared, in melodramatic suppression of trauma, "Extraordinary! The Lord has revealed to us nefarious House records. Fake cattle sales to the Mescalero Reservation in the thousands!

"And a code!" McSween read aloud: " '*T.B. Catron equals Grapes. L.G. Murphy equals Box. F. Godfroy equals Hampton. Indians equal Trees. W.L. Rynerson equals Oyster. First National Bank of Santa Fe equals Terror.*' And lastly: '*Alexander McSween equals Diablo.*' " There were angry mutterings among those listening.

"Please, please, rejoice. This is all a godsend." He waved the paper. "This is letter from District Attorney Rynerson, dated from Las Cruces, just four days ago - four days before murder." He read: "*Friends Dolan and Riley. If any resist Brady he will do right in arresting him. If Tunstall tries to make trouble, he must do what he has to. It must be made hot for them, as hot as Hell. Shake that McSween outfit up till it shells out and then shake it out of Lincoln. I will help all I can.*" McSween declared, "We've got our proof."

Optimism surged through the frightened crowd.

FEBRUARY 19, 1878   2:03 AM   TUESDAY

Laughing, Jessie Evans and his boys drove seven horses into the Feliz Ranch corral - disoriented blind Colonel having been shot - as Gottfried Gauss peered from the chosa and tearfully said to Henry Brown that all must be dead. After Jessie's gang left, Brown saddled one of Brewer's returned horses; and Gauss sadly watched the last of his young men ride northward to Lincoln in the moonlight.

By daybreak, Alexander McSween, Adolph Barrier, and Dick Brewer were at Fort Stanton, facing bull dog-featured, graying Commander George Purlington, in his Adjutant's office.

When they left, feeling confident of protection, Purlington proceeded to his actual office where William Brady waited. Purlington said, "Sorry, Sheriff. Took time to get rid of them. I got the telegraph from Tom Catron that the Lincoln County War was starting today." Purlington laughed. "How can I help?"

Maintaining a charade of fellow soldier, walrus-mustached Brady said he needed military assistance to conduct his duties. McSween had an armed mob. Purlington said, "Put that in writing for Governor Axtell, so he'll recommend it to General Hatch. Meanwhile, I'll send First Lieutenant Cyrus Delany and a cavalry squad back with you to make sure nothing *untoward* happens in town."

At 9:30 AM, in Lincoln, were two unusual groupings. The first was of sixteen cavalrymen outside the House. A few had also accompanied Sheriff Brady to the Tunstall store, where he gave them hay for their mounts from its rear shed, as McSween surreptitiously observed from the rear of his house. In front of his property was the second group: townspeople and Tunstall's men.

At 10:06 AM, James Dolan, George Hindman, Billy Matthews, and Buck Morton arrived at the House. Soon after, Henry Brown cautiously entered McSween's property from the rear, joining drifting words: "lawless ... a good man ... remember when they killed Robert Casey ... something has to be done ... his poor family."

Fred Waite called out, "Here they come!"

From the west, Billy, erect on Gray Sugar and staring ahead, led death's parade, followed by John Newcomb, driving his mule-drawn buckboard with single cargo; behind which rode the dark weathered tracker, Ramón Barágon. Some who waited had seen corpses brought in like this one. But it was Billy, with his remarkable blue eyes fixed on the unseeable, that sealed the event as momentous.

At McSween's picket fence the wagon stopped. People peered into the bed. And the blanket-wrapped body, with suggestion of head and taper of shoulders to pyramid tip of booted feet, was more gruesome than an exposed corpse; eliciting individual visions of violation.

Billy continued numbly eastward, past the store with the name of a dead man. Someone opened the corral gates in its adobe wall and took his horse. Back on the street, Billy saw the long wrapped object carried through Alexander McSween's front door. He followed.

Men filled the parlor where a carpenter's bench, incongruously present, held the form. When Dick Brewer asked Billy if he had seen the posse, Henry Brown answered: "I did. Bwen I bwas combin' back do de Ranch." Enraged, Billy snarled that he had not warned them. The barely-pigmented youth whined, "I had doe hoss."

McSween said sympathetically to Billy, "God didn't leave John Tunstall alone. He left you with him."

"I couldn't find him," Billy whispered.

John Newcomb interjected, "When we came, buzzards was circling. We heard him shooting. Told us if he couldn't find him, they wouldn't neither."

McSween said to Billy that his testimony at the Coroner's Jury Inquest that afternoon was important. Billy murmured, "I saw what they did to that innocent man." Outside sounded hammering of George Washington, making the coffin.

Disconcertingly, Billy backed to the carpenter's bench, hands wide-spread at its edge: a protector hurled back unconsciously to his mother's death; and decompensating into madness of Michael McCarty.

Newcomb eyed him warily. He said, "The boy, he took over with the body, you see."

McSween asked Billy if he wanted to prepare Tunstall. He nodded, released the rope he had tied, and spread open the blanket.

The face of the corpse was hideous: one side concave and gory, with a naked eyeball protruding from bone shards; and the mouth was painted with blood.

Bizarrely, Billy, lips in silent dialogue, raised up the dripping head, as if assisting its mute testimony.

McSween's stomach contracted. Excusing himself, he rushed through the west wing, through the wall dividing his yard from the Shield's, where the outhouse was located. Inside, he retched and vomited.

When McSween returned to metallic stench of blood, Ramón Barágon addressed him: "Señor, I say to you where Señor Tunstall was find ees not where he dies. He dies thirty yard from trail where ees blood and tracks from many horses. But they takes him then maybe a hundred yard away, and shoots hees horse."

"Hiding him," said John Newcomb. "And worse. They put his horse's privates on him. And his hat on the horse's head. Like it was all a joke."

A guttural exclamation drew attention to Billy. His face was inhuman, grimacing skin contracting eyelids to slits.

He said, "Got to ride," while unholstering his gun ominously, as the fearful men parted and Fred Waite followed protectively.

In the warehouse, Billy emptied hidden cartridge boxes into an empty flour sack. He then saddled Jim French's horse to spare Gray Sugar, and galloped west, with Fred Waite racing after.

At Deadman's Rock, Billy turned into Yginio's valley, where Waite lost him, but heard shots. Waite approached the circling galloping insanity thinking, "Hell of a risk;" and shouted, "Inquest's soon, Kid. Let's head back along the river."

In the clear Bonita, tiny gray-brown fish scattered at their striking shadows. To the boy, staring blankly, Waite said, "Here's an ol' Chickasaw story. About Death. Death demands attention. He walks around and touches people. Some run. Some fight. But one boy ignored him. So Death took someone the boy loved. Then the boy realized he was real." Sun-golden streams ran from Billy's eyes.

At two, Billy, ashen, addressed the six coroner's jurymen, seated at the McSween dining table with Justice of the Peace "Squire" Wilson. If they concluded a murder had occurred, they named those responsible. Present also were Adolph Barrier, David Shield, Harvey Morris, Alexander McSween, Fred Waite, and Dick Brewer, who had already given his testimony; as had John Middleton next to him.

With anguish, Billy said, "I saw what they did to that innocent man. I saw Jessie Evans, Buck Morton, Frank Baker, and Tom Hill chasing us. I know that James Dolan, Billy Matthews, and George

Hindman were involved. Two days before, those three came to the Feliz Ranch - probably to kill him then. But he wasn't there."

When asked by Isaac Ellis about the shooting, Billy shuddered. "I checked his pistol. A Webley Bulldog. Two shots had been fired." He sneered. "That was faked. The shells were ejected. In a gunfight, nobody ejects before firing all the rounds. It was murder."

When all were silent, wrinkle-faced jowly Wilson, with high collar and blunt-cut white hair, said, "Head to the parlor - sorry 'bout him being there, but there's a desk - and write out your report."

After they left, Wilson asked, "You got a complaint too, Alexander?" McSween gave the details of the hay stealing.

When the jurymen returned, Frank Coe, their President, read the report in his loud nasal voice: *"We, the unersigned Coroner's Jury, find that John H. Tunstall came to his death by means o' bullets shot into his head an' body. The persons reesponsible were Jessie Evans, William Morton, Frank Baker, Tom Hill, James Dolan, an' probly others."*

"Thanks," said Wilson. "I'll write out the warrants."

McSween said to him, "To serve them, I suggest that you appoint Fred Waite and Billy Bonney as deputies of Town Constable Atanacio Martinez."

Then McSween addressed them all: "The Fort Stanton Post Surgeon, Doctor Daniel Appel, has been assigned to do the postmortem - probably as a part of the assistance we requested from Commander Purlington. But just two weeks ago, he married Mescalero Reservation Agent Frederick Godfroy's daughter, Kate. Because of my public criticisms of his new father-in-law's dealings, Appel might be biased.

"So, for a second opinion, I've hired Doctor Taylor Ealy, who's just locating his medical practice here with his family."

McSween thought, "I've covered everything. Even Brady's hay theft." But he blocked recognition that he was the obvious next victim.

FEBRUARY 20, 1878   9:11 AM   WEDNESDAY

As Alexander McSween led Deputy Sheriff Adolph Barrier and Town Constable Atanacio Martinez on the street's slushy snow, he held up "Squire" Wilson's arrest warrants and said, "As evil is drawn to evil, these men are at the House;" and handed them to Martinez, who scowled at his coercion into extreme danger.

At the warehouse, they found Fred Waite shaving at a cistern and Billy with carbine ready.

Atanacio Martinez, seeing the boy's arousal, finally felt his own importance in his town's fate, and felt reconciled to his own.

Billy led them past the soldiers ambiguously loitering at the House, and into its billiard room, where Brady sprang up combatively to mask his surprise. George Peppin, Billy Matthews, and Jack Long readied for a fight. First Lieutenant Cyrus Delany, James Dolan, George Hindman and Buck Morton waited tensely at another table.

Atanacio Martinez read names. Brady answered loudly, to make sure Dolan heard, "I don't know anything about Jessie; and anything my possemen did is legal. And I say it's *you* arrre breaking the law. The law as *I* see it.

"Hand over that Winchester," he said to Billy. "We're heading to jail." To Hindman, Long, and Matthews he said, "I could use company, me boys. Town's going to see who's the law here before they appoint *escaped murderers* as deputies. Jimmy wanted you to know, *Henrrry Antrim*, that nobody escapes their past."

Townspeople watching the procession, saw humiliated Atanacio Martinez with head down, and Fred Waite's emerald eyes challenging them to act. Billy was in front, defiantly immune.

Soon, fear emptied the single street.

The group of seven passed the Wortley Hotel and the Mills and Schon houses on their left as they approached McSween's, where he was tensely observing Dr. Ealy examining Tunstall's body.

Across the street was the Stanley's adobe, then the Cisneros house.

In the warehouse, at the rear of John Tunstall's store, Frank MacNab, John Middleton, Henry Brown, and Jim French played poker, unaware of the parade of injustice.

And across the street from the store's adobe corral wall, in his little house near the southern hills, "Squire" Wilson chose to remain snugly inside.

At the vacant lot to their left, on which McSween planned to build a school and church, George Washington watched the procession from beside a long shallow hole, his angry shovel blade cutting the earth.

They passed, on their left, the old Torreon, and east of it, set back on a long path, the Baca house where Josephina was secretly looking out at Washington; and where her bearded, paunchy, bony-legged father, Saturnino, stepped out to be seen by the sheriff.

They passed the courthouse to their right; and the long, one story building, shared by Ike Stockton and José Montaño, as saloon and store respectively, where all stayed hidden.

In the McSween parlor, Dr. Ealy, washing his hands, said, "It was cold-blooded murder."

The procession of seven had passed Juan Patrón's. Beyond, to their left, was the residence and small store of Isaac Ellis.

But they were already at their destination.

George Washington continued to dig red alluvial soil from its bed of centuries, as he sang, "I looked over Jordan, / and what did I see, / Coming for to carry me home? / A band of angels coming after me, / Coming for to carry me home."

Six hundred yards due east of John Henry Tunstall's deepening grave, the three shackled prisoners sat on damp straw mattresses, buried alive in the pit jail.

FEBRUARY 21, 1878   3:05 PM   THURSDAY

When Fort Stanton's Post Surgeon, Dr. Daniel Appel, replaced its sheet, John Tunstall's corpse had additional wounds. Alexander McSween, pale with strain, standing with Adolph Barrier, asked his conclusions.

The authoritative young physician, with closely-trimmed brown beard and mustache, answered with unrestrained animosity, "I only make postmortem reports as complete documents. But I'll tell you basics.

"A bullet fractured the clavicle, cutting its attached subclavicular artery. This would have left him time to fire a weapon. A second bullet caused death by *entering* above the left eye.

"From it, radiated a fracture around the skull - which can only be accounted for by fragility of advanced venereal disease; since both wounds were made at a distance while he was on horseback.

"All that supports the contention that Sheriff Brady's possemen behaved in self-defense. That's also in keeping with bullets having been fired from the deceased's revolver. Venereal disease supports his insanely aggressive behavior."

A half mile east of McSween's house, in the pit jail's semi-darkness, Fred Waite, stroking his hat's eagle feather, said to Billy, "Letting Martinez out yesterday was a compliment: proves it was *us* they're afraid of with Tunstall's funeral tomorrow." Billy was silent.

"So your name's Henry Antrim?" Billy said it was his stepfather's; and the murder was self defense.

Waite said, "So you've met Lady Law. She looks good at a distance. But get in the same bed," he patted the stinking pad, "and you realize she reeks of corruption. She's the whore of anyone with money and power."

Billy sighed. "Remember, Tunstall said that one person can change the world. If you're true to yourself. And don't back down. And don't give up." As he repeated the words, he clung to their promise of sanity and meaning.

FEBRUARY 22, 1878   2:03 PM   FRIDAY

Like fallen clouds, snow patched the vacant lot east of Tunstall's store, where the McSween's piano perched on boards near the open, red earth grave containing the coffin. Alexander McSween thought, "I need Susan so much," while looking at the mourners: townspeople, the Shield family, and Tunstall's men.

McSween commenced with insulating courtroom fervor. "God has brought us here to celebrate the gift we're giving Heaven: John Henry Tunstall." He opened his Bible. This cue brought Susan Gates to the piano, along with Washington and his fiddle. McSween said, "In Job it is written 'If a man shall die, shall he live again?' "

The fiddle-accompanied girl sang sweetly from sheet music, "My faith looks up to Thee, Thou Lamb of Calvary."

McSween continued. "And from Corinthians: 'For as in Adam all die, even so in Christ shall all be made alive.' " Again Susan Gates sang, but joined by McSween's weak tuneful voice: "Jesus, Lover of my soul, / Let me to Thy bosom fly."

Later, above Billy's and Fred Waite's dank pit, bootsteps sounded in the jailhouse. "Funerrral's over," Brady said into the trap, and laughed. "Or maybe, me boys, they're just starting."

Up in the little adobe, Billy asked about their weapons. Brady said, "Get them at the House. But I took a fancy to your Winchester. Spoils of warrr, Kid." Billy's eyes narrowed murderously. That stolen object now embodied the lost man, who had given it to him.

FEBRUARY 23, 1878   11:20 AM   SATURDAY

Alexander McSween again faced his open front door and an anticipatory crowd. He said, "We who've just had a second martyr in Lincoln County are taking a stand. I say second, because we have not forgotten Robert Casey. We've made a Citizens' Committee. And I sent Commander Purlington a letter informing him that Sheriff Brady obstructed our making arrests. To prevent conflict, he ordered his soldiers to accompany us when our Committee repossesses the illegally blocked Tunstall store." Approval was murmured.

"There's more. The murderers made a big mistake: John Tunstall was *British*. The murder of a foreigner can bring about a federal investigation! The eyes of Washington, the eyes of our good President Rutherford B. Hayes, can now look upon our suffering."

Grandly smirking, he grasped his lapels. "So early this morning, I wrote a letter detailing the murder to the British ambassador to the United States, Sir Edward Thornton!" Some cheered.

Dick Brewer, feeling obligation as Tunstall's foreman, suggested that they go to Sheriff Brady and get an explanation. "Squire" Wilson said he had business with him too; and Juan Patrón and Atanacio Martinez could speak for their Citizens' Committee.

Alerted by the soldiers, the sheriff waited on the House walkway, holding Billy's carbine. The boy's furious eyes darted to it.

Wilson spoke first. "Brady, I'm serving you with this here warrant for theft of Tunstall property." Brady said he had a Writ of Attachment. "Not to take Tunstall's hay and use it for soldiers, Will. That's larceny. I can arrest you now; or you can post a two hundred dollar bond." Sourly, Brady agreed to the bail.

Next, Juan Patrón, on behalf of the Citizens' Committee, offered Brady an eight thousand dollar bond for McSween. After it was refused, Atanacio Martinez announced he would again conduct a search for the accused Tunstall murderers. Brady shrugged and stepped aside, knowing they were not there.

Soon, at Atanacio Martinez's request, the soldiers followed their group to the guarded store.

Billy stayed at Brady's side. He said, "I want my carbine back." The man ignored him.

All except William Brady were unaware that eighty-seven miles southwest of the town, James Dolan was galloping to Mesilla to obtain for him an Alias Warrant for the immediate arrest and incarceration of Alexander McSween for failure to post his bail.

By nightfall, in the Tunstall store warehouse, Billy had regressed back to numb oblivion, sitting on the floor, aimlessly studying his Colt .44, while hearing the others at poker: "call," "pass," "standin' pat," "fold." Fred Waite, concerned, hunkered down and spoke. Billy said he was not hungry. Alone again, he heard whooing.

Billy was outside in cold wind, which was only the dream of wind in littoral trees, with a voice that said, "Come to San Patricio."

Billy repeated "San Patricio," as if it was unfamiliar but lovely; and barely felt Yginio Salazar's embrace.

They rode together until the wind became music and he was led by Yginio into a room of music, and heard "dance hall."

Like a sleepwalker, unaware of greetings, Billy stopped at a stucco wall. Its limed bone-whiteness had dancing shadows. With them, he swayed, aware of bones in his feet: his bones on the floor of red clay. All that existed was bone, blood-red clay, and music that animated them. He turned to the room of dancers: all skeletons covered with clay. He was dancing, skeleton jointed, amidst faces which - if the music stopped - would freeze forever or shatter.

Yginio gripped his arm and said, "Billy, you have not stopped dancing." Billy saw skin moving over the skull, blue-grey eyes within their skull, jawbone of the skull moving.

Suddenly, he knew it was magnificent, and laughed and laughed.

Intoxicating spices steamed from Yginio's offered plate. Billy ate ravenously, as a pretty girl drew Yginio into the room of living flesh and notes.

Then Billy was dancing with a girl in his arms. Her skeleton was dancing with his. It was a magnificent joke, a magnificent triumph of bone and clay brought to life. When they stopped, he recognized his partner: María Montez.

Enrique Montez came to them and said, "All of us here in San Patricio know Señor Tunstall died a noble man. We will be here to help. If old Señora Sanchez had not been sick tonight with her weak heart, my wife would have been here too. Come now, María."

Yginio approached and asked Billy, "What happened? You look resurrected."

Billy laughed. "Wonderful to be alive. Dance with Death. It is all a dance."

FEBRUARY 25, 1878   8:12 AM   MONDAY

With deceptive calm, Alexander McSween, at his desk in his parlor, looked up from writing. To David Shield and Adolph Barrier he said, "Please witness my Last Will and Testament." The surprised men complied.

McSween said, "I don't like going into hiding, but you've convinced me, Adolph, that without extreme precautions, I won't stay alive." Shield, restraining a sob, said that was awful.

In defensive cocooning, McSween felt nothing. He said, "Be that as it may, David, I want to keep John Tunstall's business running while I await court. He was sending Billy Bonney with our mail to the Roswell post office, and making Peter Maxwell's regular delivery of cigars and brandy. We'll continue that.

"As for me, I'll stay in Ruidoso farms and San Patricio. John Chisum agrees." He detached his collar and left it on his desk.

Eight and a half hours later, Billy arrived at Roswell. When he had passed Brady's Walnut Grove Ranch, a shot had sounded. He had fired back at the fleeing man on his bald-faced chestnut; but the range was too great for his revolver.

In his post office, bushy-headed Ash Upson was suspiciously resealing a letter. Billy ostentatiously presented McSween's with sealing-waxed backs. Upson, as usual, said, "I'm *positive* I knew you."

Billy remarked that store goods had been added. "Heiskell Jones did that." Upson bent below the counter and held up a jar with powdery, flat, sugar hearts. He said "They're a penny for ten."

Billy gave the coin as John Jones entered by accident, hesitated uncomfortably, and said, "Us Seven Rivers boys had to ride 'gainst Chisum."

Billy said it didn't cancel his debt to their family. Relief swept through Jones. He said, "Glad you're not holdin' a grudge. You're a better shot then me."

After Billy laughed and left, Jones said, "Ash, I wish this goddamn fightin' had never started."

"Not me," the little gnome grinned. "Historians are the world's second oldest profession. I'm waiting to see which side wins. Then I'll write their version." John Jones teased that he took nothing serious. Upson said, "If you'd been doled out my combination of brain and body, you too would have learned the vanity of all human endeavors."

FEBRUARY 26, 1878   3:29 PM   TUESDAY

Billy, on Gray Sugar, was two miles south of Fort Sumner, watching, from a high ridge, the flood-swollen Pecos, crashing uprooted trees into rocks.

Suddenly he saw Paulita on Centauro, her hair wildly blowing, riding recklessly close to known sink holes. She noticed, and galloped to him, calling over the roaring river, "Race you to the water."

Close to the red torrent, she dismounted and said, "Papa loved it like this." She studied Billy quizzically. "You look older."

"By twenty-eight days! I learned new things." He glanced sidelong. "About love." Unimpressed, she looked back at the dangerous waters.

To her lovely profile Billy said, "I brought you something. Guess." Little, she said, because it must be on him. And sweet. Because he would want some too. He said, "You're so smart," and from his jacket withdrew his fist. "Say, 'Please.'"

She refused, saying it was already hers. He laughed. "Then you've got to open this."

She lifted his fist, palm up, sniffed, said it wasn't peppermint, and licked the crevice. His startled hand opened to a candy heart, immediately seized and sucked as she ran.

"Don't swallow," he called out, catching up and laughing until a new feeling placed his hands gently around her shoulders. He murmured, "Just to taste the sweetness," and bent to touch lips to hers.

Her eyes became huge as a fawn's. She said, "That felt like dancing. Can you get more candy like that?" In distracted wonderment, he walked with her, hand in hand, back to their horses.

When they neared the town, Paulita said, "A strange-looking man just arrived. The people gave him a nickname: Juan Largo. Long John. He's all legs. A buffalo hunter. I can tell I don't like him. His real name is Paul, no, Pat Garrett. I heard he's planning to stay. I wish he wouldn't."

When Billy left his Tunstall store delivery with Peter Maxwell, the man asked if the fighting in Lincoln was over. Not yet, Billy answered, and walked the southeast diagonal to the Gutierrez's front door.

Celsa, happy and welcoming, received him. She said, "Saval is away. And I have kept my promise." He did not remember one, but in the bedroom, she unrolled a long, gray, wool muffler. He teased that she had missed big parts. She feigned a pout. "I have no patience for knitting. Still, it will be warm."

Laughing, he tossed its messy webbing, lassoing her close. "Tonight there is no rush," she said. "There is a new side of beef on the north porch of the patrón's house. Cut a piece. I will fry it for you."

From the cupboard, she took out a butcher knife with a riveted wood handle. Its old blade had been honed to a concave belly leaving a rounded tip. With eerie curiosity, Billy asked whether he'd seen it before. "Probably. We cannot change our cutlery like the Maxwells."

From Celsa's door, Billy walked the diagonal northwest across the parade ground to the mansion.

Returning to Celsa's kitchen, he soon inhaled heavy aroma of the sizzling meat. She said, "So you like it almost burnt. The Padre said in the Bible were burnt offerings. Even God liked cowboy steaks." Billy laughed.

Dressed before dawn, he looked down at Celsa, still asleep, while savoring renewal. Then he left, redirecting passion to war.

MARCH 1, 1878   9:15 AM   FRIDAY

Men, assembled inside the Tunstall store, could hear workmen hired by Alexander McSween to replace his house's picket fence with a more secure, adobe wall.

Dick Brewer, overwhelmed by accidental leadership, pressed a V of index finger and thumb into its counterpart in a meaningless grip, and stammered, "S-something's got to be done." Charlie Bowdre, flat-crowned hat tilted, shouted to kill the sonsobitches. Brewer said, "We were Tunstall men. Now we're McSween's. We follow the law."

Billy asked where McCloskey was. "Doing day work at Bob Gilbert's Ranch. Near the Pecos-Peñasco junction." John Middleton asked why Chisum hadn't paid them. Frank MacNab answered that he had just gotten out of jail. Fred Waite commented snidely that they would get copies of his memoirs for pay.

Bowdre, rising on his short legs, said, "Ah want Gauss tah tell us the names o' those goddamn possemen."

Volunteering to write them down, Billy strode to the apartment for equipment. Still on the desk was the Tennyson book. He opened it to a bookmark and saw within inked brackets: "[Then loudly cried the bold Sir Bedivere, / 'Ah! my Lord Arthur, whither shall I go? / Where shall I hide my forehead and my eyes? / For now I see the true old times are dead.']"

When Billy returned with brimming eyes, the old man was behind the glass counter, leaning on both hands like a cannon on a rampart, spitting names as Billy wrote, learning new ones.

After Gottfried Gauss finished, Brewer said to all, "I'm already a Special Constable. You'll be my posse. To arrest them and bring them to jail." Fred Waite laughed, asking if he was serious. They would be in jail as long as it took Brady to ride there on Dandy Dick. Brewer studied his calloused hands. He said, "McSween asked me to be Captain. If you boys don't want me, I'll step down." All were silent.

Encouraged, Brewer said, "Then let's think up a name for ourselves." Billy said he'd also write out their declaration.

"BacSweens," called Henry Brown. "Bwhad beople 're callin' us."

"That leaves out Tunstall," said Billy, visualizing the Deadwood Dick, dime novel. He asked, "How about 'The Regulators?' Men striking blows in defense of justice." All agreed.

Billy wrote, then read aloud: "*REGULATOR MANIFESTO: We declare on March 1, 1878 that we good citizens of Lincoln County do form a group called The Regulators. This is our oath: One. We will bring to justice those who murdered John Tunstall. Two. We will bring to justice anyone who murders any of us. Three. We will never divulge anything that would risk the safety of any Regulator. Four. If any of us gets put in jail we will break them out. Five. Anyone who breaks this oath can be killed by any other member if they want.*" He added, "We could sign in blood."

Brewer said he liked it except for the last two. They had to stay legal. Charlie Bowdre said, "Signin' in blood ain' necessary, 'cause we're willin' tah die."

All gathered at "Squire" Wilson's, where, as Justice of the Peace, he prepared the additional warrants from Gauss's list. Waite asked him about legality of a posse's killing in self-defense. Wilson answered,

"Whad' you think all this rigmarole was for?" Billy listened eagerly when Dick Brewer said some of the murderers had been seen around the Peñasco-Pecos junction. And Bowdre gave his rebel yell.

MARCH 6, 1878   3:48 PM   WEDNESDAY

When Dick Brewer and his posse approached the vegetated Peñasco-Pecos junction, Billy noticed four, distant, dismounted men at cottonwoods; and cried, "Morton and Baker! With Bob Gilbert. And, Dick, I swear, *with McCloskey*!" Waite, MacNab, Middleton, Bowdre, Scurlock, French, and Brown bunched closer.

Billy broke into a gallop, howling mortal combat.

Those pursued raced toward the riverbank's acres of dense green-black giant sacaton grass. Suddenly, Gilbert and another veered away.

Billy, galloping after Morton and Baker, screamed to let those other bastards go. The Regulators followed him.

Stopping at a distance, Bob Gilbert said to William McCloskey, "I'll send word to Dolan. You go join up with 'em. You got paid well before. Right?" The grizzled man considered greedily.

In racing dustfog, Brewer shouted at Billy not to kill them, while the boy was yelling Morton! Baker! and firing reluctantly wild to keep them at an exhausting gallop.

First one of their horses dropped, then the second. Billy pursued the two running men, who scrambled into safety of the solid barrier of inch wide, giant sacaton grass blades, over six feet tall.

"Come out," Brewer, amidst the grouped Regulators, panted at the verdant wall. "I'm Constable. Got warrants."

Frank Baker's voice came: "We ain't got no chance with the Kid." Brewer told Billy to give his word. Like hell he would, Billy hissed.

The high restless grasses scraped in chill wind. Then hoofbeats were heard. William McCloskey called out, "Howdy, boys. Bob Gilbert seen ye was a'chasin Baker an' Morton. 'Cause I'ze a Tunstall man, he sen' me right pronto te help. I knows 'em."

Billy taunted that he'd been right there with them. "No, Kid," McCloskey wheedled. "Gilbert got me at the ranch."

Brewer shouted to the dark grasses: "McCloskey's here!" The vegetation lurched unnaturally. Upraised arms, and occasionally hat tops, were seen, as Morton and Baker used a cattle trail from the river. They then emerged, Baker calling out that they were unarmed.

Billy trotted to them, revolver pointed, swinging a leg over the horn to land on his feet, as Brewer cried out for him not to shoot. Sneering, Billy said, "Give me the goddamn gun, Frank." From his boot, big-jawed Baker withdrew a derringer.

Billy insolently handed it to Brewer, who said they'd camp there; and ordered Jim French to see if Morton's and Baker's horses were alive. "Here?" asked Billy. "Where all their friends know by now?" Brewer repeated here.

MARCH 8, 1878   8:37 PM   FRIDAY

In weak light of a crescent moon, twelve men stopped at South Spring River Ranch as, from outbuildings, John Chisum's cowboys materialized, carbines pointing. Chisum himself ambled up and said, "Heard ye finly hunted somethin' more profitble then wil' turkeys, Dick. I got a room ye kin use tha' remins me fonly o' the Las Vegas jail." To the armed cowboy beside him, who functioned as his bodyguard, Chisum said, "Frank, take 'em in."

Billy said he wasn't leaving them. "Suit yerself. I heard 'bout you, Kid. Didn' figer ye were wearin' tha' hogleg as a watch-charm."

Billy followed to a windowless room with cots. Chisum said to his gunman, "Tell Brewer's boys t' bed down in the secon' bunkhouse.

" 'Im, the Kid, an' you guard these birds. Oly flyin' I'd like for 'em's off a rope." Affably he added to the prisoners, "Bu' yer invited fer dinner."

After they all ate in the dining-room, Frank Baker requested his saddlebag. Billy insisted on emptying it for him on the table. There was a braided horsehair bridle, a gold watch, a pair of sox, and hobbles. "Interestin'," said Chisum. " 'Preciate seein' this."

Both men requested writing implements. Chisum smiled facetiously. "Captivity shur brings ou' tha' writin' urge." He said to his cowboy, Frank, "Git it. Low on envlopes though."

Tense Buck Morton finished quickly, Frank Baker slowly, his prognathous jaw jutting with effort. He slid his paper to Chisum, peacefully smoking a cigar, who read aloud the crude scrawl.

"*Miss Lizzie Lester, 15 Oneida Street, Syracuse, New York Stat. Dear Lizzie. I am sendin you my bes bridel that I made with my own hands and my gold watch. I will not live to see you again lest somebody gets me out of this fix. Your long time friend, Frank Baker.*"

While watching Buck Morton, pencil-mustache blurred in stubble, fold his own letter, Chisum said, "I'd 'gree yer luck's runnin' muddy, Baker. Good idea, though, not sendin' 'er the sox."

Later, alone with Brewer, Chisum observed Billy spreading his bedroll across the prisoners' doorway, and remarked, "Kid's touchy as a teased rattler. An' younger they 're, the more powerful their venom. I wouldn' make a bet on yer prisners occupyin' tha' jail."

MARCH 9, 1878   11:00 AM   SATURDAY

Complying with Buck Morton's request for mailing, Brewer was leading all to Roswell, when Billy noticed McCloskey's attempted conversation with the prisoners. He rode alongside the man and said, "I once knew a gambler. Always cheated the same way. And with the same suckers. Made money. Till he was shot, I mean."

At the post office, Billy followed Morton, Baker, and Dick Brewer inside. Ash Upson said, "An unexpected mélange." Brewer explained that they were going to the Lincoln jail.

"We ain' gonna make it," said big-jawed Frank Baker, handing Upson his addressed package. "Kid 'ill kill us. He's a murderer, Ash. Jessie tol' me; an' Dolan tol' 'im. Real name's Henry Antrim. Killt a man in Arezona Terretory." Brewer glanced askance at Billy. "'Scaped. Come here jus' five months 'go."

As slim-hipped miserable Buck Morton requested an envelope, Upson's hairy face became alive with memory. "Little Henry Antrim of Silver City! Mother a jolly Irish lady. Don't you remember me, Kid? I boarded with you. Something else. You and I have the same birthday. Old Ash is still alive and well inside this brain!"

Billy did not respond, but Upson continued eagerly, "Buck, did you really kill Tunstall?"

Billy said, "In cold blood. Along with Frank Baker, Jessie Evans, Tom Hill, George Davis, Buckshot Roberts, George Hindman, Jack Long, Billy Matthews, Manuel Segovia 'the Indian;' and behind it James Dolan and the Santa Fe Ring - with Sheriff Brady as a front."

Upson gloated, "All on your list, eh, Kid? Frontier justice. I can see it now. The loyal frontier boy avenges the death of his boss amidst the conflagration of a great range war and stampeding cattle. Kid," he said, handing him a candy heart, "I also remember you like these."

After they left, the little bearded man unfolded Morton's letter, scanned its address to Richmond, Virginia, and read: *"Dear H.H. Marshall. The 6th March I was arrested by a Constable party and accused of the murder of Tunstall. Nearly all the Sheriff's party fired at him so it is impossible to say who killed him. One man wanted to kill me after I had surrendered and was restrained with the greatest difficulty. We are enroute to Lincoln. If they kill me I want the parties dealt with."*

Next, Ash Upson jotted on a blank paper: *"Silver City, Catherine Antrim. Murder - Arizona Territory. Billy Bonney, The Kid, November 23, 1859."* He labeled a folder: *"The Authentic Life of a Kid Named Billy: A Frontier Saga of Blood, Range War, and Adventure in the Wild Frontier Territory of New Mexico, Written by the Actual Observer of All That Occurred, Marshall Ashmun Upson, One Time Reporter for The New York Tribune.*" Into the folder went the paper and a copy of Morton's letter. Upson's book was begun.

At 2:33 PM, Dick Brewer, ignoring Billy's warning, was leading his group on the main thoroughfare toward Lincoln, thirty-three miles to the west. Billy commented, "Tunstall's birthday was the sixth. Three days ago." Waite asked if he was planning presents.

An approaching dust cloud was seen. Soon, Billy called out, "Yginio Salazar. Martin Chávez. Friends." Those agitated riders, on lathered animals, spoke. Billy translated. "Dolan sent out twenty men against us. Either you shoot me, Dick; or I kill Morton and Baker; or we ride north to the Blackwater Canyon military trail."

Yginio and young swarthy Martin Chávez watched them enter the flatlands, whose only landmark was the easternmost face of the Capitan range; with its base lost in glowing mist, rendering its looming granite unattached and hovering.

Hours passed as twelve, infinitesimally small, man-horse forms marched through grass blowing reedy lament in oceanic dimensions; as twelve thousand feet above raced billowing cumulous clouds weighing almost six hundred tons.

Cloud shadows also fluctuated sunlight twenty-eight miles west of Dick Brewer's posse, in the House office, where James Dolan spoke, from behind its desk, to Governor Samuel Beach Axtell; Commander George Purlington, in dress uniform with saber and sidearm; Lawrence Murphy; David Shield; and Isaac Ellis.

As clean-shaven, almost sixty year old Axtell listened, he hunched sharp shoulders toward his ears. Puckered skin encircled his beady eyes, and his arched nose overhung purplish lips. Dolan said to that vulturous creature, "Larry has risen from his sickbed to attend, Governor."

Shield offered to summarize for Axtell the grievances, preliminary to their Citizens' Committee's meeting. Axtell responded that he had already taken the necessary measures; and addressed Dolan: "Catron got Brady's letter justifying his posse's actions. You've got my proclamation for posting on the courthouse door? And Wilson's copy?" Dolan nodded complacently.

"Your citizens' meeting's unnecessary," Axtell said to David Shield and Isaac Ellis. "But you can stay and read it." As he walked out with Purlington, Axtell said, "Give my best to Will Brady, Jimmy."

Dolan slid calligraphy, signed by the governor, across his desk. Shield and Ellis read: "*PROCLAMATION TO THE CITIZENS OF LINCOLN COUNTY. The disturbed conditions of affairs at the County Seat brings me to Lincoln. My object is to assist good* *citizens to uphold the laws and to keep the peace. It is important that the following facts be clearly understood. 1st John B. Wilson's appointment by the County Commissioners as a Justice of the Peace was illegal, therefore all his appointments are void and he has no authority whatsoever. 2nd: His appointment of Richard Brewer as a Constable has been revoked, so Brewer is not a peace officer and his appointments are consequently invalid. 3rd: It follows that there exist no legal processes except those issued out of the Third Judicial District Court by Judge Bristol, and there are no Territorial Officers here to enforce them except Sheriff Brady and his deputies."*

At 4:56 PM, Dick Brewer called out over dolorous plains wind, "We'll camp in the Blackwater arroyo. Walls are fifteen feet, so our fire can't be seen." Giant sacaton grass traced that ravine, slicing through the lowland of Blackwater Canyon, which, in spring melting and summer rains, became a conduit for massive runoff of the Capitan Mountains and eastward sloping plains.

Fred Waite said the only way through the grass was a cattle trail. For the single file, Brewer said he'd go first; then McCloskey, Morton, Baker; then the Kid; then everybody else. Ignoring Charlie Bowdre's shout that the canyon's black walnut trees were good for hangings, Brewer led, as blade-tips along the uneven path reached their waists or knees, as if they were wave-tossed vessels in a dark sea.

Brewer descended Blackwater's steep arroyo bank, rimmed by the rough-barked, twisted, lonely black walnut trees, spaced by inhibitory toxins they secreted through roots; and was relieved to see that its flat bed, thirty feet across, was dry. To his left was the junction of a comparable, but unnamed, channel, in whose deep cover they could ride westward the following day.

Once on the ravine's floor, William McCloskey immediately slipped Buck Morton his Colt .44, and spurred his horse to the opposite incline.

Following him, Morton aimed at Billy, whose revolver's front-sight blade was already a slit at McCloskey's head. At the report of Billy's gun, Morton's horse shied, deflecting his own shot.

Buck Morton lunged, with Frank Baker, up the steep incline. With a bloodcurdling yell, Billy passed tumbling McCloskey, followed by the others in pursuit of the two striving to round a small hill.

Buck Morton's last thought, before Billy's lead entered his skull, was "four bullets left." Then, hearing the boy's cry of murderous triumph, Frank Baker felt only impact of a bullet piercing his heart.

Other bullets from Bowdre, Middleton, French and Brown riddled Morton's and Baker's fallen bodies, landed with limbs in impossible positions, and soaking blood into earth so thirsty that, within the hour, it would descend one foot.

Brewer arrived at the carnage with harrowed expression. He said, "I'll ride to Lincoln. Tell Wilson they were resisting arrest. But McCloskey? What what should I say about McCloskey?"

Bowdre answered, "Morton grabbed his pistol an' shot him."

In a startlingly placid voice, Billy said, "I know a local sheepherder. He'll bury them." Brewer said they shouldn't come with him to Lincoln. "They're waiting for us in San Patricio," Billy responded. He seemed to smile, until it became a chilling sneer.

MARCH 18, 1878   10:18 AM   MONDAY

With Charlie Bowdre, Billy entered Dick Brewer's crowded farmhouse and embraced Yginio Salazar, saying, "You saved us." His thin friend smiled.

Brewer began their meeting of Tunstall employees, townspeople, and some San Patricio men with announcements, saying, "McSween came back to Lincoln last Monday - of course, with Deputy Barrier. But after Governor Axtell's proclamation, he went to Chisum's. And his wife's back too.

"And I still don't like what happened with Morton and Baker."

"Rather have 'em loose?" asked Bowdre angrily. "Shootin' at us like goddamn bounty hunter, Buckshot Roberts, jus' did at the Kid an' me." Men turned murmuring.

Brewer said, "When I got in last night, I went to Wilson's. It was the worst night of my life - besides Tunstall. Wilson couldn't believe it. What the governor did to him and us is illegal."

"It's obviouth. He'th a Ring tool," said pear-shaped Scurlock.

Brewer continued, "Here's good news. McSween told me an man's come to Chisum's named Montague Leverson - a naturalized British citizen from Colorado. Leverson knows the British ambassador and President Hayes. McSween said now we'd win.

"And the other side's having problems. Dolan broke his leg last Saturday jumping off his horse to shoot at an unarmed man. I heard it was you, Juan." Patrón, in his poor-quality suit, said he would rather not make accusations. Brewer said, "And Tom Hill's dead. Two days ago, Jessie and him were near Shedd's, at the camp of a German, John Wagner, who was bringing a herd of sheep from California. Wagner's Cherokee partner shot Hill and got Jessie's right wrist too. Jessie's at Fort Stanton for treatment."

Fred Waite joked, "Seems all we Regulators need to do is stay home." Several laughed.

"I propose," said Frank MacNab, carrying out clandestine orders, "that we let Seven Rivers boys know the Regulators stand against their Chisum rustling."

"I say it's a bad idea: making them fight us," said Billy.

John Middleton said, "Ask that bastard why he hasn' paid us."

"And don't forget," said Fred Waite, "the Kid and I were promised a ranch." Waite chuckled. "When history looks at the Lincoln County War, they can't say the Regulators did it for money."

"Libertad!" called out Yginio Salazar, as all felt the fervor.

MARCH 21, 1878   8:23 AM   THURSDAY

Riding Gray Sugar northward, over pine-covered ridges from the Coe farm, Billy was whistling "Turkey in the Straw," when shots rang out. Firing futilely while galloping in Billy Matthews's direction, he saw the man reach the main road to Lincoln.

Billy paused to stroke his mare's satin neck. "Sure wish I had my Winchester," he said, before continuing.

MARCH 23, 1878   10:52 AM   SATURDAY

"Heard you've been fighting in that Lincoln war," said gangly Bob Hargrove in his saloon. "And you're called 'the Kid'. And you're eighteen. And you've killed as many men as you've got years."

Billy smiled, and said the last part wasn't true. Carrying his coffee cup, he joined poker players, including Barney Mason, and ignored his hawk-faced expression of dislike. Exiting hours later, Billy passed an entering, extremely tall man, with a buffalo skin coat, saying to a companion, "And on that day I got two hundred buffs."

Billy walked toward the mansion. For the first time since the Morton and Baker shootings, he noticed that his woolen coat was littered with burs and spikes of needle grass from the remote site.

He brushed and picked, attempting to look more presentable. And the myriad seeds that had ridden with him for over two hundred miles became free-flying sparks of life in wind. The death of one man, which had lead to the death of three, had brought this boy here for their liberation into the current of life flowing through forty thousand miles of flatlands; theirs now for hundreds, perhaps thousands, of years.

Luz Maxwell welcomed Billy with obvious pleasure as he offered a dance lesson. Left alone in the big drawing-room while she searched for Paulita, he noticed a large oil portrait of Lucien Maxwell, and smiled at the rebellious image of the immensely rich man posing with a big cigar, untamed hair, and wide-brimmed black hat.

When Luz Maxwell returned, she said "Paulita's going out of her way to dress. Oh, my."

After the lesson, accompanying Billy back to Gray Sugar's stall in the stable, Paulita asked, "Why didn't you come for so long?" He explained there was a war in Lincoln County. "Promise you won't let the bad men kill you." He asked why she wanted that promise. "Because I'd miss you so much."

From a skirt pocket, she took a small polished turquoise nugget, and said, "This was Papa's. It's from Persia. It's the same color as his eyes and your eyes. It's for you - for good luck. It's like the sky."

Billy put it in his vest and said, "Thanks. Now I have luck and my own piece of Heaven." Forgotten were the eyes and heart of silver swallows, and the melancholy that their beauty had not prevented death. But he hugged Paulita tightly.

MARCH 24, 1878   2:23 PM   SUNDAY

John Chisum, on his chair of rawhide-bound long horns, was comparing red-headed Susan McSween favorably to fancy women he kept in Las Vegas. In purple, scooped daringly for daytime to her collar bones, she said, "It's outrageous," and glanced at the wet tip of his cigar. "Sacre bleu. That proclamation makes my blood boil."

He chuckled. "Seems yev got pleny o' heat t' boil it."

She looked to her husband, formally dressed in the safety of South Spring River Ranch, then at Adolph Barrier and at Chisum's brothers, Pitzer and James. Pitzer's round face, with handlebar mustache like John's, was directed to the window where workmen were laying monumental foundations for a new house. Coarse James, with stubbled cheeks sunken by missing teeth, drawled, "Think me an' Pitzer 'ill check the boys. One Chisum jawin' is 'nough."

Susan McSween addressed the last man. "Mister Leverson, your countryman's murder must make your blood boil too?" He nodded somberly, sparse-haired and puffing a Meerschaum pipe.

She persisted: "If Governor Axtell says that posse was illegal, it means everything Justice of the Peace Wilson did was." Her eyes flashed wickedly. "So couples he married are living in sin." John Chisum laughed. She said, "Evil men are silly."

"Evil men must be fought," said Montegue Leverson pompously.

"Men, men, men," she said with distaste, but smiled misleadingly. "There's a missing piece in men's brains. Us women have feelings; but unlike animals, *we* control them."

Chisum's eyes, with leathery splays, were merry. "But anmils shur have fun." She said that was shameful to say.

He chuckled. "Alexander, she's oly been 'ere a week, an' I'm henpecked." McSween, slumping, said she was impossible to fight; while Chisum decided he was a poor specimen of a man.

"My good people," said Montegue Leverson, "what you have endured! I visit John and learn he's been in jail. Inconceivable. Then occurs a murder implicating Territorial officials. Incredible. And ensues citizens fighting injustice. Inspiring. Consequently, I said to myself, 'This Lincoln County War's for you.'

"I see it as a grand game of chess. Against their rooks I shall move - as Alexander tried - my friend, Ambassador Edward Thornton; as well as Secretary of the Interior Carl Schurz. Against their knights, I shall move my friends in the British Foreign Office. And against their king, Thomas Benton Catron, I advance my friend, President Rutherford B. Hayes."

Chisum said he'd vote for Sam Colt and his jury of six. Ignoring him, Montegue Leverson continued, "All this is my stepping stone to New Mexico Territory's governorship."

When he exited, Chisum said to McSween, "Montague's aways 'cited 'bout some damn cause. 'Is odds o' bein' govnor 're the same as a wax cat's in Hell.

"An' seems neither o' you believes corruption's jis' 'nother word fer govment."

MARCH 28, 1878   1:17 PM   THURSDAY

Looking out through gray rain, John Chisum said, "Prolly is a good time for Alexander an' Depity Barrier t' occupy a bunkhouse. In less time then a hoss's tail flicks a fly, we'll be receivin' the Sheriff of Lincoln County with a considerble herd o' soldiers."

Shocked, Montegue Leverson hurried away also.

Left with Susan McSween, Chisum said, "Le's me an' you meet the enmy with a smile." She smiled malignantly, saying she'd meet them with what they deserved. "Bible shur doesn' constrain you - unlike yer better half."

Under the porch shelter, John Chisum and Susan McSween faced seventeen drenched men, fifteen mounted. William Brady and the sole officer sloshed to them through mud. She asked the sheriff what he was doing with soldiers. Taken aback by her presence, Brady said they were his posse.

The slim fair officer, politely touched the brim of his cap, no protection from rain dripping down the neck of his dark-blue cape. He said, "Ma'am, I'm Second Lieutenant George Smith. Seeing as Lincoln citizens refused, it fell to us. It's our intent, Ma'am ..."

"This is McSween's wife," said Brady irascibly. "I'm here to arrest your husband with an Alias Warrant for not paying bail in lieu of imprisonment."

"He's not here. And I don't know what you're talking about."

"Howdy, Brady," Chisum said. "Lieutenan', I'm owner o' this here spread."

Second Lieutenant Smith lied. "Though the sheriff called us a posse, we're here on separate missions, Sir. I'm offering Fort Stanton's protection to this lady's husband till the Grand Jury next month. Missus McSween, you can make a football of my head if a hair of Alexander McSween is injured. We'd accompany him to the fort from wherever he wants."

Brady added, "You'rrre choosing between the Grand Jury or Coroner's Jury."

"Thank you for confessing your tactics. John and me will discuss it," she said.

Before following her inside, Chisum said to the drenched men, "This might help. I deal with rain by thinkin' 'bout good grass."

Soon Montegue Leverson reemerged and contributed that Smith sounded like a man of his word. Susan McSween added that Barrier simply wasn't enough protection. "I agree," said Chisum seriously.

Back outside, Chisum said, "Brady, how 'bout yer headin' back t' yer friens in Lincoln? An' you, Lieutenan', how 'bout you an' yer boys waitin' on the road 'tween 'ere an' there, so McSween - if we fin' 'im - kin meet up with ye. An', Brady - if we fin' 'im - me, 'is wife, an' a frien' o' mine 'ill travel there with 'im in my carriage.

"John Tunstall taught us a lesson: ride with so many unarmed citzens tha', if you boys try that self-defense story agin, it 'id be deeclared murder. Murder o' the coroner's jurymen. They'd die laughin'." He walked back in, slamming his door.

MARCH 30, 1878   7:10 AM   FRIDAY

In cold pouring rain, Billy, Frank MacNab, Fred Waite, John Middleton, Jim French, and Henry Brown, were riding, at Chisum's request, from San Patricio to his South Spring River Ranch.

Billy asked MacNab why Chisum's messenger had told him that Mac was returning to Lincoln so soon. Brady would kill him.

MacNab said, "Brady can kill only if he's alive." Waite asked if that was his idea or Chisum's. MacNab responded evasively: "Only Brady and his deputies can murder legally."

By afternoon, rainwater still poured from viga beam drainspouts at South Spring River Ranch. In its large sitting-room, McSween paced, bent in weariness and agitation. His wife, sitting near Montegue Leverson, asked Chisum why he'd never married. "Haven' foun' a gal willin' t' court me 'nough." He smiled provocatively.

They heard hoofbeats. Chisum checked and said, "Our troops'. Alexander, will yer boys do whaever ye need?"

Missing the implication, McSween answered, "John once said, 'One's like black powder, the rest like lead bullets. One makes the others move.' Then I didn't know their names ..."

"Sacre bleu. Why should you, dear? They're only hired hands," said his wife.

McSween gave Billy's name. Chisum said, "I met 'im when 'is prisners could still fertell their future. Some hosses 're too rank t' break. Those need shootin'."

Susan McSween stood, patting her coiffed curls and smoothing her brown and yellow skirts with low bustle, purchased in St. Louis with assurance of its fashion come-back. She said, "Mister Leverson and me will pack, while you both deal with broncos." Her brittle laughter sounded in the hall.

"Tha' gal doesn' scare easy," said Chisum. McSween admitted that she insisted they stay. "Any more o' her bloodline where ye got 'er?"

They heard Billy, Waite, French, Middleton, and Brown, hanging tarpaulin coats on pegs.

Billy entered first, scanning.

The wide room had two windows big enough for escape. Its door was to the right, with an expanse of wall to the left. McSween was on a chair beside a big fireplace. Billy stopped with back to the wall. The others choose seats.

McSween felt the men's intense focus on him, like being encircled by wolves. His bowels spasmed. "Glad you all came," he said, rushing out.

Inside the privy building, he was barely able to pull down his pants to avoid explosive diarrhea. With buttocks trembling, he prayed, "Thy will be done."

When Alexander McSween returned, Billy, concealing rage, said, "Mac, the best man I've ever known is dead. We've got a list of those responsible. I'm trying to decide if you belong on it."

Armed, he swaggered right up to McSween. "D'you admit that keeping that Fritz money killed Tunstall by giving the excuse?"

McSween said, "Like me, John Tunstall believed we had to get rid of the Ring-connected Murphy-Dolan House. I accept that my body too may be the dam against the flow of money into its coffers of evil."

The boy's face twitched involuntarily as he asked if Tunstall had wanted that Fritz money where it was. "Yes. He knew everything I did." Saying he got his answer, with new affection for McSween, Billy returned to the wall.

Stimulated, McSween said to the group, "We are all the children of a loving father who watches over us and waits with open arms to receive us forever."

Chisum stepped in and said, "Boys, i's soundin' like a church. Go t' the bunkhouse. Cookie Sam 'ill give ye coffee. Then I'll give ye my thoughts, an' git this drive movin'."

Billy exited into the pouring rain. In concealment of a low ridge, he hunkered down and watched a red rivulet at his feet. Suddenly, his body was racked by sobs, releasing first full grief in the forty days since Tunstall's murder; and releasing his longing for that man.

Even greater depths of pain were plumbed at McSween's image of a divinity, like a father he had never known, who could wait with open arms to receive a wandering child. Billy sobbed until sorrow drained to quietness. But in the red water he saw flowing blood, and looked up. "God," he said into the storm, "I'll give you a show. Just keep watching."

For the regathered group, Chisum drawled, "Wha' we've got is the law turned upsi'down. We've got warrans; bu' *Brady* blocked 'em. Govnor Axtell made a proclamation makin' *Brady* the oly law."

Manipulatively, he eyed Billy. "An', jis' a day 'go, *Brady* was here with soldiers sayin' they'd pretect Alexander - an' convinced Depity Barrier t' leave. Git my drift?"

McSween spoke, oblivious to the violent provocations. "Myself, my wife, John, and our friend, Attorney Montague Leverson, plan to arrive in Lincoln by mid-day on the first.

"Then I'll proceed to Fort Stanton for that promised protection till my trial. The rain delayed us, and we missed that military escort.

"So I'd like you all to go to Lincoln before me. My goal, like John Tunstall's, is peace." But from his words his men received only confirmation of Chisum's message of danger. And white rage burned in Billy's brain. Its object was Sheriff William Brady.

MARCH 31, 1878   10:56 PM   SUNDAY

In darkness and torrential downpour, the six Regulators veered southward from the Capitan Mountains; their hoofbeats pounding the drowning earth, dark as butchered meat, with murderous beat of: "It is ... Bra ... dy. It is ... Bra ... dy."

Frank MacNab alone felt the brutal weather and longed for their sheltering destination: the Tunstall store warehouse.

When its door opened, Gottfried Gauss, there as caretaker, embraced Billy emotionally, saying, "But it iz too dangerous vor you in Lincoln." Billy said Mac was coming the next day. They had come to protect him from Brady. Gauss collected himself. "Yavoll. Zo my boys is back."

After they ate, Billy began to clean his revolver. To no one in particular, he said, "Sure wish I had my Winchester." But the men watched as if he was performing a ceremony of war for them all.

APRIL 1, 1878   6:09 AM   MONDAY

Extremely aroused, Billy returned through the Tunstall store's warehouse door, which briefly framed dead light of a storm-filled dawn; and said, "Best place for activity is behind that gated adobe wall. You can see the street to the east, and - though the store blocks - you can make out enough to the west."

He sneered. "Today the Regulators are going to equalize. John, you take first watch. " Let's use a two whistle signal for Brady." He made it: shrill, but bird-like.

At 7:03 AM, after Middleton's signal, the other five crouched at the corral's slatted gate and peered through at Brady arriving on his fancy sorrel, Dandy Dick. Henry Brown asked Billy what he thought.

"I'd gamble on getting a full house: waiting for the deputies. I'd bet they'll all be heading east to ambush Mac."

"You're the boss," said MacNab, as they reentered the warehouse. Chisum seemed to think he was, Billy responded. "Might. But the way he pays, he's lucky I'm here at all."

Billy's glance was so lethal that MacNab added, "I'll do my job. But it's not burning in me like you."

Billy hissed, "Fight 'cause you believe in it, or get out."

"Easy, Kid," Fred Waite said. "Save it for the enemy."

In foggy drizzle, a half mile west of the Tunstall property, William Brady was leaving his horse at the House stable.

That morning, his wife, María Bonifacia Chaves Brady, pregnant with their ninth child, had insisted that he wear his heaviest overcoat, since he had a cold. His heavy-cheeked face with huge mustache convulsed in a sneeze.

Entering the House, he was met by Dolan, using a silver-headed cane for his healing fractured fibula, and directing him to the office.

There, Brady bantered, "You've been working me harrrd, Jimmy. Nothing but a flea can be in two places at once."

"Listen to me, Will. I am at a loss. Why didn't you serve that Alias Warrant on McSween? And why wasn't he dead *before* I had to get it?" Sneezing, Brady said things were harder without Jessie.

"Let me be more clear, Will. Catron is *very* concerned, *very* concerned about McSween's increasing following, and his public targeting of himself and Rynerson." Brady grumbled that it was not his fault.

"I say it *is*, Will. *Listen to me.* Jessie may be indisposed. John Kinney is not. And Kinney has no sentimentality about women and children - *including yours.*"

The terrier-like face was aghast. "Now that you understand your job, tell me what you think about Billy Bonney."

Brady sneezed, too upset to wipe his nose, draining onto his mustache. He said, "Worst hard case I've seen. Needs brrreaking bad."

"Will, Will, you are so slow. McSween is just a bag of wind. If not for Bonney, he would have handed over the Fritz money. You fought Indians. You know that defeating the Apaches would be finished if not for Victorio.

"One man makes the difference. They are freaks of nature - like a match put to dry grass that can burn for miles. Billy Bonney is not just a hard case. He is our most dangerous enemy. He must be *killed*.

"And Saturnino Baca told me Bonney's threat to us is increasing. He's bringing Mexicans to the McSween cause. Think of this, Will. If they used their power politically, economically, and numerically, they could control this Territory. In fact, we have been saved only because Bonney is still unaware of his power."

Brady's eyes wandered in aimless anxiety. "Ah, Will, I have fatigued you. But you have a chance to redeem yourself. Our friend, Second Lieutenant George Smith, informed me that, when McSween canceled his military escort, he wrote that he would be arriving here today with John Chisum. Listen now. I *predict* two deaths in Lincoln town today."

In the billiard room, after drinking whiskey, Brady said to George Hindman, George Peppin, Jack Long, and Billy Matthews, "Jimmy's nominated us as McSween's welcoming committee."

At the House exit, he lifted a Winchester carbine from the gunrack and said, "This was Billy Bonney's. According to our grrreat leader, Jimmy, his will be a name to remember - unless we eliminate him. But, me boys, first we have other eliminating on our list for today."

It was 8:58 AM. Rain-filled wagon ruts shone like sword blades as Brady and his deputies sloshed eastward on the muddy red street which, in a quarter mile, led past the Tunstall store corral's gated adobe wall, where waited the teenager, Billy Bonney. The inhuman expression on his face would have turned them back.

Brady said, "And once again this was not the long deserved Deluge," the alcohol diminishing the sting of Dolan's words and stimulating martial enthusiasm. Playfully he rested Billy's carbine on his shoulder, as if in a marching drill. Passing the McSween house to their left, he noticed approaching townswoman, Mrs. Ham Mills. "Top o' the mornin'," he called, doffing his hat.

"And how you are, Shereeff Brady? Eet ees cold today, no?"

"Feeling my rheumatism. But as they say, 'The older the fiddle the sweeter the tune.' You must be happy tis not your husband, Ham, who's sherrriff in these wicked times." She acknowledged stiffly, ashamed of her abandonment by that absconding spouse. Brady continued, "And tired I am of being blamed for everything in Lincoln County. But the Irish only forgive their grrreat men after they're buried." Laughing heartily, he called out loudly to his men, who had continued eastward.

Billy heard him. Two whistles of a bird that did not exist sounded in the cold mist. Twenty-five feet northeast of Billy's ferocious eyes lay John Tunstall's body. He was aware of that.

Brady, catching up with Billy Matthews, just as they passed the east side of the Tunstall building, said, "At least Tunstall ..."

Gunfire cracked from five Winchester carbines and a Colt .44.

Peppin and Long sprinted to the Torreon.

One wayward missile crossed the street and ripped through "Squire" Wilson's buttocks as he bent over his onion patch two hundred seventy yards away.

Matthews froze long enough to see Brady briefly suspended, heavy body resisting bullet impacts. One entered his left temple and sprayed out brain. Brady was dead when he splashed into puddling mud.

Matthews ran westward to the Cisneros house.

Then the only sound was the groaning of George Hindman with a bullet in his chest. In adrenalin fueled run, he had managed to pass the courthouse before dropping to his rear, legs akimbo, terrified by sharp hot pain; and thinking, "I'm going to die."

Skinny-legged Ike Stockton bravely raced from the Montaño building and lifted him. A shot rang out. Hindman's head jerked. Fred Waite smiled tightly, smoke wafting from his carbine muzzle. Horrified, Stockton dropped the dead man, and sped back to his saloon.

Suddenly, the gate in the adobe wall swung open. Out ran Billy and Jim French to Brady's corpse. Billy crouched and grabbed his Winchester. He was rising, shouting glory, when Billy Matthews's shots came from an east window of the Cisneros house. Billy did not even wince as a bullet cut below his left hip. It continued through the thigh of screaming French. Billy half dragged him along the protective east side of the building and through the gate.

"Got Tunstall's Winchester!" Billy crowed ecstatically inside the corral. Then he asked, "Frenchie, can you ride?" He whimpered no, while squeezing his thigh, streaming blood.

As Fred Waite made a tourniquet, Billy shouted to the others to get the horses. He yelled to Gottfried Gauss, at the warehouse, "Get saws and an ax."

Through the back door to Tunstall's apartment, Billy hauled Jim French saying, "I'll come back for you tonight." Hoping to conceal the bleeding, Billy laid him on an oriental rug. Gauss returned.

"Floor boards," Billy said. "Hollow underneath." He stomped to find cross-supports, then deftly axed a wedge so Gauss could saw open a big trapdoor. On the dirt, French was laid, holding his Colt .44, as if in ritual burial.

Galloping westward from the open, adobe wall gate, with his triumphant fellows, emerald-eyed Fred Waite noted that Brady lay at the center of the street and center of Lincoln. "Bull's-eye!" he shouted.

Soon Billy noticed that his left leg felt wet and pants were torn. To Waite he joked, "After this, I'll need new trousers to look my best in public." He added, "Sure wish I'd had my carbine. I was trying to get Matthews, but needed that extra range." Then, under his right leg, he felt its scabbarded beloved form, smiled, and called out, "To San Patricio! The Regulators did it! Brady is dead!"

APRIL 3, 1878   8:36 PM   WEDNESDAY

High in the Sierra Blanca Mountains, west of Ruidoso farmland, Regulators and San Patricio men congregated at a bonfire celebrating McSween's return. Hunkered down with a stick, Billy aggressively poked its fire-filled logs to spray fierce sparks.

George Coe said to his cousin, "With grama grass hay to Fort Stanton going at sixty dollars a ton, I think we'll finally pay off our mowing machine. Got your corn in, Dick?"

Charlie Bowdre called, "How the hell can we farm? What with goddamn bounty hunter, Buckshot Roberts, shootin' at us."

Doc Scurlock, intoxicated like Bowdre, sang to the tune of "John Brown's Body," "Will Brady's body lieth a'molderin' in the grave."

"I didn't like what happened," said Dick Brewer. "But otherwise McSween would be dead today."

Jim French added shrilly, "An' I'd be dead if Billy hadn' come back for me. Ol' Gauss, he'd got me Doc Ealy. Ealy pusht a wrapped fire poker clear through, an' bandaged me up. Uner them boards agin, I heerd them goddamn Dolans so close I coulda toucht their goddamn boots."

"I'd 'ave shot Brady myself if I was there," boasted George Coe. "A bastard. In seventy-six - when he arrested me and Doc, saying we'd protected Freeman after that shooting he did in Lincoln - he sat us bareback on my bony old horse, and hobbled our feet under the belly; and led us to Lincoln just to torture us, 'cause there was no jail then. If that horse had run, we'da been killed."

Bowdre shouted, "We're soldiers!" He gave a rebel yell.

Billy glanced mischievously, jabbed the wood with his stick, and, into surging flames, surreptitiously tossed cartridges.

At their deafening reports, all ran in panic. Only long-haired Fred Waite, with golden eagle feather in hatband, stayed, aiming Colt .44 at the fire, while Billy laughed and called, "Army. Battle's over."

As the embarrassed men slunk back, Brown said the place had seemed safe. Billy responded, "No place is safe for a Regulator now. We're in a high stakes game. I'll bring you boys up to date. Yesterday, I rode into town with Yginio Salazar and met with Juan Patrón ..."

"In broad daylight," interrupted George Coe. "The day after Brady and Hindman?"

"Actually," Billy said, "riding out, we *did* run into Peppin. He went for his gun, but by then mine was drawn; so he decided to let us alone.

"But here's the serious part. I found out from Juan Patrón that about two hours after the Brady thing, Mac, Chisum, Missus McSween, and their friend, Leverson, arrived in town. But Peppin got Commander Purlington and soldiers to meet 'em. Peppin arrested Mac with something called an Alias Warrant; even though Mac said that was illegal, 'cause Peppin couldn't be a deputy of a dead sheriff.

"Didn't stop Peppin from arresting Attorney Shield and George Washington too. Said they helped kill Brady and Hindman. Then Purlington searched Mac's house and Tunstall's store.

"Leverson's a lawyer, so he told Purlington the Constitution prevents search without a warrant. Juan said Purlington told Leverson, 'Damn the Constitution and you for an ass.'

"Anyway, the soldiers took the men to Fort Stanton. And Missus McSween insisted on going too.

"Leverson stayed at Patrón's and wrote letters. Juan showed me a copy of one to President Hayes. It gave our side of the Brady-Hindman send-offs.

"Leverson went back to Santa Fe today. But this is our war.

"And we just got a new Regulator job. Yesterday, Tunstall's horses were stolen from the Feliz Ranch by Jessie's boys, and taken to the Mescalero Reservation or Shedd's. We should get them back."

"Long live Mac!" shouted drunken Charlie Bowdre.

Dick Brewer seconded Billy's plan. The Regulator's destination would be the Mescalero Reservation on the next day.

APRIL 4, 1878   10:17 AM   THURSDAY

Descending Sierra Blanco foothills, ten Regulators approached land purchased in 1867 by Dr. Joseph Blazer, once an Iowa dentist. Five years later, around his property, had been established the 570,240 acre Mescalero Indian Reservation.

Initially, Blazer constructed a two-story adobe with a defensive tower. Then, having built himself another house, he had leased the first to Indian Agent Frederick Godfroy, his wife, and two daughters: Kate prior to her marriage, and Louisa. Mrs. Godfroy had converted its east side to a way station; and Blazer had retained northwest rooms for his business and a post office. Down an incline, was his sawmill on an east to west creek dividing the upper property from a corral.

Unseasonably hot sun beat on the approaching Regulators, making Lincoln's mud-soiled murders of three days before seem from another world or a dream.

Their leader, Dick Brewer told them, "We'll eat at Godfroy's, then check out the Mescalero Reservation for Tunstall's horses." From the corral, he, Charlie Bowdre, Billy, the Coes, Frank MacNab, John Middleton, Fred Waite, Henry Brown, and Doc Scurlock crossed the creek's footbridge, laughing and talking.

As they entered the way station, Mrs. Godfroy repeated her hang-up-gunbelts rule, and returned to the kitchen. Soon, tight-lipped, she and her daughter, Louisa, brought out food. "Thomehow, Ma'am," said Scurlock, looking up through his round lenses, "I don't feel hothpitality." She replied that their boss, McSween, had told mean lies about her husband to the newspapers.

On a high southern ridge, Andrew "Buckshot" Roberts, on a mule, stopped to scrutinize Blazer's Mill with wary eyes of the buffalo man he had been before buying his Ruidoso farm. Spare and weather-beaten, he raised his hat brim with his left hand, since his right shoulder, with long-embedded buckshot, had limited range. He patted his mule and said, "Doc Blazer was shur my check fer the farm sale 'id be in the mail, Johnny. We's gettin' the hell outa he-ah. Dolan ain' pretecktin' us from them Regalators."

Reassured by no horses hitched at Godfroy's way station, he soon tied Johnny there, compliantly looping his cartridge belt over the horn, but pulling his Winchester carbine from its scabbard.

A voice said, "Mornin', Buckshot."

He whirled, Winchester cocking, exclaiming, "I's you, Frank! Ye liketa startled me."

Frank Coe said, "We're neighbors. I gotta tell you: the Regalators is here."

Neither noticed John Middleton, who ran back inside shouting that Buckshot Roberts was there.

Mrs. Godfroy, overhearing, rushed out to get Joseph Blazer.

Brewer said, "I've got Wilson's warrant for him." Waite laughed, asking where he'd take his prisoner. "I don't care. I'm arresting him. And if anything happens to me, I appoint MacNab Captain. With me comes John, George," he hesitated, "and the Kid."

Stolid, bearded Blazer hurried in, forbidding violence.

"Tah hell with you an' yer rats' nest o' Dolans," Charlie Bowdre shouted. Winchester cocked, he ran out, along with George Coe, who had his Colt .44 in hand. Brewer followed, calling to Roberts that he was under arrest, as Frank Coe beat a hasty retreat.

The little man waited with his carbine at his only firing position, his right hip; and shouted back, "No way, Mary Ann."

Charlie Bowdre, beside himself with rage, screamed, "Kill me fohr a hunred. Ah'll do ye free;" and fired his poorly aimed carbine into Roberts's abdomen as the man shot back.

That bullet struck the heavy brass buckle of Bowdre's cartridge belt, doubling him up, and ricocheting into George Coe's extended revolver, which wrenched, mutilating his entrapped trigger finger.

Shrieking, Coe fled. Buckshot Roberts pumped his lever again, striking John Middleton in the chest, before running along the porch into Joseph Blazer's office.

Dick Brewer, overwhelmed by the mayhem, stood screaming hysterically, "I'll kill him! I'll kill him!"

Billy acted, slipping along the building and calling, "Here, Buckshot!" Roberts fired the last of his twelve rounds. Then, having kept count, Billy rushed the doorway, carbine pointed.

With shocking strength, the little man rammed Billy with his carbine butt, throwing him backward. Knowing that Blazer must have a weapon in the room, Billy retreated to the east side.

There, Waite was demanding a wagon from Blazer for Middleton, on the ground and coughing up blood; and for George Coe, whose cousin was binding his bleeding index finger with a bandana.

A shot rang out from a firewood pile to the west of the building. Smoke hung as they saw Brewer kneel again.

Billy cried, "Buckshot 'ill know he's there!" and ran to make diversionary fire. Brewer reappeared. Roberts pulled the trigger. For a hundred and two yards, his bullet traveled with marksman's perfection, and passed through Brewer's left eye. Seeing Brewer's catapulting form, Billy halted.

As they all departed, Charlie Bowdre, bent with pain, managed to say, "Leas' I got the basthard."

Meanwhile, Andrew Roberts, grunting in animal ferocity, dragged a mattress from Blazer's cot. When barricaded behind it with that man's single shot, Springfield, hunting rifle, he heard, "They're gone, Buckshot." The dentist then was looking down.

After hearing his successes, dying Buckshot Roberts said, "Promise me, Doc, te take keer o' Johnny. He war my bes' mule ever."

APRIL 8, 1878   9:12 AM   MONDAY

On the first day of the Grand Jury, a breeze blew through the McSween parlor where "Squire" Wilson and Harvey Morris watched Billy playing marbles on a Persian rug with Minnie Shield and her six year old brother, Davie; their circle scratched in pile.

The pudgy clean-shaven intern said he felt moved by Billy's coming. "I figured I should, Mister Morris."

"Your knock on my window scared me out of my wits. Call me Harvey, though."

"Sorry, Harvey. But given the situation, the only way was from the Bonito. Anyway, it's not likely that anybody'd try anything with court going on."

Wilson said, "Isn't what Bristol and Rynerson thought. They demanded a military escort. That was a damn tragedy with Dick."

Billy's marble struck one of Minnie's. She asked how he kept it in the circle. Practice, he said.

"They buried them both right there?" asked Morris. Billy said he and Yginio Salazar had gone back late Saturday night. Two crosses were on a hill right by the way station, side by side.

Harvey Morris said, "Doctor Ealy - who's renting the Tunstall apartment now, with his family - told me he wrote a letter to Washington. His uncle's a Congressman named Rush Clark. Ealy made clear the mitigating circumstances in the Brady deaths by arguing the risk to Attorney McSween.

"And, with the Grand Jury, Attorney McSween should do well. The majority of the jurymen are knowledgeable about corrupt Santa Fe Ring tactics, and are sympathetic. And the other arrests - of Attorney Shield and George Washington - were groundless."

"Where's Papa and Uncle Alexander?" asked Davie, finally exposing his anxiety. Harvey Morris replied that they were visiting a place called Fort Stanton.

"Squire" Wilson said, "More good news. Looks like the County Commissioners will appoint John Copeland sheriff tomorrow. And seems I'm still Justice of the Peace. Nobody's abiding that fool proclamation. Good time to ask, Kid: Which of you shot me? Still can't sit easy." Billy said it wasn't him. He was aiming at Matthews.

Davie's marble struck; its object rolled out. He shouted that he'd won. Billy smiled. Wilson asked, "How are the others doing, Kid?"

"San Patricio looks like a military hospital. But Middleton's walking around and Frenchie's healing. George Coe went to Fort Stanton to Doctor Appel. Lost most of his trigger finger."

"I don't want to lose my finger," said Davie, twisting a big button fastening pants to shirt.

"You're safe," said Billy. "That's not a children's accident."

When Billy said that, one thousand four hundred nine miles northeast of Lincoln, in Washington, D.C., seven men who were gathered in the Cabinet Room, on the second floor of the east wing of the White House, were thinking about dangers in Lincoln County.

One of the men was President Rutherford B. Hayes. He sat, broad shoulders framed by his high chairback, resting forearms on their long conference table, fingertips releasing as if from prayer. Under his full beard, trailing a gray streak from each corner of his mouth, he smiled warmly at the gathered men, with an extra acknowledgement of long friendship to the one at the far end.

He said, "We have inclement weather, Gentlemen. I thank you all for braving the streets that Lord Bryce characterized as 'the wilderness of mud.' Isn't that so, Lord Thornton?"

To his right, burly dense-bearded Ambassador Edward Thornton, with supercilious shaved upper lip, said diplomatically, "I believe he spoke before the macadam and wood-block paving of your administration, Mister President."

"Ah," Hayes smiled affably, "at least we can claim some triumph of civilization." At fifty-four, his face, though pitted, was unwrinkled; and his straight, sandy hair, brushed to the side, enhanced his high forehead.

He next addressed a small black-outfitted man to Thornton's right. "And Mister Beeton, I wish your visit wasn't for the tragic purpose of the death of your nephew, John Henry Tunstall. Henry Covington Beeton, is it? And all the way from Victoria, British Columbia?"

"Yes, Mister President," answered the very nervous man. "That's where we have our mercantile business: Turner, Beeton, and Tunstall - his father, John Partridge Tunstall; my brother-in-law, John Herbert Turner; and myself."

The president sighed. "Before we proceed, I extend my sympathy and that of my wife, Lucy Webb Hayes. I've gotten many letters about your nephew's death. In their reading, I felt his admirable spirit." His dark-blue eyes saw Beeton's with tears.

Hayes glanced around the high-ceilinged room in which he and his Cabinet had met since he had assumed office the previous March twentieth. Across from him, on the wall, was a map of the United States and its Territories. Above a fireplace, a mirror reflected a profuse bouquet on its mantle. Hayes said, "And my wife arranged the flowers. She has a conservatory here. They're English roses: her tribute to your nephew.

"Now, let me make the introductions. I assume you've already met our British ambassador - your envoy - Sir Edward Thornton. To your right is Attorney General Charles Devens." That man nodded, thick white mane brushed backward and narrow beard framing his face. "And across from me is Carl Schurz, Secretary of the Interior." Rebelliously informal, he had a pince-nez clamped on his aquiline nose, and wore tan pants and a brocade vest over a white shirt. Wavy red hair rose anarchically, matching untamed beard and mustache.

"And to my left is Secretary of State William Evarts." That elegant clean-shaven man, with graying sideburns suavely tapered to jaw-angles, nodded at the visitor.

"And to his left, is Congressman Rush Clark, who wanted to attend because his nephew, Doctor Taylor Ealy, lives in the town of your nephew's store."

In front of each official were piled papers. To his secretary, at his own desk, Hayes said, "We will want a full recording."

He began. "The matter before us is of great import since it involves our esteemed ally, England. Why don't we first locate Lincoln County. Carl, do us the service."

Athletically fit, Schurz walked to the map and spoke with a slight German accent. "It is much of the lower right quarter of New Mexico Territory. Twenty-seven thousand square miles. And, almost in its center, is the town of Lincoln, where was located the store of John Tunstall. And there are almost four thousand acres of his ranchland along two rivers." He traced horizontally. "The Feliz. And the Peñasco."

The president asked Henry Covington Beeton what he hoped for. Beeton said, "Full recovery of my nephew's property. And, of course, we want the wrongdoers punished."

Subduing his famous oratorical voice, Attorney General Charles Devens intoned, "Only a little over a decade ago we poured forth our blood to fight for a county in which liberty and justice prevail."

"Speaking of our ideals," suave Secretary of State William Evarts said, "our Secretary of the Interior here, fought in the German Revolution of forty-eight; and even rescued his university professor from Spandau Prison. And he also fought for another red-haired revolutionary, Garibaldi. You've come to the right place."

Hayes said, "My goal's been to fulfill the dream of Abraham Lincoln - our assassinated, great president - to unite our country in honorable peace. It moves me that this place is twice named Lincoln, in town and county.

"Well, Gentlemen, let's review the issues and decide on a plan of action. To commence, I will bring to your attention a letter dated the first of April, which I got from an attorney acquaintance of mine named Montague Leverson, and written from Lincoln."

Hayes read aloud: *"I came to this town this afternoon and found that only a few hours previously, two of Mister Tunstall's murderers had been killed: the sheriff who employed escaped convicts in his posse and a man who was one of this sheriff's deputies on the occasion of Mr. Tunstall's murder. The state of affairs here is precisely that of the two Sicilies before they were freed by Garibaldi. The administrators of the law were the criminals and the honest men were driven to the mountains and pursued as bandits.'"*

Carl Schurz nodded sympathetically. Hayes said, "And Attorney Leverson also noted that there was an unjust arrest of another attorney, named McSween, whom citizens were trying to protect."

Ambassador Thornton said he had received letters from that same McSween, and had forwarded them to Mister Evarts. Evarts responded that he had sent them to Attorney General Devens. Devens said, "And I forwarded copies to my counterpart in New Mexico Territory, U.S. Attorney Thomas Benton Catron, and requested an inquiry and report. To date, I haven't gotten a response."

"Interesting," said Thornton archly. *"My* communications from Attorney Alexander McSween indicate that this Catron; as well as the governor, Samuel Beach Axtell; and a district judge, Warren Bristol, are *shielding* Tunstall's murderers. And *I* have already communicated thusly to Mister Evarts; as well as conveying Attorney McSween's allegations of graft in the local Indian Agency and land frauds associated with the same individuals."

Beeton spoke. "This is a bit odd. An Attorney Stephen Elkins wrote to assure me that any investigation will go well since Governor Axtell and Judge Bristol are men of highest regard."

Thornton quoted from a Leverson letter to him. *"The persons Dolan and his partner Riley as well as Governor Axtell are tools of a Ring whose head is U.S. Attorney Thomas Benton Catron "*

Blond, broad-faced, Congressman Rush Clark spoke. "Guess you could say that's where I come into the fray. After I got a letter from my nephew, Taylor Ealy - a doctor in Lincoln - I contacted a lawyer friend in Colefax County in northern New Mexico Territory: Frank Springer from Cimarron. And Springer said the Territory's a volcano ready to explode.

"He says the cause is the Santa Fe Ring, and gives all the same names as its members. And I don't know if you all remember - because it started in the late sixties and early seventies - all those questions of corruption about the county's largest Mexican land grant, the Maxwell Land Grant: two million acres in northern New Mexico Territory and Southern Colorado. Frank Springer implicates that same Catron in that mess also. Says the sums of money involved were gigantic. And claims that the crooked dealing in its sale is how that Santa Fe Ring got started."

Beeton said, "I think the grief will simply kill John's father."

"I sympathize deeply," Hayes responded. "My wife and I are blessed with five children: four sons and a daughter. But we have lived through the deaths of three sons. Gentlemen, we must admit the need for investigation."

"Mister President," Charles Devens replied, having waited for self-aggrandizing impact, "when I got no response from U.S. Attorney Catron, *I* took action. I appointed a Special Agent of the Justice Department who can also address the issues pertinent to the Department of the Interior. Here's what he's assigned."

Devens read: *"To investigate the murder of John Henry Tunstall, investigate the actions of U. S. Attorney Catron and Governor Axtell, investigate allegations with regard to graft on the part of Mescalero Apache Indian Agent Frederick Godfroy, investigate possible land grant fraud, and investigate the Santa Fe Ring.'* His name's Frank Warner Angel, an attorney of highest intellect, integrity, and vigor. And his departure is imminent."

"Gentlemen," said the president, "I am deeply moved by your efforts, all in the name of our highest ideals. As I said in my inaugural address, and feel deeply in my heart, 'He serves his party best who serves his country best.'

"I may have been elected the nineteenth president with the most uncertain margin in our country's history - with two numbers that will rule my life: one hundred eighty-five to one hundred eighty-four." He turned to Beeton. "The difference of one electoral college vote which made me President over my opponent, the Democrat, Samuel J. Tilden.

"But - like this murder in Lincoln County - those results reflected pernicious undercurrents. If the colored man, insured liberty by the Fourteenth Amendment, hadn't been unjustly deprived of his Florida voting rights, guaranteed by the Fifteenth Amendment, my victory would have been decisive.

"So, Gentlemen, to New Mexico Territory we now send a man named Angel. Let us hope that goodness can prevail thorough the working of forces sometimes beyond our comprehension."

APRIL 19, 1878   1:57 PM   FRIDAY

Awakened by Billy, Ash Upson rubbed his hirsute hungover face and stumbled through the storage room into the post office. He whispered conspiratorially, "Just bring my glass and bottle, Kid. So you're on the run, a fugitive in your own land?"

Not exactly, Billy said, and asked if he still had candy hearts. "Let this ambrosia take effect. Heard about Buckshot Roberts. Twenty against one."

"I can't say it was the Regulators' best showing; but he faced five of us." Upson asked if McSween was convicted or exonerated. "Neither. His case hasn't come up yet. Last Saturday the Grand Jury indicted Dolan, Evans, and Hill for Tunstall. But Hill's dead."

Upson asked about outcomes for the Brady-Hindman-Roberts murders. "For Brady and Hindman, they indicted me, Middleton, Brown, Waite, French, and MacNab. For Roberts, they indicted me, Bowdre, Middleton, Brewer, and George Coe."

Upson said he would be hanged. Billy answered, "There are so many indictments besides those that - if they want to - it 'ill take time." Upson asked which side was winning. "I'd say McSween's. The candy hearts were under the counter."

Upson found the jar and asked, "Had any recent escapades of single-handedly fighting off marauding Apaches - like you did in the Guadalupe Mountains last October? John Jones told me." Billy laughed, saying he'd never fought Indians.

Upson said, "If McSween wins, you'll be a frontier hero: youngest warrior fighting for justice." Billy teased about the possibility of McSween's loosing. "Just as good. Boy outlaw killing a man for every year of his life." That isn't true, Billy said. "Doesn't matter," said Upson. "It's dramatic and memorable. And I thought it up."

"You're funny, Ash," Billy said as he left.

APRIL 20, 1878   5:09 AM   SATURDAY

When Paulita secretly climbed out her bedroom window into Billy's arms, she said it was her birthday. She was fifteen. He said, "I know. I came so we could watch the dawning of your sixteenth year."

At his concealed horse, Paulita allowed him to lift her onto the saddle. Mounted behind, he pressed her close and drew aside her hair. Lost in kissing her neck's bare warmth, he heard her say they'd miss the dawn. She pressed her heels.

Gray Sugar advanced; and acres became pink peach blossoms in a pink shimmering grid of reflecting acequia irrigation ditches. "Beautiful," Billy murmured; but he meant her.

On his spread bedroll, in the orchard, Paulita said, "I have to be back before ten to go with Mama and Pete to Las Vegas. We stay with a boring family: the Jaramillos. Mama goes to the hot springs. And Pete gambles. Billy, teach me how to play poker."

"Someday." He drew her to his lips. Somewhere in the delight, he became aware of undulating peach perfume, and realized Paulita was stretched innocently along his length; and the undulating was his loins. He sat quickly, drawing her up, saying, "Changed my mind. I'm teaching you draw poker right now."

Later, Billy went to Hargrove's Saloon to gamble. Two players were wool merchants for the spring shearing; and three were Las Vegas bound for higher stakes gambling. The last, very tall, Billy had recalled from his previous visit. He gave the name Pat Garrett. When the long game ended, Billy raked in the pot, as Garrett remained.

Garrett said, "You seem young. Looking for work?" Billy denied it. "I am. Been here since February. Pete Maxwell hired me for wagon driving. Now I'm looking into hog raising with a Thomas McKinney. "Kip". His grandfather signed the Texas Declaration of Independence.

"Myself, I come from plantation stock. My Papa was a Colonel in the Confederate Army: John Lumpkin Garrett. Damn War ruined our plantation fortune. Killed him."

Absentmindedly, he scratched. "Damn buffalo lice. Spent years on the buffalo range. Stupid animals. Shoot the leader and they just mill. Then you shot the rest." Billy said it sounded like they were loyal. Garrett laughed, thinking it was a joke. "The lice live in your clothes. I can't afford new ones."

Billy offered a hundred dollar loan. Garrett said, "I'll be around to pay you back. Feels right here. I'm a follower of the atheist, Robert P. Ingersoll. He says this life is all there is. Make the most of it."

They walked out together. Garrett laughed. "I've probably gotten more women than buffs. Take these three coming. Know their names?" Billy said they were the Gutierrez sisters. Garrett said, "Bet you'd pick the real beauty. I'd choose the ugliest. They're satisfied if you just come home. A beauty's all trouble. Remember that and it will be worth ten times the money you gave me."

At Garrett's request, Billy made introductions. Apolinaria smiled invitingly. But Garrett shook Juanita's hand with mysterious final pressure. She felt dizzy with emotions.

That night, when Billy and Celsa cavorted naked, she straddled him and pinned his wrist. His free hand playfully sought her inviting wideness, but was seized also.

Earnestly she asked, "How much do you need Celsa?" He profusely assured passion. "Then I planned to ask ... to say, I must have ..." Under her, he was rising and lowering, tempting her with sweet brushings, undoing her resolve with desire.

Yielding, she soon resisted again and said, "I want your heart."

Unable to stop completely his pleasurable rhythm, Billy teased, "You have a big part of me right now. Ow!" he exaggerated, as she dug nails into his back. She persisted, asking what he would do if she refused him until she knew he was hers. "I would say you might change your mind."

Insistently, confidently, he drew her with him, until her voracious thighs became so wide-stretched that their taut sinews struck him at each deep thrust, and aroused subliminal danger that made his eyes close tightly and teeth clench, as if his face was being blasted by freezing wind. And as if penetrating a gaping arroyo, he disappeared into a blood-red land. He heard her whisper, "Someday, I will get your heart."

APRIL 22, 1878   4:21 PM   MONDAY

In his parlor, Alexander McSween was feverish with excitement. With him were Regulators and some of the grand jurymen. To hear his verdict, townspeople crowded at his open door.

Of those jurymen absent, three had worked for James Dolan; one was jury foreman, Dr. Joseph Blazer; and another was Desederio Zamora, a poor man, who had suspiciously put up the five thousand dollar bond for Jessie Evans's Tunstall murder indictment.

To his audience, McSween exclaimed, "I've been declared innocent!" Wild cheering erupted.

Outside, Gottfried Gauss startled Sam Corbett by saying, "Yustiss. Now ve finish revenge."

McSween continued, "I will read to you my jurymen's other words, that will echo through our history: *'The murder of John Tunstall for brutality and malice is without a parallel. By this inhuman act our county lost one of our best and most useful men.'*

"And they also held Governor Axtell responsible for our troubles," McSween said. "They concluded: *'Especially do we condemn his Proclamation relating to John B. Wilson.'*

"Also, John Partridge Tunstall, Tunstall's father, is offering a reward for five thousand dollars for apprehension of his son's murderers.

"So the unjust saw the writing on the wall. Judge Bristol even approved our good friend, John Copeland, as sheriff. Copeland's leaving full-time management of his ranch, near Fort Stanton.

"With the Grand Jury generated warrants, he and his just-appointed deputy, Josiah Scurlock, will apprehend *real* criminals.

"And, in two days, we're having a mass meeting. I propose making a petition to tell Tunstall's murderers to get out of our town." Again there was cheering.

"I'll end with more good news. President Hayes is sending a Special Investigator here to get to the bottom of John Tunstall's murder!" Animated talk began.

"Wait. There's more," McSween enthused. "We've also gotten a new commander at Fort Stanton: Colonel Nathan Augustus Monroe Dudley. He's higher ranking than Purlington, and was transferred from Fort Union on the fifth - obviously to assist us. Better yet, past commander, George Purlington - who understands our situation - is staying on! We've been tested. But the world is God's crucible, refining us into pure gold."

During applause, Frank MacNab said to the Regulators, "I'm letting the Seven Rivers' rustlers know we're closing them out." He left, followed by Frank Coe.

Long-haired Fred Waite looked at Billy's dark expression. "Ol' Chickasaw saying: 'Your own foolish general is more dangerous than your enemies combined.' " Billy was not listening. Dolan's promised river of blood now provoked certainty that McSween's victory would yield retaliation.

Right then, James Dolan was nine miles to Lincoln's northwest, at Fort Stanton, in the new commander's office. The tall soldier listened suspiciously to him, splendid white mustache waxed to pointy tips. Dolan said, "And we citizens appreciated your providing a military escort for Judge Bristol and District Attorney Rynerson. Otherwise outlaws from Sheriff John Copeland's ranch, right near this fort, could have ambushed them."

"And I assume Governor Axtell conversed with you in regimental headquarters in Santa Fe about our crisis?"

"Mister Dolan, I see no role in it for the military."

"Nor do I. We have excellent civilian resources." As if to rise, Dolan lifted his silver-headed cane, still needed for his healing leg. But he lingered. "Oh, I was also to extend regards from U.S. Attorney Tom Catron. He has *significant* interests in Lincoln County. So he and his Washington associate, Steve Elkins, wanted me to assure you that facts, which could undermine your credibility here, would not surface.

"By *facts*, I mean your Court Martial in November of seventy-one at Camp McDowell for numerous offenses including drunkenness on duty, for which you were suspended And just last year, your Court Martial for drunkenness and behavior unbecoming an officer, for which you were temporarily removed from your command at Fort Union.

"I know Tom Catron defended you for the latter - though it was unusual for a non-military lawyer to do so - and that he did it to protect someone of your stature, being second only to General Hatch in the Territory, from unjust accusations.

"So I'll speak freely as Tom's good friend. We know that attaining higher positions - and thus remuneration - in our peacetime army is difficult, given the reduction of the officer corps. Grateful citizens realize that it is prudent to assist those committed to their protection."

Dolan slipped an envelope from his frockcoat. "This is a token of our appreciation: eight hundred dollars." Dudley hesitated, then took it.

"Might you be interested in hearing about our additional provisions to protect law and order?"

Dudley stiffened. "Understand me, Sir, I am not interested in something that smacks of irregularity."

"Forgive me. I am not implying a bribe. We citizens realize that any efforts could burden your already extensive duties. We feel the *least* we can do is make available to you that sum on a monthly basis - to double your current salary.

"And because of the hostile partisan situation, we would place it in a factitious account set up in the First National Bank of Santa Fe. Third party drafts could then be written against it by a co-signatory."

Dudley said, "The situation is more complex, Sir, than you may realize. *You* can make recommendations. *I* will decide whether they are appropriate for military action."

"I would not have expected otherwise. I take it that we have an agreement?" Dudley nodded with restraint to show reluctance.

Dolan said, "By the way, another of Tom's friends is *George Purlington*." The hoped-for smile of dawning recognition was noted. "And some of the junior officers are friends as well: First Lieutenant Cyrus Delaney and Second Lieutenants Millard Filmore Goodwin, George Smith, and James French. And Post Surgeon Daniel Appel can be relied on too."

Dolan stood and said, "I hope I have been a service to you, to Lincoln town, and Lincoln County." The old soldier took the extended small white hand, as Dolan savored this crucial surrender.

To the alcoholic sworn to sobriety to protect his career, Dolan added, "And at a future occasion - since I come often to use the post telegraph - we can share that gift of excellent whiskey sent to you by our local innkeeper, Sam Wortley, in celebration of maintaining peace."

Dolan had taken that precaution. Commander N.A.M. Dudley's utter debasement might be necessary for his plans.

APRIL 25, 1878   3:45 PM   THURSDAY

On the north side of the Capitan Mountains, snow pillowed ponderosa pines outside the secret cave where Billy and Yginio Salazar planned for war. For his father's cause, Yginio would fight; for Tunstall, Billy would carry the standard. Stored already were hundreds of their manufactured cartridges and bullets.

Into a trunk, Billy returned the lard he had just used for boot waterproofing; and checked the cardigan sweater from Tunstall, fragrant from protective cedar strips.

"Did you know," Billy asked, "that Colt made a double action pistol? I had one for a time. Called the Lightning. Thirty-eight caliber. Soon they will have one in forty-one caliber. The Thunderer. I want one." Yginio said he preferred a .44, to have the same cartridge for pistol and carbine. "Me too. But just as a hide-away back up."

Yginio laughed. "You just want it. Like you want girls for their beauty. I will show you something." He unholstered his Colt. Billy noticed a diagonal split on its right grip, and joked that it was the one Matthews *gave* them. Yginio grinned. "Yes. But look at the left grip. I carved that up-side-down U. Someday that will be part of my brand when I own the land north of Dead Man's Rock. It is the horseshoe of Torcio, who only knows freedom."

Then, both began to clean their weapons for perfect readiness.

APRIL 29, 1878   8:16 AM   MONDAY

Alexander McSween, with Minnie Shield in the east back yard of his big house, heard his name, and nearsightedly looked to the rear adobe wall. Confident of victory, he had halted further construction.

As Billy came through its gate, holding his carbine, and with saddlebags draped over his shoulder, Minnie tossed crushed corn to their chickens; while shooing away the big Rhode Island Red rooster, with iridescent green tail feathers, who competed too greedily with his black and white Wyandotte and Plymouth Rock hens.

"Mac," Billy called, "word's out that the Seven Rivers boys are heading here." Impossible, McSween said. The fighting was over. Billy sighed at the response, as unrealistic as Tunstall's; and said, "Thought I'd spend the day. Regulators Middleton and Frenchie healed up and are stationed at Ellis's with Waite, Bowdre, Scurlock, and Brown.

"The Seven Rivers boys are calling themselves a posse to 'help' arrest the murderers of Brady, Hindman, Morton, and Baker. Seems you're a target too, Mac. War might start today."

McSween scoffed that Dolan was planting rumors because of the town's petition forcing him to leave.

Billy said, "He's still here, along with Matthews, Peppin, and Long. I scouted the House before dawn." McSween, annoyed by adolescent alarmism, said he nevertheless wanted no guard.

Billy's eyes narrowed slyly. "Actually, Mac, I came with a Bible question. My Ma got married in the *Presbyterian* Church in Santa Fe. I figured you had a supply of Bibles. I wanted to read about Abraham and Isaac." With unctuous missionary zeal, McSween said seeking Biblical truth was a sign of being elected for Heaven, and invited him to come in.

Billy shifted his saddlebags, heavy with .44-40 ammunition, and followed McSween and Minnie around to the front door, while rapidly scanning the hills across the street for snipers.

From the parlor, Minnie returned to her family's east wing for her lesson with Susan Gates. McSween directed Billy to the first bedroom in the west wing, and left to prepare a case.

At Billy's knock, Susan McSween's voice said, "Is that you, darling?"

"No, Ma'am. It's me, Billy Bonney. Mac sent me to get the big Bible." There was a pause. Yes, she could see it. Just open the door himself.

She was in a tin tub, naked back to him. " 'Scuse me, Ma'am," he gasped. She asked him to hand her the towel. She turned. In the wet pearly whiteness were two salmon-colored tips, as a glistening arm reached. Again outside the room and bright red, he heard, "You forgot the Bible."

"I remembered, Ma'am ... something I've got to do about the chickens."

Exiting the front door, Billy proceeded along the house's west side, into its back yard, where he saw George Washington leaving the outhouse in the adjacent eastern yard. The man returned through the adobe wall dividing those back areas, and perpendicular to one closing off the house's central courtyard.

At Billy's request for privacy, they walked out the rear gate beside the stable, crossed the remaining flat land, and followed a footpath descending the tiered embankment to the Bonito River.

On level ground, Billy hunkered down. With a stick, he traced random featherings on the red earth. Washington sat on firewood logs. Billy said, "George, something real strange just happened. Mac sent me to this bedroom and ... And Missus McSween said just open the door. I did. And she was naked! In a tub. Naked!"

Washington laughed. "And she acted like she was dressed, didn't she?" But he abruptly soured. "I don't know what she wants. She calls you into some damn place - where you shouldn't be alone with her -

and she's taking off or putting on some woman thing. Even has me tie the backs of new corsets while she holds her breath. Once she even had me under the dress she had on, tying some damn ribbon tapes back behind her petticoats so the skirt would lie flat in front. If anyone had walked in, I'da been lynched. I'd say she thinks I'm a nigger; same as a woman for all she cares."

Billy's stick traced a small circle in a bigger one, like the salmon-pink vision. "Seems it's not the color of our skins, but the cut of our clothes, George."

"Makes sense. All below the Saint Louis ladyship. I tell you, Kid, those white Northern folk hate us worse then Southerners, 'cause we got free to marry their daughters or get their jobs. They didn't choose our freedom. It was God's plan. Like my life.

"When I was a kid, my mother escaped a Kentucky plantation with me on the Underground Railroad to Ohio. There, she married a mulatto reverend, who'd been schooled in Wilberforce College. Wilberforce was made in fifty-six for colored folks.

"That reverend was sent there by his father, who was a Kentucky plantation owner with a pricking conscience, 'cause he'd begotten him with one of his slaves. Even bought him land before telling him never to come back. I got book-learning and Bible from that stepfather.

"My mother was a mulatto too, but could almost pass for white. Her mother *was* white - the plantation owner's daughter! That daughter begat my mother with one of her daddy's slaves - dark as me. They tried to escape to Kentucky together, but he was lynched.

"Their child, my mother, was raised on that plantation by a slave woman. When she grew, she was raped by the owner, her own grandfather. I came from that.

"I fought for our freedom. In the War, I served in the Fifth U.S. Colored Infantry. In sixty-four, I fought at Chaffin's Farm in Virginia, the War's greatest battle by colored troops. After the War, I reenlisted in the Ninth Cavalry and served in Texas.

"When I mustered out, I came here; and 'ave worked going on three years for the McSweens.

"But I'm saving to get me a farm. I just got to decide where a man with my skin can raise his children free. The night Abraham Lincoln was assassinated, arsonists burned down Wilberforce. It's rebuilt now, but I'm not putting down my roots in Ohio."

As they climbed back to the house, Washington was thinking that if he was not positive that everything was God's will, he would be destroyed by rage. But he could endure. He could forgive. And one day, he'd elope with Josephina.

He said, "Since it seems we're in our own little Civil War - at least for now - I'm willing to be here."

Billy, deeply moved, said, "My father died fighting for freedom in the Civil War."

In mid-afternoon, Billy had returned to the Regulators standing guard at Isaac Ellis's house. On its parapeted roof, he was watching George Coe demonstrate how, with bandaged hand, he could still work his carbine lever, when Coe's cousin called them back down.

Addressing the group, MacNab said, "Frank and me are heading west up the Bonito. To tell folks the Seven River boys are coming."

Billy said, "You'll pass Charlie Fritz's ranch. Where they'd stop. You could be ambushed - same as we got Buckshot." MacNab retorted that if he don't have brains to see that, he deserved to die, and stomped out with Frank Coe.

At Charles Fritz's ranch, eight miles northwest of Lincoln, black-bearded Andrew Boyle, with fierce thick eyebrows, was standing with him, Fritz's wife, and his teenaged daughter, Carolina, in front of their wood-framed residence, directing his thirty-one Seven Rivers boys; sending some to a second house on the property.

Later, when approaching the Fritz house, MacNab said, "You know, Frank, Chisum's tired of the rustling. He'll stay at South Spring River Ranch, but I wouldn't bet on him keeping cattle."

Coe's thirsty horse became restless. He laughed, saying she liked to race, and galloped ahead toward a stream near the second building.

Inside the main house, Boyle, the Olinger and Beckwith brothers, Manuel Segovia "the Indian," John Jones, and thirteen other men watched in surprise.

"The bastards made it easy," Bob Olinger said. "Was that the Kid who rode past?"

"Maybe," said Andrew Boyle. "But we've surely got MacNab. The one we wanted most."

At shots, Frank MacNab's mount bucked and felt slipping weight. In mindless panic, his rider, like a prey animal with bulging eyes, sprinted ahead of a savage pack of running men. Manuel Segovia "the Indian's" bullet hit him first.

Bob Olinger stood over their victim, unconscious, but alive. He said, "Gonna show you all the advantage of a shotgun." He pointed his Whitney's barrels at the chest and pulled one trigger. There was a bloody quivering hole. At the head, he pulled the second trigger. One side of the face collapsed.

Distant gunfire signified the response of the second group to Frank Coe. His horse was hit. He scrambled into a gully yelling, "I surrender." But shooting was resumed by the others, fresh from their kill. Coe threw his revolver over the rim, waited, and climbed out. He said, "Hell. Shur's a lot o' you. Where's MacNab?"

"Bastard's dead," said Bob Olinger. "We'll finish you in Lincoln with the rest." Wallace Olinger said he'd take him in.

One hundred forty-two miles from the Fritz Ranch, in Fort Sumner, Pat Garrett was having a nightmare about a beast, as he lay on a cot in the erstwhile barracks along the east side of the parade ground. Some, like him and the woman beside him, stealthily entered and left in darkness. Juanita Gutierrez whimpered in slumber, restless with newly torn flesh. Garrett was being stalked by a golden eyed panther. It leapt. But its eyes were blue. And it had a brand of a cross.

Lurched into wakefulness, he nudged the woman, who began to cry. He patted, like comforting a dog, and said, "You were good, Juanita. You're my girl now. Go to Celsa's. Bad to stay here. You understand?"

"I no bad." Reassuringly, he kissed her round cheek and confirmed their next assignation.

APRIL 30, 1878   6:27 AM   TUESDAY

At the House, the agitated mail rider, met by Billy Matthews, asked, "Heard the news? Frank MacNab's dead! Resisting arrest by the Seven Rivers Posse." The slab-faced man feigned surprise.

Back in the rear storeroom, Matthews made his way around bedrolls of the sleeping Seven Rivers men. On the far side, Frank Coe and Wallace Olinger sat on crates. Coe asked Matthews, "Where're the rest o' yer boys?" having decided that his captors were unaware of the Regulators' occupation of Isaac Ellis's house. He was told they were waiting east of town for the Regulators to ride in.

At McSween's house, the mail rider repeated his report to the attorney and added, "I won't deliver no mail if you're all shootin'. Want stamps?" Numbly, Alexander McSween requested nine, then stared at the departing man, and across the street to the wall of hills, experiencing their oppressive closeness.

He heard, "Mac, it's me. Billy. Step back in. I'm moving fast." From the west corner of the house, with Winchester, saddlebags, and double cartridge belts, Billy, coming from Isaac Ellis's, passed him, then closed the door. McSween said that Frank MacNab was dead, and slumped on the couch, trying to assemble chaotic thoughts.

Finally, he adjusted his collar and said, "I'll ride to San Patricio and get its Justice of the Peace, Gregorio Trujillo, to make out murder warrants for Sheriff Copeland."

"You can't use the road, Mac," Billy said. Seven Rivers boys are hiding in the House and east of town. Mind if I head to that Bible room to look out? Wouldn't want to disturb your wife though." She was dressing in the room after it, McSween said. Billy responded, "Well, we've got the east covered. And you've got me for here."

Looking out from McSween's bedroom, Billy was surprised to see Yginio Salazar near the stable, and leaned out the window motioning. Yginio entered through it, handing in his carbine and saying, "MacNab was killed yesterday at the Fritz Ranch." Billy's lips tightened at the location. "A hired man from there rode to tell me. So I went to San Patricio; and the men told me the Regulators were here for a battle."

Billy said he wished those men had come. But now, with Yginio guarding the house, he could get out and take care of the west end.

When the first shot sounded from the east, it was met by others. For miles, those poised for war knew fighting had begun. And they barricaded doors and windows. On Isaac Ellis's roof, George Coe, having fired that first shot, said to Henry Brown, "Got him. Bastard was standing on one of those bee hive boxes. Guess it was empty."

Almost a quarter mile away, two men, apprehensively glancing, dragged Coe's victim, "Dutch" Charlie Kruling, wounded through both calves. When the others joined them on the Ellis roof, George Coe shouted with surprising bloodlust, "I got one! If they got MacNab and my cousin, like the mail carrier said, I'm gonna get ten for them."

At the same time, Susan McSween rushed into the parlor, asking her husband what was going on. He said, "No need to worry. As soon as Sheriff Copeland comes, he'll put an end to it. Ruffians murdered again. For intimidation. Because of my court victory."

Eastward, lean bowlegged John Copeland, approaching Lincoln on its road, saw the House puffing gun-smoke from windows and counterfire coming from multiple locations along the northwest side of the street. Other reports sounded farther ahead. "Hell," he said, turned, and spurred his horse toward Fort Stanton.

By 3:43 PM, Second Lieutenant George Smith, with a squad of nineteen, arrived at Lincoln's outskirts. At his side was the sheriff, who had not stopped agitated chatter, as his mustached lip flashed pink gums with little teeth. Following were the cavalrymen and a mule-drawn military ambulance: a Civil War, buckboard-style wagon with squared stays and canvas covering.

John Copeland said, "So I heard gunshots. I thought, 'I can't handle this.' I only had this job since the ninth; and I'm not getting shot right off." The officer halted his men level with the House.

Billy Matthews, George Peppin, and Jack Long stepped out. Copeland called, "It's over boys. Surrender."

Matthews ignored him, saying to Smith that Jimmy was inside.

"Sir," Smith responded stiffly, having been coached by Purlington, "I'm here under orders from Colonel Dudley merely to end this civil disturbance." Leaving four mounted soldiers, Smith proceeded eastward.

John Copeland's pink gums flashed. He had only one deputy - Scurlock by name - and he didn't even know where the hell he was. The Second Lieutenant barked, "We are deploying, Sir. Place yourself behind the line of skirmishers."

As the military mass, in staggered rows of four, neared the Ellis house, gunfire there ceased. Sheriff Copeland met the owner at the door and demanded an explanation. Angrily, Isaac Ellis answered. "The bastards killed MacNab, and you're asking us? Is Frank Coe dead?"

John Copeland said, "How the hell should I know? Only MacNab's body's in the ambulance. I said, to myself when I come riding in, 'What the hell's going on?' So I went to Stanton."

Ellis said, "Wish you hadn't. We coulda finished them off today. The Kid made a plan: pin 'em till they ran out of ammunition."

Ahead, agitating brush, Seven Rivers men stood, waving white handkerchiefs, or with long guns butt up.

Copeland rushed to mount his horse and meet them.

Twenty-seven surrendering men gathered, laying their four dead beside "Dutch" Charlie Kruling, who had bandana-tourniqueted legs.

Andrew Boyle said, "Lieutenant, we're surrendering to you. The sheriff will turn us over to Brady's murderers." Copeland said irritably that he didn't want them anyway. He had no place to put them.

Smith responded, "My orders were just to stop the fighting," but was considering Purlington's anger at his failed apprehension of McSween that March at Chisum's ranch. He said, "Alright. You're all coming with me to the fort. Also, get someone at McSween's to unload MacNab. We're not undertakers."

In the House storeroom, Wallace Olinger, having received whispered communication, was speaking to his prisoner. "Soldiers rode in, Frank." He paused meaningfully. "I got to go."

As soon as his guard departed, Frank Coe tentatively opened the storeroom door, ran behind the outhouse, then climbed through the rear fencing. Gathering strength, he raced eastward.

At "Squire" Wilson's property, he rushed across vegetable beds and banged on the side door. Once inside, Frank Coe embraced his startled host, exclaiming, "I'm alive! I'm alive!"

MAY 1, 1878   8:18 PM   WEDNESDAY

At dawn, George Washington had completed a second burial. To the disturbed ground, near John Tunstall's grave, he had said, "You know, MacNab, seems this 'ill be a cemetery here, not a church or school. Man never knows his real plans. Just God does."

At the same time, James Dolan had ridden with George Peppin and Billy Matthews the twenty miles to Blazer's Mill, to Justice of the Peace David Easton, who shared Joseph Blazer's office. There, Dolan had Peppin and Matthews swear out affidavits to Easton, naming Alexander McSween, William Bonney alias Henry Antrim alias Kid, and others unknown, with murder and assault with the intent to kill. The victims were the four dead Seven Rivers men and the injured "Dutch" Charlie Kruling.

When the men left, Easton fumed to Blazer, "They just forced me write my own death sentence. In the same room Andrew Roberts died. I quit this damn job."

Now, at San Patricio's cantina, the Regulators enjoyed festivities in their honor. Absent were George Coe, who, after a tearful reunion with his cousin, had returned with him to their farm; and Doc Scurlock, who had remained in Lincoln at Copeland's request.

Alexander McSween, sitting with Billy, Fred Waite, Justice of the Peace Gregorio Trujillo, and Town Constable José Chávez y Chávez, officiously patted his document case, and said. "With these Trujillo warrants, Sheriff Copeland can make the arrests. With all twenty-seven charged with intent to kill Frank MacNab, and with my additional complaint of obstructing delivery of United States mail, justice will be done again."

He cracked his knuckles, checked his collar, and asked José Chávez y Chávez if he could avail himself of his hospitality. He had brought his travel kit.

But he needed the warrants delivered that night. To Billy, he said, "You must be exhausted after your exertions;" and chose Henry Brown, who appeared least intoxicated.

As soon as McSween left with Chávez y Chávez, Billy called out gaily, "Baile!" Without thought of a partner, he danced, calling to the musicians, "Faster, faster."

Hours passed. New musicians replaced the old. Those who had not fought, shared in Billy's exultation of first battle victory. The night faded. But still Billy danced, not knowing if the room was empty or full, because, long before, his compressing body had disappeared and he was only music and joy.

MAY 4, 1878   11:25 AM   SATURDAY

John Copeland's short upper lip was exposing gums in the office of Colonel Nathan Augustus Monroe Dudley, who said he refused to tolerate disrespect. Copeland said, "What disrespect? You're treating me bad, Dudley. I bring you them warrants two days ago for them Seven Rivers boys - with Hearings all set in San Patricio.

"But you give me warrants from Easton for McSween and the Kid, and send me back with a passel of soldiers to make sure I served 'em - making me search all goddamn San Patricio for 'em; even when they wasn't there and upsetting the citizens. I've had this job since the ninth, and I'm ready to quit like Easton."

The commander became alert, realizing, unlike the lawman, that David Easton's warrants were now invalid. Dolan's plans were foiled. Officiously, Dudley announced that he was returning the prisoners to his custody.

John Copeland's eyes narrowed. "What the hell am I going to do with twenty-seven men? You know I got no way to hold 'em to the sixth. And, to think, we signed a petition welcoming you."

As if responding to the distress, a man in Santa Fe, one hundred thirty-two miles northwest of Fort Stanton, thought, "The Lincoln County situation seems desperate." Thirty-three years old, handsome, brunette, and clean-shaven, he walked vigorously across its main plaza toward the one-story Palace of the Governors, occupying the entire north side of the square.

Accustomed to the sophistication of his New York City home, to him, its white Victorian cornices, added along its adobe roofline, appeared ludicrously anachronistic. His intelligent hazel eyes studied its front portico, with log supports so thick that wrapped arms would just touch hands to elbows. He knew that the large window to the left of its central doors belonged to Governor Axtell's office.

To his right, enclosing the eastern margin of the square, was a two-story building. He had been told it was called the Johnson Block. Its roof shaded a second floor porch. It too, though stuccoed adobe, made a bid for Victorian high style by that porch's balustrade of fanning struts, inadvertently mimicking magnified spider webs.

On a whim, he began at the Palace entry, strode left along its board walkway, crossed Palace Avenue, and walked the insignificant distance to the last door on the southeast corner of the Johnson Block. Its plaque read, "LAW OFFICE. THOMAS BENTON CATRON. SECOND FLOOR." He had noted that the building also housed downstairs the newspaper offices of the *Santa Fe New Mexican* and the First National Bank of Santa Fe. He smiled.

Next he went to an obelisk, a Civil War monument at the grassy plaza's center, while marveling at the sky's blueness and the distant purple Sangre de Cristo Mountains. He asked a passerby, "Would you know where the jail is?"

"Tourist are you, young man?"

"You could say that," he said with amusement. People frequently mistook his age. He was probably older than the speaker.

"Bad section of town. But cross the plaza," he pointed southwest, "and you'll be at San Francisco Street. Turn right on it, then left on Sandoval. Just a block, and you're at Water Street. Across is the courthouse. And just to its east is the jail. Right behind the Herlow Hotel's livery stable. It's a long building on an alley off Water. We've got better sights here, I assure you."

In less than ten minutes, the visitor was at those neglected adobes, and, satisfied, turned to go to his hotel, the Exchange, for a mid-day meal. Proceeding east along San Francisco Street, to his left he noted a perpendicular narrow lane with pack donkeys. At his right, in a doorway, stood a man of astounding physiognomy watching him.

Hatless like himself, he had a flamboyantly curled, ginger mustache. The man said, "I am Paul Herlow. I welcome you to the beginning of your journey." The visitor asked the local eccentric why he hadn't said the middle or ending. "It is my hobby to guess. Am I correct?" He nodded amiably. Herlow asked, "And your name?"

"Frank Warner Angel."

MAY 10, 1878   10:45 AM   FRIDAY

A buggy traveled north from Lincoln. Its driver said to his older companion, while adjusting that man's muffler, "It is freakish: snow this late." That older man, bundled in a buffalo robe coat, smiled vacantly, accustomed to the attentiveness. The younger noted the jaundiced pallor, not concealed by mustache and neat faded-red beard, and handed him a silver flask, saying, "Sam Wortley packed us food too."

"You've never forgotten a detail, Jimmy." A cough jarred Lawrence Murphy's painfully swollen liver. He said, "Death's not easy." Dolan lied that Dr. Appel said he would be cured in Santa Fe.

Murphy smiled. "The job of the doctor and the priest: give hope. I never understood how McSween bought Presbyterianism, with its predestination to Heaven or Hell at birth. Catholicism makes sense. You're saved if you play the game right."

James Dolan laughed. But Murphy was serious and said, "Feels strange not to lie any more. You really are like my son now." He sobbed lightly. "I want you to marry - to be safe when I'm gone."

Annoyed, Dolan clucked to the horse. Murphy persisted. "I've talked to Charlie Fritz about his daughter, Carolina: a good quiet girl."

Dolan touched the shaggy shoulder. "Think of all we've done, Larry. The sutler's store at Stanton. Remember the whiskey still in the cave near it? And our counterfeiting sideline?"

Murphy asked what happened to the press. "Three brothers, the Dedricks, bought it. Two run a livery stable in White Oaks. The third, Dan Dedrick, a while back, *'bought'* Chisum's original Bosque Grande Ranch!" Murphy laughed gleefully.

Dolan said, "But a matchmaker! A new sideline!" Murphy admitted that Charles Fritz understood a marriage would end their mortgage on his ranch. "Poor girl," Dolan said facetiously. "Chattel to her father."

"Warming to her already," teased Murphy; but returned to their prime purpose. He asked, "You reviewed with Matthews and Peppin what to say in their Angel depositions?" Dolan nodded.

Murphy continued, "Deception is an unsung art. Lying well," he paused to catch his breath, "requires saying as little as possible. Claiming to forget. Anticipating your opponent's accusations by raising them yourself." Dolan smiled, lying that he had learned so much from him. "But what a pupil I've had," said Murphy.

Dolan smiled again, but not at the compliment. The physical passion had been mere human indulgence. He was relishing a non-human attainment: Murphy's descent over years to such moral degradation that it could be called the loss of his soul.

Murphy said, "As to us, Jimmy, we say to Angel that the partnership of McSween and Tunstall *did* exist. That McSween, *not Tunstall*, started the Lincoln County troubles by embezzlement. That Axtell is a hero to all good citizens. That outlaws hired by McSween are terrifying the populace. And that McSween made up the 'Santa Fe Ring' as a smoke screen for his wrongdoings."

Dolan added, "Our being in Santa Fe now is good timing. Catron and Axtell can meet with us about that partisan ignoramus, Copeland. After that Brady tax accusation, you would have thought McSween knew that a sheriff needs to post bond as tax collector within his first thirty days. I've waited with baited breath. Copeland's time ran out yesterday! All we need to do is give Axtell our choice for the new sheriff - to add it to his proclamation removing Copeland."

Just then, thirty miles south, in Lincoln, Alexander McSween said to John Copeland, "Victory's on its way with the arrival of Special Investigator Angel. Now's the time to secure Tunstall's property. Those horses stolen from his Feliz Ranch must be retrieved. Their number is small; but the principle is great."

MAY 25, 1878   9:45 AM   SATURDAY

Back in Fort Sumner, where crowds anticipated a horserace, Billy, in the mansion, boasted to Luz Maxwell and Paulita, "When us Regulators rode into Lincoln with the rescued horses, people cheered." He omitted that, in their wake, Manuel Segovia "the Indian" - one of Frank MacNab's murderers, thief of his now retrieved mount, and member of Tunstall's assassination posse - lay bullet-riddled and dead. Paulita fingered a curl dangling to her chest, where Billy's distracted eyes discovered new fullness.

To his reddening face, her mother said, "Justice, at last," nursing her own vendettas. Paulita asked if he was the leader. Luz Maxwell laughed. "That child does not stop talking about you. Even your horse." Paulita asked if Sugar could have a baby with Centauro soon.

Billy was blurting about waiting, when Peter Maxwell hurried in, whining to his mother, "Damn crisis. Gold Dust has a problem. And this was the race to fix that Fly fiasco."

Luz Maxwell sighed. "Fly should have taught the opposite. But your father never learned either."

To Billy she said, "The famous story of Fly: It was sixty-six. Lucien had made a race course outside Las Vegas. The grand hotels like Moore's Hotsprings were not yet built; but the town was fashionable because of the waters. And Lucien had a horse that he thought was unbeatable: Fly. She was to race a bay named Bald Hornet, from El Paso. There were probably five thousand people. Our Harry Betts was on Fly. The track was a mile. For the first half, Fly led.

"But Lucien forgot that all her victories were half miles. Unfortunately, Bald Hornet was a full miler. So he won. Later Lucien admitted to me that he had lost a small fortune."

Maxwell said to Billy, "I've got a proposition: ride Gold Dust. I'll pay well."

"Do it, Billy," said Paulita. "You'll win. I'll watch." He said he would have to look at the horse first.

Behind the barn, Jesús Silva held the restless stallion, a gleaming red-gold buckskin with black mane and tail. Silva whispered to Billy, "Betts was thrown. Hurt badly. The horse went crazy." As Maxwell waited impatiently, Billy located a muscle spasm in Gold Dust's hip, making him kick out in pain. Billy agreed to ride, offered to try hot compresses, and gave no guarantee.

Then came the running, the straight track to the horizon. Somewhere in time, and through a blur of people and shouting, Billy on Gold Dust passed another horse, then the finish line; neither wanting to stop.

Reentering swarming humanity, Billy dismounted. Maxwell euphorically embraced him, and exclaimed with misleading drunken hyperbole, "I'll never forget this! I owe you. Anything you ask."

Then Billy saw Paulita. Justified in the unrestrained crowd, he hugged, burying his wet dusty face into her hair.

MAY 28, 1878   10:22 AM   MONDAY

At the Lincoln Courthouse door, Sheriff John Copeland stood with frightened townspeople looking at a nailed posting.

Under *PROCLAMATION BY THE GOVERNOR* was an American eagle flying like a harpie into their town, its open beak facing the House as if in allegiance. "Damned if I understand," Copeland replied to questions. "Some messenger from Santa Fe said it was something about taxes. Yes, it means I'm not Sheriff no more. George Peppin's your sheriff now."

Dawning on all was realization that each victory was rapidly defeated by a corrupt backlash of Santa Fe Ring power. No one said the word, but it hovered: "war." The eagle was screaming, "War!"

JUNE 2, 1878   1:10 PM   SUNDAY

When Billy rode up to the Coe cousins' farmhouse, hitched was an unfamiliar gelding: a muddy u-necked roan with worn-out equipment. Cautiously, Billy checked a window. The Coes were at their table with a husky blond youth, whose clothing gave the same impression of exposure to the elements.

Inside, Billy helped himself to beans with salt pork, and sat opposite the stranger. George said, "This here's Tom O'Folliard. Drifted from Texas looking for work. Told him we're in a war."

The clean-shaven boy, with broad-featured face, looked shyly at Billy with dull light eyes fringed with unruly brows. His thick-lipped mouth, drooping open, made a friendly smile. Large buttocks protruded over his stool.

Billy ate hungrily. He said, "Been to Lincoln. Everybody's upset about Axtell's latest proclamation about Copeland. But President Hayes's investigator will be in Lincoln this week. I signed up to give information."

"Makes you a target," said George, with timidity that irritated Billy.

Frank said, "Can' believe he's 'Angel.' We're needin' a mericle."

Billy said, "Mac - I visited him - was making notes for his statement to him. He's real confident that President Hayes will help." Sipping coffee, Billy faced the newcomer. "Interested in fighting?"

"Wouldn' min'," O'Folliard answered in a pleasant gentle voice.

Frank asked what work he'd done. "Farmin'. At my uncle's in Uvalde. 'Im an' my aun' raised me. They don' wan' me no more."

"Tom," said George. "I forgot. This here's Billy Bonney."

"Hey, Billy." Small eyes watched Billy's lips, waiting for him to speak. Billy asked if he'd want to shoot a few rounds. "Wouldn' min'," O'Folliard said.

After ascertaining his limited firearm ability, Billy spent hours teaching O'Folliard. When late afternoon, cool wind blew from high conifer-covered hills, Billy said he was heading up there to sleep out. O'Folliard said, "I been sleepin' ou' from Texas. I don' min'."

Later, with their cook fire glowing in moonless night, O'Folliard asked, "You killt anybody?" Maybe, Billy answered. "I'd too - to proteck friens like you. I never saw nobody shoot like you. An' you 'splained things good. Yer real smart. Tell me somethin'. Why 're people alays fightin'?"

Billy watched stars flickering in the high pine needles. "Some take what isn't theirs. Others have to stop them." Aware of the hero worship in the bashful eyes, Billy relaxed into familiar superiority and protectiveness with this more pleasant version of his lost brother. And Tom O'Folliard sighed with relief of a drowning man seizing flotsam and feeling no longer at the mercy of the deep.

JUNE 6, 1878   4:17 PM   THURSDAY

Inside the Lincoln courthouse, Juan Patrón, in his best suit, and holding long legal papers, entered the room where Frank Warner Angel waited with a transcriptionist. The handsome attorney watched Patrón's practiced planting of his cane to swivel and swing his paralyzed leg, whose foot then slapped lifelessly against the clay floor; and decided the precise unashamed maneuver added to his aura of dignity. Graciously, Angel said, "Your willingness to review the McSween deposition of this morning is appreciated."

Sitting, Patrón used both hands to lift his paralyzed leg into a normalized position. He said, "For me, it was a privilege to read the truth that will come to our esteemed president."

After Patrón had finished his own deposition, Angel asked about his injury. "I was shot in a failed attempt of the Dolan party to take my life. I did not say it for your writing because, if you were to hear all my words, you would see that the one hundred and seventy-eight pages of Alexander McSween would be only the beginning of what us citizens have suffered." Patrón's large melancholy eyes recognized that the investigator seemed moved.

JUNE 8, 1878   8:34 AM   SATURDAY

When Billy entered the courthouse room for his deposition, he assessed a large window for escape. The seated man, assumedly Frank Warner Angel, continued to watch the door, and said, "I'm waiting for a Mister Bonney." When Billy identified himself, Angel smiled, noting his startlingly blue eyes and said, "I was expecting an older man. That said, tell me what you understand of our preceding today."

Billy chose a chair against a wall. "To hear from me what happened to Mister Tunstall." Angel asked his age. "A hundred sixty-eight days short of nineteen, Sir."

Angel was amused. "So you were born on November twenty-third of fifty-nine." Their eyes met, acknowledging mutual ability. "Do you understand that the testimony you'll be giving today will be under sworn oath?" Billy had not, but agreed to it.

After his deposition, Billy was directed to another room to await Angel's review of the transcript. He went to its open window, which faced the south hills. Unexpectedly, Tom O'Folliard was there. Billy said, "You were supposed to be at Ellis's, watching the horses."

The heavy youth looked bashfully at his large feet. "I'm here to proteck you."

Billy left him there. On a table, were stacks which he realized were completed depositions. Billy wedged a precautionary paper wad into the hinge-side door crack. Then he read Murphy's. McSween's made a separate pile. Skimming that, he came to its Exhibits of contracts with the Fritz estate, and read their unfamiliar legal jargon: "*Know all persons by these presents that we, Emilie Scholand and Charles Fritz ...*" Footsteps interrupted. He removed his paper block.

The transcriptionist left his statement for checking, and said he was to come back and sign in front of Attorney Angel. Spidery, extremely slanting letters covered the papers. Billy read: "*William H. Bonney being duly sworn says that he is employed on the ranch of John Henry Tunstall as well as having in partnership with a Fred Waite a ranch on the Peñasco River for the purpose of cattle raising.*" Continuing, he was pleased to see recorded his meticulous detail about the murder, including his beginning sentences with "that said" in mimicry of Angel.

Next, reading Gottfried Gauss's deposition, he saw Buck Morton's quote about scalping, and slammed the pages down.

When Billy returned, so pale that Angel guessed the process had drained him, the transcriptionist gave a pen. In Billy's hand, now accustomed to revolver and carbine weight, it felt surprisingly fragile. He leaned over the desk.

Lacking needed Spencerian support for hand and forearm, he wrote, *"William H. Bonney."* It looked awkward, the *"B"* worst of all.

Angel remarked, "My understanding is that you were also on the posse to capture John Tunstall's murderers - until Justice of the Peace Wilson was removed by the governor."

Color flared. "Sir, since John Tunstall's murder, I was *always* an officer of the law. I was Deputy to Constable Atanacio Martinez this February nineteenth; and I was a member of Deputy Josiah Scurlock's posse from May fourteenth.

"I'd still be, except Governor Axtell fired Sheriff Copeland on the twenty eighth of this month. But that doesn't mean my work's done." The steely gaze was not a boy's. Angel felt surprise and foreboding.

Later, at Isaac Ellis's place, Billy introduced Tom O'Folliard as a new Regulator, and asked for writing materials. At the dining table, with O'Folliard raptly observing, Billy then created pages of rightward slanting lines, ovals, loops, and the alphabet.

Finally, in once again, fluid Spencerian script, with personal modifications, was *"Know all persons by these presents"* and *"Witnessed by,"* then repetitions of *"William H. Bonney"* and *"W.H. Bonney."* Lastly was an artistic inspiration: *"W Hbonney;"* in which "H" and the "B" were united as one.

Billy looked with satisfaction at this culmination of self-naming, and felt its auspicious power.

JUNE 25, 1878   10:00 AM   TUESDAY

In the Lincoln courthouse, James Dolan's mellifluous voice continued ingratiatingly to Frank Warner Angel, "We had all hoped you would return to Santa Fe. Larry Murphy and Sam Axtell - I know - found their chats, their depositions, with you so helpful; as did Tom Catron with his. Oh. Tom did want me to mention that his schedule delayed preparing documents you requested."

Dolan paused. "How much longer will you be in Lincoln?" The answer was till the second of July. Dolan replied, "After the interview with Doctor Appel?"

Angel felt uneasy at this private knowledge. Dolan said, "In fact, we might still be able to show our appreciation. Steve Elkins may be going to Washington ..."

Angel thought, "He's testing for a bribe. He's their messenger."

Dolan saw no fear and thought, "He doesn't realize our power."

Angel said curtly, "I live in New York, not Washington, Mister Dolan," and proceeded with the interview.

"Please give your statement as to the reasons for the current troubles in Lincoln County."

The answer was recorded: "*The sole cause arises out of one Alexander McSween trying to defraud the estate of our past partner, Emil Fritz, out of a life insurance policy for $10,000. McSween also formed a conspiracy of men, including John Tunstall and John Chisum, to ruin me and my partner John Riley by spreading false rumors about our business.*"

After the deposition's review, Dolan wrote his distinctive signature, "*Jas. J. Dolan,*" in which J's were bold, but following letters became short and squat, as if behind a façade existed a different being.

Angel said, "It seems the Lincoln County troubles may not be over. I've heard rumors that a John Kinney and his men are being sent here by District Attorney William Rynerson to aid Sheriff Peppin in an attack on McSween and his followers."

Dolan smiled indulgently, satisfied at having acquired the date of Angel's departure so the attack could be scheduled; and lied: "First of all, I know nothing of those rumors. But I do know that the McSween faction spreads false tales to case alarm."

Angel asked how he could say that with Tunstall's murder just four months past. "Because they are unrelated. Tunstall was duped by that scoundrel, McSween, into attacking our sheriff's possemen."

As Dolan left, Angel thought, "Fascinating: the criminal mind in action." He paused to savor his achievement, as the pieces were falling into place with such stark contrast of good and evil.

JULY 3, 1878   7:19 AM   WEDNESDAY

In Las Tablas, Yginio Salazar had been awakened by an exhausted rider from Mesilla sounding the alarm that John Kinney and thirty men were riding to attack Lincoln. Earlier, Yginio had heard that Sheriff George Peppin had deputized Jack Long and Billy Matthews.

Now, with zealot's fire, Yginio rode bearing these warnings to the Regulators hiding out with Alexander McSween at John Chisum's South Spring River Ranch.

At the southern foothills of the Capitan Mountains, Yginio stopped at the little, mud-walled, jacal residence of a family friend. The woman said, "The big war is coming. People are fleeing Lincoln."

Before leaving, Yginio bowed his head at her santos and painted tin retablo of the Virgin of Guadalupe.

At the town's main road, Yginio joined the agitated current of Lincoln refugees, and learned a new and dreadful rumor: the first attack would be at San Patricio.

In San Patricio, men were in the fields, their jacals and adobe brick abodes like squat loaves on hills leading up to the mesa on which were a store, the dancehall, the cantina, and the largest houses.

There, at the Montez's dining table, sat Town Constable José Chávez y Chávez, Justice of the Peace Gregorio Trujillo, Enrique Montez, and swarthy Martin Chávez from Picacho.

The Town Constable said, "Yes, Florencio Gonzalez fled to Fort Stanton. He was sure Sheriff Peppin would murder him."

Enrique Montez said they had heard Juan Patrón was killed. "No," Chávez y Chávez responded. "But Saturday they tried. He also is at the fort for safety."

To Martin Chávez, Montez said, "And McSween thought he was safe here last Thursday. But Sheriff Peppin raided with six possemen. Then soldiers joined them to help. The Regulators were shooting from various rooftops until Peppin and the soldiers left."

Martin Chávez nervously commented that in Picacho it was thought that Kinney would invade Lincoln with a hundred men.

Chávez y Chávez said, "Exaggeration. But we heard that, to kill McSween, Kinney was offered five hundred dollars and also the cattle of Tunstall. Where is your sweet daughter?" he asked Montez, who said she was with old Señora Sanchez. Her bad heart again.

Martin Chávez asked, "So you do not fear another attack here? We in Picacho are uneasy."

"No," answered Chávez y Chávez. "We are not too worried."

In an adobe on a hill below, a pudgy five month old nursed. Full, he smiled, bubbling white. "Go to Auntie Doll," his mother said, using her tiny sister's nickname, and went to a cutting board with cubed goat meat. With a large knife, she diced green chili peppers and asked, "When will Eusebio be back from Picacho?" Her sister was patting together the baby's hands to a song, and did not hear. "Eusebio, when will he be back?"

"By nightfall. With your Mateo. We are lucky. Marrying two brothers and living together. Oo, Javier. Careful. No fingers in Auntie Doll's eyes." She laughed. "Before we know, we will be at his wedding."

At the same time, a young goatherd on the highest hill above San Patricio noticed a giant dust cloud to the south. With his eight goats were three playful kids. One precociously tried to mount another, but ended up broadside, hanging. The boy laughed and forgot the odd phenomenon.

Soon after, Yginio galloped to the primary level shouting, "Attack! Attack! The posse!" Men ran from the Montez house. "Kinney! Peppin!" Yginio panted. A shot rang out. Then a barrage.

Yginio raced Torcio higher. From behind a rocky outcropping, he saw invaders streaming up the hills.

At the house of the two sisters, a rider fired into a window. They were huddled between the cupboard and stove. His bullet ricocheted with a ping off the metal. The mother felt her baby's spasm and a brushing past her blouse. The baby became limp. The man heard the sisters' wailing just as Yginio's bullet shattered his spine just below the neck. His body seemed to disappear as he slid off his horse.

Now there was only rampage and destruction. Some, with Peppin, Long, Matthews, and short muscular John Kinney, rode into the main part of the town.

Onto the goatboy's hill went one. The boy had run away. His tame animals were shot before their killer eagerly joined his companions, riding like a net through fields, leaving people and livestock dead in their path.

Next were the small houses. María Montez was in one, crouching with arms around frail old Señora Sanchez. A man entered, looming, and growled, "Where's dinero, bitches?"

The old woman struggled to rise. "Help me," she said to María. "I have savings." She led María to a crock heavy with coins. After filling his pockets, the man roughly pushed aside the old woman, who tumbled, petrified, in crushing agony of her infarcting heart.

María, brutally grabbed, struggled until dissociating into unawareness of blows, or being on the clay floor with her body forever changed.

Amidst Kinney's men, George Peppin shouted to the Montez parapets, "Throw down your arms."

Recognizing futility, Yginio departed on Torcio, tears streaming, as the murder of his father and this massacre became one.

George Peppin shouted, "Any McSween will end up a beggar." He felt pleasurable power, but was unaware that his transformation by Dolan from builder to destroyer was complete.

Kinney taunted, "And tell McSween you met up with John Kinney, head of the Rio Grande Posse. Tell him that, greasers."

In the new silence, tiny Doll stood. Outside lay a man. She knew he was her nephew's murderer. Calmly, from the cutting board, she took the knife. With it pressed in the folds of her skirt, she walked to him.

He pleaded for help. She bent.

Revenging, she sliced and sliced his throat until the red wedge gaped wide, flecked with green chili fragments.

To the dead face she then spoke in words she thought were English: "Gringo dog."

At 8:29 PM, at South Spring River Ranch, John Chisum asked laconically, "Still readin' tha' same book, Alexander?" The lawyer smiled, looking up from his Bible. "Tell me honestly. You figer ye can win?" McSween ventured that he'd hoped to get some of his men.

"Figered ye might ask. Addin' better cards. Bu' I'll show ye my hand. 'Member tha' my boys ran ou' on me in *my* war. Anyways, they're fixin' t' start a big drive." McSween struggled to suppress fear, but did not recognize the selfish treachery.

On the fortified roof above, Billy and Fred Waite stood watch as Tom O'Folliard listened to Billy explain that everything he had said to Angel went right to President Hayes.

Fred Waite said, "You finally convinced me, Kid: you haven't got a drop of Indian blood, or you wouldn't trust the Great White Father in Washington. Ol' Chickasaw saying: 'Whites go through fake legalities just before they attack.' "

Billy said, "If that's so, we don't need Washington to win. Chisum may not be paying, but we've been supported by friends. And, when the time comes, we'll have the Mexicans with us."

Waite saw a galloping horseman. But Billy was already down the ladder.

In the big sitting-room, while Yginio Salazar told about the massacre in San Patricio, the fire blazed as Billy furiously added wood. He heard, "But what's the right time?"

Suddenly, white fury obliterated everything. Billy's eyes were wild, face savage. "*Now's* the time. We fight. In Lincoln. It's war!" He faced McSween. "Are you coming?"

"Yes." McSween said, surprised at his own calm.

JULY 4, 1878   5:10 AM   THURSDAY

On the way back to Lincoln, when Billy, Fred Waite, and Tom O'Folliard, entered Roswell's dark post office, they heard, from the storeroom Ash Upson used for sleeping, clinking of bottle neck against a glass. Upson believed, if he put bottle to lips, he was irretrievably alcoholic. When he stumbled out, Billy sent O'Folliard with him to get ammunition from the Jones's side.

Waite laughed. "Seven Rivers ammunition for our war. Kid, you're something."

While O'Folliard loaded the supplies, including sacks of jerky, and Billy paid, Ash Upson said, "Heard you added more notches to your gun." Billy answered that nobody notched their gun.

Upson turned to Waite. "Do you realize that this is 'The Kid: Boy Warrior of the Lincoln County War?' The hero of the book that's going to make me rich and him famous."

As they left, Upson called, "The Seven Rivers boys are riding to kill you Regulators. That is, after McSween. Kid, if you get killed now, it won't be much of a story. I'll have to add the part about killing Indians." Waite scowled.

Several hours later, sixty-five miles northwest of Roswell, in Lincoln, Susan McSween indignantly adjusted her ostrich-feathered hat. She wore a seventeen-seam, orange silk bodice, fitting like skin over her corseted hour-glass, and flaring over a plaid overskirt, yellow underskirt, and puffy rear flounces with a train. She lifted her perfume vial for a heavy application. "Ruffians," she said, putting it back where the purloined one had stood. Without informing her sister or brother-in-law on their side, she stalked out.

Unfurling her parasol, she proceeded down her front path with little stylish strides restricted by the tied tapes pulling taut her skirt front; opened the front picket gate, and turned left.

Contemptuously, she eyed yet another fleeing family of cowards, the Stanleys, in their buckboard. At the Tunstall Store, she stepped into its porch shadow to further minimize sun exposure, before returning to the red earth street.

To her right, "Squire" Wilson, tending his vegetables, greeted her. Passing the vacant lot to the left, and trying to ignore the thought that her trailing train must be thoroughly dirty, she glanced at the crosses of Tunstall and MacNab, and ahead to the Torreon.

To its east side, and set back from the street, was her destination: the house of their tenant, Saturnino Baca. His right angled addition to the original two room structure made her think with disgust, "He married that woman when she was eleven. She's no better than a broodmare."

At the front door, Susan McSween rapped sharply, but immediately checked her kidglove knuckles for scraping. The door opened. Potbellied long-bearded Saturnino Baca, in a loose old jacket, baggy pants, and woven leather sandals glowered. She noted his large tufted ears, and thought, "The old goat." Behind him clustered children of all ages and his very pregnant wife, Juana María. He looked toward the street.

She realized townspeople had stopped to listen, but spoke even more loudly. "I heard you sent that posse to San Patricio to kill my husband." In a low threatening voice, he told her to leave his place. "Your place? You're *our* tenant. You should be punished."

"You make to threaten me or my family, Señora McSween?"

"You, not me, will have to live with your conscience, Mister Baca." Satisfied, she left the humiliated couple, whose longstanding animosity she had magnified to a vendetta.

JULY 13, 1878   9:16 AM   SATURDAY

In the Picacho house of Martin Chávez, Billy, Tom O'Folliard, and Charlie Bowdre were at a table. Men in that town, and in San Patricio, infuriated by the massacre, were preparing for the ride into Lincoln the following day. Other Regulators guarded the adobe in which McSween still slept.

Bowdre, with poised pen, said to Billy, "Yaw good with words. Ah wan' tah write Edgar Walz an' Catron 'bout how we Regalators protect people an' propahty from their Ring. An' that we'll take revenge."

Billy dictated: "*Mister Walz Sir. We all know that your brother-in-law Mister Catron sustains the Dolan party. Steal or destroy property of the poorest or richest American or Mexican and the full measure of the injury you do shall be visited upon his property. REGULATORS.*"

One hundred-twenty miles northeast of Picacho, Frank Warner Angel, waiting alone in the Las Vegas courthouse, visualized his wife's body, felt desire, and introspected. "It's all this violence I've been listening to. Unrestrained lust." On the desk were his interview questions for Deputy Sheriff Adolph Barrier.

Angel imagined Rutherford B. Hayes from a photograph and fantasized, " 'Yes, it would be an honor, Mister President, to be considered for the Supreme Court.' Tilden got 'Boss' Tweed. Hayes almost lost to Tilden. I could vindicate Hayes. Uncover the scandal of the century." British Ambassador, Edward Thornton, was praising him when the fresh-faced transcriptionist entered. Angel said, "An interesting town you have here."

" 'Specially Moore's Hotsprings Hotel. I've been there once. High class people." Observing Angel's handsomeness, he offered, "It's got beautiful women. It's in the mountains."

When Adolph Barrier arrived, Angel studied him with interest, having been intrigued by his unusual dedication. After the transcribed questioning, Angel probed. "This is not for the record. You remained with your prisoner from January fourth to March twenty-ninth. You have a wife and children. Did this represent a hardship?"

Barrier said a considerable one.

"This is back on the record. Please describe your motivation - include gain you may have accrued or been promised." And the transcriber wrote: "*My action in regard to Alexander McSween was to preserve his life and not for any pecuniary or personal considerations. I have no interest in the troubles in Lincoln County other than as a citizen of the Territory who believes that justice should be meted out to everyone without fear or favor.*"

After signing, Barrier asked, "Did you hear things got worse in Lincoln County, Sir?" Angel questioned, saying he had been occupied with several other investigations also.

"On the third, there was a raid on San Patricio, with considerable loss of life and property - said to be done by a known rustler named John Kinney, and his gang from Mesilla. I heard he was sent by District Attorney Rynerson." Angel did not reveal that he had known about that risk.

"And I've also heard that Governor Axtell removed Sheriff Copeland and replaced him with George Peppin. Peppin and his deputies rode into San Patricio along with Kinney's men. I'd say it all means that Attorney McSween's in gravest danger."

Angel said, "I'd like your opinion. Do you believe there exists a Santa Fe Ring in which Governor Axtell and U.S. Attorney Catron are participants?" Barrier said that he did. "If that's so, your actions could have - and may still - put you, your job, and even your family at risk. Why did you do it?" It was his job, Barrier answered. "But your acts violated Judge Bristol's orders."

"It was my job as a human being, Sir," Adolph Barrier answered steadily.

When Angel was again alone, gathering his papers, he thought, "And if I was tested like Barrier - to lose so much for nothing - what would I do?" Outside the bright window were purple pine-dotted mountains. Angel's only task for that day was completed. He felt restless excitement.

JULY 14, 1878   9:18 AM   SUNDAY

Hot wind, channeled by the mountains and high hills, seared the empty Lincoln street, brutally preparing it for war.

In the Wortley Hotel, James Dolan, Billy Matthews, Jack Long, and Pantaleon Gallegos listened to long-necked George Peppin, with anxiously bobbing Adam's apple, saying, "All that's left here, Jimmy, are McSween's wife and her sister, the Ealys with Miss Gates boarding with them, Missus Montaño, and Ellis and his family. José Montaño and David Shield are out of town. Baca stayed. And crazy 'Squire' Wilson's gardening. And I don't have enough men for a fight. Pantaleon, can you get some Mexicans?"

"Baca and me try. All is McSweens."

Dolan commented tartly, "George, possibly an occupational hazard of being Lincoln County Sheriff is loss of nerve.

"Have you forgotten Andy Boyle with his Seven Rivers boys at the Fritz Ranch, and Kinney's Rio Grande Posse camping near Dead Man's Rock? Are you forgetting our key ally: Colonel Dudley?"

Peppin complained that they'd just made some law that the military couldn't help civilians.

"What you are talking about," said Dolan, "is the Posse Comitatus Act, passed last month on the eighteenth. It said soldiers could not be used in civil disturbances, unless by command of the president. John Riley is in Santa Fe. He got word to me that Tom Catron found a way around it. The military still has to protect women and children. Saturnino Baca's voluminous brood is here - with his wife about to have yet another addition."

Matthews asked, "What if that investigator Angel wires Hayes and stops everything?"

Dolan sneered. "All of you, listen: I AM THE POWER." His sapphire eyes were horrible, insane, and irresistible in absolute conviction. "In this world, there is gluttony concentrated in so few, but in a magnitude beyond your conception. *I* remove the obstacles in their path. And once their power is attained - as it exists now in New Mexico Territory - *nothing* can stop it."

Peppin asked uneasily if he was joking. People had rights.

"Dead people have none," Dolan said.

Bootsteps shifted their attention. "Jessie," Dolan said warmly, "I was about to let everyone know that Doctor Appel had worked wonders on your wrist."

"Ain' no problem with the Winchester." Wrist bandaged, he swung the weapon.

A few minutes later, bald Sam Wortley ran in shouting, "Your trouble's riding this way!"

Dolan's tone was clipped and hard. "Jessie, keep them back. When you can, Jack, get Kinney and his men. Matthews get the Seven Rivers boys."

Approaching from the east, was Alexander McSween, leading his sixty-one loyalists; and excitedly misjudging the town's emptiness as retreat of his adversaries.

Shots rang from the Wortley Hotel. Billy assessed the quiet House and yelled, "They're all at the Hotel! We can finish them off!"

"No! I say, 'No!' McSween countered, suppressing trepidation that his enemies still lurked. "We stand for peace."

Little Doc Scurlock, de facto Regulator leader after death's attrition, listened with indecision. Attack was valid; but McSween's authority was paralyzing.

Ridiculously pear-shaped, with his dusty spectacles two blind moons, Scurlock called, "What Mac thayth, we follow!"

"To my house!" commanded McSween. They turned to gallop eastward, proving, but not realizing, that they had no strategy.

At his picket fence, McSween ebulliently waved his hat at his wife, emerging with Harvey Morris and George Washington. His voice rang out, "I'm home to stay! We'll hold the town till the citizens come back secure in peace!" Many of his men cheered.

"Please, Mac!" yelled Billy. "I'll do it myself. Let me get them at the Wortley."

McSween instead called, "Direct our men, Captain Scurlock!"

Billy attempted again, saying to Scurlock that Matthews and Long had already crossed to the stables to get help. Scurlock felt pressured, and mobilized. "You damn well heard Mac. When we get together again it 'ill be to thelebrate winning. You, Martin Chávez and hith men, and Fernando Herrera, and Yginio Thalathar go to Montaño'th. And Than Patrithio men go there too, and to Patrón'th."

"I go with Billy," called O'Folliard, fearing separation.

"What about Mac?" Billy called.

Scurlock realized his error. "Frenchie, you go," he said.

Billy said, "If you want it that way, we've got to distribute the food and ammunition from the pack animals. Mac 'ill need the most. And each place needs to store water for a siege."

In Spanish he said to Martin Chávez, "Go to the wall in the back of McSween's. There are two gates wide enough to lead a pack horse: one at the east yard beside a chicken coop, the other near the stable in the west yard." He then said, "Missus McSween, we've got to cut portholes in your walls."

"Alexander," she asked with dismay, "is that necessary?" Unsettled by the unexpected fusillade, combined with Billy's certainty of danger, he said it would demonstrate determination.

Doc Scurlock continued, "For the Tunthtall thtore: Henry Brown, George Coe, and John Newcomb. And for the eatht thide of town, at Ellith'eth, I want Charlie Bowdre, John Middleton, Frank Coe, Fred Waite, and anyone left. I'll be there. And put all the horthes in the Ellith corral."

At the rear of the McSween property, Billy learned from George Washington that the boarded houses immediately west were the Schon's and Mrs. Ham Mills's, and across the street was the Stanley's; as he directed the men carrying in supplies, including a six pound keg of gunpowder for reloading.

To Washington, Billy said, "Get help blocking windows with adobe bricks - damn it that the wall wasn't finished - and then shutter them."

Gray Sugar pranced restlessly, responding to Billy's frustration. Washington knowingly asked if he was angry. "We just goddamn missed such an easy win. Like getting dealt a royal flush, then throwing down your hand anyway."

At 2:40 PM, Alexander McSween, sitting in the parlor with his wife and Harvey Morris, realized he was exhausted. There had been no rest since February eighteenth. Even before, there had been that abominable Bristol Hearing. But he refused to think about the corpse that had lain in that very room. When this was over, he and Susan would go to Saint Louis to rest. The noise of the men making portholes was a nightmare.

Abruptly, McSween felt claustrophobically imprisoned. The room appeared strange; with a bizarre impression that chairs, sofa, piano, his wife, and Morris were not real - only a stereopticon picture. A shadow image sprang at the corner of his eye: Tunstall's ghost? Fleetingly, he wondered if he could go mad from pressure.

He composed himself. He hadn't had a fresh collar for weeks. He must dress properly for the townspeople when they returned. He would be a hero. He heard his wife say with exasperation, "Sacre bleu, Mister French. Please stop pacing."

"Sorry, Ma'am. Way I am. But call me Frenchie."

"Then please go to the east wing, Frenchie, and ask my sister to make you something to eat." Susan McSween watched his jerky rapid exit and said, "Alexander those men are leaving adobe dirt all over. Harvey, when that nerve-wracking boy finishes eating, get George and him to clean up."

Morris asked about storing water, like Billy said. "We can wait," answered McSween. "He's hot-headed."

After Morris left, McSween said, in his preachy courtroom voice, "Susan, I know that my labors, and the fugitive days, and the deaths were not in vain. I've gotten a confidential communication from Investigator Angel that, on June thirteenth, an inspector from the Department of the Interior was sent to the Mescalero Reservation. I anticipate Indian Agent Godfroy will soon be removed. And Governor Axtell also. I'd even predict the fall of U.S. Attorney Catron. And when Catron falls, so will his minions: Dolan, Riley, Bristol, and Rynerson. And Murphy's on his deathbed. It's only a matter of time." He felt her admiration.

"And after I write John Tunstall's father about my success, he may continue investing. Then you'll get those ruby earrings!" She laughed, having already taken the precaution, in the unexpected chaos of strangers who might be thieves, to pin the ring to her corset cover. McSween felt his earlier excitement return. This was God's purpose. This was the certainty of salvation.

Three hundred and six yards east of their house, in the Montaño store, Billy listened to swarthy Martin Chávez's high-pitched voice. "And Enrique Montez's daughter was beaten ... and other things.

Thirty-two died including the baby and the old woman. Much damage and robbery. The old woman alone had savings of four hundred eight dollars." Yginio Salazar said bitterly that all were martyrs for freedom.

That moment, Jim French ran into the McSween parlor and shockingly smashed a front window with his carbine butt, firing westward. Susan McSween indignantly demanded that he open the front door. The smell was disgusting. "No way!" he exclaimed, wildly aroused. "Seven Rivers boys 're come!"

"Good," said McSween smugly. "I've got Justice of the Peace Gregorio Trujillo's warrants for them."

French laughed at the absurdity. "Can I give George a pistol, Mac? I got me an extra." When told they stood for peace, French called, "George, we gotta brick up these windas goddamn fast."

At the Wortley Hotel, Dolan directed milling horsemen. "Put the horses into the House corral. Kinney and Boyle, I want your boys at the House for now. At the Torreon I want Long and Matthews. Bring Dummy for a messenger. They won't shoot him. With me here, I want you, George, Andy, and Pantaleon." Jessie Evans, beside him, made clear it was his place too.

After hearing French's blasts, Billy asked in Spanish, "Who is coming with me to McSween?" Five volunteered: José Chávez y Chávez, Ignacio Gonzales, Florencio Chávez, Francisco Zamora, and Vincente Romero. Tom O'Folliard joined them.

Martin Chávez remained immobilized in impotent imbalance with crossed legs, one foot humbly atop the other; just like his farmer father, ashamed of his skin color and Indio blood. As they ran out, Billy called, "Thanks for the good food, Señora Montaño."

Seeing them from inside the Torreon, Long shouted, "You're under arrest, Kid." Billy laughed and fired at Long's fortified slit.

Jim French threw open the front door. "Brought you company," Billy said to him; and to all: "We can still hold the town. The new men are trapped to the west. Those at the Torreon have got Montaño men and Tunstall men at either side."

Susan McSween asked when it would be over, just as Minnie Shield came from the east wing.

Billy said, "Can't say, Ma'am. We've got about eighteen days' supplies. As long as we've got water. 'Cause we're stuck inside."

Minnie cried out in alarm that the chickens would starve. Billy said, "They're good at finding food.

"And Missus McSween - sorry to bring this up - but we need something to put ... more than chamber pots. We can't get to the outhouse.

"And at the Montaño's they're using the bathtub to store water. We can put, uh, yours in the east kitchen for water too."

"Aren't you over-reacting?" asked McSween, affronted by the intrusiveness. "Like my embezzlement case, this is a bluff."

"Hope so, Mac. But these boys need to know where you want 'em to bed down."

As the McSweens gazed with discomfiture at the strangers, Billy noticed tearful Elizabeth Shield in the dining-room with her baby and the two younger boys. Again horror, she was thinking. That's why Miss Gates had moved to the Ealy's. Why couldn't she be brave like her sister? There was also anger. Susan had brought her to this unsafe place. No. That was ungrateful. Susan was sharing her wealth. David. He'd hear and send help. Then she visualized the shattered French figurine and trampled books. Trembling, she held baby Annie tighter.

East of the Torreon, Saturnino Baca's wife lay groaning with familiar labor contractions, as Josephina ministered and her husband avoided the suffering.

In the Tunstall apartment, dinner was being shared by the Ealy's and Susan Gates with George Coe, Henry Brown, and John Newcomb. The doctor asked, "So you believe this is the War?"

Susan Gates listened apprehensively as she cut meat for the Ealy's five year old daughter, Pearl.

"Could be," said Coe, "but they're cornered again - like on April thirtieth."

"Squire" Wilson, in his little house, was reading *History of the Great Rebellion* by Thomas P. Kettell, published in 1865. "Battle of Pittsburgh Landing," he mouthed, as he looked up from page 308. "That's the same as Shiloh." He continued. "In the event of an attack at Pittsburgh Landing, Major General Lew Wallace was to flank the rebels by marching from Crump's Landing. But, through misdirection as to the way, he never reached the battle-field until the fighting was over for the day." Wilson laughed. "Can't fight a war if your general can't find it."

Within artificial darkness of the barricaded McSween house, it had been decided that the re-arranged dining-room would be the men's quarters. Supplies were also left in David Shield's office: the first room in the east wing, and where Harvey Morris also slept.

On the parlor sofa, sitting beside Alexander McSween, his wife stitched needlepoint. He sought the distraction of her nimble fingers, but glanced at the cobweb-clumped bricks blocking all windows, and felt claustrophobic. "My dear," he said stiltedly, struggling for normalcy, "we've had so little time together. It would be a comfort to be together at night."

"And for me also." She smiled tenderly, with sexual stirrings at his new masculinity. "I've missed you." Animated voices came from the dining room. "They're gambling," she said with repugnance.

McSween answered, "Would you play the piano, Susan? I'll bring them in for that song from Psalm hundred and twenty-one: 'I to the Hills Will Lift my Eyes.' It would be a charity."

Trusting, with annoyance, her needle sideways in her hoop, she made out his "evening devotional." The men filed in; those with hopeless cards experiencing salvation.

Billy asked McSween to tell Elizabeth Shield that he'd be heading out through the kitchen. "Me too," Tom O'Folliard said urgently. "I'm protectin' you."

Once outside, Billy noted that his ungainly husky companion followed with surprising agility. They scrambled down the first tier toward the Bonito, then to its twilight water.

Billy drank and splashed his face. Tom O'Folliard copied within insect chanting of synchronous grating punctuated by surges of solo virtuosity. Billy mingled briefly with that song, then led eastward along the riverbank.

Leaving Isaac Ellis's house after coordinating plans, Billy said to O'Folliard that he wanted to check the horses. "Tha's why you got tha' feed bag o' corn from Ben Ellis? He's Isaac's son, right?"

"Yes. For Sugar." In the corral, she arched her lovely silver neck as she came nickering. After he slipped on the feedbag, she rested its bottom against his jacketed shoulder. Billy said, "Some horses put them against the ground to get the corn. She figured out she could use me instead." He laughed softly with affection.

JULY 15, 1878   6:39 AM   MONDAY

Alexander McSween awoke in his wife's dark and stifling room to thudding, and thought, "Portholes in my bedroom. All this to better appreciate what God has provided." That consolation ended with shamed realization that the men would conclude that he didn't sleep with his wife.

Sleepily, Susan McSween murmured, "I think they get wicked pleasure from ruining things." He said he was blessed that she'd stayed in town. She yawned daintily. "Of course. No ruffians will bully me out. That boy who left, did he come back?" Told very late, she responded, "He's certainly lively."

When clothed professionally, McSween left her buttoning her corset front over a chemise. Awaiting her were lacy corset cover, under petticoat, rear flounced outer one, a bodice, and layered skirts.

Yginio Salazar and Francisco Zamora, with axes and crowbars, enthusiastically greeted McSween, as hesitating notes came from the parlor. Billy was locating "Turkey in the Straw" with index fingers.

"Mornin', Mac," Billy said cheerfully to the man entering and adjusting his collar. "Seems Dolan's fighters don't miss sleep even in a war. We managed to fill the tub. And Missus Shield said the men in the Torreon didn't bother her and the children using the outhouse.

"But we've got a problem. She saw Baca's girls bringing food and a water bucket to the Torreon. I was hoping to starve 'em out. Saturnino Baca's a problem."

Anger invigorated McSween and yielded a plan. Striding to the east kitchen for breakfast, he heard the mastered "Turkey in the Straw" being played exuberantly.

Later, at his parlor desk, McSween wrote forcefully under his legal letterhead: *"Saturnino Baca. Sir. Unless you leave within three days, eviction proceedings will be instituted. You have made improper use of my property by aiding murderers threatening my life."* He directed Washington to deliver it.

When the task was completed, Baca paced in rage, deciding the time had come to perform Dolan's order. He wrote from provided notes: *"Colonel Dudley. McSween with 100 men threatens us. My wife just had a baby and is scared to death. Please let me have some soldiers to protect my family and you will confer an everlasting favor."* He told Josephina to bring it to Señor Dolan.

At the Wortley Hotel's rear dining-room, hazy with tobacco smoke, Josephina waited uncomfortably as Dolan read and Panteleon Gallegos eyed her lasciviously. "Tell your father," Dolan said, "that I will send a messenger to the fort. And that he will be rewarded. He will understand."

Five hours later, Susan McSween said to Billy, still at the piano, "If I hear 'Turkey in the Straw' one more time, I'll lose my mind." To her surprise, with the same two fingers, he played the hauntingly beautiful "Irish Washerwoman;" and glanced impishly at her as Tom O'Folliard watched him admiringly.

At Isaac Ellis's corral, his sixteen year old, tow-headed son, Ben, raking the horse droppings, smiled at Gray Sugar while deflecting her nudging head. "You're darn spoiled," he said.

A mile to Ben Ellis's west, at the Wortley Hotel, Dr. Daniel Appel rebandaged Jessie's wrist and said, "Just like a pit fighting bulldog. No pain, and healed quicker than nature intended." Bitterly, Jessie responded that his thumb couldn't work the Colt hammer.

Dolan asked Appel about married life. He answered, "Damn shame what McSween made my father-in-law go through with that

Washington inspector. He couldn't back up his bills by numbers of Indians; so he said they'd run off with Victorio; but wasn't sure he'd convinced him."

Dolan sighed histrionically. "And now McSween's turned loose his cutthroat gang. Dan, we need soldiers to protect women and children. I sent Dudley Saturnino Baca's *desperate* letter."

"That's why I'm here. Dudley called it 'fact-finding,' " Appel too was frustrated by the inexplicable impasse.

Shortly, Yginio Salazar, looking through a westward porthole, called, "Ambulance coming."

McSween met Daniel Appel and said, "Gunmen who murdered John Tunstall and Frank MacNab are threatening the town. We need military help." Pensive notes poised as Billy heard and sighed at the dangerous naivety.

When Appel stopped at the Baca house, Saturnino said, "At least take my wife and new baby to the fort," and wondered if he would be blamed by Dolan for the lack of troops.

Simultaneously, Dolan said to Peppin, "You have David Easton's warrants for McSween and Bonney," correctly assuming he was unaware they were invalid. "Get Long to serve them."

Soon, Jack Long approached McSween's front door, reliving trauma of near-death at the Brady killing. Billy called to McSween that it was an easy shot. McSween irritably countered that it was probably their peace overture, as he went to open the door.

Long said, "I'm here with warrants for arrestin' you an' ..." Billy fired wild through a porthole. Long sprinted around the west corner and scrambled down the shallow arroyo at the property boundary.

Alexander McSween was left with lurching anxiety at what the deputy had meant by warrants.

JULY 16, 1878   8:10 AM   TUESDAY

In abject terror, Alexander McSween groveled and groped along a low tunnel whose door was being pounded by an enemy battering ram. Wet with perspiration, he awoke to knocking and his wife shaking his shoulder.

"Mornin', Mac," Billy called through the door.

Rubbing his stubbled face, McSween took his robe from his wife's armoire. At the opened door, Billy, radiant-faced, with Harvey Morris, enthusiastically reported that Dolan's men were still pinned.

McSween said, "Good. That's good," and thought, "That terrible dream. Can Harvey smell me?" With Billy's water warnings, he had not bathed. Susan had, saying she would not live like an animal.

Morris - now Billy's tubby caricature in shirt and vest, and with pants tucked into ankle-high boots - said, "Mister McSween, I'd like permission to use a pistol."

When he was refused, Billy asked, "What about Harvey making cartridges, Mac? We brought thousands of bullets and shells, and a keg of gunpowder."

Morris pleaded, saying he wanted to contribute. Billy added, "He's sure picking up poker well." Morris blushed and said to McSween that it was to understand future clients.

His wife called that she had to dress. McSween closed the door behind him. Billy said, "Mac, there's a problem;" and led him to the parlor, where odor of human waste assailed him. "We've just got three buckets. We need a better plan." McSween said it probably would be over that day.

Billy ignored that and said, "We'll use that big, lidded barrel in that west storage kitchen." McSween gave permission, and decided it solved his dilemma of reactive constipation.

"And there's another problem, Mac. Only way there's through your rooms. It 'id be better if you both went to the Shield's side." McSween listlessly agreed.

Two hundred eighty-nine yards west of the McSween house, in the Wortley Hotel, James Dolan said angrily to George Peppin, "We're accomplishing nothing."

He called, "Refill, Sam. Also pen and paper." As Dolan sipped whiskey, he dictated for Peppin: "*Colonel Dudley. Sir. If you could loan me a howitzer, I am sure that parties for whom I have warrants would surrender. We are being attacked by a lawless mob.*"

By late afternoon, Commander Dudley's courier, Private Berry Robinson of the 9th Cavalry, rode, in response, from Fort Stanton. Newly recruited, the black youth still lacked formal training. His order to carry a letter from Dudley had prevented a meal of bread and stew, universally scorned, but gaining hunger's appeal.

Dummy met him at the House. Berry Robinson asked, "Y'all know where the sheriff is?"

"They killed him. Sometimes he was mean. Sometimes nice."

Robinson heard beckoning, and was met by George Peppin at the Wortley Hotel. After reading Dudley's message, Peppin exclaimed that he had refused help.

Dolan paid no attention, and invited the soldier to dinner. As Robinson ate in the adjacent room, Peppin complained to Dolan that he couldn't keep the men there much longer.

Dolan spoke instead to Jessie: "You are about to fire the most important shot of your career."

To Peppin, he said, "George, all we need is Private Robinson. Tell him to ride down the street to report back to Dudley on the state of affairs."

To Jessie, Dolan said, "Shoot at him so it looks like it came from McSween's. If you want to hit, make sure he can ride back to the fort.

"And George, the McSweens won't fire because of the soldier. That's your chance to get better positions."

Full and relaxed, Private Berry Robinson rode eastward, wondering if the town had a brothel. Suddenly, a bullet whirred between his chest and his horse's neck. The gelding reared and was thrown over by Robinson's inexperienced wrenching of the reins.

Remounted, unhurt, but panicked, Robinson galloped out of town into the setting sun.

Soon bullets rained down from the high foothills behind the Montaño store, signifying that whatever water the occupants had stored might be their last.

JULY 17, 1878   5:52 AM   WEDNESDAY

Outside was the silence between the birds of night and those of the day. In David Shield's office, Billy looked through a porthole. The McSweens were in the once-shared bedroom of the Shield children; the children themselves moved to the next room in line: their parents' bedroom. Billy whispered to Yginio Salazar that Dolan's men had not gained much. Tom O'Folliard, half asleep, mumbled that he agreed.

Bony, greasy-haired Jim French entered, urinated into a bucket, and said, "Oly place I been this long's jail. Why'd we 'ave t' put them sheets over everythin', Billy? I' looks weird."

"Missus McSween didn't want dirt." Billy grinned. "I bet if Mac let her, she'd be at her own porthole with a pistol." Yginio laughed.

George Washington came in. "Mighty quiet," he said. "Man could have gotten a good night's sleep if Harvey didn't snore worse 'en hell emigrating on cartwheels."

The door opened. Susan McSween's voice, bright and energetic, announced, "We're making breakfast. We saw Susan Gates out. We'll get more water today."

At Fort Stanton, Dudley was meeting with Purlington and Appel. His blustering breath exuded Dolan's alcohol, sent back with the doctor for him. Dudley said, "Determine who attacked my soldier."

On the high south hills, Peppin awoke to hot slanting rays and silence. He roused his four men, saying they'd might as well go down. Charlie Crawford, rolling his bedding, complained, "Andy Boyle tol' us Seven Rivers boys we'd ..." Nine hundred fifteen yards north of him, keen-eyed Fernando Herrera, Charlie Bowdre's brother-in-law, slipped the barrel of his Sharps Big Fifty rifle through a porthole in the rear of the Montaño building. Its crack and Crawford's words, "be killin'," overlapped just before a 475 grain lead slug transected his pelvis. Charlie Crawford collapsed screaming as his running companions abandoned him.

At 12:00 PM, Daniel Appel, George Purlington, and five other soldiers rode into Lincoln to gunfire staccato, as pulverulent wind skimmed the glaring street in choking eddies.

They joined James Dolan and George Peppin in the Wortley Hotel, while Jessie Evans listened. "It was an outrageously audacious attack," Dolan said melodramatically.

Purlington, as baffled by Dudley's inaction as were his listeners, said they had orders from him to interview McSween about the incident.

Dolan nodded a cue. Peppin announced, "A man's been shot, Sirs, but I can't get to him;" and prepared to advance his men using the shield of military presence. Appel responded, as anticipated, saying he had to tend the wounded man. He would take soldiers there with him for protection.

After Dudley's men had departed back to Fort Stanton, having received McSween's statement denying the Berry Robinson shooting, and having retrieved dying Charlie Crawford, the assault resumed on the besieged buildings from the south hillside vantages attained by Sheriff Peppin's men.

At 4:22 PM, inside the McSween house, lit only by oil lamps, the nineteen sweltering people breathed increasingly fetid air.

On the parlor floor, Harvey Morris and George Washington, with the keg of gunpowder, were refilling retrieved casings of the shooting men.

Nearby, on the sheet-concealed couch, was Alexander McSween, having neglected to shave, unopened Bible on lap, and distracted by a secret: the night before, an asthma attack had occurred. What if another came now? Right now?

Susan had nursed him with wet compresses on his laboring chest. Hoarsely he had forced out, "I'm failing, Susan ... In the hour of victory ... I ..." The baby's squalling had been in the next room, his wife sparing him that her sister's milk was failing. From the opposite side, the men in the parlor had been singing, at the top of their lungs, a ribald song from the Mexican independence revolution of 1866 which overthrew Emperor Maximilian and caused his Empress, Carlota, to flee. "Adiós, Mamá Carlota ... Y en tanto los chinacos / que ya cantan victoria. [*Goodbye, Mama Carlota ... And all the poor beggars / already are singing of victory.*]"

Staring at the muslin-masked ceiling, McSween had said, "In my mind, Susan ... is agony. We're trapped. In my mind ... insane words. Satan's possessing me. What if it means I'm damned?" He had sobbed, stopped only by her contemptuous reprimand to pull himself together. Regressed, childlike, he had pleaded with her not to hate him. She had forced a laugh and said, "I love you, my leader of the Regulators. And Harvey's parents will be surprised that law training included bullet making."

Now McSween noticed Morris sitting on the floor, his fat face grimy with black powder; but that reality was replaced by fantasy. McSween was again in Bristol's bedroom, but saying, "And the whole matter's before the president. Any further attacks on myself will necessitate ..." Crack! Crack! Crack! Crack! Anxiously, McSween wondered, "Can you go deaf from gunfire? If I went deaf, I couldn't practice law." There was a scaffold. A hangman tightened nooses on Dolan, Evans, and Riley. McSween's anxiety soared. "Vengeful thoughts," he said to himself. "Might mean I'm damned."

Billy entered and hunkered down between George Washington and Harvey Morris. All laughed hard.

"Billy," McSween asked tremulously, "how are things ... progressing?"

"Great, Mac. We got water. Their men on the foothills make no difference. Our men, and Martin Chávez's in Montaño's, and the men at Ellis's and Patrón's have 'em pinned."

Billy rose to leave. Panic coursed in McSween; he would be alone. He blurted whether the men were holding out well. "Sure, Mac. They've been waiting for this chance for years. You made it possible."

Relief swept over McSween. He thought, arranging his askew collar, "I made it possible."

JULY 18, 1878   8:32 AM   THURSDAY

The people in the besieged McSween house had settled into optimistic waiting. At Elizabeth Shield's suggestion, everyone was having breakfast at the fully-expanded dining table. She had regenerated herself by deciding that, though it seemed frightening, they would never murder a family in their home. She was again successfully nursing baby Annie.

Alexander McSween had shaved, and was in a fresh suit. His wife, bangs curled in stubborn refusal to compromise her standards, was beside him, watching the sweaty men eating with incorrect forks and spoons from the confusing array.

"They shot Ben Ellis yestaday," French volunteered. "I headed ou' late las' night. I says to myself, 'I don' give a damn ...' "

"Please, Frenchie," said Susan McSween. "Not with the children."

"Sorry, Ma'am. I says, 'Te hell with i'. I ain' no bird in no cage. I seen Ben. Through the neck. Ellis, he's mighty riled up."

To their east, from the Tunstall apartment, Dr. Taylor Ealy, medical kit in hand, accompanied by his wife, Ruth, supporting their baby daughter with one arm and holding little Pearl's hand, proceeded to the injured Ellis boy; watched by men in the foothills, wondering if they should shoot them.

In the House corral, James Dolan, with his silver-headed cane, was being assisted into his buggy by stocky John Kinney, who then took the reins for the trip to Fort Stanton. Dolan said, "I sent Jessie ahead with a message for Dudley that John Chisum was sending cowboys. And a cannon." Dolan smiled facetiously. "Anything is *possible*. And for our meeting with Dudley, all I need is for you to represent the law." Kinney laughed heartily. Dolan said, "The idiot must be awakened to his responsibilities."

At 4:18 PM, a mighty thunderclap drowned out Commander Nathan Augustus Monroe Dudley's words. George Purlington; Daniel Appel; and Second Lieutenants Millard Filmore Goodwin, George Smith, and James French shifted on uncomfortable chairs, all aware they were listening to a charade. "And, in conclusion," Dudley said, "we have all signed an agreement that the purpose of our Lincoln maneuver - in compliance with the Posse Comitatus Act - is the non-partisan protection of women and children; since civilian law enforcement under Sheriff Peppin is overwhelmed, even with John Kinney's Rio Grande Posse. And, on good information, reinforcements are on their way to the criminals from cattleman, John Chisum."

As Dudley completed Dolan's earlier instructions, he contemplated their threat sheathed in reassurance. Dolan had said, "We are *well* aware that you might be hesitating to protect us because you might risk conviction for treason and life in military prison if the resources of the army are used against American citizens.

"Unfortunately, refusing to send soldiers now *would not protect you*. Treason could be claimed by a vindictive person for your June twenty-eighth intervention in San Patricio with Sheriff Peppin."

Dudley's face had reddened as he capitulated to the inevitable. Intoxicated, relapsed into alcoholism to cope with the Santa Fe Ring's stranglehold, he had blustered to Dolan with self-justification: "You underestimate me, Sir. I didn't rise to this rank by being a dullard. *My* actions have protected *our* mutual interests. I *strategically* awaited sufficient evidence of need for military intervention. Neither of us wants fodder for accusations since we *both* realize that the outcome '*might*' be McSween's death."

Dolan had then expressed such effusive admiration that Dudley had actually felt soldierly zeal.

Now, as a downpour pounded, to be heard, Dudley spoke more loudly. Passing the soldiers' closed door, a middle-aged laundress heard, "Gentlemen, tomorrow we will break camp by four thirty AM and be ready to march by five. We should be in Lincoln by ten. I will lead a column of two detachments - of forty infantry and twenty cavalry - commanded by Lieutenants French and Smith respectively. We will bring a mountain howitzer and Gatling gun."

Though the laundress's ability to speak English was limited, her comprehension was good. She ventured closer. Dudley said, "Purlington, I want that blacksmith, Nelson, to work - if it takes all night - to get the howitzer ready. And I want the Gatling gun with five thousand rounds. And three days rations."

The godmother of the murdered infant of San Patricio ran toward the fort building where Juan Patrón was staying for protection. By the time she arrived, drops had ceased and the hot ground steamed.

At 9:48 PM, with rebozo over her head, the laundress trudged along the road from Fort Stanton into Lincoln. Passing the sinister House, she crossed herself.

At the big home with a picket fence, described by Juan Patrón, light slits through its walls made bars on the black ground.

When its door opened, she stepped back, repelled by rank odor. "Señor McSween?" she queried, and was stiffly acknowledged. "I no speak good Engleesh. I from San Patricio. Mañana men comes. Howzer y Gading they bring." McSween said no one inside was named Howzer or Gading. "Please to understand. Cuidado. Make to be careful. All gente, all peoples, loves McSween."

"I understand. You come from San Patricio to wish us well."

When Billy walked in, McSween said, "Something remarkable just happened. A Mexican woman from San Patricio was just here."

Billy ran to the door. She was gone. Billy said he wished he had called him. "There was no need. She was an angel of mercy sent by God to confirm our path."

JULY 19, 1878   8:00 AM   FRIDAY

Susan McSween's laughter pealed in the kitchen, expressing everyone's certainty of winning. A refreshing breeze flowed through doors of the east wing. George Washington, cleaning the stove, was chuckling as he listened to Billy's Gold Dust story. Susan McSween playfully asked Billy what happened next. Glancing sidelong, he said he had won; he knew what he could get away with.

In the parlor, Town Constable José Chávez y Chávez said to Yginio Salazar, looking out a porthole, "I knew your father well. He could have led an uprising. Not like Juan Patrón."

In the sitting-room, Harvey Morris exclaimed, "I lose? It's not a royal flush?"

"They are red, yes," said Florencio Chávez. "But the king it is diamond. Others is heart."

Yginio Salazar announced the arriving mail rider. At the door, McSween gave him a letter which said: *"Dear Ash. I suppose you hear queer versions. Right will triumph. Continue with our plans. You will be an excellent schoolmaster. Building of the church and school will soon start."*

On the roadway, four hundred yards west of Lincoln, Commander Dudley was ordering his all white infantry, all black cavalry, and four white officers to halt. He surveyed the column, a quarter mile long. Beside him, were Captain George Purlington and Second Lieutenant Millard Filmore Goodwin, in the capacity of his Adjutant. Leading the cavalry, in rows of four on their matched bays, was Second Lieutenant George Smith.

The artillery was next. The two hundred twenty pound, bronze, mountain howitzer cannon, resting on its two wheeled carriage, was pulled by paired horses. Attached was a cart carrying twelve pound lead balls, lanyards, fuses, and primers.

The huge Gatling gun was drawn by an infantryman astride one of the two pulling mules. It was a golden brass, six hundred pound machine gun: the world's most awesome weapon of war. Its attached caisson bore preloaded ammunition magazines totaling thousands of cartridges.

Two ambulances, one driven by Dr. Daniel Appel, contained hay, rations, ammunition, and tents. On foot, led by Second Lieutenant James French, the infantry followed. Four cavalrymen made the rear guard.

Dudley, with his splendid, white, waxed, pointed mustache, was in dress uniform with dark-blue jacket double rowed by golden buttons and festooned with gold cord. But he experienced his grandeur through his black domed helmet, emblazoned with a gold metal eagle and topped by a spire flaunting a dyed yellow, horse's tail.

Nodding to Captain George Purlington, Nathan Augustus Monroe Dudley, already intoxicated, resumed their eastward march.

In front of the Wortley Hotel, the troops stopped as George Peppin came out to meet him. Commander Dudley projected to his men as witnesses, "I and my soldiers have come because the current civil unrest has placed women and children at risk.

"I direct myself to you, Sheriff Peppin, as the representative of legal authority here. We will make camp to the east. Three infantrymen will take position in the center of town."

Dolan nodded subtlely, acknowledging his dictated speech and their understanding that those infantrymen would occupy Alexander McSween's west yard.

Jim French, in the west wing, saw the arriving troops first, and shouted for the others.

Dolan said to Peppin, "Surround McSween's place with men in the Mills and Schon houses, and across at the Stanley's. And hang a black flag." Peppin asked where. "Where the McSweens can see it, of course. On the Stanley house."

At the first flurry of his men, Alexander McSween rose from his desk where he had started a letter for John Tunstall's father: *"Before us is victory and ..."*

With dulling torpidity, he returned to the couch, took up his Bible, and aimlessly turned clumped pages, Old Testament to New Testament.

He heard Billy's voice ringing excitedly about a parade. Harvey Morris was looking down at him saying that military intervention under the Posse Comitatus Act was illegal.

Jim French ran in yelling, "Mac, them Dolans is runnin' like ants from a stepped on anthill! An' three soldiers stopt at our wes' side! We can' shoot!"

From his lookout, José Chávez y Chávez called, "At the house across, they ties the black flag. Like Santa Ana for the Alamo: 'No surrender. Death.' " Yginio Salazar sneered. Did they think they would fight any other way but to death.

To the women, Billy said, "Get water before they start shooting."

Soon, in the dim McSween parlor, silence was punctuated only by Jim French's pacing on the floorboards; the rug having been rolled up days before at Susan McSween's demand. Then shots came from the rear. Enraged, she ran in exclaiming, "I can't believe it, Alexander. We were getting water. Men shot at us! And some stayed at our stable. And ignored three soldiers standing there to protect us."

Minnie Shield had followed her and said, "I'll get the water, Auntie Susan. God wouldn't let them shoot a little girl." Minnie looked for reassurance to Billy, calmly checking cartridge stores.

She asked, "Is the bad man with the big mustache outside?" No, Billy said. He was in Heaven. Under his breath Yginio said that was correct, except for the direction.

George Washington whispered to the men, "Know what Dudley's brought? A goddamn Gatling gun. Invented in the early sixties by some bastard named Richard Gatling - family kept slaves; and, even though he ended up in Indiana, folks said he was a Jayhawker for the Southern cause. Colt makes 'em. Goddamn gun has six barrels you turn by a crank, and shoots cartridges the size of a donkey's cock. Two hundred fifty a minute."

The front door was banged. Alexander McSween opened to glittering accoutrements of the commander, who said, "I, Colonel Nathan Augustus Monroe Dudley, am here to describe my mission."

Susan McSween, at the east door of the parlor listened, as did the men in the shadows.

Dudley concluded: "Any act of violence directed toward us will be seen as an act of war against the United States. And I'll order my cannon and Gatling gun turned loose and tear your house to the ground. Our interview is completed."

McSween closed the door and felt an icy chill. The tone was hostile. Was it possible that in Peppin's first raid on San Patricio, Dudley's troops were helping him? But that was illegal. But what would happen if it was true? His legs felt rubbery.

McSween returned to the couch. Susan's protective sheet slid unpleasantly on its horsehair upholstery. Billy had said *you* made this possible. Then the *fault* was his. If I hadn't tried to stop the Ring ... Susan shouldn't have made me stay. Don't think like that. Accept God's stream of destiny. He opened his Bible and read softly, alone in the shrine of his suffering, "Isaiah, six, three. 'And one cried unto another, and said, Holy, holy, holy is the Lord of hosts; the whole earth is full of his glory.' " Right there, John had been on the carpenter's bench. He saw Dr. Appel pealing back scalp from skull, saw his bloody hands promiscuously probing the split-open chest. McSween thought, "If I walked out I'd be shot."

Ignacio Gonzalez whispered to Florencio Chávez, "We are dead men."

Yginio responded vehemently, "You chose to come from Montaño's. Do you now change your mind?"

Francisco Zamora and Vincente Romero denied regret.

"You really think there's that much danger?" asked Harvey Morris.

"You're learning poker," said Washington. "Our odds of winning just dropped considerably."

In the other room, José Chávez y Chávez said to Billy, "It is very bad."

O'Folliard asked Billy, "Ain' the soldiers here to proteck women an' chilren?"

"Don't worry, Tom. We're prepared to fight."

At the same time, Minnie, with rolled-up sleeves, perspiring, stopped on the path up from the river, and set down her second heavy water bucket beside the first. As she lifted one, she recited her mother's nursery rhyme for the baby: "My name is Kate. This doll is mine ..." She deposited the bucket at the top level, hooked her short damp hair behind her ears, and went back for the other one. It felt heavier. "Her rosy lips, and face so fair, / I'm sure must please you, and you'll say / 'Tis nice with such a doll to play."

As Minnie finally came through the gate, to her right was the chicken coop building. Made of upright boards and with a slanted roof, it almost looked like the outhouse at the other side of the gate, but wider.

Chickens scurried hungrily to her. Into their metal pan she poured water, and heard horses and jangling harnesses.

Thinking happily, "It's the parade!" she left her buckets at the back doorway to the east kitchen and ran to the front picket fence to watch. A man mounting a horse had a hat with a golden plume like a story-book knight's.

At that moment, Henry Brown said to George Coe and John Newcomb, "Bac and de oders are drapped. Bwe've god do helb." Coe answered that there was nothing they could accomplish except getting killed. Inside the Tunstall apartment, the Ealy family and Susan Gates were unaware of those three men's escape.

As Minnie Shield watched the grand, eastward, military procession, the Schon house became occupied by Billy Matthews, Pantaleon Gallegos, and Seven Rivers posseman; the Torreon by George Peppin, Jack Long, two Seven Rivers men, and Dummy; the Stanley house - its black flag, a shawl of Steve Stanley's wife, having been hung by Bob Olinger - received him, as well as his brother Wallace, John Jones, Bill Jones, and Jim Jones. Into the McSween stable, ran Andrew Boyle with the Beckwith brothers, Bob and John. Over the south foothills, ranged Kinney's and Seven Rivers men. And in the Mills house were Dolan, Jessie, and John Kinney.

"Mornin', Dudley," called "Squire" Wilson, shambling from a vegetable patch onto the street. "What brings you here?" After the commander's litany, Wilson pointed to Minnie. "There's a child. Don't miss her."

"Stay out of this, Wilson," Dudley menaced. But the old man refused to step back, forcing the column to swerve to the left to avoid trampling him.

At the Tunstall store, Dr. Taylor Ealy called to the commander, "There's a seriously injured boy at the Ellis house. Sheriff Peppin's forces are interfering with my treating him. And I and my family have been virtual prisoners here."

Dudley answered coldly, "I've got Doctor Appel. We no longer need your services."

The soldiers next filed past the Torreon and the house of Saturnino Baca, where the man stood outside with vindictively glinting eyes. To their right was Montaño's. Dudley ordered the cannon pointed at the long structure. Before the petrified eyes of the inmates, its four infantry gunners began its loud loading drill.

Abandoning weapons, the San Patricio and Picacho men seized any piece of fabric. The front door flew open. Each had hidden his face. All ran eastward.

Yginio, seeing them, screamed, "Cowards! Dogs! Fornicators of your mothers!"

"Why 're they wearin' sheets an' things, Billy?" asked O'Folliard.

"Because they are cowards," hissed Yginio. "How can they forget San Patricio in two weeks?" Billy said that was probably what got them running.

One infantryman said to his snickering companion, "I bet on the one with the apron."

Mrs. Montaño, at her door, addressed the helmeted man. "Why you threaten my house?" He asked if any were left inside. She merely glared and walked back in.

With boozy arousal and carelessness, Dudley then shouted an order to cavalrymen: Sergeant James Lusk, and Privates James Bush, and John Williams: "Get the hell to Sheriff Peppin and accompany him back to cut down these escapees."

James Bush, an ex-slave bearing whipping scars, and idealistic about the army, scowled at the partisan violation, but complied. To his other troops, Dudley said, pointing to the open lot across the street from the Montaño property, "We'll make camp here. But I want the Gatling and the howitzer at McSween's house."

Soon, José Chávez y Chávez said to Susan McSween that she and her sister might be permitted to leave. She said, "We will not. This is our home. And the soldiers will protect us."

Checking a porthole, she exclaimed angrily, "What's this? Sheriff Peppin's coming this way with three soldiers like they're his men. I'm going to stop that." She rushed to her room to prepare herself.

Minnie remained. "Did you see the parade, Billy? There was a knight."

"Harvey, where's the gunpowder keg?" Billy asked, and was told it was still in the parlor.

Billy said, "Minnie, could you help by picking up those shells lying around, and bring them to the room where your Uncle Alexander's reading?" She nodded and began in her serious precise way.

Susan McSween came through the parlor smelling of roses and with a magenta parasol, matching her shirts and contrasting her boldly black and white, chevron-striped top.

George Peppin and the three cavalrymen were passing the Tunstall Store when Susan McSween called to him, inadvertently delaying his pursuit of the escaping men. "Why are you with soldiers? They're not allowed to take sides." After Peppin's faltering response, believing she had achieved her goal, she strode back, unaware that the Gatling gun and howitzer were rolling after her.

In the oil-lit gloaming of the parlor, McSween's men were making cartridges. "Here's the bag of gold thimbles," said Minnie to Billy, who smiled rewardingly.

"It is strange to think," said Ignacio Gonzales, "one's last day." Francisco Zamora said he rejoiced to fight nobly. "I do not mean fear," Gonzales lied as he crimped a bullet to its casing. "Only strange to think." In English, he said, "To go to Heaven."

"Are we going to Heaven today, Billy?" Minnie asked apprehensively.

"Everybody looks healthy to me," he said. "Come here. I'll show you something." The men stopped to watch. His tongue curled to touch nose tip. Minnie tried, but hers, like most people's, was anchored by a restraining underside frenulum. Soon, all were smiling, the mood having lifted.

When Susan McSween reentered, her voice rang with indignation. "Alexander, they're pointing gigantic guns at our house." Like a somnambulist, he followed her to a strange vertical opening in his front wall. At the other side of the picket fence were two monumental carts. One was so large that the soldier, leaning against its wheel, raised his elbow to attain its height. On it was an golden tube, thick as a tree trunk. On the other, was a cannon.

McSween heard his wife. "Peppin must be behind this. With his men and soldiers in our stable yard, it's like being surrounded. Do something, Alexander."

"A soldier for the Lord," he said, shuffling to his desk. With viscously confused mind, he wrote: "*Colonel Dudley. Sir. Would you have the kindness to let me know why soldiers surround my house. Before blowing up my property I would like to know the reason. Constable Chávez y Chávez is here and has warrants for Sheriff Peppin and his posse for murder. Respectfully, A.A. McSween.*"

He tried to re-read it, but the words made no sense. His wife was gone. "Mister Bonney," he asked, as if in court, "would you review this document?" Billy said it made the point; but how would he get it to him.

"Minnie," McSween said, "be a good girl and take this to Colonel Dudley." She asked who he was. McSween did not answer. Billy said he was the knight.

Walking out, Minnie waved at the four young infantrymen beside big carts. When she showed one the addressed envelope, she was directed to the camp. That one, watching her skipping down the street, said, "I didn' volunteer to kill no white chilren. I come to fight Injuns. I heard the army's got more 'en a third bein' deserters. If they makes you kill white chilren, I ain' stayin' neither."

At the camp, Minnie was led past two ambulances on the street, past gathered soldiers in the field, through the cooking area, past the picket line of horses, to officers' tents near the Bonito's vegetation.

Inside one, she watched the recipient writing at a folding table, and wondered if he was really the knight, until she saw the magnificent helmet on a box.

He guffawed, and said to the other man, "Listen to this, Goodwin. McSween wrote, *'Before blowing up my property I would like to know the reason.'* So I answered: *'Sir. If you desire to blow up your house, I, as Commanding Officer, do not object providing it does not injure any U.S. soldiers.'* Hahahahaha." Secretly, Dudley had consumed more whiskey from his silver flask from Dolan.

When Minnie received that folded letter from the cheerful knight, she said, "Mama read me a story about a knight like you, who risked his life so people could go to Heaven."

"Take her back to the street, Goodwin," Dudley said gruffly to his Adjutant.

A half mile east of the camp, George Peppin, joined by John Kinney's men, began shooting in meaningless show at riders already across the Bonito River. Hearing the skirmish, Dudley demanded his horse and trotted to the scene.

Enraged, he shouted drunkenly at the lawman, "You imbecile! How the hell did you miss getting them after I sent for you? I even gave you these soldiers to cut the bastards down. What more did you want me to do?" James Bush glanced bitterly at fellow Private, John Williams, and Sergeant James Lusk, who refused to meet his eyes.

In the Ellis corral, Kinney's men were stealing remaining horses. When on the street, Gray Sugar made a piercing whinny for Billy. Torcio suddenly bucked, throwing his rider, and galloped westward.

Seeing him, Yginio understood and murmured, "Run, Torcio. Run to freedom."

Peppin, returning dejectedly westward with the three soldiers, was joined by Jack Long and Dummy, each with a bucket. Long leered, "Got coal oil kerosene from Ellis's. 'To start a fire."

At 12:10 PM, no wind blew through the Bonito River valley, over which scorched the sun. Within the buildings of McSween, Tunstall, Ellis, Baca, Stanley, Schon, Mills, Wilson, Montaño, and Wortley, people waited. Men also sat high on the rocky southern promontories. And the black flag, tied to a viga beam, hung a motionless marker in the desolation.

In that void, sounded six men's dust-muffled bootsteps. Commander Dudley, George Purlington, Daniel Appel, George Peppin, Bob Beckwith, and Andrew Boyle were going to Justice of the Peace "Squire" Wilson's house. He was awakened by knocking.

Peppin said, "We want warrants for McSween and the Kid. These men will sign the affidavits. For assault with intent to kill Private Berry Robinson on July sixteenth." Wilson refused.

Peppin looked at Dudley helplessly, having finally been informed by Dolan about the useless David Easton warrants, and having admitted it to the commander.

Dudley's face distorted in fury at this next impediment, knowing the whole exercise was becoming a fiasco in which he would be the focus of blame. He shouted at Wilson that he would put him in double irons in the fort. The old man understood the death threat, and responded, "I'll write 'em, but 'gainst my will."

George Peppin added, "And appoint Bob Beckwith as my deputy to serve them."

Andrew Boyle had left their group to run McSween's. At the stable, he got a crowbar. Prying open shutters at Susan McSween's bedroom, he called back to John Beckwith to get for burning.

Soon, Jim French heard Boyle shout through the window's tumbled bricks for them to surrender; that they had warrants. Firing at the impossible angle, French yelled back, "We got warrans too: in our guns, you cocksuckin' sonoabitch."

As his men ran through the parlor to the west wing, McSween gazed at their odd stop-action flickering through porthole light projections. He thought, "Was it seven?" and sought his book's first page: the seven days. He read, "In the beginning God ... divided the light from the darkness."

His wife hurried in asking what was happening. He said, "The issue before us is of extreme importance."

Billy shouted to her, "Trying to pile wood to burn the place down. But they pulled back."

Again Susan McSween went outside, tipping her parasol to block from sight the ugly implements of war.

At the Torreon she encountered Peppin, returning with the three soldiers, and said, "I demand to know why you, as Sheriff, are letting men try to set my house on fire?" He answered insolently that he was getting them all out that day - dead or alive. "And *I'm* going to Colonel Dudley to put an end to this," she said."

In the parlor, her husband murmured John, Chapter fourteen. " 'In my Father's house are many mansions ... I go to prepare a place for you.' " Washington was before him with a nauseatingly steaming bowl. Morris was, for some reason, on the floor. McSween said, "Give food to Harvey. He needs energy to argue effectively in court," and thought, "Angel is somewhere close." That name amused everyone. He laughed loudly. Morris glanced up at him. "We're well protected," McSween said.

Susan McSween was outside Commander Dudley's tent. George Purlington and Adjutant Millard Filmore Goodwin stood at the commander's side. Bored soldiers listened. She said, "And consequently I came to request your protection."

"You are harboring outlaws, Madam. And I've been instructed by a letter from your husband that he intends to blow up your house himself. Purlington, it's inside. Get it."

After reading the letter, she looked relieved. "Alexander's just saying we're afraid you'll accidentally use those scary guns. Those outlaws are trying to kill him. They were loosing mercantile competition and ... Please take him to the fort. Otherwise they'll surely kill him today."

It was a civilian matter, Dudley said. "Then why are your soldiers with Sheriff Peppin?"

Dudley turned crimson, as guilt, risk of exposure, and loathing of domineering women combined. "How dare you accuse me? Take your consequences. Your husband tried to shoot a United States soldier." She denied it. He laughed. "And you're pure as new fallen snow."

"And your words now sound very thin."

"And you, Madam, have a reputation which I've heard is sufficient to negate any common slang which you might choose to cast on myself."

To George Purlington, he said, "I've heard that she's known as the whore of Lincoln town." Purlington laughed, as did listening soldiers.

One jeered, "I'll have some of what you're offering."

She spoke with suppressed rage. "You'll live to rue this day."

"Do not threaten me, Madam, or I'll have you shot." Unintimidated, she answered that he was just a hired assassin. She turned, passing soldiers with audible obscenities.

Back with her husband, Susan McSween said, as Harvey Morris and Billy listened, "Colonel Dudley won't help. He's on Peppin's side. Poor Elizabeth. The poor children."

McSween wondered if she would cradle him like Elizabeth held Annie. He had a jarring thought that she had given birth to him. It happened, he thought: Madness. There was a sharp spasm. What if he could not control his bowels?

Susan McSween led Billy confidentially away and said, "I'm worried about the piano. Can you protect it?"

Billy's eyes shone with amusement. "You sure are something. Hear that boys," he called out, "least we can do after six days of hospitality is save her piano." There was general laughter.

By 2:00 PM, the vicinity of the McSween house swarmed with hunters of animals, some also hunters of men; while James Dolan, John Kinney, and Jessie Evans sat drinking in the Mills house.

Jessie said, "Jimmy, I don' like them soldiers here. They alays do things like somebody's watchin'." There was, Dolan said. The United States government.

"Tha's wha' I'm sayin'. Tha' black flag don' help ifen the McSweens surrenders. Dudley 'ill 'ave t' proteck 'em.

"Are ye shur the Kid's there?" He kept asking, Dolan said. Long had seen him go. He had even tried to arrest him. "Wha' 'id 'e say?"

"Obviously not yes." Jessie laughed.

Inside the stable, Andrew Boyle said to Dummy, "If you go with Mister Long and throw in this coal oil, I'll let you go back to the House."

As Boyle spoke, Minnie Shield set down her next set of buckets at the east yard gate. Careful to prevent chickens from escaping, she dragged both in. As a reward for herself, she opened the door to the coop to look at hens brooding.

Next she tried to carry both buckets. Excited chickens followed, as the Rhode Island Red male made his way domineeringly. She laughed, "I'll bring you food soon, Mister Rooster."

At the door, Davie met her. She glanced back toward the birds.

Horrifyingly, two men threw open the rear gate and ran toward her. One held high a flaming smoking torch.

Shrieking, grabbing the bucket handles, Minnie lunged inside the kitchen just as its windowglass smashed.

Coal oil was dumped through. Dummy's hideously contorted face was framed momentarily, but etched permanently in the two children's minds. Then the firebrand struck.

She was being pulled from the room. Men ran past. Guns fired. Her aunt and George Washington spilled out her buckets. Then Billy threw smothering blankets over mitosing islands of flame on water.

Davie was screaming, "I saw the devils from Hell! I want Papa. I want God." Her two younger brothers wailed.

In whizzing bullets from the broken kitchen window, Dummy and Jack Long sprinted to the nearest refuge: the outhouse. There, as its shot plank walls sprayed splinters, Long pulled the board seat off the deep latrine, and jumped into the compost of feces, urine, and lime. Dummy wailed, "I won't go," but leapt after a close miss.

Billy said, "Someone's got to stay here and keep 'em pinned. Tom, will you?"

"Would'n min'," the husky youth said placidly. They were really pals, he was thinking.

In the next room, Minnie, sobbing, clutched her mother, who held her while murmuring, "The Lord is my shepherd; I shall not want," as all three boys cried.

Harvey Morris returned to the parlor and said, "Attorney McSween, they just tried to set fire to the house again. Let me use a gun." After being lethargically refused, Morris clenched his fists, but also felt relief; and wondered if he was a coward. Billy called to him to keep up the cartridge making.

From the west side, Ignacio Gonzalez rushed in shouting, "Fire!"

Billy and Yginio ran back with him. Jim French was cursing, unable to approach a blaze in the storage kitchen because of the shooting through Boyle's breech. "No use," French said. "I's too big."

Billy responded, "We have to protect the next rooms in line;" and went back to the parlor where he said, "Harvey, if fire gets close, get that gunpowder keg out."

George Washington, with a towel-wrapped object, said he was looking for a safe place for his fiddle. Billy laughed. "Near the piano. Missus McSween 'ill fight there harder than anyone." Washington laughed too, but continued with it to the east wing.

Alexander McSween was reading Psalm 88. "Thy wrath lieth hard upon me, and ..." Shocks of anxiety wracked him. He smelled smoke and thought, "Asthma!" His chest constricted. He looked wildly around. Harvey Morris was there. He was not alone.

His wife and Washington entered. She said, "Put the piano in the dining-room. That Chávez y Chávez is big. Ask him for help."

"Susan," McSween whispered, "what if the smoke causes my asthma to ..." His mind went blank.

She said, "The fire isn't spreading, Alexander. And no matter what Colonel Dudley feels, he's got to protect our lives."

She smiled artificially to mask alarm at his deterioration and anger at his failed masculinity. But there was grim relief of drawing strength from that weakness. She was not like him. And, for the first time in her life, she realized that her possessions could be lost, but she could not be defeated.

She said, "In the Bible, isn't there something about getting through a fiery furnace?" McSween coughed, asking if she believed they were just being tested. "Yes," she said distractedly, watching Washington and José Chávez y Chávez struggling with the piano.

"What if she's wrong?" McSween thought. "I've presumed salvation. That was sinful hubris." He understood now. Abandoned by God. As if feverish, his teeth chattered.

She called to Washington and José Chávez y Chávez, "Be careful not to scratch the case."

In the yard, chickens ran frantically as loud bangs would not stop. Some escaped through the open gate. The enraged rooster strutted his yard, seeking the rival that had so stimulated his hens. A young male, immature pinfeathers studding his head, received his fierce attack. Blood flowed from his enucleated eye. Inside the coop, one hen felt painful spasms as her oviduct contracted prematurely, discharging soft eggs. Under her body, jostled by frightened others, they ruptured, oozing out embryos. She spread her wings in a futile attempt to protect them.

It was 3:42 PM. The adobe shell of the McSween house was a furnace where floors, furniture, clothing, rugs, and the roof itself - massive viga beams and cross struts - were all merely fuel.

Finally demolished, the storage kitchen ceiling collapsed; its adobe mud roofing crashing down, as scathing air rushed upward and created a partial vacuum, sucking in draft to feed the holocaust.

Eight sopping-wet men, faces covered with wet bandanas, shouted encouragement to each other in smoke of their weaponry. One voice punctuated the others. "Great shot, Yginio!" Billy yelled. Then he called out, "Someone tell Harvey to move out the gunpowder keg."

As all evacuated the front rooms, Billy heard the crashing ceiling in McSween's prior bedroom; and watched with fascination its flaming door transform into light. Then, doubling below the poisonous smoke, he rushed after the others.

In the east wing, Susan McSween was saying, "Put the piano on the wall facing the courtyard," when a deafening boom slammed the house.

Harvey Morris, in panic, had forgotten the gunpowdre keg. Its explosion demolished the parlor ceiling and part of its front wall. And the fire raged.

In the Baca house, at the blast, Josephina screamed that they were dead. Even George Washington! Her father yelled, abusive fist raised, "George Washington? You are upset about a black one? It is no problem to hang him for such a crime. Do you understand?"

In the east wing, Yginio Salazar called out that a woman was leaving Tunstall's building. Susan McSween identified Susan Gates, saying she must be going to ask Colonel Dudley for protection.

In the bedroom, Susan McSween talked with her sister and the huddled children, having passed through the adjoining room where her husband was sitting rigidly in a wingback chair.

He had made a discovery. If one barely breathed, one became a tiny nodule and felt nothing. But a horrible thought ruptured that composure: Any second that nodule could extinguish; then his mind would disappear, lost to madness.

Listening to her aunt talking about protection, Minnie asked softly, "Mama, are we going to die now?"

Elizabeth Shield said, "No, my baby, just think about God's love." Six year old Davie sucked his thumb while stroking his nose, as he had last done when three.

Inside the outhouse, Dummy whined, "I wants to go, Mr. Long." Jack Long said he'd be shot. "No I won't. God's here with me." Long said sarcastically that God wasn't in an outhouse. "Don't matter none to God. I'm holding him tight with the teeth of my soul. Now I want to go." Long told him to shut up.

At 6:17 PM, Billy's enthusiastic voice resounded through the east wing. "Fire's moving slower."

Passing seated McSween in conversation with his wife, Billy called to George Washington in the kitchen, "We might as well eat."

Several of the men, dripping with perspiration in the over hundred twenty degree heat, laughed at his incongruous gaiety.

Billy went to Tom O'Folliard, still at the shattered kitchen window, and said, "You're sure giving Long and Dummy a bad day." O'Folliard grinned.

Yginio called out loudly, "The Ealy's are getting into an ambulance wagon."

Billy entered Elizabeth Shield's room as Minnie said to her, "I know the knight. I'll ask him if we can go too." His eyes met the woman's. Minnie asked, "How do I go out? I'm afraid of the fire."

Billy said, "Out the kitchen door, then through that gate in the picket fence before the outhouse. Minnie, this is important. Don't go in. It's being used."

In the next room, McSween gave an odd giddy laugh, and said to his wife, "Juan Patrón and I can share the same cell. And write our memoirs. How they exploded our house for no reason. The world's upside-down."

On his wife's face was pity. He had to respond. He said, "Jesus, Father, forgive them; for they know not what they do."

Susan McSween said she would stay. At the doorway, Billy cleared his throat. " 'Scuse me, Ma'am. I couldn't help hearing. I've got an escape plan. It's got running. Skirts won't work."

She asked if he planned to save Alexander. "What this is all about, Ma'am." His eyes shone playfully. "Still want that piano moved along?" She glanced coquettishly, saying of course.

Minnie ran in, flushed with exertion. "The knight wasn't there; but a man named Doctor Apple said we could come if we hurried. They're bringing a sick boy named Ben. Doctor Apple said that they have an extra wagon 'cause they won't need ambulances here."

The color drained from Susan McSween's face. She leaned over to embrace her husband; but his head bowed to his book. She kissed his hair, and whispered, "I'll come back tomorrow." She did not believe she would see him alive again. He was thinking that she had failed him. He was forsaken.

All she took was her parasol.

At 7:19 PM, in the Mills house, James Dolan stared out a window at the burning McSween house as Jessie and John Kinney played poker. "Maybe they are dead," Dolan thought, then heard more gunfire. He visualized them choking in remaining rooms, and thrilled to cruel potency. "This is my creation, Billy," he said mentally. Another portion of the roof fell in with billowing smoke. Dolan tried to regain the reverie. The boy began to laugh, curls gleaming in flames which could only illuminate him.

Dolan turned back to the room. "Time to get the men ready," he said dispassionately. "If it was just McSween, he'd burn up with his house. But with the Kid, they'll make a run for it. Make sure someone lets Dudley know."

Inside the building, McSween's wingback chair had been carried to the kitchen. "Mac," Billy said, as he led the dazed man to the new location, "sorry about the piano. No use moving it more."

Billy called into the smoke, "Boys, here's our plan." They came, sunken eyes visible above protective bandanas. "Everybody bring hats and jackets." Ignacio Gonzalez asked irritably why they needed clothes to die. "I'm not planning funerals. Everyone has to drink. We may need the water for the fire. Yginio, make Mac drink."

McSween looked blankly at the glass held by Yginio. In his mind was "Holy, holy, holy is the Lord of hosts; the whole earth is full of his glory." He buried his face in his hands. When he was a little boy, he had a rocking horse on gliders. He swayed back and forth, back and forth.

Billy shook him, blue eyes fierce in soot-blackened skin. "Act like a man, Mac. Take the water." McSween did, nodding with infantile compliance; then fingered his perspiration-wilted collar, trying to make it stand upright.

"Listen boys," Billy continued, "when it's dark, we're making our run. In two groups. First is mine. Purpose is to distract 'em so Mac can escape.

"We've got about forty yards that 'ill be lit around this place. We'll head to the side gate in the picket fence. Then a diagonal towards Tunstall's corral. And keep shooting.

" That should give Mac - and those with him - enough time to head along the cover of the adobe wall and chicken coop and out the back gate. Then Mac's group 'ill do what ours will have done, which is run down to the Bonito." Tom O'Folliard said he was with him.

"And the reason you need those clothes is to make you worse targets. I'd rather have a bullet hole in my jacket or hat than anywhere more personal." Some laughed.

José Chávez y Chávez said he was with him too. Yginio said he would guard McSween.

Billy said, "There's really a third group. Whoever's left could sneak out in the confusion." Jim French joined him. Francisco Zamora and Vincente Romero chose McSween.

"I'll join your group, Billy," Harvey Morris said. "I feel miserable about the gunpowder."

Billy laughed. "Being with me isn't a punishment, Harvey. They'd 'ave burned the place down anyway. And George, I can't see as there's more for you to do."

Quietly, Washington said, "I'll bear witness, if the Lord let's me live."

"We'll back you up. But at a distance." Billy wiped his wet face. "It got too hot for us in these parts." All laughed except McSween.

"And we'll all meet up across the Bonito. I'm sure the others are there waiting for us."

Gonzalez and Chávez were silent. Billy said, "Ignacio and Florencio, seems you'd like to be in the third group. No shame to that. We all fought like men today."

At 9:00 PM, the sky was brilliant with stars, the moon golden on its fifth day after fullness. Lincoln was in darkness, except for the flaming McSween house, bright windows in the Mills and Baca houses, and the cookfires of the soldiers' encampment.

Since night's concealment had allowed closer approach to the besieged house, over two thousand rounds had been exchanged.

Far below, from the south bank of the Bonito, the howling and yapping of coyotes pierced the gunfire as they discovered escaped chickens.

At the same time, Second Lieutenants Millard Filmore Goodwin, George Smith, and James French, with their Springfield '73 carbines, marched, concealed within the Bonito River's forestation, and under secret orders from Colonel Dudley to prevent escape from the burning building. When they came to the Tunstall property, they stopped at the northwest corner of its corral.

The attackers faced a structure of two thousand six hundred square feet made of fire and soaring smoke. Many screamed challenges and obscenities as they fired their weapons.

But two men were silent and alone. Dolan remained a spectator at the Mills house. And Jessie stalked behind McSween's property.

In the west kitchen, Billy, Tom O'Folliard, José Chávez y Chávez, Jim French, and Harvey Morris waited. Billy said to McSween, Yginio, Francisco Zamora, and Vincente Romero, "When you hear shooting really start up, run like hell. Here we go!"

Billy and his group, holding their guns, slipped out the door and along the shadowed, exterior, north wall.

Then Billy sprinted northeast, toward the picket fence yelling, "Run! Run! Run!" Ahead was the margin of darkness and light, lurching in insane exuberance of the fire. Beyond the fence, in the Tunstall corral, were illuminated men. And Billy leapt, gyrating and dodging, into the pool of shimmering gold; calling "Run, run, run!" and breathing the deliciously pure air. He heard a rhythm of cracking guns. It was his music for the dance in defiance of death.

Throwing open the picket gate, he shot at the ghoulishly lit apparitions; his body, a bobbing, whirling, indistinct chimera, half light and half darkness. He was the decoy, swaggering and shooting in outrageous display of invulnerability; taunting the enemy with his dance and keeping them at bay. And he was yelling with joy and rage; but now it was fire that poured from his own mouth roaring, "Run! Run! Run!" to his four, as he veered northward. Somewhere there was a weapon that could explode golden missiles two hundred fifty times a minute. But he was a cloud of brilliant astral particles through which bullets could fly without contacting corporeal substance. "Run, run," came from that blazing self.

He saw Billy Matthews, George Peppin, and Bob Olinger firing at them. He saw the three soldiers at the Tunstall corral, blasting, in unison, a volley at them.

Then, immediately ahead, was a man with a carbine. For a moment, he and Billy were suspended in silence in which the music pauses, the virtuoso having made it part of the melody, to force dancers to find their own rhythm within an infinity of choices. Billy's eyes met those of John Jones. The finger of Ma'am Jones's oldest son rested on his trigger, as Billy safely passed the lurid light edge into night. Then the trigger-finger squeezed innocuously, and the instrument completed one intrinsic note in Billy's dance macabre.

But Billy had not seen another carbine directed at him from the darkness. Its muzzle had followed his chest in unfailing synchrony. Then its barrel swung. Jessie Evans fired. His aim was as perfect as it would have been only seconds before; but its target had changed. Billy looked back. Harvey Morris fell. Running were Tom O'Folliard, Jim French, and José Chávez y Chávez. Urgently, Billy shouted, "Run, run!"

Then Billy was soaring, dropping to the first riverbank tier, leaping off it into the Bonito's river mists below.

"McSween, you must stand," said Yginio. "You gave your word of honor." The other men moved fretfully at the open doorway.

"Yes," Alexander McSween said hoarsely. "My word ... is my honor." He fumbled for a pencil in the damp frock coat he had never removed that day, marked his Bible page margin, and laid the black marker ribbon.

He stood, placed the book in his pocket, and faced the yard, shadowed to the left along its bisecting adobe wall. Far treetops were unnaturally day-like in fiery reflection.

Francisco Zamora and Vincente Romero ran past, pausing at the chicken coop. McSween thought, "I am not alone," and walked out.

The contrasting shock of cool air contracted his bronchial tubes. Gasping, he hunched against the wall.

"He must come," Francisco Zamora whispered urgently. "The shooting is less. They will be here."

Andrew Boyle, with the Beckwith brothers, emerged from the stable and fired test shots at the east yard. In the kitchen, Ignacio Gonzalez, Florencio Chávez, and George Washington waited.

Billy, O'Folliard, Chávez y Chávez, and French splashed through the Bonito and clambered up the far bank. "Where is they, Billy?" whispered O'Folliard.

"Please, McSween," said Yginio, but the disoriented man walked back toward his kitchen door.

Behind the Tunstall corral, the three officers were returning to camp, their leader, Second Lieutenant Millard Filmore Goodwin, having decided that they had fulfilled their orders.

Emboldened by lack of counterfire, Andrew Boyle shouted, "McSween, surrender!"

From the dark corner of wall and house came, "I surrender ..." Then Alexander McSween whispered, "To the Lord of hosts. I surrender my life to him."

Bob Beckwith knew all were waiting for him to serve the warrants. Weak-legged, he stepped through the gate dividing the two yards, awkwardly extending the papers.

McSween thought, "I'm alone. Midst of my enemies. Forsaken." Cramping diarrhea purged in thick wetness.

Beyond the back wall, Jessie, observing with concern, shouted so that his powerful voice was heard by all, "No surrender!"

From all sides, men fired as they ran into the east yard.

Francisco Zamora and Vincente Romero lunged inside the coop, where panicked thick-clawed chickens, in futile flight, lacerated their hands and faces as they tried to beat them off.

Yginio Salazar ran toward the lawyer and willingly into the hail of bullets. One struck his carbine, wrenching his right hand. Another cut his upper left arm; two lodged in his right lower back.

He fell. He knew he must not move as men's boots ran past. In his mind was, "Holy mother of God, protect me. Saint Joseph protect me. Dear Lord, Savior, protect me."

He could hear a fusillade as the coop was riddled with bullets. Francisco Zamora died with eight; Vincente Romero with three.

And, at the wall and house corner, lay McSween's body, face up, five bullets in his chest. On top of him, Bob Beckwith sprawled with a bullet in his head, two in his chest, and four through his back.

Finally liberated from the outhouse, Jack Long joined the men; but Dummy turned a confused circle, saw the yard's open rear gate, and ran without stopping back to the House.

Across the Bonito River, Billy said, "We should wait longer." But there was only watery flowing and occasional whooing of an owl. Finally he said, "We have to find the others."

"And we will see if there really is anyone here for us," said José Chávez y Chávez. Billy fired two communicating shots. There were answering ones.

Soon they were with Fred Waite, Henry Brown, John Middleton, Charlie Bowdre, Doc Scurlock, and Martin Chávez on horseback. Waite asked about the others.

"We don't know," said Billy. But Chávez y Chávez said they were dead.

Canteens were given. Finally, Martin Chávez said in Spanish that he would never forget the shame. Billy said, "We all did what we could. But if they made it, we can't leave them." Scurlock said he'd stay with Martin. Then he'd take José back to San Patricio.

"How'd y'all make it out o' there?" asked Bowdre.

"Billy made a good plan," said O'Folliard. "He tol' us to run like hell. So we did."

All laughed. Billy mounted behind Waite's cantle. French joined Middleton; and heavy O'Folliard, using the elevation of a rock, finally was behind Brown.

As they rode toward the Capitan Mountains, Waite asked Billy to tell him what he really thought. "They probably got Mac. I saw Harvey go down. Yginio was with the others."

"Sorry, Kid. Still believe in the Great White Father in Washington?"

"There just wasn't enough time for that Angel Report to take effect." Waite felt Billy's arms wrap tighter. There was a snuggling and silence. He realized the boy was asleep.

The chicken yard was filling with yelling whooping men, some still firing, not wanting the excitement to end.

Through its gate in the dividing wall, came Andrew Boyle and John Beckwith, calling for his brother. Rolling the prone form from McSween's body below, he saw his brother's livid face.

Boyle shouted, "The McSweens shot Bob Beckwith! We heard that bastard McSween say he surrendered. Tricked Bob into an ambush!" Stunned, his brother followed the carried body.

Yginio Salazar was being kicked. Then someone stole his cartridge belt. Boyle said, "I'll give him one in the head. For Bob."

Billy Matthews said, "Don't waste a cartridge. He's dead."

Inside the kitchen, Ignacio Gonzalez, trembling in terror, had followed Florencio Chávez, and had angled McSween's big chair in hope of concealment.

As Washington retrieved his swathed fiddle case, he heard Bob Olinger call out, "Let's make a bonfire, boys."

There were shouts. Smoldering wood was heaped on McSween's body. Someone approached. One joked that now McSween was burning like his house. Washington heard James Dolan asking, "Has anyone checked inside?" Then Washington heard, "Kid?" John Jones said that he got away.

Washington knew his risk was tremendous, but he called out, "There's only me here." Dolan said, "George Washington! And what is that you're carrying?"

"Just my fiddle, Mister Dolan."

"Just what we need. A fiddler for our celebration." As Washington came out, he glanced leftward, where clothing flamed and flesh sizzled. "This way, George," Dolan said. "To the stable yard." Washington saw Yginio crumpled at the wall. Quickly he eyed the gapping picket gate and saw a form lying beyond it.

Dolan called out to the men, "We're bringing kegs from the Wortley! We're having a celebration!"

And, from the banks of the Bonito, coyotes detected the burnt offering of the body of a man. They salivated, howled into the bountiful night, and knew it was good.

At 10:41 PM, from a vantage high above Lincoln, could be seen a fiery three-sided shape, as if communicating a message to the heavens. And in the 125,000 square miles of New Mexico Territory, there was no object more bright on the dark land.

Along its roofless chambered arm, to the west, were jostling forms joined to ectoplasmic shadows, kicking up dust as ashy as if their dance was in a crematorium.

And George Washington, fiddling, sitting on the adobe wall, was above delirious bleeding Yginio Salazar on its other side; in whose mind were jumbled his own words and those Washington was forced to sing by demanding drunken voices. "From this valley they say you are going ... Though I walk through the valley of the shadow of death, I will fear no evil ... But remember the Red River Valley ... thy rod and thy staff they comfort ... I shall miss your bright eyes and sweet smile."

With clumsy battering boots, Dolan's victorious men danced, some partnering each other, unaware that the fiddler above them saw purgatory. Washington watched those beside the kegs gorging on liquor, and some retreating to vomit or urinate before returning to debauchery.

"Oh Susanna!" was yelled.

Yginio heard footsteps. Ignacio Gonzales and Florencio Chávez dodged quickly through the picket fence, then ran toward the river. Soon, from across the Bonito, a few shots were fired and answered.

Only one man, moving among his minions like the Prince of Darkness, paused and listened. He glanced at Washington, but he sang more loudly, "I come from Alabama wid my banjo on my knee' / I'm g'wan to Louisiana, my true love for to see."

"Make a lovin' song," shouted one of John Kinney's men.

And George Washington sang, "O Shenandoah, I love your daughter. / Away, ye rolling river."

Behind the north wall opposite the McSween stable, Jessie Evans sat with his bottle of whiskey and listened to the familiar words. Looking to the faraway north, he experienced yearning whose unconscious object was Billy. Jessie rubbed himself. "O Shenandoah, I'll ne'er forget you, / Away, my rolling river! / Till the day I die, I'll love you ever." Jessie's head arched back against the cold mud wall as his body released tension which had mounted throughout the day.

Men were stumbling to the street, joining others who had been looting the Tunstall store. All went westward to the House.

Jessie, aware of that migration, adjusted his pants, and entered the west yard. Washington watched its two remaining figures blurring together in smoky obscurity as the night claimed its own; and Dolan and Evans disappeared.

After stretching his stiff body, George Washington deposited his instrument in its case and walked to the empty Tunstall warehouse.

JULY 20, 1878   12:35 AM   SATURDAY

Yginio Salazar opened his eyes. Above, clouds, silver-edged by the hidden moon, were protecting him with darkness's cover. He touched his aching left arm and blood-saturated sleeve. Searing of right wrist returned memory of his carbine's torsion. Sitting made a stabbing pain through his midback. He thought, "Father give me strength. I have been shot there too."

Staggering, he stopped at the body. "McSween," he said, "you have conquered. The Devil lost Heaven long ago. He has only dirt and ashes." Water. He must have water.

He stumbled into the smoky kitchen. Cups of last water were still on the table. Now he must go home. He thought, "Madre must think I am dead."

Crossing the yard, where injured chickens crawled and flapped aimlessly, Yginio went through the open gate toward the river, then westward. Occasionally, supporting tree trunks saved him from falling in syncopal waves of nausea.

The town receded, but getting home was impossible. Close was the jacal of the Oteros, remembered friends of his father. With renewed energy, he supported his shot left arm by slipping its hand into his waistband.

Inside that Otero house, husband and wife were still awake. All day, they, and their now sleeping children, had stayed in, as gunfire had echoed. "We need water," said Esperanza Otero. "It is safer for me to go than you." Her husband reluctantly agreed. At the little altar table she crossed herself, then lifted a bucket and a dipper, and walked out to the barrel cistern.

"And what they did to the people of San Patricio," she thought with escalating fear as she ladled, pausing to listen. From Lincoln, a pack of coyotes howled. That was all. She lifted the bucket after slipping the long dipper handle under her arm.

She opened the door. One apprehensive backward glance showed a shadowed man. She gasped, "They are coming!" and slammed the door, which, to her horror, could not close because of the dropped dipper's handle. She threw herself against it.

Into the open crack came, "In the name of God, let me in. I am Yginio. Son of Teofilo Salazar."

The couple lay him groaning on their straw mattress. Cutting away his shirt, they found a band of clotted blood compressed between underwear bottom and pants waistband.

When they, at last, stopped their ministrations, he was asleep. Esperanza whispered, "They will come and kill him. And us too. In San Patricio they killed even children. Please, Reynaldo, take him away."

"Where? To the coyotes? God brought him to us. He was protected by the same hand of the Lord that will protect us."

At dawn, George Washington, lying on the floor of the ransacked Tunstall warehouse wrapped in an old tarpaulin, awoke to the crowing of the McSween rooster. He sat and coughed. His chest felt heavy from smoke inhalation. A dream about a square dance lingered. On the stove was Gottfried Gauss's pot with coffee of indeterminate age. Washington poured some. There had been men dancing on a sheet of fire. The song was in his mind: "Lou, Lou, skip to my Lou; Skip to my Lou, my darling."

The rooster crowed again. Washington rubbed his face. "George," he said to the hand, "today you're going to be burying." He sighed deeply. "Couldn't kill that old rooster," he thought and murmured, "Fly's in the buttermilk, shoo, fly, shoo;" but failed to resist blurring tears, and said, "Lord, you sure don't give much room for comparison between down here or up there with you." He searched the looted area for something to wrap bodies. There was only the tarpaulin.

The sky was still colorless as he walked west. To his rear, were drifting voices of encamped soldiers. Scanning the grassy expanse toward the Bonito River to his right, and the open area ahead, he recognized Harvey Morris. "You poor soul," he said. The rooster crowed again. "Yes," he said, "couldn't kill old Mister Rooster."

Entering the yard, he saw the bullet-riddled coop; and through its kicked-in door, discovered bodies of Francisco Zamora and Vincente Romero as timid hens ventured out. Others were in clusters throughout the yard. He felt odd relief that so many had survived, before he realized they were pecking at their dead or dying fellows.

Then he faced the corner. "My God!" he exclaimed in horror, running to it. Chickens clustered on McSween's corpse scrambled away, squawking and flapping indignation. The starving dehydrated creatures had eaten the eyeballs.

Washington covered his own eyes and said, "You sure don't spare a man, Lord." Remembering where he had seen Yginio, he turned back. Along the dividing wall was a trail of blood that had dripped from the boy's left arm. Washington considered searching for him, but decided the bodies required burial before further desecration.

With that momentum, he got a wheelbarrow, planning to bring Morris and McSween to lie beside Tunstall, while waiting to see if relatives would come for Zamora and Romero.

As he grasped McSween's corpse under the armpits and dragged, he smelled feces, and experienced pity so sharp that he understood the word heartbreak. As he arranged the body in the barrow, he said, "Don't you feel bad, Mister McSween. Even Christ had his bad moment up there on the cross, thinking his father had gone and left him. But now you're where you belong: with Him."

Washington's hurried trenches were shallow and beside John Tunstall's and Frank MacNab's. He remembered McSween's Bible. At the ribboned page, was the man's penciled line. "We got our service," Washington said. "I'm just sorry I've got you no coffins." With his folding knife he slit the tarpaulin to blanket each from dirt.

At their feet, he said, "Lord, receive the bodies of these two good men. Alexander McSween he chose your words from John: 'In the world ye shall have tribulation: but be of good cheer; I have overcome the world.' " He slipped the book back in its place in the frockcoat.

And as he shoveled the red Lincoln earth over yet more graves, he heard wagons. Three rolled from the House, lent by Dolan to the Seven Rivers men to continue their looting of the Tunstall store. The other was a donkey-drawn carreta cart with Vincente Romero's brother, coming to take him and his brother's friend home.

In the camp of the soldiers, Nathan Augustus Monroe Dudley said to George Purlington that they would stay till afternoon. Their mission had been successfully completed. Purlington left to inform the troops present, indifferent as Dudley to other soldiers on their way to the Tunstall store to participate in further plunder.

JULY 25, 1878   10:40 PM   THURSDAY

A decisive battle is merely a harbinger of defeat. True defeat occurs in fighters' hearts. To that debilitation Billy was immune. The magnitude of their opposition had confirmed for him the grandeur of their cause. But his losses, amassed beyond grieving, could only be mitigated by a new direction in the struggle.

As he and Tom O'Folliard rode north along the Pecos River, he followed the Milky Way: his spiraling galaxy of two hundred billion suns, flowing white and seen edge-on by him, two thirds from its center, and in the cosmic cycle dated by Fred Waite to July.

O'Folliard glanced frequently with adulation. "Billy," he said, "tha' Chisum fella, we jus' saw, didn' seem happy we was alive."

Billy sneered. "That's 'cause I told him I'm equalizing. He's gonna pay in cattle for not paying us Regulators. Tunstall and McSween counted on him. I blame that bastard for us loosing - more than I blame Jimmy Dolan and the Santa Fe Ring."

"Bu' you been payin' me an' Charlie."

"Like John Tunstall would have. He kept his word. Remember when we went to the cave in the Capitans to get money? That's why we're going to Sumner. To get more by gambling."

"What 'id Chisum mean by 'times changin'?"

"He believes the Frontier's passing. Shorthorns from the East will replace longhorns, and railroads 'ill end the drives - like barb wire will end the open range. Said next month he's sending herds to Texas."

" 'Splain why Kinney didn' kill Yginio after he trackt 'im by 'is blood."

"Remember when Mister Otero told us that Appel had doctored Yginio, and told Kinney they'd killed enough Mexicans without killing him? Anyway, Yginio's in hiding now in Sumner's sheep camps. We'll visit him. Too bad about that fake affidavit in the *Mesilla News*. Its a Ring paper. Said Yginio'd sworn that Mac forced him and other Mexicans to join an illegal posse so Mac could keep money he'd embezzled."

When in sight of Fort Sumner, Billy said, "Tom, I was thinking that you could stay in those barracks near the stable - to keep an eye on the horses - 'cause there's somebody I need to meet with ... uh, to fill in about the war."

Soon Billy was at Paulita's open window, gazing at her asleep. Only days before, he had run unhesitatingly into bullets, but was now stopped in awe. A boy - it seemed so long ago - had once cried with joy and astonishment "silver and gold" to another young girl. But now treasure was here, precious because it was inviolate: proof that he, like Tunstall, was truly good. "Paulita," he whispered.

She sprang up as he climbed into her room for the first time. Holding her delicate body in its nightgown, he felt her sobbing. "Pete said they burned down the house you were in. And everybody died. And today's the third anniversary of when Papa died. So Mama and me cried all day.

"Mama said July's cursed. First they killed Papa, then ... Stay with me, Billy." Pulled toward her bed, he retained the presence of mind to turn the key in her door.

Sitting primly at the edge, he held Paulita sideways on his lap. And, as they kissed, owning the same breath, he discovered it was enough - not need, not urge, but contentment.

Finally, beside her in bed, fully dressed and taking precaution, he said, "It would be nice if you turned around." A great horned owl on the roof-top whoo'd, answered by another. "They found each other," he murmured.

When her sleeping nestled warmth permeated him, he whispered to her for the first time, "I love you, Paulita."

JULY 29, 1878   4:04 PM   MONDAY

In cottonwood refuge at the Pecos bank, Billy and Paulita sat on his blanket spread on Earth's fragile paint of life, atop a twenty mile deep crust, on an almost two thousand mile thick mantle, surrounding a red-hot nickel-iron core.

As Billy angrily described the war, he mounded scrabble: gray limestone, two hundred fifty million years old, and red sandstone, only thirty million years younger. Lobbing those shards, he sliced the turbid red river with skipping flares. "If Dudley hadn't brought in soldiers ... Anyway, we didn't lose. It's not over."

Paulita said, "Deluvina told me a secret. She says *you're* Dragonfly. So I checked Papa's book called Wood's *Insects at Home*. It had dragonflies, but nothing about saving the world."

Billy said a bug collector wouldn't know about Deluvina's Dragonfly.

"That explains it. Mister Wood wrote that the beautiful color of their eyes disappears when they're dead. He kills them. You have beautiful eyes, Billy. Are you Dragonfly?"

Not listening, he unbuttoned his shirt. "I want you to feel this," he said romantically, glancing sidelong, taking her hand. She asked why he wanted her to feel his underwear.

He laughed uproariously. "No! My heart. You make it beat like that. What I want to say is: I love you, Paulita."

"I know," she answered with a child's innocence of passion. "Look, Billy. Twinkley lights all over you and the blanket."

"Uh, d'you love me?"

"From the day we met."

Projecting through their cottonwood's leaves, flickered over them incandescent multiplications of the crescent sun. That star, eight hundred sixty-four thousand miles across, exploding light in fusion of hydrogen and helium, and hurling it ninety-three million miles to them in eight minutes and twenty seconds, was being encroached upon by darkness. The moon, four hundred times smaller, and only six thousand seven hundred ninety miles away from them, was cutting into its western margin in its ten mile per hour progression, blocking its light.

Billy laughed. "You love me!"

They kissed in scintillations of that eclipse, while the four-and-a-half billion year old rotating sun, with its rotating and revolving planets and moons, continued their journey of two hundred twenty million years around their whirling galaxy, within their universe, 13.7 billion light years across. And each light year was six trillion miles. That spinning was the infinite vortex of consciousness, in which scale is only the illusion of inward and outward swirling awareness by one pervading intelligence; momentarily localizing in flesh in its dance of forever.

And, for Billy and Paulita, energy had solidified into matter so, in that dance, one could dance with another and for another.

Eighty-eight miles southwest of the Pecos River banks, in Lincoln, James Dolan was staring out the east window of his House apartment at the burned-out shell of McSween's building, when the startling shadow of the eclipse passed over; sweeping darkness toward its destination.

Soon, two hundred miles northwest of that town, in Santa Fe, a massively obese man rose ponderously from his desk in his law office, as daylight abruptly dimmed. Intrigued, he strode to the second story porch.

Alarmed people clustered in the plaza below, pointing to the heavens and praying against evil in Spanish.

Samuel Beach Axtell rushed out from the Palace of the Governors, calling up to the porch, "What is it?" to Thomas Benton Catron.

The behemoth was silent, as if absorbed in an intrinsic role. As the artificial night of total eclipse descended, he checked his gold watch. It was 4:37 PM. Stars appeared. The black circle of the moon, overlapping and obliterating the sun, was rimmed with its fiery corona. The gluttonous creature looked into that flaming eye, as complete occlusion of light was achieved with Santa Fe and himself as the epicenter of darkness.

A smile arched his precisely clipped mustache. He was reliving the gratification of ten days before when, also triumphant in darkness, he had received the telegraphed news from Dolan that McSween was finally dead.

AUGUST 17, 1878   7:52 AM   SATURDAY

Back in the Capitan Mountain cave, Billy gazed outward at a peculiar vision. During the night, countless newly-hatched spiderlings, each casting a silken tether, windblown, had criss-crossed the pines with a swaying, iridescent, filamentous maze.

Tom O'Folliard said to him, "Yginio's mom is good folks: stickin' tha' ax inta the stump so's we know i's safe hereabouts.

"An' tha' lady in Sumner shur was nice te give you a haircut at two AM." Billy smiled, saying her name was Celsa. She'd told him Pat Garrett had proposed to her sister, Juanita.

O'Folliard laughed. "I's funny how people there calls you two Li'l Casino an' Big Casino 'cause o' the poker playin'. You keep loanin' him. Does he pay back?"

"Not so far. But he keeps other people in - plays so badly that he puts money in their pockets."

"I don' unerstand why they'se sayin' you killt some clerk in the Injun resarvation las' Monday. We was jus' gettin' back them hosses they stole from us in Lincoln. A' leas' lookin' for 'em; an' takin' wha' we ended up with."

"I sure wish I'd found Sugar. But we got two of Dick Brewer's that Jessie stole from the Feliz Ranch. Brewer was a murdered Regulator. Had a farm near the Coes."

O'Folliard asked if it was true that the Coes were leaving that day, and did not notice the wince of abandonment. "Yes. To the San Juan Valley in the Farmington area. Northwest corner of this Territory. Going back to farming.

"But about that man who was killed - Morris Bernstein - he worked for that crooked Indian Agent, Frederick Godfroy. Seems he was shooting at some of the San Patricio men who rode in with us. I was probably blamed 'cause my name's known from the War."

O'Folliard asked if Yginio was going to live. "Yes. But they couldn't get those two bullets out of his back."

"Billy, them's real fine gloves you got in yer trunk. An' I never seen no sweater like that."

"They're from Tunstall." Billy blushed. "Mean a good deal to me."

"You figer Sumner's safe?"

"Sure. And from there we can go to Tascosa, Texas, to sell stock. Like Charlie told Catron in his letter: we Regulators will collect payment from him and other Ring men. It's part of the War.

"And I'll take you to a lookout to watch Chisum's big Texas drive. I once did cowboy work for him in Arizona. But I had to leave. A year ago today. Guess a lot's happened since then."

At that moment, in Washington D.C., one thousand five hundred twenty-one miles northeast of the Capitan Mountains, Frank Warner Angel paused at the threshold of the Cabinet room where five men awaited him; and tightened his grip on the handle of his carrying case with New Mexico Territory reports, before entering with habitual brash confidence.

Memorizing details to tell his wife, he got an unexpected memory of Ella, the exquisite woman in Moore's Hotsprings Hotel. In his wallet was her carte de visite photograph, naked except for a diaphanous shift.

The president sat at the head of a long table, a small flower-filled vase before him, and said to the secretary, "Mister Rogers, you can go now. We won't need a record of this meeting."

Affably, Rutherford B. Hayes continued, as Angel took a seat, "Your journey was a long separation from your wife and daughter;" surprising him by this kind awareness.

"And we are impressed, young man," said a lanky speaker, with startlingly wild, red hair and beard, sitting at the far end of the table. Before him and the others were piled Angel's forwarded copies.

Angel answered that he was actually thirty-three. Hayes chuckled. "To us, I'm afraid, that *is* young. I'll make the introductions. To your left is William Evarts, Secretary of State. Across from me is Carl Schurz, Secretary of the Interior and our resident fiery liberal. Carl works harder than any of us. With his one secretary and one clerk in the Patent Office Building, he manages the Office of Indian Affairs, General Land Office, Pension Funds, Patent Bureau, Census Bureau, and Bureau of Education.

"Across from you is Attorney General Charles Devens of the Department of Justice. And to my left is John Sherman, Secretary of the Treasury and our champion of the greenback." Hayes chuckled again. "It seems that counterfeiting is the only thing you didn't find." Angel laughed.

Hayes continued, "You shed light on a part of the country as remote to us, in many ways, as Darkest Africa. We were pleased that you provided us with your tentative reports ..."

"Tentative?"

"So we can discuss your findings confidentially."

Hayes turned to John Sherman. "Our Angel is like one of your Secret Service operatives." Angel expressed curiosity about the unfamiliar entity. "That question will take us to the heart of your findings.

"But first, I want to make some relevant points. Our great War wasn't just about slavery, but about the role of federal government. In the South, people were willing to die to maintain states' rights.

"Now that the central government won, it's my duty not only to protect citizens of all races, but to protect states' autonomy. Hence my slogan: 'Put aside the bayonet.'

"For example, once I realized that the newly-elected Republican governor of South Carolina, D.H. Chamberlain, needed federal troops to stay in power, I asked him to defer to his defeated Democratic opponent, Wade Hampton - who's now governor. I felt home rule would help the healing. The colored people didn't need Chamberlain. They've got the Fifteenth Amendment now."

Angel said, "But I've been reading about the Ku Klux Klan and ..."

"I'm not denying problems; but my conscience is clear. Our country needs help healing from the Civil War. Since the panic of seventy-three, what the American people want is economic stability. Everyone knows I'm not running for a second term. My legacy will be prosperity and a strong Republican party.

"And part of recovery is also restoring confidence in the federal government after the Grant administration's scandals. As you know, when Samuel Tilden lost, he said I'd won by fraud. And he had the credibility of having exposed New York's corrupt "Boss" Tweed Ring. And Tilden's persisting. This May, he tried again to question my legitimacy.

"I'm convinced that those Grant scandals added to my close vote. Actually, their sad litany is crucial for our meeting today. In sixty-nine, Jay Gould and Jim Fisk - in collusion with Grant's brother-in-law - cornered the gold market to inflate prices.

"In seventy-two, there was the Crédit Mobilier scandal in which Union Pacific Railroad Corporation owners were also stock owners in its construction company, named Crédit Mobilier. Their profits were rumored to be in the millions from falsified building costs. And they'd been subsidized unwittingly by the federal government under the original Congressional Act for construction; but kept that money coming through bribes of corporation stock to congressmen.

"It's been called the biggest financial scandal in our history, but, to be fair, there weren't any convictions. And, as loyal partyman, James Abram Garfield - in the House of Representatives since sixty-three and a Crédit Mobilier stockholder - told me: the scandal was exaggerated.

"Meanwhile, Ulysses S. Grant's Secretary of War was being bribed by merchants at army forts; and post office contracts were going to men who paid the right government official. Even Grant's private secretary was in the Saint Louis Whiskey Ring Scandal in which tax collectors were bribed with millions.

"So I'm determined to cleanse our party of that unsavory reputation.

"But to return to the Secret Service. It's a federal organization formed in sixty-two."

John Sherman added: "From the beginning, it's operated under the Department of the Treasury. In Lincoln's day, over half the paper money, and a good deal of coinage, was counterfeit. The Secret Service is a secret federal police force with power to go anywhere in the country to fight counterfeiting."

Hayes said, "And I joked that you were like an 'operative,' Attorney Angel, because its agents - called that - are as good at finding wrongdoers as yourself."

"Wrongdoers, indeed!" Frank Warner Angel said. "When you speak of scandal ..."

Hayes interrupted. "And, as to our Indian policy, we clearly can't tolerate agency funding scandals while we're trying to eliminate renegades like Victorio. Though it's a digression, I'll tell you that I'm considering a law to get rid of Reservations. I want to put Indians on farms with a twenty-five year title. That way, we can give that valuable land to our settlers. And now, let's turn to your findings."

Construing Hayes's tone as noble, Angel formulated his presentation accordingly. "Mister President, you've proved your lofty ideals by the very issues you've empowered me to investigate. As a staunch Republican, that emboldens me to speak without restraint. So I'll begin with my conclusion. I say this, not in vanity, but in moral indignation: I've discovered in New Mexico Territory, in the investigation of the murder of John Henry Tunstall, the largest scandal ever to come to light in our land, a scandal of proportions that would dwarf all the others. This scandal has occurred," he smiled, "possibly on soil never trod by your Secret Service operatives. Had it not been for this single act of murder, what I found would have remained concealed by sheer distance alone.

"For in that Territory - so gigantic that Lincoln County, in which the crime occurred, could fit Massachusetts, Connecticut, Vermont, Rhode Island, and Delaware - there exists a land grab scheme in which one man has amassed six million acres. His name - as stated in my reports - is Thomas Benton Catron, New Mexico Territory's U.S. Attorney.

"What I've stumbled upon is well known to the local citizenry, but unknown to the national populace. Its name is the Santa Fe Ring; and it runs the Territory as its fiefdom with Catron as king.

"Its consequence is unprecedented disenfranchisement, not only of the land owning, pre-Territorial, Mexican population, but of the Whites who've settled there. To the visitor - as I was - what is noteworthy about New Mexico Territory is not their strange mud-brick buildings, but the economic pall which hangs over it, because all money is sucked into that Ring.

"And the Santa Fe Ring operates like other Rings: by financial rewards and favor to politicians, judges, and law enforcement officers.

"But more perniciously, it operates by fear: intimidation, false arrests, removal of legally elected officials, illegal search and entry, and use of the military to enforce its power. And, Gentlemen, it operates by murder of its opponents.

"In fact, last month, as I was preparing my reports, that Ring staged a retaliative massacre of Mexican people - men, women, and children - in a town called San Patricio, near the town of Lincoln.

"Soon after, an attorney named Alexander McSween, who had been openly opposed to them, was murdered by that Ring, his besieged house burned down around him, his wife, her sister and her five little children, and the men trying to defend them. All this was done, I have been told, while a Colonel Dudley, commander of the local fort, participated as a Ring partisan, in violation of the Posse Comitatus Act. And the perpetrators of all those crimes were also the murderers of John Henry Tunstall."

Angel's handsome features contracted in a scowl. "Thus, these moral monstrosities completed the elimination of the only resistance to arise against their might." Angel smiled cynically.

"Though you could say there's one survivor: an eighteen year old boy, the youngest of my deponents - Tunstall's employee and witness to his murder. A William Bonney. In fact, I heard he was one of McSween's few defenders to escape from that burning building."

Hayes spoke sympathetically. "I realize it's hard to know so much and not feel so much."

Angel felt an embarrassing urge to cry, so great was his yearning for goodness after wallowing in New Mexico Territory's evil. Angel said, "Gentlemen, I'm moved to share my deepest concern. We recently passed our Centennial: our celebration of the greatest democracy in history. In a mere four generations, have the seeds of its destruction been planted? Because Thomas Benton Catron has reinstituted the machinery of tyranny."

Hayes sighed deeply and said, "Attorney Angel, you've given us far more than we could have imagined. Am I to understand that all your reports were directed *solely* to Attorney General Devens and Secretary of the Interior Schurz?"

"Yes, Mister President," said Angel, noting nothing ominous about their questioned exposure. "For the Department of Justice, I provided my overview of Lincoln County issues titled '*In the Matter of the Lincoln County Troubles.*'

"A second report covers the murder: '*In the Matter of the Cause and Circumstances of the Death of John H. Tunstall, a British Subject.*' That one I divided into three questions: one, the cause of death; two, the circumstances of it, and, three, whether it was brought about by the lawless and corrupt action of U. S. officials.

"There's a separate report just on U.S. Attorney Catron." Angel turned to Carl Schurz. "And for the Department of the Interior, I addressed the charges against Governor Axtell ..."

The president interjected smiling, "And don't leave out your almost four hundred page transcript of your depositions with Exhibits which you gave us all - just on the Tunstall matter. And your Uña de Gato land fraud investigation, your report on Surveyor General Henry M. Atkinson, and your Mescalero Indian Agency fraud investigations."

Hayes addressed the others. "Gentleman, we certainly have enough information to decide on a course of action. I call special attention to the section entitled '*Third*,' in Attorney Angel's second report to Devens, because it's about John Tunstall's death."

They leafed through their copies and read: "*Third: Was the death of John H. Tunstall brought about by the lawless and corrupt action of United States Officials? After diligent enquiry and examination of a great number of witnesses, I report that his death was the result both indirectly and directly of the lawless and corrupt conduct of United States officials in the Territory of New Mexico.*

"*As to indirect causes, it is my finding that John H. Tunstall, through his large and new mercantile endeavor and his recently acquired land holdings, which would have controlled most of the cattle range between the Mescalero Indian Reservation and the Pecos River through water rights to the Feliz and Peñasco Rivers, presented a financial threat to the existing political-judicial-economic alliance known as the Santa Fe Ring, whose leadership constituted the highest level of New Mexico officials: U.S. Attorney Thomas Benton Catron and Governor Samuel Beach Axtell.*

"*As to direct causes, it is my conclusion that the murder itself was a premeditated act done in compliance with directives, incentives, and promise of immunity from said Santa Fe Ring and its leaders. The act was committed under a guise of a local posse action to give it a screen of legality. Its organizer was a James Dolan whose business holdings were in competition with Tunstall's. And its promulgator was Lincoln County Sheriff William Brady, who employed known murderers, rustlers, and escaped convicts to do the deed.*"

When the cabinetmen finished reading, the president was rotating his little vase, peacefully studying its blossoms.

Carl Schurz said to Angel, "If only you were not still in diapers during our revolution in Germany. Things would have turned out better." All laughed.

Avuncular, bearded Hayes, smiling benevolently, said, "As you know, on June thirteenth, in response to your information,

Department of the Interior Inspector, E.C. Watkins, was sent to the Mescalero Reservation. His report was forwarded on June twenty-seventh to Ezra A. Hayt, Commissioner of Indian Affairs.

"Watkins found that Agent Frederick Godfroy had, in Godfroy's own words, 'loaned' government supplies to that same James Dolan, his partner John Riley, a Doctor Joseph Blazer, and a known rustler, a John Kinney. In addition, Agent Godfroy was billing the government for rations for fifteen hundred Apaches, but could demonstrate only a few hundred. Obviously, Godfroy's removal is imminent.

"In the matter of the Uña de Gato Land Grant, we also agreed with your findings of fraud. Appropriate action will be taken."

"Thank you all," said Angel, welling triumph barely concealed.

Hayes continued, "But to return to your other reports - which you wisely introduced as having extreme implications - the matter is more complex. My inaugural slogan, which has apparently captured people's imagination - 'he that serves his party best serves his county best' - is crucially applicable. You are young, Attorney Angel, your intelligence and competence notwithstanding."

Hayes sighed and turned to the little vase of flowers, slowly dying in dismemberment, as they futilely soaked up water. "Part of being young is the belief that truth is enough. To a degree, we here have already discussed the issues you raised. And - *if* they could be proven - what you've discovered would, in fact, be a scandal to rock the county. That's why I reviewed past troubles of *our* party.

"Do you realize," Hayes's voice was assuming harsh firmness, "that *if* this scandal were exposed, it would not just dwarf - as you say - those scandals of the Grant administration, it would *destroy* this one?"

Angel felt his fingertips become cold. "Tilden would initiate my impeachment. And there is more. What you've discovered would give the next election to the Democratic party; and would also cause a major international incident with our important ally: England.

"This Tunstall report was initiated at the request of Ambassador Edward Thornton, beholden to Queen Victoria, who, after the death of her spouse, Albert, is fetishistic about mourning. I wouldn't like consider our political and economic ramifications." Secretary of State William Evarts nodded grimly.

"What our country needs now is the continued guidance of the Republican Party. And, Tom Catron, this *possible* leader of this *possible* Santa Fe Ring, is a Republican. I may add that he is a man who was a Democrat, but once in New Mexico Territory, espoused our party as the one to receive his great power and influence - of which you may have discovered one unfortunate aspect.

"And that Territory's becoming a state is delayed only by resistance of us in Washington to accepting so many Mexicans - people of mixed race - into our country. But the time will come. And a man like Catron will insure the direction of its vote. And, as you know, Catron gave you a deposition; but, to date, did not supply the extra information requested. So we can say we've got no proof."

Angel struggled to resist the progression. The president was saying, "And a position of Assistant District Attorney for the Eastern District of New York State is available by November - under three months. We here feel that your promotion would enhance your state."

With subdued voice, Angel said, "Thank you, Mister President."

"And we've prepared a revision for your Tunstall report to submit to you for your consideration. We hope you'll find in your heart that to serve the American people is to protect the Republican Party."

Hayes removed a sheet from his own stack and read it aloud: "*Third*: *After diligent inquiry and examination of a great number of witnesses, I report that the death of John H. Tunstall was not brought about through the lawless and corrupt conduct of United States officials in the Territory of New Mexico.*"

Angel's face colored, then paled. "But what about the reports I submitted on Axtell and Catron? They contradict that."

"That's an excellent question," said Hayes. "It can be addressed. Samuel Beach Axtell was appointed governor of Utah Territory by President Grant. There he became so embroiled in the Mormon conflict that when New Mexico Territory's governor, Marsh Giddings, died in office, it was thought best to transfer him there; where he got himself into trouble again. So in Axtell's case, we can act.

"And, as to contradictions, putting together a puzzle is a delightful parlor game. My wife and I often leave one out on a small table. But before the pieces are assembled, the picture doesn't emerge.

"As you said, your reports went *solely* to the Departments of Justice and the Interior. Those on Axtell, Catron, and Atkinson will be stored in the Interior's offices. Those on Tunstall will go to the Department of Justice and to Ambassador Thornton.

"The pieces will *never again* be joined. So, one can say, for all practical purposes, '*No contradictions exist.*'

"And we'd like your *final* reports presented by October - just before that position of Associate District Attorney would begin.

"But we want to know *today* if our dedication to what's right for this country meets with your approval."

Secretary of the Treasury John Sherman said, "I want to repeat, Attorney Angel, that today's discussion is secret. It's a matter of national security, far beyond ..."

"I understand," said Angel and thought, "If I told this story, who would believe it? They'd deny this meeting. There's no record of it. My career would be ruined."

He said quietly, "It appears that there's only one choice. I'll use this ... additional information." He signed the false document as a demonstration of intent.

"Well now," said Rutherford B. Hayes, again affable, "I imagine after our labors, you, like the rest of us, are hungry." He chuckled. "Be forewarned that with the temperance views of myself and my wife, Lucy, we've got a liquor-free household. 'Lemonade Lucy,' I've been told she's called. And we're simple people. You're invited to our luncheon. It consists every day of bread, butter, and cold meats." He laughed. "I've already had my vice of the day."

"And that is?" asked Angel, tension dissipating with his decision.

"My one cup of coffee at breakfast," answered the president.

AUGUST 31, 1878   1:10 PM   SATURDAY

On a mesa, as Tom O'Folliard with Billy watched Chisum's giant cattle drive below - a plodding passive departure eastward, like innocence lost - Billy spoke excitedly about rustling plans.

But they were glarrrious raiding of Cú Chulainn, transposed to the Lincoln County War, where, in archetypal recesses, waited the giant red bull fit for a queen. That same red bull, millennia before, had been captured in ochre and charcoal on cave walls in god glory awe; was later challenged by bull dancers in ancient Crete; was sacrificed in temples of Greece and Rome; and now, Billy's day, was murdered, pouring blood for spectators in Spain and Mexico, so his elemental powers could assuage humanity's impotence.

Billy said, "I've found stock outlets who aren't Ring men. Between Sumner and White Oaks - a town north of Lincoln - there's 'Whiskey Jim' Greathouse. He's got a way station and ranch. The Ring's biggest competition is Pat Coghlan. In the Tularosa area.

"And I'm still trying to meet a Dan Dedrick at his ranch called Bosque Grande. He somehow works with Coghlan. Also, Charlie and Doc will ride with us. They're moving to Sumner to fight the War too."

The outcome of that freedom struggle depended on a meeting then taking place one thousand four hundred thirty-five miles to the northeast of Chisum's herds, in Washington, D.C., in the White House Cabinet room. There President Rutherford B. Hayes addressed Secretary of the Interior Carl Schurz, Secretary of the Treasury John Sherman, Attorney General Charles Devens, and George McCrary, the clean-shaven, gray haired Secretary of War.

Hayes said, "U.S. Attorney Catron is a lucky man. The brazen illegalities in Governor Axtell's Lincoln County Proclamations justify his removal, and overshadow any need for action other than choosing a new governor. For that, we'll meet here at three."

Only Carl Schurz stayed. Confidingly he said, "Rutherford, my friend, *you* - as well as Tom Catron - are lucky. Providence protects you: in your election and in this Axtell.

"I would not like to contemplate the outcome if our Angel had known about the letters and petitions we have gotten over the past two years from Cimarron, in Colefax County, where that Santa Fe Ring is the pet obsession of the citizenry - including that fanatical newspaper woman, Mary McPherson. The one Tom Catron wrote to us to disregard as 'a crazy person.'

"And, fortunately, our young blood-hound also did not sniff out that, in seventy, our very own William Evarts was lucratively employed as an attorney by his *good friends*, Catron and Elkins, to add prestige - of his having been Attorney General the year before - to his legal opinion for them that the Maxwell Land Grant's title was sound for its sale - to get around Elkins's brother's questionable survey."

Schurz added, "As President Johnson's Secretary of the Navy, Gideon Wells, said, 'Evarts is a man who accommodates himself to any set of principles.'"

"What of that?" Hayes declared irascibly, revealing the ruthless arrogance of his immense inherited wealth, and seen only by his intimates.

With acceptance of futility, which he rationalized as mankind's foibles, Schurz sighed. "Merely that from our Olympian heights we are privileged to observe the irony of history unfolding."

From his papers, Schurz withdrew a document. "This letter to us is from April of seventy-seven, only a year and three months before their war in Lincoln County. From Mary McPherson. Last night I check-marked this paragraph. That Ring was no secret to us at all!"

Hayes read: *"To the President: The undersigned in behalf of the people of the Territory of New Mexico herewith present the following Charge: that U.S. Attorney Thomas B. Catron, Judge Warren Bristol, Chief Justice Henry Waldo, and Governor Samuel B. Axtell have conspired together in a group known as the Santa Fe Ring for the purpose of corrupting justice so as to deprive citizens of personal liberty and the right of fair trial, and to compass the revenues of the Territory and the property of its citizens including large land grants for purposes of private gain. We citizens therefore respectfully request their removal from office."*

Schurz continued, "Mary McPherson's son-in-law, Raymond Morley, a railroad engineer, joined with Cimarron attorney, Frank Springer, to buy the *Cimarron News and Press*. Morley's wife is McPherson's daughter. So every corrupt move the Santa Fe Ring made, they printed it in that paper. A local young gunfighter named Clay Allison even championed their cause. He reminded me of that young William Bonney, who so moved our Angel.

"You may recall that one of the first things *you* did as president, as a favor for Tom Catron, was authorizing Fort Union troops to enforce warrants issued by his loyal Ringman, Territorial Chief Justice Henry Waldo, to kill Morley and Springer if they resisted a falsified arrest - shades of Commander Dudley in Lincoln!

"Of course, Tom Catron and Sam Axtell were unhappy when that plot failed, but eventually they succeeded - by another murder."

Carl Schurz handed another Mary McPherson letter with a check. "*An outrage was the assassination of a Methodist minister named Franklin J. Tolby, who was fighting the stranglehold of the Santa Fe Ring on our Territory. They murdered him after warning him to leave Colfax County which he refused to do.*'

"Doesn't that remind you of the murdered Tunstall and McSween a year later? The Morleys and McPherson even printed in their newspaper that Clay Allison refused seven hundred dollars from Catron to do that Tolby deed.

"And look at this petition to us from McPherson last May. A list of charges identical to the ones Angel found against Axtell."

Hayes said sarcastically, "We're ousting Axtell. What else do you want? Exposing how I got my winning electoral vote in Florida? But Hayes had learned to tolerate idealism from this stingless gadfly.

"Only to contemplate, Rutherford. In Colefax County was no organized uprising; though they called it the Colefax County War. How did these people in Lincoln County make all this progress against the Ring one year later? I decided we missed something. I re-read McSween's pedantic deposition to Angel. I was not ready to fight.

"So I concluded that there still remains *alive* the *real* leader of their Lincoln County People's Revolution. And you know, as well as I do, that was what it was."

Their eyes met, both aware that in place was the next potential enforcer: the Secret Service, poised, if needed, for political murder if the unrest continued and threatened the Ring. Hayes had already informed its Chief about the Lincoln County situation.

Thus, Frank Warner Angel, naively by his reports, had not only established that Washington was merely one more link in the Santa Fe Ring; but also had left its participants there poised for future lethal action.

With his Cabinetmen reassembled, Hayes began by asking what they knew about Lew Wallace, his prospective pick for governor.

Secretary of War George McCrary said, "Ulysses S. Grant detested him after Shiloh. And in July of sixty-four, Lew Wallace initiated the battle at Monocacy Junction without orders. Later, he claimed it saved President Lincoln from kidnapping. He once said to me, 'Washington lay exposed in its nakedness.'"

Carl Schurz joked: "The poet who was a general. Or the general who was a poet."

"Gentlemen," chuckled the president, "let's go over the specifics and make our decision. Troops won't kidnap me, but my wife will - for dinner." They laughed.

Schurz said, "I have taken a special interest in Lew Wallace. Do not forget that I rescued my old professor from Spandau prison. I have a weakness for intellectuals." He adjusted his pince-nez and straightened his notes. "My assignment was to interview him. This is what I learned.

"Louis Wallace - who renamed himself 'Lew' because he thought it sounded better - was born in Brookville, Indiana, on April tenth of eighteen-seventeen. His father was the Governor of Indiana in thirty-seven. Lew became an attorney. For a wife he picked a very rich girl. In the War - probably because of his father - Governor Oliver Morton of Indiana made him Indiana's Adjutant General with the responsibility to raise troops. Then Lew was made Colonel of the Eleventh Regiment of Indiana Volunteers.

"It was for this regiment that this poetic romantic - so dashing that the paintings of him imply broken hearts - designed the Zouave costume. With the red pantaloons, tight green jackets, and little caps, to me the pictures look like organ grinder monkeys."

Hayes smiled. "It wasn't as bad as that, Carl. But they did stand out in parades."

"That I can imagine. And we will see how eccentric is this Lew. We come to the battle of Shiloh in Tennessee. Do not forget - because we have seen such horrors later - Shiloh, in sixty-two, was the biggest battle ever fought on American soil. Twenty-three thousand seven hundred forty-six casualties; more than the total casualties of your Revolutionary War, War of Eighteen Twelve, and the Mexican War combined.

"Originally it was called the battle of Pittsburgh Landing. Wallace was positioned at Crump's Landing six miles north of Pittsburgh Landing, near the north to south Tennessee River.

"In my mind, the key to Shiloh is not often mentioned, which is that, through his own spies, Lew Wallace learned that the Confederate army under General Albert Sidney Johnston was approaching. Did he inform General Grant? No. Why? He has said he assumed Grant would know something that big. Well, he didn't. And, the month before, Wallace had again been promoted - this time to Major General: the highest rank a man could reach at the time.

"Back to Shiloh. Two main routes went to Pittsburgh Landing: one direct - the River Road - one indirect, the Shunpike Road. With the terrain, the River Road went a bit east before going south. The Shunpike went quite west before looping back.

"Then came April fourth. Wallace's scout, Bell, reported to him that the rebel army was heading from Corinth to Pittsburgh Landing.

"So Wallace wrote a note - probably poetic - and gave it to his orderly Simpson to inform Grant. But - as revealed in the intense controversy that followed - Wallace told Simpson if he couldn't deliver it directly to Grant, he should *mail it*. Gentlemen, Simpson mailed it!

"Ulysses Grant said he never got the letter, which can be believed since - as you say in this country - 'all hell broke loose' two days later on April sixth, when everyone was asleep, except for the Confederate army. Wallace was awakened by his sentinel, who told him he heard guns from the south. So Wallace did the natural thing: went for breakfast on a steamboat on the Tennessee River.

"At eight-thirty, Grant's boat, the Tigress, passed his. Grant asked Wallace if he had heard gunfire. Wallace answered *only* that he had. So Grant told him to hold in readiness.

"At eleven-thirty, Grant sent Captain Baxter, his Chief Quartermaster, to tell Wallace to come to Pittsburgh Landing for a battle. Poor Baxter wrote those orders from Grant on a paper picked up in the Tigress's ladies' room. History has not told us what he was doing there. The note - whose penmanship Wallace criticized - Wallace later said he had lost. More unfortunate was what came next.

"Wallace had those two roads to get to the battle. Guess what he did?" The men were smiling. Schurz was their eccentric. "He had lunch. After that, he took the longer Shunpike, having decided that, by then, Grant must have the enemy retreating westward - which was where that road would first put him. In reality, a Confederate artillery of sixty-two cannon were firing on desperate Union men trapped at Pittsburgh Landing.

"Soon, Wallace was met by a messenger from Grant saying, 'Hurry up;' and, strangely - to Wallace - departing eastward.

"Nevertheless, Lew Wallace blithely proceeded west until met by another Grant messenger. When that one also left in the 'wrong direction,' it occurred to Wallace that *he* had made a mistake. So what did he do? Stopped to wait for his stragglers.

"Then came two more couriers who reported that they were losing at Pittsburgh Landing, and pleaded with him to release troops. He refused. He felt it would make a bad impression if they did not arrive as a unit. But he did proceed southeast.

"That left Wallace with Snake Creek to cross. It was a bog. So he and his men descended waist deep. He later revealed that he decided not to worry about their uniforms. That is fortunate or this might still be a slave owning country - though poor Abe Lincoln might still be alive.

"At that point, Lew Wallace was only a half mile from the battle. Since he was not Alexander the Great, famous for his lightning marches, he chose to bed down in that bog. He leaned on a tree. Sleep was further interrupted by mournful cries of the wounded at the adjacent battlefield.

"Wallace did arrive the next morning. Union General Buell had already crossed the Tennessee River with eighteen thousand more troops for Grant. As you know, that day, Grant won.

"Then, not surprisingly, Grant removed Wallace from any future command of troops. Maybe he hoped to humiliate Wallace into leaving the army; but it only stimulated his flurry of writing, in which he denied wrongdoing, but concluded that the war was young and they were all still learning

"But Lew was bored. So, in August of sixty-two, when his friend Governor Oliver Morton summoned him to assist in organizing the defense of Cincinnati, Ohio, he went - obviously alone. By coincidence, heading in that same direction were Confederate troops under General Kirby Smith.

" When Wallace found out, he took over Cincinnati without asking anyone, declared martial law, and composed a literary piece of sorts: a proclamation demanding that all inhabitants defend their city.

"Unable to get rid of him, the army next tried sending him to miserable Camp Chase, which held five thousand, renegade Union soldiers. His assignment was to prepare these derelicts to fight Indians in Minnesota. To everyone's surprise but his own, he did shape up and send off this criminal crew. I do not know, however, if they merely deserted again.

"Then came Lincoln's reelection. Wallace was sent to Baltimore, Maryland, to protect poling places. He got carried away, as usual, and was about to hang four men - declaring, without proof, that they were Confederate spies - when Lincoln leashed him.

" Then April fourteenth of sixty-five passed at Ford's Theater. Because he was an accomplished lawyer and a loyal Republican, Wallace was appointed by President Andrew Johnson as judge in the assassins' military trial.

"But it has been the conclusion of our less hysterical times that Wallace bullied and hampered their lawyers. And making the eight defendants wear bizarre pointed caps covering their heads, does smack of his costuming dramas. As you all know, the hanging of the defendants, David Herald, George Atzarodt, and Lewis Payne, has left people uneasy because their fellow gallows victim, Mary Surratt - John Wilkes Booth's landlady - was considered innocent. The so-called accomplices, Doctor Samuel Mudd, who set Booth's broken leg; Edward Spangler; Samuel Arnold; and Michael O'Laughlin were also sentenced - again at Wallace's adamancy - to life in prison on the Dry Tortugas in Florida. President Johnson pardoned them later; though, by then, O'Laughlin had died of yellow fever.

"But this courtroom experience prepared Lew Wallace for his next assignment: heading the Andersonville War Crimes trial against Confederate prison keeper, Captain Henry Wirz, in August of sixty-five. Wirz too was hanged, though without public regret.

"And Wallace continued to wax poetic. On July fourth of sixty-six, he presented his old friend Governor Oliver Morton with the battle flags of the Indiana regiments and said ..." Schurz took up a paper: " *'In the armies of Persia was a chosen band called the Immortals bearing spears pointed with pomegranates of silver and gold. We, too, have our Immortals! And instead of a king to serve they have for leader that man of God and the people, Lincoln the Martyr.'*

" This writing makes me miss Abe even more. Gentleman, how do you point a spear with a pomegranate?" Several laughed.

"Then comes Mexico. Wallace had earlier convinced Lincoln and Grant that the Texan Confederates planned to join French Imperialists under Napoleon the Third's puppet king, Archduke Maximillian of Austria.

"So, in late sixty-five, Lew did an arms running scheme for anti-imperialist Mexicans. They graciously took the arms and ungraciously never paid him.

"It is true that Lew Wallace has never shown venality. He has barely shown practicality.

"In sixty-six, he made an even stranger Mexican plan: offering their then president, Benito Juárez, to import American colonists to defend their border from Indians in exchange for free land. Can you imagine Juárez wanting to give up more land to Americans?

"But Wallace happily declared that the experience helped him finish his novel on Mexico, *The Fair God* - which has gotten so much literary acclaim.

"In seventy, Wallace ran for the House of Representatives from Indiana. The Democrats made much of Shiloh and the hanging of Missus Surratt. He lost, but blamed election fraud.

"Since seventy-four, he has engaged in private law practice back in Crawfordsville, Indiana, and is working on a book on Jewish history called *Ben-Hur*.

"And, as you all know, he campaigned loyally in Florida for Rutherford's presidential bid."

Suave William Evarts said, "He almost got his reward this year. He was offered the ambassadorship of Bolivia, but refused. Probably the low salary."

Schurz laughed. "Not the five thousand dollars. He didn't like the landscape."

"So he might accept the Governorship of New Mexico Territory, which pays only two thousand six hundred dollars a year?" asked John Sherman.

"Apparently, yes. He thinks New Mexico Territory will look like Jerusalem and assist in completing his new book."

"Thank you, Carl," said Hayes, smiling. "Informative and amusing. Is Lew Wallace right as its next governor?"

"I will be a more serious," said Schurz, adjusting his pince-nez and reverting to token idealist. "This Lew Wallace, as I said, reminds me of my old professor. Then I risked my life to rescue him. Now I would let him stay. Intellectuals ruined our revolution. They were all mind and no heart. They cared only to act clever - not to act. I left the country in disgust.

"And, with Lew Wallace, possessing a mind able to be a lawyer, a general, and a writer, only gave him vanity to override orders with his own incorrect decisions, and to become despotic with horrible consequences like Missus Surrat. Does this bother him? Not at all. Because he feels nothing. We would send into this faraway battleground the opposite of our Angel. Please excuse my pun."

"Carl," smiled Hayes, "I'll continue that pun. We don't want an avenging Angel sent. This war needs to stay in darkness. I'm confident that Lew Wallace won't embarrass the Republican Party."

"And how many more will die?" asked Carl Schurz, exaggerating melancholy resignation.

"As many as have died likewise through history," said Hayes. "And now it's time for dinner."

SEPTEMBER 2, 1878   8:05 PM   MONDAY

Billy, finishing his plate of tortillas and beans, told Celsa he had to leave immediately to help Charlie; his wife, Manuela; and Doc. They were moving into the east barracks. She purred, "And leave me?" From behind, she massaged his shoulders. "Do you remember our first dancing?" She drew him up to voluptuous rhythm.

Finally beside the bed, Billy's eye was caught by a little paper-framed tintype on the side-table. "Barney Mason?!" he exclaimed. On its back was written, *"To Celsa. Unfergittible."* Billy doubled up laughing. She mumbled nervously, afraid of repercussions, "Marriage gives a woman nothing. Take poor Juanita. Miserable. And married to Garrett only a few weeks. But *you* are the one I wait for."

Billy's eyes were still laughing. "A between times wait?"

Misinterpreting indifference as leniency, she teased, "So you see Celsa can be naughty."

Later, lost in wetness of intertwined bodies, the tintype was crushed beyond recognition. And Celsa was again convinced of her hold over Billy.

SEPTEMBER 6, 1878   3:29 PM   FRIDAY

New Mexico Territory wept in rain splashing wind bemoaning fleeing Regulators. Like the Coes, they fled, not in cowardice, but convinced of futility and wanting a new life. Even Susan McSween, having moved with her sister's family to Las Vegas, merely ruminated about revenge.

Inside the Capitan cave, Billy and Tom O'Folliard watched Fred Waite, with his long black hair and hat with golden eagle feather, pack for Oklahoma Indian Territory, to which he planned to take Jim French. O'Folliard said he'd miss him; he was good folks.

Emerald-eyed Waite said to Billy, again facing paternal abandonment and gazing at flames boiling coffee, "Remember, Kid, about the Seven Deadly Sins? Here's an eighth: Resignation. Mine. I realized Lincoln County is a moral proving ground. Evil here's so powerful it breaks people where they're weakest.

"I know you won't give up the fight - Tunstall's 'don't back down' - so I'll give you this ol' Chickasaw warning: 'A traitor is a gambler: betting the other side will win.'

"Or call it 'Thirty Pieces of Silver.' That was all it took to get Christ crucified: the bribe one of his men got to give away his hideout - probably about a hundred dollars our money. His name was Judas."

Billy smiled. "So Judas lost. People to this day know he was a rat. He can never escape!"

Waite shook his head ruefully. "You'll never change. Me, I'm through with my White side. My direction's Indian now. If Whites take over the country, nothing will be left. In the end, there'd just be the glutton, Thomas Benton Catron, owning a wasteland.

"And all you'll get, Kid, is being branded an outlaw - if they don't kill you - like they'll kill Victorio." At those words, Waite realized the deadliness of his own sin. The boy faced the same death penalty indictments he did. If a trial ever came, he would not risk himself by attempting aid. Worse, he sensed that, for the rest of his life, he would keep secret his connection to the Regulators.

Heavy with guilt, Fred Waite held up an elaborately adorned, tobacco pouch and said, "Once I counted. Six thousand beads. An Indian masterpiece. Ol' Chickasaw saying: 'Objects hold memories.' Yours now, Kid. To remember this ol' Chickasaw."

Billy thanked him and remarked that the following day he'd be equalizing from the Ring. Waite smiled. "Guess Oklahoma Territory newspapers will keep me up on your progress. Ash Upson might even write your book. 'Boy hero,' wasn't it?"

Billy, laughing at the dime novel irony, said, "Or outlaw - if I lose."

SEPTEMBER 13, 1878   5:58 AM   FRIDAY

Black clouds like dismembering night were in dawn's gray as Billy rode northward along the Pecos River on a magnificent sorrel gelding whose mane and tail flagged white streamers.

With satisfaction, Billy looked back at sixty-five horses being herded by Regulators Charlie Bowdre, John Middleton, and Henry Brown. Renewed was war's daring, but in skirmishes linking Mackie's petty thievery with a cause. And there was confidence that soon Angel's reports would bring presidential intervention permitting them all a law-abiding life.

Tom O'Folliard, riding at his side, asked Billy how far Tucumcari was. "About sixty miles northeast. Almost at the Canadian River - or Red River. Then it's east fifty miles to Tascosa, Texas. We were lucky. Charlie Fritz was holding Dolan's best horses. And Walz's Carrizozo ranch - really Catron's - 'ill be good for cattle. But I heard there's a horse shortage in Tascosa." Billy sneered, patting his sorrel's shoulder. "This here's Dandy Dick. Belonged to a deceased sheriff named Brady."

Thinking about retribution, one thousand three hundred seventy-one miles northeast of their herd, in his Patent Office Building professional quarters, Carl Schurz was sitting with Lew Wallace. Schurz asked him whether - after reading the Angel reports - he still wanted to be governor of New Mexico Territory.

The long-limbed graceful man, with military erectness, nodded grandly. His gray-woven black hair still had the profuse forelock of his youth; and his united mustache and long rectangular beard, in imagined style of an Abyssinian king, had likewise been sported for thirty years. Schurz complimented his book, *The Fair God*.

Wallace added that it was being called the great American novel. His next, set in ancient Jerusalem, was the telling of Christ's coming.

"And the governorship would not interfere with that coming?" red-headed Schurz smiled.

"Indeed, not," said Wallace. "And I would step into paternal gubernatorial footprints, confirming, at fifty-one, that I am at last a man. Well I know the yoke of parental authority. My father - as Indiana Governor only about a decade after Tippecanoe and the killing of that fanatical Tecumseh - was well-respected, and, at home, a taskmaster. Even my blessed mother - who died when I was but five - had her stern ways. As to punishments, she was as creative as I was incorrigible. She would tie me to a bedpost or dress me in a girl's frock. She was as determined to make a man of me as was he."

"And you served your country well. President Hayes wants to remove any last obstacles to your reward."

"Shiloh," Wallace answered bitterly. Drawn heavy brows accentuated his indignant brown eyes. "Someone had to bear blame for that first day. It enables me to write from experience about Jesus - the greatest martyr of all - having myself also tasted the gall and vinegar of injustice."

Carl Schurz asked, given that perspective, what had been his impression of the Angel reports. Without telling Hayes, he had rebelliously provided Wallace with copies of them all.

Wallace said, "Voluminous but fascinating. Change names and weaponry, and one would have ancient combatants with pagan gods appeased by blood sacrifice. My own Mexico experiences revealed to me the primitive Christianity left by Hernándo Cortés - my 'fair God'- after he defeated Aztec Emperor Montezuma. And recall: the Christ casted out demons. Now I too shall have the opportunity to dwell in a land where the Devil still walks the streets." He chuckled. "A privilege few authors of biblical tales receive."

Schurz asked if his wife would mind living in that backward place. Wallace said, "Susan loves adventure - as I do - but not privation. It may be of historical fascination to reside in the Palace of the Governors - which I read was built at the start of the seventeenth century by Don Pedro de Peralta, Spain's first governor. But then it really was a palace. Now it would be rather like taking her to live in the ruins of the Coliseum. Pre-wife repairs will be paramount.

"As to my own pilgrimage to that unholy land: if I have not brought peace to Lincoln County in the sixty days following my October first swearing in, I shall be ashamed of myself. After all, I shall be residing in Santa Fe, in the valley of a mountain range known as Sangre de Cristo: 'Blood of Christ.' What better place to both write about, as well as bring forth, a tale of redemption and salvation."

OCTOBER 10, 1878   10:35 AM   THURSDAY

At their Tascosa, Texas, campsite, in a golden leaf canopied corral of rope tied to cottonwood trunks, Billy curried Dandy Dick. He told Henry Brown, readying one of the eight other horses in that enclosure, to trim hair under the jawline. It made the head look better.

Tom O'Folliard commented that the mail rider they'd met had given good advice on their location. Billy said, "Henry Hoyt's his name. Lives here. Sure was riding a sorry specimen. Maybe he'll buy."

When locals finally approached, they were lead by clean-shaven Hoyt, with red curls, whose friendliness contrasted his compatriots' hostility. Two were superintendents of big ranches: a wall-eyed man from the LX and the other from the LIT. An LX foreman, in hairy buffalo hide chaps, gave his name as Charlie Siringo. Hearing they came from New Mexico Territory, he growled, "There's a war there. We don't want trouble here." Billy said they were just selling horses.

Henry Hoyt contributed that, except for their local lady rancher, Miss Lizzie - who had a racing mare named Spider and was famous for wearing trousers - Billy now had before him the area's best citizens. Hoyt introduced Jim McMasters and Jule Howard, who ran the local saloon and store.

Charlie Siringo interrupted, "How much you sellin' these up here for? Jus' askin', 'cause I got me my Whiskey-peet." That gelding was a platter-hoofed Roman-nosed bay.

"Thirty for those below," Billy said. "But I'm not sure yet about selling these up here. I realized they're exceptional."

Hoyt asked if they could try them anyway; that sorrel was one splendid animal. Billy said they could ride any horse; but he would probably keep that sorrel for himself.

After the Tascosa men rode off, each sampling a "special" horse, Middleton said, "They couldn' survive a day in Lincoln County."

Henry Hoyt returned first on Dandy Dick, exclaiming, "Absolutely superb. Someday I hope to afford a horse like this. My current abode is a mattress pad on Howard and McMasters' floor. It turns out that John Chisum's advice that I come here for my medical practice was not correct."

Charlie Bowdre asked if he was a doctor. "Rush Medical College. But I was too effective here in their smallpox epidemic. I put myself out of business.

"I'd met Chisum in seventy-seven when I came to at Fort Sumner. In fact, I vaccinated the Maxwell family there to prevent smallpox. I remember their beautiful daughter, Paulita."

Billy's ears turned red. He asked, "Uh, when you vaccinate somebody, where d'you do it?" In their home, Hoyt said. "What

I mean is, where on their, um, body?" Hoyt said on the arm, like Edward Jenner, who developed the concept. Billy sighed with relief.

Later, as his four laughing companions slapped Billy's back, Bowdre, with his Cavalier-style mustache and goatee and tipped flat-crowned hat, said, "Goddamn it, Kid, ye sold these up here fohr a fortune! Even tah Siringo." Billy's eyes shone. He said to bring up more so he could decide if he could part with them. But they had to stay on best behavior. Those men were a nervous bunch.

Two hundred fourteen miles due west of Tascosa, in Santa Fe, at his polished desk, Thomas Benton Catron sat with enraged jaw contracted over the roll of fat bulging from his collar.

Passing his hand over his gray hair pomaded to conceal a bald pate behind a full front, he noticed that its palm-down print on the mahogany expanse had left watery beading beside two sheets of paper.

He sniffed, wrinkling his small nose, and rose grunting to lock his door while flapping back his frockcoat and confirming a tell-tale obnoxious odor. As he lumbered to a cabinet, his sox became soaked by sweat glands discharging in sympathetic nervous system over-activity: the incurable syndrome of hyperhidrosis. To that sweat, bacteria added putrefaction. Concealing this stench was Catron's obsession.

Carrying a glass bottle and a cloth from the cabinet, he pushed aside the two papers which had stimulated the response. From the bottle, wafted scent of formaldehyde. Wiped on his palms, its drying effect was immediate. Then came the laborious task of exposing his feet, almost unreachable over his gigantic belly. The ablution was completed after unbuttoned access to adipose-buried armpits.

But through habituated olfaction, when he sat again, he was oblivious that his office now smelled like it contained the embalmed body of a rotting corpse.

He tore up the two papers into his waste basket.

The first had been a letter dated September 24, 1878. It had said: *"Honorable Charles Devens, Sir. I will be in Washington next Monday, September 30th, and I would like to meet with you to make a statement on Mr. Catron's behalf. With the facts I know, it can be clearly established that bitter political and personal enemies have assailed him and the charges in the report of Investigator Angel are unfounded. I have also written to the President today to the same effect. Very Respectfully, Steven B. Elkins."*

The second had been Catron's decoding of a telegram from Elkins, dated the day after that meeting with Attorney General Devens. It had stated: *"President advises too much to lose. Evarts warns too close to Maxwell Land Grant questions. I concur. Risk extreme."*

Then Catron waited, staring with his soullessly blank, dead-fish eyes. "Come in," he said to a knock. His secretary set down his newly dictated letter and exited. Catron proof-read: *"Honorable Charles Devens, Sir: In accordance with a purpose which I have long entertained I hereby tender my resignation as U.S. Attorney for New Mexico Territory to take effect November 10, 1878."*

Catron signed; then he whispered, "Every last one will pay."

OCTOBER 12, 1878   3:13 PM   SATURDAY

At a saloon table in Howard and McMasters, at Tascosa's plaza, Henry Hoyt, red curls tousled, animated and intellectual, vaguely like Tunstall, was impressing Billy, in the throws of new paternal transference, as Tom O'Folliard listened and Charlie Siringo drank.

Hoyt said to Billy, "When I was at the University of Minnesota, I was trained in sprinting by the famous professional runner, Ned Moulton. Have you ever competed in running yourself?" O'Folliard said proudly that Billy ran good. In Lincoln he was in front.

"To get back to my story," said Hoyt. "On my way to enter Rush Medical College, I visited the Centennial Exhibit in Philadelphia. There I met the great Joseph Lister, the father of antiseptic surgery. He discovered one could prevent infection by killing tiny invisible beings called germs." O'Folliard asked how tiny things could hurt you.

Billy said, "It must depend on numbers. Like coral insects spitting out enough shells to make islands."

Hoyt said, "Ah, you know science. I'll confess: I'm an evolutionist." Billy looked puzzled. "Why, it's the greatest discovery of our lifetimes: evolution! Charles Darwin discovered that we're descended from apes. His book in seventy-one, called *The Descent of Man*, convinced me. While reading it, I looked at my hand, and, by golly, it was a monkey's." Billy laughed.

Suddenly Middleton shouted bestially at his poker-playing townsman tablemate, teeth bared, "You sonoabitch! Let's fight!"

Billy sprang up snarling, "Light out for camp, John, or fight *me*." Middleton backed, palms open placatingly, mumbling about Billy's being edgy, and rushed out.

Billy sat, again a pleasant boy. He said, "I promised no trouble."

Henry Hoyt commented, "You've got quite a combination: intelligence and power over men. The world is your oyster! But we've just witnessed evolution's tragedy: We still act like apes."

Siringo slurred, "Tragedy's that you both don' drink." He looked around. "Town's goin' to hell. Lowlife wolfers is comin' in."

To Billy's questioning, Siringo answered, "End o' the buffalo herd. "See tha' filthy tramp? Wolfes an' coyots come fer rottin' meat on them thousans o' bufflo carcasses left by the hunters. Wolfers poison those critters fer their skins."

"A cruel death," said Hoyt. "Along my mail route, I've seen wolfers' victims in the acres of slaughtered buffalos. Strychnine rat poison is used. It kills by exciting the nervous system to agonizing muscle contractions till suffocation. That human sitting there would embarrass our ape cousins."

Billy sighed, and changed the subject, asking about local dances. Hoyt said they were on Saturday nights. At Romero's dancehall. But Pedro Romero had strict rules: no weapons.

Billy said nonchalantly, "Why don't you ride Dandy Dick more?" Concealed was his attempt to prolong contact with the world of the intellect, long lost to him.

OCTOBER 19, 1878   8:12 PM   SATURDAY

In crisp night, arriving at Romero's dancehall at the plaza, Billy greeted clean-shaven Henry Hoyt, as Tom O'Folliard, Charlie Bowdre, Henry Brown, and John Middleton entered. Billy told Hoyt that they'd be leaving soon; all the horses had been sold. The doctor said he'd be departing too, having been hired for a mail route between Fort Bascome and Las Vegas.

Then Hoyt inhaled vigorously and challenged Billy to a footrace.

When Billy agreed, Hoyt took him to Howard and McMasters, where he proudly donned his old, spiked, sprinting shoes.

Back in the plaza, Henry Hoyt established their destination as the dancehall. At his own count, he leapt forward. To his surprise, Billy kept pace.

Just before the entrance, Hoyt slackened, realizing the imprecise stopping point. Assuming it was inside, Billy continued; but his heel struck the threshold, and he sprawled onto the dance floor.

Instantly, he was surrounded by his men, unsure if he had been shot, secreted Colt .44's bristling.

Furious, Pedro Romero rushed screaming, "Out! Out! And never come back!" Leaving, Billy said to O'Folliard that he didn't know if he had won the race.

At the same time, one hundred ninety-two miles due east of Tascosa, in Santa Fe, Lawrence Murphy was dying. James Dolan sat at his bedside, listening to the stertorous breathing, and smoothed covers over the fluid-distended belly with its cirrhotic liver. Jaundiced Murphy mouthed, "Lamy."

Dolan reassured that he was coming. The Saint Francis Church was close. After grooming Murphy's faded reddish hair and beard,

Dolan placed the comb on the bedside table; arrayed, as Murphy had requested, with a blessed candle, a glass of well water, and a tablespoon. Purposefully omitted by Dolan was a cross.

There was knocking. Dolan braced as if for a mighty struggle.

"This way, Jean-Baptist," Dolan said demeaningly to the entering gentle, slender, white-haired, French prelate, in a knee-length white surplice over a dark cassock, and carrying a black Extreme Unction box. From his neck hung his large pectoral cross, received when he was consecrated as Vicar Apostolic in Rome by Pope Pius IX. On June 16, 1875, Jean-Baptist Lamy had then become an Archbishop.

Dolan said, "Major Murphy appreciates your coming this late. His big contributions to building your Saint Francis Church apparently bore fruit."

Unaware of the snideness, gentle Jean-Baptist Lamy said the Lord chose the time; he was but his servant.

Removing the irreverent comb, Lamy set down his box and took out bottles of holy water and blessed oil, and the Eucharist wafer in a leather pyx container. The odd lack of a cross was remedied.

Lamy knelt and became lost briefly in adoration of his God, unaware of Dolan's cold stare of hatred.

Standing, he prayed and sprinkled the holy water on Murphy, on his final bed, and on Dolan, concealing a cringe. For Murphy's confession, Dolan left at the priest's request.

Murphy struggled to speak. "Fear Hell, Father. Used Jimmy ... for sin ... selfish needs."

Compassionately, Lamy granted absolution of that guilt which he sympathetically misconstrued as "possessive love of an adopted son."

Lamy then called Dolan back.

Into Lawrence Murphy's moribund lips was slipped the Eucharist, miraculously transfigured, as the priest knew, into flesh of a man who had died for him one thousand eight hundred forty-five years before. Lamy sighed in suffusing joy at another victory over perdition.

For the final sacrament of Extreme Unction, Lamy, with holy oil, daubed eyes, ears, nostrils, lips, hands, and feet to forgive their sins; and cleansed his own fingers with the well water and cotton.

After Dolan had impatiently shown Archbishop Lamy out, he announced loudly, "Everything's ready, Larry. Full Masonic ceremony. With Catron, Axtell, Bristol, Rynerson."

Murphy whispered, "My Will, Jimmy. Everything left to you. More ... money ... stolen from Fritz ... than ... you knew. I tricked them all. My blue ... eyed boy."

Dolan smiled sardonically, certain that Murphy was still his. With a collector's avarice, awaiting this soul's departure, Dolan thought, "It is time to find another."

OCTOBER 24, 1878   10:19 AM   THURSDAY

In Tascosa's Howard and McMasters Saloon, Billy, with titillated excitement, watched Henry Hoyt packing, and announced, "I decided to give you Dandy Dick for your new mail route." Billy blushed fondly at the astounded man, though unaware that bestowing his sole trophy of the Lincoln County War was like a son's rite of reciprocity.

Billy added, "I want this real legal." At the bar, he wrote, "*Tascosa Texas. Thursday Oct. 24th, 1878. Know all persons by these presents that I do hereby sell and deliver to Henry Hoyt one Sorrel Horse Branded BB on left hip and another indistinct Brand on right Shoulder for the sum of Seventy five $ dollars. In hand received. WHBonney.*" He had Howard and McMasters witness it.

Hoyt asked, "Have you read law?" Billy smiled, saying with a legal Angel. Hoyt fumbled in his pocket for a small return, presenting his gold pocket watch with braided horsehair chain.

After Billy and O'Folliard left, Henry Hoyt said to Charlie Siringo, "I'll wager that this bill of sale is worth more than the horse. I'm keeping it. That boy is special."

"Hell he is," said Siringo. "I'll sell ye my old boots. So, when *I'm* famis, ye can say they was from a real cowboy spendin' his days on the hurricane deck o' a Spanish pony." Both laughed heartily. But Hoyt carefully rolled up Billy's paper.

Eighty-one miles due west of Tascosa, in Las Vegas, Susan McSween, in widow's weeds, was then meeting with a broad-chested sandy-bearded attorney, Huston Chapman; her age, but just opening his practice. David Shield, to her concealed anger, had recommended him after cowardly refusing to represent her on pressing probate matters. It was just as well. David might have seen through her scheme. Self-justified by losses, she was keeping her dead husband's Emil Fritz insurance money, while requesting reduced legal fees.

Adding to her discomfiture, were traumatic associations from Huston Chapman's empty left jacket sleeve, the arm amputated after a gun accident when he was thirteen.

She concluded her disjointed account: "My mind's not logical like Alexander's, but - I mean to say - the house was burned down because of Colonel Dudley. Sacre bleu! Even our chickens were pure bred. And our piano was lost too." That epitomized her devastation. "I tried to stay in Lincoln; but I heard Colonel Dudley would kill me."

To Chapman, her incoherence was feminine; her refinement confirmed by obsession with obscene insults in Dudley's camp. But her indignation concealed her greatest secret. Even McSween, even her sister, were unaware of how she had once used her milk-white skin and lovely bright red hair. By coincidentally adopting the townspeople's jealous slur, Dudley had exposed her, as once she had been exposed to lascivious men while the French madam, in her St. Louis girlhood, bartered for revolting acts; and bequeathed only her exclamatory 'sacre bleu' as imagined sophistication.

Chapman said, "To me, this case far exceeds probate matters, Missus McSween. My deceased father was one of Portland, Oregon's founders. He created its first newspaper: the *Oregonian*. He would have published your tragic story. And its villain is Colonel Dudley."

Chapman was contemplating his luck: just starting out and getting a big case against an officer. There would be newspaper coverage, even local fame - if she could be convinced to pursue it.

He said, "With Governor Wallace taking office this month, you've got recourse for protection and for justice - against Colonel Dudley. For murder of your husband and arson of your house, Dudley could be hanged. We could get indictments in the Lincoln Grand Jury next year, in April. But immediately, I can inform the governor of your plight - maybe get Dudley removed."

Her eyes became alluring. Huston Chapman was unmarried, professional. Only one arm was not so ugly. She said, "Sacre bleu! You're so clever. Colonel Dudley *is* a terrible man. Do everything you can." Her wrath now had an object.

She said, "My sister's oldest children, Minnie and Davie, still have nightmares about fire. And, at Colonel Dudley's orders, one of our killed attackers, Robert Beckwith, was buried at Fort Stanton with full military honors. Can you believe that? Sacre bleu!"

"Indeed. I understand injustice and challenge - living with one arm being my teacher. In fact, besides my law degree, I've got one in engineering from Portland Academy. Until two months ago, I worked for the Atchison, Topeka and Santa Fe; bringing tracks into this Territory from Colorado, over the Raton Pass through the old Maxwell Land Grant - culminating that railroad's far-sighted land purchases there in seventy." Neither she nor Chapman understood that he had naively enriched the Santa Fe Ring, the Ring that neither understood they were about to oppose.

They were interrupted by hurried entrance of a spindly round-shouldered man with dark fringe beard, hair transecting bald crown, and lugging a stuffed briefcase. He said, "Oh, excuse me, Huston. Didn't realize you were having a meeting..."

"Excellent timing, Ira. This is David Shield's sister-in-law. Missus McSween, my associate: Attorney Ira Leonard."

Returning to their discussion, Chapman asked her, "Those fighters in your burning house, what became of them? They'd be useful for court testimony."

"I have absolutely no idea. They were just Mexicans and hired hands: not the sort I associate with. But there was one - young and lively - Billy Bonney. I remember that name."

OCTOBER 25, 1878   11:42 PM   FRIDAY

In the Fort Sumner barracks, Pat Garrett, naked, listened to Juanita Gutierrez's snoring with disgust. "Married only about two months," he thought, "and the bitch already got fat as a pig." In sleep, she brushed him. He felt a stirring and thought, "All I'm getting from her is 'I'm feeling sick.' " The pressure felt insistent. "Damn. I'm not doing myself with a wife right here."

He said, "Juanita," pulling up her nightgown, waking her. "What the hell?" he exclaimed. "It's not that time. You've got rags in there. You did it to keep me out." He slapped her fat cheek.

"Please, no. Eet ees for a leetle of blood." Pulling out the tamponading cloth, she fingered it for secret hemorrhaging. She removed the nightgown, fireplace ember-glow enhancing her breasts.

Stimulated, easing himself in, he heard her groan. Never had she been vocal. He thought, "Needed that slap. Religion ruins them." Her stridulent squealing in pain was misheard as passion; and, vigorous with sexual success, Garrett squeezed bruises onto her sweating fat.

Within her rammed uterus was a three month old, female fetus, slit mouth of her humanoid head opening in silent wail as her placenta, disastrously implanted at the cervix, was tearing away.

With Garrett's withdrawal, Juanita whispered weakly, "Please to remember ... I love you."

As he turned his back and dozed, she thought, "Blood is running out now. The cloth is necessary." But the effort was too great.

Garrett awoke in darkness. Juanita was asleep and naked. He smiled thinking, "First time she didn't dress." Again, he slept. Clarissa pleaded, "Pleeease come back, Pat."

Awaking at dawn, Pat Garrett thought, "Strange. She didn't move." He touched Juanita's arm and recoiled from cold stiff flesh. With his panic returned Joe Briscoe's branded cross and murder.

Dressing to escape, Garrett looked back. Between Juanita's legs glistened gore. Beside her was red-stained fabric. He thought, "The bitch was bleeding;" and felt vindicated.

Then he thought, "The rags could be evidence I knew. Bitch, you gave me this misery."

After the cloths were concealed in his saddlebag, Pat Garrett calmed and thought, "I'll be pitied, widowed so soon;" and blanketed her neatly before emerging to seek sympathy.

NOVEMBER 5, 1878   9:58 PM   TUESDAY

In her house, Celsa said to Billy, "It has rained since Juanita died. And Apolinaria follows Garrett like a she-dog." Celsa lowered her voice. "One could suspect the evil eye. The doctor cleared Garrett of suspicion. But envy and witchcraft go together."

Billy went to the window. The dark mansion was obscured in pouring. "Are you paying attention?" He returned to the table. Celsa asked, "Was your business a success?"

"Got you a present." She received Hoyt's watch, exclaiming it was real gold.

Billy smiled distractedly and said, "I have to go. Just riding in like this ... Things I must do."

He walked out onto the splashing imaginary lake of the parade ground to walk a northwest diagonal.

Soon he was in Paulita's room, her arms around his neck, her bare feet dangling, both laughing and kissing and saying they had to be quiet. She locked the door while he pulled off wet coat and boots.

Embracing him, while they sat near the fireplace, she asked what was lumpy. "A money belt. Money from Tascosa."

In mock attack he pressed her to the warm carpet, nuzzling her neck, expecting a playful tussle. Instead, she languorously extended.

Immediately, he sat to her objections that she wanted more kissing. "I could tell. Brought a surprise. Find it."

His vest yielded a packet of peppermint balls from Howard and McMaster's Saloon. But she also held the Persian turquoise nugget. "You're a pick-pocket! he exclaimed to her giggling.

She asked, "Will you keep it for always?"

"My whole life." He returned it to his vest's upper left pocket.

He said, "I learned something interesting from a doctor in Tascosa: Monkeys are our relatives 'cause we look similar."

"Oh, Billy. Then we're related. Could it get in the way of getting married?"

He blushed and teared. "Wouldn't interfere. Uh, I just remembered, he gave you a vaccination." She rolled up her nightgown sleeve, revealing her naked arm to him for the first time, before he covered its tiny pitted oval and temptation.

"And I raced a lady who wears pants like you." Jealously Paulita asked if she had liked him. "Not a bit. I beat her and won a big bet. The money goes for Yginio's doctor. And for people in San Patricio. And to Regulators like Doc and Charlie and Tom."

Billy sighed. "We lost John Middleton. He joined a Hunter and Evans cattle drive. And Henry Brown headed to Kansas."

"But you're winning the war. Mama told me and Deluvina that they fired the bad governor and the bad man Catron who made Papa die." Billy smiled, saying he had just heard that from Doc Scurlock.

Paulita said, "And after the war, we'll move to Cimarron. And never ever be apart."

"Yes, Paulita, my precious," he responded, not to her fantasy, but to the beauty of her huge dark eyes.

NOVEMBER 9, 1878   8:00 AM   SATURDAY

In Hargrove's Saloon, Billy and Pat Garrett had played through the night, while seated Tom O'Folliard slept. When Bob Hargrove served breakfast, Garrett told him to put it on his on his account.

Gangly Hargrove said it was just as well he'd be tending bar there; he'd take it from salary. "Not fair," said Garrett.

To Billy, Garrett said, "Shouldn't play when I'm behind. But I'm determined to get revenge."

Nonchalantly, Billy asked if he had money. "Some. Like I told you, I've been working for that Kip McKinney at his hog ranch."

As they ate, Billy ventured that he was sorry about Juanita.

Abruptly, Garrett remembered the bloody cloths and said, "Kid, after that, I could use a long ride alone. Know an isolated place to spend a night?" Billy described Stinking Springs.

Garrett said, "What's helped me is the writings of that famous atheist, Robert G. Ingersoll. Get on with life; it's all there is. He proves Christianity's a hoax; the Bible's absurd.

"For example, like the Devil tempting Jesus by offering him the world. Why would Jesus be tempted if he made it himself? Same with crucifixion. If Jesus was God, he knew there wasn't death; so crucifixion was no big deal."

Billy said, "I'd figure it differently, Pat. Seems Christ took on a human body. That must include the mind. So, like any man, he'd have to face temptation and death. He couldn't be a hundred percent certain."

Garrett felt humiliated. "You missed the point: Priests push fake superstition."

"Is this Inger fella alive?" O'Folliard asked. Garrett nodded. "I was thinkin' that bein' in Heaven mighta changed his mind."

Billy looked into Pat Garrett's gray eyes, with their peculiar combination of rage and lonely pain, and said placatingly that Ingersoll must make people think.

Relieved, Garrett took a paper from his wallet. He said, "I copied this from a book of his. I want it read at my funeral." His cramped script was illegible, so he read it aloud after Billy handed it back.

"Life is a narrow vale between the cold and barren peaks of two eternities. We cry aloud, and the only answer is the echo of our wailing cry."

Billy said, "Sounds real moving," as Pat Garrett wondered where in Fort Sumner he could get a short-handled shovel to dispose the last of Juanita's evidence.

NOVEMBER 13, 1878   10:57 AM   WEDNESDAY

To his young, clean-shaven, chinless secretary, mincingly entering his office with a recopied document, Lew Wallace said, "How did Samuel Axtell tolerate these malodorous, vermin infested quarters, Henley?" The fellow shrugged noncommittally.

At distant hammering, Wallace added, "Hark, the sound of the carpenter. Soon this palace will not be a burlesque of its name, and will be fit for my wife's arrival."

"Here's your finished 'Amnesty Proclamation,' Governor."

"Your calligraphy is excellent, Henley. I'd surmise that losing your services was one more sad blow for my predecessor." Tim Henley waited subserviently, left hand raised limply at the wrist.

Wallace said, "This proclamation should end Lincoln County squabbling. I only regret President Hayes's refusing me martial law. Utilizing General Edward Hatch in his capacity as Head of the Department of the Southwest would have simplified solutions."

Henley reminded him of his meeting with Hatch that afternoon, and asked if he wanted the boxes of reports from Washington unpacked.

"No," Wallace said. "They're by an investigator named Angel - of all things. My proclamation will make the past irrelevant.

"But do sit. Some questions preoccupy me." Henley asked if he wanted his opinions about the troubles in the Territory. "Actually not. I am curious about an odd encounter I had, on a recent morning stroll, with a fellow resembling a circus strongman. He introduced himself as Paul Herlow. I said I was the new Governor. Oracularly he pronounced, 'Now everyone is in place.' "

Tim Henley said, "He's been here long as I remember. Owns a hotel on San Francisco Street. Strange but harmless."

"Next, I wanted your opinion on a letter I received. It is from a Las Vegas attorney named Huston Chapman, and dated the twenty-fourth of last month." Wallace read aloud: *"My Dear Sir. Assuming your earnest desire to see Justice done, I am writing you in regard to Colonel N.A.M. Dudley, Commander of Fort Stanton. I am in possession of facts which make him criminally responsible for the killing of one Alexander McSween in Lincoln.*

And he still represents a threat to McSween's widow, my client, Mrs. Susan McSween. Owing to the very partisan manner in which he has acted in civilian affairs in Lincoln County, I urge that you place a limit on his power to do harm."

Wallace asked, "Do you know about these McSweens?" Tim Henley shook his head. "To me, these claims seem preposterous against a commander. Anyway, my proclamation will suffice."

Before signing, Wallace read it again, checking and recalling his the Civil War proclamation rousing the citizens in Cincinnati. *"AMNESTY PROCLAMATION AND PARDON. For the information of the people of the United States, and of the citizens of the Territory of New Mexico in especial, the undersigned announces that the disorders lately prevalent in Lincoln County have happily been brought to an end. Residents who have been driven away are invited to return under assurance that ample measures have been taken to make them secure in person and property.*

"And that the people of Lincoln County may be helped more speedily, the undersigned, by virtue of authority in him vested, further proclaims a general pardon for misdemeanors and offenses committed in connection with the aforesaid disorders between the first day of February 1878 and the date of this proclamation.

"And it is expressly understood that the foregoing pardon is upon the conditions and limitations following: It shall not apply to any person already under indictment nor operate for the release of any already undergoing penalties."

Wallace looked up. "As to the last sentence, Henley, it bears my wisdom born of wartime: swift hanging guarantees swift peace.

"Now, I'm off to lunch with Tom Catron. He generously invited me to the Exchange Hotel to explain the problems here."

Later, when returned to his office, Lew Wallace prattled to full-bearded and balding General Edward Hatch: "I am writing a religious history of sorts. It is a curious leap from that to quelling citizen unrest, to facing red Indians on the warpath."

"Glad you prioritize the Indian problem, Sir," Hatch said gruffly. "Victorio must be eliminated. He's been attacking our settlers since I chased his Mimbres Apaches out of Ojo Caliente in this Territory. He refuses to go to the San Carlos reservation in Arizona Territory."

Wallace, ignorant of specifics, said for effect, "Hernándo Cortés - my well-known novel's fair God - ended Aztec barbarism, foreshadowing your mission. I concur with your policy."

Three hundred twenty miles southwest of Santa Fe, in New Mexico Territory's Black Mountains, Victorio's band hid. There, an eight year old was saying to his teenage companion that he remembered the soldiers' attack at Ojo Caliente, and how his grandmother had hidden him in a ravine.

"Many died," the youth answered. "Ussen gave us fertile Ojo Caliente. We will never go to the desert of San Carlos and starvation. Before that, Victorio said we would die fighting."

The child asked, if that was so, how had their cousin died without bullets.

His cousin answered, "You have known only death by bullets, Kaywaykla. Before evil soldiers like Hatch, our people died whenever Ussen called them - like our cousin. But Victorio will lead us to freedom: freedom of life or freedom of death."

NOVEMBER 23, 1878   1:13 PM   SATURDAY

"The Lincoln Proclamation!" shouted skinny Yginio Salazar, bursting from a sheep camp line shack, fist pumping high to Billy and Tom O'Folliard. The shepherd, Francisco Lobato, waited with his black-and-white herd dog, wagging his feathered tail in recognition.

"Come," Lobato said, "inside is Martin Chávez with the news."

With Chávez was a stranger: a dark hair-lipped youth, with ragged serape and old sombrero. "Juan Rioval," announced Yginio to Billy. "He is working with Francisco." Rioval muttered sullenly and slunk out. "Hates Anglos," said Yginio.

Martin Chávez said to Billy, "I came from Lincoln. Nailed to the courthouse door, from the new governor, is a proclamation of amnesty for the War." Billy asked if they were pardoned. "Maybe not," said Chávez. "Only yes if you are not indicted or not in jail."

Billy laughed. "No one is in jail. Almost everyone was indicted in April's Grand Jury. So it means everybody or nobody!"

Chávez laughed too. "There is more good news. Peppin talks of giving up his sheriff job for fear of," he put one ashamed foot on the other, "*us* Regulators. People say that George Kimbrell - an honest man married to a Mexican woman in my town - would be appointed as the new sheriff. And the wife of McSween is returning to Lincoln with a Las Vegas lawyer to continue the fight."

"Billy," said Yginio, "I just remembered. Today is your birthday."

Billy sneered. "Seems I got Lincoln for my nineteenth."

One hundred thirty-eight miles northwest of Francisco Lobato's sheep camp, in the Palace of the Governors, Lew Wallace reviewed the copy of his letter sent to Carl Schurz the day before, as Tim Henley entered, announcing that Schurz had just forwarded a letter from Frank Warner Angel.

Wallace said, "Put it in the boxes of other Angel papers."

He re-read his own letter to Schurz: "*I have the honor to inform you that since the posting of my Amnesty Proclamation there has been no report of violence. The result will doubtless be gratifying to the President. It certainly is to me.*"

The unread Angel letter said: "*62 Liberty Street, New York. September 6, 1878. Honorable Carl Schurz, Sir. This is to document that I have just had a visit from District Attorney William Rynerson. He desired to know what grounds I reported for Governor Axtell's removal. I declined to answer. He is that man's appointee and a member of the Santa Fe Ring. It remains a matter of concern to me that he and many others involved in the Tunstall murder remain unchecked in New Mexico Territory.*"

One hundred thirty-four miles southeast of Santa Fe, Attorney Huston Chapman gripped the reins of a trotting horse pulling the buggy bearing himself and black-clad Susan McSween westward into the town ahead. "Lincoln," she announced tartly. "You've driven with one arm better than most with two."

Chapman forced a smile. "But less than talkative. A bad tooth. Is there a dentist here?"

"Sacre bleu! There are *no* amenities at all. But here now, to your left: that adobe with two doors in front. That's Juan Patrón's - where you'll be staying. I'll be in the house of our past tenant."

Chapman asked if the return to Lincoln was difficult. She said, "I'm not here to reminisce."

Impressed, he responded, "Nevertheless, Colonel Dudley's a danger. For security, you should locate past employees, Susan ... Missus McSween."

"Use 'Susan.' The other is so dreary - like 'Widow McSween.'"

Having become aware of townspeople's stares, she straightened her black hat with its black-dyed sparrow. She said, "Those men will probably ride in anyway. Gossip is a fact of life here. They'll soon know I'm back."

NOVEMBER 29, 1878   3:38 PM   FRIDAY

Over snow-mounded flatlands, Billy and Paulita raced northward on the four mile stretch of old military road, bordered by fat-trunked bare cottonwoods. He was exercising one of her brother's race horses; and she was on Centauro.

After passing the leafless peach orchard, to their left, and skirting acres of fallow corn fields, they let the animals relax.

Billy squinted into the horizon and said, "I'm heading back to Lincoln town soon," avoiding her sad face.

"I'm also taking some cattle to a Pat Coghlan in the Tularosa Valley. They're John Chisum's 'payments' to us Regulators."

"Please be back by Christmas. We have big parties. The Jamarillo family comes from Las Vegas. They're Mama's friends, Papa's too."

Evasively, Billy promised dancing lessons before he left.

Ninety-five miles to Fort Sumner's southeast, in the past house of the Baca family, broad-chested sandy-bearded Huston Chapman, stood before Susan McSween, and said, "By Christmas, we should have progress. The locals I interviewed gave me more ammunition for arguing Dudley's removal." He rubbed his cheek. "Blasted tooth.

"Listen to my letter: *'Dear Governor. Pardon me for presuming again upon you, but I tell you candidly that the people here in Lincoln live in fear of more outrages from Colonel Dudley. I can also assure you that they take no stock in your Amnesty Proclamation, since it neglects to distinguish the acts of molestation and murder done by criminals from the justifiable responses of their victims. And they think that you have been derelict in your duty by not visiting. I am hoping that this will convince you to come at last and take action.'*

"And here's the notice I'm putting on the courthouse door: *'There will be a mass meeting here of citizens on Saturday, December 7th, 1878 to draft a petition to President Hayes about the crisis.'* "

Susan McSween's approval radiated seductive admiration.

DECEMBER 7, 1878   3:37 PM   SATURDAY

Entering Susan McSween's reclaimed Baca adobe, Huston Chapman angrily brushed snow from his overcoat and said to her, "Nobody came to my meeting. What's wrong with them here?"

"They're cowards. They ran away before Alexander's war too."

In the Palace of the Governors, Lew Wallace was saying to Tim Henley, "Yet another letter from that nuisance attorney named Chapman. Why can't he and that woman, McSween, just let sleeping dogs lie? I need peace there in Lincoln County.

"Take this dictation for General Hatch: *'I am forced to request that Colonel N.A.M. Dudley be replaced. He has excited animosity in Lincoln County to such degree as to have become an irritant.'* "

One hundred thirty-two miles southwest of Santa Fe, at Fort Stanton, Commander Dudley, in his office, addressed James Dolan; George Peppin; Second Lieutenant James French; Jessie Evans; and Jessie's replacement for dead Tom Hill: Billy Campbell, as fair and porcine as his predecessor. Intoxicated, in guilt-ridden anxiety, Dudley asked, "Jimmy, you got th' aff'davis on tha' bish, M'Sween?"

Dolan, relishing the man's degradation, said, "Yes. Tom Catron feels they are effective protection if she makes that rumored criminal case against you in next year's April Grand Jury. But the real instigator is her troublemaker attorney: Huston Chapman."

Dolan leafed through the affidavits. "Nonetheless, for the widow, this is what George said: '*I would not believe her even under oath;*' and: '*I know her to have been false to her marriage vows, having seen her in immoral contact with a well-known citizen.*'"

Dudley guffawed and asked Peppin who he had seen. Peppin mumbled John Chisum, embarrassed by Dolan's concoction.

"And," continued Dolan, "a John Priest, deputized by George just two days ago, gave us this statement: '*Missus McSween is not looked upon as a virtuous woman.*'

"Also, a farmer, Francisco Gomez, said she approached him in, I quote: '*a lewd and libidinous manner and had frequent acts of sexual intercourse with him when her husband was still alive.*'"

"Some greaser said 'em big words?" asked Billy Campbell. Jessie scowled at him.

Dolan said, "Gomez is Saturnino Baca's son-in-law. And Baca himself stated that Susan McSween was '*a prostitute in the past.*'" Dudley snorted that at his tent he'd called her a low type himself.

Dolan said that the Affidavits would be forwarded to Governor Wallace also.

"Good," said Dudley. "Bu' wha' I really need is her damn loyer sis feet uner. Fr God an' Counry."

"Is 'ere money in tha'?" asked Billy Campbell.

Jessie Evans said, "Keep yer goddamn ears open. Wha' the hell ye wan' Jimmy t' say?"

DECEMBER 27, 1878   2:12 PM   FRIDAY

Two hours earlier, a storm had obliterated Capitan Mountain peaks, and stark white sky had turned contrasting snowflakes into gray cinders that had turreted the McSween ruins into nature's folly.

Inside the House, Long said anxiously to James Dolan and Billy Matthews, "Peppin was right to quit. No purpose dying for nothing."

Dolan smiled condescendingly. "'Nothing' is the key word, Jack. As sheriff, he had been paid *nothing*. With the troubles, Lincoln County affairs are in chaos."

Dolan withdrew his pearl-handled Lightning from his shoulder holster and studied it with aesthetic appreciation.

That stimulated Matthews to say it was too bad that Lieutenant French had been too drunk finish off Chapman and Susan McSween on the twenty-first. Dolan sighed and agreed.

With vagaries of New Mexico weather, snow clouds had split with hot interstices, so galloping hooves to the east splashed red slush of Lincoln's street. Billy, in front and wearing his brown Irish cardigan, shouted, "Freedom!"

Following him, rode Yginio, Tom O'Folliard, Doc Scurlock, and Martin Chávez. Charlie Bowdre, last, square-crowned hat tilted, fired into the air. Billy shouted, "Damn it, Charlie. I said no shooting."

"Was that a shot?" asked Dolan. Jack Long sneered and called him as jumpy as them.

The Regulators stopped at Isaac Ellis's. The man yelled, "Don't set a foot here. Ben almost died. I don't want no more trouble."

Billy said to the others, "I bet Jimmy's in town."

Bowdre called, "Let's shoot those basthards right now!"

Billy responded, "In July it was right, Charlie. Now it might be bad for Missus McSween."

George Washington was running to them, calling, "Welcome back! Come to Baca's old place!"

In her small sitting-room, disdainfully eyeing the rough arrivals, Susan McSween, her widow's black, but defiantly baring too much chest, haughtily said to Huston Chapman that she would let Billy do the introductions of the hired men, and excused herself.

Sandy-bearded Chapman said to him, "Forgive her abruptness. She and I have been through a harrowing experience. Last Saturday, while illegally claiming to be assisting Sheriff Peppin - before he quit - a Second Lieutenant James French accosted both of us here." Chapman laughed. "But he was too drunk to murder anyone."

Billy, impressed by the lawyer's doughtiness despite maiming disability, said he had heard they were in the same game: not backing down. So the Regulators would protect them, like they had Mac.

Cautiously, Huston Chapman asked about their testifying against Colonel Dudley. "I would," said Billy. "Testify against him and his soldiers - who I saw shooting at us in the War."

DECEMBER 31, 1878   9:04 AM   TUESDAY

In the waiting area outside the Cabinet Room, Secretary of War George McCrary encountered Carl Schurz and said, "Your new governor's already acting like Angel."

Schurz asked what happened, adding that Lew Wallace was *theirs*, not his. McCrary said, "He wanted Hatch to remove the commander of the fort near Lincoln; said he's an irritant.

"Hatch passed the request to General Sherman, who rejected it. We want to quiet that place, not add fuel to the fire."

"That analogy would not be unappreciated by the family whose house was burned down," said Schurz.

"Let Wallace use fancy words for his books," said McCrary. "I back Hatch and Sherman's protecting their officers."

JANUARY 4, 1879   4:29 PM   SATURDAY

As Billy and Martin Chávez rode southward from Lincoln in lowering sun glaring on marbleized ice, they excitedly anticipated a San Patricio baile.

Martin Chávez continued happily, "So George Kimbrell, our friend and from Picacho, is now our sheriff. And Lincoln is ours."

A rider burst from roadside scrub, carbine pointed at them.

Chávez grimaced in terror.

A second rider trotted out to their rear. "Evenin', Jessie," Billy called placidly to the first, while ignoring shouts of porcine Billy Campbell, likewise armed.

Jessie's murder-face twitched in emotional storm. "My man said drop them guns, Kid."

From concealment of forestation across the road, Yginio Salazar shouted at the startled attackers, "You drop them, Satan's spawn!" as he, Tom O'Folliard, Charlie Bowdre, and Doc Scurlock rode out, guns drawn.

The attackers' carbines thudded down.

Billy snarled, "Dismount, you two. Jessie if you're bringing a message from Jimmy, tell me. If you just came to shoot, I'll return the favor."

Yginio took their cartridge belts, finding in Jessie's waistband a concealed revolver. He handed it to Billy, who taunted, "Just what I've wanted: a Colt Thunderer. Jimmy's so generous." He thrust the blued, double action, .41 caliber revolver, with checkered rosewood grips, into the left side of his gunbelt.

"Jimmy wans t' talk peace," Jessie said sullenly; that having been Dolan's second option if murder failed. "Was times I could'a killt ye, Kid, an' I didn'."

"Makes us even then," Billy sneered. "All right, boys, take their horses. Jessie, think of 'em as two Tunstall horses you just gave back. Now start walking; but keep those hands up."

"Wha' should I tell Jimmy?"

"That I'll think about it."

Billy watched them departing and called out, "Hope you're both wearing socks!" Jessie's affectionate smile was invisible in the fading light.

When Billy and the others finally neared San Patricio, wind drowned music. Inside the dancehall, Billy saw María Montez for the first time since the massacre, and shuddered.

Embarrassed, she looked away to conceal her disfigured face and said, "It was God's will, Billy."

At the same time, Billy heard Martin Chávez say to José Chávez y Chávez, "We would be dead except for Billy's precaution for the others to follow in hiding. Again ambush and murder."

"Ambush and murder," Billy repeated with flaring white rage, losing himself in dancing bodies, feeling crushed into the earthen floor by tremendous weight of rage; while screaming insanely and pounding furious boots in rage, as if to crack through to molten depths and release volcanic explosion.

But soon, with streaming perspiration, ran his tears. His feet had found a solid core ending his plummeting. He could hear music. Softly Billy whispered, "San Patricio, San Patricio," as finally he danced weeping on the sweet perfection of the living globe.

And others in San Patricio began to grieve, joining his catharsis for them all.

FEBRUARY 10, 1879   10:04 AM   MONDAY

Juan Patrón, with his melancholy eyes, commented to Billy and Huston Chapman, at his dining table, "You both really believe James Dolan would make peace with the Regulators?"

The boy answered that people did not fight wars forever.

"And what have we Mexicans had but one for hundreds of years - with the Spanish, with the Anglos?"

Chapman said, "Look at the evidence, Juan. I'd say James Dolan's scared. He already made a peace agreement with Missus McSween. He knows our Dudley case is unbeatable. And I've heard Dudley's so scared, he's resorted to absurd affidavits about her chastity. As if that would work in court!

"Anyway, I'm going back to Las Vegas to confer with my more experienced colleague, Ira Leonard, about these developments."

Chapman rubbed his cheek. "And to take care of this blasted painful tooth."

Billy, after listening to Chapman with admiration and some filial attachment, took a paper from his coat and said, "I wrote this."

He read: " *'James Dolan, Sir. I learned from Jessie Evans that you want a Peace meeting with me. That said, I know you signed a Peace Agreement with Missus McSween on January 18th. So I wrote out a Peace Agreement you can all sign before that meeting.*

Tell Squire Wilson when and where the meeting will be. He will tell me. Respectfully, W HBonney. P.S. Right before the meeting meet us at the Tunstall corral at the adobe wall. The Regulators will be ready for Peace or War.'

"And here's the Peace Agreement: *'The Dolan party and the Regulator party agree to this. One. Both parties will stop fighting. Two. Neither party will kill anybody in the other party without first giving notice that he withdrew from the Agreement. Three. No one is to be killed for any act previous to the date of this Agreement. Four. If any member uses this Agreement as a trick to kill someone in the other party he can be killed at sight.'*"

Huston Chapman was impressed and amused, and even more certain that his McSween case would prevail.

FEBRUARY 18, 1879   5:02 PM   TUESDAY

Waiting behind the Tunstall store's adobe wall, with Winchester carbines ready, were Billy, Yginio Salazar, Tom O'Folliard, and Doc Scurlock.

Yginio, crouching, peered through its gates' slats toward the store's westward obstructing wing. He said, "A bad angle, Billy. No wonder Brady's deputies escaped. Today is worse. They know we are here."

Billy responded only that he was glad Charlie had signed the agreement before returning to Sumner. To Yginio's bitter comment about Bowdre's irresponsibility, Billy sighed, saying he missed Manuela; and repeated the plan: "I'll stick close to Jimmy."

O'Folliard said he was staying with him. "No, Tom. We may need different actions. Jimmy, Jessie, Matthews, Walz, Campbell, Peppin, and Long signed. Peppin definitely won't come. And Long probably not. Good odds."

Yginio asked, "Do you believe in omens, Billy? It is a year today that they murdered John Tunstall. For me it is an evil sign."

Billy said, "Tunstall would not mind. He wanted peace. And think of it this way: we might get our first meal at the Wortley."

Yginio asked, "When does Chapman return to Lincoln?"

"Any day. With Juan Patrón. Juan went with him to Las Vegas on business."

Boots thumped on the store walkway. Jessie Evans swung around the east corner, muzzle of his new carbine aimed. Snub-nosed Billy Campbell followed.

Billy said, "I'm glad your wrist works in cold weather, Jessie, but let's get on with this." Billy swung open the gates as portly gopher-cheeked Edgar Walz toddled hesitantly from the porch.

At the Wortley Hotel, as coats were being removed, Edgar Walz entered the warmth and paneled elegance of the dining room, squeaking, "Jimmy, they're here," and smoothing his silky beard.

Dolan was seated at the head of two joined tables draped in a snowy tablecloth; and was clad in purposeful sartorial elegance; with a new frockcoat in his consistent black, but nip-waisted and with a scarlet satin lining, unseen unless unbuttoned in lascivious display. A pocket held sleeping salts for a possible completion of his aborted seduction of the boy.

Slab faced Billy Matthews, already at a place, scowled with tiny eyes as Billy entered and glowered back at him.

Dolan rose, oozing smarmy charm. "Billy Bonney. So good to see you," and motioned to the chair closest to him; scrutinizing the boy's face for response.

Without hesitation, Billy sat, while introducing Dolan to wide-eyed Tom O'Folliard. Dolan smiled, sensuous lips enhanced by carmine dye. He said to Billy, "Your friend looks like he's meeting the Devil." Yginio made a derisive sound.

Dolan continued, "Sam, you now have here more Billy's and more carbines than ever in the Wortley's history."

The bald innkeeper's beetle-like mole crawled nervously. He said, "They can't shoot in here."

"We are celebrating peace," said Dolan, and asked Billy if Susan McSween's lawyer had written his peace treaty.

"I did myself," the boy answered with surprising self-possession.

As Sam Wortley served laden plates, Dolan ventured, "I see you still wear my hat." Billy said merely that it had lasted. Dolan found the lack of animosity unexpected but hopeful.

As pies followed and whiskey flowed freely, porcine Campbell exclaimed, "I'm toastin' Colonel Dudley!"

"Quiet!" Dolan said, fretting that the mood would be broken.

"For God and country!" Campbell called drunkenly.

Dolan sprang up, pulling his concealed Lightning and shouting, "I said stop!" To Jessie he said, "I'll kill your fool."

Jessie countered that it was his fault for getting Campbell out of jail after a murder, as Dolan returned the gun to its shoulder holster.

Tense silence clinked with utensils. Dolan, to subdue mounting desire, drank heavily. To Billy, with teary mawkishness, he said, "Your sweater reminds me of Ireland. Where did you get it?"

"Tunstall," the boy said placidly.

Dolan, further reassured, stood unsteadily with his shotglass, and bizarrely extended his arms over the long white table surface, sprinkling liquor as Archbishop Lamy had holy water; and intoned, "Behold: forgiveness of sins."

"I never seen you like this, Jimmy," Jessie muttered uneasily.

Dolan sobbed lightly. "The miracle of the blue-eyed boy ... the return of the prodigal ... son."

Yginio Salazar, revolted by the mock religiosity, walked out.

"An excellent suggestion," said Dolan. "A stroll after a fine meal. Sam," he held out his silver flask, "fill this for the road."

Dolan whispered to Billy, "And you'll forgive me? It all had to be done."

"I'll walk the street of Lincoln with you, Jimmy," he answered with tantalizing ambiguity.

A mile east of the Wortley Hotel, Huston Chapman, halting Susan McSween's buggy at Patrón's house, said, "Juan, it was my mistake not to go to a dentist. Pain's worse. I'll let you off here." He rubbed his swollen face. "I'll bring back the buggy and tell Susan my progress. Then come back to bed."

Almost invisible in darkness of the new moon, Yginio angrily seethed at the street-end of the path as the Wortley Hotel's door opened and closed. A voice asked, He-nio. "Call me Salazar, Evans. Yginio is not for you to use."

The others, startled by the pitch blackness, hesitated before proceeding. Campbell joined Jessie. Dolan, clutching Billy's coat sleeve, staggered beside him, as Edgar Walz chattered to O'Folliard, "So Tom said, 'Do you realize how much money ...' My God, it's dark!"

O'Folliard called uneasily to Billy. Dolan answered, "Myself and Billy are walking the street of Lincoln ..." He added in sing-song baritone: "in peace."

Through Billy's bootsoles, the frozen corrugated ground felt like scattered bones. He looked upward at glittering grains of stars. Gathered, they would be a fraction of the moon, yet they shone defiantly in the void; whose vastness felt to him not remote, but protective of those tiny lights and possessing a consciousness pervasively intimate, like the a face of a beloved so close that it encompassed him in tender presence.

Penetrating the street of darkness, grasping Billy's arm for support, Dolan slurred, "When Jessie firs' brought you, I said to myself: pasience. He'll see."

Ahead were the uncertain masses of McSween ruins. Dolan sang, "We'll let them know, before we go, we'll fight until we die, / For Irishmen when at the wors' would rather fight than fly."

George Washington, unhitching Susan McSween's buggy horse at the Tunstall store's lean-to, heard the singing.

Dolan sipped from his flask. "Billy, you need a new coat. This is made from some cheap Mexican blanket.

"After this, you'll come back to the House. I'll give you ... so much." He squeezed Billy's arm and brayed into the night, "Some of you will fall, / For here we stand true Irishmen that never fear'd a call."

At the previous Baca family house, Dolan halted. To Susan McSween, somewhere inside, he said, "Our las' problem;" and tugged Billy along.

Jessie asked where they were heading. "Fine walk for us Irsh. Go 'way." Dolan leaned closer to Billy and whispered, "Murphy lef' me so much. We can star' over."

Susan McSween, after looking out a window, said to Huston Chapman, "I'll make a hot bread poultice for your face;" and added scornfully that Dolan's drunks had passed.

"*You* made peace," he said. "Our strategy is to show that your case against Dudley will bring peace here."

She called back from the kitchen that his news about Governor Wallace coming to town was promising, and returned with linen for his wrap.

Chapman said, "Also, the attorney I sub-let from, Ira Leonard, told me about something called the Santa Fe Ring. The politics involved may account for Colonel Dudley's partisan actions."

Chapman wished he did not feel so ill. She looked so attractive. He said, "Excuse me for presumption, but have you considered - I mean to say, someday - remarriage?" He felt foolish, face all lopsided, but, after all, he did well with only one arm.

She fingered her ruby ring and said Alexander wouldn't have wanted her to remain alone.

Dolan's group passed the Montaño building. "To Patrón's!" Dolan said. "Tell him about peace."

Assuming the knock was Chapman's, Juan Patrón immediately opened the door; then contained his alarm.

The small room filled with the men as Patrón's wife, Beatriz, disappeared through the inner doorway.

"Damn greaser!" Billy Campbell shouted at Patrón. Yginio lunged; but Jessie Evans, grinning, blocked him.

Billy signaled Doc Scurlock to the back doorway.

Billy Campbell, brandishing his revolver, yelled, "I'm killin' this greaser for Colonel Dudley."

Edgar Walz, in that line of fire, screamed a high-pitched "eeeee" that made Jessie laugh uproariously.

Jessie called, "Hell, Campbell, not now."

"We came in peace," chanted Dolan drunkenly. "And we leave in peace."

Outside again, the blinded group, now without Doc Scurlock, stood in confusion. "Back to Wortley's," directed Dolan, leading them through darkness beside Billy Campbell.

Jessie angled closer to Billy and said, "I heerd how ye got yer carbine back. Matthews couldn' believe i'. 'Im shootin', an' ye runnin' ou' anyways. You's somethin'."

Billy said, "It wasn't much risk. Matthews can't aim."

Jessie laughed. "I'da done the same. An' Brady never got nothin' right." Succeeded in killing Tunstall, Billy said. "I ain' talkin' fightin', Kid." Jessie lowered his voice. "Jimmy, wasn' too sad 'bout Brady …" Billy did not answer. "Ye ain' talkin' much. Hell with ye."

Someone walked toward them in moonless obscurity. Vague bandaging circled the face.

Billy Campbell called, "Who the hell 're you?"

"Huston Chapman. Am I speaking with James Dolan?"

Jessie stepped forward. "You's speakin' t' Jimmy Dolan's frien'."

"An' I'm Billy Campbell, Colonel Dudley's frien'. I says dance."

"I refuse," said Chapman, annoyed by the foolishness.

"You refuse!" hissed Dolan savagely. "You goddamn troublemaker." Infuriating him was more than a potential case against Colonel Dudley. It was the return of a Tunstall of a McSween, each competing with him for Billy's soul.

In the opaque shadowing, Dolan seemed to fumble with his coat, then to poke his hand angrily against Chapman's chest. Instead, the unseen grasped Lightning fired bright explosion, bursting Chapman's coat into flame.

Chapman staggered.

Campbell successfully shot also before their victim fell.

Billy, signaling to Yginio and O'Folliard to leave, heard Chapman gasp, "I'm killed;" and saw his stump arm flapping its coat sleeve like a dying bird's wing.

Dolan jeered, "Burn, McSween, burn," pouring from his flask, but only drowning the flickering fire.

"Jessie, Campbell, help me," he ordered. They emptied their flasks on Chapman, as Dolan dropped matches into witchy lurid light, in which, for a second, Billy saw the blood-scarlet lining of his open frockcoat.

Billy Campbell shouted, "I promist Colonel Dudley I'd kill tha' bastard. For God an' country!"

"Let's go, boys," said Dolan exuberantly. "Finally, we're finished."

Nearing the Wortley Hotel's path, Dolan said, "Ed, I forgot. Take Campbell's gun. Put it in Chapman's hand."

Walz backed timorously. Billy volunteered to do it.

Billy's last image of those grouped at the Wortley Hotel's bright open door was of Dolan's face fixated on him with eager promise of love.

Billy ran.

Passing the rear of the Tunstall corral, Billy made low hooting signals. Yginio, on Torcio, with Tom O'Folliard and Doc Scurlock, emerged leading his horse. Billy mounted, racked by nausea and horror. All galloped away.

And in Lincoln again was odor of burning human flesh; and again human blood soaked the red street; and frightened townspeople huddled in their houses, as again a murdered man lay mutilated and alone throughout the night.

THIRD CYCLE

FEBRUARY 27, 1879   2:09 PM   THURSDAY

In his newly decorated office in the Palace of the Governors, Lew Wallace basked in adulatory attention of his attractive petite wife, her brunette center-parted hair dipping and pinned back in the style of Lucy Webb Hayes. He said, "My dear, writing *Ben-Hur* is transforming me. I - like some dirt-encrusted seventeen year locust crawling from ignorant underground slumber - am emerging into cleansing airy light to become a true Christian."

"Oh Lew, here I was feeling self-pity last month when I arrived in this ugly city that looks like a big brick-yard, and you've been finding God."

"An achievement needed by the rest of this Territory's quarreling citizens to end my woes. Added to their roster of foul slayings has just been an attorney named Chapman."

Susan Wallace asked, "What are they all fighting about?"

"You alone shall hear my confession: I have no idea. Behold those stacked boxes. They bear reports ad infinitum generated by an investigator sent here by Hayes. To feign diligence, I glanced at a few pages prior to my interview with Carl Schurz. Any further reading was unnecessary.

"I knew the solution. Pardon most. Get martial law so the military could round up those already indicted; then hang the lot of them.

"To that effect, once here, after posting an Amnesty Proclamation, I further requested removal of a local irritant: a fort commander. But at every move, I have been thwarted by Hayes and military higher-ups - all afflicted with General McClellan-like indecisiveness that nearly cost us the Civil War.

"So I - participant in history's great events - must descend to petty mediation in little insignificant Lincoln, center of the strife.

"However, I formulated a clever plan: to offer rewards to induce its citizens to themselves capture the outlaws and rustlers who, according to Tom Catron, are the cause of unrest. By the way, he invited us to the Exchange Hotel to dine in your welcome.

"And, recall, my additional Herculean task is to eliminate the elusive and bloodthirsty renegade Apache Chief Victorio."

She teased that the Bolivian ambassadorship now sounded better. "But, my dear, then you would have lost the boast that your husband had transported you to a palace." Both laughed in shared love and utter indifference to his constituents.

One hundred fifty-two miles southeast of Santa Fe, in Fort Stanton, James Dolan was also laughing, but in response to Nathan Augustus Monroe Dudley's confided fears. Dolan said, "After Wallace requested your removal, Tom Catron met with General Hatch. Tom wants you reassured that your past feuds with Hatch are outweighed by his detestation of Wallace. Hatch served under Grant in Tennessee the year after Shiloh. No one forgives Shiloh.

"So Tom and Ed Hatch came up with this. If Wallace forces Hatch to act, they want *you* to immediately contact the Adjutant General in Washington and request a military Court of Inquiry ..."

"Even with my two Court Martials - remember, one was just the year before I was transferred here?"

"Those concerned personal peccadilloes. *This* Court of Inquiry concerns violation of the Posse Comitatus Act. The person who stands to be most embarrassed is Hatch himself. He has ultimate military responsibility in the region. So I am to give you this." Dolan handed a paper. "It is a suggestion for *your* letter to be sent to the Adjutant General - if needed."

Dudley read: "*I have been informed that General Hatch stated to an officer that he did not believe Governor Wallace could sustain his allegations against me. I respectfully ask that a Court of Inquiry meet to thoroughly investigate my conduct.*"

Dudley said, "Hatch be damned. *I* would lose."

Dolan smiled. "In fact, loosing is impossible. Tom has already lined up his good friend, Henry Waldo, to be your defense attorney. Waldo is the most esteemed trial lawyer in the Territory and was Chief Justice a few years back." Dudley said that didn't eliminate facts. "But the three Court of Inquiry judges *decide* on the facts.

"The Court will be scheduled based on availability of the highest ranking, local officer to be its Chief Judge. That soldier *happens to be* your best friend from Fort Union, Colonel Galusha Pennypaker, Sixteenth Infantry. Whose side do you think *he* will be on?"

Dudley finally relaxed and chuckled.

Dolan said, "And your vindication can later be presented as evidence to any civilian court if the widow still attempts a criminal case against you. Any jury would bow to that military verdict." Dudley laughed so hard that he spilled some of his drink.

MARCH 13, 1879   11:11 AM   THURSDAY

After Huston Chapman's murder, Billy had relapsed into madness of Michael McCarty, and had been patiently nursed in the Capitan cave by husky Tom O'Folliard, with his big-buttocked sincerity and his naïve assumption that the incoherent cries and shivering seizures meant "a mighty big fever."

Decompensation had begun during their dismal ride from dark Lincoln, on Capitan Gap crossing the Capitans; Doc Scurlock having already left for Fort Sumner. Yginio had shouted at Billy that he had been a fool to trust Dolan and his stinking ejaculate, Evans. What if the lawyer had not been killed? Would he have joined that Devil's coven?

Furious, Yginio had ridden ahead toward Las Tablas, leaving Billy shaken and O'Folliard saying he agreed that Dolan wasn't good folks.

Suddenly, Billy had uttered an inhuman howl and had fallen from his horse, writhing on the dirt.

Inside the Capitan cave, Dolan's hallucinated hungry fingers had pierced Billy's coat sleeve, like talons sinking into his flesh. Dolan's breath had inflamed his face, as demonic desire possessed his mind, unable to break away from the only man who had wanted him: the son being claimed in love.

Madness is not of a moment, it is a tectonic disaster known also to the Earth, whose fragmented rock plates drift slowly; but once meeting in crushing compression, can roil land and raise tsunami seas of devastation. For Billy, Yginio's intolerable truth had collided his boundaries of Good and Evil, booming into awareness his soul's recognition: he could have rejoined Dolan.

That truth racked him - like the death rigors of his mother - in agony of aftershocks reverberating damning grief, not for noble Chapman, but for Dolan, whom Billy sought in a landscape deliriously changing; until unfurling enveloping scarlet satin became a door of solid flame - the door in the burning McSween house - and he plunged through and downward and yielding with vertiginous spinning, stopped only by agonized contracting; balling up as in a forgotten alley of childhood, and vomiting bile as in purging or exorcism.

Billy was yelling, "Mister Tunstall," into the strange night, until he heard his own voice - or was it Tunstall's answering voice - and felt the man again catch him after a swooning. He sat up and wept.

O'Folliard was tenderly wiping his foaming drool. He asked, "Wan' some taters, Billy? You been callin' yer Ma te make 'em like in Ireland te save you from starvin'. Yginio brung some."

"Is he still angry?"

"No. Oly said you was a fool."

"I do want potatoes," said Billy, rubbing wet eyes.

He realized that everything was now so simple, like gazing at an unobstructed view. He said, "I'm the witness to Dolan's murder of Chapman."

Later, in the Salazar house, Billy decisively folded a letter as O'Folliard and Yginio watched. "I will deliver it," said Martin Chávez, one foot humbly atop the other. "But how can you write to his Excellency the Governor? You are nothing to one so high." Billy laughed, saying he was worth a thousand dollars.

"Wallace is the one worth nothing," said Yginio. "He proved that in his public meeting in Lincoln. He called us outlaws and set rewards. How can you trust him? Do not be a fool again."

Billy winced, but held firm. "Because he seems like a good man. He arrived only a week ago, but talked to everybody. And when he found out people were too afraid of Dudley to make affidavits against Dolan, Jessie, and Campbell for Chapman's murder, he had "Squire" Wilson make out warrants. And he had them arrested at Catron's Carrizozo ranch, and put in Stanton along with other murderers and rustlers from the War. And, only three days after arriving in Lincoln, he even got Dudley removed."

Yginio countered scornfully that Wallace had also used Stanton soldiers to try to capture *them*. "But that was nothing," Billy said. "We heard about it immediately. Wallace just needs more information.

"And think of this: our wins are adding up. They got Chapman on the eighteenth. Eighteen days later we got Dudley. We got Morton, Baker, McCloskey, Brady, Hindman, Manuel Segovia 'the Indian,' Buckshot Roberts, Governor Axtell, U.S. Attorney Catron, Sheriff Peppin, and now Colonel Dudley. Dead or removed.

"And Dolan, Jessie, and Campbell are - at this very minute - prisoners at the fort; along with fifteen Seven Rivers murderers of Tunstall, McSween, and MacNab. And Chisum, Walz, Catron, and Charlie Fritz are 'helping' to pay our bills.

"And Wallace and Sheriff Kimbrell have their jobs because of us Regulators. And I'm not just writing to our governor. I am speaking to President Hayes. Wallace must report back like Angel."

Billy laughed. "I'm a Gatling gun cranking away." He stood and shouted, "Bang! Bang! Bang!" into their laughter. At last he knew which side he was on; at last, he fully belonged.

That afternoon, fourteen miles southeast of Las Tablas, Lew Wallace and Juan Patrón sat at the small dining-table in "Squire" Wilson's house, as the wrinkle-faced man, dressed in antique frockcoat formality, hunched in his old wingback chair, with his jowls skeptically retracted into his high collar. Wallace continued, "My labors are being rewarded, as confirmed in our mass meeting by Mister Saturnino Baca's revealing to me the hideout of the notorious outlaw called 'The Kid;' thus allowing me to direct troops there right after offering my thousand dollar reward for him.

"And on March seventh - maintaining my insistent momentum - I finally succeeded in obtaining General Hatch's removal of your irritant, Commander Dudley." Wilson asked who would replace him. Wallace said, "His next ranking officer: George Purlington." Patrón interrupted Wilson's grumbling about that choice by saying that all efforts were deeply appreciated.

"And yesterday I initiated my plan to end rustling by providing Commander Purlington with a list of all recorded brands which I obtained from the County Clerk's office. Recovered animals are to be kept at John Newcomb's, to whom I gave the title Cattle Keeper of the County."

Wilson guffawed. "Newcomb would need Chisum's Pecos range to hold 'em. Wait a minute! *You're* the one at Shiloh who couldn't find the battle!"

Juan Patrón said with alarm, "Please, 'Squire,' we should talk of pleasant things before His Excellency returns to his room at Montaño's." Patrón added placatingly, "I predict people here will name buildings and erect statues to you in praise and in thanks."

Four hundred yards to their west, in the previous Baca House, Susan McSween was reading a letter. "*And I have enclosed a copy of the missive which I sent on March 4, 1879 to Secretary of War George McCrary to confirm your retaining of myself as your lawyer and your instruction to me to proceed with the case against Colonel N.A.M. Dudley begun by my deceased colleague, Huston Chapman. I will arrive in Lincoln on April 11th to make plans with you. Respectfully, Ira Leonard, Attorney at Law.*"

At the same time as she finished reading, "Squire" Wilson answered a knock at his side door and said, "Yeah, I'll give it to him. Night, Martin."

Wallace received the paper and read: "*To his Excellency the Governor. General Lew. Wallace. Dear Sir. I have heard that you will give one thousand $ dollars for my body which as I can understand it means alive as a Witness. I know it is as a witness against those that murdered Mr. Chapman. If it was arranged so* *that I could appear in Court I could give the desired information. But I have indictments against me for things that happened in the Lincoln County War and cannot give up because my Enemies would kill me. The day Mr. Chapman was murdered I was in Lincoln to meet Mr. James Dolan so as to be able to lay aside our arms and go to Work. I was present when Mr. Chapman was murdered and know who did it and if it were not for those indictments I would have made it clear before now. If it is in your power to Annul those indictments I hope you will do so as to give me a chance to explain. Please send me an answer telling me what you can do. You can send the answer by bearer.*

"*I have no wish to fight any more. Indeed I have not raised an arm since your Proclamation. As to my Character I refer to any of the Citizens for the majority of them are my Friends and have been helping me all they could. I am sometimes called Kid or Antrim but Antrim is my stepfather's name. Waiting for an answer I remain, Your Obedient Servant, W HBonney.*"

MARCH 15, 1879   12:53 PM   SATURDAY

Insensitive to the tense atmosphere caused by Billy Bonney's dangerous offer to testify against Santa Fe Ring murderers, Lew Wallace conversed grandly in Juan Patrón's house.

"Señora Patrón, your traditional Mexican cooking links me to Aztec days shrouded in mists of time." To her husband, he said, "And I am naming you Captain of the Lincoln County Riflemen, my volunteer force for capturing criminals. I created the same with great success in Cincinnati in the War." He glanced with brief curiosity at a sombrero and serape clad youth standing across the room.

Patrón asked, "You have the letter, Excellency, for delivery?"

"Yes. Let me read it to you since it is intrinsic to our plans: '*W.H. Bonney. Come to the house of Squire Wilson at nine o'clock next Monday night alone. Follow along the foot of the hills south of the town and knock on the east door. I have authority to exempt you from prosecution if you will testify to what you say you know. The object of the meeting at Squire Wilson's is to arrange the matter in a way to make your life safe. To do that the utmost secrecy is to be used. Don't tell anybody - not a living soul - where you are coming or the object. If you could trust Jessie Evans, you can trust me.*'

I signed it merely 'Lew Wallace' not to intimidate him."

"And our messenger?" Juan Patrón nodded to the youth. "Ah, that exotic fellow. Tell him that this cannot be a matter of mañana, mañana."

Patrón limped with the paper to the boy. "Your letter will be delivered," Yginio Salazar said coldly, and walked out.

MARCH 17, 1879   8:35 PM   MONDAY

"Want whiskey, Govnor?" "Squire" Wilson asked Lew Wallace, who was pacing in his little adobe. "Not the best, but does the job on a cold night like this."

"Yes. In my campaigning days, I had no pretensions of the gourmand." Wilson presented a bottle and unwashed glasses. "In sixty-two, I lunched with General Grant at a house of a Missus Crisp he was using as a headquarters ..." Flatulence sounded from the old man, who said dried beans did not agree with him. Just fresh vegetables.

Wallace, with Abyssinian beard carefully brushed, asked, "Do you have a weapon, Wilson? We're about to meet with a desperado."

"You're afraid of Billy?"

"Of course not. Tested by battles, my fearlessness is proved. As I was saying: for that lunch, they set up a board ..." Wilson asked why the lady wouldn't let them eat at her table. "That is *not* the point. The point is that, with this great general, I shared a lunch of biscuit hard as ice, beans boiled with flitches of salt pork, and pickled cucumbers acid enough to parboil your throat. Thus, your whiskey requires no apology."

Wallace watched the fusty old man downing glassfuls. "Please avert intoxication. You are the witness."

"I hold liquor good. And it helps my nerves. Fact is, one of them boys shot me clear through the posterior." Wallace asked if it had been yet another murder attempt. "No. Stray bullet. Billy and the rest were busy killing the sheriff and trying for the deputies. If I'da known, 'course I woulda waited inside before hoeing."

Wallace sighed at comedown from General Grant to bumpkin, and asked, "Have I mentioned I'm writing nothing less than a book about the Christ?"

"Nope." Wilson looked out a window. "No lights. People musta heard the Kid's coming." Surprised, Wallace said it was secret. Wilson laughed. "Ain't no secrets here. What's your book's name?"

"*Ben-Hur: A Tale of the Christ*. Ben-Hur is the name of my main character: a Jew. Through him, the reader can follow two paths of suffering to the seat of God: one of a simple man; the other of God's son, the Christ."

Wilson said, "The simple man's still suffering. Mind if I use my easy chair? This hard one gets my shot posterior to aching." He considered precautionary options for gunfire in case Wallace had planned an ambush, and dragged it behind the potbellied stove. He said, "I can hear if you talk loud. I'm going deaf."

Wallace continued, "For your edification, I can reveal that my book raises the great Christian question: Could I recognize the Christ myself? For we are each Ben-Hur. Can we recognize a good man?"

Outside, Billy whispered to Tom O'Folliard, "Yginio's on the south hills. If he signals, get ready to shoot anyone coming here. Especially soldiers." O'Folliard anxiously fingered his carbine, saying Yginio figured it was a trap. "We'll know soon enough," said Billy.

At 9:00 PM, at a soft rap, Lew Wallace rose majestically and thought, "Here I am, the Governor of a vast Territory, meeting in secret rendezvous a savage outlaw."

At the open door stood a slim youth, a Winchester carbine under his left arm and his cardigan's side pulled back intentionally to reveal a holstered Colt .44 and second cartridge belt.

"Are you Governor Wallace?" he asked. When assured, he said, "I'm William Bonney. Are you alone?"

At "Squire" Wilson's name, Billy did not move. Lew Wallace asked his concern. Billy said, "He writes arrest warrants."

"That is beside the point. I chose this location for privacy." Billy entered.

"A strikingly handsome lad," Wallace thought. "It seems so long ago that I too was a beardless boy." He said, "We can sit at this table."

"I'm staying here, Kid," said Wilson. "Ain't Dudley being kicked out somethin'?" Billy said it did not leave him sad.

Billy took a chair opposite Wallace at the table and stared into his face with such intensity that the man thought, "Insolent rogue;" and said, "I presume you understand that my promise of pardon is based on your claim of witnessing the Chapman murder?" Billy nodded. "And you also witnessed Colonel Dudley's actions here last year?"

"From what I could see, Sir, since I was with others besieged in the McSween house by Sheriff Peppin and his men. And, when I escaped at nightfall, I could see the area through which I ran."

Wallace's eyebrows rose at the articulateness. He asked Billy's age. "Nineteen and about four months."

Wallace thought, "Strong jaw. Unusual lips with deep corners in seeming smile. Scornful?" He asked, "Have you participated in court proceedings? I mean other than being indicted."

"Yes, Sir." There was suspicion. "If you read the Angel report you know I gave him a deposition in a court - at least the courthouse here." Lying easily, Wallace said he had, of course, read everything. "Then you know I witnessed the Tunstall murder too - at least its beginning and end. Have you ever met with James Dolan?"

Wilson answered, "He sure did. At the Wortley. Just before he sent Jimmy to Stanton. Sam told everybody. Two govnors eating at his place in twelve months."

Wallace anticipated the boy's leaving. Instead, Billy asked softly, "Where's Chapman buried, 'Squire?'"

"What'd you say?" called Wilson. "Right with Tunstall, McSween, Morris, and MacNab."

Billy's face tightened bitterly. He began by describing the Dolan peace meeting. "That connects," he said, "because it brought together Chapman's murderers and me." Wallace questioned whether he had participated in the murder.

"Of course not. Chapman was Missus McSween's lawyer against Dudley. I'm on her side. That's why Dudley wanted Chapman killed. Dudley had already tried to kill him and Missus McSween last December thirteenth with a soldier from the fort."

After Billy's rendition of the Chapman murder, Wallace questioned people's positions. Billy offered to draw it. Wallace responded that as a writer he could visualize. Soon he stopped Billy, saying he had left out Scurlock. Billy smiled for the first time, exclaiming that he had remembered. Of course, Wallace said. He was also an attorney.

Impressed, Billy said, "You're a general, a writer, a lawyer, and the governor;" and almost mentioned that his father had fought in the Civil War too, but did not. He continued, "I had Scurlock leave Patrón's to get our horses. The mood was unpredictable."

Wallace asked if he could be as precise with regard to Colonel Dudley's actions in Lincoln. "It was night when we escaped, but the fire made it light as day for about forty yards through which we ran. So I easily saw Dudley's three soldiers shooting at us."

Wallace said, "District Court begins April thirteenth. You would testify about the Chapman murder?"

"In exchange for the pardon, Sir. That includes Buckshot Roberts and Sheriff Brady and Deputy Sheriff Hindman."

Wallace asked facetiously, calling it idle curiosity, whether he *had* murdered them. "No, Sir. I tried to shoot Roberts, but he knocked me before I could. And I wasn't aiming at Brady or Hindman. I was trying to get Deputy Matthews. But I only had my Colt .44 and didn't have the range."

Incorrigible rogue, Wallace thought, and asked about any other indictments.

"I'm not rightly sure where I stand on Buck Morton, Frank Baker, and Manuel Segovia 'the Indian.'

"But as you know from Angel's report, I'd been a Deputy Constable and then a posseman under Constable Dick Brewer with the Morton and Baker capture. I shot at them with other possemen while they were resisting our arrest. But I never shot at Manuel Segovia 'the Indian.'"

With surprise, Wallace questioned deputizing. "I was made one after John Tunstall's murder. That was on February nineteenth of last year, under Town Constable Atanacio Martinez.

"Then I became a posseman - like I said - under Brewer. That began on March first of last year. That May I also was a posseman with Deputy Josiah Scurlock under Sheriff John Copeland."

Wallace felt anxiety. To unravel the claims and counterclaims of lawlessness and lawfulness would require immense labor. He thought, "My plans could be ruined. Physically impossible to finish my book. I could end up trapped in these backwaters."

Angry that his fate was linked to this ruffian, he mumbled wearily, "In return for your testimony in District Court I would let you go scot-free with a pardon in your pocket for all your misdeeds."

"What?" queried "Squire" Wilson, behind the stove. "I can't hear."

Billy said, "Then you'd have to arrest me so they won't expect my testimony. Otherwise they'd kill me long before Court. I'll send you a letter on how to do it."

Wallace said he was curious about his choosing this dangerous option, since others under indictment had simply left the Territory.

"Because I deserve the pardon. I'm no different than a soldier or lawman. They don't back down. And I want Chapman's murderers to pay the price." Billy stood. "You'll hear from me in a few days."

After Billy was gone, Lew Wallace said to Wilson, "What a rogue."

Dragging his chair back out, Wilson said, "Billy? He's a good boy. Gave the people here hope against the Santa Fe Ring."

Wallace was not paying attention. From his frock coat, he took pad and pencil, as insulted pride stimulated restorative inspiration. He jotted: *"The galley-master says to the slave, Ben Hur, 'Do not be overconfident about my words. Perhaps I do but play with thee.'"*

MARCH 18, 1879   1:15 PM   TUESDAY

In José Chávez y Chávez's house, Billy, after writing a letter, listened to Yginio Salazar's outrage at having to deliver it. "You are a fool to continue this, Billy. There is no secrecy like you think. You believe it is coincidence that the day after you meet with this fool, Wallace, that Evans and Campbell escape from the fort? Or coincidence that this soldier with the name 'Texas Jack' helps them? From the same pocket that last year paid Evans's five thousand dollar bail for murdering Tunstall, came the money to pay 'Texas Jack.' From that tick swollen with human blood: Catron.

"Now Evans will ambush you." Billy disagreed, betting Jessie and his boys would leave the Territory. Catron had been using John Kinney anyway. Yginio sneered. "So you think you have no worries about this testifying?"

Billy blushed, already liking the man; and said, "I trust Wallace. But after the escapes, he might back out of our deal."

Tom O'Folliard asked anxiously, "Billy, you shur I can be 'rested too, te go te jail with you?" Yginio ridiculed that plan, but was moved by O'Folliard's solemn answer: "I protecks Billy. We're usin' my hoss rustlin'. Billy, read me your letter. I can oly make ou' li'l words."

"Friend Wilson. Please tell you know who that I do not know what to do now that those Prisoners have escaped. Send word by a bearer. If he still wants it the same send a note telling me what to do. Send one of Kimbrell's deputies to the junction of the road to Lincoln and the road into San Patricio. Someone will get the note to me. W HBonney. P.S. Do not send soldiers."

Four hours later, "Squire" Wilson, having received Billy's letter from Yginio, delivered it to Lew Wallace at the Montaño house.

The governor then wrote a response. The old man read: "*William Bonney. The escape makes no difference. I will comply with my part, if you will with yours. To remove all suspicions, I think it better to put the arresting party in charge of Sheriff Kimbrell. If I don't get another word from you, the party will be at the appointed place by three o'clock on March 21st.*"

MARCH 20, 1879   3:16 PM   THURSDAY

Governor Wallace addressed his two man audience while rhythmically swooshing a writing-covered paper, like manning an oar of a tyreme slave galley, the image in his mind.

"And I say to you, Señor Patrón and Sheriff Kimbrell, I am not tricked by a face too young for mark of depravity within."

The lawman objected that the boy was still willing to go through with the fake arrest. Wallace chortled. "Is the informer to be respected? Is he not willing to give evidence against men whom he said were his allies by written agreement?"

"But, Governor," objected George Kimbrell, "that doesn't rightly fit. Billy Bonney's testifying would be 'gainst those he's been fighting; they killed two of his bosses."

Wallace sighed. "From my perspective, I am being asked to find honor among thieves." Compact Kimbrell, irritated by the pompous maligning, angrily compressed his lips, drawing his little chin up toward his handlebar mustache.

Wallace said, "I shall read to you my latest missive from that young rogue. You judge. As with the others, it was delivered by a Mexican - the faction that seems loyal to him." Kimbrell glanced at stone-faced Patrón. "It gives his address only as *'In Camp.'*

"It states: *'Sir. I will keep the appointment I made, but be Sure and have men come that you can depend on. I am not afraid to die like a man fighting but I would not like to die like a dog unarmed. Tell Kimbrell to let his men be placed around the Montez house and for him to come in alone and he can arrest me. In the Fort I might be poisoned or killed through a window at night. But you can arrange protection against that. Watch Lieutenant French. He would not hesitate to do anything. There will be danger of somebody waylaying us to kill us on the road to the Fort. Also you will never catch those fellows Evans and Campbell on the road. Watch Fritz's Ranch. From there they will likely go to Seven Rivers on the way to Texas. Give a spy a pair of glasses and let him get on the hills back of Fritz's and watch. If they are there provisions will be carried to them. It is not my place to advise you but I am anxious to have them caught and perhaps know how men hide from soldiers better than you. Please excuse me for having so much to say and I still remain, Yours Truly, W HBonney. P.S. I have changed my mind. Send Kimbrell to Martin Chávez's at Picacho. I was told yesterday by a man I know to be a friend of Evans that I should leave town since you were doing everything to catch me. It was a blind to get me to leave. They must be worried that I might testify. Tell Kimbrell not to come before three o'clock since I may not be there before.'* "

"Excellency, if I may humbly suggest," said Juan Patrón, "he mentions the fort. Among my public offices is Jailer. He will be safer in the jail here in Lincoln."

"As you wish, Gentlemen. The management of the incarceration I leave most gratefully to you."

MARCH 21, 1879   5:26 PM   FRIDAY

Seven shadows made by the low sun flickered westward over the red earth road. To funereally plodding hooves, was added clinking of wrist shackles. Watching people from jacals in the Capitan foothills stood tight with emotion on dry, bristling, roadside grass. Their children, excited by spectacle, waved at this strange parade of Sheriff George Kimbrell, Billy, Tom O'Folliard, and glum guards, not privy to the pardon plan.

To Tom O'Folliard's distressed question, the sheriff answered, "Don't worry, boy. You're arrested. Just couldn't find your warrant in the house. My children got into my papers."

The group passed the Brady ranch, then the original cemetery of La Placita del Rio Bonito, on the north side of the street, where Billy told O'Folliard that Yginio's murdered father was buried.

Juan Patrón met them at the pit jail, upset that it was so cold and mildewed. George Kimbrell's brows tented. "Kid, you really believe Wallace 'ill give you that pardon?" Billy answered that he had given his word. Kimbrell glanced at Patrón, then walked out.

It was not right, Patrón said. He would go to his Excellency and offer his house for the jail.

After he left, Billy said to O'Folliard, "Juan's holding our guns; but I kept the Thunderer."

A hundred thirty-four miles northeast of Lincoln, Paulita was pacing in the mansion's drawing-room. Her mother looked up from her embroidery at the discontented girl, and decided it was time to embark on a difficult subject. "Dear, I've invited the Jaramillos for your birthday. And their son, José, why you've practically grown up with him. He'll be twenty this year."

Paulita taunted that he looked like a monkey. And was always whining to his mother. Luz Maxwell answered, "They did perhaps overindulge him - living in Las Vegas in such luxury. Any girl would be proud to marry him," she proclaimed; attaining the first step of her purpose. "A Jaramillo. One of the famous names in the Territory - like the Ortegas and Perezes."

"Did you marry Papa because of the name Maxwell? No, not a monkey. A mouse."

Paulita noticed Deluvina, outside the doorway, then withdrawing into the hallway of chandeliers. She followed whispering, "Something bad is happening to Billy. Last night, I dreamt he was riding on a narrow road to a terrible dark place. I was afraid."

Deluvina said, "Today Winter released Spring. Come outside so our feet can touch the waking Earth and gain life's power.

In moonless dark, a great horned owl flew from the mansion's roof, briefly blocking stars. Deluvina sighed at death's omen and said, "If you are afraid for Billy Bonney or for yourself, you never understood his joy of the birds. Your path will be wide with crowds of others who fear criticism, fear loss, fear enemies, fear fighting, and finally fear being killed - and feel only self-pity.

"Billy's path is narrow, because it is for the few, like him, without any fear, because certainty of their correct direction leaves only joy."

Paulita said her dream's darkness and danger were frightening. "On the path without fear, they are as nothing, child. Shadows of clouds. Do you think Lozen or Victorio see danger and darkness? No. Because they can live without any fear, they can fly free."

Paulita said she hated the uncertainty: waiting for Billy to come. "I listened," said Deluvina. "If you want certainty, you are fit only for the mouse. Today Billy Bonney is possibly far from here; but in the night, you were with him. To love someone joins the spirits. Only the bodies are apart."

"You know I love him!" Paulita, leaping like a fawn, ran back to the mansion against a firmament of rare shooting stars, arcing willingly toward earthly annihilation. And Deluvina comprehended subliminally what she could not admit.

MARCH 23, 1879   9:13 AM   SUNDAY

From an open window in his Lincoln quarters, Lew Wallace, anticipating an interview with Billy Bonney, heard nearby guitar music and voices. To Mrs. Montaño he said, "You will be proud to know that last night, in your very house, for my new book, I wrote the beginning of the path to Golgotha."

When he emerged into the sunny day, Mrs. Ham Mills approached saying, "Good morning, Excellency. For my part, I thanks you for capture of thees keeler of good Shereeff Brady. I am last person to talks to him." Wallace smiled with grand benevolence and continued his eastward stroll with military grace.

Curiously rounding the Patrón house, he was startled by a crowd, including the musicians. From an open window, came a gay call of "Turkey in the Straw," as Billy leaned out, shackled wrists dangling.

At the door, Juan Patrón met Wallace, and said they eagerly awaited his arrival. "Indeed," Wallace said. "I already saw one of your eager prisoners." Patrón smiled nervously, saying the boy had many friends. "I have just spoken to Missus Mills. I would not name her one." And many enemies, Patrón said.

Later, at the dining table, Wallace completed copious notes of Billy's responses to questions about rustling, though no explanation had been offered as to their reason. But to Billy's fertile imagination, it was as if his heroic lost father had now joined him in battle for freedom. Billy added, "So the Seven Rivers boys lived off that rustling. That's why they sided with Dolan. But that's probably in your Angel report with all the connections to the Santa Fe Ring."

"Of course," Wallace lied, and sought relief from boredom. "I have heard that you are a crack shot. With permission from your jailer, I would like a demonstration."

Behind the house, facing the flat land extending to the foothills, Billy fired his carbine again. To Lew Wallace's praise, he answered modestly, "Some bottles were just grazed, Sir. D'you want to try?"

After misses, Wallace said that the Colts and Winchesters from seventy-three felt different than Civil War models. Billy experienced that as profound, and happily volunteered, "And individual guns also need familiarity to aim perfectly to compensate for ..."

Wallace interrupted competitively. "So you'd say it's like pointing your finger?"

Billy sighed, sustaining his first disappointment in the escalating glorification.

That night, Wallace wrote a progress letter to Carl Schurz. After informing him of his ongoing arrests of *"the instigators and perpetrators of the recent crimes in Lincoln County,"* he concluded: *"And today I interviewed a precious specimen named The Kid, whom the sheriff is holding here and is an object of tender regard. I found the minstrels of the village serenading him in prison. The atmosphere of moral degeneration here quite reverses the order of the civilized world."*

APRIL 12, 1879   1:25 PM   SATURDAY

John Chisum stood on the railed porch of his newly-completed South Spring River Ranch mansion, squinting at light reflected off its idiosyncratically abutting, artificial lake. To Pat Garrett, beside him, he said, "Jis' stocked i' with trout. I'll fish from here. My idea. Bu' I've still got no job fer ye, since las' time ye were here lookin' fer work."

Garrett said, "Just checking. Anyway, I'm managing a saloon in Sumner; and I'm in the hog business with a certain Kip McKinney. And I made plenty on the buffalo range." Chisum asked how he was with a gun. "Been shooting all my life. Ours was a plantation family. I'm like you, Mister Chisum: ready for opportunity."

"So yer like me?" Chisum faintly mocked. He lit a cigar. Garrett said it reminded him of home: the best cigars, being born to money. "Makes er ruins a man. Shootin' buffalo ... Shootin' *men*?"

Garrett glanced at him. Chisum noted a new stony coldness. "Feel like a ceegar?" Chisum asked; and watched its practiced handling. "Had a man, MacNab, fer a cattle deetective. Killt las' year. Thomas Benton Catron in Santa Fe. Know that name?" Garrett lied that he did, but tried to remember it. "I gotta protek my stock fer Hunter an' Evans. Rustlin's gettin' worse."

Garrett tapped his cigar on the railing, its striking ash causing fish to dash hopefully; and said shooting could be expensive, given MacNab. "No triggers 'volved. Fer now, paymen's 'nothin'. Bu' fine numbers could be in fron' o' zeroes if yer eyes kin see." Garrett tested, saying he was going to Santa Fe; some names there kept coming up. "Yer free as the wind," said Chisum. He could not be intimidated.

Chisum continued, "I've got curosity 'bout a Billy Bonney. Spens time in Sumner. Nickname o' Kid. Know 'im?" Garrett nodded. "Us cattlemen got a rule: 'liminate the bad uns, an' you 'liminate stampedes."

Thirty-eight miles west of South Spring River Ranch, Billy, in manacles which he had quickly donned, was opening Juan Patrón's front door to knocking. In a rumpled sack suit was a dismayed, spindly, button-nosed man, bald in front and fringe bearded. He asked, "Where's your jailor?" Saying he was out, Billy scratched near his concealed Thunderer. "I'm Ira Leonard: Susan McSween's new attorney." He wheezed from his concave chest. "Excuse me. Asthma. Not bad; just the late journey. Arrived last night from Las Vegas.

"I'm here to see a Mister Bonney." Identifying himself, Billy led him to the dining-room. Leonard asked, "You prisoners are alone?"

"I stays with Billy," O'Folliard said proudly. "My name's Tom."

Billy brought coffee to the kind-eyed man, who said, "I spent the morning with Governor Wallace. He told me you'd be testifying in the Grand Jury about Huston Chapman's murder. Huston and I shared an office. We'd conferred about his Dudley case just before he was killed."

Billy asked why he was doing it. The man smiled wistfully, rubbing his dark-circled eyes with sparrow frail fingers. "Certainly not money. The widow told me she has none left. But Huston was a special man. Winning this case would honor his memory." Aware of his intellectual limitations, Leonard used generosity to satisfy impecunious clients, who later, more easily, forgave courtroom defeat. He added, "Governor Wallace wants justice."

Billy said, "He should. We replaced that crook, Governor Axtell, with him." Leonard looked perplexed. "Wallace didn't tell you? Did he explain that I'm testifying about Attorney Chapman in exchange for a pardon for my fighting in the Lincoln County War?"

"No. But today was just our first meeting. He also said you might be willing to testify against Colonel Dudley in a Court of Inquiry about his actions in Lincoln. It starts at Fort Stanton next month. Would you?"

Billy held up his shackled wrists. "I'm not doing much else." His blue eyes flashed playfully.

Leonard's breathing relaxed with relief. And he liked the boy. He said, "Wallace told me that Dudley initiated that Inquiry last month, rashly thinking he could clear his name. I'll be assisting the Prosecution myself. And Wallace decided to testify against him. He told me the citizens' complaints convinced him that Dudley was as bad as the Civil War villain, Captain Wirz of Andersonville."

APRIL 13, 1879   8:40 PM   SUNDAY

   As Juan Patrón led Ira Leonard into his dining room, where Billy and Tom O'Folliard were playing cards, he admonished the lawyer about walking alone in darkness. Leonard nervously rubbed his button nose with his frail sparrow fingers and said, "Necessity overrode caution, Mister Patrón. You all need to know what happened today, since Mister Bonney will be testifying tomorrow when the Grand Jury starts. It's bad."
   Leonard sat at the table with them all and said, "Everyone Governor Wallace imprisoned in Fort Stanton is loose: everyone awaiting indictments. That means James Dolan on Chapman's case, and men from Seven Rivers on Lincoln County War murder and rustling charges." His dark-circled eyes met Patron's frightened ones. Billy asked if they had escaped like Evans and Campbell.
   "No," said Leonard. "It was legal. Three top attorneys - Albert Jennings Fountain, Simon Newcomb, and Sidney Wilson - went to Fort Stanton to represent them with Habeas Corpus petitions. Habeas Corpus is Latin meaning 'possession of the body.' An attorney can argue that a man - a man's body - can't be imprisoned too long while he's awaiting possible indictment. That's what they argued today to Judge Bristol and District Attorney Rynerson. And Bristol accepted bail from the men instead."
   Leonard sighed and said to Billy, "It sounds worse than it is. Testimony's the key to winning. Here's what will happen tomorrow with you. The district attorney explains the case to the jurymen. For this Grand Jury, it's William Rynerson. The judge is Warren Bristol."
   Billy said that was a joke: Ring tools. "That makes no difference," said Leonard. "All Rynerson can do is cross-examine you after you give your testimony. The jury indicts. Then, all Bristol can do is set a trial date and its location - or venue. And the public's not allowed in."
   "You will be alone," said Patrón, "with dangerous enemies."
   "Not alone," said Billy. "I'll be with jurymen who know about the War. Attorney Leonard, did Governor Wallace mention my pardon?"
   "No. He was too outraged by the Fort Stanton releases to talk about anything else."

APRIL 14, 1879   10:22 AM   MONDAY

   Inside the Lincoln courthouse, black-robed Judge Warren Bristol, sitting behind a table, and with over two hundred cases awaiting on the docket, gave his introductory address. "And I say to you, Gentlemen of the Jury, we all know that partisan feeling here has been intense and bitter. I admonish that you not permit it to influence you. The first case you will consider is the Territory of New Mexico versus James J. Dolan, William Campbell, and Jessie Evans for the murder of Huston Chapman."

The Clerk of Court directed the fifteen jurymen through an open door. Billy, in manacles, the only witness, followed as District Attorney William Rynerson, with ursine mane and massive beard, glared at him. When Billy finally addressed the seated group, he saw John Newcomb nodding solemnly and recognized other McSween sympathizers. He was asked by Isaac Ellis, to repeat what Campbell had said. Billy quoted: "I promised Colonel Dudley I'd kill Chapman and I did it for God and country."

The jurymen murmured. Rynerson said, "Now I'll take my prerogative. For this case, you've got only this witness. And the only true thing he said was that the night was dark. What else is true is his testimony's worthless. He's like that night - everything's hidden, including his identity. 'William Bonney's' just an alias along with Henry Antrim, Kid, and probably others. Why? Because he's an indicted multiple murderer whose *known* victims include this town's sheriff and his deputy. He's even on the run from a murder indictment in Arizona Territory." Jurymen fidgeted uneasily. "And he's on the run here - evading setting of his trial dates - because he knows he'd hang.

"But let's get back to the Kid's lies in this case. He says it was moonless dark; but he can describe everybody's actions with daytime's precision. As to motive for the murder, he says only that Chapman refused to dance! As to murderers, he accuses James Dolan, an upstanding citizen; as well as a drifter, Billy Campbell, whose claimed service of doing the killing for Colonel Dudley is absurd, since Campbell was as likely to meet the commander as I am to meet Queen Victoria.

"So it's left to me to shine light on the truth. Don't forget that this whole case rests on the victim's being unarmed - meaning *only* that no gun was found on Chapman. I say that this boy stole it.

"And here's what really happened: Huston Chapman came to this town as a troublemaking outsider looking for a fight. He'd already tried to assemble townspeople to re-instigate last July's bloodshed. He'd already attacked a Lieutenant French from Fort Stanton.

"And, that fateful night, I say that Huston Chapman, fully armed, roamed Lincoln's street, probably drunk. And he homicidally threatened the town's upstanding citizens, in whose company this so-called 'Billy Bonney' happened to be.

"Chapman's intended victims, James Dolan and Billy Campbell, responded by shooting back - as would any of you. And Jessie Evans, also falsely accused, was simply an innocent bystander.

"Gentlemen of the Jury, the only guilty party in this case is the justly deceased Huston Chapman. What about the motive for Bonney's lies? I say it's revenge: framing James Dolan for defeating his criminal employer, Alexander McSween, last year.

Left alone, twenty minutes later, the jurymen reemerged. Before Judge Bristol, Isaac Ellis read their findings: *"Indictment of James J. Dolan for the murder of Huston Chapman. Indictment of William Campbell for the murder of Huston Chapman. Indictment of Jessie Evans as accessory to the murder of Huston Chapman."*

APRIL 20, 1879   3:57 PM   SUNDAY

In Juan Patrón's presence in the dining room, Billy introduced Ira Leonard to Yginio Salazar, who said, "I have heard about you. How you risk your life with courage."

Self-effacingly, the slight and balding fringe-bearded man smiled and sat, saying that was far too dramatic. He added that Wallace had left Lincoln to prepare for the Dudley Court of Inquiry.

Billy said, "I kept testifying. Including for your case for against Dudley and Peppin for the War's murder and arson."

Leonard smiled. "And I've heard the rumor that your testimony gets indictments." Yginio's shining eyes met Billy's.

Leonard studied his delicate hands. "But I'll be frank. I'm getting uneasy about your pardon. Was Wallace's promise in writing?"

"Sure. When I wrote asking for it, he wrote back on March fifteenth: *'I have the authority to exempt you from prosecution if you testify to what you say you saw.'* When we met on the seventeenth, he said he'd give me a pardon in my pocket. And on March eighteenth he wrote: *'I will comply with my part if you will with yours.'* I sure did that."

"Was testifying in Dudley's Court of Inquiry part of the agreement?"

"No." Billy sneered. "That was part of my own plan."

Leonard handed him a letter, saying he'd decided to help him.

Billy read aloud: " *'Governor Lew Wallace. Sir. I am writing in confidence to bring to your attention the fact that District Attorney Rynerson is bent on going after the Kid. He is trying to destroy his evidence. He is defending Dolan interests.'*

"Thanks, Attorney Leonard. But the jurymen all know that Rynerson's a liar."

"You doubt this pardon?" asked Yginio.

"I'd be happier if the word 'pardon' was in writing."

"Then you are honest," said Yginio. To Billy he said, "You must leave immediately."

Billy said protectively, "Governor Wallace must be doing it this way to make my testimony look good. He's on our side."

"I agree with Billy," said Tom O'Folliard.

One hundred eighty-two miles northeast of Lincoln, in Fort Sumner, Paulita in a lovely taffeta dress, was standing petulantly in the mansion's drawing-room where a nervous youth, with macassar-oiled black hair, sat on a couch. She said coldly, "I don't know where everybody went, José; but I'm leaving."

"Wait." Clean-shaven, he wore a black velvet suit with a heavy-linked gold watch chain ostentatiously arced twice across his vest. "I brought thomthing for your birthday." He spoke English with an affected lisp imitating elite high Spanish. Sulkily, she snatched his offered velvet pouch and peeked at the content. She asked if his Mamma had picked it out.

"Of courth. It ith a girlish thing." He eyed her peevishly from lids made oriental by creaseless continuation to sparse eyebrows. "Thit," he cajoled. "And let me thee it too." She tossed the pouch as she threw herself onto a chair, and giggled as he missed and groped awkwardly between his legs. "You act like a child," he said, extracting a gold pin with two hearts and a big pearl.

"Tho you are thixteen. Here ith your gift back." He walked to her and leaned just as she started to stand. His teeth struck her forehead. Both recoiled.

Angrily Paulita said, "Don't you *ever* try to kiss me again."

He laughed. "How do you know about kithing? Thoon you will be old enough to marry," he added hurriedly, remembering his mother's coaching. "Doth your family thill own parths of the Grant, the two million acerth?" Maybe Cimarron, she said and restlessly scanned the room. "I am thorry your father died. My mother thaid you have no dithiplin."

"And I thay to you," she mimicked, "I hate you, José Jaramillo." She left, skirt swishing like her mother's.

In Lincoln, alone with Tom O'Folliard, after Ira Leonard, Yginio, and Juan Patrón had left, Billy paced like a caged animal, while looking out the back window. He said, "Today's April twentieth. See those peach trees all pink? In Sumner there are acres and acres, all blooming." O'Folliard asked if trees knew dates. "Yes," said Billy distractedly in lowering light projecting lace curtains' webwork on his skin, grown pale with confinement.

That night, night-black Centauro and his rider galloped along the Pecos River, roiling with snow melt. And Paulita hurled José Jaramillo's heavy, velvet, gift pouch into its raging waters.

APRIL 25, 1879   9:18 PM   FRIDAY

In her cramped sitting-room, Susan McSween listened with satisfaction from the sofa as Ira Leonard, on an armchair, said excitedly, "And then Governor Wallace promised me the District Judgeship after he removes Warren Bristol. And he's motivated to win the Dudley Court of Inquiry. With it starting May second ..."

An explosive crack shattered the window at Leonard's back. The bullet struck the wall beside Susan McSween.

A second shot was fired. Leonard fell.

She extinguished the lamp. The broken pane was black in the fourth night of a new moon. "Murder! Help! Murder!" she screamed out the front door. The unseen perpetrator reholstered his pearl-handled Colt Lightning and rushed away. Townspeople had heard the shots. They bolted their doors.

Back in the dark room, Susan McSween heard Leonard's voice from the sofa. "I dove down. No paragon of courage I'm afraid."

"Could I relight the lamp? The assassin must be gone."

"Let's wait ... and call him the *failed* assassin." She sighed and said he'd have to decide about staying. If she lit a lamp she could make tea. "How about you?" he asked. She'd have coffee, she said.

Soon, sipping his beverage, Leonard said, "I'll stay," and laughed. "Here I am with a major case, no pay, and spared death by inches. You couldn't get a replacement! And you'd definitely need to keep Huston a secret."

"Thank you." She sighed again. "Do you realize there'll be more gossip in town about you sleeping here than about another murder attempt?" Where else, he asked. Ellis had refused. Wallace was at Montaño's. Patrón's was a jail. The Wortley was a Dolan den.

There was loud knocking. She rose. He heard, "Thank you, Mister Patrón. No one was hurt. Bonney wants to come? Certainly not. Please go home. To be out in Lincoln on a moonless night is very bad luck." She strained a laugh to conceal her new trauma.

APRIL 30, 1879   8:42 AM   WEDNESDAY

Tom O'Folliard studied his five poker cards for the draw, and asked for three replacements. Billy remarked that he shouldn't stay in with just two sixes. Unless he had a pair of eights or better, he couldn't improve his hand. O'Folliard said, "Thanks. Hey, how'd you know I got a me a pair o' sixes?"

Billy said they'd been doing considerable practicing. And, after this, they'd work the gambling circuit from Sumner and Portales to Anton Chico to Las Vegas.

Gottfried Gauss entered with a covered basket. "I zaid to myzelf, 'Billy, he alvays likes my zourdough biscuits.' " They ate and talked. "Zo today de Grand Yury vill vinish. People zay it vill be good vor our side. But it vas bad mit dem tryen to kill dis new attorney."

"Less risk without Jessie," said Billy.

They heard the front door and Patrón's tapping cane. "Want one, Juan?" Billy asked. The man's large dark eyes were frightened. He said he was to take him to the courthouse. "Why d'you do look worried, Juan? It's probably for my pardon."

Soon, entering the building, Patrón said, "May God be with you." The Judge's table was partially blocked by William Rynerson's massive back. The District Attorney turned. His powerful voice echoed in the room of empty chairs. "You can leave now, Patrón."

Billy saw Bristol staring at him from sunken sockets, his bald head hovering like a disembodied skull over his black costume.

Rynerson's laugh rumbled mockingly. "William Bonney! *Once again* in our Court."

To the court reporter, Rynerson said, "Please begin. Case of the Territory of New Mexico versus William H. Bonney alias Henry Antrim alias Kid, indicted by the Grand Jury of the Third Judicial District the tenth of April eighteen seventy-eight for the murders of William Brady, George Hindman, and Andrew Roberts."

He paused. "It has come to our attention that a governor's pardon was a possibility. But none has been presented to this Court. So the indictments stand.

"Also the Court takes this opportunity to inform the honorable Judge Warren Bristol that extreme partisan divisions in the County of Lincoln, where said murders were committed, makes a fair trial impossible; and consequently moves for a change of venue to Doña Ana County."

Bristol responded as prearranged: "The date of trial is to be set for the twenty-seventh day of June, eighteen seventy-nine, in Mesilla, Doña Ana County. You, William Bonney, will be held in custody till then."

That evening, at Patrón's, round-shouldered Ira Leonard spoke indignantly, saying he'd inform Governor Wallace about Rynerson's and Bristol's action. Juan Patrón responded, "His Excellency will certainly give the pardon after he hears the Grand Jury results. A miracle is accomplished. Almost two hundred indictments. More than one hundred for murder - many from Billy's testimonies."

Billy laughed. "Dolan and Campbell for murder and Evans as accessory, Seven Rivers boys for Mac, and Peppin and Dudley for arson and murder!"

"Even though they le' me off, I ain' leavin," added O'Folliard.

Ira Leonard asked Billy, "And you're still willing to testify at Dudley's Court of Inquiry?"

"Sure. I'll have to wait for my pardon anyway."

MAY 8, 1879   7:19 AM   THURSDAY

In the Fort Stanton officers' quarters, Colonel Dudley listened to Commander George Purlington, who was unaware of General Hatch's machinations. Purlington said, "Jimmy told me that Bristol's helping by changing the venue of your Lincoln Grand Jury indictments to Doña Ana County. The people there know nothing about the Lincoln County War. They're no risk.

"And for the Court of Inquiry, there isn't much worry either. The prosecuting attorney's a Captain Henry Humphreys, Fifteenth Infantry, out of Fort Bliss. Tom Catron checked. He's a nothing. The widow's new lawyer's helping him. A nothing too."

Dudley cursed Wallace for planning to testify against him. "Jimmy said your attorney, Henry Waldo, isn't worried about that. And during all this tomfoolery, Victorio's declared war - right when we're boxed in with over a hundred witnesses."

Five thousand one hundred twenty-nine miles northeast of Fort Stanton, in London, at his desk, John Partridge Tunstall sipped tea, having refused food. Since his son's death, he had aged shockingly. When he brushed his hair, clumps filled the boar bristles. Dundreary side-whiskers, puffed eccentrically to beard length, had turned white. His full mustache quivered. From his tweed jacket he took a handkerchief and daubed tear-swollen eyes.

To his wife, watering a potted fern, he said, "Emily dear, it is rather peculiar that Investigator Angel personally mailed me copies of his reports. Rather like sending baby Moses adrift into the hands of Pharaoh's daughter. Be that as it may, I maintained his requested anonymity in presenting his critical information to Lord Salisbury. Do listen to my letter.

"*My Lord Marquis of Salisbury: Even at this critical moment in public affairs I feel it necessary to draw your attention as Secretary of Foreign Affairs to the murder in the United States of my only son, John Henry Tunstall, on eighteenth February eighteen seventy-eight, in the Territory of New Mexico. At present, the matter is under the consideration of Her Majesty's Envoy at Washington, Sir Edward Thornton, who has received a written report on the matter from Presidential Investigator Frank Warner Angel, though no convictions have been made.*

"Fortuitously, a friendly source provided me with copies of two additional reports by Investigator Angel. Unlike the first one supplied to Lord Thornton and myself claiming no culpability of United States officials, they prove quite the contrary. They establish indubitably that my son's murder was in fact committed by conspiring United States public officials.

"This new information leads me to seek your involvement not only because it concerns international relations, but also because it was withheld in an apparent attempt to impair my quest for justice.

"For completeness, I am enclosing the first report by Investigator Angel as well as the other two. Those latter ones establish the guilt of a Samuel Beach Axtell, the Governor of New Mexico, and of a Thomas Benton Catron, the U.S. Attorney of that same Territory.

"I also draw your Lordship's attention to an additional crime following my son's murder, that being wholesale robbery from his dry-goods store by Governor Axtell's appointed Sheriff, George Peppin, and his possemen under the eyes of the local fort commander, Colonel N.A.M. Dudley, and his soldiers.

"I pray that you will convey to her Majesty these terrible crimes. I am confident that with your Lordship's interventions and with Her Majesty's tender sensibilities I shall obtain convictions as well as compensation from the U.S. Government in atonement for the misdeeds of its servants in New Mexico Territory."

John Partridge Tunstall blew and wiped his nose. "Finally, Emily," he said, "I feel confident of retribution."

MAY 10, 1879   9:42 AM   SATURDAY

The military tribunal was assembled in the Adjutant's office at Fort Stanton. With Presiding Judge, Colonel Galusha Pennypacker, was the prosecutor, Captain Henry Humphreys, and the two additional judges, Captain Henry Brinkerhoff and Major Nathan Osborne, who functioned as quasi-jurors.

At a table beside the prosecutor's, sat Nathan Augustus Monroe Dudley, in full dress, with his attorney, Henry Waldo.

Tall slim Henry Humphreys, next to Ira Leonard, began the Court of Inquiry, soporifically droning the introduction.

At the same time, at Juan Patrón's, Billy invisibly squeezed the top half of his deck, leaving a lengthwise bend that united cards above it in subtle tenting, before he handed the pack to Tom O'Folliard for the cut.

As Billy hoped, the cards broke at the bottom-most crimped one: an ace, above which he had secreted three others. When O'Folliard unknowingly put the rest on top, all four aces were on the bottom for Billy's deal.

Nine miles to the west of Lincoln, Prosecutor Humphreys was reading: *"These are the charges. First: That Colonel Dudley on the nineteenth day of July eighteen seventy-eight, without authority of law, did take a column of armed soldiers numbering sixty, with four other officers, also one cannon and one Gatling gun, to the town of Lincoln, and there gave aid to an armed band of outlaws, and thereby brought about the killing of one Alexander McSween. In addition, Colonel Dudley aided in the crime of arson by causing the house of said McSween to be set on fire, and, at that time, there were present two defenseless females and five children, so his conduct was inhuman and unbecoming a soldier and officer.*

"Second: That Colonel Dudley maliciously and corruptly, for the purpose of giving a color of right to his wicked and unlawful actions, did compel one John Wilson, Justice of the Peace of Lincoln, by threat of double ironing and imprisonment, to issue warrants for the arrest of said Alexander McSween and other citizens.

"Third: That on the twentieth day of July eighteen seventy-eight, soldiers under the command of Colonel Dudley entered the Lincoln store belonging to the estate of John Henry Tunstall and purposefully plundered it.

"Fourth: During the months of November and December of eighteen seventy-eight Colonel Dudley did procure men to make false and slanderous statements against the character and virtue of Missus Susan McSween, the widow of said murdered Alexander McSween, for the purpose of destroying her influence in seeking redress.

"Fifth: That on the thirteenth day of December eighteen seventy-eight, Colonel Dudley ordered Second Lieutenant James French to go to Lincoln to illegally assist the sheriff; and, while there, French, in a drunken debauch, did threaten the lives of Missus Susan McSween and a Huston Chapman."

Attorney Henry Waldo intoned, "Objection raised to charges related to the conduct of Lieutenant French as being irrelevant to the conduct of Colonel Dudley in the matter at hand." Galusha Pennypaker sustained the objection. The fifth charge was dismissed.

In Lincoln, Tom O'Folliard showed his winning hand and said, "I never got me four aces." Billy said that was how luck worked: hard to predict.

MAY 16, 1879   7:06 PM   FRIDAY

Tom O'Folliard watched Juan Patrón attempting to find Billy's ace among three Monte cards. Ira Leonard entered to their laughter. He said, "If jail was always like this, people would volunteer for it."

He sat, dejection becoming obvious in his dark-circled eyes, and said, "Wallace's testimony's over. From Monday to today. Said he felt like Henry Waldo was prosecuting *him*."

Billy asked if he fought back. "Well, not exactly. Waldo was humiliating, saying Wallace had only hearsay evidence, and hadn't come to Lincoln County from arriving last October until this March."

Billy asked Leonard how he'd questioned Wallace to bring out the truth. Leonard said, "Since it's a military court, Captain Humphreys questions. I just advise him. And, for some reason, Waldo's objections are sustained by Judge Pennypacker, and his aren't.

"But I'm optimistic. We've got so many other witnesses to prove our case. But poor Missus McSween. I decided not to tell her how brutal Waldo is."

Billy asked if Wallace had mentioned his pardon. "No." Leonard could not look at him.

MAY 23, 1879   10:00 AM   FRIDAY

Captain Humphreys questioned black-dressed Susan McSween on the witness stand as she nervously patted her red curls, aware of Colonel Dudley's glaring. "Yes, Sir," she said. "I'm his widow."

She was asked to explain the commander's role in the death of her husband and the burning of their house. She said, "On the day Alexander was murdered, that morning, Colonel Dudley came into town. Oh, I forgot. He came to our house and said things to my husband. Well, soon afterwards, some of his soldiers stopped at our stable and men ran down the street. I mean the sheriff's men."

As her disjointed testimony continued, Henry Waldo, realizing that his objections added to her confusion, peppered her with them. She struggled, "So ... where was I? Oh, I said to Colonel Dudley ... I mean after the little girl took him the letter ... that the sheriff's men are outlaws trying to kill my husband. I mean to say I was in his camp. He said that my husband shot at a soldier. I told him he didn't. It was all a mercantile competition."

With exaggerated boredom Attorney Waldo objected that her testimony made no sense and was wasting their time, and spit tobacco juice irately into a spittoon. Pennypacker instructed her to respond more directly. "Then Colonel Dudley showed me a letter saying 'blowing up my house.' I pleaded with him to protect it and send soldiers to rescue my husband. Then he used bad language unbecoming to me - or any lady - that I can't repeat. So I finally saw through it and realized he was there to help Peppin." She concluded with, "And they sh-shot constantly at us in our burning house till I left with my sister and the children."

She was asked to state what she knew about Colonel Dudley being involved in looting the Tunstall store. "I came back the next day, and had to stay in Juan Patrón's house because our house was burned down. I saw Peppin's men at the soldier's camp in suits from the store. Colonel Dudley was with them."

That evening, as Ira Leonard drove her buggy back to Lincoln, she said, "I'm sorry. I'm doing badly. It's Alexander." Her voice had the hysterical edge he had heard during her testimony.

"The memories. Alexander," her voice caught, "was devastated. Can you believe that when I was testifying I smelled burning horsehair? Our furniture was covered with horsehair. I felt like choking. I feel exhausted. I mean, a bit tired. I'll do better tomorrow."

MAY 24, 1879   2:35 PM   SATURDAY

Susan McSween watched Attorney Henry Waldo's short gray beard hairs rising like hackles in mocking cross-examination. In lieu of using a spittoon, he carried a clear glass into which he dribbled disgusting, brown, tobacco slime.

Waldo said, "You keep talking nonsense, Missus McSween. You have no way to prove that clothing was from the Tunstall store." She stammered about recognizing it; and he rolled his eyes theatrically. "Do you swear that Colonel Dudley actually refused you protection?"

Her mind went blank. She said, "No, I don't remember that he had, for I never asked for it." She had no idea what she had said, but was remembering, from childhood, a dowager handing her a coin as if she was a little beggar.

That evening, in the Baca house, she watched Ira Leonard drag a chair so that it backed against a wall before he sat. She said, "I got very confused. Have I damaged the case?"

He said, "You're doing fine. Any man with a heart would be convinced of Colonel Dudley's criminal cruelty simply by watching his attorney's vicious treatment of you."

"I'm only used to dealing with gentlemen," she said, and felt better. Neither realized, however, that he and the prosecutor, Captain Henry Humphreys, had done nothing to demonstrate Henry Waldo's misleading statements; nor had they drawn out her truths.

MAY 28, 1879   11:16 AM   WEDNESDAY

On the witness stand, manacled, Billy calmly gave his testimony to Captain Henry Humphreys, who asked, "Where exactly were you on the nineteenth day of July last, and what - if anything - did you see of the actions of the troops in the town of Lincoln?"

Billy said, "I was in the McSween house and I saw soldiers come there from Fort Stanton. The sheriff's posse joined them west of the McSween house at the area of the Wortley Hotel. That said, the soldiers passed the house in a group, except for three who headed to its west side and stayed at its stable with Sheriff Peppin's men.

"Soon, three more soldiers walked east on the street with Sheriff Peppin, while some of Peppin's men used that chance, when we couldn't shoot, to occupy a house across from McSween's, and two others to its west. Then the same three soldiers headed back with Peppin to the Wortley. Then they went east with him again - like a guard. Four soldiers were also positioned in front of the McSween house to man a howitzer and a Gatling gun.

"Mister McSween wrote a note to Colonel Dudley to find out what the soldiers were in town for, and why they had that cannon and Gatling gun pointed at his house. I know because he showed it to me. When Colonel Dudley first came past, he stopped at the door, and I heard him say to Attorney McSween that if a shot was fired at his soldiers, he'd order the cannon and Gatling gun turned loose and tear his house to the ground. That's what Attorney McSween was worried would happen.

"When I escaped with others from the burning house, three soldiers fired at least one volley at us from the Tunstall store property: the northwest corner of its corral. That's what I know in regards to actions of soldiers in the town."

Humphreys asked who escaped. Billy said, "At the same time as me, they were José Chávez y Chávez, Tom O'Folliard, Jim French, and Harvey Morris. After us, the men who escaped - or attempted escape - were Attorney McSween, Yginio Salazar, Vincente Romero, Francisco Zamora, Ignacio Gonzalez, Florencio Chávez, and George Washington."

Henry Humphreys questioned whether he knew how many were killed and who killed them. "I saw Harvey Morris shot down. Later I learned that Attorney McSween, Romero, and Zamora were killed and Salazar was wounded. I don't know whose bullet or bullets hit Morris or the others."

For cross-examination, Attorney Henry Waldo brought his tobacco juice-splattering bulk intimidatingly close to Billy. He asked,

"Were you not engaged in resisting arrest by the sheriff at the time you were in that McSween house?"

"Objection," said Henry Humphreys. "The Court has already ruled that nothing extraneous from Colonel Dudley's actions is admissible." This was sustained.

Henry Waldo found himself involuntarily avoiding the boy's intense eye contact. Waldo asked what direction he ran when escaping. Billy said, "A diagonal towards the northeast corner of the Tunstall property, was fired at by the soldiers and others, and there turned due north towards the cover of the Bonito River."

Mockingly, Waldo intoned, "Soldiers seemed to go in threes that day, didn't they?"

"Yes," Billy answered unfazed.

Waldo persisted by asking how he could make out soldiers at night. Billy said, "The fire made it almost as light as day for a distance around the burning building; so I could see their uniforms."

Waldo spit tobacco juice, and asked if he expected the Court to believe that, in agitation of perilous escape right into gunfire, he could distinguish the cut of a man's clothes. Billy answered, subtly sparring. "I don't know what your question is." Waldo requested their actual description, including whether they were Negro or White.

Billy said, "All three White. They had dark jackets with a row of gold buttons down the front and chevrons on their sleeves. They had caps and a black leather strap crossed their chests. They had light pants. They fired in unison from Springfield carbines."

Perspiration trickled down Waldo's face as he comprehended the implications: the attackers were officers; the volley meant under Dudley's orders.

He said, "Mister Bonney, your so-called observations are preposterous. Did you see a guard at the entrance today?" Henry Humphreys objected to irrelevancy. Waldo said, "Demonstration that this boy lacks observational skills is critical, since it is the crux of his claim of seeing soldiers firing on civilians."

Galusha Pennypacker allowed Waldo to continue.

Waldo said, "Describe that soldier." Without hesitation, Billy answered, "He was about five feet six inches tall, had a cap with crossed rifle insignia, and had a brown mustache. His dark-blue jacket had five gold buttons with eagles; and pale blue pants were over his boots. He had a red scar on his left cheek. His right little finger was mostly gone. As we came in, Commander Purlington passed and he saluted. I saw it then."

Henry Waldo asked for the soldier to be brought in. There was impressed murmuring of the judges. When asked, the soldier showed the deformity. Billy saw Ira Leonard's smile.

JUNE 17, 1879   6:44 PM   TUESDAY

Dispiritedly, Ira Leonard said to Juan Patrón, Billy, Yginio Salazar, and Tom O'Folliard, "I was positive things were going well. Last month, I even wrote to Lew Wallace that Dudley's face looked as red as the wattles of an enraged turkey gobbler because we were pouring so much hot shot into him. By the end of the month, we had Private James Bush saying he'd heard Dudley shout at Peppin: 'How did you miss getting those escaping men after I sent for you? What more did you want me to do? I even gave you soldiers.' " Yginio said he pitied Bush.

Leonard sighed. "But since last week, there's been one anti-McSween partisan after another." His twig fingers brushed his button nose. "All lying under oath. Still, their collusion must be obvious to the Judges." He wheezed. "Like James Dolan last week. Too bad Pennypacker barred us from admitting his indictment for Huston's murder. Dolan's a master of deceit." Yginio said snidely that he should not be surprised by Satan's skill. Leonard continued, "He even denied that there *existed* a Murphy-Dolan faction!

"And a Saturnino Baca said he knew his wife and children were in danger from McSween, because McSween's wife had threatened to have him and his family killed; so he sent Dudley a letter asking for protection.

"Then a John Kinney said his men were a posse to apprehend the murderers of Buckshot Roberts, who were in McSween's house. We objected to irrelevancy, but Pennypacker denied us by saying that since we'd claimed that the sheriff's posse had outlaws and murderers, Defense had the right to show that the McSween party were actually murderers.

"We tried to turn that to our advantage by asking about the causes of the Lincoln County War. But Waldo objected that it was irrelevant. And Pennypacker sustained it.

"Then there was Sheriff Peppin. He lied poorly." Billy laughed, saying he would end up being the Territorial expert in lying. Leonard smiled ruefully. "Peppin said Dudley told him that he'd come to protect women and children. Peppin also said Private Bush had lied, and Dudley had never sent him any word at all about escaping Montaño men. And he said the only looting of the Tunstall Store was done by Mexicans who'd been told to take what they wanted by Susan McSween.

"And Billy, I'd say your testimony gave them the most trouble." It was the first time Leonard had called him by his first name. The boy smiled. "But I'm letting Wallace know that the whole procedure of this Court is repugnant to anyone of conscience."

"Any word from him on my pardon?" Billy asked. Not yet, Leonard said and sighed.

Martin Chávez, standing guard, called, "Kimbrell comes."

The short man rushed in, dusty, his small blocky face contracted with urgency. He panted, "Messenger showed up at my house. Gave me a paper from the Mesilla Court saying Bonney's to be transferred to jail there to await trial for the murder of Brady, Hindman, and Roberts. Tomorra they're sending an ambulance from Stanton and guards to transport you, Kid. Said you're dangerous. And partisans could try to rescue you. Trial starts next week."

Billy said, "That means the trials for all the others too."

"Might be," said George Kimbrell. From his averted head, his eyes looked up, furrowing his forehead. "Kid, if you was to testify against Dolan and the others, they'd hang. You don't have a chance." He braced his compact body. "Wanted to give you the news. That's all." He hurried out.

Patrón said with uncharacteristic firmness, "Attorney Leonard, I must ask for you to leave. As Jailor, I must prepare."

Standing, Leonard told Billy he would represent him after the Dudley trial. "Thanks, Ira," he answered, informal also for the first time. Patrón followed the attorney out.

"And now," said Yginio, "you must leave. And, of course, from that liar, Wallace, there is no pardon." Billy repeated Kimbrell's statement that if he testified the men would hang.

"Listen, if you do not leave, I will give you my own gun to shoot yourself and spare them the trouble of hanging *you*. Or, if you want to pretend you are Christ - like those fanatical Penitentes - I will get you one of their full-size crosses and a hammer and spikes. Attach yourself. Juan has done what he could. As you see, he has not returned."

Tom O'Folliard asked if they were leaving. "Yes," said Billy.

JUNE 20, 1879   8:18 AM   FRIDAY

Dwarfish bushy-headed Ash Upson wobbled to his post office counter with glass and whiskey bottle after letting in Billy and Tom O'Folliard. Billy asked him for candy hearts. "Got to partake first, Kid," he said. "Also hungry. Get some crates of oysters and tomatoes from the Jones's side. We'll share." They ate from cans in the crates on which they also sat. Upson finally said, "Put coffee on the stove. Use your crate for firewood. What I do. Totally self-sufficient."

Blinking, he said, "My rousing brain just realized: you've escaped three months of prison's steely clutches." Billy laughed.

Scratching his coarse beard, Upson said, "You don't recognize your potential. Buffalo Bill's making a fortune. Prentiss Ingraham even wrote a play for him: 'Buffalo Bill's Best Trail.' Right on stage they bring wild Indians, bears, buffaloes, and jackrabbits; and people flock to see what the West's really like. Can you get a buffalo?" Billy shook his head, still laughing.

"I met someone who might. He was asking about you. Pat Garrett. Said he was an authentic buffalo hunter. He was visiting Chisum. Mailed a letter. To Santa Fe.

"I heard that the dime novelist, Ned Buntline, found Cody. Consider it, Kid; I could find *you*. With them probably closing this post office, I need a job option."

Asked again about the hearts, Upson found a few and said, "Tell me about this latest escape against all odds in which you were either breathtakingly brave or criminally conniving - depending on how the story's told."

"I just slipped off the wrist shackles and rode out." The little gnome asked if he could do that because of double-jointed thumbs. "Sure, Ash," Billy teased. Upson asked if Sumner was his hide out. Again Billy laughed. "No. It's for gambling. Part of the circuit."

Upson asked Tom O'Folliard, "Have you murdered anyone or done daring acts? For my book on the authentic West."

"I ain' killt nobody. Bu' I unce got a skunk out from my uncle's house by pushin' 'im in a box with a shovel. An' he never did spray me. My uncle said it were the damndes' thing he ever seen."

JUNE 23, 1879   12:00 PM   MONDAY

Following a plan arranged by Deluvina when he found her in the vegetable gardens beside the mansion, Billy rode searching through the peach orchard, inhaling summer breeze assuaging lost spring's longing.

Then, in the distant rows, was the blowing white dress. His "Paulita," and her "Billy, Billy" blurred joyfully until she was with him in his saddle, and he was saying, as she laughed, "Today's April twentieth on June twenty-third. Happy birthday! Close your eyes. Open your mouth." In went a candy heart with excuse to kiss.

On his spread bedroll, under peach trees with newly blushing, downy fruit, she asked why he hadn't been given the pardon. "Probably not the right time. But we're winning. The Ring men will have to stand trial. And it makes no difference what the military court does; we got Dudley out of Stanton. And he'll stand trial in Mesilla along with the rest. And Fort Sumner will be home.

"Here's our secret." He whispered, "Billy Bonney loves Paulita Maxwell." Then he gave her Fred Waite's tobacco pouch and said, "For holding memories. Six thousand beads. Each says, 'I love you, my precious Paulita.' "

In the bright happy heat, she slipped off satin slippers and ran to an irrigation channel where, lifting white skirts, she stepped into its shallow water, curling her toes in muddy clouds. He said tenderly, "Your Ma told me your Papa did that too - in Cimarron acequias. To feel the earth."

Carrying her back to the blanket, her bare feet dripping, he lay with her, as rebelliously free as himself, her eyes trusting, and gently traced her beautiful lips, murmuring, "Honey. Sweetest honey. Taste the honey."

Yes there was sweetness; yes, through her sun-drenched closed lids was honey gold. "Something wonderful," she whispered, taking his hand to her white skirt, to peach blossom cupped hollow of April's desire and her new wanting; until, with honey's sweet shudderings, she gazed into his blue blue knowing loving eyes with revelation. Then she hugged him so hard, a child again and awkward, but no less loving, no less his.

JUNE 27, 1879   1:20 PM   FRIDAY

Drinking coffee at Hargrove's Saloon, Billy and Tom O'Folliard listened to Pat Garrett, behind the bar. "Yes, June fifth. Twenty-nine. Next year thirty. I'm ready for real money."

Men at a table signaled. Garrett ignored that interruption of his first clandestine interrogation of Billy and said, "Heard you've got a big rustling operation. I'd like to join"

Billy said, "You heard wrong. The major rustler is John Kinney out of Mesilla. He was called the 'King' even before I came to this Territory in August of seventy-seven." Garrett said he was surprised; his reputation made it seem longer. Billy laughed. "Depends on who you talk to. Ash Upson told me you'd spoken to John Chisum. I'm taking his cattle as payment.

"There's a war going on: the Lincoln County War. Chisum promised to pay our side. He didn't. My bosses - John Tunstall and Alexander McSween - were murdered because they relied on that traitor's help. Our side is fighting the Santa Fe Ring. It's a bunch of crooked politicians, lawmen, and soldiers trying to control the Territory. It goes from the head in Santa Fe - an attorney named Thomas Benton Catron - down as low as you want to go."

Garrett persisted, asking how many hundreds of head he'd taken from Chisum. Billy said, "About sixty." Garrett asked, if there were so few, why was Chisum angry at him. " 'Cause I'm also telling everybody that he was a traitor. Garrett asked if he rode with others. O'Folliard said it was him. Billy added Charlie Bowdre and Doc Scurlock. Garrett questioned outlets. Billy said, "Pat Coghlan: Kinney's competition. Not a Ring man."

Garrett changed the unproductive subject. "Heard the talk about me and Apolinaria? Marry a girl wanting you that much and you're still a free man." Billy said he'd already told him the same thing about ugly women. Garrett's face heated. He said, "Wasn't sure you remembered. Is your rustling business with anyone else?"

"I'm trying to meet a Dan Dedrick - twelve miles south of here at Bosque Grande Ranch. Recently, I heard that he and his two brothers, Mose and Sam - who've got a livery in White Oaks - move rustled stock to Pat Coghlan in the Tularosa Valley. But I also heard that Dedrick's a counterfeiter. I'm not interested in that." Garrett asked about Texas connections. "Tascosa," said Billy. Garrett asked for names. Billy said, "An LX man: Charlie Siringo. He gets around."

Garrett said, "I went to that Stinking Springs rock house you told me about." Billy answered that it was a good stop-over, but a hell of a place for an ambush with that big arroyo. Garrett colored. He had buried the guilty rags in it. He said, "I understand Chisum's grudge against you, but does that Santa Fe Catron have one too?"

"I'd say he might since last October."

Two hundred six miles southwest of Fort Sumner, in the Judge's chambers in Mesilla, black-robed Warren Bristol, creating an official record, addressed James Dolan and District Attorney William Rynerson in a Hearing. He said, and the clerk wrote: "*You, James J. Dolan, are to be released pending bail of three thousand dollars for the murder of Huston Chapman. The date of trial will be set later. Other defendants, William Campbell and Jessie Evans are absent, being rumored to have left the Territory.*"

After Dolan provided the pre-arranged amount, Rynerson said that the Court had nothing further to add. He would accompany Mister Dolan outside.

At the threshold of the courthouse's oversized doors, Rynerson smoked a cigar and said, "Tom telegraphed his regards to you, Jimmy. And he received a letter he asked me about. From a man named Pat Garrett. Garrett says he's got information on the Kid."

Dolan said, "Everyone seems to have stories about Billy Bonney. Pat Garrett. Time will tell."

Rynerson said, "None of us were happy with Bonney's testimonies. And Waldo is still dealing with the problems he caused in Dudley's Inquiry case.

"Anyway, here's the strategy Catron came up with for Bristol to deal with those Lincoln Grand Jury indictments of our friends - and *yours*. They all depend on having trials. Trials need prosecution witnesses. No one will dare come forward. Then Warren can dismiss each case in response to a motion I'll make requesting that the indictments be quashed for lack of evidence. Consider yourself a free man.

"Free except for goddamn Bonney; he'd probably testify. If the bastard hadn't escaped, we'd have hanged him next month. I'll be telegraphing our progress to Catron. Have any messages for him?"

Dolan smiled. "Yes. Tell him James Dolan is about to become a married man. Charlie Fritz's daughter, Carolina. I'm rehabilitating my image." He laughed.

Rynerson laughed too, aware of rumors concerning him and Murphy. "Congratulations! Something else, now that I think of it. One of Catron's code letters. Kimbrell. For the next election, Tom wants us to find a new Lincoln County sheriff.

Rynerson continued. "And now that we've crushed opposition in Lincoln County, Catron's planning ahead. Eventually, he'll reposition Sam Axtell as Chief Justice. And no one thinks Wallace will stay long. Catron will move his friend, Lionel Sheldon, into the governor slot. So we'll all be back in business again.

"Tom's even thinking ahead to statehood - wants to be the first senator. And he's even drafted a unique state constitution for the future. It keeps power with the governor by purse-string control, and keeps the legislature weak so they can't interfere. Then, big money can control the governor and pay off bottom feeders - like sheriffs. Catron named it The System: codeword COW, as in cash cow. Said it could last generations.

"But that record of the April Grand Jury - especially with Bonney's testimonies - could ruin everything. So Bristol's choosing the right time. Flooding a room. A fire. Paper's easy to destroy."

Dolan smiled. "Like a man, William. Like a man. If Billy Bonney does not wisely leave the Territory, *he* will be our new sheriff's first priority." Final smoke exhaled from the fierce tangle of beard; and Rynerson tossed his cigar stub at the threshold. As if marking a place, it stimulated Dolan to say, "I'll be there for his hanging."

JULY 5, 1879   10:03 AM   SATURDAY

Henry Waldo stood for his closing argument, his demeanor mingling gravitas and indignation to Presiding Judge Colonel Galusha Pennypacker, and the two additional judges, Captain Henry Brinkerhoff and Major Nathan Osborne. Waldo spoke.

"Gentlemen, from the time this Court began, the Prosecution has acted with undue hostility: as if *this* was a Court Martial. That stance - combined with the fact that Ira Leonard worked so closely with Governor Wallace - left me, at least, suspicious about a hostile conspiracy. I wondered, who is this Attorney Leonard giving services without financial remuneration? If only Charles Dickens had conceived such a hero for a book." He rolled his eyes heavenward.

"As to the charges: all are patently absurd against a man of Colonel Dudley's unblemished reputation. Ridiculously, he is accused of aiding in killing one Alexander McSween and causing his house to be set on fire. But who were the witnesses? John Wilson, an ignorant old man who says he was menaced by the commander for not issuing warrants against outlaws besieging the town."

Waldo strode, slapping leather soles angrily. "Another was Sue McSween. She contributed nothing. As to Colonel Dudley's conduct, all she told us was that she couldn't repeat his language when she accosted him in his camp." He smirked. "Our affidavits as to her character prove that it was *she* who *did* unmentionables.

"And as to the testimony against Commander Dudley by the hired man, George Washington, all we can say is that dull Negro never conceived those lies. They evince wicked help - for example, by a white attorney from Las Vegas.

"My good and patient soldiers, how your months have been wasted! There was a William Bonney alias Henry Antrim alias Kid, a murderer by profession, and accessory to the attempted murder of Special Courier Private Berry Robinson. His testimony was brief, yet he signalized his opening sentences with a lie. He swears that troops fell in with both the sheriff and his posse. Yet Sheriff Peppin; his deputies, Jack Long and Billy Matthews; his possemen, Robert Olinger, John Kinney, and Andrew Boyle; and the honorable soldiers themselves - Lieutenants Goodwin, Smith, and French; and the current commander, Purlington - all attest that it did not occur.

"This boy also swore that three soldiers fired at him when he was escaping from the McSween building. It is sufficient to say that if he lies once, he would do so again.

"But let's examine that matter more closely. In the deceptive glare of the fire, it is doubtful that anyone could identify a man's clothes. This difficulty would be enhanced in the Kid's case, because he was looking from the center of the light out at the darkness - which is important. Toward the McSween building, objects were plainly discernable; so the opposite follows when conditions are reversed.

"Besides, it is certain that soldiers were not present, since the sergeant doing roll call testified that at a quarter past eight all the men were there. Yet the escape was then.

"In addition, Andrew Boyle informed us that some of his Seven River's possemen were dressed in soldier jackets and pants. To be generous, I can say that as the Kid fled he may have seen *them* and *thought* they were soldiers."

Performing, Henry Waldo was enjoying himself. Tom Catron would be amused when he told him. Dressed *like* soldiers! That had been Jimmy Dolan's idea, given to Andy Boyle for testimony.

"And those guns - the Gatling and howitzer - that supposedly intimidated citizens. About them, from whom did we hear? Missus Montaño. Her lie was just her jealous Spanish pride because the soldiers had camped closer to the house of pretty Missus Baca." There was chortling from Osborn and Brinkerhoff.

On and on Henry Waldo spoke, mucoid tobacco spittle accumulating in his glass. "Suppose that Colonel Dudley addressed Sheriff Peppin *exactly* as the *Negro* soldier, Private James Bush, stated. It would simply show the Colonel in sympathy with the Sheriff's attempt to carry out law. Implying otherwise shows only malicious intent by a *Negro* Private against an officer."

Two hours passed. Still Waldo continued. "When we look at the honest, brave, and resolute white faces of the sheriff and his posse, and think of the miserable horde of Mexicans and cut-throats who opposed to them, and when we reflect upon the skill shown by the sheriff's posse in isolating the criminals to the house of McSween, we know that no power under heaven could have prevented them from accomplishing their goal. Troops made no difference. Then where is the blame? There is none.

"As to Tunstall Store looting - an army officer accused of that!

"But now I must come to the regrettable testimony of Governor Wallace. I would suggest that he was trying to blame someone for the failure of his Amnesty Proclamation, since what the McSween villains needed was gallows, not a pardon."

Henry Waldo mopped his face as if ending a long, but well fought, battle. "Gentlemen, the foul conspiracy to disgrace and ruin Colonel Dudley, concocted by Lew Wallace, Ira Leonard, and Sue McSween, has ended in failure. Colonel Dudley comes forth unscathed. All that remains is to thank the Court for its patient attention."

After their midday meal, Captain Henry Humphreys gave his closing presentation to the three judges yawning with postprandial lassitude. "Good Sirs, we have listened to the seemingly endless words of the Defense, and recalled wise words about one guilty: 'He protesteth too much.' " The tall slim Captain, with ill-fitting jacket making him appear unable to fill its space, spoke with deep sincerity. "So we'll just state the truth."

Neither he nor Ira Leonard had realized that their last hope was forcing that truth on recalcitrant listeners.

"We contend that we've already proved each of our charges. And, we contend that witnesses brought by Colonel Dudley for refutation were merely partisans of the Murphy-Dolan faction - including James Dolan himself.

"And one needs no more proof of the dire consequences of Colonel Dudley's partisan intervention than the fact that Dolan party efforts had been unproductive from the fourteenth of July to the nineteenth when Colonel Dudley arrived and turned the tides.

"And we have shown the absurdity of Colonel Dudley's claim that his only purpose was to protect women and children. In the burning house were Missus McSween, her sister, and five children.

" Thus we have shown that Colonel Dudley's criminal acts make him unfit for service in the noble army of the United States and subject to Court Martial. Thank you for your time."

Presiding Judge Colonel Galusha Pennypacker announced adjournment for discussion with his fellow judges.

At four thirty, Galusha Pennypacker read the judges' decision: *"The following is the Opinion of the Court: In view of the evidence adduced, Colonel N.A.M. Dudley is not guilty of any violation of law or of orders. And his act of proceeding to the town of Lincoln was prompted by the most humane and worthy motives and by good military judgment under exceptional circumstances. Proceedings before a Court Martial are therefore unnecessary."*

JULY 13, 1879   11:15 AM   SUNDAY

The young priest, Reverend J. S. Tafoya, having arrived in Lincoln County the night before from Santa Fe, observed the bride and groom before him.

Quite short, the sapphire-eyed man was impeccably dressed in black. The homely face of the girl, half his age, was little concealed by a filmy veil. Heavy-chinned masculinity contrasted her small body, sheathed modestly in dove-gray silk.

When first approached, Reverend Tafoya had encouraged a church marriage, but Bishop Lamy had prepared newcomers like himself for compromises; and he was now resigned to the family home.

Hosting the service, were the bride's father and mother, Charles and Catherine Fritz. The bride's fat aunt, Emilie Scholand, was there from Las Cruces.

But toward the groom, Reverend J. S. Tafoya felt inexplicable and embarrassing revulsion.

He proceeded with the holy vows. In a tremulous voice, the girl repeated, "I, Carolina Francis Fritz, take thee, James Dolan, for ..." She stopped.

Tafoya prompted, "My lawful husband," assuming virginal fear, though she had merely forgotten the long sentence.

Finally, Tafoya said in Latin, "I join you together in marriage, in the name of the Father, and of the Son, and of the Holy Ghost." With holy water he sprinkled them, and blessed the ring presented by the grotesquely scarred best man, Jack Long. Smiling warmly, Reverend Tafoya concluded, "You can now kiss your bride."

Dolan lifted Carolina's veil, laid stiff palms on her shoulders, and touched dry lips to her cheek. Congratulations resounded.

Dolan's lightness of mood combined sheer disinterest in possessing a soul so simple, with anticipatory lust for some unmet object worthy of his eternal passion to ensnare.

In desert heat ninety miles northeast of the Fritz ranch, at Fort Sumner's outskirts, Billy and Paulita were racing toward the vast cornfields. There they tied their horses. When she was little, Paulita said, Deluvina would take her to that growing corn; and she would pretend its green walls were her secret house.

As they walked between rows, Billy said, "Someone I knew - he was part Chickasaw - once told me about corn and July." Billy hunkered down in the clodded, moist, red earth. Maturing ears, tight green bundles, spilled lush tassels from upturned erectness. "Chickasaws believe people help corn to be fertile." Paulita did not know the word. Billy blushed and said, "To grow good."

Paulita broke off an ear, peeling back wing-like sheaths, bit pale naked kernels, and handed it to him. Milky juice glistened on her lips. "I never tasted corn this young," Billy said. "For the Chickasaws, it's forbidden to eat till they're ready." Paulita asked if he meant the people or the corn.

Overwhelming were waves of desire. "Uh," Billy said, "both." He took off his hat and gunbelt. He said, "Blessed. They blessed the corn. Wet ground," he said, and pulled her protectively to lie on him within the secret walls of green.

Her kisses tasted of new corn as, without awareness, his yearning hand mounded soil, then stroked deep a cleft, as he became an unbearably tight sheath filled with nectar, while young yearning plants urged consummation. His errant hand rose to embrace, sprinkling Paulita with its red earth, until all became corn's moon-silver wet in golden sun.

In a dreamy voice, Paulita asked if then the Chickasaws ate the corn. Within bliss, Billy said, "Yes. So pure and filled with love."

JULY 17, 1879   1:42 PM   THURSDAY

Thirty miles north of Fort Sumner, gambling at an Anton Chico saloon, Billy saw a bid and raised it. Through windows, came river alkalinity of the Pecos below the mesa on which most of the town stood. Tom O'Folliard folded and whispered, "Billy, you still got a bounty on you? Tha' man there's followin' us. I seen 'im in Portales."

The man lumbered to their table. In a tobacco roughened voice, he rasped to Billy, "Deal me in." Slovenly, with paunch puckering vest buttons, he wore a carelessly knotted tie on a collarless shirt under a green-plaid jacket. Congealed gray-streaked hair framed his broad grizzled face, sprouting a big handlebar mustache and shaggy goatee. He sat, scrutinizing Billy with bushy-browed eyes with dissipated pouches. But he lost frequently and left with the others at dusk.

Outside, on the porch walkway, Billy watched O'Folliard crossing the street to get their horses. Suddenly, the unkempt stranger stepped from hiding. O'Folliard turned back and saw him beside Billy, but was unaware that he was pressing a gun into his side.

Calmly, Billy said, "You've only got time for one, Mister." Then, his hand slashed.

The man yelped. Rubbing his wrist, he rasped, "Anything but my hands, Kid. Your top card was gathering dust. Shame to be put out of business so early. You needed a scare."

"Thanks," Billy said snidely. "Not many would risk their life just to scare someone young."

The man laughed, extending an oversized grimy hand. "Sorry. Misjudged you. Name's Dave Rudabaugh, known as 'Dirty Dave.' Shake it gentle; it's had a bad experience.

"How 'bout talking in my room?" O'Folliard said he was probably a robber. Nonchalantly, Rudabaugh pulled out a bill wad larger than his fist.

Billy asked, "Where's your gun?" Dave Rudabaugh flicked his arm. From its plaid sleeve dangled a derringer on a woven elastic band. He said, "Enough range for my line of work."

As they approached Dave Rudabaugh's frame hotel, painted women hailed him familiarly. He unlocked his room to tobacco and body odor. A table with chairs and a whiskey bottle was below a hanging lamp, which he lit, before putting his ear to the walls saying, "Seem empty. But I don't want eavesdropping. I'm paying for the rooms at each side." Still suspicious, Billy accompanied him.

When they returned, Rudabaugh sat at the table with Billy and O'Folliard, and took a handful of pre-rolled cigarettes from a jacket pocket, proceeding to smoke one after the other, while dropping ashes on the floor. From another jacket pocket came a deck which he shuffled with previously concealed, masterful ease.

To O'Folliard, Rudabaugh extended its downward-facing fan, having him pick a card, then telling him to remember it and return it to the pack. He reshuffled, set down the deck, and said, "Start at the top; turn over one card at a time while spelling out yours. Like: a-c-e-o-f-s-p-a-d-e-s. At the 's' turn up the card."

O'Folliard said the game was too hard. With surprise, Rudabaugh asked Billy if they were partners.

"We're pals," said O'Folliard proudly.

Billy did the maneuver. The last letter was the card. He smiled.

From the green-plaid jacket came another deck, still in its wrapper. Its new card sequence was shown before lengthy shuffling. Rudabaugh showed the cards again. The original order was retained. His baggy eyes flicked to Billy's delighted face.

O'Folliard, like the man, was taking swigs from the bottle. Rudabaugh said to Billy, "I've seen your Three Card Monte, Kid. Nice." From his vest came three cards. "I'll pay a hundred for my ace. Miss it, I get the money."

Rudabaugh stood to adjust the sooty hanging lamp. The ace, when shown, was smudged. O'Folliard, seeing the accidental mark, eagerly said he would do it. His pick was a queen. Crestfallen, O'Folliard paid a stack of twenty dollar gold pieces, and said the whiskey had made him sleepy. Soon he was snoring on the bed.

Rudabaugh slid Billy the coins; but he offered to play a round of Monte for them. Wiping off the ace, Billy turned to check O'Folliard, and inadvertently bumped its edge. But when Rudabaugh turned that creased card, it too was a queen.

The man returned the money smiling, but suddenly his face darkened dangerously. He growled, "Wait a minute. Are you a professional suckering me? Knew all this already?" Billy said he'd just copied him: do damage, then switch.

Reassuring himself, Rudabaugh said, "Don't drink when the game's for real," and took another mouthful.

Puffing a cigarette, he said, "I've been a gambler since I was fifteen. Broke my mother's heart. Only person who ever loved me. Believe it or not, I'm like her: I hate gamblers. They're sick; they'd starve their families. I get pleasure destroying them.

"And I play high stakes. I've played for twenty thousand; each man ready to plug you for one wrong move. I convert fear into challenge." Scornfully he added, "Credulity and chicanery: the way of the world. I profit from the suckers - just about everybody. They'd cheat you themselves if they knew how. I hate them worse than gamblers.

"Back to you: You've got a few tricks. Bottom dealing. Nullifying the cut with a bridge crimp to protect your little arranged group."

"Hard to say," Billy said.

Rudabaugh laughed. "You're a natural. Face innocent as an angel. Impossible to read. But you need variety. Watch."

He shuffled, then dealt, face up, a game for five. "Number three will probably fold if you and me keep raising. But you'll figure I'm bluffing. Poor clumsy 'Dirty Dave.' Got the idea?"

Billy nodded and asked how he'd dealt those hands. Rudabaugh, gathering the cards, said, "Some would pay anything for that answer."

"But here's a question. Remember our hands?" Billy gave his own and Rudabaugh's. "The other three?" Billy hesitated. "Don't worry. Hard question."

"Order dealt, or just what was in them?" When told, Billy recited all without hesitation.

"Hell, now I know why I picked you! I lost my partner to a Vegas jail after I shot the deputy while failing to break him out.

"Okay. Here's a test. Fan the whole deck. Remember what you can." Billy scanned, restacked it, and identified each card as he turned it up. Rudabaugh said, "Only other man I know who can do that is me."

"There are only fifty-two," Billy said.

Rudabaugh laughed and rasped, "What I'll show you took me twenty years to learn; but it's only four parts: location of cards, stacking, false shuffling, and negating the cut.

"As to your opponents - leaving out the suckers - you've got gamblers on three levels. At the top are professionals like me. Basically play with fair cards and skill in their hands and brains. Next are bottom dealers ... like *someone* you may know. Then you drop to thieves: show a hand, and call out what they don't have. It passes.

"First take location: putting cards in place. For that, I bet you memorize discards; and, when you gather 'em for a deal, you bottom stack a few. But you can also arrange for five players - twenty-five cards - ready for your deal!" The baggy brown eyes flicked to grinning illumination.

"But less skill necessitates more crudeness. Like those cards I just dealt: strippers." Billy looked stumped. Rudabaugh slid his chair back. "You're making me uncomfortable. It doesn't hang together. How can you be so smart but not know stripped cards?"

"No teacher, Dave. I even paid someone for his deck - saying it seemed lucky - but couldn't find anything. Anyway, yours was a new deck."

Rudabaugh guffawed. "New! Watch." From the green-plaid jacket came a boxed pack labeled "Andrew Dougherty Company, New

York." Rudabaugh then spread open the jacket to reveal a pocket-filled lining and said, "Tailoring worth its weight in gold.

"Forgot my manners. I'll make coffee." He placed a pot on the potbellied stove. Soon he said, "Proof this deck's new is its tax seal, right?" He passed the box through spout steam, and, with a folding knife, lifted the seal off for easy replacement.

He handed over the deck, while pouring the inky beverage into crusted tin cups. "Seem virgin, Kid?" Billy examined and nodded. "Hand them back ... sucker."

Rudabaugh stroked the deck and turned over his hand. In his large grimy palm were anchored four aces and four kings. "Strippers. Edges are trimmed; making some too big, some too small. This deck's like some 'virgins': get to the crucial spot, you realize somebody beat you to it." He tapped the sides, and gave Billy the pack. Edges of the largest stuck out. Those were kings and aces. Shadow lines from smaller, indented ones were queens, jacks, tens.

Rudabaugh said, "After location, you stack. You arrange your groups by touch and arithmetic in your first shuffling. For example, with overhand shuffling - if I want aces - I put them on the bottom of the pack in my left hand. Then I snap off the top and bottom cards together. That leaves one ace with one card on top. It's obviously called 'milching.' I then snap three more cards on for a first stack of five. And repeat. To suckers, it just looks like I'm shuffling by dropping cards from one hand to the other.

"The other stacking is during riffle, or butt-in, shuffling: half the deck flicked into the other half. Most men have to repeat running the right number off their thumb. I can do it in one. Called interlacing."

As he spoke, Rudabaugh had riffle shuffled the deck. He handed it to Billy. It was arranged for five hands, one with four aces.

He said, "But you can save the trouble." He retrieved the pack, coughed, and hacked into a handkerchief from his jacket. When he handed the deck back to Billy, its arrangement was different. He said, "Substituted in the handkerchief. Called 'cold decking.'

"After you've got your stacks in place, you do false shuffling: just a show of more action.

"Next, you negate the cut - so the cutter doesn't put ruin to your work. That's when *you* put in your bend. Right? But there're other ways. Simplest is to pick up the cutter's two halves, and slap the top *right back* on the bottom." Billy laughed. "Suckers don't expect the obvious.

"And, with a partner as cutter, you just need *one* bent card. They cut to it. But watch this. The cards are legitimate, but my partner's left me a little step between halves. I take that deck, and, with my little finger, push down the step. Quicker than the eye can see, I flip the two halves back to uncut order for my deal." Billy whistled through his teeth.

"Then there are cruder tricks. Ever seen a marked deck?" Billy said he'd guessed the 'lucky' deck was. From his vest, he took that deck, whose backs had rows of little asterisks. Rudabaugh checked it.

"You're right. Watch the test." As Rudabaugh flicked the cards, some asterisks spun. He said, "Those petals are marked clockwise, each slightly shorter to give number and suit. Formula's usually along the top, and from left to right: ace, king, queen, jack, ten, nine, eight, seven. Down the left side's hearts, diamonds, clubs, and spades.

"But look at *my* deck." Rudabaugh took out one with red-and-black plaid on white. "Called 'sorts.' No card backs are exactly the same. So you buy fifty packs and sort them by differences into any system you want. Undetectable.

"Also, you can mark in play, called daubing." He touched his lip for tobacco juice to stain a back. "Or there's 'nailing': jabbing your thumbnail to nick a high one.

"Of course, there's always bottom dealing." The baggy eyes flicked to Billy. "But second dealing's my preference. It's from the top. Since you're just selectively handing out cards, it removes the need for fake shuffles or fake cuts. But you do need marked cards or peeking while dealing.

"Here's how to second deal. Holding the deck in your left hand, you pull back the top card with your thumb, and deal out the card below it: the second. You can also deal off that top card whenever you want. You can even add bottom dealing if you've got a stack there - or if you bottom peek also." He dealt. "You detect it by watching a spot on the top card. If the spot stays put, it's 'cause it's 'gathering dust.' To peek, you slip the top card forward with your thumb, and use your index and third fingers to bend downward. You'll see the upper right corner upside-down. You can peek the bottom similarly."

Billy sipped his coffee. Rudabaugh puffed his cigarette and rasped, "You're ruining a peeking tool. Pass a card over that cup." Billy exclaimed that it was a mirror. "Called a 'shiner.' Anything reflective works." Rudabaugh slid off a wide silver ring from his left little finger. "Put it on with its flat polished side underneath. Hold the deck in your left hand, and deal over it by pulling the card back to yourself." Billy did it and grinned. "It's yours. To a sucker, it's just gambler's jewelry.

"But any other machinery gets you killed." From a satchel, Rudabaugh pulled out a brass Jacob's ladder. Elastic straps attached it to his arm under his jacket sleeve. It shot a card into his palm.

He yawned. "I've got the mental energy, but the physical's gone to hell. I'm ready to turn in. You boys can use one of the other rooms. Tomorrow, let's talk about partners."

Rudabaugh reached into a vest pocket. "One more thing: my most important piece of equipment: my Fugio cent. Remember that game for twenty thousand? I won. The loser threw it in. Had been his lucky piece." It was copper and an inch across. "First coin issued by the U.S. government. When our country was still full of hope - like all suckers."

Billy examined it. Thirteen linked rings framed the perimeter. The reverse had a sundial and sun, with "FUGIO" and "1787" around the margin, and "MIND YOUR BUSINESS" in the center. Rudabaugh said, "Fugio's Latin for 'flies.' Like 'time flies.' And 'Mind Your Business' was a Ben Franklin slogan meaning 'keep on making money.' Good mottos for a professional.

"But my favorite's the chain. Its the original thirteen states. Reminds me of jail shackles; and that I've always broken out, dug out, bribed out." He growled, "Means suckers can't hold me. Means chains can't keep you from freedom. It's the one thing I'd never part with."

Billy asked, "The coin or the freedom?"

"The luck," said Rudabaugh.

JULY 18, 1879   10:04 AM   FRIDAY

As they ate breakfast in his room, "Dirty Dave" Rudabaugh, with tortilla dough and bean juice carelessly sticking to big mustache and goatee, asked if they had slept well. Tom O'Folliard said he had, but Billy had been up playing cards.

Billy fanned a pack and did the spelling trick with Rudabaugh. The man felt moved, and again asked about partnership. Though Billy's response was non-committal, Rudabaugh, while rolling his day's pile of cigarettes, proceeded to extol its advantages.

He said, "With a partner, you can do 'cross fire': raise till everybody folds except you two. Then one of you 'wins' the pot.' " O'Folliard yawned and said he'd clean their guns. And the food was almost as good as Patrón's in Lincoln.

"Lincoln?" asked Rudabaugh. "Still got a war there?"

"Yes," said Billy.

"Anyway, what kind of evidence is this?" Rudabaugh curled upward the right side of his big mustache. Other signals showed suite, value, yes, and no; and reminded Billy pleasantly of Josie.

"And you can use them in play to get cards to your partner. Let's say he's got two high pairs and wants a full house. He signals. I've got the needed card. I fold; throw down four, palm one. Meanwhile, his hand happens to pass over the discards. He's dropped his worthless card. When he calls, I say, 'Wait a minute! Let's see that hand;' and reach over to his cards. Then he's got his five.

"But what I like best is the science. Called probabilities. The odds of getting each possible hand have been figured out. I've memorized the tables. Turns out there are two million, five hundred ninety-eight thousand, nine hundred sixty different poker hands. You can figure your own odds by knowing your hand. Helps knowing everyone else's too!"

Rudabaugh stretched. "There's one thing I'll probably never tell. I call it the 'Rudabaugh Move.' I can locate *any* card in the deck." He saw such admiration on Billy's face that pride swelled.

Immediately, it was undone by his thinking that if the boy realized that his winnings were always lost to whoring, faro, and dice, he'd be as disappointed in him as had been his mother.

Billy said, "Dave, maybe you can help with this: I need boys for cattle work."

"Billy Wilson and Tom Pickett. They work for Dan Dedrick, a friend of mine. I sometimes use them as partners if I keep things simple."

Guessing the work was illicit, Rudabaugh made a face-saving proposition. "That Vegas murder's been a handicap. Great gambling, but if I went there I'd be lynched by Mexicans. That deputy was one. So I'd help you too."

When Billy added that he had been trying to meet Dedrick, Rudabaugh promised to arrange it, and confirmed that man's rustling and counterfeiting.

Fifty-one miles northeast of Anton Chico, in Santa Fe, Pat Garrett was walking its streets lost. He stopped at a man with impressive physique to ask for help in finding the office of an Attorney Catron.

Paul Herlow responded with peculiar familiarity, "It has taken you a long time to find your way."

"You're mistaking me for someone else." After getting directions, he said, "My name's Patrick Floyd Garrett."

"But is that how you want to be remembered?"

"Pat Garrett," the tall man answered, and smiled uneasily.

AUGUST 25, 1879   4:17 PM   MONDAY

"I envy your equanimity, Henley," Lew Wallace said. "Calm even after copying for Carl Schurz that Dudley Court outcome."

He paced angrily. "The outrage: even after my demanded review by Secretary of War McCrary and presentation of damning evidence, Dudley remained exonerated and was even put in command of Fort Cummings!

"At least this invidious injustice yields fodder for literary output. You may recall I told you that the mother and sister of Ben-Hur were released after eight years of imprisonment. To dramatize the injustice, I too was feeling, I made them lepers from jail contagion! And I wash my hands of Lincoln County."

Tim Henley asked, "What about that letter from Attorney Ira Leonard, Sir? He's requesting a pardon for someone there."

"Do not impose distraction. Reminder of that vile place blocks creative juices for my evening's writing. Add it to the Angel reports."

AUGUST 26, 1879   2:09 PM   TUESDAY

With the close Pecos slapping placidly, Billy, in long-john top, dozed in the sun. "Look at me," Paulita said. She had on his shirt over her clothing. He joked that two of her could fit in. "There's only one me. Can I see your chest, Billy? I saw muscles moving when you breathed." Blushing, he gave her two minutes.

"Oh, Billy! You're beautiful. Let me look longer and I'll show you mine." His mouth opened, but no sound came out. Instead, he attacked in tickling, until her own tickling became caresses and he surreptitiously adjusted his pants.

Finally, he whispered that the time was long up. As he put on the long-john top, she said, "I never knew you and I were different." Red-faced, he asked if she wanted to pick flowers. She persisted. "It's like Centauro. I've seen him with the mares; how his ..."

"Not really," Billy interrupted. "He's a horse ... and being a horse, it's not the same." He glanced hopefully, but she insisted on knowing whether she was right.

"Maybe. Somewhat. But love makes it different. And love's what we've got. It makes things happen at the right moment. Like poker probabilities. They're based on arrangements of just fifty-two cards arranged in fives, and *they* make millions of hands. So I figure that since the beginning of time, millions and millions of possibilities happened to bring us together. And now that we've made it, I figure we have forever."

OCTOBER 17, 1879   11:05 AM   FRIDAY

The clean-shaven even-featured man spoke languidly as he puffed a cigar and addressed six others in his home. "I'd say it 'ill work just fine." Like them, he wore his Stetson rebelliously angled, but cream-tan, it expressed the wealthy self-indulgence of the rest of his cowboy-style clothing. Billy, like the others, sat on an old cushioned chair left by John Chisum when he sold the speaker this Bosque Grande Ranch.

Dave Rudabaugh, smoking, rasped, "Dan, I knew you and the Kid would see eye to eye."

Dedrick answered with his drawl of perpetual boredom and moral indifference, "I've got no problem dealing with a small operation. Suits me and Sam and Mose just fine."

"Tom Yerby shur ain' complainin'," said Charlie Bowdre. "Ah've been workin' at his ranch three months now; an' we're keepin' some cattle there. An' some at Greathouse's ranch north o' White Oaks."

"The work's okay with me," said a rawboned youth with blond mustache and severe acne. O'Folliard said he forgot his name. "Tom Pickett. Tom. Same as yours."

Dedrick continued to Billy, "You can drive the cattle to White Oaks to my brothers. The numbers are about what Mose and Sam can handle in their new butcher shop there."

Pickett said that they might as well expand with all the miners moving to White Oaks; what with gold there in the Jicarilla Mountains. And miners lived on beef.

"Never can tell," said Dedrick. "But at their livery, they're selling any horse that can walk."

An ugly black-haired youth, with oversized broad face and a continuous black eyebrow said, "How'd Sam lose that arm, Dan?"

"When he was twelve. In a cane crushing machine. Forgot to introduce you. This here's Billy Wilson."

"And I'm riding too," said Dave Rudabaugh with the noblesse oblige he had settled on. "But I miss Vegas. With the railroad there since the fourth of last month it must be Gamblers' Paradise."

"It *is* something," said Billy. "Across the Gallinas River from Old Town in East Las Vegas - they're calling it New Town - is the best gambling I've seen."

"Heard you lost a man, Kid," drawled Dan Dedrick to say something. Billy named Doc Scurlock, saying he'd moved to Texas to become a teacher.

Having paid no attention, Dedrick continued with his mercenary interests. "We're thinking - Mose and Sam and me - of buying cattle in Mexico to sell here. Be interested, Kid?" Billy felt distaste at the implied cheating of Mexicans with counterfeit money.

Instead, he answered that he and Charlie might open a stage station in Portales; and added that he was using Pat Coghlan too for buying. "A good man," said Dedrick. "But we do business of a different sort."

Rudabaugh said, "The Kid knows about the counterfeiting. Not interested."

Dedrick yawned and drawled, "Heard the news? John Jones was murdered." Billy winced unnoticed.

"Interesting story. On August twenty-sixth, him and John Beckwith argued about stolen cattle. Beckwith drew. Jones beat him. Then Jones decided to turn himself in, but stopped at that cow camp that used to be Jimmy Dolan's. Didn't know they were sentimental about Beckwith. Anyway, one of the boys was in bed sick. Called Jones over. Shook his hand, but held tight while Bob Olinger shot him twice in the back and twice in the head.

"Gives me conclusions. Bob Olinger's a coward. And dumb. The first, 'cause he shot Jones in the back. The second 'cause he forgot his friend was in front. So a bullet got him too; ruined his hip. And lastly, Olinger likes to kill. One to the head would have been enough."

Obviously agitated, Billy said that John was Ma'am Jones's oldest. Dedrick shrugged. "Sorry I mentioned it. Thought it was funny."

Billy asked about writing a letter. Dedrick said, "Desk's in the next room. Don't get carried away by the stacks of hundred dollar bills. They're only worth the labor of printing."

There, Billy wrote, "*In Camp. October 17, 1879. Ma'am and Heiskell Jones. I heard about the murder of John by Bob Olinger. Tell your sons I will take care of it. I have not forgotten all you did for me. Respectfully, W HBonney.*"

Dedrick entered, read it over his shoulder, and said, "We'll do well together. Can't beat loyalty. Think I'll give you something." From a small rosewood box, he took a tintype of himself. "Token of friendship," he said without sincerity. Billy's neutral expression as he pocketed it, hid his feeling of repulsion

OCTOBER 25, 1879   1:11 AM   SATURDAY

Billy and Paulita were on a high mountain looking northward to Cimarron. Then, holding each other, they careened off, floating to and fro like overlapped autumn leaves.

Abruptly Billy woke and realized he was curled around Paulita's sleeping form. He eased off her bed and hurried from temptation.

On Fort Sumner's parade ground, Billy was alone under an illusory dark dome, as the earth, slanting twenty-three and a half degrees on its axis, faced a changing band of sky: twelve major constellations viewed in progression of zodiacal journey around the sun. Burning brightest was Sirius, the Dog Star: blue-white, fifty-three trillion miles away, and almost twice as hot as the sun.

Burning too, Billy strode the diagonal across moonlit ground toward the southern row of buildings. At its rear, he looked into the third house. Celsa Gutierrez was alone and asleep, as if waiting.

OCTOBER 29, 1879   3:09 PM   WEDNESDAY

The sapphire eyes were studying the very long-legged man seated awkwardly on a low slipper chair, when a small woman wheeled in a cart with sponge cake and tea service. James Dolan said, "Why, Lina, thank you. Pat, this is my bride: Carolina Fritz Dolan." A blush suffused her homely heavy-chinned face before she meekly left. Dolan smiled, having discovered social power as well as camouflage in his new status.

Eating the cake, Garrett encountered an extremity of baking soda. "And do call me Jimmy. Tom Catron wired me. You made an excellent impression on him." Dolan waited. Garrett experienced uncomfortable silence, and said valiantly that he would like more cake.

Dolan watched him stand and said, "You are an impressive man, Pat. Impressive in what Tom has told me, and impressive in appearance. Tom said you had a career as a hunter."

"Harvested buffs till seventy-eight. Earned respect of the best - like John William Poe."

"I too had an associate talented in firearms. A Jessie Evans. Unfortunately he relocated to Texas. Tom mentioned that you arrived in Fort Sumner in February of last year." To get more out of life, Garrett responded. "Ah yes. More. More whiskey?" Garrett accepted. "The best," said Dolan. "From Tom. He cares about his friends. And is fierce in opposition to his enemies. Fierce."

"You need that. Or you lose everything. Like to my Papa. Before the War, we had big plantations. In Alabama and Louisiana."

"Ah, yes. The War that stole birthrights." The gray eyes glanced eagerly. "Lost wealth," Dolan tried. Excitement waned. "A life of prestige and respect." Dolan saw anger ignite and said, "I sympathize with those plantation owners, because we good citizens of Lincoln County went through something similar. Tom mentioned that the Lincoln County War was not that familiar to you. The leaders - McSween and Tunstall - you know those names?"

"No," Garrett answered, having forgotten Billy's past mention.

"No matter. They were criminals killed resisting arrest along with their gang of Mexicans and Negroes. It was like the great War: pitting the *dark* races against our *superior* stock. If the local fort commander and his brave soldiers had not saved us, our town would have been burned down by them. After that, the scurrilous survivors tried to implicate me - one of Lincoln's original *white* settlers - in a murder of a corrupt attorney trying to incite further rioting. They even tried to Court Martial the commander for saving us. From all that, I learned an important lesson." Dolan smiled ironically. "Evil must continuously be fought. Do you agree?"

"Why not? Add superstition and you've summed up mankind. I'm a follower of Robert P. Ingersoll."

Abruptly, the alabaster face became alert, dormant craving aroused. Dolan said, "Ingersoll is very close to my *own* heart," now recognizing a soul yearning for him. "In fact, we are seeking a replacement for Jessie Evans to protect us from that gang."

"It's got a new leader?"

"That answer is one reason why Tom found you promising. You know him. Billy Bonney."

Garrett laughed. "The Kid? That's flat wrong. He's a generous sort. People in Sumner like him." Dolan patiently asked if he could, nevertheless, find out more about him.

Garrett hesitated, unsure if they were aware of his Chisum meeting. He said, "I keep my eyes open. The Kid sees me as a friend. Depends on what you're offering."

"Also Charlie Bowdre, Josiah Scurlock, Tom O'Folliard, Dan Dedrick, Pat Coghlan?"

"Scurlock left the Territory. I know Bowdre and O'Folliard. And the Kid told me he's doing business with Dedrick and Coghlan."

"Interesting. Dedrick engages in counterfeiting. Is Bonney involved in that?"

"Didn't seem so. But if you want a killer, it doesn't appeal."

"Of course. I now see that you are made of finer stuff. Finer stuff, Pat. What we citizens of Lincoln County need is a good sheriff. We suspect the current one is colluding with the Kid."

Dolan sighed histrionically. "Listen to the truth about Bonney. He has warrants for the cold-blooded ambush murder of the town's beloved sheriff, William Brady, and his loyal deputy who died at his side defending him. And so many others.

"And to think: the injustice of someone of your high born status reduced to tending bar and raising hogs. The sheriff's election isn't until next November. But the sheriff must be a resident of Lincoln County. You now have friends to help you move - there and upward. Exciting isn't it? Filled with what you deserve." The glazed, gray, longing eyes were locked into his sapphire gaze. "Answer me, Pat," he heard in reverie.

"Yes, Jimmy." A smile flashed under the slick black mustache.

After Garrett left, rattling teacups brought back Dolan's attention. He said, "Lina, my dear, what I am is beyond your conception."

The inhuman look in his eyes was so startling that she stepped back. "You have married a fisher of men. And today I set my hook well. You don't understand, but that is why I am content." She smiled hopefully.

"And you and I have only to anticipate a pleasant future. About six more months for the baby, Doctor Appel said. If only Larry were here to see it all. But he never lost faith in me." From her position, she could not see the sneer that exposed a strangely pointed canine tooth.

NOVEMBER 23, 1879   2:24 PM   MONDAY

Approaching an opulent saloon on Main Street in East Las Vegas with Tom O'Folliard, Billy stopped at a hitched, bay, quarterhorse mare. Her mahogany-red coat contrasted glossy black legs, mane, and tail. Billy said, "Look at those hindquarters, Tom. I bet she can really run." Playfully, the bay mare pushed his chest. "Remember when Sugar did that?" O'Folliard did not, but commented that he had sure tried hard to find her. Billy deflected layered sorrows, including her resemblance to Long Tom, as they entered the smoke-filled room.

Billy picked a table with prosperous-looking men, one raking the pot to himself, cigar in teeth, as his companion said, "You win again, Ellison." Billy asked to join. Ellison said that it was a high stakes game.

"Youngster," added another with a trim white beard, "the buy-in's two hundred. Also, no I.O.U.'s. What we've got is what we're playing."

"No problem for us," Billy said, and was invited to sit by a clean-shaven player, introducing himself as Taylor Jackson, and still crestfallen by his big loss. The last player was thin and had an air-swallowing habit. The white-bearded man said he was Louis Haby, and gave the name Ed McBee for the one with aerophagia, who belched: the byproduct of his affliction.

"Beginners?" Ellison asked. Billy interrupted O'Folliard's denial, saying yes, but with some recent good luck. Both bought chips.

Taylor Jackson nodded toward Ellison and said, "Luck here's picked Jacob. He's running as good a streak as his horse. That race track here. The famous one built years ago by that millionaire, Lucien Maxwell. Yesterday was a big race. You're looking at the winner."

Jacob Ellison boasted that her name was Dynamite Doll; hitched outside: a bay quarterhorse mare. Billy's dark brows rose.

Infrequently, Billy or O'Folliard won. Food was eventually brought. Billy occasionally fingered a silver ring on his left pinky. Ellison's chips gradually diminished. At midnight, all agreed to keep playing. Ellison said, "You boys must *really* have had luck."

Billy gushed, "I did, Jacob. A royal flush! With a huge pot!"

By two in the morning, O'Folliard was snoring. Ellison asked the bartender to get a message to his groom to return Dynamite Doll by midday. Breakfast passed. Jacob Ellison's ill fortune persisted for hours until a deal by Billy; then Ellison's eyes darted slyly.

After McBee, Haby, and O'Folliard folded, Ellison said to Billy and Jackson, "I've got a proposition. Hitched outside, by now, I've got an easy thousand dollars in horse-flesh to add to my bet. Gear thrown in free." Jackson folded.

Billy saw the bet and added to the big pot. Ellison smiled. "Showdown, boy. I call." Confidently, he displayed his four aces and a king. Billy became flustered, saying he could not remember if one suit in order was better than four of a kind. He shyly displayed queen, jack, ten, nine, and eight of spades. Haby exclaimed that it was a straight flush; he won. McBee made a colossal eructation.

"Win some, lose some," said Jacob Ellison with surprising equanimity. Billy smiled sweetly and asked for owner's papers.

As they rode out of town, Tom O'Folliard said, "This new hoss you got shur is purty. Tha' man a' the livery was good folks te buy yer ol' hoss. Are you gonna call her ... Wha'd the man say?"

"Dynamite Doll. No." In his soft blurred voice, Billy said, "I'll call her Cimarron. Nice birthday gift. I'm twenty today."

NOVEMBER 24, 1879   5:23 PM   MONDAY

In his Old Town, Las Vegas office, Ira Leonard uncomfortably greeted Billy and Tom O'Folliard, ashamed of the run-down district, all he could afford after Chapman's death and his impecunious cliental. Billy's presence also salted traumatic wounds: Huston's murder, two shots and near-death in the Lincoln night, and legal defeats.

Leonard said, "So you heard about Susan McSween's case?" Billy shook his head. Leonard sighed. "The Court of Inquiry cleared Dudley. Then, our civil case against him was scheduled in Mesilla for the tenth of this month. But she got so many death threats that we got a postponement till last week. The defense told the jurymen that the military court had already cleared Dudley of murder and arson. So they declared him innocent also. That change of venue saved him; Mesilla jurymen didn't understand the Lincoln County War."

Leonard sighed again and said, "Lew Wallace is still trying to replace Judge Bristol with me."

Billy asked if he had mentioned his pardon. Without looking at him, Leonard said, "No. I urge you to leave the Territory. With your trial set for a triple murder, you'd be hanged."

"I can't. The War's not over."

Leonard lit another oil lamp, saying it felt too dark, and asked why he'd come. Billy said, "In Lincoln, you offered to be my lawyer. Are you still willing? For money. If I need it."

The man resisted fear, and said, "I'd be honored to represent you."

DECEMBER 23, 1879   9:10 AM   TUESDAY

Having checked a hog-tied, stolen, Chisum, yearling calf, and watching him scamper away over frost-dusted Yerby ranchland, Billy, leading Cimarron by the reins, answered Tom O'Folliard's question about the healed brand. "It's G upside-down U. The G's for 'Genio': what his Ma calls Yginio. The U's for Torcio's horseshoe. Yginio's planning a ranch someday outside Lincoln, along the Bonito. Calls it Salazar Canyon. Right now, all he's got is the upside down U carved in his pistol grips."

Charlie Bowdre, listening, patted the shoulder of his shaggy brown mustang-cross. "Me an' Rebel like the cattle business; though Ah'm hopin' fohr that stage station in Portales. It's hard leavin' Manuela in Sumner. An' y'all are invited tah our place fohr Chrismas."

"An' Pat Garrett almost missed that holiday. Manuela tol' me that fool walked intah a pen where a sow'd just had a littah at Kip McKinney's. She 'bout killed him. But Manuela says he'll get a wife out o' it. Apolinaria Gutierrez's been nursin' him."

"Remins me. Manuela said Garrett's been askin' 'bout us 'round Sumner. An' spendin' time with another fool: Barney Mason."

"An' Manuela said visitors are comin' to Sumner fohr Christmas. A rich Jaramillo family from Vegas." Billy was checking Cimarron's front cinch. "Know who's livin' across the parade ground from Manuela an' me? Manuela says she's the riches' heiress in the Territory. Whoever marries her, 'ill have money fohr a few lifetimes."

"But Manuela says it's already set up." Billy, with pupils dilating, asked whose marriage. "Pete Maxwell's sistah: Paulita. To the Jaramillo's son, José. He's rich, but not as rich as that little bitch, who's ..."

"Shut up!" Billy shouted. Hook-nosed Bowdre asked why he'd care where some rich bastard stuck his cock. Billy punched at his mouth; but short-legged Bowdre dodged; and O'Folliard seized Billy. In blind fury, Billy pulled away and struck O'Folliard in the stomach.

Doubled up, thick lower lip quivering, O'Folliard asked, " 'Re we still pals, Billy?"

Gasping for air, Billy felt faint. " 'Course, Tom. Pals."

Bowdre said, "An' come fohr Chrismas dinnah. Loco ohr not."

One hundred and eighty miles southwest of the Yerby Ranch, James Dolan's wife said to him that she didn't understand the special paper he held; only that her father said Mister Winters owed him a favor. "I'll explain, Lina." Her eyes became vacant with anticipated incomprehension. "This is your Christmas gift: consequently our mutual property. Gold was discovered in White Oaks. This paper is a deed made out to you for three hundred fifty feet of Jack Winter's North Homestake Mine." She asked about feet. "That is the length of the shaft. Any gold found there is yours. Ours."

"Shaft? James, you do it." From her knitting basket she took a tiny sweater in progress. As her needles clicked, she said in her hesitant voice, "I forgot to tell you: we need more sugar." He asked if she would like her own store. "If it would make you happy, James." Her lips were repeating the formula of her stitches. He said he had been thinking of taking over the abandoned Tunstall store. "Tunstall? Wasn't he the partner of the man trying to steal Uncle Emil's money?"

"My dear, you continuously impress me. Yes. McSween. And you remind me about an unpleasant aspect of that property."

"If the baby's a boy, could we name him Emil?"

Inattentive, Dolan said, "There are several graves to its eastern side. Bad for business. I would have all sign of them obliterated."

DECEMBER 24, 1879   11:55 PM   WEDNESDAY

Feverish with jealousy, Billy had spent the day spying on the guest-filled Maxwell mansion. In the afternoon, Lucien Maxwell's grand coach had drawn up, and, along with Luz Maxwell, from its front door had emerged an elegant middle-aged couple accompanied by a youth, foppishly dressed in a sable coat and calling peevishly.

To the threshold had come Paulita, in garnet satin, answering: "I *said* I'm *not* coming, José;" as Billy insanely aimed his Colt .44.

After nightfall, there had been dancing, but rashly peering into windows, Billy had not seen her. Finally, light came from her room.

When Billy was inside, seeing the now-hated garnet dress on the floor in ravished nakedness, seeing her in a nightgown that another might also see, he found her remote, though only with anger at family pressure; but to him confirmation of his rival's success. Unaware of his despair, Paulita urged him to her bed.

Fully dressed, Billy lay stiffly beside her and whispered, "If I was killed, what would y'do?"

She'd die too, she said. "Kill yourself?" She said she'd probably just die. "It doesn't happen that way."

She sighed, wanting only his hugging and talk of love. She said, "I'd be like Mama: waiting till my body was in the ground close to yours, and going to you in Heaven.

"But in between?" He braced. "What would y'do? Marry?"

She sobbed, "Nothing would matter. Nothing could ever take my heart from you. Oh, Billy, don't get killed. I can't even stand weeks when we're apart."

Only true love could make those words, those tears. He sobbed too. "Paulita, Paulita, precious Paulita," he said, realizing how much he needed her. "It's not my time."

He collected himself. "The War depends on me. I know that now."

New pain pressed for recognition; one agony gone - his rival - but replaced by one worse: Death.

Tunstall's grievous wounds returned. Again Billy wept. Without words, he realized one gave one's self as an offering, as Fred Waite had said. It was like picking up a fallen standard-bearer's flag and granting him continuance within you. Thus could Tunstall, McSween, and Chapman - good men - even Frank MacNab and Harvey Morris - still fight. He was now the bearer for them all.

Paulita said, "Billy, after the War, we'll move to Cimarron."

"Just got a horse named Cimarron," he said. "We'll ride, Paulita. Ride. And they'll never catch us; never separate us. Ever."

DECEMBER 30, 1879   9:09 AM   TUESDAY

At his desk, a man sipped coffee. His cup's unmatched saucer had a stained crack, which he liked as affirming austerity. He fingered blond fringe around his prematurely bald, long head. In emulation of his Chief and that man's four predecessors, he lacked sideburns. And, like all but the first Chief, he had a wide mustache, though personalized by its precise chevron astride his pointed chin.

Adorning his Spartan office, was just a framed assembly of four etched portraits of the Chiefs labeled, "William P. Wood 1865-1869, Herman C. Whitley 1869-1874, Elmer Washburn 1874-1876, and James T. Brooks 1876."

As was his habit, he re-read the report he had just completed on his preprinted form.

U.S. Treasury Department
SECRET-SERVICE DIVISION
New Orleans District

James J. Brooks,
Chief U.S. Secret Service

Sir: I have the honor to submit the following, my report as *Chief* Operative of this District for *Monday* the *29th* day of *December,* 18 *79,* written at *New Orleans, Louisiana* , and completed at *9* o'clock *A* M on the *30th* day of *December,* 18 *79*

It detailed his activities and those of his Assistant, Dave Raynor, now in Texas. The document was signed, as were thousands of his prior ones, with his bold *"Azariah Wild, Special Operative."* There were only forty of that highest rank in the country.

JANUARY 3, 1880   4:59 PM   SATURDAY

As lights of Fort Sumner came into view, Billy told Tom O'Folliard that Pat Coghlan was sure he would get the Mescalero Reservation beef contract. That meant Catron and the Ring would lose out: Just what Tunstall and McSween had wanted.

Both noticed a small group of cattle and a glowing campfire ahead. Two of four herders loped to them. Billy said one was James Chisum, and called out to that stubble-faced man; whose companion responded hostilely: "I'm Jack Finan. We got us some rustled Jinglebob calves here. Somebody's used a runnin' iron on 'em. John Chisum'd say it was you. No one'd question my ..."

Billy's Colt .44 pointed. He smiled pleasantly, saying no one would question self-defense. He added that he didn't see jinglebobed ears, but wanted to see the brands.

Soon Billy laughed and said, "James, I'm downright insulted that you'd accuse me of such a pathetic job. But your brother knows he's paying up for the War." Chisum muttered that John said he was gunning for him. Billy answered, "That's his guilty conscience talking. But to guarantee a peaceful evening, I'm giving you both a *strong* invitation to ride with us to Sumner."

When the group of known adversaries entered Hargrove's Saloon, the crowded din nervously subsided. But at the bar, one inebriated stranger, called for more whiskey. Gangly Bob Hargrove ignored him and asked them, "What'll it be?" Billy ordered the best he had - for a Chisum. The red-mustached drunk yelled, Chisum!

The bartender said, "Easy, 'Texas Joe' Grant, " to that cowboy, whose old leather chaps cupped his thighs.

Joe Grant called, "I been to Seven Rivers. They'd pay good fer shootin' tha' varmint." Three men, an inadvertent buffer, retreated from the bar. "Ye got a fancy gun, ye rish Chsm bastard," Grant exclaimed, noticing Finan's pearl-handled revolver. Handing him his, he grabbed it from its holster.

Billy said, "That's not John Chisum. It's his brother."

Blearily, Grant asked *his* name. "William Bonney." To Finan and Chisum, Billy said, "Seems a good time to leave."

"Bonney?" exclaimed Joe Grant. "You're the Kid! Man shoos you'd be famis."

Billy smiled, saying they wouldn't. He was almost at the door, purposefully behind the others, when Grant shouted his name.

The pearl-handled revolver clicked as its hammer slammed an incompletely turned cylinder.

Billy whirled. Two bullets penetrated Joe Grant's forehead as Tom O'Folliard ran back in, gun drawn.

Spectators crowded around the dead man.

Sneering, Billy joined them. He said, "It was just a game of two; and I got there first."

With O'Folliard protectively behind, he walked out to awed repetitions of "Kid. The Kid."

JANUARY 14, 1880   3:26 PM   WEDNESDAY

"Glad you could make it here to Alabama, Raynor, Azariah Wild said, clicking teeth biting words. His plump assistant asked anxiously if Chief Brooks was satisfied with his reports. Wild said, "He's got more important things on his mind with the election coming. The platform's sound money. Republicans want results."

Azariah Wild's chevron-framed lips pursed aggressively. "You're raw, Raynor. Know how I know?" The young man's tongue slipped out to lick mustache hairs nervously; irritating Wild intensely. "I know because you talk like an ordinary citizen. Not like one of us SS men. Want to improve?"

"Yes, Sir. The men and women I interview ..."

"Start improving now. Not 'men and women.' Dregs. It takes SS ingenuity to bring these vermin to grief. When I'm back in my New Orleans office, I'll send you a book by Captain George Burnham: *American Counterfeits*. He knew our second Chief: Whitley. Gives cases of shovers of the queer."

Dave Raynor looked at a loss. "Can't infiltrate counterfeiter gangs if you can't speak their lingo. Burnham can. First I thought the Chief should ban the book. But it doesn't give inside information."

Raynor's wet active tongue had bunched mustache hairs. Wild decided the habit looked so idiotic that it provided camouflage.

"Here's inside information: how the SS started. The Civil War. With our first Chief: William Wood. With the McCormick reaper case. Back then, counterfeiting was a major problem. Lincoln knew something had to be done. Edwin Stanton was his Secretary of War. Stanton knew Wood. How? In fifty-four, Stanton was a lawyer. Had a client accused of patent violation. Patent was on the reaper invented by Cyrus McCormick. McCormick was suing Stanton's client who manufactured reapers. Looked bad. Case rested on a divider blade. McCormick's was curved. Night before the client's reaper was brought to court, Wood, a private detective, paid it a visit. Hell of a job to straighten the blade, I heard." Teeth clicked. "So Stanton's client won.

"Stanton remembered. Brought William Wood to meet Lincoln. Wood wasn't taken in by all that Lincoln blabbing about freedom. Wood knew the real problem wasn't counterfeiting. The federal government needed more power. He demanded the right to detain anyone he felt was a danger. Lincoln granted it. Wood didn't want Congress knowing about him and his men. Lincoln granted that. And Wood thought up our names: 'United States Secret Service' and 'Operative.'

"The real secret is *our* power. Example from Burnham's book. Whitley's day. Sweetest family. No one would suspect them. Problem then and now is counterfeiting laws are too lax. Require a witness to passing 'the queer.' The Operative needed one. Had an old coneyman in jail - so far gone with consumption he was called 'The Skeleton.' In court, 'The Skeleton' testified that family were the worst counterfeiters. All went to jail."

Raynor asked if it was true. Wild said, "They're all expendable. If one rat was eating your sack of flour, and you killed another, you'd save trouble later on.

"And we're on our own. Yes, we write reports to Brooks. But take that second rat. Say he's eliminated. But the wrong man. No problem. Brooks said in his seventy-eight 'Circular' that, as Chief, he'd decide what to tell the public. Not much. He knows we're the patriots protecting democracy like the law can't." Wild's jaw bit shut.

"Back to our reports. Whitley, the second Chief, decided on daily ones. He was grand. Six feet ten. A Lieutenant Colonel. Union side. Don't get the wrong idea. Before the War, he'd relocated from New England to Kansas. Kansas had fugitive slaves snuck through into Iowa by antislavery types like John Brown. Whitley captured those niggers for their masters. Better, he perfected our use of informers: threatening any way we want till they squeal on their pals.

"Down to brass tacks, Raynor. Our target is 'The Principal.' Usually has a gang passing or 'shoving' the 'queer': the bills. Our job is to get names. We use local law enforcement if they're not on the take. We pay informers and make the buys to incriminate. These are old rats that can't be caught with just any cheese. But a dog returns to his vomit."

Wild looked out the window into the dusk. "Once had a dream. I was standing at a long trench. In a forest. Lined up were vermin. Our men had revolvers. I said, 'Fire,' and watched those subhumans fall in. Then niggers shoveled dirt. Then they were gone too. Us SS men stepped forward; and that dirt was already covered with grass. So everything was secret."

"That's inspirational, Sir," said the youth, bright-eyed with contagious sadism.

"And we're part of that dream. Remember that, Raynor."

FEBRUARY 23, 1880   7:17 AM   MONDAY

Beginning their return to Fort Sumner across the Llano Estacado from successful Tascosa horse sales, Billy and Tom O'Folliard chose a new route, and soon noticed distant whiteness that was not snow.

"Bones!" Billy exclaimed. "Those are acres of bones! And men loading them."

They approached with curiosity, having to force their skittering mounts between huge buffalo skeletons whistling wind ululations through cages of bleached ribs.

Billy and O'Folliard stopped at a wagon with two men throwing in the heaviest parts. O'Folliard asked what they were doing.

One said, "We's boners, boy. Sell 'em back Eas' fer ferteelizer. Git ten dollars a railcar load - tha's nine tonz. How 'bout workin' wit us?" In the stench of final putrefaction, Billy felt like vomiting.

The man said, "I read in some newzpaper tha' if a railcar's fordy feet long, there's 'nough bonez in Texas te fill two trains lined side by side from San Francisca te Ne' York." Impressed, O'Folliard said he didn't know they made trains that long. "Not the trains, boy. The bonez."

Leaving that plain of slaughter, O'Folliard said to Billy, "Hell mus' look like tha'."

Billy sang, " 'O bury me not on the lone prairie' / These words came low and mournfully / From the pallid lips of the youth who lay / On his dying bed at the close of day." O'Folliard said it was sad. "But a real pretty melody," Billy answered, not yielding to death's pull.

FEBRUARY 24, 1880   1:24 PM   TUESDAY

As Billy neared Fort Sumner with Tom O'Folliard, a blast of wind wrenched off his hat. He galloped after it through scrub, in futile search. At the stables, he left O'Folliard and took his Winchester.

Approaching the parade ground, Billy saw, in front of Hargrove's Saloon, a small congregation at a wagon bearing a red slope-roofed house, whose white lettering advertised: "PROFESSOR VIRGIL PUTNAM. TINTYPES." Lowered steps led to a rear door.

A canvas backdrop had been attached near the saloon entrance. Suddenly, the long, narrow, canvas reflector, leaning against the canvas, slammed down. Spectators jerked at the mimicked gunshot.

Professor Virgil Putnam, in a chemical-stained frock coat, opened the door, white hair blowing, calling patiently to his boyish orange-haired assistant, retrieving the reflector: "Freddie, don't leave the camera unattended."

Billy, closest, was examining that large cherrywood box on a tripod. At its back, flapped a light-excluding cloth, and, in front, on a black bellows, was mounted a board with four lenses in a square.

The Professor addressed his meager audience. "Twenty-five cents to be remembered by loved ones and history." Men were leaving. "I'm using the Anthony Multiplying Camera. Stand for one, but get four identical ferrotypes on a five by seven, thin-rolled, *iron* plate, merely called, in error, *tin* types. Get two for half price."

Virgil Putnam wiped his spectacles. "You've got too much dust here," he remarked to a blond youth, his only remaining potential subject besides Billy.

"This ain't my place. But I live in dust. Cowherding." To Billy, the friendly blond, so similar in appearance as to seem a brother, said, "Way you're dressed, reminds me of when I didn't have a dime either." He called, "I'm paying for him. We'll get the two. Mine's proof to the family that I'm above ground. You go first," he said to Billy.

The Professor descended and said to Billy, "You do seem less than your Sunday best. Freddie, get that new style hat that's so popular back East: the Carlsbad."

Billy dubiously received the black chapeaux with absurdly high crown and narrow brim; and, balancing his carbine, dented in its dome to a jaunty angle; and donned it, right-tilted.

The Professor commented that he seemed padded, asking if it was regional undergarments - like animal pelts. Billy laughed as he walked to the metal posing stand. He said, "It's cold on the Llano. From skin out: long johns, two pairs of pants - not easy to stuff into your boots - two bib-front shirts, vest, bandana, and the cardigan. Can you include my guns?" Of course, the Professor said. Weapons were so fashionable that he carried some as props.

"Then hold up a minute." Billy pulled back his cardigan to expose the holster. Then, in a trick he had devised, he folded under the right edge of his vest to rigidify the panel for unimpeded access to the high Colt butt. He added the gambler's ring to his left pinky.

Next, the Winchester was displayed standing flat to the camera at his left foot, muzzle grasped in his left hand. As the Professor proceeded to camera's rear, Billy cocked his right hand at the revolver.

Freddie raised the canvas reflector with usual incompetence. Putnam noticed that both it and Freddie's hand would be in the picture, sighed, and called from under his tenting, "One, two ..."

Instantly, Billy completed his pose with insouciant head-tilt and sneer. When the Professor reemerged, Billy swung the carbine by the barrel, buttstock arcing to his right hand, thus revealing that it, like his Colt, had been exhibitionisticly positioned for immediate firing.

As Virgil Putnam pulled out the camera's light-protected plate holder, he invited his subjects to watch production. Only Billy followed him inside to chemical odors in the bottle-filled single room with yellow window-glass and front heaped with bedding. "Before you, proclaimed the Professor, are my magic chemicals, discovered in the fifties. You'll assist."

As Billy unstoppered the indicated bottle of developer for him, Virgil Putnam slid out the metal plate and puddled on it that combination of distilled water, ferrous sulfate, and glacial acetic acid; before spilling it off into a waxed wood sink. The resulting four ghostly images were then rinsed, before being dipped into the fixing solution, called by the Professor "the agent of death that grants to you perpetual life: cyanide of potassium." Washing followed.

Billy said, "I can even see the nicks on the carbine stock from its hard fall in Lincoln. And even wind: the bandana's blowing. Wait! Everything is reversed."

Virgil Putnam said, "Right to left, but nevertheless you. After it dries, I will varnish it with gum sandarac, alcohol, and oil of lavender, before snipping apart the four copies.

"Now we must prepare a plate for your friend." He took out one, commercially pre-coated with black asphalt tar. "To this, I add iodide of ammonium and bromide of cadmium in colloidion, whose ether and alcohol are perfume to my nose. But the magic is in its nitrate of silver. It excites the plate to light."

As they exited, Billy vigorously exhaled the noxious air. The blond youth was saying to Freddie, "Abilene, Kansas was getting too settled up, so us cowboys headed west." Freddie said, " 'Cowpuncher' is the new name for drovers, Professor. Mister Blue told me."

"Abbott. 'Teddy Blue's' my nickname. 'Cowpuncher' came with the railroads. Us boys use a pole to punch up cattle that lie down in cars. To pack 'em in."

Boyish Abbott walked to the posing stand. "Wait for me," he said to Billy. "I'll buy the drinks too."

Inside Hargrove's Saloon, Billy sat with his back to a wall. "Teddy Blue" Abbott asked, "Been here before?" but continued, "My first time too. Came to these parts to work for a John Chisum."

He called to Bob Hargrove, "Bottle of whiskey for us." When the man brought it, Billy ordered beans and steak.

"Figure we're 'bout the same age," said Abbott. "I'll be twenty in December." He downed his first drink. "No worse 'en anywhere else." Hargrove returned with the food. Billy ate ravenously, and soon requested more. Abbott asked, "Found any working girls here?" Billy shook his head.

Abbott poured his next glassful and said, "In Colorado, I heard 'bout Chisum. But when I come here, his cowboys told me, 'You've got to be either for Billy the Kid or 'gainst him.' Heard of him?"

Billy's dark brows rose in surprise. "Not by that name."

"Chisum's boys say he's partial to Mexicans. I sure ain't. And I ain't rough as him: killing a man for every year of his life. They say Chisum's afraid he'll be next. Fact is, I heard somebody was shot right here by Billy the Kid. And lisen to this. All five bullets went through the same hole in his head. So I'm not staying. You staying?" Billy nodded. "Which side you gonna take?"

Billy's eyes sparked playfully. "Billy the Kid's. 'Cause of basic similarities."

After Billy left, "Teddy Blue" Abbott asked the saloonkeeper, "Know tha' tramp boy's name?" Hargrove said Billy Bonney. And he had taken care of paying.

Having picked up his two tintypes, Billy noticed, across the parade ground, a sombreroed old peddler beside a laden donkey cart from which hung straw hats. Billy went to him, asking in Spanish for one in felt. The peddler's black canny eyes flicked covetously to the tarpaulin cover, lashed down by a net. Billy commented that he had not seen him before.

The man said, "I come from Chihuahua. Near Tres Castillos. My name is Abrahán." As if divulging a secret, he said, "I *do* have a hat. One I did not intend to sell. It was to be for my special son, born late in life to my spouse."

Untying the bindings, he withdrew a tan felt sombrero, it's brim not extreme. Abrahán said, "With gold or silver trim it would be a nobleman's. Three dollars." Three dollars! Billy laughed; saying that was how he sold horses. The one he saved, sold best.

Abrahán laughed also, and repeated, "Three dollars." Deftly he knotted on a wide green band. "Now it is like no other. It was meant to be yours." Billy smiled as he paid the exorbitant price.

APRIL 20, 1880   8:56 PM   TUESDAY

From her open bedroom window, Paulita watched a distant silhouetted rider, complaining to Deluvina that she could not tell if it was Billy. He wore a sombrero.

Deluvina responded that Navajos never cry; but today Paulita had wasted many tears. "I wanted Billy to come. My light! It must be my light!" Paulita lowered its wick. "Yes! He's coming!"

Embracing Deluvina's round soft arms, Paulita said, "You'll protect us?"

"I protect what I can, my child: your freedom."

When mounted with Billy, Paulita said she had the whole night. With the almost-full moon, they raced past the peach orchard, past the cornfields. When they slowed, Billy said, "Your hair's all moon silvered. There was a tintype Professor in Sumner. He said a picture is made by silver getting excited by light. I got two from him. I gave one to a man I'm doing business with, named Dan Dedrick. He gave me one of himself; so I figured he likes 'em. I lost the other."

He kissed her. "Seventeen," he said, and sang, "But, my darling, you will be, will be, / Always young and fair to me."

When they were on his bedroll, Billy said her birthday gift was a surprise, and handed her his newly purchased field glasses, explaining that after he realized tintypes were just light and dark, he'd checked out the moon with them. Paulita looked and exclaimed, "Oh, Billy! Giant oceans, mountains, and plains."

He said, "I give you the moon to watch over you, precious Paulita," himself feeling its watching presence.

He drew her with kissing into its phosphorescence until he was caressing warm moon mounds and moon crevices; and she said, "Let me too, Billy. It's like being married." And it was impossible to say no. And stars poured golden into their silver sea.

Billy awoke to Paulita asleep against his side, relieved that only clothing was in disarray. "My love," he whispered. "My wife."

MAY 31, 1880   9:45 AM   MONDAY

Alone behind Hargrove's bar, Pat Garrett, guzzling whiskey to anesthetize recrudescence of Joe Briscoe memories, was startled by the coincidence of Billy's laughing and talking entrance with Tom O'Folliard.

Serving them coffee, Garrett said, "Even though you look like a Mexican with that sombrero, Kid, I'd recognize you by your voice. Is it a disguise?" Billy only laughed at the absurdity.

"Haven't seen you since I married Apolinaria on January fourteenth. Double wedding with Barney Mason in Anton Chico."

Garrett leaned forward confidingly. "I heard her sister Celsa's sex-mad like the father. And jealous! Apolinaria says Celsa even tried to stab a man for being unfaithful. And she's married! Explain that."

Billy smiled blandly. Garrett said, "Play your cards close to the vest, don't you? Well, I've got the years on you, anyway. Thirty next month." He sipped his whiskey. "Heard about Joe Grant. Some say you're the best shot in the Territory."

"If his gun hadn't misfired, they'd just say I died young."

Garrett pressed on. "I went to Texas recently, looked up that LX man, Charlie Siringo, you recommended. Siringo said his spread and the LIT are having rustling problems. For protection, they've made the Panhandle Cattleman's Association.

"Also, I tried to find my best friend from my buffalo hunting days, the greatest of them all: John William Poe." Garrett had grown so accustomed to the lie, with its thread of truth being their single meeting, that he believed it. "Found out he'd been a Deputy U.S. Marshal in Fort Griffin." Meaningfully, he eyed Billy. "Him and me know that hunting an animal is the same as hunting a man.

"Now Poe's working as a cattle detective for that Association. And I did get together with one of their detectives: a Frank Stewart." Garrett paused. "How's your work with Dan Dedrick coming?"

"He takes some cattle. And horses at his brothers' White Oaks livery." Garrett asked about counterfeiting. "Like I've told you, I don't like the idea of passing bad money to honest citizens."

Garrett said, "Wouldn't bother me. They just pass it themselves. Fact is, Barney Mason wants to work with me and you. How about introducing him to Dan Dedrick?" Billy nodded.

Garrett smiled broadly at this success and said, "Me, I'm probably moving to Lincoln County, being married and all. To Roswell. Ash Upson will board with Apolinaria and me - what with his post office closing.

"And Lincoln's settling down. Someone named Dolan just opened a big store there." Billy asked if he had met him. Evasively, Garrett responded, "He had a son this month. Seemed a nice sort."

Billy sneered. "If you can say that about a mastermind of murder. And that store - it's stolen from one of his victims: John Tunstall. I already told you about the Santa Fe Ring headed by Thomas Benton Catron. Dolan's its enforcer.

"Jimmy Dolan's behind murders of Robert Casey, Dick Brewer, Frank MacNab, Attorney Alexander McSween, Francisco Zamora, Vincente Romero, and Harvey Morris. And over thirty men, women and children massacred in San Patricio. Dolan was indicted for killing John Tunstall and also an attorney, Huston Chapman, who tried to bring justice to Lincoln County. Dolan's only failures are Juan Patrón, the Mexican leader in Lincoln, who ended up just crippled. And bullets accidentally missed another attorney, Ira Leonard, who replaced Chapman."

Billy sneered again. "Dolan's only other failure is *me*. He hasn't found the right hired gun yet."

Garrett gulped more whiskey as the words "hired gun" undid his new self-esteem. He slurred, "If i's like you say, you can't win."

"But we are. After Lincoln County Sheriff William Brady - in cahoots with the Ring - died in the War, and another Ring sheriff - George Peppin - quit, we got an honest sheriff now: George Kimbrell. And we got rid of Governor Axtell - a Ring man - and got Lew Wallace in as governor. Wallace even promised me a pardon."

"He'll be pardoned!" Garrett thought, panic flaring as when fleeing Joe Briscoe's murder, the murder of an innocent.

O'Folliard called out, "Hey, Charlie!" as Bowdre with tipped, flat-crowned, black hat entered; and Garrett slurred greeting.

Hook-nosed Bowdre said, "Get me stahrted, Pat. Ah'll try tah catch up." Noticing a fine new jacket on a wall peg, Bowdre asked, "Where's the fancy gentleman?"

Arrogantly, in drunken carelessness, Garrett said, "I's mine. From Jimmy Dolan."

Bowdre pulled a big gold watch from its pocket and wiggled his volatile brows teasingly. Garrett forced laughter, said the truth was that someone had forgotten it; and glanced nervously at Billy, who was not paying attention.

AUGUST 26, 1880   10:42 AM   THURSDAY

At Beaver Smith's, Billy and Tom O'Folliard were playing poker with two strangers, when Dave Rudabaugh, in his green-plaid jacket, joined them and motioned to shaggy side-burned Smith for a bottle. As the game progressed, Rudabaugh, in a cloud of his cigarette smoke, drank heavily and shared the whiskey with the two strangers.

Tongue loosened by alcohol, one boasted, "We're from White Oaks. New Englanders like most there. We may have come for gold, but we're making a proper town. Even attracting the best sorts - like this newly married couple. The woman was a widow. Married an attorney in June." His friend asked if he meant that Susan McSween Barber and George Barber. "Yes. Heard a rumor that John Chisum paid her off in cattle to avoid some sort of litigation. People are calling her the 'Cattle Queen.' But the Barbers keep to themselves." The man cut the deck handed by Rudabaugh.

Rudabaugh sneezed into a grubby handkerchief before dealing from it. Having been blue-and-white plaid-backed, it was now red-and-black. Billy cleared his throat in warning, but drunk baggy-eyed Rudabaugh seemed oblivious. After several rounds, one White Oaks man said, "I'd swear this was blue-backed."

His friend teased about keeping secret his drinking from the town's temperance women.

Two hundred thirty-six miles due south of Fort Sumner, in Fort Davis, Texas, Ranger Charles Nevill, in a room over a pit jail, said to his fellow guard, "This here's that letter we intercepted. By the prisner tha' murdered Ranger George Bingham when him an' his men caught their gang. Looks dangrous. I wrote headquarters for reinforcemens."

The other read the penciled note: "*Augus 25, 1880, Fort Davis Jail, Texas, Billy Bonney Kidd, Fort Sumner, New Mexico Territory. Rember the peace promiss you writ in Lincoln. They got me in Fort Davis in the Bat Cave. Wors jail in Texas. They ambusht us and killt George Davis but we got a Texas Ranger. Come before they send me to Huntsville Prison. I got Charlie Graham to write. He writes a better hand. But these words is mine. I never tol you. Davis was my brother. When I sees you I will tell you his real name. Evans aint mine neither.*"

Nevill said, "I been hearin' rumors 'bout that Billy Kidd from LX and LIT men, and the Panhandle Cattleman's Association. Rustlin' an' murder. Leas' we gained us time."

SEPTEMBER 5, 1880   9:10 PM   SATURDAY

In the erstwhile Tunstall apartment, now his office and banished of lamplit profusion, James Dolan spoke ingratiatingly. "Pat, I see you share my preference for darkness. But coming tonight at my request - all the way from Roswell - is admirable. We are advertising that dedication, your dedication to law and order - particularly in White Oaks where most are newcomers, ignorant of our past troubles, but now constituting a third of Lincoln County's voters. Hopefully the horses and equipment we provided were satisfactory?"

"No problems. Got me to Texas. And I did what you said there: told LIT and LX boys that the Kid's a major rustler. Even called him "Billy the Kid" - what he's being called." Garrett concealed learning the name from Chisum, to whom he was still secretly reporting.

"Next step depends on *if* I make Sheriff. I'd use Texans for my posse. And Panhandle Cattle Association detectives. I met with one, a Frank Stewart. And John William Poe, another, is my good friend. I don't want New Mexico sentimentalists interfering."

Dolan smiled sardonically, saying they *did* have similarities. But he knew of a John Kinney and a Bob Olinger, who were trustworthy. And *when* he was sheriff, he would need deputies from the Territory. Garrett said, "That brings up a question: money. I've been working hard."

"Ah yes, money," said Dolan." He displayed a hundred dollar bill, then smiled. "Pat, your face betrays you. This is not payment. It is our means to our end." Beside it, Dolan laid another for comparison. Garrett noticed no difference. Dolan's lips pursed scornfully, reminded of his final meeting with equally stupid William Brady. Then appeared Billy, that first day, breaking the Catron code: lost Billy, the brilliant blue-eyed boy.

Dolan sighed and said, "First, share with me the best Kentucky bourbon. A visitor from New Orleans is coming; and I wanted him to enjoy southern amenities." When Garrett was swirling his snifter, Dolan said, "The first bill is counterfeit. I happen to know that there is a press in this Territory. The bill was printed on it. Notice the line of tiny perforations. A telltale defect in its rollers. That bill was paid to me in this store by a Billy Wilson - in the company of a Tom Pickett."

"But all that has nothing to do with the Kid."

Dolan sighed histrionically. "Details of no interest to history. And history is merely the story people are told, then retell.

"I joke that I am a fisher of men. This bill is my hook, the hook to complete my work. Tom Catron, through his past law partner, Steve Elkins, now in Washington, has informed the federal government of this current threat to our financial stability.

"There exists a Treasury Department division to track down counterfeiters, which is appropriately named the Secret Service, since it operates outside scrutiny - and with as much federal money as we need. We are beginning this country's biggest manhunt. And, with Secret Service backing, *you* will be its leader."

Dolan saw the expected smile, but also a perplexing flicker of guilt. He continued, "An operative - as Secret Service agents are called - named Azariah Wild, has been assigned to investigate.

"And you have already convinced the Panhandle Cattleman's Association that the Kid has a gang of cattle and horse rustlers rampaging throughout Texas, this Territory, and Old Mexico. The link to Billy Bonney will be Billy Wilson, passing bills as a member of *the Kid's gang*."

"But once this Wild talks to ..."

"Pat, let's consider who Azariah Wild talks to: me, *our* sheriff, and those I *helpfully* recommend."

"But it will just lead to Dan Dedrick and Pat Coghlan: a real counterfeiter and a real rustler."

"Pat, I do appreciate your anticipating obstacles. But who would least want to be implicated? Dedrick and Coghlan will want to *help* authorities apprehend the *true* ringleader. And who is this Billy Bonney alias Henry Antrim alias Billy the Kid whom Azariah

Wild will learn of? A leader of a huge gang of at least sixty cut-throats and desperadoes, with murders too numerous to count. A man who only months ago escaped trial for the cold-blooded murders of our sheriff and his deputy, and the thrill killing of an aged farmer named Andy Roberts. And he continues to maraud by rustling and counterfeiting. Do you now understand?"

"The locals know different."

"But newspaper owners care about our plight. Tom Catron's friends own the *Santa Fe New Mexican*. And Albert Jennings Fountain, an attorney in Doña Ana County, has the *Mesilla Valley Independent*. Last year, Attorney Fountain even rescued me from unjust imprisonment at the hands of the very sheriff - George Kimbrell - whom you will run against. And the venue for Bonney's murder trials is the *Mesilla* Court. When Bonney is apprehended, Doña Ana citizens - including his jurymen - will read the truth for his hanging. *If Bonney is not shot resisting arrest.* Do you now understand, Pat?"

Garrett wondered if the single lamp had gone out. Darkness was absolute. Or was he asleep? Or the bourbon so strong? Was it Dolan's voice? "Follow me. Follow me." Was he following? Or falling? "Tell me you understand." Light blinded utterly as darkness, but as flames howling agony of incineration. Was he howling? Were his lidless eyes forced to see, in a hell of forever, bullet-torn flesh and flaming revelation of McSween burning, of Chapman burning, of Tunstall's flaming hair around sizzling skull hole, of flaming Briscoe's halo; all within an endless panorama of naked writhing bodies, all howling agony; while Dolan, clothed in scarlet flame, walked over them - them trying to kiss even his feet in brief distracting adoration - while Dolan was saying, "Do you now understand?" And there appeared a wound penetrating the left breast of Billy.

Dolan was beside him, hand on his shoulder, sapphire searching his eyes. From amnesia - the alcohol was unexpectedly strong - surfaced tight-groined excitement of squealing Juanita, but freed surprisingly from guilt at killing. And the shame of murdered Briscoe was also lost in redemptive relief of newly leached conscience. Garrett, aware only of swelling power, said gratefully to his savior, "Yes, Jimmy. I understand. My job: He has to die."

SEPTEMBER 11, 1880   10:38 AM   SATURDAY

Billy, Tom O'Folliard, Charlie Bowdre, and Yginio Salazar sweated in parched land. "Goddamn drought," said Bowdre. "Ol' man Tom Yerby's loosin' stock. An' they're sayin' this winter will be the worst evah seen. Fire an' ice. I's turnin' intah Hell here.

"What do y'all think o' Garrett runnin' fohr sheriff?"

"It is bad," said Yginio. "Already people of Las Tablas are being threatened by Dolan men.

"And there is more talk about you, Billy. That you are the biggest outlaw." Billy laughed, saying nobody would believe it.

Bowdre scratched his chest, and felt his wallet. "Wan' tah see how Ah'm spendin' mah fohrtune?" He removed a small photograph. "Carte de visite. Got it in Vegas of Manuela an' me at a high class photographer's: Furlong's. Pretty, ain' it?" The guns looked great, Billy said. "I mean Manuela. Ah'm not carryin' guns at mah heart." Billy laughed, saying he looked like a Regulator with those two cartridge belts, that Winchester across his lap, and the Colt leaning out for cross draw. "Ah did feel like one. But look how proud Manuela's standin'. Said it was her happiest day - 'cept fohr our weddin'."

Eight hundred fifty-seven miles southeast of the Yerby Ranch, in New Orleans, Azariah Wild, stroking his chevron mustache, wrote his daily report to Chief Brooks. *"I have the honor to acknowledge the receipt on the 7th of this month of your communication relative to my trip to New Mexico Territory with your enclosed letters from local citizens victimized by counterfeiting. I expect to start next Wednesday September 15th. I have spoken to the U.S. Marshal for such articles as I may need like bracelets, etc."*

SEPTEMBER 26, 1880   4:18 PM   SUNDAY

At his entrance door, Paul Herlow observed the approach of two men, overdressed for Burro Alley, but appearing in their element. Dust smoked about the black-suited legs of one and the brown-plaid ones of his companion.

The latter said, teeth snapping, "You've been valuable, Mister Dolan. Meeting here with me and U.S. Attorney Sidney Barnes."

"I had to. Sidney Barnes is my friend, and a friend of the past U.S. Attorney, Tom Catron. You can imagine my alarm, as owner of the biggest store in Lincoln, when I was paid a counterfeit bill. You bring us all hope, Mister Wild."

Flattered, as intended, Azariah Wild responded, "If, like you're saying, counterfeiting's just part of a plague of lawlessness, I can extend my powers." Having crossed San Francisco Street, Dolan and Wild were passing Herlow.

The muscleman said, "Most satisfactory, is it not?" Dolan asked what he meant, smiling despite himself. "Perhaps it is the *affinity* I sense between you both." Wild asked if he knew Dolan. "Not by *that* name. And *he* now meets me as *Paul Herlow* at my hotel."

Dolan said, atypically mischievous, "If you'd like, Mister *Herlow*, since I deal with the public too, I will let people know about it."

"I thank you. But, as you know, the public finds some businesses themselves. Like mine. What is *your* business *now*, Mister *Dolan*?"

"Mercantile. Tempting free will: the sport of Fate or the Devil."

"Ya. *That* is our affinity: influencing direction. One could say from Heaven to Hell. But I have detained your progress long enough. You still have work to do."

Later, in his room at the Grand Central Hotel, Azariah Wild, while reviewing his reports, thought, "That merchant Dolan will be more valuable to me than he imagines." He scanned entries, delayed in their mailing to headquarters because of his travel.

From New Orleans he had documented twelve days before: "*As I was about to leave I had a present made to me of 100 Havana cigars and two bottles of French Cognac Brandy by F. Pinta. I make mention of this as I may be charged with receiving bribes.*"

For the twentieth he had written: "*In Santa Fe, New Mexico: From 7:30 to 8 o'clock AM at the office of the U.S. Attorney Sidney Barnes in consultation about the counterfeiting cases in Lincoln County. He will send for U.S. Marshal John Sherman to act in concert for arrests.*

"*I also met here this day with the merchant on whom a counterfeit note was passed. His name is James J. Dolan, a prominent citizen of the town of Lincoln, who informed me that Billy Wilson and Tom Pickett who passed the bill are among the worst characters in Lincoln County where multiple murders have been committed within the past two years, but because of corruption not a single arrest has been made. Therefore, without my assistance there would be little hope of arresting them.*"

Lastly Wild read the one he had completed at 5 AM that morning with regard to the past Friday: "*I have this day consulted in company of U.S. Attorney Sidney Barnes with several reliable men who are doing business in Lincoln County. Merchant James J. Dolan was helpful in bringing them together. Among them were a business associate of his in Santa Fe, John Riley; the most prominent Mexican of the area, Saturnino Baca; and a rancher named Edgar Walz.*

"*I will now proceed to Fort Stanton where James J. Dolan recommended I stay, then to the mining town of White Oaks where I have been informed some of the counterfeiters do business. I have purchased me miner's clothes at an expense of $10.75 which was necessary to keep from being suspicioned. I will charge them to the Division under Incidentals.*"

SEPTEMBER 27, 1880   8:51 AM   MONDAY

Azariah Wild, in his miner's disguise of bib-front denim overalls and a dark flannel shirt waited as the driver of a run-down buggy, hired to take him from Fort Stanton to White Oaks, loaded his heavy canvas satchel containing manacles; a trunk with the Havana cigars, bottles of cognac, and daily report papers; a small traveling case; and a miner's pick.

Uninterested in passing scenery, Wild then sat swaying while he removed, from a leather case, his latest report, written at his preferred dawn hour, and read: *"I have been informed by James J. Dolan that my route is much exposed to Indians and considered dangerous without an escort, but the troops are all out seeking hostile Apaches escaped from Reservations. He has generously offered to advise me of risks before I undertake any future travel."*

Four hundred seventy-one miles south of Azariah Wild's road from Santa Fe, in Mexico's Chihuahua City, in the province of Chihuahua, American Consul Louis Scott was writing a letter to Secretary of the Interior Carl Schurz.

"Sir. For the President's use in this election year I provide this progress report on our Victorio War which we date to May 7, 1879 when this renegade chief commenced murder of settlers and theft of their stock and eluded capture by crossing here into Mexico.

"Before the current involvement of our military, action against Victorio had been taken by the Volunteer Mesilla Scouts, a group assembled by New Mexico Territory attorney, Albert Jennings Fountain, owner of the 'Mesilla Valley Independent' newspaper and a well seasoned Apache hunter in his younger days as well as sworn enemy of all outlawry.

"This report documents our new plans. It is agreed by all that this problem can be ended only by a War of Extermination. Central to that is a mutual agreement with Mexico for our pursuit across their border.

"Of course we have to contend with the American public being misled by the hostile Northeastern press. For example, the 'New York Sun' decried an 'inhuman policy' in which Victorio's band had been torn for no reason from their homeland in Ojo Caliente. The truth comes from a white man planning to settle there. He states, 'The life of one citizen laboring to develop the lands or mines of our Territory is worth more than their whole race.'

"As to extermination, General Hatch believes the best way is to use their own people. That policy showed its effectiveness this May. Apache Scouts located Victorio and his band in the Black

Mountain range near Silver City. In a surprise dawn attack they successfully killed several bucks, squaws, and children. The scouts reported that squaws shouted if Victorio died they would eat him to save his body from Whites. I offer that as proof that these people are not human.

"At this point in time soldiers from most forts in New Mexico Territory have been deployed and will cross the border since we believe Victorio is again hiding here in Chihuahua. And from Mexico, Joaquín Terrazas, a cousin of Chihuahua Governor Louis Terrazas, the major landholder and stockraiser here, will lead Mexican troops. Joaquín Terrazas is a known scalp hunter. The amount offered for Victorio's is two thousand pesos, less for that of bucks, squaws, and inevitably children since their scalps pass for females'.

"So I conclude with all optimism that the end is near for this savage beast. Victorio said that he would fight to the death. Tell the President we will soon grant Victorio his wish."

OCTOBER 1, 1880   11:12 PM   FRIDAY

"I could sell this hair for a lot of money," Celsa said as golden-bronze ringlets fell. "Billy the Kid. Everyone is talking about you. But you still like Celsa?" As she leaned to kiss, the cold scissors carelessly pressed Billy's neck. He reached, but she stepped back purring, "But, no. I must finish. So I can say Celsa Gutierrez cut the hair of the famous outlaw."

Billy laughed and said, "At least, take off the blouse." Close golden nakedness took all attention as metal again snapped until, with his insistent kissing, Billy heard the scissors clatter to the floor.

OCTOBER 4, 1880   9:58 AM   MONDAY

At a barrel cistern behind the Dedrick's White Oaks livery, Billy, stripped to the waist, washed himself. Tom O'Folliard said with surprise, "Yer all scratched up, like fallin' inta cactus patch." Billy blushed as he dressed. "Why'd tha' messenger come to us in Sumner?"

"Yginio sent him. Ira Leonard was in Lincoln last week and got word to him. Ira said it was real important that I meet him here at the Oaks today."

As they walked down White Oaks Boulevard, pigeon-toed Lincoln County Deputy Sheriff Will Hudgens stopped them to say: "We'd like you to do your business elsewhere."

After Hudgens walked on, O'Folliard asked why he was unfriendly. Billy said, "Talk about me being an outlaw makes 'em nervous. They remind me of a murdered Regulator named Dick Brewer. Honest men trying to build a future."

Billy turned onto Main Street at a blacksmith shop, saying, "I want to make sure Jim Carlyle has time for our horses." Billy asked a boy straightening horseshoe nails whether he could have Jim do Billy Bonney's and Tom O'Folliard's horses at the Dedricks'.

"Sure. But be careful. People are saying Billy the Kid's in town."

Billy and Tom O'Folliard met Ira Leonard in a rooming house on Jicarilla Street. His sallow beard-rimmed face, with dark-circled eyes, was strained. "I didn't want to alarm you," he said. Billy said he had assumed it was about his pardon.

The man hesitated. "Actually, it may be. If we take the right approach. It could involve you testifying again. At Lew Wallace's request, I met here this past Saturday with a man sent by Washington to investigate counterfeit bills. Named Azariah Wild. He works for the Treasury Department in a Secret Service.

"Wild mentioned a Billy Wilson and Tom Pickett. Do you know them?"

O'Folliard said, "Shur. They rustles with us."

"Two-bit drifters," Billy said. "How'd that Wild hear about them?"

Wheezing, Leonard gave Dolan's name. Billy laughed. "Jimmy Dolan was a counterfeiter himself in the early seventies. With his partner Lawrence Murphy. They had a press in a cave near Fort Stanton where they made whiskey too."

Leonard smiled wanly. "Yet it was - according to Wild - upstanding merchant, James Dolan, who - not mentioning his indictments for murdering Tunstall or Chapman - reported his 'distress' at being paid worthless currency by Wilson and Pickett."

Billy responded that it seemed Dolan was running out of steam for making trouble. "On the contrary," said Leonard, "a Lincoln citizen doesn't contact the Washington Chief of a secret organization. But a man like Thomas Benton Catron could - and did."

Billy said, "The Ring might try that bluff; but I know their cards."

"And that, my client, is your clue as to their motivation - especially with your past testifying."

"Get me."

"Correct. Tell me about Wilson, Pickett, and counterfeiting."

"The bills are made by Dan Dedrick at his Bosque Grande ranch. Dedrick's in the cattle business too, rustling with Pat Coghlan in the Tularosa area. Coghlan gets cattle in Texas from the big ranches - like the LX and LIT - and throughout this Territory."

Leonard asked if some were from him. "If you call about five hundred - my total to date - any contribution to thousands."

"I take it that you have no strong loyalty to these people?"

"I'm not sure what you're getting at; but they don't care about the Lincoln County War."

"Hear me out then. Governor Wallace has gotten more friendly with me. He got me a judgeship - though not Warren Bristol's. So this is my advice as your attorney. This Secret Service investigation gives me an opportunity to send Wallace another request for your pardon. Counterfeiting is a new embarrassment in the light of his failure to get a single conviction for any offenses - civilian or military - committed in the Lincoln County War. But now, with you being called an outlaw, he'd look foolish for pardoning. I want to tell him you'll testify against these men. The publicity would let him save face when pardoning you.

"Wild is staying at Fort Stanton. His contacts are controlled by Dolan. But at my meeting with him, Wild asked me for information. He wants to meet again with me in Lincoln this Wednesday. For that, I want to give him a letter from you stating you'd testify to show your reform from outlawry. In exchange for the pardon."

"I'd do that - even though the outlawrey is a lie. I don't like counterfeiting."

"I'm relieved." The sparrow fingers flitted nervously over the button nose. "A last question. Wallace told me that you gave him a shooting demonstration. Did you say it was as easy to kill a man as to point your finger?"

"No." Billy concealed an inward recoil. The pardon had melded with his quest for fatherly love. He said, "Truth is, *he* said aiming was like pointing a finger. That's probably why he's such a bad shot."

After Ira Leonard reviewed with admiration Billy's completed letter, the boy asked nonchalantly, "Does that Azariah Wild write reports like Investigator Angel wrote to President Hayes?" Yes, weekly, Leonard answered. Billy said, "They're probably carried by the mail coaches passing Sumner. There's a post office a few miles north of there: at Sunnyside."

Paying no attention, Leonard inhaled with relief. He said, "Let's both meet back here with Wild on Thursday the twenty-first."

Meaning well, Ira Leonard had focused on Billy's pardon; but had not comprehended the additional spectacular opportunity. In two days, he would meet with a federal agent having unlimited power. Leonard possessed credibility both professionally and from Lew Wallace's backing. Just by talking, Ira Leonard could destroy the Santa Fe Ring; whose colluding perpetrators he could name; whose heinous crimes he could list. In two days, Ira Leonard alone could win the Lincoln County War.

Even more obvious, was his chance to warn Azariah Wild about James Dolan and to clear Billy of outlaw accusations. None of this occurred to his mediocre mind. Instead, unsuspectingly, Leonard was merely maneuvering Billy into harm's way.

OCTOBER 8, 1880   12:16 PM   FRIDAY

Reviewing his latest reports, bundled in a winter jacket which Dolan called a "loan," to avoid Secret Service policy against accepting gifts, Azariah Wild, unaccustomed to winter, looked resentfully at snow covering the Fort Stanton parade ground before re-reading his reports to Chief James Brooks.

For the one of October fifth, he had written: "*The following new information is from the merchant James J. Dolan. His contacts have informed him that besides Billy Wilson and Tom Pickett more men may be involved in the counterfeiting plague here. One is an outlaw who came here from Arizona after committing a murder there named Henry Antrom alias William Bonney alias Billie Kid from whom cattle thieves may get counterfeit money. Thus far I have found no evidence to support these suspicions.*

"*The problem has been that U.S. Marshal John Sherman has not yet issued the warrants for Wilson and Pickett. But James J. Dolan has already recommended a Robert Olinger as being the best man to be commissioned as Deputy U.S. Marshal for arrests.*"

The report of the eighth stated: "*I left Fort Stanton at 7 AM and reached Lincoln at 8:30 AM. The object of my visit was to confer with Judge Ira Leonard. In meeting with him the following information was obtained. In my report of October 5th I spoke of an outlaw whose name was Henry Antrom alias William Bonney. During the Lincoln County War he killed three men. Governor Wallace had issued a proclamation granting immunity for participants, but as Antrom had already been indicted it did not cover his case and he has been hiding out as an outlaw ever since.*

"*According to Judge Leonard, who is Antrom's attorney, Governor Wallace had promised Antrom a pardon, but has failed to put it in a shape that satisfied the court. Antrom wrote a letter to Judge Leonard which he showed to me in confidence that leads me to believe that we can use Antrom in the counterfeiting cases. Judge Leonard has arranged for a meeting with his client and me on Thursday, October 21st in White Oaks for* *me to discuss participation with Antrom. If Antrom will be of value, I can arrange the pardon as long as I have your approval to proceed in that matter."*

Accidentally, innocently, fortuitously, on his own initiative, Azariah Wild was poised to change Billy's life. Accidentally, Billy's pardon loomed along with another chance to break the Santa Fe Ring. Accidentally, after such long exertions of blood and war, victory was eminent through chance alone.

Eighteen miles northwest of Fort Stanton, in White Oaks, Deputy Sheriff Will Hudgens was calling out, "Quiet down now," to twenty-eight men. "This may be a saloon, but it's our meeting house too. Let's give Jimmy Dolan our attention."

Dolan, in his usual black, stood up, gratified that absent were the Dedrick brothers and Susan McSween's new husband.

He said, "Thanks, Will. First I'll apologize that I'm no public speaker. I'm just a hard-working merchant, trying to make a good life for my dear wife and infant son. But - what with my ownership, along with Jack Winters, in the North Homestead mine - I feel like a White Oaks citizen myself. I care about this place.

"I want to save it from what we went through in Lincoln. Our town was invaded by an outlaw gang which took it over and murdered our beloved sheriff - a father of nine. We needed Fort Stanton soldiers to save us.

"So I'm here with a warning: that gang is on the rampage again. And you know the leader. Back then, we did not. He'd fled hanging in Arizona Territory after a cold-blooded murder there.

"By now, he's killed a man for each year of his life. He even runs a counterfeiting ring. Can you imagine getting worthless bills for your gold? And you know his name: Billy Bonney."

Deputy Sheriff Hudgens called out, "I warned him to keep away - after you warned me."

Dolan said, "Our murdered sheriff, *Will* Brady, did to." He paused. "*Will* Hudgens. I guess I forgot to say that Will Brady's assassin was Billy Bonney. Known as the outlaw, Billy the Kid."

"Are you sure?" asked Carlyle. "I shoe his horses. I'm a reasonable man, Jimmy . . ."

"That's why we like you," a man called out.

Dolan smiled sympathetically. "Jim Carlyle, I'd say *you* are in peril. Billy the Kid's Arizona victim was a *blacksmith*.

"But that's the nature of deception. If the Devil didn't know how to be appealing, he'd have no following!" There was laughter.

Scrawny-necked James Bell asked, "Is that the kid who hangs around the Dedricks' livery?"

Dolan nodded solemnly and said, "But I'm here to give hope. The real problem is that the current Lincoln County Sheriff, George Kimbrell, is afraid of Billy the Kid - maybe even partisan.

"So we citizens found the right man to run against him next month: a family man willing to risk his life for law and order - Patrick Floyd Garrett; or 'Pat' as we call him. Pat Garrett will put the noose where it belongs.

"But before election day, remember this: Billy the Kid is an escapee from our jail. And Will Hudgens, as Kimbrell's deputy sheriff, can form a posse *on his own* to capture him.

"But heed my words: Billy the Kid is dangerous. Capture is provocation. So remember: any coroner's jury accepts killing in self-defense." The sapphire eyes looked at the frightened faces and knew each man was his.

OCTOBER 16, 1880   2:41 PM   SATURDAY

In the huddled horseback group behind a little hill, Rudabaugh rasped to Billy, "Land here 'round Sumner's so flat they'd name an anthill a mountain." Tom O'Folliard, Charlie Bowdre, Billy Wilson, and Tom Pickett listened. "I'm telling you again, Kid, I've done stages; nobody takes the mail. It's the payrolls."

"I'm paying for the job, Dave," Billy responded. "I hear it, boys! When they stop to remove the brush, we move out."

"You're about to ruin your reputation," Rudabaugh joked.

In the mail sack, thrown down from the top rack by Pickett, Billy located a thick packet addressed to Washington, D.C. for James J. Brooks, U.S.S.S., U.S. Treasury Department.

"Just stay put," Billy said to the drivers, as they all prepared to ride away. "I shoot backwards real well."

When they stopped, Pickett, squeezing an acne pustule, said, "Dan Dedrick may be doing a big cattle deal out of Mexico. Interested?"

When Billy declined, Wilson said, "Don' matter. Dan's got a Barney Mason to carry the queer. Mason said he was a frien' o' yers."

"News to me. But I heard Barney might visit Dedrick. You boys interested in a horse job next month? I heard a way station keeper in Puerto de Luna, 'Padre Polaco,' got some rustled from Chisum. We can sell 'em at White Oaks."

Wilson and Pickett agreed before riding southward to Bosque Grande. Rudabaugh asked Billy about staying with him. "Sure. We're going to Stinking Springs. For the night."

Later, in the rock house's windowless darkness, with Bowdre, O'Folliard, and Rudabaugh asleep in their bedrolls, Billy read Azariah

Wild's reports in candlelight. They began with one for October eighth. Billy skimmed complaints of the cold and of problems getting aid from U.S. Marshal Sherman.

He came to, "*And on this day the Lincoln merchant James J. Dolan brought me to the property of the cattle rancher Edgar Walz. He estimates his losses of both cattle and horses to the gang at almost a thousand head.*" It concluded, "*There is one thing certain: New Mexico Territory is the center of a gang of rustlers and counterfeiters.*" It was signed, "*Azariah F. Wild, Special Operative.*"

Billy next read, "*The following is a copy of a letter written by me to U.S. Attorney Sidney Barnes in Santa Fe on October 6, 1880. 'Dear Sir. Judge Leonard has confirmed my meeting with William Antrom alias Billie Kid for the 21st of this month. If I can get him to give information, his outstanding pardon may be arranged and a large number of arrests will likely follow.'*"

When O'Folliard, waking, went out to check the horses, Billy was reading the report for the twelfth. "*James J. Dolan believes that the Sheriff of Lincoln County, George Kimbrell, is either partisan or a participant in the gang.*" Billy whistled softly through his teeth.

The last report was dated the fourteenth. "*When James J. Dolan was told about my plan for Antrom's pardon, he confessed that he had been afraid to tell me earlier that William Antrom (whose correct alias is Billie the Kid) is very active in all activities of the rustling and counterfeiting gang and comes into nearby towns to play cards with Sheriff Kimbrell. Based upon this new information it may be better to arrest Antrom at that time of my meeting with him and later decide how to utilize him.*"

Billy re-read the last sentence before finishing the conclusion: "*James J. Dolan also reports that his contacts have given him names of other gang members now congregated at Fort Sumner with Antrom: Charles Bowdre and Tom O'Folliard.*"

When O'Folliard returned, his talking awoke the others. Billy said, "Seems Jimmy Dolan's trying to convince a Washington investigator named Azariah Wild that we're part of a big gang. And seems Wild was planning to jail me when I met with my lawyer in the Oaks next week. I figure I'll disappoint Wild on that one."

OCTOBER 21, 1880   2:17 PM   THURSDAY

James Dolan, behind his store counter, appraised Wild staring miserably out at the snow, and decided to pounce. Nature, in its freezing brutality, had conspired with his own manipulations to wear down the operative. Wild had turned to him for solace, incredibly calling him "Jimmy;" and, more incredibly, revealing

Billy's possible pardon, thus enabling its sabotage. "Azariah," Dolan said with silky, subtly demeaning informality, catching his eyes, "Listen to me. I can help you more, help you more."

The eyes were held, waiting and needy, and being trained to fall under the spell. "I have some fine Kentucky bourbon," Dolan said, aware of Wild's refusal to drink on the job. "Here we use it to keep warm." Dolan smiled. "And consider your French cognac and the Havana cigars adequate barter."

"Yes, Jimmy," Wild said dejectedly. "After I'll go to your office. Do my report."

In that apartment, calmed by the alcohol, Wild finally wrote his humiliating entry to Chief Brooks. *"I respectfully call your attention to the fact that the mails have been robbed on the night of the 16th of this month. In this mail I had several reports. The plans of my mission here are now as well known to the gang as to myself."*

Then Wild asked Dolan for more of the 108 proof whiskey.

Ninety miles northeast of Lincoln, Billy and Paulita were walking the Pecos bank past skeletal cottonwoods. Billy said, "I found out that the Santa Fe Ring's so scared of us Regulators that they're trying to frame us to a Washington investigator by pretending the War's just outlaws making trouble."

"But why didn't the governor just give you the pardon?"

"Remember that horse I rode after Sugar was stolen, and before Cimarron? Never could beat Centauro in a race. Wallace is like that gelding: doesn't have heart." Billy hesitated, unwilling to abandon hope in the pardon or the man. "So, when he needed my help in testifying again, I decided not to - until I get it." In his eyes was yearning, not for her, but for the last man he would try to love.

OCTOBER 25, 1880   11:03 AM   MONDAY

Ignoring Yginio Salazar's warning that he risked his life to come to Las Tablas, Billy, in his green-banded sombrero, was there campaigning for George Kimbrell.

To O'Folliard, Billy said, "Charlie told me that Manuel Brazil - that rancher east of Sumner - bought our latest Chisum cattle without questions. Here comes a buckboard! Prospective voters!" Billy called out, "Mornin'!"

A fair man beside a dark-skinned Mexican driver returned the greeting. Billy said he hoped the snowstorms wouldn't keep them from voting. The passenger laughed. "I always do. Name's George Curry." His gloved hand shook Billy's, warm in its gauntlet glove from Tunstall.

Curry said, "I plan on going into politics myself." In that case, Billy answered, he'd recommend re-electing Sheriff Kimbrell. He backed the people. Curry said, "I'm for Pat Garrett. Heard he'll bring in that Billy the Kid and his gang."

In Spanish, Billy addressed the other man. With lowered eyes, he answered in English, "I must ask Señor Curry, my patrón, for advising." In Spanish, he said, "I am sorry."

After Billy and O'Folliard rode away, George Curry said, "You're voting for Garrett, aren't you?"

His worker responded only, "Señor Curry, that was Beely the Keed."

Later that day, fourteen miles south of Las Tablas, Dolan, Wild, and Garrett were in the store office drinking the French cognac. Wild said, "Jimmy told me good things about you."

Dolan laughed jovially. "It took time to get Azariah to call me Jimmy." He glanced at Garrett, sullen at being on display, and brought him the bottle. "Pat, have more, even though you're not a drinker - unlike Sheriff Kimbrell, a notorious drunkard. Pat's as formal as you are, Azariah. Southern aristocracy."

Garrett stretched his long legs. Wild thought, "Reminds me of that tall SS chief, Herman Whitley." He said, "Jimmy told me you've infiltrated the gang in Fort Sumner." Garrett nodded. "Did Jimmy tell you why I'm here?" Garrett said to get money. "Yes. But this is confidential: we can eradicate those vermin - any way we want." Wild's teeth clicked.

"Azariah," gushed Dolan, "what a relief. By the way, has that loan horse been helpful: that bald-faced chestnut?" Wild said he was, but insisted on a daily rental of a dollar. "Of course. Interestingly, the gelding connects to the gang. He belongs to a Jacob Basil Matthews. His ranch on the Peñasco River had been stolen from him by one of its deceased members. Attorney Tom Catron recently returned the title to him. That same criminal once claimed to own this building.

Dolan continued, "By the way, a Las Tablas citizen named George Curry just got word to me that he'd sighted Billy the Kid there. And he is in Mexican disguise with a sombrero."

Wild said, "Something doesn't fit. The Kid knows about me. Why doesn't he just escape to Old Mexico?" Dolan caught his eyes and stared intensely, saying Chief Brooks would resent doubts. There was no need to doubt. No need to doubt. Wild heard himself repeating, "No need to doubt," before his mind went blank. He asked, "What were we talking about, Jimmy?"

Dolan's tight smile was the only sign of his intense exertion of will. "Our new sheriff," he answered.

OCTOBER 28, 1880   10:18 AM   THURSDAY

In the Plaza in front of the Palace of the Governors, on a bunting-covered platform facing a large crowd, Lew Wallace sat with his wife; with Lucy Hayes, her once lithe figure corseted to compress hundred and seventy pound bulk; and with her sons Birch and Rud - the other children, Fanny, Scott, and Webb, having remained in the Hayes family's Ohio mansion, Spiegel Grove.

American flags flapped gaily from the Johnson Block's second story, where a grotesquely obese man listened under roof shadowing.

Full-bearded President Rutherford B. Hayes, standing on the platform and radiating fatherly warmth, continued, "Being the first president in the West, I report no wild Indian attacks." Several of the largely Hispanic audience laughed. "I'm not here politicking. Everybody knows our *Republican* administration has brought peace and sound money. And our *Republican* governor, Lew Wallace, has brought peace here too."

Thomas Benton Catron lumbered back into his second story office, satisfied that Hayes was doing his job to protect the Ring.

"To finish my chat with my inauguration promise: 'He who serves his party best, serves his country best.' And the man for that now is James Abram Garfield!"

As the group left the platform, Paul Herlow, in the audience, said to himself, "Each looks and is identical: Grant, Hayes, Garfield."

Following the crowd, Herlow heard a woman say to Lew Wallace: "And I read ... parts manuscript ... wife Susan showed." He heard Wallace answer that it had made him a true Christian. Next month *Ben-Hur* would be released by Harper and Brothers in New York.

One hundred and eleven miles due east of Santa Fe, Billy was hungrily eating spicy beans and tortillas in the Maxwell mansion's kitchen, while noticing Paulita's and Deluvina's dejection.

He said, "That Secret Service man is a bad investigator. I'm sure the president won't take him seriously."

Paulita's eyes brimmed. "You don't know."

"Victorio is dead," said Deluvina.

"On the fifteenth," the girl sobbed. "Deluvina, I'm not a Navajo. I can't help it."

"It is all right, child. It is very sad." To Billy, she said, "In June, General Hatch's men killed his son, Washington - the future chief Victorio named for freedom."

Billy asked where Victorio had died. "In Old Mexico. Do you know where Tres Castillos is?" Billy remembered Abrahán, and answered, Chihuahua; but asked what Tres Castillos - Three Castles - was.

Deluvina said, "They are three small mountains on land as flat as here. The highest, Cerro del Sur - where eagles nest - is where Victorio made his stand. He did not know of the agreement that Mexico would let American soldiers chase him over the border. With him were one hundred and forty-six: sixty-one warriors, the rest women and children." Paulita sobbed that one must have been his sister Lozen; and all were scalped.

Deluvina said, "Victorio did not know how many hunted him. From the American side came over two hundred men and Apache scouts." Bitterly she added, "His own people. And from the Mexican side came Joaquín Terrazas, with over three hundred and fifty. And, from the mountain, Victorio saw their dust coming to that destination chosen by Ussen, the Great Spirit of his people. When Terrazas and his men surrounded his mountain, Victorio had no ammunition." Billy sighed. "Just before midnight, Victorio began the death song. And when dawn came, death came."

Billy said, "Victorio died free. Same as I'd want."

Paulita accused Deluvina of crying. She stiffened. "No, child. It is just water from my eyes."

From her apron Deluvina took a torn-out column from the October twentieth *Las Cruces Thirty Four*. Billy read its oversized headline: "GLORY! HALLELUJAH!! VICTORIO KILLED, WAR ENDED!! PEACE!"

Paulita said, "I want to burn it. How do you open the firebox?" Deluvina smiled, saying it was a good start for cooking. She hooked off a flat lid. Paulita dropped it in.

Deluvina watched Billy. He said, "Burned up in a moment, but people will never forget what Victorio fought for. Exactly what he wanted." Deluvina shuddered, reliving the chill at first telling him the tale of Dragonfly.

OCTOBER 29, 1880   8:27 AM   FRIDAY

Eating eggs and bacon in the paneled dining-room, Azariah Wild said to Dolan, "Good of that Sam Wortley to offer me a free room here last night. Even stored my miner's pick in his lodgings in that building across the street - the one you had before the gang stole it. But, Jimmy, are you positive I'm not suspicioned?"

Dolan smiled imperceptibly at the dependence. "Not only is your disguise excellent, but the locals are preoccupied with next week's sheriff's election.

Dolan continued, "So much connects to that gang. Even your eggs. They are from chickens I gave Sam along with their coop. It needed repairs. Bullet holes." Wild looked up.

"It was July of seventy-eight. That gang of sixty rode in like Victorio's marauding Apaches and took over this town. Back then, their leader had a walled-in stronghold here. A notorious embezzler, he lived with a woman of ill-repute. He and his gang blew up that building to start their burning of the town. Thank God, that criminal was killed resisting arrest. But Billy the Kid - who was right there - escaped, vowing revenge. That's when he became the gang leader. I apologize for not telling you sooner exactly who he was. But I am terrified of him. That is the reason we here call it the Billy the Kid gang. At last, you know our whole story."

Azariah Wild looked at his eggs. "Ah yes," said Dolan. "At that embezzler's house of infamy was the flock. I am tender-hearted - my Irish nature. I rescued them."

Later, in his room, Wild wrote for his report: "*I am now perfectly confident that there is a counterfeiting and rustling gang of at least sixty here as I am of anything that I have not seen with my own eyes. They congregate at Fort Sumner, but have two ranches: One at seventy-five miles from there (the Pat Coghlan Ranch), the other at twelve miles (the Dan Dedrick Ranch). At the Dedrick Ranch they have the plates and press. They also have a band out stealing horses and cattle and robbing mails, while others guard the stock they have stolen. And the leader is William Antrom alias Billie the Kid.*"

NOVEMBER 2, 1880   10:10 PM   TUESDAY

With excited voices and Havana cigar smoke behind him, James Dolan stared out a Wortley Hotel window into new moon darkness.

Serving tables, Gottfried Gauss, working locally as a handyman, was a hired helper. Sam Wortley called, bald head gleaming, "Ready for champagne, boys? Any minute, "Squire" Wilson and the County Clerk will be finished counting ballots." "

Bob Olinger shouted that they were already celebrating, and was joined by laughter of George Peppin, Jack Long, and Billy Matthews. At another table were George Curry, Dr. Joseph Blazer, and Dr. Daniel Appel.

Dolan returned to his table, joining Wild; Garrett; and Kimbrell, with small contracted face. Dolan said, "Not drinking, George?" Kimbrell answered that he had a long ride back to Picacho. Anyways, he didn't drink much. Dolan raised black brows at Wild.

To Pat Garrett, Dolan said, "Same day as choosing the president. Do you think Garfield or Winfield Hancock will win?" Garrett stupidly asked who Hancock was. Dolan saw Wild's shock and said, "That's Pat's sense of humor."

The vote counters entered. Billy Burt, the County Clerk, read, "*Patrick Floyd Garrett, three hundred fifty-eight. George Kimbrell, one hundred forty-one. Total ballots cast, four hundred ninety-nine. Our new Sheriff, Patrick Floyd Garrett!*"

Wilson glumly shuffled out as the room erupted in shouting, while Gauss cleared dishes and bald Wortley served more champagne. Billy Burt, urged by Dolan to join them, said, "Las Tablas went thirty-nine to one to you, Pat." Gauss listened. "Almost no votes at all from San Patricio or Picacho. But big turn out in White Oaks for you."

Peppin called for a speech. Pat Garrett stood reluctantly. "Thanks, boys."

In the din of applause, the front door was not heard. Stocky muscular Kinney strode in with two, carbine toting men, who departed when Dolan nodded. "Pull over a chair, John," Dolan called. "Next to our new sheriff!"

Kinney smiled, then said to Kimbrell, "Me and my boys just came from Picacho. Course we know San Patricio better. But the citizens agreed that snow kept 'em from voting."

Dolan stood. "All right, boys. Time to go. We've got some official business now." Kimbrell rose. "Not you, George. You're staying." Blanching, Kimbrell sat as sounds of departing men echoed.

Dolan called, "Bob, Bob Olinger, we need you here too!" He looked at the others remaining - Wild, Garrett, Kimbrell, and Kinney - and said, "This is a momentous day for Lincoln County. All of you - except you, George - know that Azariah was sent by Washington."

Wild said arrogantly, "To eliminate that huge gang of desperados." Kimbrell glanced at Kinney, who smiled back superciliously.

Confused, Kimbrell asked Wild about his mining business. "There is none." The teeth snapped. Wild said, "I demand your oath of secrecy." Kimbrell gave it.

Wild took a paper from his carrying case. "I wrote out your appointment of Patrick Floyd Garrett as your deputy until he takes office as sheriff in January. But from today he'll *act* as sheriff. And you'll stay in your house.

"And, Kimbrell, if you pass on information to the Kid or his gang, I'll arrest you as a member. We're finished now." George Kimbrell walked out dazed. Wild said, "Brazen isn't he? Like I said in a report, 'the worst nest of criminals in the country.' Now for the real business."

Bringing a new champagne bottle, Sam Wortley passed Gauss and told him to start the dishes, thus ending his eavesdropping.

Azariah Wild removed two more papers. He said, "By not responding, U.S. Marshal John Sherman caused delays. But I finally got the commissions for Deputy U.S. Marshals. Carelessly, both were made out to Robert Olinger." Wild handed one to him. "So I changed the other to *Patrick Floyd Garrett*. "Pat," Wild said smugly, "as a Deputy U.S. Marshal you have authority *anywhere* in the Territory. Not just Lincoln County."

"What an impressive surprise!" said Dolan.

"We're powerful," Wild mumbled, feeling the champagne, and left to his room. As the others followed suit, Dolan asked Garrett to stay.

Behind the Wortley, a waiting rider saw a figure emerge. Yginio Salazar hooted the signal, and Gottfried Gauss, after trudging through the snow, gave the tallies, adding: "Und der iz a big man von Vashington." Impatiently, Yginio said they knew. "Vait. He tells Kimbrell to ztay in his house. Zo Garrett iz zame as sheriff now."

Pat Garrett, alone with Dolan, opened a gifted pasteboard box, revealing a blued Colt .44 with a seven and a half inch barrel; and said he'd already given him one. Dolan responded, "But it was not new. A shooting accident made it useless to its owner. This is not a token of congratulations. It is to prevent misfiring. I ordered it from Benjamin Kittredge and Company in Cincinnati. And I checked its serial number. Fifty-five-o-ninety-three. It will make history: the gun that killed Billy the Kid."

NOVEMBER 3, 1880   2:22 AM   WEDNESDAY

In freezing blindness of moonless dark, Yginio Salazar, tense with bad news, climbed the snow-covered north face of the Capitans on Torcio. When he dismounted, tying reins by touch, to his astonishment, he heard, from within the cave, exuberantly trilling "rrrr's" and "ay, ay, ay's" of a fiesta baile. "Billy," he called. A glow appeared.

Inside, Billy was dancing. Tom O'Folliard added wood to the fire. "No," Billy panted. "Dancing with Darkness." Wet with perspiration, he was stripped to his shirt.

O'Folliard scraped dirt onto the nascent flames and whispered, "Sit with me, Yginio. 'Bout 'leven, Billy says, 'I gotta dance. Kick ou' the fire.' So I does."

Billy had realized that Darkness, somehow solid, unseeable, was dancing with him. From its gaping maw came icy blasts of infuriated hunger; but dancing away, he had laughed at its inept starvation; until new warmth made him shed clothing, as if finding sun's power in night. And his striking feet had increased grand celebration until he had called out, as Yginio heard; and Darkness was forgotten. Then firelight appeared, confirming ancient fears of

Darkness, making it bold. But he had spoken, and the flame had disappeared; instead rushing upward through him, pouring sparks of light. He was filling the sky with stars; so not only the Darkness was forgotten, but the Self.

Far away, Billy's name was called. He was shivering, muscles fasciculating in sidereal ecstasy. His coat was being put on, the fire lit, hot tin cup of coffee held; and he knew Yginio was there. Peacefully, he asked if the election was over.

"Pat Garrett won," Yginio said. "And they made him a deputy to replace Kimbrell immediately. You must leave."

"No."

"That makes no sense."

"It does. Let them call me 'Billy the Kid' if it means freedom; if it means not giving up or backing down. There are different ways to win. Now, staying is one."

O'Folliard asked Billy if he thought Pat would shoot him. "First he'd need the chance. Second, it would depend on his conscience."

NOVEMBER 21, 1880   8:43 AM   SUNDAY

Azariah Wild peeked out the Tunstall store's office at shopkeeper, Sam Corbett, and asked Dolan if he could be a Kid gang spy. From his desk, Dolan reassured him and added, "With Garfield's victory of seven thousand three hundred sixty-eight votes, and his electoral college win of two hundred fourteen to fifty-five, we have no Hayes-like uncertainties to interfere with our plans."

Wild responded: "Scale of this operation here exceeds anything the Chief's ever done," and smoothed his perfect chevron mustache around his sly smile. "Finally got the warrants. Thanks to your recommending Judge Warren Bristol.

"So Garrett and me formulated a three pronged attack on the gang." His teeth snapped. "One. White Oaks posse arrests, kills, or runs the gang to their Sumner headquarters. Two. Garrett and his Texas men - I'll ride there - attack at Fort Sumner. That posse includes Garrett's friend, Frank Stewart, a stock detective for the Panhandle Cattleman's Association. Three. Other Texans finish off any vermin left trying for the border.

"Should mention, Stewart knows another Garrett friend, an Association cattle detective named John William Poe - a past Texas Deputy U.S. Marshal.

"Poe's already checked the Pat Coghlan Ranch. Found fourteen hides with the LIT brand. Strange number with the thousands involved."

Dolan said, "A gang that big has them butchered fast."

"Makes sense. Should mention this. I just got a helpful letter from a cattleman named John Chisum." Dolan concealed surprise at the unexpected ally. "Said when Garrett told him about the queer, he remembered someone to whom Billy Wilson passed a hundred dollar bill. Strange that we've got only two bills total." Dolan reassured him that people in the Territory couldn't tell good money from bad. Others were afraid to talk. "Makes sense," said Wild.

Wild continued, "And Garrett's Fort Sumner infiltrator, Barney Mason, met with me yesterday. He's uncovered a huge plot. I put him on a regular salary. Know anything about him? Foreman for a certain Peter Maxwell."

The sapphire eyes briefly ignited. Dolan said, "What I do know is that Maxwell owns Fort Sumner; and his father, Lucien Maxwell, bought that property from the federal government in a sale involving Tom Catron. You may recall that man, Herlow, in Santa Fe, who saw our affinity. I too like information. I will get more on Maxwell." Impressive, Wild said, the way he worked without remuneration.

"Knowing that I eliminated …," Dolan stopped, "that I played a small part in protecting our populace from Billy the Kid will be reward enough."

"Then you'll soon be paid, Jimmy."

Wild, no longer circumspect, in front of Dolan wrote his report of the twenty-first: *"The informer Barney Mason stated that a Dan Dedrick proposed to him as follows: 'I want to employ you to take counterfeit money to Mexico to buy up a herd of cattle to bring to New Mexico to me and my brothers. When I agreed, he brought $30,000 in counterfeit money which he gave me to do it.'"*

NOVEMBER 22, 1880   6:16 AM   MONDAY

Relaxing at their campsite in Coyote Spring after selling horses at White Oaks, were Billy, Tom O'Folliard, Dave Rudabaugh, Billy Wilson, and Tom Pickett. A quarter mile south, five White Oaks possemen were waking, while bow-legged Deputy Sheriff Will Hudgens, his brother John, and Jim Carlyle guarded their prisoner: Mose Dedrick. The deputy said to Mose, "We know you're getting stolen stock from Billy the Kid."

"And I'm denying it again," he answered wearily. "The court will decide."

"We don't need a court," said Hudgens's brother. "Like Jimmy said."

"Be sensible," said Carlyle, as the others joined them.

"Wish we could make a fire," said James Bell. "Hard to start the day just with jerky."

"Can't take chances," said the Deputy Sheriff. "We're a real posse."

As the men ate, James Bell tried to explain to another how to cock his brand new Colt .45.

"Daylight soon," said Will Hudgens. "The gang will outnumber us. There'll probably be a fight."

All were ashen with fear. Before his brother left to take Dedrick back to town, he asked again: "Mose, you're sure they're at Coyote Spring?"

"That's where the Kid told me they'd be."

Later, still at Coyote Spring, Billy was saying, "Those sixteen rustled Chisum horses we took from Padre Polaco's were all good. I'm glad I rode the buckskin today. I realized he's worth more."

"Hoss I got's the bes' hoss I ever got," said O'Folliard.

"Why'se he called Padre Polaco?" asked Tom Pickett, picking acne scabs.

"In Poland he studied to be a priest," said Billy. "Name's Alexander Grzelachowski. I sure wish Ira'd been in the Oaks yesterday. Maybe I got my pardon. Anyway, Jim Greathouse buying horses from us helped: bringing ten to White Oaks instead of sixteen. Today we'll sell those left at the livery."

"Where's your gloves, Billy? Ain' you cold?" asked O'Folliard. Billy said they were in his saddlebag. "Figer I'll call this hoss Red; 'im bein' red."

All heard snow-muffled hoofbeats.

Eight riders dashed in, firing wildly. "To the horses!" Billy shouted, just as his and Wilson's were accidentally hit.

Billy leapt up behind O'Folliard. Pickett rescued Wilson. "To Greathouse's," called Billy. O'Folliard said they weren't following. "Didn't figure they would," Billy said. "But what the hell were those White Oaks men doing?"

NOVEMBER 27, 1880   3:16 PM   SATURDAY

Will Hudgens looked back at his new posse of fourteen, while listening to Jim Carlyle tell him and stringy-mustached James Bell that the deep snow was like Massachusetts. Hudgens said, "And tracks show. Only possibility's Greathouse's. We'll capture them in the morning."

Eight miles northeast of the posse, was the adobe ranch house and way station of "Whiskey Jim" Greathouse and his partner, Fred Kuch. Five of the horses in their corral were saddled and bridled: three, the survivors of Coyote Spring, two repurchased.

At a table, Greathouse, a bearded bear of a man, sat with Kuch, Billy, Dave Rudabaugh, Billy Wilson, Tom O'Folliard, and Tom Pickett. Joseph Steck, the slow-moving cook, with nose pointing over limp black hairiness, listened.

Billy said to Greathouse, "I sure wish you'd had a spare carbine and gloves. They got mine," giving no clue that lost were two cherished possessions: both Tunstall's gifts. "In the morning we're heading to Sumner. No use risking the Oaks."

Greathouse said, "Hell no, boy. Can't even think of that. Right, Fred?"

"Yeah, Jim." Small-boned and energetic, blond Kuch contrasted his partner.

"I still don't know why they attacked us," Billy said. "I even saw Jim Carlyle."

"They're crazy, that's why," said Greathouse. "I'm from Arkansas. Totally different. These White Oaks fellas, they're New Englanders. Descended from people so crazy that England kicked 'em out. Called pilgrims. Soon as they settled, out came the craziness: they decided their grannies were witches and burned 'em up. They're still witch hunters. And you're the local witch: Billy the Kid. Greatest outlaw ever!" Greathouse threw back his laughing head and spread big hands over his belly. "Come to White Oaks to spook 'em. Goddamn fools."

Billy said that it made no sense. "How come you think things make sense? How old are you?"

Twenty-one four days ago, Billy answered. "Old enough to know better. World makes no sense. People are fools. And the worst crooks win. Now you know everything you need." Billy laughed.

Greathouse said, "I've held stock for all of you: Kinney, Evans, Coghlan, Dedrick. I know you're not doing much. But you've made more enemies then a man could without trying. Least you made John Kinney happy. With cover of your reputation, he's working backtrails so hard they'll lay railroad tracks on 'em."

Forty-five miles southeast of Jim Greathouse's ranch, in Roswell, Azariah Wild, at Pat Garrett's house, was listening to Ash Upson say, "I agree that Missus Garrett is shy. I've been a boarder here for months. Years ago, I was a boarder at the home of Billy the Kid in Silver City. He was bloodthirsty even then." Wild looked astonished.

Upson asked, "As a miner, would you read a book on Billy the Kid?" If it ended with his death, Wild responded. "That goes without saying. If Joan of Arc had died falling off her horse, or Christ from dysentery, their stories would be forgotten." Probably true, Wild said, and decided not to risk his own life on Garrett's posse.

NOVEMBER 28, 1880   6:35 AM   SUNDAY

At first light, Joseph Steck went to feed the horses. Unfastening the haybarn door, he was accosted by two revolver-brandishing men, and exclaimed, "What you want, Mister Bell?" Embarrassed at being recognized, James Bell directed him through drifted snow to the Hudgens brothers and Jim Carlyle.

Carlyle volunteered to send back a note. Removing gauntlet gloves, he took out a little account book and pencil, and wrote on a torn out page: *"We are White Oaks posse. Place surrounded. Surrender immediately."*

Back inside, Joseph Steck handed it to Billy, who announced calmly, "Boys, we've got White Oaks visitors again. Say they'd like us 'to surrender.' " Billy Wilson asked what for. Jim Greathouse repeated that they were plumb crazy.

Billy wrote on the back, *"If you are a legal posse what are your legal papers? Send in your leader to show them and talk. Respectfully, W HBonney."*

Joseph Steck proceeded back into the gray light. "This way," a voice called from below the rise. Behind a shed, Carlyle waited with James Bell and two others. Steck handed him the response.

"It's from the Kid," reported Carlyle. "Wants to talk to our leader. I'll do it." Bell said to get a trade; otherwise he'd be killed.

The damp page tore under frightened lead. *"To the Kid. I, Jim Carlyle am a Community leader. I will come. But we want an exchange."* Bell told him to add that, if they heard a shot, they'd shoot their man. Carlyle wrote, dizzily imagining his murder.

After Billy read it aloud, Jim Greathouse said, "I'll try to talk 'em out of this. Just don't fire off pistols. They'll be edgier than a mare with a newborn foal." He put on his coat and hat, and walked out.

"Morning, boys," he boomed amicably. Jim Carlyle emerged and passed him, trudging up the incline to the house. Greathouse called after him, "Which way?" But with distraction of someone climbing gallows, Carlyle did not answer.

Stringy-mustached James Bell beckoned from behind the shed. Greathouse invited them in to eat. Bell said they only wanted surrender.

Entering the ranch house, Jim Carlyle, confused by the unexpectedly small number of men, as his gun was taken, coughed nervously, putting gloved hand to mouth. Billy shouted, *"You're* the one who stole my gloves!" Furious, Billy took them and asked, "Where's my Winchester?" Carlyle stammered that he didn't know.

"Let's eat," Billy said grimly. Jim Carlyle sat frozen. Billy said, "You look like you need a drink. What kind of leader are you?" This challenge had effect. Carlyle accepted bottle and shotglass.

At the adjoining table, unperturbed but bored, Rudabaugh, Fred Kuch, Pickett, and Wilson smoked and played poker. "Don't make it a long day, Jim" said Billy. "Do you have warrants? Are you sure you don't have my Winchester?"

Carlyle poured a second glassful and pleaded, "Kid, I don't know about your gun." He glanced around. Across the room was a large window, once a door. "We've got no warrants," he said dully.

"Then what the hell are you all doing? Ambushed us. Stole from us. Killed two of our horses. Go out and explain that to your boys."

Carlyle saw a doorway behind the bar, decided the gang lurked there, and slurped another glass.

Billy called, "Fred, I'm sending another letter." He wrote, *"To the Citizens of White Oaks. Your leader Jim Carlyle says that you have no warrants. You are just a mob. We will send him back and you send Greathouse back to end the game. We want no trouble. And we never made trouble. Respectfully, W HBonney. P.S. Whoever stole my Winchester I want it back."*

When Fred Kuch returned, he reported, "Deputy Hudgens said maybe you already killed Carlyle." Rudabaugh growled that they were trying to shoot "Whiskey Jim."

"No!" yelled Carlyle, springing up. "Don't shoot!"

Nobody was shooting, Billy said. But he might have to be their cover for escape. Carlyle sat, sobbing drunkenly, back heaving, saying, "I know you're a giant gang."

Billy wrote, *"Sirs. Carlyle is no help. If Greathouse wants to stay he can. But we need Deputy Hudgens instead. We have no gang. We just want to be on our way. W HBonney."*

Fred Kuch presented that note to Will Hudgens. His brother said, "I don't like it. Jimmy told us the Kid's a sheriff killer. He's trying to get you. Kuch, tell him - if they won't surrender - to release Carlyle in five minutes or we'll shoot Greathouse." Kuch left.

At the shed, John Hudgens gave that news. "Five minutes, you say?" asked James Bell. "And we shoot him?" Apprehensively, Bell looked at the big prisoner, full of life.

After Hudgens labored through deep snow to tell the others, Bell, taking off a glove, unholstered his new Colt .45, its freezing metal sticking to his sweaty skin. He put on the glove again, clutching the weapon awkwardly.

Jim Greathouse said, "You'd shoot a man in cold blood?" His three guards were silent. Then all stomped to ease numbing feet.

Inside, Fred Kuch told the conditions. "Surrender like hell!" exclaimed Billy. "Get ready to leave, boys. Take 'Whiskey Jim's' gunbelt. He'll need it." Jim Carlyle listened horrified.

Outside, James Bell said, "Nothing's happening. Clumsily, he pulled back his Colt's hammer with gloved thumb. He lost hold. The revolver dropped through the snow, struck a rock, and fired. Embarrassed, Bell retrieved it.

Inside, at the shot, Jim Carlyle screamed, ran, and plunged through the big side window.

The possemen saw flying glass and an escaping figure, and fired. Three bullets, one James Bell's, hit Carlyle, while "Whiskey Jim" Greathouse bolted away.

Without hesitation, Billy and his followers raced through the back room and out to the corral. "To 'Old Man' Spencer's ranch," Billy called. They galloped northeast.

By the time Fred Kuch and Joseph Steck arrived outside, Jim Greathouse had saddled and bridled his horse. All three rode away, though no possemen were seen during the escape.

In flight, the posse had abandoned dying Jim Carlyle.

DECEMBER 7, 1880   4:38 PM   TUESDAY

Tom O'Folliard, coming from Manuela Bowdre's house in the Fort Sumner barracks, met Billy at the stable, and said, "Somethin' strange happent. When I was ridin' to Yerby's ranch te tell Charlie we was back, men chased me. I know un was Pat. He's too big for a hoss."

Billy answered, "Chisum must have hired him as a stock detective till he became sheriff."

O'Folliard said, "Ain' right the way them Oaks men come back an' burnt down Greathouse's place an' tha' ol' man's too."

" 'Old Man' Spencer. They're a mob. But I still can't figure what made them so violent. Anyway, Jesús Silva said Missus Maxwell wanted to meet with me. I'm heading there now."

In the drawing-room, Luz Maxwell extended her hands warmly to Billy and said, "We've heard dreadful rumors. And then that dreadful newspaper article. Peter, do get it." When Maxwell returned, she said, "It's an editorial from the *Las Vegas Gazette* written by its owner, a J. H. Koogler. Last week on the third. One of our men brought it. Unfortunately it's all smudged."

Billy made out: "a gang of outlaws harassing the stockmen of the Pecos and Panhandle country, and terrorizing the people of Fort Sumner and vicinity. The gang includes over sixty men ... is under the leadership of Billy the Kid, a desperate cuss ... Are the people of San Miguel County to stand for this any longer?"

She asked if he was this Billy the Kid. "I've heard the name," he said. "But the information's fake."

"Of course. I wanted you to know that we offer you what protection we can."

"*You* insisted, Mother," Peter Maxwell clarified resentfully.

Sixty miles due south of Fort Sumner, in Pat Garrett's house, Azariah Wild was reviewing reports. In escalating anxiety, he had atypically written two the Friday before, succumbing to paranoia through Dolan's manipulations. He scanned the first. *"Information has reached me this day that a part of the Billie the Kid gang numbering at least 20 were run by the White Oaks posse to Greathouse's Ranch. Their leader was induced to go in and was immediately murdered and the Kid and his gang made their escape."*

The second, prepared only an hour and forty-five minutes later, was uncharacteristically scrawled. *"Large numbers of the Billie the Kid gang may be very near here. I am trapped and unable to get out of this place with safety."*

At 10:16 PM, in Paulita's bed, Billy declared, "We're still winning. They're all running so scared that even five of us seems like an army."

DECEMBER 12, 1880   11:13 AM   SUNDAY

After spending the night at the ranch of Manuel Brazil, Billy and Tom O'Folliard, having been joined by Charlie Bowdre for the ride back to Fort Sumner, rode west along the snow-covered road. Billy said, "Manuel's real helpful. Interesting how he came from Portugal. I'd bet that after he worked for Lucien Maxwell, he rustled Chisum cattle - like everybody else - to start his ranch."

Bowdre sighed. "This deslate land remins me how much Ah've lost. Ah've got a confession, Billy. Pat Garrett foun' me at Tom Yerby's las' Sunday, an' took the two mules we were holdin' there. Said they were rustled. Said I should leave y'all.

"Pat's actin' so uppity that I decided tah write him fohr a pahdon. Mahby when he's sheriff, he can get it."

Ahead was the Maxwell cemetery. He sighed again. "Ah've been thinkin' that we each got a dyin' place. Comes a day, an' yaw there."

Billy said, "Better to think about living. Let's head to Hargrove's. See how the boys' game is going."

"Firs', Ah got business with Manuela." Charlie Bowdre laughed to dispel depression. "We always agree on business."

Billy and Tom O'Folliard entered the saloon to uneasy silence. At a table, were Dave Rudabaugh, Billy Wilson, and Tom Pickett, along with two Maxwell employees: Pedro Lucero and José Valdéz.

Billy asked Hargrove for writing materials. At an empty table, he said to O'Folliard, "Too bad Bob just has red ink. Tomorrow, we'll ride to Sunnyside and get Milnor Rudulph the Postmaster to mail these."

He wrote: "*Governor Wallace. Sir. I noticed in the Las Vegas Gazette a piece which stated that Billy the Kid, the name by which I am sometimes known, was the Captain of a Band of Outlaws. There is no such Organization in existence. So the Gentleman must have drawn very heavily on his Imagination. My main business at White Oaks at the time I was waylaid and my horse killed was to see Judge Leonard who has my case in hand. After mine and Billy Wilson's horses were killed we went to a way station forty miles from the Oaks kept by Mr. Greathouse. When I got up the next morning the house was surrounded by an outfit led by one Carlyle, who came into the house and demanded a surrender. I asked for their Warrants and they had none. So I concluded it amounted to nothing more than a mob and told Carlyle that he would have to stay and lead the way out that night. Soon after a note was brought in stating that if Carlyle did not come out inside of five minutes they would kill the Station Keeper (Greathouse) who had left the house and was with them. In a short time a Shot was fired on the outside and Carlyle thinking Greathouse was killed jumped through a window and was killed by his own Party thinking it was me trying to make my escape. The Party then withdrew. They returned the next day and burned old man Spencer's house and Greathouse's.*

"*During my absence Deputy Sheriff Garrett probably acting under John Chisum's orders went to Mr. Yerby's ranch and took a pair of mules of mine which I had left with Mr. Bowdre who is in charge of Mr. Yerby's cattle. Garrett claimed that they were stolen and even if they were he had no right to confiscate any outlaw's property without legal papers.*

"*I have been at Sumner since I left Lincoln making my living Gambling. The mules were bought by me the truth of which I can prove. John Chisum has benefited by the Lincoln County War and is now doing all he can against me. There is no doubt but what there is a great deal of stealing going on in the Territory. But me being the head of a Gang is untrue and would be proven if some Impartial Party were to investigate.*"

Next, in a letter to Ira Leonard, Billy recounted the same incidents, but concluded, "*The pardon is necessary to end these mob attacks on me and my friends,*" thus leaving that mundane matter to his lawyer.

Billy stretched luxuriantly. Writing the first letter had been another rite of passage, re-establishing connectedness to Lew Wallace, not as a petitioner for pardon, but as a reporter in their mutual fight against injustice.

DECEMBER 15, 1880   8:12 AM   WEDNESDAY

Outside Comstock's Saloon in White Oaks, thick snow fell steadily. Hitching posts were crowded with horses of Pat Garrett's thirty-two possemen inside. All were Texans, except for Barney Mason; and none of the traumatized townsmen had come.

Garrett sat with the Panhandle Cattleman's Association detective, Frank Stewart; Barney Mason; Charlie Siringo, representing the LX men; and Bob Roberson from the LIT.

Siringo said, "We're chasin' a meerage. Not one cow round Sumner. Oly two mules at Yerby's. Like I firs' tol' ye, Garrett, I met the Kid in Tascosa in seveny-eight; he wasn' doin' nothin.'"

Bob Roberson drawled, "Men don' move cattle in the snow."

Frank Stewart with round, brown-mustached face and a truncated chest making his gunbelt look high-waisted, said, "Poe found fourteen LIT hides at Pat Coghlan's ranch."

"Mons ago," said Roberson. "An' fourteen's nothin'. Garrett, ye ever workt cattle?"

Stewart, beside Garrett, slapped him encouragingly on the back and said, "You boys don't go out in this kind of weather. Takes a buffalo hunter like Pat to get the job done. Right, Pat?"

Garrett glanced thankfully and said, "We're hunting men, not cattle."

Wanting to escape additional humiliating lying, he added, "We're riding out."

Charlie Siringo announced that he and the LX boys were heading to Anton Chico for supplies. Bob Roberson joked that they'd never see him again, what with cash in his pocket and saloons for gambling.

Pat Garrett rose, imposing in a long black overcoat from Dolan, and said, "I'm going to Puerto de Luna. Then Sumner. Who's riding with Mason and me?" Frank Stewart confirmed.

Loud talk was of men avoiding the foul weather. Bob Roberson said, "I'm sendin' my LIT boys: Louis Bozman, 'The Animal,' an' 'Poker' Tom Emory." Charlie Siringo called that LX men wouldn't come in second, and volunteered Lon Chambers, Lee Hall, and Jim East.

Bob Roberson asked if there'd be a supply wagon. "No," Garrett said disdainfully. "We're moving fast. Puerto de Luna's about a hundred miles. I want to be there by late tomorrow."

Frustrated by lack of more volunteers, Garrett said, "We've got our posse." He, Frank Stewart, Barney Mason, Lon Chambers, Jim East, Lee Hall, Louis Bozman, and Tom Emory walked out.

Eighty-seven miles northeast of White Oaks, in Fort Sumner, Billy, Tom O'Folliard, and Charlie Bowdre were eating in Beaver Smith's Saloon. Bowdre said, "Ah couldn' sleep. Ah wrote Pat mah lettah fohr a pardon, all the while thinkin' death's terrible."

Billy said, "It isn't, Charlie. It's your final weapon. Once you're willing to die, nothing can stop you. And I'd bet, even after I'm dead, our War will fire up some new Regulator who'll keep it going if we haven't won yet. But what 'ill you do if there's no pardon?"

Bowdre grinned: a cavalier with tilted hat and drooping mustache and goatee. "Then, goddamn, Ah'm proud tah ride with y'all."

Sixty-eight miles south of Fort Sumner, in Roswell, Azariah Wild said, as Ash Upson was writing his book at the Garretts' dining-room table, "I'm leaving." Asked if the mining was finished, Wild responded, "Mining? Oh, yes. It worked out."

DECEMBER 16, 1880   10:33 AM   THURSDAY

Having traveled through another snowstorm, Pat Garrett and his seven possemen had arrived at Puerto de Luna, which consisted of a few adobes around a plaza, one side being the way station of Alexander Grzelachowski, "Padre Polaco;" its overhanging porch with unexpectedly imposing posts.

Inside, the "Padre," a short, broad, curley-bearded man with bulbous meaty-nostriled nose, was in jovial conversation with his unexpected bounty of guests. "Zo, you cum frrom Vhite Oaks," he said to Garrett with guttural singsong.

Paying no attention, Garrett asked if he'd seen the Kid lately. "Not zince he stal my zixteen horrses."

Garrett asked the hare-lipped, sullen, young server if he understood English. Dark-skinned Juan Rioval nodded and took their order for more whiskey.

Returning, Rioval heard Garrett say, "Padre, I need someone who wouldn't make the Kid suspicious."

"Vere are you goink frrom here?"

"South. To Los Ojitos: John Gerhardt's Ranch. For the night." When the owner entered the kitchen, Juan Rioval whispered, "For thees ees money?"

Garrett did not look up. "Two fifty dollar gold pieces. When I get the information."

"Some gringos they cheat Mehican. Feefty dollar now ees good."

"Some Mexicans cheat gringos. I'll be at Gerhardt's bunkhouse. I want to know if he's in Sumner."

"You weell tell 'Padre' for to let me go. And to geeve me good horse."

Twenty-five miles southeast of Puerto de Luna, Billy, Tom O'Folliard, Charlie Bowdre, Dave Rudabaugh, Billy Wilson, and Tom Pickett were playing poker at Hargrove's Saloon when Saval Gutierrez, Jesús Silva, Pedro Lucero, and José Valdéz entered. Silva came to Billy before returning to the others. Billy reported, "Jesús says no one's seen Pat for a while. But Texans were scouting around recently. It might not be safe here."

Later, Billy checked the parade ground in flake-filled twilight, and noticed a rider enter the quadrangle and cut its deep snow sheet in ultramarine wake. Soon, a split-lipped dark youth entered, shaking snow-laden serape and sombrero, and went to Jesús Silva and his companions.

To his tablemates, Billy said, "Snow's picking up. After we eat, I say we head back to Brazil's." Short-legged Charlie Bowdre, feeing uneasy, said he'd ride with them.

Soon Jesús Silva brought the youth, telling Billy he had requested an introduction. Billy stood, saying in Spanish that they had already met at the sheep camp of Francisco Lobato. In November, two years past, when Yginio Salazar was staying with people he trusted. Juan Rioval flushed with shame and said, "Yginio ... he is very brave;" extended a clammy hand; and felt confused, hoping for a mistake. He said, "You are called 'Keed?' " Billy smiled and nodded. Again Rioval reached out, before hurrying from the saloon.

Tom Pickett said, "Hell of a lot of handshaking. Like sealing a big deal."

On the way out, Billy stopped at Jesús Silva's table and said to the four, "We will be at Manuel Brazil's."

At almost two in the morning, Garrett opened John Gerhardt's bunkhouse door and looked down at goat-faced Juan Rioval. "Thees Keed ees een Sumner," he croaked, raw-throated from freezing air.

Two coins clicked on his dark palm. He turned, but felt a restraining hand. "If you warn him, I'm a sheriff and marshal. I'll arrest you."

Back in his bunk, Pat Garrett listened to the snoring men as he reached in his pants, feeling excited by the fear in Rioval's eyes, but seeing them as blue; seeing horses straining through snow, bits pulled tight. Control so complete. His saddlebags were heavy with Wild's shackles. Inescapable. A buffalo staggered, spraying blood. Engorged pleasure erupted in echoing "hunter, hunter."

DECEMBER 18, 1880   11:02 AM   SATURDAY

In gusting blizzard, beside the Maxwell family cemetery, Pat Garrett waited, mounted, squinting over a masking muffler.

Finally, hawk-faced Barney Mason appeared, shouting that the Kid had been there, but was gone. And most of the men were out taking care of the herds; winter lambs were freezing.

They rode to Beaver Smith's Saloon where that muttonchopped man in his empty saloon said, "Come te pay yer bill, Garrett?"

Garrett laughed. "Why I froze my cods off. Seen the Kid?"

"I ain' gettin' paid te track 'im," answered Beaver Smith.

Outside again, Mason said, "The stables. Always workers there."

They entered moist warmth and sweet vegetable smell. "Who's here?" Garrett called. Jesús Silva emerged with a curry brush. "Anybody else?" Only José Valdéz, Silva answered. "Wouldn't know where the Kid is, would you?" The denial was suspiciously immediate.

Meanwhile, Barney Mason had proceeded down the corridor and turned in at a distant stall. When Garrett approached, he heard, "No, Señor. Heem I does not know."

Mason said, "You've been here a few years. You're lying." José Valdéz, seeing Pat Garrett at the stall exit, realized he was trapped. "Silva can't hear," Mason added.

Garrett unbuttoned his overcoat, took out a pouch, and exposed gold coins, saying he was a sheriff and marshal, and asking Valdez how long it would take him to earn a hundred dollars. "Years, Señor. And I owes patrón's store. Who knows?" Garrett said it would be his for one day's work.

José Valdéz walked to the halfway point and asked, "What ees thees work?" It was to deliver a letter to the Kid. Then come back to tell him.

"This Keed he ees wanting by the law?" For murder and rustling, Garrett said.

In Peter Maxwell's tack room, Valdez sat at the desk, penciling his version of Garrett's dictation. " *'José Valdéz write to tell Sheref Garet y his men go to Rozwel. Now in Sumner it is safety.'*

"And eef I find heem, where I find you, Señor Shereef Garrett?"

"In my sister-in-law's house."

"Please no tell Saval or Celsa. Eef this Keed murder like you say, I protects my life."

After José Valdéz left, Garrett said to Mason, "When he comes back - and, sure as hell, he knows where he's going - I'll ride back to Gerhardt's and bring back the men."

That night, at the Gutierrez's table, Garrett drank whiskey and said, "So Saval's out with the shepherds?" Celsa stretched languorously to raise her blouse-hidden breasts, and asked if he was hungry. He smiled. "Hope Saval appreciates what he's got." She said an old man was always tired. But *he* also was away from home. Garrett's face closed. "I'm there as much as I can." Beginning to prepare food, she said sometimes he looked sad, and glanced hopefully. But preoccupied with overwhelming responsibility, he was drinking heavily.

Six miles due east of Fort Sumner, at the Brazil ranch, Billy, O'Folliard, Bowdre, Rudabaugh, Pickett, Wilson, and the owner were at a long table. Juan Gallegos, the cook, brought more food. Billy said to small, bearded Brazil, "So one of your hands said José Valdéz gave him this note, Manuel?"

"Yes," Brazil answered. "How did he know you were here?" Billy said he'd told him and other friends in Sumner. "So you go back tomorrow? You think Garrett will not search for you? He is sheriff."

"Of Lincoln County," Billy said. "He's got no jurisdiction here in San Miguel. And, by next month, he'll be too busy. Anyway, Sumner's safe because of our friends."

At the same time, at Celsa's, Pat Garrett responded to a knock. José Valdéz stood in moonlit albedo of snow. "Yes," he whispered.

DECEMBER 19, 1880   6:18 PM   SUNDAY

Besides the saloonkeeper, in Beaver Smith's, the only occupants were Garrett, his possemen, and Barney Mason. Frank Stewart and Lon Chambers sat together drinking coffee, while the others continued a poker game, started in mid-morning when they had arrived. Outside, Lee Hall stood watch.

Chambers asked Stewart, "Ain't this is excitin'? Gettin' Billy the Kid?" The short-waisted cattle detective said it was just part of his job.

Billy had watched the early darkness, only sixty hours before winter solstice when the northern hemisphere, tilting farthest from the sun, left darkness ascendant on the year's shortest day. Snowfall had stopped, but clouds sank to earth in listless opaque miasma of the full moon. He said, "Might as well head out for Sumner."

Lee Hall reentered. "Can' see," he said. "Fog's come in heavy."

Garrett sent out Lon Chambers for the next watch. Tom Emory asked him, "Really think the Kid's comin'? Not that I min' poker with you, Pat. I'll be playin' it in Hell if Satan doesn' have a better game." Garrett said he'd come, and called and raised two dollars.

Due east of Fort Sumner, Billy and the five others rode in hushed insulated anticipation. Billy said they'd be there in a few hours.

Lon Chambers paced the snow-drifted saloon walkway. Past the empty dance hall, was the fog-shadowed entrance road. In the saloon's light, he checked his pocket watch. 8:29. Inside, Tom Emory said, "Hell, Pat you've got a winnin' streak."

Billy sang, "One word more, our signal token, / Whistle up the marching tune, / Hurrah, my boys, for Ireland's freedom, / By the rising of the moon." Rudabaugh asked if he was Irish. "American. My Ma was Scotch-Irish."

Barney Mason grumbled, "They won't ride this late."

"I'm standing pat," Garrett said, looking at his cards. Pat's pat, joked Tom Emory.

Billy sang at 9:08 PM, as they turned into the town's entry road, plowing through snow, "Turkey in the straw, haw, haw, haw. / Turkey in the hay, hay, hay, hay, / Roll 'em up and twist 'em up ..." His voice, muted by the nimbus, echoed off the adobe-walled narrows.

Lon Chambers rushed into the saloon shouting, "Riders comin'!"

"Home!" called Tom O'Folliard at Billy's right, and enthusiastically spurred Red to the lead. Glancing left into the fog, he saw, backlit by the saloon's windows, shadow men.

"Ambush!" he yelled, wrenching Red's reins leftward to block Cimarron; then swerving to become Billy's shield.

Pat Garrett's perfunctory shout of "Surrender, throw down ..." was lost in deafening gunfire which he initiated.

One bullet struck Dave Rudabaugh's horse, who bucked a single jump, but galloped with the others back down the corridor.

"Hell," cursed Jim East, "they got away."

But slowly, a horse meandered into the light, his husky rider slumped. Garrett grabbed the slack reins. With disappointment, he said, "It's Tom O'Folliard."

Lois Bozman and Tom Emory pulled him off, but unprepared for his weight, merely broke his fall as he screamed in pain. He was lifted.

At the door, Beaver Smith said, "I don' wan' blood in here. He's the oly un?" Frank Stewart said they had his tarp.

At Pat Garrett's direction, O'Folliard was laid beside his chair. Garrett knelt and opened the boy's coat.

He informed him, "Bullet's at the heart. Won't take long;" and sat, saying, "My turn. I call and raise two dollars."

O'Folliard asked where Billy was. "Dead outside," Garrett said. "We got him."

O'Folliard struggled to rise, crying, "No! I protecked ..." frothing blood.

Lee Hall said that was cruel. Someone dying deserved the truth. "Boy," he said loudly, "the Kid got away." Tom O'Folliard relaxed, smiling into death's tremor.

"Barney," Garrett said, "do me a favor. Head to Maxwell's. Ask Pete what to do with him."

Beaver Smith said, "Joe Gran' got a hole ouside o' town."

DECEMBER 20, 1880   3:18 PM   MONDAY

Heavy snowfall left no visibility from windows of Manuel Brazil's ranch for Billy, Dave Rudabaugh, Charlie Bowdre, Billy Wilson, and Tom Pickett, now trapped after their desperate return ride from the ambush.

Early that morning, before the storm's arrival, Brazil had left, volunteering to check Fort Sumner for Garrett's presence.

Now, serving them coffee, Juan Gallegos asked apprehensively why José Valdéz had written that Garrett had returned to Roswell. Billy answered, "Maybe Garrett *was* going, but the last storm stopped him. Valdéz knows about the War. It would be like going against his own people, if that's what you mean." Rudabaugh rasped that it wouldn't be the first time. The bastard could even lead Garrett back.

"Soon as the snow lets up, let's cle-ah out," said Bowdre. "Head to Portales, then Texas."

"I need a horse," said Rudabaugh, smoking one cigarette after the other. "Lucky mine made it a ways. And lucky Wilson's horse managed the two of us. Unlucky that this is the last of my tobacco."

"But why 're they chasin' us?" asked Wilson, with oversized broad face and a continuous black eyebrow. "An' killin' Tom for nothin'."

"We don't know he's dead," said Billy. "Maybe we should part ways. They're after me."

"Kid," Rudabaugh teased, "you may feel famous, but that sucker, Carlyle, thought we all are."

"Then we'll ride tomorrow," Billy said. "Juan, we'll need provisions. And I'll pay for a new horse for Dave."

At Fort Sumner, Manuel Brazil, snow-crusted and with ice-coated beard hairs, was hurrying anxiously into Beaver Smith's Saloon where townspeople, in agitated conversation, avoided Tom O'Folliard's transitory memorial of disturbed sawdust on the floor.

At the bar, Brazil asked Beaver Smith for privacy, and was taken to a back room, where he said, "I need to find the sheriff Garrett."

Smith said, "Eas' barracks. People 're angry. I'd watch my step."

Riding along the white-drifted rear of the joined adobes, Brazil saw two strangers walk out and reenter. There he knocked.

Lon Chambers opened the door, Colt .44 in hand. "Pat," he called. "Greaser to see you." Garrett, stooping at the low doorway between rooms, came out.

Brazil said, "Sheriff, I come to say the Kid came to my ranch last night with a gang. To stay, they threatened my life and spoke of Greathouse and Spencer. I do not want burned down my ranch."

Garrett said, "Tomorrow, when this weather lets up, you'll lead us back. I'm not walking into an ambush."

One hundred twenty-eight miles northwest of Fort Sumner, Lew Wallace, in his office, said to his secretary, "Possibly being a writer should be a prerequisite for being a governor, since writing occupies all one's time." Tim Henley waited attentively with bent limp-wristed arm. "As I as saying, when *Ben-Hur* came out last month on the twelfth, the reviews were superlative. Sales promise soon to exhaust the printing of five thousand."

"By the way, Sir, I left you a letter. I reviewed it. Dated the twelfth, from William Bonney."

Wallace laughed. "Yes, yes. I saw it. Another bloody murder committed by him, and I receive its denial and the rogue's lament that an outlaw's property is sacred before the law."

Henley said, "Also, it's been impossible to get a copy of that Lincoln County District Court transcript for April of seventy-nine, where he testified. I contacted Judge Bristol, who said - at least temporarily - it's lost. I ..."

"Waste no more time. As to that court's indictments, I gather that - except for Bonney's own and his outlaw compatriots' - Judge Bristol dismissed them all in the October session of the Doña Ana District Court. Did you draw up my notice for J.H. Koogler for his *Las Vegas Gazette*?" The secretary located it, saying it was to appear on December twenty-second.

Wallace read: *"BILLY THE KID. $500 REWARD. I will pay $500 reward to any person or persons who will capture William Bonny, alias The Kid, and deliver him to any Sheriff of New Mexico. Satisfactory proofs of identity will be required. Lew Wallace, Governor of New Mexico Territory."*

Henley cautiously interjected, "But didn't you promise him a pardon for his testimony, Sir?"

Wallace answered, "Alongside the Christ, were crucified two thieves. Of Him, one demanded rescue. The other accepted his transgressions and said, 'Lord remember me when thy comest into thy Kingdom.' And Jesus answered, 'Verily I say unto thee, today shalt thou be with me in paradise.' Bonney is unrepentant as the first miscreant. The Christ knew that salvation, a pardon, comes from acceptance of guilt. Christ made his choice. I made mine: I shall not pardon William Bonney."

DECEMBER 21, 1880   6:03 PM   TUESDAY

In landscape of snow, Billy and the others rode eastward in plowing slow escape, with Dave Rudabaugh complaining that they would freeze to death before Portales and his rheumatism was killing him. They had to stop. And no one knew where they were anyway. Charlie Bowdre, Tom Pickett, and Billy Wilson agreed.

Billy sighed and said, "It's Stinking Springs then, boys."

Seventy-eight miles southwest of their group, Azariah Wild, departing the Territory, was sitting beside a toothless wagon driver as two bony mules plodded, and asked if he had heard any news about recent attacks by the Billy the Kid gang. "I don' know nothin' 'bout sitch things," gummed the man. "I'll be stoppin' soon. This was a hell of a storm. These is the oly mules I got."

At 9:32 PM, Pat Garrett and his six horsemen waited in arctic cold, with faces too numb to feel occasional striking flakes, and watched Manuel Brazil's return from checking his ranch. They were gone, he called. Garrett and his possemen followed him back to his corral. Trampled snow outside its gate made a dark pool. The waning moon, lacking only its right edge, allied with reflective land as if compensating for the failing sun which, at this day of winter solstice, shone less than eight hours. But only darkness flowed through the fresh trench: a line unfurling like a huge black rope attached to the riders. Garrett smiled. "We've got our tracks."

Eight miles east of Manuel Brazil's ranch, in the rock house of Stinking Springs, the betraying path ended. Alejandro Perea had fit its flat rocks, as if attempting to restore the sedimentary sheets of the lost ocean's bed, and had chosen to orient the structure in exact harmony with the four directions. Walking deep in the big arroyo fronting it, he had lifted a golden-tan stone, whose mica flecks reminded him of stars. And in that empty flat land, Alejandro Perea's little building was man's only creation, an inadvertent temple immortalizing minute marine organisms in stone.

Now, tied to its hitching post, in snow to their hocks, stood five horses. Closest to the door was Cimarron. To her left was Wilson's horse, followed by Bowdre's Rebel, then Pickett's, and, last, Rudabaugh's sturdy black provided by Juan Gallegos.

Inside, all were asleep except for Charlie Bowdre mentally obsessing, "Even with pickaxes Tom's grave would be shallah in frozen ground." Bowdre went to the stove and put in their last wood.

DECEMBER 22, 1880   1:16 AM   WEDNESDAY

Charlie Bowdre had finally fallen asleep as seven riders approached in darkness. "This is it, boys," announced Garrett. "No windows, no portholes. Just one door. Stewart and Chambers, guard the back. The rest of us will be hidden in an arroyo up front. Remember: the Kid wears a Mexican sombrero with a green band."

When Bowdre awoke to dawn's gray light, he realized his face was stiff. "Like de-ath," came to his mind. He looked at Billy and was surprised to see his eyes open, head pillowed on bent arms.

Dave Rudabaugh moved and groaned, "Son of a whore rheumatism. Neck feels like hell. If I hadn't tried to rescue my partner, and if that goddamn Mexican deputy hadn't gotten in the way of my bullet, and if they wouldn't lynch me in Vegas, I'd have gotten rich there."

Billy rolled his bedding, laying his sombrero to the side. "Where's the corn?" asked Bowdre. "Ah'll feed the horses." Billy pointed. Tom Pickett shook Billy Wilson awake.

Charlie Bowdre asked, "Where's mah hat?" No one answered. He put on Billy's sombrero, slung over his arm two canvas nosebags with corn, and walked out.

They could hear him say, "Rebel," and nickering. The other horses jostled, so Bowdre freed his thick-coated brown mustang and slipped on the bag, walking him toward the doorway.

From the south, came a cough. Bowdre grabbed his Colt.

As in a nightmare, men's heads hovered above the snow. Their gunfire shattered the silence as the eastern sky burst into gold.

Billy, crouching at the doorway, blocked by Bowdre and Rebel, could not shoot. Lying flat, he slipped out and caught Rebel's dangling reins; calling, "Charlie, this way."

Instead, in confusion of pain and blood loss from the two bullets in his chest and one in his left thigh, Bowdre, coughing redness onto snow, stumbled toward the invisible arroyo.

Using the concealment of the entering horse, now pulled by Pickett, Billy freed Cimarron and Wilson's. His mare came in, but Wilson's gelding balked.

Charlie Bowdre was walking to Manuela. The possemen, inexperienced with killing, except for Garrett, watched fascinated. "I wish ..." Bowdre said to her as he toppled into the abyss.

Billy saw Bowdre's fall into the illusion of nothingness, then grabbed the reins of Wilson's gelding.

"They're leading the horses in," shouted Jim East. Garrett fired into the gelding's shoulder. An immediate second made a diagonal into the heart. The fallen animal, partially inside, blocked the door.

"Damn," spit Billy in fury; but called sociably, "That you, Pat?" Survival would now depend on manipulation.

"Yes," Garrett shouted back. "Thought it was you in that sombrero, Kid."

"Easier ways to get a hat."

"Why don't you surrender?"

"A possibility. How'd you find us?" To the answer tracks, Billy called, "Makes no sense."

"You're surrounded. Come out and talk."

"Rather not. You're shooting anything that might be me. Even a horse."

There was silence.

Bowdre's body was dragged to the gully floor. Garrett sidestepped down. With satisfaction, he checked the bullet holes in the vest, claiming them as his; and took from the wallet a carte-de-visite. He said, "Got his genuine blood on it. Could be valuable." Louis Bozman, watching him pocket it, felt disgust.

Billy shouted, "Pat, thought your jurisdiction was Lincoln County."

"I'm also a Deputy U.S. Marshal." He confirmed having warrants.

Bozeman asked Garrett about rushing them. "No purpose. They'll come out eventually. Jim, go back to Brazil's. Get a wagon for that." He gestured with his head to Bowdre's corpse. "And food and firewood."

"I see it this way," Billy said to his companions, "with Charlie, I'd bet Pat's embarrassed. And our chances 'ill improve by nightfall."

"With no cover and two horses for us four," said Dave Rudabaugh sarcastically.

Within their dim, cold, crowded stone box, as the sun made its arc, Billy struggled to tear out the stovepipe for access to the roof, while Wilson and Pickett controlled the frightened horses and Rudabaugh complained about absurdity - especially Billy's alternative plan to jump his mare over the dead horse. "Zero chance," Rudabaugh said; adding, "It's suicide;" while the door's bright opening taunted with a mirage of freedom.

In evening, the wagon returned. Bowdre's body was loaded. Cooking odors wafted. "Any coffee, Pat?" Billy called from the interior, in which the men could barely see each other.

"What worries me," said Rudabaugh, "is going to the Vegas jail. I'll be lynched." Billy sighed and said it could be their condition of surrender. "Then I'll go out," said Rudabaugh.

He tied his handkerchief to a manzanita twig, followed Bowdre's crushed path to the arroyo edge, and said to Pat Garrett, "We're sticking together. If you take us to Vegas, the Mexicans will lynch me." Garrett agreed to Santa Fe. Rudabaugh said they'd still pass through Vegas. "I'll make sure you're protected. Tell the Kid to send the horses out first."

When Rudabaugh reentered, all the gear and weapons had been neatly piled. Struck on their rumps with hats, Billy using Bowdre's black square-crowned one, the horses leapt over their dead. Hopeful squeals came from the other two horses, still tied, hungry and thirsty.

The four captives clambered, hands up, over the equine cadaver, the moon casting their progressing shadows, as five men with carbines rose in the blue-white wasteland. "Evenin', Pat," said Billy, wearing Bowdre's hat. "How 'bout dinner?"

As the captives ate, the Texan possemen kept glancing at Billy, Barney Mason having remained in Fort Sumner after the first ambush. Frequently, Billy met their gaze and smiled pleasantly. Jim East finally said he couldn't believe he was so young. "Getting older all the time. Where d'we head from here, Pat?" The answer was Brazil's ranch. Then Sumner.

When the caravan of captors and captives departed Stinking Springs, followed by the wagon driven by Lon Chambers, they left one dead horse and, from the small stone structure, a shadowed furrow which ended abruptly in the moon-silvered land, as if the walkers had suddenly, bird-like, become airborne. But from above could be seen the gaping, black, serpentine ravine with a cookfire dying within.

DECEMBER 23, 1880   11:12 AM   THURSDAY

The journey had begun. After departing Brazil's ranch in howling air, in the wagon Billy sat shackled, right wrist to Rudabaugh's left, beside the blanket-wrapped corpse; with Billy Wilson and Tom Pickett likewise chained together.

Pat Garrett and his possemen rode guard, Frank Stewart on Cimarron.

"Manuel," Billy called, "why'd you take back Dave's horse? I paid for it." Brazil pretended not to hear. Already received by him from Garrett were gold coins, partial payment to transport the prisoners to Las Vegas.

The first destination was the rear of Fort Sumner's eastern block of barracks. Garrett said, "I'll talk to Bowdre's wife." Finally, he reemerged. "I didn't tell her what we were bringing in; so be prepared." After a few minutes, they exited with loud laughter.

Soon, Beaver Smith brought plates to the saloon table with Garrett; Billy; Rudabaugh; Frank Stewart; Jim East; and Barney Mason, who had joined them. At another table were Billy Wilson and Tom Pickett with Lee Hall, Lon Chambers, Tom Emory, and Louis Bozman.

Garrett was in barely controllable hypomania at the magnitude of his achievement. He said to Mason, "So we'd frozen our cods off in that wash. They didn't expect a thing." He turned to Billy. "Did you?" No, Billy answered, eating hungrily. It was a complete surprise.

Garrett continued. "Out walks someone in a sombrero. So I cut him down. Thought it was the Kid."

"Thanks, Pat," Billy said. "Where's my hat anyway?"

"One of the boys took it. Because it was yours." Billy said it still was. Garrett scowled, and continued to Mason, "At Manuela's, I've never seen a female that mad. She came at us with a poker. We dropped him. Frozen stiff. Hit the floor like a log." Garrett laughed as Billy became pale. "So I said I'd pay for a burying suit. She didn't even thank me."

Mason said he'd heard he'd paid for O'Folliard's coffin. Jesús Silva had dug the grave and had told him.

"So Tom is dead," Billy said, masking pain. "Where's he buried, Barney?"

"Listen to this, Pat," the hawk-faced man said, ignoring Billy. "You won't believe it. The Maxwells put him in *their* cemetery. Even had Jesús Silva make a cross."

Billy smiled wistfully. "That means Tom's right there with Lucien Maxwell. Goddamn."

Garrett called out, "Beaver, we'll need supplies. Want to make Gerhardt's ranch tonight."

Beaver Smith came to their table. "Now tha' yer rollin' in money, Garrett, might as well pay up yer bill here. I'd like a suit 'for I'm dead." Garrett laughed and said he could tell people someone famous ate there.

"Who?" Smith asked spitefully. To Billy, he said, "Ye got an owstandin' bill too, Kid."

Billy said, "These boys were wanting my Colt .44 and Thunderer. You can have 'em. White Oaks boys already stole my Winchester."

"Kid," said Stewart, "that bay mare of yours. I'd like her."

Rage surged, but Billy said, "As a *loan*, Frank." Stewart glanced mirthfully at Garrett, hanging being inevitable, and said it was a deal.

Deluvina's entry distracted attention. She stopped expressionless beside Garrett and said, "Missus Maxwell asks for Billy Bonney to be brought to her home for a farewell."

Garrett slid his chair back and said, "Frank, you and East come with me." Rudabaugh said he wasn't invited. "Sorry, boys. Harder for two to make a break than one."

Town residents had gathered. Billy's eyes met those of Jesús Silva; Pedro Lucero; Paco Anaya; and Saval Gutierrez with Celsa, concealing emotion. The visiting Sunnyside postmaster, Milnor Rudulph, had joined the curious as Billy led the procession across the parade ground with Rudabaugh, followed by their captors.

At the mansion's picket fence, Garrett slowed with confusion. Billy said, "Entrance is at the southeast corner, Pat. Used to be Lucien Maxwell's room. Now it's Pete's office and bedroom."

Deluvina opened the front door to the hallway of chandeliers. Distant festivities could be heard. Billy flushed, knowing among Christmas guests would be José Jaramillo.

In the drawing-room, Billy's sole focus was Paulita, blanched with terror. She and her mother approached with her brother shambling reluctantly to Pat Garrett and extending his soft hand. "Nice of you to indulge the whim of the women. I've got guests to see to," he said and departed.

Luz Maxwell said to Billy, "I want you to know that Charles Bowdre will be buried beside that other man."

To Garrett she continued sweetly, "I do not want my daughter exposed to a common criminal. So, if you please, unchain Mister Bonney to say goodbye."

Self-importantly, Garrett announced he was too dangerous. Her voice became venomous. "Then give us privacy."

As Dave Rudabaugh teared up remembering his mother's love, Luz Maxwell squeezed Billy's free hand, while Paulita wept. But Billy smiled, put his arm around the girl, and whispered, "I'm here ..." His warm sweet breath brushed her cheek. "With you ... Now."

"Alright," called out Garrett. "Let's go."

"Billy," Paulita said, "one more goodbye."

He looked sidelong, dark-lashed eyes flashing, and playfully said, "I'll be back."

By the time they were on the porch, Pat Garrett's mood had plummeted at the unexpected rejection. He felt reduced to a manufactured sheriff of a bogus case.

Inside, Luz Maxwell was praying to Lucien to protect Billy; while Paulita and Deluvina returned to the room where the three had hoped to take him, where outside waited a saddled fleet horse.

One hundred eight miles northwest of Fort Sumner, Azariah Wild was reviewing his report at the Santa Fe Grand Central Hotel. "*Arriving in Santa Fe I visited the banks and found there were no complaints of counterfeit money. Information has reached me that Fred Kuch (one of the Billie the Kid Gang at Greathouse's Ranch) has left for South America. I am also in receipt of information that U.S. Deputy Marshal Pat Garrett has killed at least one of the outlaws and is in pursuit of the balance. Also Jessie James is surely with them under the name of Campbell. I have that on good information.*"

DECEMBER 25, 1880   3:13 PM   SATURDAY

Waiting for their turn at Alexander Grzelachowski's Chrismas dinner, Billy and Dave Rudabaugh looked out a rear window where their captors' horses tantalizingly stood. Their guard, Jim East, sat beside a fireplace to their left.

Over their days of attachment, Billy and Rudabaugh had devised wrist iron communication by staccato jerks. Now, the metal tapped, making Rudabaugh eye the only door.

Jim East said, "They're taking long enough to eat. Was a goddamn long ride from Gerhardt's." He lit a cigarette. Billy asked about sharing tobacco. "Shur." The two walked toward him as he reached for his pouch. Suddenly East was aware. They were between him and the door, their chain taut-stretched between encircling irons. "Strangle me," he thought, and yelled, "Stop!" Both waited. "Ow!" he cried, singed by his forgotten cigarette, fallen on his thigh. Hearing footsteps, Billy said it was too late, but his offer sure was in the spirit of the day; and he smiled ingenuously.

Entering the dining-room, Billy noted that the far wall had a large window, a fragile barrier covered by lace curtain web. When Alexander Grzelachowski returned with more dishes, lifting his big bulbous nose, he said to Billy, "And vod did you do vif my zixteen horses, eh?"

"Helped you return 'em to their rightful owners, Padre." Tom Emory, guarding Wilson and Pickett, stifled a laugh.

Jim East said, "This here's the bes' Chrismas dinner I ever had."

Alexander Grzelachowski noticed Billy breaking bread, and thought, "Then Judas, which betrayed him, answered and said, 'Master is it I?' " He felt shame at being part of the capture and murmured to East, "Tank you. It iz our repootation."

"You said it, 'Padre,' " replied Billy to the man whose guilty retreating back was to him.

DECEMBER 26, 1880   1:53 PM   SUNDAY

The wagon driven by Manuel Brazil approached sprawling Las Vegas from the southeast, its two tired mules splattering red slush onto horses of Pat Garrett and his four remaining possemen, Lon Chambers, Lee Hall, and Louis Bozman having departed for Texas.

Rudabaugh said morosely, "Overnight's enough time for lynching. Ever see that giant windmill in Old Town plaza, Kid? Built years ago for some well. Those four posts going to the platform are over twelve feet tall. And another fifteen to the top of its tower. You get to that platform by a ladder thorough an opening. String a man up on the tower and make him jump into the hole.

"These goddamn bastards enjoy doing it so much that even on July fourth last year - when the Atchison, Topeka, and Santa Fe had their big celebration for the opening of the tracks - they hanged two men. Then they cut 'em down so the railroad committee could decorate the thing with bunting." Billy laughed, saying Pat would protect them. He'd given his word. Garrett heard as intended.

Rudabaugh taunted, "Like goddamn Brazil here. Goddamn Benedict Arnold. And Mason's another one. And goddamn my partner J.J. Webb. I never told you, Kid, but after all I did, the bastard wouldn't leave the cell! Tells me he wants to wait for the outcome of his appeal on his death sentence. And it wouldn't look sincere if he escaped. And I don't even want to think about Sheriff Romero. Antonio Váldez was his deputy. Mexican loyalty."

With Tom Pickett squeezing pimples beside Billy Wilson, lying lethargically on the bedrolls, they traveled along the Gallinas River, New Town to their right across it. "First time I ever intended to stay in custody," Rudabaugh rasped. "But if I don't get a cigarette soon, I'll ask them to hang me."

"Here comes the bridge," Billy called out, wearing Bowdre's black square-crowned hat at the same rakish angle as the murdered man. Through Garrett's mind passed, he can't be killed.

As their group clattered onto Bridge Street, people rushed to the spectacle. Pickett shook his companion's arm, but Wilson retched and spit up, not caring where it soiled. They heard, "Where's the Kid? Lynch Rudabaugh! Kid! Billy the Kid!"

Suddenly, a pug-nosed man rode up, threw into the wagon an opened newspaper, and said, "I'm J.H. Koogler, Kid. Own the *Las Vegas Gazette*. You're in it." Billy saw Lew Wallace's $500 reward notice. "I'll interview you tomorrow."

Pat Garrett, nodding grandly, was thinking, "The hero, the success. Papa, if only you ... Apolinaria." He pictured Dolan, Catron, and Chisum; all smiling.

The adobes of the original village on North Mexico Avenue, South Pacific Street, and South Gonzales Street, gave way to pretentious structures of the railway-induced boom. Seeing the plaza ahead, Billy said to Rudabaugh, "It *is* a natural gallows." Thanks, Rudabaugh responded. He needed that.

The wagon passed the plaza's west perimeter, turned left at its northern side, and proceeded onto a short road which led to Valencia Street and the dilapidated San Miguel County jail. From its heavy door, came squat, black-mustached, Sheriff Desiderio Romero, who announced officiously that he was receiving *his* prisoners.

Garrett, towering freakishly, said, "As Deputy U.S. Marshal, they're mine. And I'm protecting them."

Billy smiled meaningfully at Rudabaugh, who was too unnerved to notice. Billy called to Sheriff Romero, "Where's Deputy Sheriff Barrier?" Romero said he had moved - became a house painter.

Finally, they were led into a cell. Before Garrett left Stewart as guard, Billy flattered him with profuse thanks, as Pickett, chained to Wilson, was forced to sit on the cot beside his fetally curled body.

Billy began to pace, making Rudabaugh follow. At the walls, he surreptitiously pressed his boot; then said "We'll have to use your cards, Dave. The boys stole mine. Pickett, make room so we can play."

Stewart asked Billy how he managed to keep his spirits up. "Clear conscience, Frank."

DECEMBER 27, 1880   7:03 AM   MONDAY

At the cell bars, joining that day's Winchester-bearing guard, Tom Emory, stood a slim man with a pad, looking competitively over his shoulder. Billy sat, on the outer of two joined cots, right arm extended to Rudabaugh, lying on his back.

The visitor said humorlessly, "I'm Mister Kistler. Beat the *Gazette* reporter. My *Las Vegas Optic* usually does. Koogler says he made up "Billy the Kid." Is that true?"

"No," said Billy. "I heard it before his December third article. How about getting Sheriff Romero to unshackle me so we can go to a room and talk?" Tom Emory refused the request.

With pencil, Kistler jotted, "*Kid is about twenty years of age and has a bold and yet pleasant cast of countenance*;" and asked, "How'd you get your reputation? It's second only to Victorio's."

Billy laughed. "Thanks. I know what they did to him. The reputation is all lies. There's no gang. These men captured with me - and the one murdered in cold blood - Charles Bowdre - were employed at ranches. Three days before, the same possemen murdered my friend, Tom O'Folliard, in an ambush when we were riding into Fort Sumner for business."

Barry Kistler wrote, "*He laughed heartily when informed that the papers had built him up a reputation second only to that of Victorio. The Kid claims never to have had a large number of men, and that the few who were with him when captured were employed on a ranch. This is his statement and is given for what it is worth.*"

Angry voices could be heard. Kistler hurried. " 'Dirty Dave,' how do you feel about possible lynching?" Rudabaugh asked what the hell he thought he would feel. Kistler wrote, "*Dirty Dave' Rudabaugh, dressed and groomed as befitted his moniker, said he feared citizens would lynch him for his vicious cold-blooded murder of their deputy sheriff, Antonio Váldez, during an attempted jail break.*"

A man carrying food was let into the cell. In Spanish, Billy criticized the gritty beans. The man answered, "The people are with you. Many will come to the station."

Tom Emory asked what the greaser had said. "He's wanting you to open the door so he can leave," Billy answered. As it was relocked, Billy, with Rudabaugh in forced mimicry, crouched at the pot and spooned out platefuls. Billy said, "Mister Kistler, no wonder you had a desperate jailbreak. It was the beans."

Pat Garrett entered. Billy greeted him effusively and reported that the food was inedible. Garrett said, "There's a man out front with new suits for each of you. A mail contractor named Mike Cosgrove."

"Trying to get his name in the papers," rasped Rudabaugh. "It's a political appointment."

"Get the hell up to go out," said Tom Emory to Billy Wilson, and stepped inside with his Winchester. Garrett growled for him to back out, seeing the opportunity at the same time as Billy.

The prisoners were escorted by Emory and Garrett into draft blowing along the hallway from the open outside door, guarded by Barney Mason, Frank Stewart, and Jim East.

A striding pug-nosed man called out to Billy, who answered, "Mornin', Mister Koogler."

Fidgety Mike Cosgrove approached. He said, "Marshal Garrett, these are the new suits," but faced the newspaperman. "Bought with my *own* money. I'm the Mail Contractor." Ginger haired and middle-aged, he became distracted by curiosity. "Which of you's Billy the Kid?'" Billy smiled, saying he was; they'd met many times in Fort Sumner, Anton Chico - all along the Pecos. Cosgrove exclaimed, "Billy Bonney?! You're the Kid?!"

"I'm Billy Bonney." He laughed. "I didn't make up the rest. You've got Mister Koogler here to thank for that. And some other folks," he said more seriously, "who had a game of their own."

J.H. Koogler, holding a pad identical to his rival's, jotted: "*Mike Cosgrove, the obliging mail contractor, who often met the boys while on business down on the Pecos, came with bundles of new clothing. Outside a large crowd strained their necks to get a glimpse of the prisoners, who stood in the passageway like children waiting for Christmas gifts.*"

Cosgrove said to Garrett, "Could they put them on? To show people of San Miguel Country that …" The tall man reluctantly unshackled the prisoners. They rubbed sore wrists.

Koogler said, "Seems you're in a bad fix, Kid. You could be hanged. But you take it so easy."

Billy, smiled. "No use looking on the gloomy side just because the laugh's on me this round of the game." Koogler took the quote.

To Cosgrove, Billy said, "I'll save mine for later, Mike," as the others stripped to long underwear.

"Billy! Billy!" a female voice called, continuing in Spanish. Laughing, Billy walked outside with the tenacious reporter. The pretty girl called, "I love you." He tipped his hat, Charlie's hat, then stomped snow from his boots.

Koogler saw crying Mexican women and wrote, "*Billy the Kid was the attraction of the show. One would scarcely mistrust that he was the hero of the 'Forty Thieves' romance which this paper has been running in serial form for six weeks.*"

Billy said, "I was starting to think they'd convinced people I was a wild animal."

Koogler jotted, " '*There was a big crowd gazing at me, wasn't there,*' *he exclaimed, and then smilingly continued,* '*Well, perhaps some of them will think me half man now; everyone seems to think I was some kind of animal.*' "

Koogler realized he had never seen eyes that color of blue, and wrote, "*He did indeed look human. He looks like a schoolboy with silky fuzz on his upper lip, clear blue eyes with a roguish snap about them, and light hair. He is, in all, quite a handsome fellow. He certainly has winning ways.*"

Billy called to his audience, "Anyone know if the jail in Santa Fe is bad as this?" It was the same, someone answered. "Then I'll have to play that hand," he said. Some cheered.

Back inside, Billy picked up his paper-wrapped bundle. Wilson and Pickett had packaged their cast-offs in the wrapping paper; but Rudabaugh's old clothes lay in a rancid heap.

Sheriff Desiderio Romero, with freshly-polished badge, faced Garrett with premeditated challenge. "Deputy Marshal, you can take 'the Kid' and Wilson only. Rudabaugh stays for the murder of

Antonio Váldez." Rudabaugh's flamboyant mustache and big ragged goatee jerked apprehensively.

"And I checked your warrants. There is none for Tom Pickett."

"You got no warrant on me, Garrett?" the youth exclaimed. "You'da killed me if I'da walked out 'stead of Bowdre."

Angrily, Garrett loomed over the short sheriff and said, "There are federal charges against Dave Rudabaugh for mail robbery and counterfeiting. Those go above Territorial ones. He's mine."

Romero wheedled: "Leave Rudabaugh and I'll give you Pickett," awkwardly addressing the underside of Garrett's chin.

"Rudabaugh comes with me. Shackle him to the Kid, boys."

From outside, came muffled shouts about lynching. Garrett said, "East, Stewart, and Emory, I'll still need you for the train. Barney, you ride with us to the station. We may have a fight." Billy rewarded him with a filial smile. "Brazil's wagon is ready. Sheriff Romero, they're your citizens and you're the law." Resentfully, the squat man strode past, flaring his arms to exaggerate his puffed chest.

Tom Pickett and Mike Cosgrove remained. The mail contractor said, "You can keep the suit," precipitating, to his discomfiture, the youth's cathartic sobbing, face buried in hands.

As the three prisoners were loaded, Manuel Brazil said fearfully to Pat Garrett, "I heard the talk. A Mexican mob is at the station."

Coldly, Garrett asked for his money back. Already on horseback, Barney Mason, Frank Stewart, Tom Emory, and Jim East brandished their carbines. Garrett mounted as the crowd gave reluctant clearance and the mules again began their patient journey.

Billy whispered, "So digging out could 'ave worked?"

Rudabaugh whispered, "Yes. Ground's soft at those adobes with white flakes. The suckers don't realize that water's seeping in. Anything metal works. Sharpen it by scraping on the bricks."

Billy said that was good news. Seemed the one in Santa Fe was like it. "Wondered why you were asking. But I'll never see it."

Teasing, Billy said, in that case, it was time to teach him the 'Rudabaugh Move.' Rudabaugh chuckled. "Not a chance. If I make it, we'll be playing poker. My only advantage now."

"Glad you're not folding yet."

Billy said to Wilson, "They let Pickett off. Probably you'll get off too." The boy lay with his bundle clutched to belly. "Didn't figure you'd take it this hard."

Rudabaugh said, "Injustice, betrayal, and threat of hanging does that to some people, Kid."

Again they crossed the Gallinas River. Billy said, "I've never been on a train before. Always wanted to."

He called to Frank Stewart, on a different horse, "Where's Cimarron?" Stewart lied that he'd left her at a livery.

Bridge Street, continuing eastward, became National. "This is all real familiar," said Billy to Rudabaugh. "New Town." Crossing Grand Avenue, the street angled southward and intersected Railroad Avenue, as the district became one of saloons, shacks, and warehouses.

Manuel Brazil slowed the team at the sight of the distant crowd, but was forced by Garrett to proceed. A train bound north for the Raton Pass was exiting, bell clanging. Its locomotive's smoke stack, belching a black cloud, flared six feet above the long cylindrical boiler body with mounted bell and steamdome. Below the front's big headlight, the ribbed cowcatcher jutted, skimming the iron rail tracks. Billy waved at the engineer in the square wooden cab. Following was the tender with coal and water; and, behind that, the baggage car and passenger ones.

Manuel Brazil, with difficulty, controlled the fearful mules as the vehicle rumbled past, trembling the ground.

The mob, shouting threateningly, stood beside the two story, red-brown, depot building with shingled slanted roof. Brazil demanded payment. Garrett gave him two fifty dollar gold coins and said, "Drive closer. We'll hitch our horses to this."

Alongside a passenger car, the prisoners were brought down. Garrett ordered Brazil, "Wait for Stewart, Emory, and East in town. They'll be back tomorrow."

The prisoners and guards rushed up a passenger car's metal steps and through its narrow rear door, frightening passengers, who hurried to other cars, except for two drunken men with Sharps rifles. One called to Garrett. "Ain' had a chance to shoot a greaser in weeks."

Directing his charges, Pat Garrett paid no attention. Billy smiled at him sweetly, eliciting confusing affection. Garrett said to him, "If I have to, I'll arm you all."

At a seat to the left, Billy opened the window to see the mob as Rudabaugh groveled to the floor. Billy announced excitedly, "They're rough. Wish we had 'em in Lincoln in seventy-eight. Pat, arm us now." Garrett merely smiled.

Billy waved his free hand and shouted, "Mornin', Mister Koogler!" Having run past the shouting men in the tracks, the reporter panted that it looked bad. Billy said, "Pat Garrett gave his word he'd protect us. But damn being in these;" and raised his right hand with the wrist iron, which forced Rudabaugh up. "He said he might arm us all."

J.H. Koogler wrote: *"We saw Billy the Kid again at the depot where the crowd presented a warlike appearance. He leaned out* of the train and told the reporter that the prospect of a fight exhilarated him, and he bitterly bemoaned being chained and lamented, 'If I only had my Winchester, I'd lick the whole crowd.' The burden of his desire was to be set free to fight on the side of his captors as soon as he should smell powder." Koogler said, "All I want's the truth."

"Sure," said Billy. "You'd need to understand our freedom fight against the Santa Fe Ring. They killed or ran out of the Territory most of our side except for me."

Koogler wrote. "*He said, 'I wasn't the leader of any gang. I was for Billy all the time.'* What about the thousands of head of cattle and horses the Billy the Kid gang rustled?"

"That was a lie to cover up Ring crimes. And I couldn't clear my name 'cause Governor Wallace - who'd promised me a pardon - never put it in proper writing. They pulled me into court in Lincoln on old warrants from the War there, and changed the venue to Doña Ana. So I skinned out."

Koogler wrote, "*I went up to Lincoln to stand my trial on warrants out for me, but the Territory took a change of venue to Doña Ana so I skinned out;*" and asked, "What about your capture?"

"Last week, Pat Garrett and his men ambushed us in Fort Sumner. So we decided to leave the Territory till things quieted down. The storm stopped us at Stinking Springs. He ambushed us again there."

Koogler wrote, " *'They wouldn't let me settle down so I was going to leave. If they hadn't ambushed us I wouldn't be here today.'* " Koogler asked, "If you were free, should certain men fear your revenge?"

"No. But John Chisum's responsible. He let our side down."

Koogler wrote, "*Chisum got me into all this trouble and then wouldn't help me out.*"

There was angry mob shouting, as an armed man entered the locomotive. "That's J.F. Morley!" Koogler cried. "Was a Deputy U.S. Marshal." Flat-footedly he ran in that direction.

As the engineer cowered, Morley released the brake, then pushed the Johnson bar lever forward, opening the steam valves. Pulling the throttle back with his other hand, he released steam to the cylinders. With wheels activated, the great machine chuffed smoke and engaged the tracks. Koogler saw Billy waving Charlie's black hat and shouting, "Write the truth, Koogler. Adiós!"

The mobbing crowd leapt out of the rail bed. The reporter scribbled, "*As the train rolled out, Billy the Kid lifted his hat and invited us to come and see him in Santa Fe, calling out, 'Adiós.'* "

Billy turned to Garrett, sitting with Mason in the seat behind, and asked, "How fast d'you figure we're going?" Garrett answered that, at other times, the conductor said thirty miles an hour. "You've already ridden this train to Santa Fe?" Billy asked with surprise.

There was an image of Catron stacking gold coins. Garrett thought, "And no one knows about Chisum." He responded, "When campaigning for sheriff." He called out, "Good work," to J.F. Morley, entering their car. Morley asked, to Garrett's irritation, if he'd be getting some of that reward money he would be pocketing.

Across from Billy and Rudabaugh, were Tom Emory and Billy Wilson. In front of them sat Jim East and Frank Stewart, whose phrase, "the bay mare," Billy heard.

Windows across the aisle blurred passing Sangre de Cristo Mountains. Checking his own view, Billy was startled to see, descending from the sky, a gigantic spider; before realizing it dangled, as an illusion, close to his face, but against the outside panorama. She had waited to meet him for two hundred and fifty million years of progenitors, first in Permian seas, then on exposed dry land. Seeing with four eyes, she reached eager pincered legs. But a jolt frightened her, and she somersaulted upward along her dragline as the train rattled southwest into snowfall.

Billy slid up the window and thrust out his hand, telling Rudabaugh, "The wind lifts you. A bird must feel firm as in water."

Rudabaugh said, "Keep thinking. In the Santa Fe jail we'll fly out." Billy laughed.

They were following the old Santa Fe Trail into a snowstorm and upward through the Glorieta Pass, at over seven thousand four hundred feet. They followed the conquistador explorer, Francisco Vásquez de Coronado, searching for cities of gold three hundred thirty-nine years earlier.

Then they labored up the grade and over high trestle bridges on tracks disappearing under snow.

The whistle blew to halting wheels.

The conductor entered, announcing, "Stuck! Waiting for a crew to dig us out! Could be hours!"

Dave Rudabaugh asked him about the tracks getting to Santa Fe that year. "February ninth. But only to Lamy. There's a spur line into Santa Fe." Billy questioned Mesilla. "Not yet, boy. Only made Albuquerque April tenth." He left.

Billy said to Rudabaugh, "Plenty of time in Santa Fe. Unless they use a wagon."

"Too much risk of rescuing you. And my trial's there. But for no hanging offense."

One thousand six hundred fifty-three miles northeast of Glorieta Pass, in his New York City apartment, Frank Warner Angel, in an easy chair, with the *New York Sun* on his lap, was starting to doze.

His wife Sadie, on a settee, reading to their seven year old daughter, noticed and said, "You must be the hardest working district attorney they've had."

"Assistant District Attorney," he said. Alert again, his attention was caught by a headline: "OUTLAWS OF NEW MEXICO. THE EXPLOITS OF A BAND HEADED BY A NEW YORK YOUTH. THE MOUNTAIN FASTNESS OF THE KID AND HIS FOLLOWERS – WAR AGAINST A GANG OF CATTLE THIEVES, MURDERERS, AND COUNTERFEITERS."

Reading, Angel realized the long melodramatic story was about Billy Bonney. It concluded, "About three years ago a difficulty arose in Lincoln County between the stockmen and the Indian agent on the reservation. Nearly every man was under arms, and troops were called out by Governor Wallace to quell the disturbance. Billy the Kid was mixed up in the affair and had some narrow escapes. On one occasion he was obliged to take refuge in a house which was surrounded by solders. The house was set on fire and the Kid escaped firing his Winchester. There is no telling how many men he has killed. Governor Wallace has offered a handsome reward for his capture. It is not expected that he will be taken alive. He will fight to the last."

The misinformation surfaced Angel's repressed feelings about Rutherford B. Hayes, along with a new conclusion. He thought, "They knew all along. I was their dupe." Billy Bonney's words, "My work's not done," came back. Angel thought, "He'll be the last of the Ring's opposition to be killed. Am I to blame?"

That guilt brought back beautiful Ella in her nakedness. Mournfully, he said, "Oh, Sadie, Sadie, the world has so much badness." She smiled, shook her pretty blond curls, said he was making it better, and got up to make him tea.

Hearing her gay chatter with their child in the kitchen, he called, "I don't need any. I feel like ... sleeping."

In the bedroom, Angel's clarity increased about Hayes's evil: purposeful undermining of Reconstruction which could paralyze the Negroes for generations, the attempted extermination of the Indian race, and the cover-up of the Santa Fe Ring. Then Angel realized: Hayes *was part* of the Santa Fe Ring! He should have been impeached. Hayes's true legacy would be continuing decay of democracy through covert collusion of political and judicial power with robber barons - backed by law enforcement thuggery. Bitterly, Angel thought, "And the cover-up is so complete. He'll be untouched by history - seen as honest and well-meaning."

He remembered his own words about Ring members to Hayes and his cabinet: "moral monstrosities." That's what they all were. But Billy Bonney was not captured. And he'd sent John Tunstall's father his reports on Catron and Axtell. He'd done what he could. Speaking out now would only endanger Sadie and his daughter - all their futures. His mind turned to an upcoming case. And again he forgot.

At 7:53 PM, Billy, dragging grumbling Dave Rudabaugh by their mutual manacle, bounded with Mike Cosgrove's bundle down the metal steps to the platform of the Santa Fe depot. Rudabaugh commented, "At least this crowd's here to see you and not to lynch me."

A ruddy-faced man strode to Garrett saying, "U.S. Marshal Charles Conklin here. We've got the ambulance you ordered."

Billy Wilson fearfully repeated the word, his single eyebrow contracting over bloodshot eyes. "To pull down the canvas," Billy whispered, "So the good citizens can't see us."

A prodigiously muscled man in the crowd purposefully caught Billy's eye. In the amber artificial light, his crescented mustache was red-gold. He stepped forth, making an odd gesture: curling his fingers into a spyglass. Through it, Paul Herlow viewed the boy who looked back unflinchingly into that cyclopean pupil.

Garrett ordered Herlow to back up. The strongman did not move. He said, "So, Pat Garrett, you are back. But this time, you bring together Billy the Kid and Santa Fe. Now nothing can be changed till the end of time."

Billy, Rudabaugh, and Wilson were directed onto one of the ambulance's seats running along each side.

They traveled northward along Guadalupe Street, turned eastward at Montezuma; then crossed Aztec, Anallo, and a bridge spanning the creek-like Santa Fe River. Their street became Bridge. It ended at Water. There they turned left, and left again, into an alley.

Once out, Billy examined the run-down adobe jail before realizing that, across its street, stood the same remarkable-looking individual. Contact confirmed, with unexpected grace, the man bowed. Billy smiled gently, as if in forgiveness. And Paul Herlow did what he had done very few times in his career: he smiled back warmly, as if at one he had chosen.

They entered the office of a long-faced man, who pompously identified himself as Sheriff Romulo Martinez. A lanky, mustached individual with him was Deputy U.S. Marshal Tony Neis. Martinez asked for the shackle keys. Garrett realized he had no idea where they were. Those commercial cuffs, provided by Azariah Wild, used a tiny two-pronged one. "Look like a goddamn fool," he thought.

"Sheriff," he said demeaningly, "We've had a long delay. And almost fought a battle to bring these men in. I'll take care of that later." Billy asked about food. It was too late, Romulo Martinez responded. "I'll pay for it," Garrett said. "They haven't had much for days. I want special rations."

Billy, Rudabaugh, and Wilson were led by Romulo Martinez and Tony Neis through a door and along a linear block of cells. They stopped at the fourth. Neis said, "Kelly, you got company."

The barred door in the barred wall clanged shut behind them. At each side, were bunk beds. Under the single window on the far wall was a low cot with a seated occupant. To its right was a chair and a small table with tin candle holder.

"E'ward Kelly," announced the shriveled inmate with skimpy black beard and mustache. "Bu' I'm callt 'Choctaw'. " Though he did not appear Indian, he had knee-high buckskin boots and shoulder-length, greasy, black hair.

Wilson immediately flopped on the bunk to the right.

Billy tossed Mike Cosgrove's package on the upper level of the other bunk and said, "I'm Billy Bonney. This here's Dave Rudabaugh. And that's Billy Wilson."

Kelly asked, "Any o' ye got tobaccee?"

"I wish," rasped Rudabaugh. "If we'd gotten East, I'd have grabbed his pouch first, Kid."

Kelly said, "Ifen yer callt Kid, I'll call ye Kid an' 'im Billy."

Outside with his men, Garrett said, "We deserve the best," and forgot about the keys. "The Exchange Hotel. Meal's on me, boys. So are our rooms there."

After Kelly and Wilson were asleep, Billy said to Rudabaugh, "Wonder where the food is?"

In the office, Sheriff Romulo Martinez, Deputy U.S. Marshal Tony Neis; Deputy U.S. Marshal Charles Conklin; and jailer, Enrique Silva were finishing the plentiful repast. Neis asked, "You're positive we don't get any of the reward for the Kid?"

"Our reward," Martinez said, picking his teeth with the overgrown nail of his right little finger, and gesturing to the empty plates.

DECEMBER 28, 1880   8:13 AM   TUESDAY

Billy pivoted to face the barred window above sleeping "Choctaw" Kelly. Without opening his eyes, Dave Rudabaugh, on his back and handcuffed to him, whispered, "Now I wish they'd lynched me. Starving to death is worse."

Rudabaugh joked, "But we could eat 'Choctaw'! Like the cannibal Donner party in forty-seven. Got snowed in crossing the California Sierra Nevadas. Embarrassing when rescued." Billy laughed.

Down the corridor, the door opened. Pat Garrett was saying he'd come to check. As soon as he and Romulo Martinez were at their cell, Billy complained that they'd gotten no food. Martinez said, "Perhaps we thought it was for us. For waiting so long."

Aware of Billy's expectant gaze, Garrett experienced invigorating power and said, "The Kid's mine. You better keep him in good health. Get it now. This time I'm waiting." Unperturbed, the long-faced lawman shrugged, and sauntered back down the corridor.

Billy asked, "Pat, can you get word to my lawyer in Las Vegas - Ira Leonard - to let him know I'm here?" Garrett lied, saying he would try; he would be in Vegas the next day.

Billy asked, "How d'you get to the Palace of the Governors from here? I remember it was close."

"You just head east on Water, north on Ortiz, and cross San Francisco Street. Right there's the Plaza. Got the biggest lawyers in Santa Fe in the next building. Men like Thomas Benton Catron ..." He realized his faux pas.

To his relief, Billy just laughed and said, "I'm not figuring on Catron taking my case."

They could hear the door, then irregular footsteps. A big-eyed thin youth came into view, a club foot deformity shortening his right extremity on which he balanced, toes downward. As well as a bucket, he carried three tin cups. "Where's the food?" asked Billy.

The black-haired boy answered in Spanish that it was at the door. He opened a panel to give the water bucket and cups.

Billy, Rudabaugh, and "Choctaw" Kelly, who had his own cup, drank greedily. Billy and Rudabaugh brought the last cup to Wilson.

Garrett gave Billy the tiny key, which he used to unshackle them all as the club-footed youth returned and slid in a food tray.

"Thanks for everything, Pat," Billy said. The man absorbed the appreciation, but his discomfort at seeing the boy caged disappeared only when he exited the building.

The club-footed boy asked Billy, "Do the other two understand?" Billy shook his head. He said, "I am Nico. Many pray for you."

Entering the spacious hallway of the Palace of the Governors outside Lew Wallace's office, Pat Garrett was met by Tim Henley. When told Wallace was in Washington, Garrett said he'd come to get the Billy the Kid reward money. Henley claimed no authorization. Rage welled in Garrett. "Then telegraph Wallace that Marshal Patrick Floyd Garrett was *very* dissatisfied by the treatment he got."

Soon, inside Thomas Benton Catron's Johnson Block office, Pat Garrett sat facing the big desk, behind which mounded the lardaceous attorney, who immediately questioned precautions against escape; and was reassured that he had checked the Kid that morning.

The behemoth pushed back his oversized seat, grunting while reaching into a side drawer. From a stack of hundred dollar bills, he dealt five, and slid them with backs of fat fingers as Garrett detected a fecal odor. Because of his obesity, sometimes Catron failed to successfully wipe defecation.

Catron said, "I'm not finished, Pat. I'm adding a private reward." Fifteen more hundred dollar bills were added. "It's a long way from here to Mesilla. And there will be more for you after he's hanged."

Garrett said, "Something worries me. I've heard about some pardon Governor Wallace promised. What if I do all that work, and then Wallace ... I mean, my final payment if the pardon ..."

"Do you play chess, Pat?" It was denied. "The object is to block your opponent. Jimmy will show you our *New York Sun* article on the outlaw captain, Billy the Kid. Can Lew Wallace - who, I may add, is now in Washington seeking an ambassadorship to exit our Territory as soon as possible - humiliate himself nationally, thereby destroying his own ambitions, just to keep a promise to this outlaw known coast to coast? It's called checkmate."

Garrett leaned back, reassured by the confidences. "Tom - between you and me - there never was any gang. Took some doing to take in Azreeah Wild and those Texas boys."

The grotesquely bloated face darkened with horrifying abruptness. Catron sprang up, gelatinous neck flopping. He leaned forward on splayed hands and hissed, "*No one* gets in our way, Garrett. That boy is the most dangerous person here - the most dangerous to *us*.

"We made you. We can destroy you." Sweat oozed from Catron's palms over the mahogany. "Now get out."

Garrett did not move. "Tom," he said steadily, "I'm a deputy sheriff and deputy marshal. I'm no hired killer."

The hulking form sat, staring with his dead-fish eyes. Then he began to laugh.

JANUARY 1, 1881   1:00 PM   SATURDAY

Standing on "Choctaw" Kelly's cot, Billy looked through the cell window. The others were on a blanket spread on the floor, playing poker with Dave Rudabaugh's cards and pebbles from the dirt floor as chips. With boot pressed to the wall, Billy pulled the cylindrical bars.

Kelly glanced up, saying he'd tried that. " 'Choctaw', what's outside?" Billy asked. "Looks like an open lot and then a building."

"Courhouse." Kelly studied his hand. "Damned ifen a man don' worry 'bout rocks same as money."

"Kid, why'd ye wan' two extree chamer po's from Nico?"

"Good to have," Billy said; and removed from his vest a spoon stomped flat with his boot-heel, rubbing its bowl against the wall's brick. "What 're you in for, 'Choctaw'?"

"Some sez I murded a ceertain John Reardon. In a saloon. Playin' cards. I called 'im a goddamn cheat. He started te stan', so I shot him. Later I heerd he didn' have no gun. Ifen he did, I'd be deed; an' 'e'd be 'ere talkin' te ye."

Steps could be heard. Jailer, Enrique Silva, let in a stranger. Dark-suited, he had a leather case and center-parted hair. "Choctaw" Kelly said, "This 'ere's my lawyer, 'pointed by the Court: Edgar Caypless."

Caypless asked for a David Rudabaugh. Groaning, he stood, saying jail was for the young. "I came today, Mister Rudabaugh," Caypless continued, "because I was informed yesterday that I'm appointed to your case and that of a William Wilson." The boy scrambled up hopefully.

" 'E's sumtin'," said Kelly. "Santa Fe half deed wit New Year's celabratin', an' he's workin'." That was overstated, Caypless said. He had no choice. Mister Rudabaugh's trial was Monday.

"Monday!" exclaimed Billy.

Edgar Caypless glanced with disinterest at him, and took the chair. "Railroading bastards," said Rudabaugh; and asked, "What 're my charges?" as the lawyer took writing implements from his case.

Billy Wilson asked when they were doing him. Caypless looked through papers. "The twenty-first. Only a Hearing before the judge."

"It appears," he was reading his notes and directing his attention to Rudabaugh, "that you have charges of mail theft, train robbery, counterfeiting, and rustling." He appraised his client, the new suit already rumpled and soiled. The man looked as surly and rough as the crimes implied. "And your response?" Rudabaugh claimed alibis for the robbery charges and denied counterfeiting or rustling. Caypless sighed when he said his occupation was professional gambler.

"Excuse me, Attorney Caypless," Billy asked, "d'you have an extra pen and paper?" Receiving them, he lay on his belly on the blanket, ink in his cup. He wrote the recipient's name as Governor Lew Wallace, and continued: *Sir. I am presently being held in the Santa Fe jail for the indictments for which you promised me a pardon. If you can spare the time please come to see me. I have also tried to get word to my attorney Ira Leonard whom you made a Judge. I need to meet with him also about my case. Respectfully, W H Bonney."*

Folding it, Billy returned the pen to the attorney and initiated a poker game with "Choctaw" Kelly.

When Edgar Caypless prepared to leave, Billy ascertained that he knew Ira Leonard by sight, and asked, "Maybe you could help me with a case of my own.

"A valuable mare was taken from me on December twenty-second by a certain Frank Stewart. Also the best quality saddle and bridle." Caypless asked if it was replevin: a rustling charge. "Hopefully not. Maybe he'll give her back if he hears from a lawyer. I need to sell her to pay Attorney Leonard, who I also need to contact. She was raced under the name Dynamite Doll. My name's William Bonney."

"I'll try. By the way, have you all heard that Billy the Kid's in this jail?" "Choctaw" Kelly asked who the hell that was. "Just the most famous outlaw in the country. Captured after the biggest manhunt."

As Enrique Silva arrived, Billy asked, "Attorney Caypless, could you possibly bring this to Governor Wallace?"

When the man took the letter, Billy said, "Just to let you know, a name I've been called *is* Billy the Kid." The man's eyes widened with sudden interest, as the boy gave his ingenuous smile.

JANUARY 3, 1881 2:19 PM MONDAY

Dave Rudabaugh's shoulders stooped uncharacteristically as he entered and lay on his bunk. Finally he said, "Guilty. Robbing the U.S. Mail. Ninety-nine years. Sentenced by Bristol."

Billy Wilson shuffled to his cot and covered himself completely, including his head.

At three, the jailer walked the corridor, which he also did at eleven in the morning and eight at night.

As soon as Billy heard the outer door close, he levered the end of his sharpened spoon to break his cup's handle.

At five, when Nico delivered their trays, Billy requested a new cup. Then, only he and "Choctaw" Kelly ate. Billy said, "Ninety-nine years is a long time without food." Rudabaugh laughed.

Billy said, "Boys, I need you in good shape. I've got an escape plan. Wilson, you'll feel better if you eat." He mumbled about being sick. "Just means you're hungry."

Lethargically, Wilson joined them. "What d'you figure the odds 're of them sentencing you to hanging, 'Choctaw'?" Billy asked.

"Tryin' te ruin my appetite an' git my food? I shur don' like Dave's sentence. Tha' Brisol's a hangin' judge. An' Reardon's wife 'ill be there aweepin'."

Billy said he'd heard about a man whose friend tried to break him out. But he wouldn't leave. "Then he war plumb loco," said Kelly.

Billy Wilson said, "Tha' Caypless ain' worth a cow patty. Woner wha' Pickett's doin' jus' now."

"Is he un te get us ou'?" asked Kelly.

"No," said Rudabaugh. "Just Lady Luck's best friend. I'm ready to toss that damn Fugio out the window. Biggest manhunt in the country, and you're the one I was riding with."

Billy said, "Well, here's the plan: digging out with chamber pot lids and the extra cup. And we've got cross-boards from the cots. Garrett left the bracelets: good hooks for rocks. And I happen to have a knife to cut open our mattresses to hide the dirt." He displayed the sharpened spoon. "We can dig under your cot, 'Choctaw'. And put the boards and dirt over the hole."

"Ye didn' seem the schemin' sort," said Kelly. "Jus' a nice boy."

"I am," Billy said, blue eyes mischievous. "One who likes his freedom."

JANUARY 21, 1881   11:16 AM   FRIDAY

The sound of the opening cellblock door precipitated coordinated movements. Billy laid concealing boards; "Choctaw" Kelly added dirt from the chamberpot lids; and Dave Rudabaugh pushed the cot back to the wall. The three rushed to the blanket for their cards.

Billy said, I call, as Enrique Silva opened their door for Billy Wilson, who reported, "Nothin' happent with me. Caypless was there. He used bad words with Judge Brisol: like 'hab ass' an' 'corpse.' Meybe he was angry. Bu' Brisol, he says he wans bail o' five thousan'. So I says, 'I ain' got nothin'. Then they sens me back."

Billy said, "Too bad about hitting that big rock. But a strong foundation will hold up the wall while we work." Rudabaugh responded that optimism might be a sickness, making a man crazy.

Later, behind the cot, Billy announced they were around the rock. "Quick," said Rudabaugh, standing guard. "Someone's coming." All sprang to their bogus poker hands. The sheriff and, to Billy's delight, Ira Leonard were outside. Long-faced Martinez spitefully gave his lawyer only a half hour.

Leonard said, "At court today Edgar Caypless said you wanted to see me;" and went to the small table. Billy sat on the cot, and asked if Caypless had gotten back his horse. Leonard said Garrett had informed Caypless that a Frank Stewart had sold her in Las Vegas to the owner of Moore's Hotsprings Hotel, Winfred Scott Moore, as a gift for his wife Minnie, who named her Kid Stewart Moore. "Damn, Ira, that mare wasn't his to sell. She was my only hope to pay you."

The dark-circled eyes welled. "No money's necessary."

Billy thanked him and blushed at the implied affection. "If they keep me here too long, can I get out on Habeus Corpus like they used at Stanton?"

"Tha's it!" exclaimed Wilson. "Wha' they wouldn' give me: a corpus."

Leonard said, "Bristol would never grant it. And you'll be moved by train. The tracks won't be finished till spring."

"What about my pardon?"

"Wallace is in Washington promoting his book till next month."

"What about Susan McSween? She knows everything."

Leonard looked away with discomfiture. "I talked to her in White Oaks, with her new husband, George Barber. About you. She said she couldn't remember who you were."

"Even after what I did with Dudley ..." His voice softened. "Guess that's all she had in her. She was brave enough back then."

Leonard stood. "Also, Sheriff Martinez made it almost impossible for me to see you. But I promise, when the time comes, I'll be with you in Mesilla."

FEBRUARY 10, 1881 9:10 AM THURSDAY

Lew Wallace announced cheerily: "Just back from Washington and off to Silver City later today, Henley."

"Sir, I wanted to make sure you knew that William Bonney is in the jail here. And that you saw his letter requesting a meeting with you with regard to his pardon."

"Yes. I saw it. That reminds me," Wallace said, as both sat. "Our jail! A book possesses tales known only to its author. You will be surprised when told that the scene most moving to me involved the jail holding Ben-Hur's mother and sister. To me, it epitomized injustice.

"For its model, I used our *actual jail* on Water Street. I even drew its cellblock for my publisher to reproduce in my book. You may recall that the mother and sister became lepers. It transpired thus. And, even now, it brings tears to my eyes. Purposefully, they were placed in a cell of contagion by the nefarious Roman, Messala, to accomplish murder by disease without taint to his hands. Thus, a remote cell called Number Six was walled off; the only access being the adjoining one inhabited by a blind tongueless wretch obligated to pass sustenance, but unable to be a witness.

"And, in our wretched jail here, there is a corridor with *six* cells. The sixth, windowless, was my inspiration for horror. Sunk in its earthen floor is a metal stake with a ring, to which a prisoner is chained in utter darkness."

Three hundred seventy-six yards southwest of the governor's office, in Cell Four, Billy said, as he handed a laden pot lid to Billy Wilson, "If it keeps up like this, boys, we're out in only a few days."

FEBRUARY 28, 1881   10:57 AM   MONDAY

"Choctaw" Kelly walked between long-faced Sheriff Romulo Martinez and Marshal Tony Neis back from the courthouse saying, "How the hell 'id Bristol think I'd git a bond fer eigh' thousan' dollas?"

Neis responded that it was a good time to talk. In his office, Martinez said, "Judge Bristol spoke to us about you, 'Choctaw'. He knows about Reardon's popularity here. So a change of venue would help you: for example to Las Vegas where prisoner Rudabaugh will be transferred next month on the seventh for a murder trial. In exchange, Judge Bristol needs an informer for escape plans."

"Choctaw" Kelly thought, "Oly a few days an' ou'." He said, "I don' know nothin'."

"Here's something else about murder trials," said Martinez. "The judge gives the jury instructions. First degree murder gets hanging. Self-defense and you go free. Judge Bristol could instruct the jury that a murder could not be first degree *unless* the assailant was *positive* the victim was unarmed. Or, that they *had* to call it self-defense if the assailant *believed* the victim had a gun."

"Les jus' say there war some plan. Where'd I be kept?"

"Cell Two has only one inmate. Feebleminded. In for disorderly conduct."

Kelly pictured them all standing uncertainly outside their hole. He said, "They been diggin' a tunnel. Near te finisht."

After the jailor, Enrique Silva, completed his three o'clock walk-through, and Billy started the digging, "Choctaw" Kelly complained about being sick and remained on his moved cot.

Soon Wilson warned of people coming.

When Romulo Martinez arrived with Tony Neis and Enrique Silva, he ordered them up from their poker game saying, "You've been here two months. Routine check."

Silva and Neis dragged the bunks and "Choctaw" Kelly's cot from the walls.

"Pull off the mattresses," Martinez said, perspiring heavily. To Silva's surprise, rubble spilled from slits.

"There must be digging," said Martinez. "Get a shovel, Enrique." The jailor returned, striking the blade's staccato at the south side. "Damn it," said Martinez, "why the hell would they tunnel into Cell Five?"

At the correct wall, there was hollow resonance, then scraping. Neis looked. "There's a major tunnel here, Sheriff," he said and ordered Silva to see how far it went. Silva scowled at the derogation, but soon emerged saying it was almost outside.

Martinez shouted, "You goddamn bastards. We're separating you. Neis, take Kelly to Cell Two. Silva, get cuffs for them; and a pair of leg irons too." Neis returned with Silva, who was rattling chains and proclaiming he was not to blame. "Shut up," Martinez yelled, horrified at how close he had come to ruin. "Just goddamn put on the wrist irons. Neis, take Rudabaugh and Wilson to Cell Five." Rudabaugh's baggy tear-filled eyes met Billy's.

Enrique Silva knelt at Billy to attach the leg shackles. Martinez ordered, "Take him to Cell Six."

"You did not say to bring the padlock," said the jailor.

"Then go the hell and get it. Meet us there."

When Enrique Silva returned, he objected that he could not see in the darkness. Martinez swung open the door maximally, which revealed a mattress on the dirt floor. Releasing pent-up rage, Martinez struck Billy on the back, propelling him inside.

Kneeling again, Silva passed the arc of the padlock through the iron ring in the floor and the mid-point of Billy's leg chain, and exited. Martinez slammed shut the heavy door.

Billy saw dim light in the door's small square. He heard departing voices before total silence was partnered with total darkness.

At 5:22 PM, Nico unbolted a floor-level panel in Cell Six. A tray scraped and the panel closed.

Blindly Billy walked to the limit of his chain, bent, groped with joined hands, and fingered the contents. There was a tin bowl of soupy beans, no utensils, and a tin cup of water.

Nico's face blocked the square. Billy whispered, "Can you get me paper, a pencil, a candle, and matches? I will be careful with the light."

"Maybe from the garbage at the Exchange, paper for wrapping meat. When you finish, push the tray back so I can reach it. My family will pray for you."

Billy sat on the mildewed pad, sighed, and drank off liquid from the beans; then fingered in mouthfuls, spitting out grit.

Then he manipulated the tight leg irons, unable to relieve his bootleather's chafing ridges. Next, he tapped the padlock repeatedly with a wrist cuff, attempting, in vain, to release its mechanism. Reaching through coat and cardigan to his vest, he got Garrett's tiny key, which proved useless for these Territorial manacles requiring a big, screw type.

Then Billy stood to walk the circle of his tether, within the circumference of which were mattress and chamber pot. Pacing, he repeatedly, in vain, tried to compress a hand to slip it out.

Finally he lay down, looking up into absolute blackness, which could have been the ceiling of a jail or the infinity of a starless night sky.

MARCH 2, 1881   1:05 PM   WEDNESDAY

In light from Nico's candle, and with the tray turned over on his lap, Billy smoothed a paper spotted with grease and blood. With Nico's pencil he wrote: *"Dear Sir: I wish you would come down to the jail and see me. It will be much to your interest. I have your letters which date back two years and there are Parties who are very anxious to get them but I will not dispose of them until I see you. That is if you will come immediately. Respectfully, W HBonney."*

On the folded outside he wrote *"To Governor Wallace."*

Next he wrote to Leonard. *"Ira. Please come to the jail immediately. I have been taken from the cell in which you saw me and chained in a terrible place without any light and without edible food. It is necessary to do all you can for they seem determined to kill me before my trial. Respectfully, W HBonney."*

On its folded back he misspelled phonetically, *"To Attorney Caplis,"* and added a star.

The candle was then hidden.

Hearing voices, Billy stood.

The door swung. Long-faced Romulo Martinez, holding a rifle, proclaimed, "I have brought businessmen from New York to see you, Billy the Kid." Five top-hated individuals peered in. The long-faced sheriff exhibitionisticly pointed the rifle at him before the door closed.

Hours passed until the awaited footsteps. "Listen, Nico," said Billy. "Under my bowl will be two letters. Give the one with the star to the lawyer who comes here: Caypless. And the other take to the governor's office. Tell them it is from William Bonney. Are you afraid Martinez will find out?"

"No. I carry messages for various people." With the tray was spicy fragrance. Nico said, "From my mother. I told her they feed you nothing. They are her empanadas, but little. Each dough is filled with raisins and apples. And sugar for your strength. My father laughed. He said it is manna from Heaven. Also there is a packet with crushed chilies. For the beans.

"They said to tell you we have family in San Patricio. The Lord will judge."

MARCH 4, 1881   3:22 PM   FRIDAY

Writing after Enrique Silva's rounds, Billy heard voices, and just managed to hide his writing equipment before the door opened to rifle-brandishing Sheriff Romulo Martinez with two men, and, to Billy's surprise, an elegant woman with a little boy. The lawman said, "This is Billy the Kid. He is so dangerous that ..." The woman complained that the smell made her faint. As the door closed, the child's voice called out, "Goodbye, Billy the Kid."

Billy paced angrily before sitting again, and, with blindman's skill, lit the candle. Before writing, he gave himself luxury of staring at its restless spear of light. Lew Wallace was again the recipient.

"*Dear Sir. I wrote You a little note the day before yesterday but have received no answer. I expect you have forgotten what you promised me, this month two years ago, but I have not, and I think you ought to have come and seen me as I requested you to. I have done everything that I promised you I would, and you have done nothing that you promised me. I think when you think the matter over, you will come down and see me. It looks to me like I am getting left in the cold. I am not treated right by Sheriff Martinez. He lets in any Stranger see me through curiosity, but not my Attorney. I guess they mean to send me up without giving me any show but they will have a nice time doing it. I am not entirely without friends. I shall expect to see you some time today. Patiently Waiting. I am very truly yours, Respectfully, W HBonney.*"

Billy smiled at having proven both obligation and consequences of betrayal. The pardon was secondary to this victory.

Quickly, he studied the ground ring and leg chains before pinching the wick, enjoying its retinal after-images before testing an hypothesis. He lifted the leg chain. Each link was an oval with a solid weld. Isolating one, he joined together its two mates at its rear, and slid its curved front though the floor ring, until stopped by those back links. Into that front protrusion, he slipped his fingertip. *There* one could crack a chain!

When Nico received the dinner tray, he said, "My mother sent you a biscochito. It broke in my pocket, but I did not eat even a piece." Billy laughed, and asked if he could get a metal rod. "Aye, no. Please. If I was caught ... We pray for you every day."

After the panel bolt re-engaged, Billy stroked the tray to collect what had been a wheat flour cookie made with leavening, salt, lard, sugar, eggs, anise seeds, and cinnamon. He took the chili packet from his vest, added that flavoring with its high vitamin C content, and began with the beans.

One hundred thirty-two miles southwest of Santa Fe, a banquet was in progress in the Wortley Hotel, where Dolan stood at the head of joined tables. He said, "For the first toast of the evening, I propose we drink to our hero, who made Lincoln County what we wanted."

Bob Olinger shouted, "Pat Garrett for president!" and swallowed champagne. Garrett, beside him, smiled and adjusted the cuffs of his dandyish, custom-tailored, brown-plaid suit.

Dolan continued, "And we welcome Lincoln County's newest deputy, James Bell: member of the Carlyle posse and witness to the last of Billy the Kid's atrocities." The scrawny-necked man, with stringy mustache and thinning dark hair, flushed in shy pleasure.

After many courses and drinks, talk became more animated. John Kinney called down the table to Edgar Walz, "I hear Catron sold the House to Lincoln County as its new courthouse."

George Peppin said to Dolan, "Bet you and Murphy never thought you'd build *that*."

"*You* did," Dolan answered. "And now you are its renovator. Larry must be looking down from Heaven smiling to know that our private apartments will be the new jail." James Bell said he could only picture him living in his big house.

Kinney teased, "Jimmy, he's ready to buy the town. Aren't you?"

Dolan said he could not deny his good fortune.

"Goddamn," said Bob Olinger, "ain't even a word for Dolan luck. We all know you been offered two hundred thousand for your share in the North Homestake Mine."

Peppin said, "Pat, I'm putting your office beside Jimmy's old apartment."

Dolan joked, "And now we can control the Territory right from this room. We have the law: Garrett, Olinger, and Bell."

In his cell, Billy decided to eat biscochito pieces, parsing out his meager fare. Aftertaste of anise remained pleasantly when he lay back and sang softly into the darkness, "If you will answer these questions for me ..." He smiled and said, "This very day I'll marry with thee." Unbathed for so long, he raked fingers through grimy hair.

In darkness, where it made no difference if the lids were open or closed, transition into sleep was sometimes imperceptible. Billy was with Yginio Salazar. Both were naked. They dove into the Bonito River, rippling in moonlight. Billy surfaced, running fingers through his clean hair, then dipping his head into the water. It was a cistern at Tunstall's Feliz Ranch. Gottfried Gauss said to Billy from the chosa, "Eat. I make you more." Again Billy was in the river. Paulita, underwater like him, was laughing. Above them was dazzling sun-sheeted surface. "We have to wait," he called, but she reached out sun-dappled arms. "But the darkness," Billy said. It was an inverted triangle against her white flesh. There was an etching of a body cut in half. "It's the womb," he said and heard her say, "Like being married. This very day I'll marry with thee." Afterimages flashed in a black void. "Inside, Billy," she whispered. "Inside the darkness is life." And he passed from darkness through an opening into freedom and rapture.

MARCH 9, 1881   11:37 AM   WEDNESDAY

From his desk, Lew Wallace said to his secretary, "Alas, Henley, even with Tom Catron's sage advice, I appear not destined to make my fortune in Silver City with the ore promised by seductions of its name." He stroked his Abyssinian beard. "Put this letter from president-elect Garfield, praising my *Ben-Hur*, with the Territorial papers I'm saving. Garfield has promised me - once he is president on the twentieth - an ambassadorship to Turkey.

"As to my successor, Tom Catron recommended a Lionel Sheldon. Apparently Tom's one-time partner, Steve Elkins - our past Territorial Delegate to Congress - has already extolled him to Garfield. I have heard that Elkins is a veritable Midas, with so grand a fortune in land, railroads, mines, and finance that he and his wife, Hallie, eat with golden utensils off gold dinnerware. And I, of course, shall give testimonial for you to Sheldon."

"Thank you, Sir." Tim Henley paused. "In your papers for today, I put two letters which I recopied because they were on soiled paper. From William Bonney."

"Ah yes. I recall that his transport to Mesilla awaits railroad completion. By the way, make sure that in my 'Report of the Governor' is included that, in my administration of but two years, the Atchison, Topeka, and Santa Fe completed five hundred fifty miles of track in this Territory."

Henley said, "I was reading in the newspaper, Sir, that yesterday was the hammering of the silver spike at Deming. It was an historic day. The tracks forked at Rincón to get there. And the other branch joined the Southern Pacific from the west coast. We've got our second transcontinental now. From Rincón they're building south to Mesilla, then El Paso." With veiled provocation, he added, "So Bonney will be moved soon *unless you pardon him.*"

Wallace located the two recopied letters. "And did that rogue think he could blackmail me? And does he really believe that I have any obligation to him? 'Promises,' he says. Put these with Garfield's. I'm saving them to write a fascinating saga: my autobiography." He chuckled. "Sometimes I feel as if I am living a tale I am writing."

In his cell, Billy had finally softened with spittle the boot-leather under his painful ankle irons. Satisfied, he transversed the perimeter of his bondage point. Then he began to dance, using the chains for music and rhythm, resounding the darkness with clattering red-rusted iron; with thumping of boot soles on the red, iron oxide-stained earth; with drumming in his ears of blood pumping iron-protein hemoglobin in red corpuscles; and with echoing from iron-red adobe walls. And from deprivation of seventy-three days of incarceration and inadequate food, he felt lightness of flying.

Two hundred sixty-seven miles southeast of Santa Fe, in his Roswell house, Pat Garrett, drinking whiskey, said to busily writing Ash Upson that he was taking the book seriously. "Of course," Upson said. "Once the Kid's hanged, everyone will rush out their version.

"And I'm realistic about sales. The author will be Pat Garrett himself. The title is *The Authentic Life of Billy the Kid: The Noted Desperado of the Southwest, Whose Deeds of Daring and Blood Made His Name a Terror in New Mexico, Arizona, and Northern Mexico.* What do you think? You'll be the hero."

The gray eyes looked disdainfully at the humped little man. Garrett said, "I *am* the hero."

In Washington, D.C., one thousand five hundred seventy-nine miles northeast of Roswell, in one of five official offices adjacent to the Cabinet Room, suave Secretary of State William Evarts, handed Stephen Benton Elkins a copy of the letter which he had sent to Ambassador Edward Thornton two days before.

Almost Catron's twin, huge-bellied Elkins differed only in being clean-shaven. He read Evarts's words: "*It is scarcely necessary for me to recall to the worthy Representative of Her Majesty's Government that the laws of our States and Territories are exercised by them without interference by the federal government. Attorney General Charles Devens has assured me that should the indicted murderer Jessie Evans be arrested he would be brought to justice. Sympathizing with the father of the deceased John Tunstall in his bereavement, I would be happy to see him receive some compensation. But I regret that there exists no federal fund from which such a gratuity could be paid.*"

Elkins asked, "What about James Dolan's indictment? And Tom told me that Evans is in Huntsville Prison for killing a Texas deputy."

Evarts, a close friend since working with Elkins and Catron on the Maxwell Land Grant, smiled superciliously. "Of zero concern, Steve. Warren Bristol not only destroyed all the seventy-nine Lincoln County Grand Jury transcripts, he took care of Dolan's seventy-eight one for Tunstall also. So Dolan's indictment can't even be proved.

"As to Evans: his whereabouts are unavailable to Thornton. Additionally, the Texas D.A. requested only second degree murder, since Evans was not the certain killer of that deputy - being in an attacking group. So he got twenty years. And Dolan is arranging his escape. Better yet, Thornton's quitting his ambassadorship. He's succeeding Lord Dufferin as Envoy to Russia.

"Even Lord Salisbury - whom the Tunstall family also contacted - left as Foreign Secretary last year. Anyway, Salisbury had put his famous red S on the Tunstall documents: meaning 'requiring no action.' As a wise statesman, he knew that after the pro-Confederacy stance of his country, it was time to court us. They'll want our alliance if Bismark's strength and the German Republic's imperialism continue to increase after that Franco-Prussian War victory.

"And the Tunstall family also turned to Prime Minister William Gladstone, but hit another wall. Right now, Gladstone's negotiating with us to provide Marines for his hoped-for invasion of Egypt - advancing Britain's colonial ambitions while pretending to help weak Khedive Tawfik against a possible coup by the Orabi led army.

William Evarts continued. "That Tunstall family made a bad mistake. We actually have *no* problem granting reparations for murdered foreigners. But their linking of settlement to accusation of U.S. officials required our concomitant admission of their guilt. Obviously impossible. So we sunk the whole case.

"The real problem, as you know, are those Angel reports. Rutherford knew their risk to all of us - and let his good friend Garfield know. After all, after the twentieth, you and Tom will be working with *him*. And with my replacement as Secretary of State: James Blaine!"

Elkins's big down-curved mouth raised in a smile. Evarts continued, "Your backing of Blaine's past presidential bid, of course, *guarantees* that he'll continue our suppressing of this Tunstall case.

"By the way, Steve, I heard that you were in the Department of Justice asking about Angel's report on Catron." Elkins looked surprised. Evarts said, "Someone in the clerical staff told me. Since Charles Devens was the only one unaware of our relationships, Rutherford wanted it in a more secure place. It's with Carl Schurz's Department of Interior files in the Patent Office Building.

"In case you need to *check it*, I had a key made for you to Schurz's filing cabinet in Room twenty-eight, to the left of the Library. Use the main F Street south entrance after closing time at four fifteen. Here's a pass signed by Schurz for the watchman, authorizing you to remove departmental property ... if you need to. Catron's report is next to the Angel one on Surveyor General Henry Atkinson. None of us would regret its *loss*.

"And you may be interested to know that Schurz couldn't stomach these realities. He's leaving political life and going into journalism. But he's too deep to ever say a word.

"Well now, bring me up to date on your plans."

Blubbery Stephen Elkins said, "Of course, Tom and I are continuing our New Mexico endeavors. When statehood comes, he told me he's ready to spend a million for his senatorial campaign.

"And recently, my father-in-law, Senator Henry Davis, and I bought eighty thousand acres of coal deposits in West Virginia - to make railroad deals like Tom and I did in New Mexico. Also, Hallie and I are building another house in Deer Park like the Newport cottages on Bellevue Avenue. Calling it Halliehurst.

"And Tom and I have opportunities for you again, Will. Giving up your big bucks law practice for this measly ten thousand salary must make it hard to keep up your houses here and in New York, and that six hundred acre Runnymede estate in Windsor, Vermont.

"So here's a word to the wise: there's a three hundred acre tract - twelve miles south of here on a Potomac branch and across from Mount Vernon - called Mount Beverly Farm. Its rich in marl fertilizer. Natural resources are the wealth of the future. Something to buy cheap now for *your* future. Tom and I like to keep our friends happy."

Elkins added, "That reminds me, we've got one last problem in New Mexico Territory: that William Bonney - who already testified against our friends, and still can. Hayes did the trick for his capture by contacting Chief Brooks for Tom, and getting the Secret Service involved. Now Bonney's in jail awaiting murder trials.

"But - like you mentioned with Jessie Evans - all his shootings were in a group - only second degree. Tom and Warren Bristol are strategizing that legally. He must be hanged."

Suave Stephen Elkins smiled. "In Washington we all know that Hayes's slogan - 'he that serves his party best serves his county best' - just means: 'Serve your friends.' " Both men laughed heartily.

MARCH 17, 1881   4:48 PM   THURSDAY

"Finally in writing, Henley," said Lew Wallace. He held President James Abram Garfield's acceptance of his resignation as governor and his appointment of Lionel Sheldon. "With pride, I declare that I have left the Territory - which I found in lawless turmoil - in a state of peace, with justice honorably meted out."

Unnoticed was Tim Henley's scowl.

Six hundred yards away, Billy tried to wash himself. Nico had brought him a rag, which he dipped it into his cup of water, and rubbed his face, savoring cold evaporation. Under clothing, he ran it over his body. The last drops, he rubbed through dirty curls.

Lying back, Billy faced absolute darkness. He was looking out a train window when the panorama was obliterated by a spider of human size. She clasped front-most legs into a circle through which she stared at him before pointing upward. Billy said, "Yes." Extending from her was a riata, which became a coil hanging from Cimarron's saddle as, mounted, he faced a narrow doorway. But there was no need to crouch when his mare leapt through, because above was not a lintel, but the sky. They were racing to the riata hanging through clouds. Billy caught it and began to climb. Deluvina said, "Blessed as I found it. You know you do not need the rope." He looked back and saw his long iridescent wings. Deluvina whispered, "Dragonfly. Fly. Fly." Cold air beat his palms. "Yes," he called. "I can see the opening."

He looked down. Darkness was pooled on the land, like the oceans of the moon. It could not follow him. And his desire became so intense that he knew nothing could stop his upward propulsion or prevent his climax into bliss.

MARCH 27, 1881   1:31 PM   SUNDAY

Billy re-read his just completed letter to Ira Leonard. *"Tomorrow I hear I am being taken on the railroad to Mesilla for the trial. I know that you have not visited me again because they would allow only those who they were sure had no help to offer me. I will write again to Governor Wallace about my Pardon. It is important for you to ask him again also. Respectfully, W HBonney."*

On the folded outside he wrote *"Caplis,"* and put a star.

The wick protruded from its final wax sliver. Billy wrote to Lew Wallace: *"Dear Sir. For the last time I ask. Will you keep your promise? I start to Mesilla tomorrow. Send Answer by bearer."*

Later, at the familiar sounds of the irregular club-footed step and the moving bolt, Billy said, "These letters are important, Nico. Tomorrow I leave. Enrique Silva told me."

Nico answered that he now understood. His father had said they were waiting. Billy said, "Tell him the time is now."

MARCH 28, 1881   6:12 AM   MONDAY

Nico whispered, "They are coming," while reaching in for Billy's tray, then sliding it back saying, "Rincón," and rushing away.

Billy smelled the biscochito and smiled. Soon, his door swung open to pearlescent stirring dust. Silva knelt to free his legs from the floor ring, murmuring to the boy, whose face was now lean with jawline in sharp definition, that he was not to blame.

Billy said, "I know, Enrique," and saw the doorway blocked by three figures: Sheriff Romulo Martinez, Deputy U.S. Marshal Tony Neis, and Bob Olinger. "Get the hell out," ordered Olinger, as Billy concealed surprise. "We got orders to shoot you for any reason."

Billy entered the corridor sliced by light shafts projected from the remaining five cells' windows; and squinted through pupils in spasm of maximum dilation after twenty-eight days of darkness.

"Ambulance is outside," said Neis. "Wilson's already there. He's going to Mesilla too." Billy asked long-faced Martinez for his hat, Charlie's hat, and Cosgrove's package, and was told they were lost.

The cell block door gaped wide to the front offices. Romulo Martinez opened the one to the street.

Billy was transfixed by the sky. A flock of bandtail pigeons circled as he slitted his eyes to endure the luminosity which he could feel. Ahead was an ambulance.

Billy Wilson, on its bench to the right, stared blankly ahead beside a short blocky stranger with a Winchester carbine. Tony Neis motioned Billy to the left side, and Bob Olinger joined them. The vehicle shuddered as the two mules pulled its large wheels from suction of springtime mud.

The stranger identified himself to Billy as Deputy U.S. Marshal Francisco Chávez; and noticed Olinger's Whitney double barrel shotgun. He said, "Haven't seen one of those since they came out in seventy-four. Once knew a farmer who had one."

"Ten gauge," said Olinger insulted. "Not much left of a man once he meets up with it."

Finally, the ambulance stopped at the train station. Tony Neis assessed a huddle and called back that they were just locals. Once out, Bob Olinger menaced an approaching spindly, balding, button-nosed man. Neis told Olinger to take it easy. It was Judge Leonard. He was coming with them. Followed by Olinger, Leonard kept pace at Billy's side, telling him his trial began as soon as they got there.

"Get the hell in," said Olinger as they neared the passenger car. Billy ambled provocatively slower, saying it seemed if a man was made a Deputy U.S. Marshal he would want to talk like one - instead of like a common murderer.

Billy chose a seat at the right. Ira Leonard joined him. In front of them sat Francisco Chávez and Tony Neis; across the aisle were Bob Olinger and Billy Wilson.

With ringing bell and screeching whistle, the locomotive rolled south with a protective barrier of noise in which Billy asked Leonard if he'd gotten his letters. "Yes. Though they wouldn't let me see you. Why are you so much paler than Wilson?"

"I got the worst room in the hotel. Could Caypless sell my horse?"

"He's trying. The Scott woman says she'll fight it. But you can tell the Judge you've got no money; and I can be appointed your attorney through the Court. I get some payment that way."

Leonard whispered, "Did you kill Roberts, Brady or Hindman?" Billy said no; but they should demand the pardon. Leonard said, "Wallace resigned. He's just waiting for his replacement to arrive."

"Then we still have time. The more I hear - like today, seeing they appointed Bob Olinger - shows that only criminals are against me. Same War. Same reasons."

Leonard said tenderly, "But its got just one soldier left."

"No, Ira. The people are just waiting for a chance."

Their train passed Albuquerque. At times, the red Rio Grand was seen in their southern course. At the San Marcial depot, Billy learned from Leonard that Rincón was two and a half hours away. He smiled and stretched. "Food sure is good at these stops. I like riding trains. Some day I'd like to fly in a hot air balloon. Except you wouldn't get the full effect. I'd imagine having wings is better."

Leonard thought, "So young. So unfair. There's no hope."

As they entered the Rincón station, Billy saw that further tracks, still under construction, were blocked by flatcars laden with steel rails, cross ties, and kegs of spikes. Tony Neis exited.

Then Billy noticed men riding out from behind the stationhouse. One horse was a palomino. Tony Neis began to shout. Bob Olinger leapt to the seat behind them.

Eight men approached the train, Yginio Salazar in front.

Billy thrust fisted hands high out the window. Olinger yelled, "Goddamn cocksuckers, come closer and I shoot him."

Billy said, "Ira - go out last. I remember you don't enjoy flying bullets." When they were on the platform, Olinger put the double barrels to Billy's head. Billy said loudly, "I'd be careful, Neis. The last time Bob tried this maneuver he shot through his victim and crippled his friend." Yginio translated. The others jeered.

When prisoners and guards entered the stationhouse, Neis showed his badge to the reluctant station agent, and said they would pay for rooms in his upstairs quarters.

Suddenly, the door opened. Olinger and Chávez took aim. Billy called out, "Ira, we're spending the night. These men need to rest their trigger fingers."

MARCH 29, 1881   3:32 PM   TUESDAY

The four horse stagecoach traveled southward as Billy, in the middle row, looked out. Carpeting the hot flatlands were extravagant spills of golden-orange Mexican poppies, blue flax, and white asters. Beside him was Ira Leonard. The front seat held Bob Olinger and Tony Neis. In the back, was Francisco Chávez with Billy Wilson, whose head jostled in passive escape of sleep.

Billy asked Leonard who the district attorney was. "Their top man: Catron's replacement, U.S. Attorney Sidney Barnes - his good friend." The jury decides, Billy responded.

Billy Wilson awoke with a start. Initially confused, he stared wildly at Francisco Chávez, then leaned toward Leonard, asking if he was his lawyer. "No. Yours is still Edgar Caypless. Arraignment and trial for you is tomorrow." Wilson wanted to know if they could hang you the same day. "No. First the jury decides guilt or innocence; later the judge sets the penalty." Wilson again sought oblivion.

Leonard said to Billy that Dan Dedrick would be a witness. Billy answered that he could straighten things out. Leonard said, "First of all, he's been arrested himself. They indicted his brothers too; but they escaped the Territory."

Leonard whispered. "Dan Dedrick will be a witness against Wilson. The district attorney must have made a deal.

"More to the point, for your case: what do you know about Doctor Joseph Blazer's property?"

"Just that he owns the mill, the post office, the way station, and land around them. That's got something to do with the Roberts indictment?"

"Possibly. But let me go over some basics. You'll go through an arraignment. They read out the indictment, confirm your name, ask whether you understand the charge, and ask what your plea is."

Billy asked who said not guilty. Leonard smiled. "I do. I'm there with you."

At the Las Cruces stage stop was a small crowd of curiosity seekers, with dress representing the local cultural mix: primarily Mexican, with a few Indians and Whites. A muttonchopped man in a brown suit and with a pad spoke to Tony Neis, who was signaling to the waiting ambulance, which would carry them the final few miles to Mesilla. Bob Olinger exited; next Leonard with his leather case, but forgetting his traveling satchel. His head jerked back. Billy had it. Someone called, "Which of you's Billy the Kid?"

Billy placed joined hands on surprised Ira Leonard's shoulder, saying, "This is the man."

The *Daily New Mexican* reporter stepped closer to the balding man. "Kid, I've got some questions." He rapidly wrote, *"Older than expected. Pale and skinny after his long imprisonment."*

Billy laughed. "He's the Kid," said Tony Neis. "Make it fast."

"Least that makes more sense," the reporter muttered. "Tell me about your murders." Billy claimed innocence. "But haven't you shot and killed men?"

Billy became serious. "Almost two hundred indictments - a hundred for murder - came out of the Lincoln County War over the past three years. I was involved in the death of only a few men, and only in a group as either a Deputy Constable or a posseman; though attempt was made to say otherwise through the illegal acts of partisan Governor Axtell, who was removed by our efforts."

The reporter wrote: *"At least two hundred men have been killed in Lincoln County during the past three years, but I did not kill all of them."*

That night, Billy Wilson slept while Billy looked out their barred window facing an alley, dark on the night of the new moon.

MARCH 30, 1881   10:21 AM   WEDNESDAY

Billy Wilson was brought back to the cell, big head drooped. "Yer case is nex'," the jailer said. "Is yer name Billy the Kid?" Billy shook his head. "I made tha' bet. Ye don' look like no Billy the Kid."

"Thanks," Billy said as the jailer left. He asked Wilson, lying and facing the wall, "How'd it go?"

"Dedrick was there. If I'da had me a gun I'da shot 'im. He said I was a counerfeita. An' the judge - same ugly ol' man as in Vegas - says rustlin' - an' mail robbry too. An' rape. I ain' even had me a girl in a year. An' every time Caypless talks, this lawyer, Barnes, says 'objeck.' An' the Judge says 'sustemed.' Then Caypless stops talkin'. Mus' mean 'shut yer mouth.' " Wilson retched. "Bu' the goddamn judge, he let Barnes an' goddamn Dedrick talk an' talk. Then the jury they goes ou'; an' then they's back. Said I was guilty o' everythin' 'cept rape."

Bob Olinger, Tony Neis, and Francisco Chàvez approached their cell with the jailer. Olinger said, "Time for your hanging, Kid."

"This 'ere's the Kid?" asked the jailer. "Why'd you say you wasn'?"

" 'Cause that's not my name."

Billy and his guards proceeded out into intense sunlight of the hot day, on the street unchanged since September of 1877 when he had approached the oversized courthouse doors where Tom O'Keefe had found the cigar stub. Billy noticed one, as if marking his circular trajectory.

Inside, spectators, crowding the long, sweltering, viga-beamed courtroom, quieted to stare. At the far end, was a platform with black-robed Judge Warren Bristol behind a table. To its side was the witness chair. Another table was for Clerk of Court George Bowman. Along the white-washed wall to the right, were rows of jury benches. Opposite was open seating, where men vied for places.

Ira Leonard, flushed with excitement, strode to Billy and pointed to the empty bench in front of the jury section. Sitting beside Billy, he said, "I've got a few minutes to explain what's happened." The three guards, displaying long guns to the crowd, stood behind them.

Leonard said, "Bristol accepted my motion to quash the Andrews case! That means throw it out!" He hugged his leather satchel to his chest. It held documentation for what he considered the most clever argument of his career. He said, "For the Hearing on that, there's just you, me, Bristol, the clerk to record it, and U.S. Attorney Barnes." For the first time, he put an arm around Billy, who smiled with pleasure.

Bristol called the court to order. People swatted at flies attempting to land on their perspiration-wet faces. In a deep singsong, the Bailiff announced, "Case Number four eleven: United States versus Charles Bowdre, Josiah Scurlock, Henry Brown, William Bonney alias Henry Antrim alias Kid, John Middleton, Frederick Waite, Jim French, and George Coe for the murder of Andrew Roberts."

Billy and Leonard walked to the platform where hatred glinted from the sunken eyes of the judge, whose bony fingers arched high on his papers like spider legs. After establishing name, receiving the plea of not guilty, and watching the Bailiff direct Billy back to his seat, Bristol requested Leonard's argument.

"Your Honor," Leonard drew in a deep breath, "I contend that the plea of 'not guilty' is unnecessary in this case of the United States versus my client, because the United States - the federal government - has no jurisdiction over land that is *privately* owned in a Territory.

"My client's indictment is based on the *erroneous* statement that the death of Andrew Roberts occurred on the Mescalero Reservation. But the property where it *did* occur - known as Blazer's Mill - was purchased by a Doctor Joseph Blazer in eighteen sixty-seven from a George Nesmith, prior the reservation's establishment by President Ulysses S. Grant on May twenty-fourth eighteen seventy-two. So, from the time of purchase to the present day - including the day of Andrew Roberts's death - the property was in private hands.

"Since the federal government has *no right* to promulgate a case against my client, I request that Mister Bonney's indictment for the murder of Andrew Roberts be quashed."

Spectator volume rose, most not understanding the argument; and some asking another to repeat it in Spanish.

U.S. Attorney Sidney Barnes was next. The prosperously rotund prosecutor, with gray fish-tail mustache like his friend Catron's, looped a thumb in a vest pocket, and strode along the platform. "Your honor," he said in Kentuckian drawl, "we are talking about a heinous crime committed just one county from ours: A crime in which the defendant - with an outlaw gang - murdered a lone elderly man.

"To argue that the government of the Untied States cannot protect its citizens is absurd. And the technicality that the Blazer property is immune to the jurisdiction of the federal government is also absurd.

"The Mescalero Reservation is approximately five hundred seventy thousand acres. *Within it,* is the acreage used by Blazer. I contend that the reservation is defined by its *boundary perimeter*. And all Indian Country is under the jurisdiction of the federal government.

"Therefore this case of the United States Government as plaintiff is both valid and necessary to provide justice in this foul crime of murder."

The judge thanked the big man and postponed trial for deliberation.

The guards assembled around Billy, leaving Ira Leonard to follow them out.

As the spectators jostled, a note by someone unseen was pressed into Ira Leonard's hand; a gun jabbed his back. The pushing crowd kept him moving. When outside, he read the scrawled scrap. "*We wont miss the secon tyme. Git off the Kid case.*" It was signed "*X.*"

After nightfall, when Leonard entered his cell, Billy grinned broadly. "That was great, Ira. And with Brady, I wasn't even shooting at him." Leonard handed him the note. Billy smiled scornfully. "Good. They're running scared."

The man could not look at him. "I came to tell you that, when this Roberts case is over, I'm requesting that another court appointed attorney be assigned. I'm sorry. I ..."

"I understand." Billy's blurred voice was soothing as he collected himself. "They play real rough. Figure it this way: they probably mean it. A dead lawyer couldn't help me much." The blue eyes appeared to Leonard strangely iridescent as they looked into his own.

"D'you know who I'd get?" Leonard said it was Albert Jennings Fountain. Billy sighed, saying, "One of the lawyers who got Dolan and the others out of Stanton in seventy-nine."

Leonard said, "Fountain has a co-counsel: an attorney named John Bail - from Silver City." Billy asked about the jury. "Twenty-one have been selected: all Mexican. Twelve would sit for your case."

"Do they know anything about the Lincoln County War?"

Leonard studied his delicate hands. "Only what's in the papers."

"But when I take the stand I'll explain. D'you know when I go back to court?" It was toward the end of the week. The district attorney would be Simon Newcomb. Billy said, "Newcomb was with Fountain at Stanton. Anything else about him?"

"He's District Attorney Rynerson's close friend." The boy was quiet. "Forgive me, Billy."

"Nothing to forgive, Ira. I figure we probably won today. We'll see about tomorrow when it comes." He then asked, "No chance of Edgar Caypless?"

"No. He left right after Wilson's case to go to Las Vegas for the Rudabaugh murder trial."

Billy hid response at the discovery. He said, "Well, Caypless still has my replevin case."

After Ira Leonard departed, Billy was left with an image of the Fugio cent as he struggled to suppress pain about its owner.

APRIL 6, 1881   2:48 PM   WEDNESDAY

Billy and Ira Leonard stood before Judge Bristol as he read his Andrew Roberts case decision. " *'It is therefore the finding of the Court that no private property in New Mexico Territory can be considered Indian Country to the extent that it is governed by the laws of the federal government, rather than the Territorial laws. Therefore the indictment is quashed and the case is dismissed.'*

"In addition, the Court accepts the petition of Attorney Ira Leonard to step down as the attorney of William Bonney, and now appoints Albert Jennings Fountain as counsel and John D. Bail as co-counsel for said defendant."

As they exited with the three guards, Ira Leonard said to Billy, "I cut this from *Newman's Semi-Weekly* from April second. What your future jurors are reading."

Billy scanned. "**Billy the Kid is a notoriously dangerous character and has on several occasions escaped justice where escape appeared even more improbable than now, and has bragged that he only wants to get out of jail in order to kill Governor Wallace. We hope that legal technicalities will not set him free.**" Billy crumpled and dropped it for a grinding turn of his bootsole.

Leonard watched the boy as his guards forced a path through the curious. "I'll never see him again," he thought. "He has to know there's no hope now." Tears came to his eyes. He crossed the street to the Corn Exchange Hotel to gather his belongings for his return to Las Vegas. He felt defeated, but relieved. The pressure beginning with Huston Chapman's murder was finally over.

APRIL 8, 1881   9:09 AM   FRIDAY

Billy Wilson, on his cot, asked Billy if they were going to hang him. "First have to convict me of something you can hang a man for."

They heard people. Two strangers in well-tailored conservative suits were let in by a new jailor. The younger of the two, in his early forties, had plain features; a brown mustache to his jawline; and short, light brown hair, brushed back from balding temples. "Which of you's the Kid?" he asked, glancing with cold intelligent eyes hooded by loose skin. Billy responded. The man said, "I'm Albert Jennings Fountain. This is my co-counsel, John D. Bail." Gray-haired, Bail had a large mustache, almost white.

"Know anythin' 'bout my case?" asked Billy Wilson.

"No, boy," said Fountain. "Kid, yours follows the one being heard now. That's enough time for what we need to do." He chose the spindly chair at the small table.

Billy sat on his cot. Bail joined him at an obvious distance. Billy asked icily, "Do I have any other choice besides you?" Fountain said no. Billy asked, "What d'you know about the Lincoln County War?"

"A lawless element attempted to take over that county. Their violence, combined with the depredations of Victorio, kept our Territory from becoming a state. I'm proud to say that I've not only written about the issues in my paper, the *Mesilla Valley Independent*, as part of my war against outlawry, but I organized the Volunteer Mesilla Scouts to kill Victorio."

"Seems you put me in the outlaw category. And you think you can defend me?"

Pompously and unfazed, Fountain answered, "Without the slightest doubt. The judicial system of our great country is based on providing every defendant with an advocate as well as a prosecutor. Why I volunteer my services is not to protect you per se, but our democratic rights."

Billy's expression did not soften. "Are you a member of the Santa Fe Ring?" Fountain answered that there was no such organization. "Are you a friend of Thomas Benton Catron?"

"I am, like him, a Republican, and active in the Party; and, like him, a member of the Masonic Lodge. Conspiracy or collusion - if that's what you're implying - is pure fabrication."

"Mister Fountain, I'm about to go to trial for murder. I'm trying to figure how you'll handle my case. What about the fact that Governor Wallace promised me a pardon in exchange for testimony which I gave? Did Ira Leonard tell you that?"

"He did. He also told me that Lew Wallace never prepared a document of pardon. It would be inconceivable to a jury, first that the Governor would make such a promise to an outlaw, and secondly, if made, that he hadn't carried it out. You'd seem a liar."

"Then I want to testify. They changed my venue because Lincoln County citizens understood the War."

"That venue change was *precisely* for that partisanship. If Judge Bristol believed a fair trial would have been possible there, he wouldn't have granted a change."

Fountain looked at John Bail, staring vacantly. "We'll decide whether the Kid takes the stand."

Bail guffawed. "Who else would? Simon Newcomb isn't going to call him."

Billy said, "Before we go into court, would you like to ask me if I shot Sheriff Brady?" Fountain said it was unnecessary. "Attorney Fountain, whether you want to know or not, I did not shoot him. And for that matter, I didn't shoot Deputy Hindman either. I never even aimed at them."

"And who, perchance, *were* you aiming at?" Billy said Billy Matthews. But Brady had stolen his Winchester and he needed a carbine's range. Fountain smiled condescendingly. "Perhaps you'd like to tell the jury that?"

"I'd like to tell them the truth: that I didn't murder Brady. And that Brady was killed to protect an innocent man he was going to murder within three hours: Alexander McSween. Just like he murdered John Tunstall forty-two days before. And McSween was murdered anyway by the Ring - using Stanton soldiers under Colonel Dudley - a hundred and nine days later. And I was there too - still protecting McSween. He stood for the people."

Skeptically, Fountain asked about protecting. "Yes, Mister Fountain. Me and others risked our lives or died in the Lincoln County War, fighting to protect freedom, rights, and property."

John Bail spoke. "I've been thinking, Kid. I'm a Silver City man. I saw one of your aliases is Henry Antrim. You're not related to a Henry Antrim from Silver City, are you?"

"Antrim is my stepfather's name. I've been called that."

"Then damned if I don't remember about you. Albert, listen to this. Harvey Whitehill - he was Sheriff in Silver City back then - still tells the story. And this here's the very boy. You wouldn't know it now, but years ago, he was a little fella. Harvey, he put him in jail there. This boy was around fourteen or fifteen. He'd killed a local Chinaman. Stabbed him. And know what the little rascal did? He wriggled up the chimney and escaped. Whitehill always said that boy would be hanged. He even tried to drown Harvey's son."

"Mister Bail, the only true thing you said was that I escaped through a chimney."

Both men laughed. "We're wasting our time," said Bail. "Let's go to Court."

As they stood, Billy asked Fountain, "Could you argue for a verdict of 'innocent,' and set free the person you most want to see dead," he sneered, "now that Victorio is."

"Of course. I'm your defense attorney." His face grew hard. "But if I was the prosecutor, I'd see you hanged."

Into the dry, red, heat-shimmering street, Billy led the procession that was his march to the courthouse. Milling people struggled to glimpse him. Swaggering heavy-bodied Bob Olinger repeatedly called out, "Get back. Dangerous," as Deputy Marshals Tony Neis and Francisco Chávez followed.

The wide-open doors of the courthouse revealed a solid press of humanity inside. Everywhere the word "Kid" echoed in other babble.

As the path cleared into the stifling chamber, Billy could see, across the long space, the black-robed judge facing him. Near his table were three standing men: Albert Jennings Fountain; John Bail; and the district attorney, Simon Newcomb. Fountain was laughing, his friendly hand on Newcomb's shoulder.

Spectators pushed for places on benches. Those defeated, stood along the left wall. At the entrance, more men clogged, making it impossible to close the oversized doors. The only emptiness was the jury seating.

On a bench closest to the judge, a short man sat, sapphire eyes brilliant. Billy met James Dolan's gaze fearlessly, and the man's expression of vindictive triumph faded.

Beside Dolan was Saturnino Baca, grown heavier, his protruding belly forcing him to spread thin thighs. His long beard had become almost white. To Baca's left was slab-faced Billy Matthews, who glared at Billy before turning to Isaac Ellis, ostentatiously holding his subpoena as if it forgave his presence.

The Bailiff recited in the din, "Cases five thirty-one and five thirty-two: Territory of New Mexico versus John Middleton, Henry Brown, Frank MacNab, Fred Waite, Jim French, and William Bonney alias Henry Antrim alias Kid indicted for the murder of William Brady and George Hindman. Case five thirty-one to be heard first."

The Bailiff called twelve Hispanic names. The crowd took up the call for a missing member. Finally, a middle-aged man with sombrero and serape rushed in saying to the judge, "Pleese perdóneme. My God ... How you say eet een Engleesh?"

Bristol began. "Case five thirty-one. Present William Bonney, indicted for the murder of William Brady." His skeletal blue-veined hand warded off a fly. It alighted on the docket paper. He crushed it.

"William Bonney," he said to the boy standing before him, "what do you plead?" He brushed the dead fly to the floor.

"I plead 'Not guilty.' " Billy looked at the twelve jurymen. None met his eyes.

When Billy sat with his attorneys, behind them stood the three armed guards. Billy leaned toward Fountain. "I can hear the jurors. They need a translator." Fountain did not respond.

The judge called on District Attorney Simon Newcomb. The small gray-suited man walked forward, holding high his square confident head. The same age as Fountain, his bald crown made him appear older, as did his blunt mustache and gray goatee.

Nodding to the judge, he then faced the jury of uncomfortably hot men. Difficult, he thought, looking at Billy. So young. Looks innocent. Dolan should have warned me. Bristol knew too. Newcomb felt angry, then decided it would make no difference.

He began. "Gentlemen of the Jury, I come before you on behalf of the Territory of New Mexico to present the charges against William Bonney, who uses the aliases Henry Antrim and Billy the Kid.

"The Territory of New Mexico makes the following charges. First: That on the first day of April eighteen seventy-eight, without motive of self-defense, acting as their leader, he brought five other men to Lincoln to waylay in ambush William Brady."

Billy whispered to Fountain, "I was never appointed leader." Fountain made a nonverbal acknowledgement, and continued to focus on the prosecutor.

"Second: That William Bonney did murder, by one or more gunshot wounds, said William Brady.

"Third: That he had premeditated intent to commit such murder.

"Fourth: That he was fully cognizant that said William Brady was the Sheriff of the County of Lincoln."

"The shereeff!" Billy heard a juryman exclaim.

"Fifth: That William Bonney was under the employment of a criminal whom said Sheriff Brady was attempting to arrest.

"Sixth: That he was a gunman hired for the purpose of intimidation and murder."

Without rising, Albert Jennings Fountain spoke. "As counsel for the defendant, I object to the prosecution's allegation that my client had any role as leader." When it was not sustained, Fountain continued, "Further objection is made to the prosecution's allegation that the defendant was hired as a gunman."

After that was denied, Fountain said, "I now petition the Court for a translator so that the defendant can be assured of jury comprehension."

Judge Warren Bristol said, "Petition denied."

Bristol continued, "The prosecution is now requested to present witnesses."

Isaac Ellis was called. In a cheap sweat-wrinkled suit, he nervously sucked saliva for his dry throat.

Simon Newcomb's questioning began. "To the best of your recollection, were you present in the town of Lincoln on the first day of April in eighteen seventy-eight?" Ellis described mending his corral fencing. "Do you know the defendant, William Bonney?"

"Depends on what you mean by know," Ellis responded warily. When told recognizing, he said, " 'Course. That boy with all those men with guns." Some spectators laughed. When asked if he had seen William Bonney in the town on that day, Ellis answered, "Yes. After the sheriff got shot people went out; so I went out. With the men riding away, I saw his gray mare."

Simon Newcomb said somberly that Ellis had been a member of the Coroner's Jury, and requested his description of Sheriff Brady's wounds. Ellis said, "Bullet holes. One in his head. Eight in his chest."

At Fountain's turn, he said, "Mister Ellis, you have convinced the Court that you saw the body of William Brady. But the fact that he was dead is not in question. I ask, 'Did *anything* occur to your direct observation - other than viewing a horse's posterior - to link the defendant and the death?" Isaac Ellis's denial was followed by spectator laughter and jurymen urgently asking others to translate.

After the midday recess, Saturnino Baca was on the stand. Simon Newcomb asked if he was present on the day of the murder. "Yes. There I lived with my wife Juana María Chávez and our nine children." Noting that he had said lived, Newcomb asked if they had moved. Fountain objected to the irrelevance, but was not sustained.

Baca whined, "Because I feared for my life and the life of my children. Billy the Kid had a hatred of us because we are Mehican."

Albert Jennings Fountain said irritably, "Objection! This is prejudicial to the defendant."

"It can be shown, your Honor," said Simon Newcomb, "that the statements address the motivation for the murder."

Newcomb was allowed to continue. "Mister Baca, how did you learn about the risk to your family?"

"From the wife of McSween, who hired the Kid to kill us. She came to our little poor house near her big rich house and said that, if we did not leave, we would be killed by Billy the Kid."

"Billy whispered to Fountain, "That's all lies. Like what he tried in Dudley's trial."

Simon Newcomb asked, "Mister Baca, does this relate to the murder of William Brady?"

"Yes, Señor Attorney. Even though the sheriff was Anglo, he had a Mehican wife; and, like me, nine children." Bristol allowed angry talking among the jurymen without admonition.

At cross-examination, Fountain asked, "Mister Baca, can you link the defendant to the murder?"

"Yes, Señor. The sheriff he was my friend. One time - maybe a week before the murder - he says to me, 'Saturnino, you and me should fear. The Kid he has sworn revenge against us."

"Mister Baca, when did you move your family from Lincoln?" He gave the month as September. "You waited *five months* before you so-called 'fled' for safety?"

Baca's sly eyes glinted. "Yes, Attorney. Possibly you do not understand that Mehican people are so poor that to get enough money - even to save our lives - can take months." The jury as well as the spectators made low angry conversation.

"Notwithstanding your claims, Mister Baca, did you witness the murder, or did you have any knowledge that the defendant, William Bonney, was in Lincoln?" Baca denied both.

Billy Matthews was next. In answer to Simon Newcomb's questioning, he stated that on the date of the murder he was a Lincoln County Deputy Sheriff. Describing the meeting with Brady the day of the murder, he answered, "Will told us deputies that he had to post a notice on the courthouse door to tell jurors ... Wait.

"I got to say there was a mix-up about the start of the spring session of District Court. So we all had to go to the courthouse to put up a notice." During this lie, he glanced frequently at Dolan, who had coached him.

Matthews was asked about any other official business. "Well, it's a long story. Sheriff Brady had this warrant for McSween, who was an embezzler, who hired the Kid ..."

To Fountain's interruption of irrelevance, Matthews was told to be more specific. "You could say that if Alexander McSween came to town we'd have to arrest him on that warrant. Anyways, we - I mean us deputies and Will Brady - headed to the courthouse.

"I remember Brady stopping to talk to a *Mexican* lady. Then we came to this adobe wall and all hell broke lose and Brady and Hindman were murdered and ..."

"Objection to the mention of other murders," said Albert Jennings Fountain, and was sustained.

Billy Matthews resumed. "I saw Brady go down, and ran into the house of a *Mexican* family."

Matthews was asked by Newcomb if he had seen the defendant. All waited breathlessly. "Yes."

Asked to elaborate, Matthews said, "To explain rightly, from that house, I was looking down the street to the east. Brady was lying in the middle. There was this building - now it's the J.J. Dolan Store - that came up to the street. The adobe wall was set back to its east side. So, from where I was, I couldn't see the gate and the adobe wall. But out runs the Kid with Jim French to the sheriff's body. And I saw him give orders ..."

"Objection," interrupted Fountain. "From the distance and position of the witness, anything about 'orders' is pure conjecture, and cannot be considered evidence."

Matthews was allowed to continue. "They were orders 'cause the Kid was pointing at the body. Then I saw French moving his head like 'yes.' Also, I was shooting at them. I wasn't just watching. And then I saw the Kid look in Brady's pockets for that McSween arrest warrant; 'cause McSween couldn't be arrested without it."

At his turn, Albert Jennings Fountain began, "If I understood your testimony, Mister Matthews, you believe the defendant was involved in the murder of William Brady. Did you see the defendant when the fatal shots were fired?" He admitted he had not.

"Mister Matthews, you have told the Court under oath that, on that day, Sheriff Brady's first order of business was to post a notice. At the time you and the three other deputies accompanied him were you armed?" This was confirmed. "Was it customary for the sheriff, when posting a routine notice, to take with him three armed guards?"

Matthews thought and swatted at flies. "Well, like I said, we were worried that the Kid gang could attack or we might have to arrest McSween." He saw Dolan's encouraging nod.

"What became of that notice?" Matthews's slab-like face colored. He admitted to never having seen it.

"Mister Matthews, was the day cold?" He acknowledged that. "Do you recall if William Brady had on an overcoat?" After the positive response, Fountain asked and received confirmation that the coat was buttoned, and raised his eyebrows in skeptical exaggeration.

"Mister Matthews, you have told the Court that it was your observation that the defendant 'looked in' the pockets' - to use your words - of said William Brady, in your supposition, searching for an arrest warrant. I find it impossible to believe - even assuming that the defendant has courage surpassing that of any man known, and foolhardiness of the same degree - that he would neatly unbutton a man's overcoat, and possibly jacket, while all the time being subjected to the repeated firing of a determined assailant."

The courtroom burst into laughter. Billy Matthews glanced bitterly at James Dolan.

After court, Albert Jennings Fountain and John Bail, talking and laughing, walked ahead of Billy and his guards.

The crowd parted, as many, Billy noticed, eyed him with hostility.

"Attorney Fountain," he called out. Fountain stopped. "There's no way this jury can understand my case with all the lies. Your arguments are good, but the jurymen need information. I want to take the stand."

Fountain said impatiently that no one would believe him. "I'm for trying. There's just this case. Then Hindman."

"Let me give you the plain truth, boy, since you just don't give up. Ira Leonard got the case of the *federal government* versus you dismissed. But he missed that all they need to do - and will do - is make another case for the *Territory of New Mexico* against you.

"And if Brady's case goes out on a technicality, they've got Hindman. And I've heard talk of a Morris Bernstein, killed on the Mescalero Reservation, with you as the suspect. And there are Frank Baker, William Morton and Manuel Segovia. There's a warrant for attempted murder of Private Berry Robinson. And rustling and counterfeiting. I'm just telling you the truth. Now you must excuse us." The guards led Billy away.

Across the street, Simon Newcomb called to Fountain and Bail, "Ready for our dinner at the Corn Exchange?" James Dolan, beside Newcomb, was smiling at a comment. Fountain answered yes; just an unforeseen delay.

APRIL 9, 1881   11:11 AM   SATURDAY

James Dolan was on the stand. "And your occupation?" District Attorney Simon Newcomb asked. The answer was merchant.

When Dolan was asked the reason for his relocation from his previous store, Albert Jennings Fountain objected to its relevance. Newcomb continued after Bristol denied the objection.

Dolan dabbed his eyes with a handkerchief. "My business failed because of the state of fear caused by the Billy the Kid gang. And I had tried so hard to help the Mexican farmers."

Asked if he knew Sheriff Brady, the handkerchief muffled a tremulous: "Yes. "I loved him like a brother."

"Mister Dolan, you have mentioned the defendant. Are you able to identify him?"

"Yes." Dolan pointed at Billy, and was startled by returned grief at forever-lost heights.

In answer to a question about meeting with Brady before the murder, Dolan gave a fabricated version. "Will said, 'Jimmy, if Billy the Kid kills me because of my Mexican wife, promise you'll take care of my family.' His wife, *María Bonifacia Chávez* Brady, was about to give birth to their *ninth* child." And right after he was killed, that baby was born without a father. A jurymen loudly blew his nose.

When Fountain replaced the prosecutor, he established that James Dolan had neither witnessed the murder nor seen the defendant in town on its day.

At 2:12 PM, Judge Bristol banged his gavel for his reconvened court. After Albert Jennings Fountain denied having witnesses, Bristol said, "Gentlemen of the Jury, I now give you my instructions. The defendant, William Bonney, has been indicted, with others, for murdering William Brady by gun shot wounds from a premeditated design. If true, that constitutes murder in the first degree.

"To find William Bonney guilty of murder in the first degree, you must believe, from the evidence, the following propositions.

"First: That he either inflicted one or more of the fatal wounds causing death; or that he was present and encouraged, aided in, or commanded such killing.

"Second: That such killing was without justification.

"Third: As to premeditated design, I inform you that if that plan existed in his mind for *even a moment* before murder, it would still be premeditated. In fact, that plan can be considered to exist if the defendant was *merely present* at the murder, and would make him as guilty as if he fired the fatal shot.

"Fourth: As to the fact that the defendant was in a group with others who may also have been shooting at the victim, I inform you to disregard that, and consider that each was behaving as an *individual;* and the defendant was therefore the same as a *lone gunman*." The last point was Thomas Benton Catron's contribution to counter a possible defense argument of second degree.

"And, to justify a guilty verdict, you must be satisfied from the evidence beyond reasonable doubt. But I instruct you that 'reasonable doubt' does not mean that you must believe William Bonney's guilt with *mathematical certainty* as you would two plus two are four. If the evidence leaves you with a *moral certainty* that he is guilty, this is sufficient proof of guilt.

"I emphasize that murder in the first degree is the greatest crime known to our laws. If you believe that the defendant is guilty, you are also saying that he will suffer the punishment of death by hanging."

Some jurors and spectators glanced at Billy, expressionless and straight-backed, manacled hands on lap, with three, ominously armed lawmen behind him.

Bristol said, "The Bailiff will now translate my instructions." For the first time, the jurymen received the proceedings in Spanish.

Next, Simon Newcomb began his closing argument, pacing with light-footed step. "Gentlemen of the Jury, you have just heard the honorable Judge Bristol remind you that the crime committed by this defendant is the worst that a man can commit. We even needed three armed men to protect us here. And, at this very moment, in Lincoln, Sheriff Brady's widow is weeping and remembering that, almost to the day three years ago, she was told her unborn baby's father was murdered by this Billy the Kid. Billy the Kid is a man whose only occupation was as a gunman to commit murder. For so the witnesses have told us. And, Gentlemen of the Jury, we are also talking about the murder of a sheriff.

"I say to you, in conclusion, that there is absolutely no doubt that William Bonney is guilty of all charges. And I say, 'Thank God that Billy the Kid has been captured before any more fall as his victims.'

"And I say that - based on the instructions of Judge Bristol - there is only *one possible verdict*: guilty of murder in the first degree. I thank you all. I rest my case." The room was frozen in silence.

When Albert Jennings Fountain was called, a jurymen swatted at a wasp; those nearby cringing in fear that the insect, if merely wounded, would sting, as if embodying the dangerous boy.

Fountain's eyes wandered without attempt to achieve rapport. "Gentlemen of the Jury," he said, "anyone accused has the right to have an attorney. That is my job.

"I emphasize the following: First, by the evidence, you must either find the defendant guilty of murder in the first degree or acquit him. Second, that you cannot find him guilty of murder in the first degree unless you are satisfied that he fired the shot or shots, or assisted in the firing of the shots, that caused the death with a premeditated design. Third, if you have any reasonable doubt, you must give a verdict of acquittal."

After the jury left for deliberation, and Fountain and John Bail walked away, Bob Olinger taunted, "Want to bet how fast those greasers 'ill hang the Kid? Kid, want to join our bet?"

At 5:16 PM, the jurymen returned. Their Foreman stood, awkwardly clutching excess garments and a paper. It fluttered to the floor. When it was retrieved, the Bailiff bore it in brief importance to Warren Bristol, who perused it and said, "These are the findings in Case five thirty-one: *'We the Jury find William Bonney guilty as charged in the murder of William Brady.'* "

Spectator cheering erupted. Through the doorway, the cry of guilty poured into the street. Bristol banged his gavel and said, "Defendant William Bonney is to return for sentencing before me on Wednesday, the thirteenth of April, eighteen hundred eighty- one."

Then the chaotic throng pressed to the exit. The guards and Billy struggled through the people, who were just parts of bodies and clothing, flashing eyes, bared teeth, and moving tongues.

On the street were shouts of "Leench Beely the Keed! Revenge for Mehican Shereeff Brazos!"

Later, inside their cell, Billy Wilson was blanketed completely, facing the wall.

Billy sat on his own cot and watched the candle dripping moon-white wax. "They gonna hang you?" Wilson asked.

"Seems they want to," Billy answered, examining his wrist cuffs.

APRIL 13, 1881   4:14 PM   WEDNESDAY

On the courtroom bench between Albert Jennings Fountain and John Bail, Billy watched the backs of another defendant, F.C. Clark, and his attorney as they faced Judge Warren Bristol. When the departing prisoner passed, Billy could see jail pallor coupled with terror. He was called next.

Bristol's long yellow teeth were exposed in an involuntary spasm of gratification as he spoke. "The Court asks William Bonney if he has anything he wishes to say?"

Billy was silent, defiant eyes never leaving the morbid head. "The Court considers that the defendant has chosen to make no statement.

"The Court will render its sentence. It is decided by the Court that William Bonney alias Henry Antrim alias Kid be taken to the County of Lincoln and there delivered into the custody of the Sheriff; and that he be confined in jail until Friday the thirteenth day of May in the year of our Lord one thousand eight hundred and eighty-one.

"And that on the day aforesaid, between the hours of nine of the clock in the morning and three of the clock in the afternoon, he be taken to some suitable place of execution by the Sheriff and there be hanged by the neck until his body be dead."

Billy and his guards exited amidst babbling spectator bloodlust. At the street, Billy stopped Albert Jennings Fountain and asked, "If I appealed that the jury needed a translator, would it delay the hanging?" He nodded. "Are you the only attorney who'd take my case?"

Their eyes, narrowed in mutual dislike, stayed in contact. "I'd say I'm the only one commanding enough respect to do anything for you. I'd take your case - but only for money."

APRIL 15, 1881   11:06 AM   FRIDAY

Billy Wilson asked why the jailer had gotten him paper and ink. Billy said, "Wish he'd been on my jury. He knew the truth. He also said everyone's been told I'll be moved next week. "I'm writing to Attorney Caypless. D'you want me to write something for you?"

"Ain' no purpis. They aw lie. If we'd agotten through tha' tunnel, I'd be far 'way. Bu' firs', I'd ashot goddamn Dan Dedrick."

No longer paying attention, Billy wrote his address as the Mesilla jail. He continued: "*Dear Sir. I would have written before this but could get no paper. My United States case was thrown out of court and I was rushed to trial on my Territorial charge. I was convicted of murder in the first degree and am to be hanged on the 13th of May. Attorney Fountain was appointed to defend me. He is willing to carry the case further if I can raise the money. The mare is about all I can depend on at present. So I hope you will settle the case right away and give him the money. Please write to Lincoln in care of Sheriff Pat Garrett. Excuse bad writing. I have my handcuffs on.*"

They could hear people approaching. Quickly Billy signed, and wrote on the folded outside, "*Attorney Edgar Caplis, Las Vegas, New Mexico Territory.*"

When the jailer returned, he brought a boyish freckled reporter from the *Mesilla News*, who said to Billy, "You just put our town on the map! What's your opinion of the verdict?"

Billy handed his letter through the bars to the jailer, and said, "I should have been declared innocent. The jurymen were not given the facts; and the witnesses were all partisan and lied. But unlike in Lincoln County where people knew the truth, the jurymen used those witnesses and newspapers, which had more lies. That's why I got a rough deal in my trial."

The reporter wrote, "*I got a rough deal on my trial;*" and asked, "Any paper in particular that you think turned people against you?"

Billy smiled faintly. "My reading's been limited. But Simon Newman's article in *Newman's Semi-Weekly* on April second was trying to incite a mob. I think it was a dirty trick when I couldn't defend myself. Seems he wanted to give me a kick downhill." The youth copied that verbatim and asked for a statement about his dire fate.

"It's unjust that I should be the only participant in the Lincoln County War to suffer the extreme penalty of the law. And, in particular, that everyone on the side of the Santa Fe Ring not only went unpunished, but profited. That includes getting away with murder and robbery of land, livestock, and possessions."

The reporter said, "If that's true, great injustice took place."

Doubt clouded his freckled face as he considered his editor's response. He wrote, *"Kid thinks it hard that he should be the only one to suffer the extreme penalty of the law."*

He then asked for Billy's final statement. He said, "Advise persons never to engage in killing." It was recorded without comprehension of ironic intent.

The reporter pocketed his pad and said, "I ... I just wondered ... It's only twenty-eight days till ... I'd be ... Are you scared?"

Billy smiled. "Why? Twenty-eight days is a long time."

APRIL 16, 1881   10:02 PM   SATURDAY

In semi-darkness of the narrow corridor, Bob Olinger and four others waited as the jailer fumbled with the lock, having just learned the secret transport plans. Billy Wilson fearfully asked if they were taking him. One answered, "I'm Sheriff here in Doña Ana County: James Southwick. Just the Kid."

The jailer held new arm and leg shackles. Billy Matthews stepped forward. Billy ignored him and concentrated on flexing his ankles in hope of looser cuffs.

James Southwick said, "Seemed like justice to me, Kid. The man you almost murdered bringing you to your hanging."

With wrists briefly free, Billy slipped on the cardigan. When his hands were joined again, the increase in weight was dramatic.

Olinger said, "Made just for you. Fourteen pounds of iron."

Billy Wilson watched with the relaxed curiosity of the immune.

Southwick added that he and some of his deputies would be riding guard. And they all had orders from high up to kill him in any rescue attempt.

Billy was then hurried out the door before he had a chance to get his coat. His anger focused on awareness that in its pocket were Tunstall's gauntlet gloves.

Wind pummeled them and rebounded helplessly from walls. At the mouth of the alley was an ambulance. From its interior, a short muscular man looked down with a nasty smile. He asked, "Remember me, Kid? *Deputy Sheriff* John Kinney."

Billy climbed up. His adapting eyes made out an additional chain. Kinney padlocked that tethering one to his wrist irons. Matthews, and Olinger joined them.

The ambulance began at a brisk trot as the maddened wind attacked its livid canvas panels, slamming concavities between the upright struts. Then the vehicle halted. A flap was rolled up. Sheriff Southwick called in, "Doing a favor for Simon Newman, boys."

Over the wind, Newman asked Billy if he was afraid of being killed on the long journey. He answered, "My guards said they'd only kill me if a rescue was attempted. And they're all real peace-loving."

Simon Newman heard Billy's laughter and wrote: *"Said he was sure his guards would not hurt him unless a rescue should be attempted. Kid says he wants to stay with the boys who're guarding him until their whiskey gave out, anyway."*

Newman asked, "What's your opinion about the hanging?"

"Wasn't my choice. Got to see if I get to Lincoln first. Can't hang a dead man, can you?"

Newman wrote, *"Says it's a stand off whether he's hanged or killed in the wagon.'"*

APRIL 19, 1881   1:59 PM   TUESDAY

As Billy's convoy skirted White Sands, John Kinney said to Billy Matthews, "Pat Coghlan's still under indictment for rustling." He turned to Billy. "Once you're hanged, he'll be let off. Wouldn't look too good to hang the rustler leader, then try Coghlan for the same thing."

Kinney chortled, "The Billy the Kid gang! Why didn't you leave? Other than a piece of lead, you couldn't get a clearer message."

Billy said, "They tried that. Ask Matthews. But he couldn't aim." Matthews scowled. Billy asked, "You'd have left the Territory?" Kinney said he'd never considered it. It was his home.

"Same with me," Billy said. "Answered your own question."

John Kinney scrutinized him, the answer unfathomable. To Bob Olinger, Kinney said, "Garrett's at Stanton?"

"Yeah. We take the Kid from there to the House in Lincoln."

Billy looked surprised. Kinney said, "It's the courthouse-jail how."

Olinger said, "And I'm a Lincoln County Deputy Sheriff on top of Deputy U.S. Marshal. I'll be your guard."

"Give us time for you to tell me all about your shooting John Jones in cold blood."

Kinney laughed. "Can't say as I don't admire you, Kid. I couldn't head to my hanging with a sense of humor." Billy asked if he was thinking about real justice.

Matthews said, "Garrett's got James Bell as deputy sheriff too."

"Bell?" Billy asked. "Isn't he a White Oaks man?" Not only that, Matthews said, but he was on the Carlyle posse.

Billy laughed. "So Garrett's got a deputy who shot his own leader and then had to blame that embarrassing mistake on me.

"And for company now I have the three of you good citizens: Bob, who murders a held down man; John, the rustler king; and Billy, the killer of Tunstall and McSween." He continued to laugh.

"Laugh now, boy. The law's on our side'" said Kinney.
"That's what's so funny, John. That's the joke."

APRIL 21, 1881   4:18 PM   THURSDAY

Approaching Lincoln, the two horses pulling the buckboard trotted briskly, leaving a gritty cloud captured in small dust devils. Invisible fingers of wind tossed Billy's hair in playful abandon, as he sat on random wagon-bed contents, and quickened his body by currents of freedom. His heavy chains rattled, the tethering one now locked to a tie-ring for lashing loads. The driver was James Bell. Alongside, rode Pat Garrett and Bob Olinger. From Fort Stanton, Billy Matthews had departed for his ranch; and the Doña Ana guards had begun their journey home.

The high hills to his right, and the more distant Capitan Mountains to the left, were taking Billy into their embrace. All plants were in commotion of swaying whipping recklessness of wind-driven new life. Bursting out in promiscuous profusion, spring's young cottontails scampered across the road. The wagon clattered past Dead Man's Rock. Billy looked to the left, to the valley of Yginio, and heard its pandemonium of bird calls and the swollen Bonito waters. Nearer, wind carried pink petals of townspeople's last-blooming peach trees; and his pale cheeks flushed with desire.

He was drawn upward. Here was freedom: here they had fought for freedom; here they had died for freedom.

"Damn it, Kid, sit," said Garrett. James Bell stopped at the House. The sun, behind Billy, burnished his hair gold and his chains silver. Bob Olinger opened the gate in the perimeter fencing.

"Stay back," commanded Garrett to those gathering.

Billy saw José Montaño; Fred Schon; "Squire" Wilson; Sam Wortley; Steve Stanley; Juan Patrón, who had driven his buggy in which sat Florencio Gonzalez; George Washington; Sam Corbett; Dummy; and Martin Chávez with a stranger, a youth, a new Lincoln County resident: Miguelito Luna.

Dummy, smiling broadly, waved at the procession. He said to Sam Wortley, at whose hotel he now worked, "That's Billy. Say, 'Hello,' " as the wagon turned inward at the fenced destination.

In a low voice, Martin Chávez said in Spanish to Miguelito Luna, "That is him." Luna waited until the buckboard receded toward the stable before getting on his horse and loping westward. When out of sight, he spurred him into a full gallop.

As Billy and Garrett walked to the House's reincarnation, Billy said, "Town looks the same. Can I use the public outhouse, Pat?"

Billy entered the left door of two facing the building. The other pair, sharing the same pit, faced the back. Quickly, he manipulated his wrist and leg cuffs, sighed at failure, and looked through a crack between boards at Bob Olinger with his Whitney shotgun and James Bell with a Winchester carbine. He then exited.

As the four walked toward the House's larger section, Garrett said it looked like he had lost weight. "Hope to gain it back under your care. Where does the food come from?" The Wortley, Garrett said. They'd bring it to him. Billy asked, "Are other prisoners here too?"

From behind, Olinger said, "Got a room just for you."

Garrett said, "I've got five others in another room. Fought over water rights. Tularosa Ditch War. Wortley's been serving them. They get taken across the street."

Billy studied the rear façade. "Outside's been stuccoed," he said. "Used to be exposed adobes." Garrett, preoccupied with responsibility, directed him to the board walkway.

The side door, which Billy had first entered when escorted by Jessie Evans, swung inward to the prior storeroom, now containing two cots. "Someone lives here?" he asked.

"Caretaker," said Garrett. "Named Goff. Or maybe Gauss. And Sam Wortley bunks here too." Billy noticed that one cot was covered with a red blanket. Against the wall, beside the other, was the miner's pick left by Azariah Wild.

Billy was becoming aware of numbers. "Turn left," said Garrett. "Along the landing." Three strides with clattering chains. "Up that back stairway." James Bell was in the lead.

"Only way to the top floor," Garrett announced. It had sixteen steps. They arrived at a hallway transecting that upper story.

To the right, Billy saw closed doors and asked, "Are those parts of the jail?" eyes innocently wide and illuminated by panes in the double doors leading to the front balcony.

"He depends on me entirely," thought Garrett. "No. I put in an armory. Wait up, Bell. I want to show him." Four strides rightward from top of stairs to its door. Garrett opened it. Billy's pupils dilated.

The walls were covered with racks of Winchester carbines and rifles. Glass cases held Colt revolvers. On wall pegs, hung bullet-filled cartridge belts with holsters. Crates had ammunition. Garrett smiled patronizingly. "And the room across will be the courtroom."

Together, he and Billy turned back toward the stairway. After passing it, Billy knew there were seven strides from the armory to the doorway on the right, where Bell and Olinger waited.

They all entered it. Garrett said, "This is my office." Present were a rolltop desk with disorderly papers, its chair, and another. A long coiled rope lay meaningfully in a corner. Bell proceeded across the room to another door. Billy noted that Garrett left two large screw keys on his desk.

Billy, Garrett, and Olinger followed Bell; eight strides from door to door. This big, freshly white-washed room, like Garrett's office, had a cathedral-like ceiling, its batten-board surfaces slanting almost another story to the rooftop.

Straight ahead, was a deeply-recessed window five feet high, four feet wide, and elevated less than two feet. Facing east, it had attracted Billy's attention on his first tour with Dolan. With upward-sliding sash, it had two sets of six glass panes. Catty-corner, was its street-side counterpart.

Between the two windows, lay a mattress pad. Two chairs and an oil lamp on the floor were present. That was all. There was no chamber pot. The deep corners of Billy's lips rose.

"Twenty-two days to hanging," said Bob Olinger. "See that ring there?" With Whitney muzzle he pointed. The east window's light brightened a steel loop hammered into the plank floor. "Where you wait for your ticket to Hell."

Billy walked. Fourteen strides from the hall doorway of Garrett's office to that metal. James Bell crouched, using the padlock from the wagon to fasten his leg chain to it. Garrett said, "Bell and Olinger will be your guards. Taking turns - twenty-four hours a day."

Olinger said, "An' see that chalk line? My idea." Bisecting the room from north to south was a dusty thread-like trail. "Cross it without permission and we shoot you."

Billy ignored him and asked Garrett where the other prisoners stayed. He said, "Across the hall. Bob, let's go to the Wortley. Get the Kid's food, eat ourselves, and bring some for you, Bell."

Billy discovered that his chain almost reached the east window, its ledge broad enough for a seat. Through it, he watched Garrett and Olinger cross the street at a diagonal to the Wortley Hotel. Eighty-four strides.

Later that evening, after he and Bell had eaten, Billy, on his chair beside the steel fastener, said, "That sure was good." Stringy-mustached James Bell fidgeted, back aching from the hard-bottomed seating. Billy said, still fact-finding, "Guess Garrett sleeps someplace better?" Bell said the Wortley; but he and Olinger slept in a room on the far west side. He'd heard Dolan once had a Masonic Temple there.

"Real interesting, Deputy Bell," Billy said, eyes barely in control of flaring anticipation. "Seems I need to," the crucial words echoed in the cavernous space, "use ... the ... outhouse."

James Bell sighed. "Part of my job."

As Bell knelt to open the padlock, the boy's eyes darted first to his back, then to his Winchester carbine, left carelessly on the chair.

Billy said, "Maybe it would help if I stand." And his lantern-lit shadow loomed twenty feet up the wall and cathedral ceiling.

APRIL 25, 1881   1:20 PM   MONDAY

As James Bell struggled to stay awake in the tedium, chained Billy observed, out the east window, an overweight young woman, head draped with a rebozo, plodding to Bob Olinger, exiting the Wortley Hotel with his five prisoners. Olinger pointed at the courthouse.

Billy said, "Food's coming." Bell stood, rubbing his aching back.

Billy said, "I enjoyed hearing about your Massachusetts family. We could also play poker if you got a small table and cards."

As a negative excuse, Bell said they needed Garrett's approval. Billy responded manipulatively: "Your friend, *Jim Carlyle*, sure liked to play poker," achieving reddening of his guard's face with its stringy mustache. "Sometimes I wonder, Deputy Bell, if people in Heaven - where Jim Carlyle would end up - keep track of their murderers." Uneasily, Bell said he'd ask about cards.

Pat Garrett, told by Bob Olinger about a woman on the front porch waiting to see him, was opening the door as officious Billy Burt, the Court Clerk, joined him saying, "I wish they'd bring the records from the old courthouse here. This constant back and forth ... I never know whether to leave my horse here or there. And it makes no sense to have Collie saddled all day just waiting."

Realizing that Garrett was not paying attention, he said, "At least we have the stable here;" and veered around an obese perspiring girl.

The girl got Garrett's acknowledgment that he was Sheriff, while shyly watching her dusty toes in sandals. She said, "I comes from San Patricio for to marry Beelly Bonney." Garrett grinned, saying his Mexican wife joked like that too. "Pero, I no joke, Señor. He ees to be hang, no? I hear eef he marry, he no hang. So I, María Montez, comes. But please, with priest."

Contemplating her grotesquely scared face, dissipated Garrett's brief diversion. He said nothing stopped the hanging.

As Garrett climbed the back narrow stairway, Bob Olinger, in the hallway and taking the Tularosa Ditch War prisoners to lunch, asked, "What did that fat greaser want?" To see the Kid. Name of Montez. Olinger said, "Ugly as sin."

Garrett laughed as he crossed the hallway toward his office, and heard Olinger descending the stairs and saying, "Goddamn it, old man. Get out of our way."

Gottfried Gauss soon entered Pat Garrett's office with a dust rag and broom. Efficiently whisking, he furtively watched the tall man go through the far door. "Sheriff, you vants I clean your desk?"

"Good, Goff. Do that," Garrett called back.

On papers, lay two cylindrical screw keys. Neatening the stacks, Gauss left the keys. James Bell emerged from the far door, saying, "Gottfried, we need something to use for a small table." The eyes of the caretaker flicked to the carbine which the deputy propped beside the desk. While leaving, Bell said, "Garrett gave me the afternoon off."

Gauss carried in one of the two office chairs. The boy was laughing. Gauss cleared his throat, meeting Billy's eyes.

He said, "Herr Sheriff, dis iz not table, but iz flat." Gauss saw the shackles and thought, "Keys!"

Garrett said, "Don't be afraid, Goff. He's chained." Realizing he had no inkling of his relationship to Billy, Gauss set down the chair with exaggerated trepidation.

Garrett said, "See that chalk line? If he crosses it, we shoot."

"But mit you here, maybe I sveep here?" He got permission and fetched his broom. As the two began to play cards, Gauss neared, saying to Billy, "Please, yust to stand." Billy made the floor-ring the apex of a triangle with his leg chains. The broom passed over it; an examining boot-toe struck to test firmness. "I am vinish," Gauss said and left.

Shuffling the cards, Billy said, "You sure were brave protecting us in Vegas," and dealt Garrett four aces. Later, as outside light faded, Billy said, "You've got no stake in me being killed."

Garrett laughed. "Just realized, you're trying to sweet-talk me into helping you."

Billy laughed too. "I don't need a yes, to get things done."

"No way out of this. Sure as that chalk line." They both looked. Gauss had swept it away.

After a few more hands, Billy asked, "Did you ever wonder if I'd 'ave shot you?"

"Didn't think about it." The blue eyes seemed dewy, almost loving. Garrett felt uncomfortable. "I mean, we *were* friends ..."

"I'd say we still are." Billy smiled. "Remember Big Casino and Little Casino?"

Garrett saw the boy running to him like a son, curls windblown. He thought, "Like rescuing Joe Briscoe. I didn't want this, Billy; I don't want you to die. You crazy Little Casino."

In silence punctuated by words of the game, Garrett recalled Ash Upson's recent admonition: I need more about childhood; more about murders. Garrett said to Billy, "I'm interested in your past."

After they ate food brought by Dummy, and Garrett had listened to the boy's humorous dramatizations, Billy asked, "Could you do me a favor, Pat? With the weather turning, it's too hot in this cardigan."

Garrett got the screw key from his office. As the wrist cuffs were removed, Billy asked, "Who made these anyway? The left hinge is rough. If you don't move right, it cuts. Best cuffs I ever saw were those you had in Stinking Springs."

"Azareeah Wild" came to Garrett's mind; then: "Just stop thinking."

APRIL 26, 1881   10:42 AM   TUESDAY

A small, disc-wheeled, carreta cart, pulled by a shaggy donkey, clattered on the Lincoln street. Its open bed had wares of firewood; long twine-tied ristras of dried, red, chili peppers; and earthenware vessels. The driver was Miguelito Luna. Beside him sat a slim girl whose rebozo demurely concealed her face.

The young couple stopped at the new courthouse-jail as Gottfried Gauss led out a white pony.

"Buenos dias!" called Miguelito Luna. "Maybe you buys from my girlfriend and me?"

"Zo, den let me hitch Collie vor Herr Burt vhen he comes here von de odher court. But it iz noting I need." High-strung little Collie balked at the strange vehicle, eyes rolling whites.

The long-skirted girl climbed down, clutching closed her shawl, and moved aside the cart's chilies, exposing a flattened newspaper-wrapped parcel to Gauss. In English she whispered, "These are very hot chilies, Señor. Can you take the heat?"

"Ya. Gut." Gauss's expression hardened. "I tell you, I am ready vor hot." She drew aside her reboza. "She" was Yginio Salazar.

Then the young laughing twosome trotted the donkey westward, finally able to return him and the wagon to the San Patricio owner.

As Gauss ostentatiously swung his bunched chilies and reentered the corral, he saw Billy going to the outhouse with James Bell. He called out, "Guten mornen, Deputy Bell."

Immediately, Billy saw the flat parcel.

Bell asked if he'd gotten himself some Mexican chilies. "Ya. Gut vor very hot cooken."

Quickly, Gauss patted the parcel and stared intensely at the rightmost of the two outhouse doors.

Billy entered there. From the interior both heard, "Thanks for keeping me company. An outhouse can be lonely without friends."

APRIL 27, 1881   9:08 AM   WEDNESDAY

Collecting poker discards, Billy eyed the heavily-used Winchester lying across Garrett's long thighs. He said, "Been meaning to ask you, Pat, that carbine looks familiar." Garrett said it should; it was Billy Wilson's. "You kept it - like Frank Stewart kept my horse?"

"Didn't think about it like that. I got it at Stinking Springs. Looked for yours. The Kid's Winchester." The blue eyes lacked the amusement Garrett had insensitively anticipated. "What happened to it?" he finally asked, cupidity evident.

Billy felt the earliest flare of anger. He said that the White Oaks boys had already stolen it; after killing his horse when ambushing them for no reason. He should ask Bell who got it.

Garrett, now irritated and provocative, said, "Carlyle died for it."

Billy sneered. "He just stole my gloves. I doubt his men shot him to avenge me. For a time now, I've wanted to ask: is it weighing on you - killing Tom? Seems it would feel like murder."

Joe Briscoe's brand of the cross appeared. Angrily, Garrett stood.

"And Charlie: killed because he had on my hat. And me, Pat? What are you going to tell yourself about me?"

Enraged, but attempting to sound caring, Garrett said, "I meant to ask if you had any next of kin you want notified after ..."

Billy watched his twitching right eyelid, and answered, "No. Anyone who wants, can read about Billy the Kid, leader of his cut-throat gang of hundreds, in the newspapers. But maybe you'll recite that little prayer you carry around. By the man who doesn't believe in God and keeps writing about it: Ingersoll."

Garrett walked out, slamming the door.

In his office, Garrett's mind raced with curses, images of Apolinaria naked in bed, and surging guilt and humiliation. From a desk drawer he grabbed a gift bottle of Dolan's whiskey and quickly drank. He had to escape.

In the armory, he found James Bell and said, "I'm leaving for White Oaks till Saturday. To collect taxes. The Kid's desperate and dangerous. Don't either of you take him for granted."

Bell said, "Not disagreeing. But fourteen pounds of shackles and chained to the floor. Twenty-four hour guard. Only one stairway to get to him. Can't see much need for worry."

Garrett said, "I'll feel better when the hanging's over."

Hearing talk, Bob Olinger came in. Bell repeated that Pat was leaving for three days; and they should keep a close eye on the Kid.

Olinger laughed and said, "He's got no more chance of escaping than going to Heaven."

When his guards entered, Billy was standing at the east window. Olinger said, "Garrett's gone to the Oaks. Lost your protector."

After James Bell left to take the Tularosa Ditch War prisoners to their Wortley lunch, Bob Olinger said, "Down there, they'll be building your gallows. Know much 'bout hanging?" Billy was silent.

"Only seventeen days till you find out. 'Course, if it's done wrong, it's slow strangalation. But break the neck right, the sonoabitch jerks around like some puppet. And comes in his pants. A goddamn puppet drippin' scum."

"Thanks, Bob. That's real interesting."

Olinger's blocky jaw pressed belligerently into his goiterously thick neck. He strode to his shotgun, leaning to the right of the door to Garrett's office, and pointed it at him.

Billy ignored that, and picked up the deck from the chair. Olinger said, "I've heard you've got a hell of a temper. I got me three days to be the one who got the Kid."

His hairy fingers laced through the Whitney's cheap, flat metal, trigger guard, within which were three triggers: the front-most dropping the barrels to add cartridges; the two behind for firing.

He said, "Fact is, I loaded extra heavy with buckshot just for you."

Placidly, Billy asked if he wanted to play poker. Olinger sat and said, "Ever seen anybody hit by a Whitney?"

"No. Never knew anyone needing a one foot spread to hit their mark."

Bob Olinger's face flared. "Turns a man's chest to jelly or blows off his head."

An excellent hand distracted Olinger, but he soon tried, "Heard you weren't a great shot. Just a made up repatation." The boy seemed unperturbed.

"Heard you'll be leaving behind a broken heart." Billy flushed. Olinger noticed and carried away the chair with cards and matchstick chips. "Some girl named Montez. How could you stick your cock into that ugly piece of meat?" Billy's lips tightened.

Abruptly, Olinger left and returned with a screw key, saying, "For your leg irons." He put it in a vest pocket. "And I'm making you a new death line." He dragged the chalk close to Billy's feet. "Now we got one that makes sense."

Resuming his chair, with shotgun on lap, Olinger continued, "I been askin' 'round - like a back-East detective. I heard a broken heart's in Sumner." Red streaking on Billy's neck surprised him.

"Six days gone," he thought, "and he was so easy to get going." He withdrew the padlock key from his vest. "Let's even out this game. Get up." When Billy sat again, his leg chain was free.

Olinger taunted, "Daydreaming 'bout ballin' that little whore?"

Unable to control his growing conflagration, Billy, in a gesture appearing casual, lay his left hand on his thigh. Slowly, he rocked its wrist side to side against the sharp hinge. But rage left it numb. "And I got her name." Pig-eyed as blacksmith Cahill, Olinger shimmered in scorching waves, while provocatively offering his shotgun.

Billy licked dry lips. "Lay off. Trail leads no ... where."

"Maybe. I'm your detective. An' we know you needed Sumner. How about this? Celsa Gutierrez."

Olinger pulled forward his chair right to the chalk line.

"Or who'd be the prize?" Billy's eyes worshipped the gun. He heard "... and Jim East said that Miss Paulita Maxwell had to say farewell to sweet Billy. How 'bout Miss Paulita Maxwell spreading her sweet legs for sweet Billy? Isn' that right, boy? Fox in the henhouse."

Olinger lewdly masturbated the Whitney barrels. Flames blurred Billy's vision - flames from the gunbarrels. "Come on boy. You're so close. I got your key. Try for this gun."

A puppet jerking on a rope was sinking into a flaming ocean of blood. Nothing mattered but to have that gun. And to murder. To turn living flesh into bloody pulp. A trench, running in darkness, gushed slaughterhouse blood. Sweet hot need lusted for finger on trigger and tremendous explosion of release. That was the freedom he wanted. Muscles muscle contracted to spring.

Billy's face transmogrified, humanity departing. The ghastly creature leaned forward.

Olinger recoiled, churning bowels releasing fumes. Billy sucked in scent of fear; that distraction permitting another: pain at his wrist, pain flowing into the white glare, pain quenching it in agony against desire. Billy sighed. Without his awareness, his left wrist had never ceased its side to side movement. Beneath it, his dark pants were wet with blood.

Bob Olinger began to doubt both his effect and his danger. Irascibly, he said, "You've got more of a repatation than your cock can support."

Billy's lids lowered in briefly drifting consciousness, but when reopened, his eyes were bright. He said, "Jim East saw the *whole* Maxwell family giving Pat Garrett some hospitality. Being chained to another of his prisoners, I couldn't much help being there.

"If you figure that's romantic, *you'll* be getting a reputation, not me. And, if I were you, I wouldn't let Pat hear that kinda talk about his wife's *married* sister: Celsa."

Both heard James Bell's approach. He said he would take over.

After Olinger left, Billy stared at the shotgun, again beside the door. Enraged passion was dissipated, but not its murderous urge.

APRIL 28, 1881   11:54 AM   THURSDAY

After having dealt James Bell another tempting hand only to have him fold, Billy said it seemed he played a cautious game. Bell answered that his mother, who'd raised him after his father died, was a religious Methodist, who felt gambling led to other vices. Billy said, "I can see how a Ma could worry. But to me poker's like living: how you play the hand you're dealt." He was riffle shuffling to minimize movement of the left manacle. The sleeve of his long underwear was now glued by dried blood to his lacerated skin.

At the same time, Bob Olinger, in the hall and at the stairway, saw Gottfried Gauss coming up, but sent down the five prisoners anyway, trapping him against the wall. "Vere you tink you komm mit all dat rush?" asked the old man, uncharacteristically obstreperous. He watched the group turn left on the landing, disappearing to exit the side door.

Billy and James Bell heard knocking. Their door opened. Gauss held his broom and a dust rag. He said, "Guten day. I komm to tell dat Deputy Olinger took de Tularosa men to de Vortley."

Bell rotated, and winced at pain radiating down one leg. "Why tell me?" He opened his tin-lidded pocket watch. "He does that every day around this time."

"Javoll, Herr Deputy." Flustered, Gauss glanced at watching blue eyes. "I cleans de Sheriff's office. Und den ... here." The door closed.

Inside Garrett's office, Gauss saw only one key. The rag reentered the pocket. The key was gone. With agitation, he pushed papers aside and opened drawers. "Mein Gott," he thought, "wo ist der andere Schlüssel?" Finally he abandoned his search for the second key.

He returned, sweeping in forceful exaggeration. James Bell was considering his cards. Gauss said, "It iz varm today. But dere iz big vind. Zo I vill leave de front vindow closed zo no dust vill come in."

Next he pushed up the large lower casement of the east window, met Billy's eyes, and said, "*Dis* iz de *good* vindow."

Gauss continued talking to James Bell, who was unaware that the loquaciousness was odd. "Deputy Bell, I vas tinking, maybe I tell you a vunny story von de old days. Vone day, der vas much shooten here - like a vor. Zo everybody runs und hides. Dummy und anoder - Herr Jack Long - dey jumps inside an outhouse hole."

Gauss forced a laugh. "Two." He repeated, "*Two*," eyes flicking to Billy's. "Understand, *two* vas hidden dere in de hole ... vor der escape ... von death." Bell chuckled.

"Life iz vunny. Maybe it iz all big yoke zo Gott can laugh mit his kinder he loves. His childs dat he ... loves." Gauss's cheeks colored.

His voice became insistent. "Now I make de horse ready vor Herr Burt. He iz in der oder courthouse. Zo I vill hitch him here. I even check de shoes vor long ride." He rushed out.

Billy smiled. "Sorry to bring this up, Deputy Bell, but that outhouse story inspired me. Think I'll pay ours a visit. Let's leave our cards." Billy smiled again. "When we come back, maybe luck will have changed."

Crouching painfully at the boy's feet, James Bell said, "Must be rheumatism. All this sitting and bending's hard on my back. My mother had it bad before she went."

"Sorry to hear that," said the boy, whose heart pounded as he looked down on the narrow back and lowered head with scalp showing through sparse dark hair. When Bell stood, Billy asked, "What time's it?"

One, two, three ... seven seconds, the watch dragged out on its imitation silver chain. Eight, nine, when opening the lid. Ten, eleven. Checking. Twelve. Thirteen. "It's twelve sixteen."

Billy lifted his leg chain, stopping at the door. "Can I go through now?" he asked in the ritual dictated by Garrett, noting the Whitney shotgun still at its right side.

In the hallway, Billy's back was to James Bell, who could not see his eyes dazzling with arousal. Twenty-seven to the top of the stairway's sixteen steps. Sixty-eight: down to the landing. "Wait up," called Bell. By seventy-six, the man was at his side. "Go on now," Bell said. Seventy-nine. A stop as Bell opens the side door. Over the threshold. Eighty-six. A minute and a third.

Thirty-four strides across the property to the outhouse. After entering the door to the right, Billy groped inside the seat hole with shackled hands. At the rear, where a horizontal cross-board supported the platform seat, his fingers touched cold metal. It was a Colt .44, hanging from a nail by its trigger guard. Seizing it, his caressing thumb felt a pattern in its walnut grip.

It was an upside-down U. Billy smiled. Masking sound by coughing, he opened its gate, half-cocked the hammer, and spun the cylinder with six, dull golden flashes before the weapon was concealed in his waistband and under the vest. One.

Billy reached back into the hole. On a second nail was a screw key. When it would not open the leg shackles, he visualized Olinger putting one in his vest pocket. "Goddamn," his lips mouthed fiercely.

He screwed opened the wrist cuffs, but re-engaged their claw tops. Into newsprint, he balled the key, dropped it into the depths, and stepped out.

"That was fast," said James Bell.

"Some things that give a man great pleasure happen *real* fast," said Billy. Bell laughed.

As Billy walked, he glanced toward the stable where Gauss was beside a saddled and bridled white pony. Giving no sign of noticing, the man thought, "Nun est alles in seinen handen, Gott. In your hands," he whispered, as ill-tempered little Collie laid back ears and pawed.

It was 12:36 PM. Billy was aware only of the gun's rigid mass with each stride. At the entry door, he stopped as the deputy opened it.

"Bell," he murmured. The man turned to him questioningly. Billy smiled strangely, and took the two strides to the landing, the one step onto it, the two across, and mounted the stairs.

At their top, Billy looked back. Pain slowed climbing James Bell. Billy disappeared leftward: the correct direction to Garrett's office. The fingers of Bell's left hand, thumb downward, curled around the edge of the wall, pulling himself up the last step to the hall.

The boy's voice asked, "Sorry to bother you. The time?"

As James Bell watched his emerging timepiece, a dark form passed. He looked up. The boy was between him and the stairwell. Then he saw the Colt .44. Billy said, "I don't want to hurt you. Get those hands high." He wore no wristcuffs.

"Don't kill me, Kid," Bell gasped, eyes darting wildly.

Billy said, "I'll just tie you with Garrett's rope."

Bell exclaimed, "I'll tell the truth about Carlyle." As the boy took his revolver, Bell bolted. Billy blocked him, striking a glancing blow to his head with the gun barrel, hoping to stun him.

Clutching the bleeding gash, Bell leapt into the stairwell, stumbling with gory hand against the wall to his right, while running down.

Billy fired just as Bell tripped and almost fell, the bullet passing over him and exploding a crater in the wall at the base of the landing. At the last step, turning leftward, Bell again lost balance, arms flinging upward.

Billy fired, this bullet passing thorough Bell's chest sideways, and splattering the blasted whitewash red.

James Bell staggered toward the exit, but the boy did not wait. With lifted leg chain, he ran into the armory and grabbed a holstered cartridge belt which he strapped on over Bell's revolver, and put Yginio Salazar's Colt in it. With a Winchester carbine from the gun rack, Billy smashed one of the glass cases and took another Colt .44, which he slipped into the cartridge belt. From an ammunition crate, he poured cartridges into each vest pocket.

Next he ran through Garrett's office, grabbed the Whitney shotgun, and raced to the east window, propping the Winchester against the wall, and climbing inside its deep recess.

On its ledge, with back pressed to its right side, boot soles braced against the opposite one, he depressed the Whitney's first trigger and released the barrels to check the loads. A cartridge was in each.

Downstairs, Bell saw the door open. A man was leading him out behind the building. Gauss looked down at the exsanguinating man without pity. Then he ran toward the Wortley Hotel.

As Gottfried Gauss came into view, the boy whispered, "Good," his high-perched panther body, waiting panther-eyed. "Goood," he purred, feline and lethal.

Gauss's agitated behavior attracted passersby. Inside the hotel's dining room, he found Bob Olinger and gasped, "Herr Deputy ... Bell iz shot. Go qvick. De *eazt* zide."

Olinger sprinted, followed by the five Tularosa Ditch War prisoners, who halted in confusion at the street. Charles Wall said, "Let's make a run for it." Augustin Davales objected that it was loco to think of escaping with leg chains. Alexander Nunnelly, John Copel, and Marejildo Torres agreed.

Olinger's thudding boots made intoxicating rhythm for one waiting with lips so tight that teeth were fully exposed. Olinger slowed, holding his Colt .44. When he was the end of a trajectory twenty-six feet long, the other end being the muzzles of his own shotgun, he heard, "Look up," sounding so calm that he squinted uncertainly into the sun, almost directly overhead.

Billy leaned, lowering his right leg down the outside.

"Kid!" Olinger cried out.

The right barrel blasted. The exploding swarm of pellets ripped open his chest, ricocheting destruction within. The boy yelled, "Olinger!" as he fired the second barrel into the supine body, which then contained three ounces of buckshot.

Men were running as the news was shouted: "The Kid's shot Bell! Shot Olinger!" Like a crystal precipitating a supersaturated solution, the original nidus of Tularosa prisoners became the gathering point.

Unaware, Billy was in murderous frenzy. "Olinger!" he screamed at the body, "goddamn cocksucker, die!" the killing already achieved.

Grasping the heavy weapon by its barrels as he would an ax, and with the tremendous strength of rabid paroxysms, Billy swung it over his head as if slashing the Celtic sword of Cú Chulainn. Its butt struck the windowsill, shattering off at its waist. Berserk, Billy hurled down the barrels and frame like a spear, striking the corpse.

Shrieking, "Die, die, you cocksucker," he next hit the corpse again with the severed buttstock. Leaning far out, he said, "You're dead, Olinger. Dead," finally satiated.

Noticing the clustered people at the Wortley Hotel for the first time, Billy saw Gottfried Gauss and remembered the shackles. Lifting his chain, he ran into the hallway, glanced at the manacles on the floor beside its west wall, flung open both doors to the balcony so wildly that their glass panels shattered, and rushed to the balustrade high above the street.

Waving Yginio's Colt, he shouted, "You, Mister Gauss, get me that miner's pick in the storeroom. But don't go near the back stairs. I'll kill anyone who comes near me. Hand it up to me here." The clustered people watched with fascination.

Billy saw "Squire" Wilson; Sam Wortley; Juan Patrón; John Newcomb; and George Washington, approaching with José Montaño and Ike Stockton. There were Sam Corbett, Isaac Ellis, Steve Stanley, and Harry Schon. Beside Martin Chávez was the boy he did not know: Miguelito Luna.

Billy yelled, "I didn't want to kill Bell. He wouldn't let me tie him. I had to. It's just me now. I'm standing pat against the world."

Soon, there was movement to the left. Billy swung around and aimed. Gauss stopped on the porch under the front edge the balcony and, holding the miner's pick by the center of its double-pointed arc, extended upward its three-and-a-half foot wooden handle.

Billy shouted, "I've got to go back in, you people. Got to break this chain. But I can see through the windows. I'll shoot any man that comes closer."

Holding the chain, he ran to the steel fastening ring and lay the pick beside it. As in the dark Santa Fe jail cell, he chose one oval link. He slid its end through the steel floor ring. The pick was then passed through that protruding link, held by its two rear mates.

Leaning because of the short handle, Billy pulled back to make the hook-like point rise with the head pivoting on the anchoring ring. The floor ring held firmly.

Again and again, Billy hauled back the handle as the tip rocked upward, impacting the link. Twenty times. Forty times. Soaked in perspiration, he continued to wrench, oblivious to blood running from his reopened wrist wounds.

But when he checked, the link seemed unchanged. Billy licked his finger and touched. The link was burning hot. Trying even harder, he used his entire body. Suddenly the pick point snapped. He careened backward, howling in rage.

Back on the balcony, Billy shouted to the crowd, "This will take longer. Mister Gauss, get me a horse. Put a blanket around the saddle. 'Cause of the chains."

Dummy, exiting the Wortley Hotel, called, "Hello, Billy!" waving and laughing.

Billy suddenly realized that, if the people had wanted, they could have prevented his escape. It was more than waiting. He called to them, "We're going to win this War in Lincoln! There are different ways to fight." Miguelito Luna lifted his fist as if stretching. Billy saw it and knew he was connected to Yginio.

With renewed energy, Billy put his hands on the railing, leaning closer to his people, his soldiers. He shouted, "They didn't dare have my trial here 'cause you good citizens know the truth."

"A .. men," murmured George Washington as he watched the boy running back inside.

Now, repositioning the link and using the remaining point, Billy yanked the miner's pick again. This time, however, he yelled, "The War! The Lincoln County War!" pumping and slamming his metal against the enemy metal: his curved horns of the giant bull of Cú Chulainn, goring enemy flesh as each impact of metal on metal became thrilling: a thrusting and thrusting of the point.

The pick was soaring upward as his legs were backward stumbling. Almost at the north wall, he stopped. There were two trailing lengths of chain.

On the balcony again, Billy yelled to the people, "Victory! Freedom!"

Hitched at the post below was the white pony with Gauss's red blanket tied over the saddle. Joining the crowd, County Clerk Billy Burt called up to Billy, "That's my horse."

Billy panted, "I'll send him back ... I've got to ride. To ride!"

Racing back inside and leaping as the trailing chains tried to trip him, he laughed at their game. At the east window, he seized the Winchester carbine and noticed the distant pick. "It's all silver and gold!" he called to it.

Setting the carbine on the floor, he wound each chain around its ankle, ran to the hallway, and bounded down the stairway, hundreds of bells sounding at his feet.

Outside, he saw James Bell's body and said, "You didn't have to kill and you didn't have to die;" before racing to the street, sun throwing his long shadow on its blood-red earth skimmed by strong wind coursing eastward. Gauss was leading the white pony to him.

As Billy slid the Winchester into the scabbard, the pony's crimson blanket blew wildly. Billy sprang up, seeking the stirrups.

Collie knew the clattering metal and red flapping were an attack. Terrified, he bucked. With no traction, Billy slid off, landing on his rear.

Laughing, he jumped up. But his audience was silent, watching with grim enthrallment.

Gauss caught the small animal. Billy asked his name. His life depended on this being. He mounted and said, "It's the wind, Collie. Easy, Collie;" turning him sideways, so the blanket merely flattened. Collie looked back, frightened eyes examining, relaxing. "We're going to ride, boy. Ride to freedom."

Then the white pony's trot became a gallop, and the racing air carried back to the people the words the boy was half singing and half shouting: "Glory, glory hallelujah! Glory, glory, hallelujah! His truth is marching on. Glory, glory, hallel ..." And they were left with only the sound of wind and the vision of sun-spangled dust.

The crowd viewed the House: monument to greed, corruption, hubris, and oppression; conquered in hours and transformed into a symbol of freedom. George Washington, tears in his eyes, murmured, "So David prevailed over Goliath. And no jail could hold him, no hand of man could shackle him. Billy of Lincoln town."

APRIL 30, 1881   8:56 AM   SATURDAY

Billy awoke to sharp resinous pine and crunch of rocky scree. The stiff form under his blanket indicated his drawn gun. In Spanish, he heard, "So you will shoot Yginio?"

Billy sat in brief disorientation, grinned, and asked, "How long have I been asleep?"

From the cave interior, a voice called, "Is he awake?"

Yginio Salazar said, "Yes. And finally not loco." To Billy, he said, "This is Saturday. You crossed Five Mile Gap on Thursday. Do you remember?" Billy smiled vacantly. "You saw our signal ax on the stump well enough, and came to this cave. You were singing. Very loud. It was difficult to make you quiet. I brought a file from home.

"What did they think you were? A bear in a circus? But you would not take off the boots. You said, 'I need to run.' "

The other person came out of the cave. "I recognize you," Billy said. "From the crowd in Lincoln."

Yginio said, "This is Miguelito Luna. He came recently from Mexico."

Miguelito said, "And I have heard the stories about you from Yginio. But I have seen the best."

"Maybe now you will give me back my gun?" teased Yginio. "I think you are finished with it, no? And you have two more and a carbine. I think that is enough for even a famous outlaw."

Sheepishly, Billy handed it. Yginio said, "So now I own the mystery gun that all in Lincoln are talking about. A mystery they will never solve." He laughed.

Billy walked alone through melting snow and past early budding, gambel oak bushes to urinate. Straining, as if to hear a distant melody, he gazed northeast.

When he returned, the two had spread food on the blanket. "And you refused to sleep in the cave," said Yginio. "You said, 'I must be free.'" Miguelito said he would have been the same. After prison so long. And only days to hanging.

"What happened to your wrist?" asked Yginio.

"Oh that. Shackle hinge was rough."

"And you told me I had to soak the bandages in salt."

"Prevents infection. Yginio," Billy exclaimed, "the horse! I promised the man ..."

"We know. You kept saying that too. Miguelito led him to Capitan Gap. We did not want him near Five Mile Gap. He will make his way home."

"Thank you both. We won, Yginio. You know that?"

"Yes." Yginio grinned. "And when you are ready, we have safe houses for you. One is the ranch of John Meadows on the Peñasco.

"And Miguelito has people waiting in Mexico. And that pony was not for Billy the Kid." Yginio laughed. "A fine horse is ready. His past owner, Andy Richardson, is too rich. He needed to learn more about charity. We helped him. This horse - like Cimarron - can race. His name is Don. Will you come into the cave?"

Billy was already lying on the blanket. "No. No walls." He yawned. "Guess I forgot the cardigan."

"We have new clothes for you. Sombrero, serape. For your disguise."

"Good." He heard spring runoff. "Later I will take a bath. Need a bath." When Yginio was wrapping a new wrist bandage, he was already asleep.

Eight miles southwest of the Capitan Mountains, Pat Garrett was riding to Lincoln, smiling as he thought about White Oaks: people congratulating him, thanking him.

But the memory of Governor Wallace's unpaid reward returned with anger. And John Chisum: paid a thousand, but had promised double. Bastard. Said after the hanging.

As Garrett hitched his horse at the courthouse, Dummy walked out, smiling broadly, and said, "Hello, Sheriff Brady. There was a funny horse with a red blanket. Then Billy fell off. But he got back on. I helped Mister Gauss rake dirt over all the blood. I did it good, Sheriff Brady."

Garrett rushed past him through the front door. He turned left through the old Dolan offices and then to the right, through the previous storeroom. At the landing, he saw the ravaged wall. High on the stairwell's left wall were violent brown-red hand-prints.

"Olinger!" he called. "Bell!" There was silence.

The rear door opened. "The Kid?" he asked Gottfried Gauss.

"Maybe no vone veels zafe to ride to Vhite Oaks. He made escape. Und Deputy Olinger und Deputy Bell he shot. Herr Vortley, he keeps de oder prisoners in his hotel.

"Me, he vorced mit a gun. Nobody knows ver he got dis. He zaid I must get him horse or he vould kill me."

Garrett tried to collect his thoughts. "Goddamn Olinger. Goddamn Bell. Goddamn Kid. Failure. Can only get so far, then it slips away." He said, "I'll have to make a report."

At his desk, he wrote with his barely legible, cramped script on the back of Billy's court documents: *"I certify that I rec'd the within named William Bonny into my custody on the 21st day of April 1881. And I further certify that on April 28th he made his escape by killing his guards James Bell and Robert Olinger in Lincoln Co. N. M."*

It ended with his incorrectly calculated sum for fees as: *"Boarding Prisoner and two Guards 8 days - $40.00. Guarding and transporting from Fort Stanton - $69.00. Returning Writ - $.50. Total: $109.00."*

One hundred thirty-four miles northwest of Lincoln, in Santa Fe, Lew Wallace signed a document bearing the Territory's great seal.

He said to his secretary, Tim Henley, "I've completed enough of these execution mandates to set a record." Addressed to Pat Garrett, it restated Judge Warren Bristol's order for Billy's hanging, and ended with his personal request for report of its completion.

Henley's subserviently limp-wristed hand lowered to his side as he thought, "Bonney testified. He deserved the pardon. This man is a vile hypocrite." That conclusion settled his long deliberation. He thought, "I will not grow a beard like his."

At 9:35 PM, the sapphire eyes watched Pat Garrett as he said, "So I came as fast as I could. To ... to warn you that he's lose."

"Warn *me*?" James Dolan smiled condescendingly. "Unnecessary. I am indestructible. But I would think *your* humiliation would be extreme." Garrett's mood plummeted, the ruse having failed.

"The sheriff who could not keep a boy in his jail longer than eight days. And not even that.

"But out of curiosity, he did have guards twenty-four hours a day and was chained to the floor, wasn't he?" Garret said nothing. The voice became harsh. "Wasn't he?" Garrett nodded reluctantly.

"Then escape was impossible. Or we have been dealing with a spirit, a demon wraith. Pat, you are omitting something.

"Was he ever unchained?" Garrett admitted for the privy.

Dolan's voice rose theatrically. "The House's public privies? To which *anyone* - in Lincoln, in the Territory, in the country - could come. Had none of you heard of a chamber pot?" Dolan laughed heartily. "Humans never cease to surprise me. They are such fools."

"I just came to report. I'm not staying if that's ..."

"Pat, please, of course, you are invited to spend the night. You trusted Bell and Olinger possibly too much. And, being unfamiliar with the partisan citizens, you could not tell the degree of risk."

Dolan's lips twisted with uncontrollable derision. "But you are Sheriff, and your job - our job - is not finished. It is as simple as that. He must be found and killed immediately. We are no longer bound by law. Where do you suppose he is?"

When Garrett answered Old Mexico, he was startled by Dolan's response: "Why go there if you have no thought of being caught?

"Conceive of how you would act if you could say, 'I have no fear. What can man do to me?' What I mean is, he could be anywhere. It would merely depend on where he wanted to be."

Dolan laughed. "Forgive me. I am not laughing at you. So Billy Bonney escaped from my House." He laughed more, long canine teeth exposed.

Finally Dolan stopped and sighed, no longer speaking to his listener, but to the faraway boy. "So he will die a death more of his choosing. That will be our compromise."

To Garrett, he continued, "I will send out some men tonight. Catron must be telegraphed.

"And I have gotten acquainted with John William Poe, who moved to White Oaks in March." Again there was scorn. "It seems you did not know him *quite* as well as you had led me to believe. I like what I saw. I want you now - in truth - to get acquainted with him. And Azariah Wild might again be of help."

Garrett flushed with embarrassment and hope.

MAY 6, 1881   12:14 PM   FRIDAY

Billy, wearing sombrero and serape, was riding southward to Mexico, having traversed the mountains at Capitan Gap and brazenly crossed the main road to Lincoln. His bay gelding's long strides had carried him past the farm that had been Dick Brewer's, over the Ruidoso River, and along the trail through the clearing where they had all waited as four shots sounded. When he approached Tunstall's murder site to its south, he had glanced into that sparse forest, but had continued, red mud accreting on Don's hooves as it had on Gray Sugar's.

The next day, he had come to the Feliz River, where, at Tunstall's prior ranch, the original chosa remained with its sandbags now rotting. His route had continued southward to the Peñasco River, then eastward, where he camped on land that would have been his. His destination was John Meadow's property near Paul's Ranch.

Billy now ate as the sandy-haired man said, "Here's 'nother on the escape. *Daily New Mexican's* making its money offa you, Kid." Billy laughed. "From this Wednesday. Listen here: 'The above is the record of as bold a deed as those versed in the annals of crime can recall. It surpasses anything of which the Kid has been guilty so far that his past offenses lose much of their heinousness in comparison with it and settles the question of whether the Kid is a cowardly cut-throat or a thoroughly reckless and fearless man. Bob Olinger used to say that he was a cowardly cur. This has taught Olinger by bitter experience that his theory was anything but correct..'"

Meadows asked, "What do you say to that?"

"Got more coffee?"

Billy, intoxicated with freedom, having heard nothing, was abandoned to peace so profound that it mingled him with the sweet air washing through open windows.

John Meadows poured and said, "I remember when you and that half-breed came hereabouts. Recently, I said to a fella 'bout you: 'when he was rough, he was rough as men get to be.' And that was 'fore the great escape."

Billy said, "My trial was a joke. And Bristol scheduling the hanging so I wouldn't have time to appeal."

He noticed in the *Daily New Mexican* of May third, a reprint of Lew Wallace's reward notice, and said mockingly, "Doesn't look like he plans on my pardon."

John Meadows said, " 'Squire' Wilson told me 'bout him. Fool in Shiloh, fool in Lincoln County, liar every step of the way. Well, you've got only eighty miles to Juarez, Chihuahua ..."

They heard rapping. Fear distorted Meadows's face. "Wasn't expecting nobody."

"I'd see who it is then," Billy answered, continuing to eat.

A young couple was revealed, a baby in the woman's arms. Meadows called, "Mexicans of mine to see you. Don't know how they knew you were here."

Billy came. The mother asked him to bless their baby. He blushed and said playfully, "May all the little señoritas love you;" but saw the parent's sincerity and felt tightness in his throat. Tousling the boy's already thick, black hair, he said, "May you have freedom all your life."

MAY 9, 1881   10:09 AM   MONDAY

In sombrero and serape, Billy had set out from John Meadows's house, not south, but north, returning to the broad red scar extending eastward to Roswell and westward to Fort Stanton.

He crossed that dark road, which also bisected Lincoln, and loped the long-legged bay into grassy terrain while singing contentedly in bright morning sun, "Mind the music and the step, / And with the girls be handy."

When their route placed them twenty-five miles northeast of a steel loop in a floor board on the second story of an enormous building, Billy saw acres of black-green giant sacaton grass where twelve riders had entered and only nine departed. Within it were Blackwater Canyon and an equally large arroyo, now named Deadman.

To his left, was the eastern terminus of the Capitan Mountains, beyond which seemed endless flatland. Billy became aware of flowing water whose eastward route had been fated 20 million years earlier, and whose patient mineral-dissolving erosion had created the bed for the Pecos River 5 million years before. "Red water," he said to the horse. "Running red from Lincoln town. A secret river pumping with the heart of the people. Bigger than those Ring men ever realized. Some day, it's going to wash 'em away."

Over seventy miles due south, was the Guadalupe Mountain wilderness ending at Seven Rivers. But Billy rode northward over layers of eons; over spear points of hunter gatherers lost thirteen thousand years before, buried when mankind had no doubt that a spring, a mountain, a tree, the earth, or the sky was holy.

Eight thousand generations had passed since the first ones discovered otherness in Africa; and lingered there for five thousand six hundred before beginning their diaspora throughout the world. Altruistic and cunning, they bore fire, dancing, loves, fears, tools; until accumulated genius found gods, cultures, husbandry, and cultivation forty thousand years before, but only as accretions around original voracious greed and exterminating instincts. That innate gluttonous destructiveness he had fought.

Yet now, only important were acres of white primrose, purple locoweed, yellow coneflowers, and riotous red-orange Indian paintbrush. Overhead, eastward-bound waterbirds - egrets, herons, and ducks - made dark banners.

"Freedom," he murmured. "This is freedom;" and viewed terrain simplified to a disk, the more important world being the sky. In the silence, he felt intensity of being, like a ship on an ocean: one microcosm on liquid immensity.

As the temperature rose, Billy removed the serape from black vest and white shirt. "Going to Sumner," he murmured. And said, "Paulita." "Paulita" reverberated with aching longing.

He whispered, "Paulita," and it became an answer. "Yes," he said. "Yes." All the flowing, flying, gusting forces were to her. He laughed because it was all so easy. The wind, hot as if fanning a fire, was an immersion, a cleansing, a purifying.

"All this is mine," he said softly, but did not claim it; rather it claimed him, absorbing him into itself. "Yes," he said, as effortlessly he gave himself; and "Yes, Paulita," as he dissolved into the sunlight.

On they continued, his and the horse's shadow lengthening to the right. But there was no impatience, no struggle against the pace of time, which he now knew was a current lovingly carrying him as land flowed by, leaving only an evanescent past.

In that long monotony, he could have seen images of John Tunstall, Alexander McSween, Dick Brewer, or Frank MacNab. He did not. With gusto he sang, "The cabin was afloat and his feet were wet, / But still the old man didn't seem to fret." He could have heard thousands of shots or seen the light of a fiery building.

But he did not. He could have visualized William McCloskey, Buck Morton, Frank Baker, William Brady, George Hindman, Buckshot Roberts, Manuel Segovia "the Indian," or Joe Grant. Instead he sang, "But the old man kept on a-playing at his reel, / And tapped the ground with his leathery heel."

He could have pictured a room in rosy light where a woman said, "You're half boy and half man now;" or envisioned Windy Cahill's blood on his hand and gun. But he sang, "Now old Dan Tucker is a fine old man / Washed his face in a fryin' pan." Far to his right was the Pecos River's ribbon of life. He sang, "Now old Dan Tucker is a come to town / Riding a billy goat leadin' a hound." Images of James Bell, Bob Olinger, or Pat Garrett were not there, only the song.

He could have imagined, from high southern hills, tiny buildings along Lincoln's red street, or stood on that street and felt the closeness of those same hills and parallel mountains. Or there could have been remembrance of a high balcony and people gazing upward, or the exaltation of the moment in which a single link of chain broke; but he fingered the black mane that could have been the dark-gray one of a mare named Gray Sugar, or the identical manes of Cimarron or Long Tom. But more poignantly he sang, "Goodbye, Old Paint, I'm a leavin' Cheyenne."

At a small spring, he dismounted. "Peaceful here, boy," he said. "Freedom's here." From camouflaging vegetation, Billy watched a few pronghorns, their population of almost fifty million already decimated by unrelenting hunters to near extinction. One suddenly communicated alarm, erecting white rump hair. Immediately, all sped away at sixty miles an hour. "Freedom," he said to them.

Again Billy rode, lost in motion of clouds, plants, animals, and air. He could have conjured up Tom O'Folliard or Charlie Bowdre or a stone structure without windows and only one doorway, but he did not. Instead he sang, his tenor lovely in the crystalline air, "Oh bury me not on the lone prairie / Where the wild coyote will howl o'er me." But he heard only the sweet melody. When he whistled "Silver Threads Among the Gold," the bloody blue cloths or the cachectic creature lying so still could have appeared, but they did not. He could have seen Mrs. Sarah Brown or Sheriff Harvey Whitehill in his jail, but he did not. Neither did he feel the acrid narrow escape chimney, nor visualize fingernails torn away to bloody rims.

But he said, "Ma." Then "My precious Billy," and wiped stinging eyes. "Silver and gold, Ma," he whispered into the wind moaning day's passing. And a forgotten song of hers returned: "She is far from the land where her young hero sleeps / And lovers are round her, sighing; / But coldly she turns from their gaze, and weeps, / For her heart in his grave is lying."

From its only other remaining fragment, Catherine spoke to him as if confirming his hero journey fulfilled: "He had lived for his love, for his country he died, / They were all that to life had entwined him."

Then, with longing and passion he uttered, "Paulita."

The reins hung loosely while he slapped a rhythm on his thigh to accompany his song. "Roll 'em up and twist 'em up / a high tuck-e-haw, / And hit 'em up a tune called Turkey in the Straw."

Later, he watched the sky drain pale, as the western horizon layered crimson and saffron, and the eastern dome became indigo punctured by constellations. Finally, his cookfire was the single spark in the night land, as crickets began their brittle stream of tiny strident vibrations receding into distant oblivion. After he ate, he lay back to swim in the Milky Way and diaphanous halo of the three quarter waxing moon; while fireflies flickered star-like around him.

Eight hundred thirty-eight miles southeast of Billy, in New Orleans, Azariah Wild was distracted by the noise of teeming humanity outside his open office window, through which humid air stank of garbage. He scanned his report to his Chief. *"I respectfully enclose a letter from my informant James J. Dolan of New Mexico Territory dated May 5th which gives an account of the escape of William Antrom alias Billie the Kid. The crime for which he was convicted was Territorial murder and not a crime against the U.S. Government. But from other letters received I believe there is an effort being made to have me return there."*

MAY 13, 1881   11:16 PM   FRIDAY

Outside her window, Billy stared at the moonlit sleeping girl under her violet satin bedspread. Clutching the frame so tightly that splinters cut, he pressed his forehead to the glass, sobbing until cooling night air made him realize the wetness. He pulled up the lower half. "Paulita," he whispered. She awoke, looking toward the ceiling. "Here. I'm here."

Inside Billy clasped Paulita. She sobbed, "Mama said today ... you'd be ... hanged."

"I forgot. I spent the day checking. There's no danger here. Barney Mason's gone."

"I know. Mama made Pete fire him for what he did to you. He's in Roswell, far away. Now Jesús Silva's foreman again - like for Papa. Oh, Billy." She wept, hugging him.

"We'll never be apart again. I've got a horse outside."

On his bedroll, they lay beside the river. She said, "And when they brought you that day, we had a horse waiting for you." He laughed about having to take the other man too. "I only remember you. Now we'll go far away."

She snuggled against him. "When you were away, I had a dream. There was a giant flooding of the Pecos. You were on one side. I was on the other. There was no way to cross. Logs were crashing. I felt ... I don't know the word." She sighed deeply. "Pain like today. Despair. That's the word.

"Then I was screaming 'no' at the whole world, and anything that would dare keep us apart. And the water got so quiet and shallow that we knew we could walk across whenever we wanted. You called out, 'It's just forty strides. We'll be together forever.' "

He said, "Forty strides takes only seconds," laughing softly in rapture. "Peach blossoms," he said. "Tomorrow afternoon, I'll meet you in the blooming peach orchard." She said they were not blooming anymore. "There's enough time for our blossoms."

He stroked her hair. "I figure I'll talk to your Mama and brother. Let them know I'm here." Quietly, she lay in his embrace. "Breathe in the freedom, Paulita. Every breath is freedom, sweet freedom."

MAY 14, 1881   9:25 AM   SATURDAY

When Luz Maxwell entered her drawing-room, lacy curtains, vivified by wind, danced spectrally between drawn-back, velvet draperies. "Mornin', Ma'am," said a familiar voice. A shadow figure emerged. With a chill, she asked what he was; he was dead.

"No, Ma'am. I believe I'd know that."

"God, in Heaven. They didn't ..." She embraced him. "And it's almost July. When Lucien died." She stood back. "The pardon? You were found innocent?"

"Well, not those particular ways. I escaped." That was dreadful, she exclaimed. He said, "Seems satisfactory, given the option. And you and your son once made an offer ..."

"Protection? Of course. He's in Lucien's room. We'll go together right now."

At the same time, Paulita said to Deluvina, "And I heard he escaped." Deluvina answered that it was not his time to die, and smiled, saying it seemed she had heard from him directly. Deluvina lifted the girl's telltale muddy boots.

Luz Maxwell and Billy entered her son's room through a door which Billy noted was at its far end and catty-corner to a wall with a fireplace. To the left, was an ornately carved bed beside a large window facing the parade ground. At its high footboard was a wingback chair followed by a baroquely carved desk at which Maxwell sat. He glanced at the sombreroed youth and said, "Mother, we don't need any more hired help."

She whispered unnecessarily, "It's Billy Bonney;" and motioned him to the wingback chair.

At the same time, Celsa Gutierrez, draped with her best rebozo shawl, joined a group of neighbors as she walked to the mansion. One asked, "You heard? Beely the Keed, he escaped. The reward is hundreds of dollars dead or alive. But it is from the jail of your sister's husband. You know more?"

"How should I? I have seen Apolinaria not once since she moved to Roswell."

Luz Maxwell asked her son, "So you think Francisco Lobato's sheep camp is best for him?"

"That Salazar boy was there for six months without any problem. But I don't want our town to get the reputation ..." She stopped him, saying Billy had fought for the cause for which his father gave his life. Maxwell retorted, "Father died of dropsy."

Billy said, "I sure appreciate you both burying Charles Bowdre and Tom O'Folliard in your family graveyard."

"Mother insisted. It seemed, at best, controversial. I remember now. Horses. Maybe you can do training." Maxwell added, "I have one condition, Mother: if I send for him, I want him to come. We can't possibly foresee the complications of having someone this notorious on our land."

Deluvina returned with the cleaned boots and said, "My child, you must now be cautious."

"He's with Mama and Pete. To tell them. At Pete's room."

"Then go. If there is a time when you are both together …"

"And they saw us, they wouldn't be suspicious. But I … this is a big secret, Deluvina: I'm leaving with him. Soon. Mama talks about that horrible José Jaramillo, but that's only because she doesn't know about us." Deluvina said she had seen the dancing lessons. "What could she see from that?"

Paulita reached for a large flagon on her dressing table, a clear glass cylinder with a domed top and raised designs of bees and honey combs. Its label, with an eagle, said, "IMPERIALE" and "Guerlain." Lifting off its opalescent sphere stopper, she poured the perfume on her hand and stroked her neck. "Doesn't this smell good, Deluvina?"

"Yes, child. It is very rare. Very expensive. It is the top you use to put it on."

"But this way I get more. It's got hisperides and neroli. They must be flowers from India or China. And rosemary and lavender and citrus. After we see Mama and Pete, could you make food for a picnic? Enough for two." Paulita laughed. "For more than two."

As Paulita, with Deluvina, entered the hallway of chandeliers on the way to her brother's room, they heard knocking. Deluvina opened to Celsa, who said, "I bring message for the patrón. From my husband." Paulita stepped forward, saying he was busy.

Celsa shifted enviously, and fingered her shawl to display its excellent embroidery. "Then I tell you. Saval he say he will be at Francisco Lobato's camp. But what is this I smell? So beautiful."

"Perfume Mama bought me in Las Vegas," Paulita answered impatiently.

Celsa addressed them both. "You hear Billy the Kid is escape?"

"Billy the Kid? I never heard of him," said Paulita.

"Here he is Billy Bonney. There is big reward dead or alive." Repeating dead, Paulita swayed and grasped the doorframe.

Celsa said, "Please, permit me to smell again. Yes. I say never I smell so beautiful perfume."

That afternoon, Paulita, on Centauro, rode beside Billy between peach tree rows, arguing that blossoms were impossible. "Evidence." He opened his hand. Delightedly, she inserted the flowering sprig into her hair.

"Look," Billy said. Between two mature trees was a newly planted sapling. On spindly branches, leaves, new fruits, and blossoms mingled in innocence. "Peach blossoms for Paulita."

She said, "I still have the sunflower from October." He laughed. "The people in town are talking. Are you called Billy the Kid?"

"Only by enemies. And newspapers. They're like dime novels."

They rode in silence, turning westward. She talked about their leaving. Purposefully he interrupted, "Let's head through here; we'll follow the river. Find a place."

In a grassy glade, they spread bedroll and picnic. He said, "I never smelled that perfume before."

"Mama bought it for my birthday. Its called 'Imperiale.' The man who sold it wrote down the story. It's from Paris. Made by somebody imperial: Emperor Louis Napoleon the Third for his wife, Eugénie. He told a Mister Guerlain what to put in it. His brother was Napoleon Bonaparte."

Billy said those were her Papa's names. "That's why she bought it. And the salesman said Napoleon the Third wrote a book about Providence, because he believed everything happens for a purpose. And on the bottle he put royal symbols: an eagle and honeybees."

Billy said, "He must have loved Eugénie very much. And when he held her, he must have smelled the perfume, sweet honeybee perfume."

"Do you remember my birthday and the honey love?" He smiled tenderly.

They ate in a silence, because by eyes, gestures, and certainty of intent, all was communicated. Separation had held them prisoner. Now, only gentle barrier of clothing restrained their reckless spirits. Together they cleared the blanket. His vest was slipped off. She opened her shirt.

It was not the wind but her fingers that caressed; and he and she were on his blanket in living leaf light and living water sound and the perfume that was everywhere. "Inside?" he whispered, and heard, "Yes." Flooded by revelation from the jail cell of darkness, he murmured, "Life. Inside it's life." And he experienced excruciatingly tender love for new life that could defeat mortality, as his entire being pressed into her, exhaling ecstasy.

And he heard, "My precious, Billy" as she enveloped him saying, "Yes, Billy. Life;" as last separateness dissolved. Then there was only freedom; and they were dancing, dancing, dancing.

MAY 15, 1881   2:04 AM   SUNDAY

Paulita, fitfully sleeping, had been dreaming about a colossal wind in which she and Billy struggled to keep hold of each other.

Her eyes opened. Actual wind slammed and wailed. A figure was leaving her window. Striding away in light as revealing as day, Billy wore no concealing serape; only black vest over white shirt.

She climbed out into blasting dust. To her billowing nightdress, he turned, warning about the moon, and lifted her to run back.

Inside, they held each other, unaware of blowing curtains lashing their bodies. "Billy," her mind was in a turmoil of fear and desire, "you said ... Lobato's."

"Started ... Couldn't leave. All that matters. Being with you ..." She said they would leave that night.

He was not listening. Yielding to passion like his, her fear dissolved. She was being kissed in flooding wind and was on her bed with him kissing and both freeing of clothes.

"Your hair," she whispered.

"Wet." "Washed. Went to the stables. Washed for you. In a cistern." But people must have seen. "No. Yes. A few. Friends. Doesn't matter." His body shimmered in moonlight.

"Billy, your wrist!" She saw the scabbed wound. He shifted, and high on his thigh was the long scar of Matthews's bullet; but she heard, "All that matters is now."

And the caressing was now; his lips were now. She heard him murmur, forever. She finally understood, and whispered, " Forever, Billy, and now."

MAY 30, 1881   6:38 PM   MONDAY

In the vegetable garden to the south of the mansion, Deluvina picked the season's first squash. Periodically, she glanced westward to high tangled vegetation, and gazed at the low orange sun thrusting crepuscular rays in soaring display.

She said to the boy, who had thought he was unnoticed, "There is great beauty in life. You come often and with danger of death." Into rustling leaves, he said not to Paulita. "To her heart. If you are killed." Friends would warn him, he said.

"You know the true danger, but you stay."

Billy's voice said, "There's no place safe for anyone with me. Not in the Territories. Not in the States. Not in Old Mexico. You know what happened to Victorio. Not just him, everyone with him. And to Charlie and Tom for being with me."

"I can't put her at that risk. With time, things may change."

He knew they would not, Deluvina said, and asked if this was enough. She heard, "It's the hand we're dealt. Life."

Again there was silence as sky colored the land red. The wind became stronger. His voice rode it. "We won because I won. And the memory of people is stronger than death."

"Then it is as it should be. It is your path, Billy Bonney. A good path. A blessed path."

JUNE 3, 1881   11:17 AM   FRIDAY

Petrified, Manuel Brazil asked goat-faced Juan Rioval if he was positive. "Yes, patrón," the boy lied. "I have spoken with Beely Keed. He threatens revenge. You must leave.

"But I can be your eyes and ears. For this I think a hundred dollars is fair."

When Brazil refused, Rioval put on his sombrero and said, "I wish you luck that Shereef Garrett finds him before he finds you."

Manuel Brazil offered fifty dollars and a horse for carrying messages. He had family in Anton Chico. He could go there.

Juan Rioval said, "There, I say, you would be safe."

One thousand twenty-eight miles northeast of the Brazil ranch, in his Crawfordsville, Indiana, home, Lew Wallace, on his favorite easy chair, with his oversized writing board inventively balanced on its arms, said to his wife, "Susan, we are almost at the Holy Land.

"Back just yesterday and off to Constantinople by the end of the month. You must be curious as to these jottings I began in the cinder-infested bowels of our Indiana, Bloomington, and Western passenger car." She smiled lovingly and said of course.

"The angel of inspiration alighted on the first leg of our journey on the Atchison, Topeka, and Santa Fe line. It occurred to me that a legend is but truth writ bold. You may recall that I had mentioned a Billy the Kid, whose escape, just before hanging, is now fodder for newspaper reporters from coast to coast.

"I decided, who better to create the legend of Billy the Kid than the man at its center: myself? And rather than just use the tale as a chapter for my autobiography, I may someday turn it into a book. Tell me what you think.

He read aloud: *"Upon coming to the untamed wilds of New Mexico as Governor, with the mission of preserving peace, life, and property, I soon learned about Billy the Kid, the most notorious outlaw of the West and the quarry of every sheriff from the Rio Grande to Death Valley. I determined to rid the Territory of this scourge and end his spree of rustling and killing as many men as his twenty-one years of life. I knew I had to risk my own and arrange a face-to-face meeting.*

"With much difficulty I had him contacted and set the rendezvous in a lonely hut on the outskirts of Santa Fe. He arrived holding Winchester rifle and six-shooter, and though a stripling, had the cold piercing eyes of the hardened murderer. Using the pretense that I was working to solve the murder of an attorney to which he was a witness, I offered him a pardon in his pocket

if he would testify and then leave the Territory. I arranged his arrest to keep secret our plan. He even demanded that he be kept in irons so as not to lose his reputation as a desperado. But he soon tired of the confinement and, without testifying, slipped off the manacles in front of his terrified guards and left.

"After a series of at least thirty-nine more murders he was brought again to jail by the brave sheriff, Pat Garrett, surrendering at the point of fifty guns and having shot down three of his pursuers. From jail he sent me a note saying I had promised him a pardon and he had letters to prove it to everyone. But I thwarted his purpose by myself explaining to the newspapers the circumstances of his not keeping his side of the bargain.

"Of course he was sentenced to be hanged. To the judge he said, 'That frightens me not a bit. Billy the Kid was not born to be hung.' Nine men were placed to guard him in jail. The day before the hanging he dashed out the brains of the guard with him and seized his revolver and killed the others who ran to their comrade's assistance.

"Once more he was lose, and the one man on whom he swore a vendetta was myself and made the boast, 'I will ride to the Plaza in Santa Fe and put a bullet through Governor Wallace, who is responsible for my fix.'"

"Oh, Lew," exclaimed his petite wife, "I never imagined your danger. I would call it *The Legend of Lew Wallace*."

Abruptly, Wallace returned his notes to their folder. Her repeating "legend" had forced associations to "fable" and "falsehood," undoing the purpose of his fiction. He visualized the actual William Bonney, now relentlessly hunted, felt the unpleasant pang of his own perfidy, and decided that in future versions he would leave out the part about the pardon, because it obscured the drama.

He said, "Before we leave for Turkey, I shall contact the Crawfordsville *Saturday Evening Journal* and give them an interview about this fascinating exploit of mine."

JUNE 7, 1881   3:10 PM   TUESDAY

In the shelter of forested Pecos River banks, Billy had lain barefoot, head on Paulita's lap, as she questioned about Old Mexico; and, like him, refused to experience their countdown to doom. He had said, "We'll have a big ranch with herds of cattle;" and had caressed her belly in small cherishing circles engorged with fertility. "And you will be Señora Bonney."

When she left, he had remained, looking through leaf patterns at gusting clouds.

Now, riding the roadway to Fort Sumner, he approached a youth on a familiar horse, and, like him, wearing serape and sombrero. "Good afternoon," Billy called in Spanish. "Nice horse you have, Juan Rioval." The goat-faced boy sputtered, saying it was only a loan from his patrón, and asked if it was him, Bonney. He was not certain. Billy said, "You should be. We have been introduced enough times. Who is your patrón?" Manuel Brazil, Rioval said, but added that it was only day work. Billy said, "He stole that horse from a man named Dave Rudabaugh."

"I know nothing," Juan Rioval said; and ventured, "But I hear you want revenge on him."

"This is my revenge: he will live. And know he sold his honor." Emboldened, Rioval asked, "And where is it you stay?"

"No place in particular. I like Sumner though."

The boy ventured, "Señor Maxwell knows you are here?"

"Of course. There are many good people and few bad ones." Juan Rioval was silent, heart thumping at this astounding discovery to tell Manuel Brazil.

Ninety miles southwest of the roadway, at his home, James Dolan was pacing, saying that they had been receiving increasing rumors from Fort Sumner.

Pat Garrett answered, "And from just about every place else in the Territory. But I sent Barney Mason to Sumner like you wanted. Of course, he found out nothing. Everybody's too scared of the Kid."

"Pat, Pat, save that for newspapermen. If Billy Bonney is there, he is being protected. You need an informer." Garrett said Manuel Brazil was a possibility; but wasn't Catron bringing back that Secret Service man. Dolan said, "Through Azariah Wild's Chief, we learned that without a federal crime there is no justification. The use of Brazil has appeal. I want you to write to him."

Garrett objected. "Pat, this reluctance brings to mind a lingering question. In your campaign, I recall the awkward issue of your literacy. Let me be more clear. We will prepare letters and documents for you. I only ask for your indulgence, your agreement." Moodily, Garrett gave it.

At his desk, Dolan wrote to Manuel Brazil: " *'Sir. It has come to my attention that the escaped prisoner William Bonney alias Billy the Kid may have come to the area of Fort Sumner. Your past services were of great value. What is needed now is information as to his whereabouts.'*

"Pat, see if this meets your approval." Dolan watched the man read, lips occasionally moving. "I did mean to comment that those new boots suit you well."

"Thanks. I went to the bootmaker you said. Carved lasts for me personally. Anything else?"

"In fact, there is. Tom just confirmed for me some interesting information about Fort Sumner, since he was involved in Peter Maxwell's father's obtaining the town. Tom's past legal partner is now our Washington contact: Stephen Benton Elkins." Garrett stifled a yawn. "You may find, Pat, that this will be of value.

"Peter Maxwell does not own the land, solely the buildings. Since seventy-four - first his father and now he himself - have been in fruitless litigation with the U.S. government to obtain it.

"If we need Maxwell, I now have bait for my hook. He is a profligate spender and gambler, and has already brought the family to a more dangerous precipice than they - or even he - realizes. Unless he gets the land, he will be the ruin of his family. And, through our friends in Washington, we could save him."

The long legs drew in to stand. Dolan said, "A final matter." Unlocking a desk drawer, he took out two papers. One was in Spanish. Garrett read the English one, its translation. It was a template for a Coroner's Jury Report. It concluded: *"And our verdict is that the act of Pat Garrett was justifiable homicide and we are unanimously of the opinion that the gratitude of all the community is due to the said Garrett for his deed and he is worthy of being rewarded."*

When the man looked up, Dolan said, "Not a man in the Territory would dare say otherwise.

Dolan continued, "One more thing. I have been to White Oaks. Though you have still neglected to meet John William Poe, I am impressed. His mind is like Azariah Wild's. He will be your deputy and will work with you to finish this task."

Garrett said he didn't like being told what to do. "Pat," said Dolan, "let me make myself *more* clear. You have long ago sold ... the right to do anything other than what we say." Garrett was unsure if he had heard or imagined "sold *to me*." But his expression became vacant, sapped of will.

JUNE 9, 1881   4:37 PM   THURSDAY

In Pat Garrett's Roswell house, Juan Rioval lied to Barney Mason, "I am sent by Señor Manuel Brazil because he know I help Shereef Garrett before. Señor Brazil hides with fear from Beely Keed vengenza, revenge." As hoped, Mason asked if he knew anyone in Sumner for a spy. "It is possible. I hear a man borracho, drunk."

Mason asked the name; and said they'd pay him a hundred dollars to be a go-between to that man. Rioval said, "José Valdéz." Mason said now he knew he wasn't lying. The boy grinned, hair lip split wide, and said, "But of course, Señor."

Sixty-eight miles due north of Roswell, in Fort Sumner, Paulita was sitting at her dressing table as Deluvina brushed her hair and said there was a great miracle: flowers growing there. Into her upturned palms Deluvina emptied those heralds of summer. Paulita giggled. "I didn't know he did that. He was playing with my hair. I'll keep them forever. Each holds memories of him."

"And I finally decided how I can fight too," Paulita said. "When Billy came back, I thought that we should leave. But he kept changing the subject;" she blushed, "or making me forget. He said, 'I won, because I wouldn't run away.' So I realized I had to let him stay. I just have to be brave about bad people who are so afraid of him, that they, that they ..."

"I understand, my child. Few can fight evil, because, like Dragonfly, they must be willing to give up everything. Even life. Very few can walk that path to the end."

"But, Deluvina, that's too sad. Dragonfly wasn't sad. He became stars in Heaven. Billy didn't think it was sad. Recently, he reminded me about the joy of the birds. Birds know that being afraid of death just keeps you from life. And Billy said death is just one second; and there are thousands and millions of moments to be alive."

Deluvina asked if that meant they were not leaving. "For now, we're supposed to be here." Paulita's cheeks flushed; her huge eyes were wide. "He says it's safe here ... but if ... if anything happened, there'd just be waiting; then I'd be with him forever."

JUNE 21, 1881   1:57 PM   TUESDAY

Lying on his back, Billy listened with amusement to Paulita read a newspaper aloud. "The *Las Vegas Daily Optic* on June twentieth writes that you said to four cowboys, 'Are you working for John Chisum?' One said yes, so you shot three, and told the last to tell Chisum that you'd fought for him in the Lincoln County War and he'd agreed to pay you five dollars a day, and you hadn't gotten one cent. So you said, 'I will credit him with five dollars for each of his men I kill.'"

Billy laughed. "Since Chisum's only got about fifty boys now, I've got no hope of settling his Regulator debt. Bad writer. It should say that I'd keep shooting Chisum's cowboys, *until* he paid. You'd figure if I was going to the trouble, I'd at least try for the money."

"And then it says, before you'll leave, you'll get even with all your enemies and depopulate Lincoln County."

Billy laughed again. "If you add my enemies, and if each equals a day, I'd be gone in a few weeks. And the only place I'd depopulate is the Wortley Hotel."

"And other papers have untrue places people have seen you."

"Give them to me." He shredded and released scraps. "Blowing words," he said.

They lay as he stroked her forehead's miniature curls. He said, "I've been getting a feeling like cattle must feel in a drifting herd. The drift's so strong that the boys don't even try to stop 'em. I feel this big direction; and I'm heading with it."

She said, "Maybe the new president will give you the pardon." He kissed her lovely lips. "Billy, I feel the moth." He laughed gently. Then they were in the magnificent drift of love.

Seventy-two miles due south of Fort Sumner, in Pat Garrett's Roswell house, Barney Mason and Ash Upson were with him at his dining table. Writing, Upson occasionally listened. Mason said he was convinced the Kid was near Sumner. Garrett said, "I'm waiting to hear from Brazil. I don't trust Rioval or Valdéz. But I'm appointing deputies: John William Poe and my friend, Kip McKinney."

Ash Upson said, "Fort Sumner's good for the story. The daring-do." Garrett asked if he thought the Kid was there.

"How should I know? But I like it. I'll use it as a chapter," the hairy face looked up at his benefactor, "or as the conclusion."

JULY 1, 1881   9:57 PM   FRIDAY

Manuel Brazil wrote at the table of his relatives as Juan Rioval waited: *"Sheriff Garrett. My answer to your question if Billy the Kid is at Fort Sumner is to say this is the truth. And I can tell you he is under the protection of Peter Maxwell."*

Forty-eight miles southeast of Anton Chico, Billy was riding Don toward the Maxwell family cemetery in light rain. He entered its picket fence, going to the only two crosses in the northwest quarter. From the foot of their long low mounds, he looked southeast to the magnificent tombstone of Lucien Maxwell. He removed his sombrero and said, "Hey, Tom," facing the wood cross to the left; and, "Rebel, you old Rebel," to the one on the right. Hunkering down, he pressed the earth on Bowdre's grave, solid as had been his wiry muscular shoulder. "You boys sure are in good company."

He looked upward to the darkness, letting raindrops mix with tears. He said to them, "Not easy to give it all up. Feeling. Seeing. Dancing. But victory sure is sweet. And they'll damn well remember what we did."

JULY 3, 1881   8:47 PM   SUNDAY

At Pat Garrett's house, Juan Rioval delivered Manuel Brazil's letter to him and Barney Mason. Garrett then woke Ash Upson in the alcohol-permeated air of the spare bedroom. Gnarled feet thrust from thrashing covers and rested on the clay floor beside his whiskey bottle and glass. Upson rubbed his face and said, "Great whiskey. I'd be Sheriff too for that whiskey." Leaning, he said to himself, "Careful, Ash. Don't spill the liquor of the Gods."

Too intoxicated to realize he could barely see, he splashed himself. First sipping the brimming surface, he threw back the entire contents. "I'll tell you an important lesson I've learned, Pat. When you're too drunk, just drink from the bottle. Used to think it meant drink controlled you. Doesn't. Just means you don't spill it."

Garrett asked where the writing things were. "Your desk. Did what you wanted: burned all the papers in it. Letters from Catron, Dolan, Chisum; receipts for their payments to you; copies of your letters to Wallace. Wallace should have paid you the reward." Garrett said he wasn't supposed to read ... "I'm a writer. Words jump into my eyes. My lips are sealed. History's loss is your gain."

Upson held up the bottle to doorway light and said, "One must plan for the future. With President Garfield assassinated, I say ... I'm going to lie down." Garrett said he wasn't dead, just shot. Pulling up covers, Upson said, "Our Billy the Kid story is better. After Abraham Lincoln, presidential assassination is an anticlimax."

At his desk, Garrett read Brazil's letter. On its bottom, he wrote: "*Meet me at the junction of Taiban Arroyo and the road from Stinking Springs an hour after dark on the night of 13th July.*"

From his jacket, he removed another letter, which had been delivered to him before he had left Lincoln. Folded over it, was a note which stated, "*Enclosed is letter to Maxwell. Must be given directly to his hand. Sign your name.*" In James Dolan's precise upright handwriting, it was, to Garrett's disconcerted surprise, on his own sheriff's department stationery.

Garrett read: "*Sir. I am writing to you in my capacity as Lincoln County Sheriff. It has come to my attention that you may be harboring in the town or vicinity of Fort Sumner the escaped murderer William Bonney alias Billy the Kid. I am, however, writing this not as a threat of the full action of the law which I can, as both Sheriff of Lincoln County and a U.S. Deputy Marshal, initiate against you as an accomplice to his crimes, but to give you an opportunity both to respond to these accusations and to possibly be of service to you in the resolution of issues with regard to* litigation in which you are currently involved. It is my hope that you will comprehend the seriousness of your current risk in the eyes of the law, as well as to see the opportunity to settle a continuing problem of your own estate.

"I therefore request your presence at a meeting with myself in Las Vegas at Moore's Hotsprings Hotel on 9th July, 1881 at 12:00 noon. This meeting must be treated with complete confidentiality. Written response must be given to the deputy who will bring this to you."

Garrett returned to Juan Rioval and Mason, handing Brazil's letter to the former. After the hair-lipped youth left, Garrett said, "'Barney, I need you to take this one to Pete Maxwell. Then I need his written answer brought back. We've got to work fast."

"Doesn't bother me to set out tonight. With Lionel Sheldon taking over as governor tomorrow, he'll probably take care of the damn reward, so you can pay me. But it takes everything in me to watch that greaser getting the kind of money you and me never see."

"Not coming out of our pockets. Apolinaria, is the food ready?"

"It is almost finish," she answered subserviently from the kitchen, with the undertone of adulation that sustained them both.

Garrett said, "In my opinion, this whole thing's a waste of time. Why would the Kid go to Sumner? But I've been meeting with my new deputy - Poe - in White Oaks. He says he's keeping an open mind."

JULY 5, 1881   9:38 AM   TUESDAY

Peter Maxwell, at his desk, annoyed, spoke to Barney Mason, sitting on the wingback chair between it and the high footboard of his bed. "Do me a favor. Instead of my writing a letter, just tell Sheriff Garrett that I know nothing."

"After you fired me for no reason, I can't see as you'd expect anything from me. But I'll tell you this: If you're involved with the Kid, he's got enemies more powerful then you know. They want to make sure he's finished off. I'll wait while you do that letter."

With a tense expression, Maxwell took stationery and wrote: "*Sir. I am in receipt of your letter dated 3rd July. I fully deny any allegations implied by it. But out of courtesy and as proof of my commitment to maintaining law in my own town as well as the Territory, I agree to attend the meeting as requested. But I cannot restrain myself from expressing outrage at the maligning of the name of Maxwell which, as you well know, is among the most illustrious in the history of New Mexico Territory. Respectfully, Peter Menard Maxwell.*"

An hour later, Celsa stopped at the vegetable garden beside the mansion, where Deluvina dug onions. "Good morning," Celsa said loudly. The heavy woman came to the picket fence.

Celsa said, "I see Barney Mason come to this house. But he does not visit me. And why visit Celsa? For my brother-in-law, the sheriff, he works. And his wife, Juanita Madril, she was my friend. So to myself I say possibly this is something about Billy Bonney."

"You can keep a secret?" Deluvina asked who she would tell. The young woman laughed. "Yes. Who you know? A slave." Celsa held two slats and lowered her voice. "If Billy come to Sumner, I, Celsa Gutierrez, would know. He can not stay from me. Celsa is the one he love." Deluvina asked if he had told her that. "It is not necessary. It was before I marry." There was a teasing laugh. "And after."

"Today, when I see Barney Mason, I thinks, 'How famoso is my Billy.' And I must tell, so someone knows Celsa owns what other women want."

Deluvina said, "There must be a reason your path led to me. So I say that you speak like a young brave who finds a dead eagle and plucks feathers. He has only feathers; the Spirit of the eagle has not chosen him."

"But no. I catch the eagle." Celsa laughed, flashing white teeth.

"Then tell me how this is love; so I can get wisdom."

"It is simple, because men they are simple. They are like stray dog you feed good and they comes back.

"But I come now to you, because I get this hunger for Billy so strong it is loco."

"Then walk the path. What would you do if you learned his love was not yours?"

"If he trick me? I hear talk. Others say he come to them. But it is still for no meaning." Celsa whispered, "I also have sometimes a man, but it is for no meaning."

Realizing she was unsure of the expression in Deluvina's eyes, shaded under her puffy hat's floppy brim, Celsa said uneasily, "Maybe you have jealous? Age it gives no difference with a woman."

"No. I do not want to own Billy Bonney. But you do. And if you lost him?"

"If he die - if they kills him - they takes from Celsa a jewel."

"But lost him to another? Walk that path you call love."

"My father, he was big liar. From my mother he makes a fool. Even to our house, he bring womans. From Juanita and Apolinaria he makes secret, but not from Celsa. Or it is possible he want to show me." She rolled her lips inward and compressed them with her teeth. "One time he walk naked, to show me what the putas want." Her face distorted with revulsion.

Deluvina asked if her mother believed he loved her. "Till she die, she say nothing. But it is possible she know the truth. She is sick, always sick; and no doctor find why."

"But, Deluvina, to see my father. So handsome!"

Deluvina said, "I know what happened to him."

Celsa was shocked. "How is this possible? We do not live here then."

"There were once visitors here. When you are a slave you are invisible."

Celsa looked away and spoke. "The husband he come to our house. My mother she is only just in the grave. He ask for José Gutierrez. I show to the room where he sleep."

Deluvina said she knew he was shot with a rifle. "Yes, I see this in his hand. No one I tell before." Deluvina said she made no judgment. "Then I say, 'Everything was finish. It was not necessary to worry again what sin he makes.'"

Deluvina looked at massing clouds. "And if you were betrayed like your mother?" Celsa hissed that she would kill.

"So tell a foolish old woman, is this love?"

The voluptuous beauty laughed sardonically. "Yes. When you permit for nothing between you and the one who is yours. Even if it is the same man. Let him die."

Both stood in silence as clouds blocked the sun. Celsa raised her rebozo shawl over her head as the first drops fell, warm as blood. "Deluvina, what I say is secret. No?"

"You have told me what is yours alone. It is your life-way and your path. And it is like one strand of spider's silk, weaving together with all the paths in all the worlds which have been and which will come. For that it has its purpose, and can be no different from what it is."

JULY 7, 1881   3:21 PM   THURSDAY

Beside Paulita on his bedroll, Billy said, "Francisco Lobato told me that it meant a good deal to people that I wouldn't leave." Her face involuntarily showed distress. "Least for the time being. "I never knew love worked like this. Each day more and different."

Paulita said she missed him so much when he was at the camps. "I figured I'd let the rumors settle down. Anyway, we'll be together again tomorrow."

"With Pete and Mama gone to Las Vegas it makes it so easy."

He nestled his face against her cheek and said, "I had a strange dream last night. I was on Cimarron. I saw two horsemen coming at me in full gallop. They were Tom and Charlie. I said, 'But you're dead.' Charlie said, 'No. We're here to ride with you.' I said, 'We won.

And you're in the best company.' They laughed and Charlie said, 'This way. You're heading in the right direction.' "

Paulita asked what he thought it meant. "Just a dream about how good it feels to be a Regulator. To never back down. And right now it means the whole day is ours, my precious Paulita."

JULY 8, 1881   6:48 PM   FRIDAY

Through Paulita's open window the day's intense heat still flowed. Brushing tendrils of perspiration-moist hair, she became aware of a presence, but outside was only sky with huge lobulated clouds.

"Paulita," she heard, sounding from the land, and climbed out in a linen dress and satin shoes.

Around the northwest corner of the porch, she found Billy, wild-eyed, hatless, serape-less; face radiant. Behind him, slowly swinging on its rope, was the white-shrouded, almost meatless, beef carcass, now narrow as the body of a man. Her voice was alarmed. "You said you were leaving."

"A giant storm's headed this way. I came back to get you. You wanted to see lightning all around. Remember? Long ago. Don's down by those trees."

When she was in the saddle in front of him, Billy said, "I realized while I was riding, time's not clocks, days, hours. No straight line at all. It was all a dream." He laughed. "We've been swimming in all time that ever was and ever will be.

"So I came ... because the storm's for us. Coming this way. We'll meet it where the light meets the darkness."

They entered the twilight vastness of the Llano Estacado where columns of hot moisture-laden air a mile across fanned them in soaring updrafts. Ahead were gray-black sky mountains, towering fifty thousand feet in a twenty mile parade; drifting toward them and rent by jagged cracks of light.

"Danger," Paulita said. "So much lightning."

Billy shouted, "No danger! Death, you can't touch us!" He panted with excitement. "I realized ... death comes only when it's supposed to. Not one second before. Before that moment it's *impossible* to die ... That's why we're totally free to live. And then, that second, it's life's. Not death's. Makes it all complete. Exact moment when you've finished what you set out to do." He laughed. "And it's not today."

Within the towering, cumulonimbus cloud formations raged nature's cataclysm, created by air hurling upward vapor, which condensed then froze, fulfilling water's trinity: gas, liquid, and solid. Maelstrom collisions sundered those ice atoms into charged particles which polarized thunderheads, so that their bases swept the distant ground in negative electrostatic repulsion, leaving it positively charged.

Into new night's chaotic disequilibrium, Billy and Paulita rode. He shouted, "Victory! Freedom!" as their skin's tiny hairs tingled with static electricity.

Thunder followed lightning, sound waves lagging five seconds behind for every mile the light traveled to them. "Coming close!" he yelled into blackening sky, as branching channels of negative charges coursed downward with a hundred million volts, five times hotter than the sun's surface; and exploded superheated air with booming shock waves.

From the land, the positive ions, yearning for lost harmony, raced to the clouds at a third the speed of light. Some joined electrons, while others, still bereft, continued ascent with hungry fiery bolts. Again and again, these lusting elemental strokes fell and rose in dazzling orgiastic frenzy.

Leaving Don, they walked in drenching rain onto the dark flatland where earth flared blood-red in lightening. "Look!" Billy exclaimed. Bolts, blown laterally, made golden ribbons; while others faded piecemeal as transient strings of radiant beads. She shouted that it was wonderful. He called, "I love Paulita!" into the bedlam.

Five hundred yards away, one electron stream, craving the reciprocally charged top of a cottonwood, struck, gouged, and spiraled down its trunk, vaporizing moisture to explode its wood in fatal consummation and thunder crash.

Again, lightning struck near them, blasting a crater with flash so bright and detonation so loud that Billy and Paulita were momentarily blinded and deafened while thrown; him cushioning her as both splashed in sheeting water and onto conductive wet soil through which the superheated bolt plunged thirty feet, branching like the light pattern it had been, and melted silicon into a fused glass pertification of energy: a fulgurite.

While ground vibrated with thundering raving tempest, the passion was their own until they became aware of discrete drops. She sat. He lay, splashing. "You're getting me wet!" she yelled, teasing. He helped her up. Clinging to her legs, her skirt was still bunched high.

Buckling on his gunbelt as he looked toward the horse, he exclaimed, "Paulita, look!" Everywhere, at points made by any object - the ears of the horse, the tips of grass blades, the edges of leaves - was a ghostly corona. Remaining sky electrons were flowing into these last concentrations of positivity.

Lifting her by the waist, Billy said, "And for her eighteenth birthday - though somewhat late - I give my precious Paulita foxfire and lightening."

Ground rippled light of the moon only three days from fullness. To the water-land he lowered her. Embracing and kissing, they stood as the storm raced toward Fort Sumner.

JULY 9, 1881   11:49 AM   SATURDAY

"Maxwell probably won't show," said Pat Garrett, and checked his ostentatious gold watch, before replacing it in his vest, matching another new plaid suit. His boots had been polished the evening before when he and John William Poe had arrived in Las Vegas and had taken their rooms at Moore's Hotsprings Hotel.

Poe, seated, like him, on a brocaded chair in the Hotel's smoking room, looked up from an issue of the *Las Vegas Daily Optic* and said, "Wouldn't worry. Jimmy showed me that letter. Maxwell's got no choice."

"Goddamn," Garrett thought. "Dolan had to embarrass me ..."

"Fine letter you wrote. Jimmy said he made the copy to show me. You covered all the angles.

"Hard to believe, isn't it, about President Garfield? Just reading this July second edition: day of the shooting. Charles Guiteau. A madman. And in a train station. In full daylight. According to Jimmy, we're lucky that this Billy the Kid didn't assassinate Governor Wallace. White Oaks citizens are still living in fear of his retaliation. Heard you once knew him."

Somewhat, Garrett said. "When doing business in Sumner."

"Jimmy told me you had money to invest after your success on the buffalo range." Garrett decided Poe had forgotten their meeting in Fort Griffin. Poe continued, "Made money myself. But I'm satisfied now with this cattle detective work.

"Incredible how the Kid escaped." Garrett flushed. Poe said, "Jimmy told me how those guards paid the price for not following your orders."

Garrett said, "I told Dolan it makes no sense to me that the Kid would be in Sumner."

"Your man Mason's convinced. And we're making Maxwell an offer he can't refuse."

"He's coming," said Garrett. Poe observed a man in a gray and black striped suit, with pants baggy to compensate for fat thighs. Only Poe stood, and extended his big hand to the man with freshly barbered, reddish hair and mustache.

"I'm running a bit late," Maxwell said to Garrett. "I had to make arrangements for Mother. She's staying with a family here." An approaching waiter greeted Maxwell by name, drew up a chair, and adjusted a small table beside it. "Do you feel this is private?"

"Nothing unusual about a meeting of guests staying in a hotel," Poe answered. Maxwell's pale brows rose in surprise, and he asked Poe his role. "Deputy to Sheriff Garrett. We're working on this Billy the Kid case together."

"Pete," said Garrett irritably, "is the Kid in Sumner?"

"As my letter said, I don't know. You referred to our land?"

"His body for it."

Poe observed nails bitten to the quick, at which the man was picking, and said, "Seems that without intending, Mister Maxwell, we may be insulting you. Let me say something that might help. We don't have to question *you*. Some of your Mexican workers might be hiding him without your knowledge."

"You could have someone send for him," said Garrett.

Maxwell made a high-pitched laugh. "And if they're so loyal to him, they'll immediately give him away because their patrón asked them too?"

"What if we had someone contact him?" asked Poe. "And lead him to a trap."

Maxwell asked, "That's enough for the benefits?" Garrett nodded. Maxwell sipped his whiskey. "But the finger could still be pointed at me if he was found." Poe smiled affably, saying that made sense. He had to be protected from slander. "Slander! My life would be in danger. Do you realize how many friends he has ..."

"Friends?" asked Poe, glancing uncertainly at Garrett.

"He means troublemakers. Other members of the Kid gang looking for revenge."

"I understand. How about this, Mister Maxwell? I'm a resident of White Oaks as well as a cattle detective. Among the rustling cases I've investigated, there was one involving the Dedrick brothers. They've moved away, but their livery was a meeting place for the Kid's gang. So I'd say that, while doing surveillance, I heard a conversation that the Kid was in Fort Sumner."

Maxwell said that sounded good. Poe continued, "You mentioned that your mother came with you. Could you return?"

"I'm here to look at some racing stock. But I could rearrange my plans."

"We'll be in Sumner on the fifteenth," said Garrett. "Next Friday, with another deputy of mine: Kip McKinney. Has a ranch outside Sumner. People don't know him or Poe."

"You mentioned my Mexicans?"

"José Valdéz," said Garrett. Maxwell looked surprised, but said he had to leave. None of it involved him directly.

"There *is* one part," Poe said. "It connects to the offer of land."

Garrett, feeling like he looked through piercing eyes of sapphire blue, said, "Pete, you'd have to tell Valdéz to call him in. We'll be there on the fifteenth. And if the Kid's not, you'll be answering questions from the people who hand out indictments. But if things go right, you've got yourself thousands of acres."

"Then carry out the dictates of the law," said Maxwell.

JULY 12, 1881   10:52 PM   TUESDAY

The moon, a day after fullness, was obscured by clouds, leaving three riders in darkness. Pat Garrett said to his companions that the Brazil ranch was ahead.

John William Poe said to McKinney, "So your grandfather died at the Alamo, Kip?"

"Shur did. We're damn proud o' it." The rangy man ran a ropy hand over his dark handlebar mustache and rubbed his nose, wide in contrast to his narrow bony face. "On top o' the res', the Kid's a greaser lover. Us Texans hate Mex-cins."

Poe asked, "You think Brazil will be there, Pat?"

"Too scared," answered Garrett. "My letter set the meeting with him for tomorrow, five miles from here - where the main road meets Taiban Arroyo."

Encountering their group at the ranch house door, Juan Gallegos nervously said, "But Shereeff Garrett, Señor Brazil he ees away. You stay long?" Garrett lied that he'd be returning to Roswell the next day. Poe added that he was heading back home to the Panhandle.

Garrett asked, "Is there a Juan Rioval around?" They were directed to the bunkhouse.

As they walked, Poe said, "Can't be too careful. I'm sticking with my Panhandle story."

When Juan Rioval was summoned outside the building, he drew back from their combined authority.

"Tonight," Garrett said to him, "ride to Sumner and give this message to José Valdéz: Tell the Kid to come there the morning of the fifteenth - this Friday - to meet with Pete Maxwell."

"But, Señor, Fort Sumner eet ees beeg, no? Where Valdéz say he come?"

Garrett thought, "Stable's in a remote area;" and said, "The stables."

JULY 13, 1881   10:00 AM   WEDNESDAY

As Peter Maxwell entered the stable, his head pounded with a hangover from his heavy drinking the night before when he had arrived back from Las Vegas. Assaulting his senses, was jangle of his father's ornate silver spurs, which he wore. He told Jesús Silva that he wanted to ride.

Silva replied that his visit had been rapid, and asked if he had seen the horses. "Too much business. Get Campeón with a fixed spade and the silver saddle."

"But, patrón, Betz he say it is maybe six month before Campeón is ready to ride. He is very young stallion. Very spirited. Possibly you choose another?" Angrily, Maxwell repeated his demand.

"Yes, patrón. Possibly a different bit? You remember, in Cimarron, a man cut through the tongue of a horse? Perhaps ..."

"Damn it, Silva, I didn't come to hear stories about the old days. Get him ready," Maxwell said, tapping his leg impatiently with his fancy, two thonged quirt.

Maxwell watched the old man struggle with the heavy saddle, over which he had laid a braided bridle of multi-colored horse hair with its huge silver contraption: the spade bit.

When the saddle was placed on the dark-chestnut stallion, he pawed the clean straw of his stall.

Silva said, "It is beautiful, no, patrón? This saddle was your father's pride." Bristling, Maxwell said it was his, squeezing throbbing temples. "But of course, patrón."

As Jesús Silva lifted the bridle, the spade bit caught ambient light. Its engraved silver, cheek piece bars would extend from above the corner of the animal's mouth to a half foot below, each suspending a chain to add more weight. Within a rectangular frame joining those two bars, was the bit's complex mechanism. A sharp spoon-like piece, the spade, extended backward. In front of it, was a little ridged wheel: the cricket, a diversion for the restricted tongue.

Style was the objective; this bit forced the horse's head tight to the neck. But throwing the nose could shear the tongue or ram the spade up into the bony roof.

Jesús Silva slid it in. Almost immediately, the cricket clinked.

Once mounted, Campeón recognized less experienced hands on the reins, and shook his head with metallic rattlings. Rowels dug into his sides. He trotted as Peter Maxwell growled, "I'm the master here," and pictured Pat Garrett's insolent face.

Soon they were northward bound on the cottonwood bordered road of the original Navajo and Apache concentration camp.

Seven and a half miles north of the town, Billy, Francisco Lobato, and Saval Gutierrez were at a cookfire near a sheep camp wagon. Billy, sipping coffee with the others, said that it was peaceful there. Gutierrez agreed.

Francisco Lobato said, "For me, I prefer sheep to Maxwell's cattle." His black-and-white long-nosed herd dog lay alertly at Billy's feet. "Mancha is so smart," Lobato commented.

Saval Gutierrez asked, "But tell me, Beelly, you have no fear to stay in Sumner?"

"Why should I? Feels like home." Billy changed the subject. "So the president did not die, Saval? Seems like he was shot in the same place as Yginio. And Yginio says it does not bother him."

"Wait till he gets old. Then everything hurts. But I tell you this: You have given much pride to our town. Bob Hargrove he said, 'Saval, this Beelly the Keed he is our hero.'"

Mancha sprang up, pricking his lopped ears and growling. A distant, small, dust plume was on the flatlands. Soon Billy said, "José Valdéz. A friend."

The three rose as José Valdéz dismounted. His dark eyes flicked to Billy and he thought, "Why would they summon him?" For the first time, he thought, "Ambush." The boy asked about Garrett. Valdéz thought, "If I speak, it will be your death. I could just take the horse and not return. No. They would hunt me." The dog raised black lips in a snarl. Quickly, Valdéz said, "Sumner is safe. My message ..."

Suddenly, Mancha leapt at him with teeth bared. Billy caught Mancha's scruff; as barking, he pulled against that restraint.

Francisco Lobato exclaimed, "But this I have never seen. Mancha is a good dog." He lifted him by chest and hindquarters, as he would a young sheep, and carried him to the wagon.

José Valdéz angrily said, "I would shoot him. Shoot him like an outlaw."

Billy laughed. "If we use my judge, he would hang."

Valdéz did not smile. "The patrón said you must meet him Friday in the morning. At the stable." Asked if it was about horses, Valdéz almost screamed, "I know nothing."

"Thanks, José. Tell him I'll be there." The man rushed to his horse to escape the loud accusatory language of Mancha the dog.

At the same time, Peter Maxwell was mentally revising his experience at Moore's Hotsprings Hotel. "I know all about you, Garrett. Working for the Ring. A gunslinger behind a badge."

Maxwell realized he was fighting something: the horse's head. He lashed his quirt, and the creature half-reared, as plains wind sprayed back froth from his dripping mouth.

Maxwell wiped his splattered face and saw his yellow deerskin riding glove laced with blood. "Damn," he said, loosening the reins. "Betz. What will ... Hell with Betz. My horse. I own Sumner."

In the distance, Maxwell saw a wagon, and remembered he had been riding past cattle, some of his herd of four thousand on the range along with his fifty thousand sheep. Wondering if the horse's injury would be evident, he hesitated. "Probably nothing serious," he thought; but was distracted by a scene ahead.

Two of his men had roped a yearling calf. Before he had departed for Las Vegas, he had left word that a new side of beef was needed for the north porch. They each had a riata around the animal's neck; one was mounted, and the second, on the ground, was pulling from the opposite direction. But what seized Maxwell's attention was the creature's spotless whiteness, a perfection exaggerated by the sun. When closer, he could see that its eyes were startlingly blue, the same color as the sky.

"Patrón, you will decide," called out the standing Antonio Savedra. "Pedro, he is sentimental." Lucero added that this one was different.

"Albino," said Maxwell. "What of it? They can't take the sun. Get eye problems."

But Pedro Lucero could not contain his dread. "Patrón, maybe God make this calf for a sign ..."

"Kill him."

"Patrón," said Antonio Savedra, "we save the skin for you. It is very beautiful."

"I'll do it. I own all this," Maxwell said vehemently.

"Perdón, Señor?" asked Savedra, confused. "But you are dressed so fine."

Maxwell tied Campeón's reins to a wagon wheel, grabbed an ax from the bed, and returned.

"This I do for you, patrón," attempted Savedra, reaching for the tool.

Maxwell disregarded him. Impetuously, he swung, intending to crush the frontal bones with its blunt side. Instead, the impact was glancing. The calf stumbled. Blood poured over his milk white head.

Savedra rushed forward, unslipped his rope, and ran back, looping the hind legs. He nodded to Lucero, who dragged the neck noose as he pulled backward. The animal collapsed, bleating high-pitched calls to his mother, instinctively regressing in terror.

Again and again Maxwell beat the head, tossing in agony. With trembling hands, Savedra unsheathed his knife and said, controlling his voice, "Thank you, patrón. Only please ... a moment." He slit the throat. Pouring shone crimson on the red earth.

Pedro Lucero dismounted and removed his riata. From the wagon bed, he removed the meat saw: a two foot strip of serrated steel with a wooden grip at each end. As he returned with expressionless face, he prayed silently, "Forgive us, Lord. For even the beasts of the field are yours."

He and Antonio Savedra rolled the young male, never branded or castrated, onto his back. Savedra sliced open the hide, which, stripped away, became a ground covering for the meat.

Savedra beheaded; and Pedro Lucero severed the legs at the knees, placing these parts with the abandoned entrails. The carcass was next sawed along one side of the backbone, which would hold together the side of beef.

Maxwell returned to Campeón, who appeared to be grazing. Then he realized the grass glistened. Blood dripped from the lowered head. The spur-raked flanks were also gory. Tempted to ask the men to take him back and lead the horse, he decided it would elicit town gossip, mounted, and dug his spurs into the injured sides so his exit could be at a brisk authoritative pace.

When Maxwell was at a distance, Antonio Savedra said, "He is not a true son to that father."

Pedro Lucero answered, "What will happen now at Fort Sumner is God's will."

After deciding that the horse would be able to sustain the return journey, Peter Maxwell let his mind wander. Scanning the land, he spoke. "In two days this will finally be mine." He laughed softly. "Something you, Father, could never do."

At 10:48 PM, the moon, two days past fullness, hovered close to the eastern horizon with an arc of ascent so steeply north that it skimmed the Earth as if unwilling to separate.

In its light, three riders were waiting past the scheduled time of their secret rendezvous. "Bastard isn't going to show," Pat Garrett concluded.

"Them Mex-cins is all liars," said Kip McKinney. "Pat, you paid this Brazil?" He said no, but he'd paid him well for Stinking Springs. "There you got it. Oly thing git's 'em off their lazy asses is money. An' I'll bet Valdéz is in Mex-co with the Kid, gruntin' an' poundin' their señoritas' an' makin' fools o' us."

"I say we go back to Roswell," said Garrett. "Brazil would have come if the Kid was here. He wants him dead as much as we do."

"Fear makes a man foolish," said John William Poe. "One more day here won't hurt. No one knows me in Sumner. I'll go to town tomorrow; talk to the locals; see what I find out. And there must be a post office near. Postmasters know the local gossip."

Garrett said, "Seven miles north. Sunnyside. It's Milnor Rudulph. His son Charlie was on one of my posses. Might as well camp closer to Sumner tonight."

They rode in silence until Poe asked, "Where should we meet up tomorrow? Give me till night - say nine. Somewhere close to town, where we won't be seen."

Garrett said, "Punta de la Glorieta. Got cornfields there and a peach orchard. Old military road with cottonwoods cuts through. Right where the main irrigation ditch, Acequia Madre, crosses it."

" 'Punta de la Glorieta' you say?" asked Poe. "That means Glory Point. Think of it this way, Pat. If we kill the Kid, it's *our* Glory Point."

If Valdéz did his job, Garrett said. Poe chuckled. "Life's just ifs. These are just hours out of our lives, but maybe his last."

Fifteen miles northwest of Taiban Arroyo, Billy was sitting on his bedroll. Francisco Lobato was asleep, but Saval Gutierrez was smoking. Billy said, "I will go to Sumner tomorrow. To talk to people myself. Then meet with Maxwell the next day."

"Then, tomorrow night, stay at my house. Celsa says she cannot believe rumors you are here. I say nothing. Celsa's temptation is gossip. So I save her, at least, from that.' "

Billy laughed and said, "The moon looks good; so big like that."

"I had not seen. Yes. So low. Like the Lord's face watching."

JULY 14, 1881   5:29:02 AM   THURSDAY

In silver land, Billy was riding south to Sunnyside, marveling at the gigantic moon staying at the southeastern horizon and hovering in night songs of wind, crickets, cicadas, and coyotes; which were only the foreground of another sound, so distant that he strained to hear. "Something beautiful," he murmured as night's edge rippled westward over the planet rotating toward day; as the disk of his galaxy revolved in its two hundred million year cycle. He and Don glided in sublime resplendence, not of music, but of exquisite harmony arising everywhere: outside and inside himself.

In rapture, Billy removed the sombrero to run fingers through overgrown hair. Voice blurred in ecstasy, one part of the wind, he whispered, "Yes. So, so, beautiful. So free."

Looking up into the pellucid dome, he realized the music beyond hearing was luminescence, and gasped; its magnitude and magnificence, stunning him as he comprehended the Great Awareness: the watching consciousness that was everything, everywhere, and always. He was that Awareness: continuous, forever. Tears streamed, and he laughed and laughed.

As if recognizing that a moment had come, Billy looked to his left, north of the summer-golden moon. High in that eastern sky was a miracle. Three close stars made a horizontal line, rivaling the moon in brightness. On this dawning day, Jupiter, left and most brilliant, Mars next, then palest Saturn, had come into rare alignment in relation to the earth. He smiled, not surprised. It was as it should be.

Don proceeded, and Billy knew his long lope was a dance: brief touchings to the ground and release into the sky; the suspended, weightless, submersion in time's ocean of eternity.

Twenty-six miles southeast of Billy, John William Poe glanced at his two sleeping companions as he sat at the cookfire and inhaled aroma of boiling coffee. With his methodical unhurried manner, he prepared his breakfast, while appreciating facilitation of moonlight.

At 6:31:20 AM, Milnor Rudulph was unlocking the door of his small Sunnyside Post Office, adjoining his house, when he heard hoofbeats. From the sombrero and serape, he decided the rider was a local Mexican. Inside, he lit an oil lamp just as the door opened. The entering youth removed his big hat.
Panic seized Rudolph. He thought, "The gun. Goddamn. Keep forgetting to bring …" He stammered, "K-kid," and thought, "Only one door. I'll make a back one." He blurted, "Garrett forced Charlie to ride on that posse. Take out your revenge on me, not Charlie."
Billy said, "Can't a man come to your post office without getting g a full confession? I'm hoping you stock candy hearts." Rudolph had none, but offered as many free stamps as he wanted. Billy laughed. "I'm not doing letter writing. Seen Garrett or his boys?" Rudolph denied it, but said he had good whiskey in the house. Billy's face became frightening. He said, "I'd bet you've got a gun there too. Feel like trying for that Billy the Kid reward?" Rudolph said never. "Bad liar, Milnor."
"I swear, Kid, to my dying day, I'll never say I saw you."

Three miles southeast of Sunnyside, John William Poe was riding to Fort Sumner and experiencing the vague excitement he always felt when hunting an animal or a man.

At 7:55:59 AM, the sky was cloudless azure as Billy rode south along the Pecos, watching crimson flashes of red-winged blackbirds.
Then, with delight, he saw Centauro and his rider, as Paulita saw him. Soon they were in each others arms. She said, "I thought you'd wait for rumors to go away. Pete's back."
"I know. He sent for me. To meet tomorrow."
"He tried to make me go to Las Vegas today to be with Mama.

"Billy, I have a bad feeling. Don't come to Sumner. Let's leave now. Please."

"I promised Pete I'd come if he ever sent for me. And I figured I'd go around town today to hear what rumors people are saying about me. Tonight I'll meet you at nine, at the north end of the peach orchard. The moon's so beautiful. We'll watch it rise."

"If you won't leave, I'll be with you. Wherever you are."

He said, "It has to be this way." She asked if he believed what she had said.

"I believe everything you say. But we're together now. We'll be together tonight. And I'll love you forever."

She asked if he felt something too. He smiled enigmatically. "Maybe. Everything flowing smooth and easy. Feels like foxfire. The storm's over. What's left is something beautiful.

"I saw the brightest stars before dawn this morning: three in a row. Deluvina would laugh. They look like Dragonfly's tail. I'll meet you again just before dawn. And give you those stars. The proof that we won."

At the same time, Poe, riding, was remembering other plains once covered with thousands of buffalo. He felt nostalgia, not for their passing, but for the blasting, as their falling bodies shook the earth and blackpowder smoke filled his nostrils. "Those were the days," he thought, without experiencing murder, holocaust, or guilt.

At 9:02:21 AM, Jesús Silva, hearing an entering horse, called to a youth in serape and sombrero, "Use the corral." Billy lifted the brim and laughed. The old man exclaimed in surprise, "So it is true!"

"José Valdéz did not tell you? He came to tell me that Pete Maxwell wanted to meet with me tomorrow."

"Valdéz? He sees the patrón? But what do I know? It is not the same as the days of the patrón's father." Silva sighed. "Yesterday, there was a horse ... terrible. This morning I had to shoot him. Spade bit. But let us not talk of such things.

"Yours is a fine horse, Beelly. But that bay mare, that was a horse." Billy said he had a case going against the posseman who stole her. "That is good. They who call themselves the law are the criminals." Silva led Don into a stall. "But they will get God's judgment. All you have lived through. You are now how old now?"

"Twenty-one years, seven months, seven days."

Jesús Silva sighed. "They want very much to kill you."

"I finished what I had to. They cannot kill that. But they needed one more lesson. You cannot chase a man from the land where he belongs." Billy paused. "Is Manuela Bowdre still here?"

"But no. She is gone. I do not know where."

At Hargrove's bar, Billy revealed himself to the shocked gangly saloonkeeper, saying he'd come for breakfast. He commented on the full house and asked who the two strangers were. Bob Hargrove said, "Colt salesmen. For Maxwell's store;" and whispered, "Fella came by late last night. Thought he saw Garrett and two men at Taiban Arroyo. Be careful, Kid. Only a cat's got nine lives."

"Probably 'cause they don't keep count."

Billy walked to the two salesmen's table. Eating hungrily, he listened. One said, "Arnold, now that the five Colt Allies disbanded their monopoly last year, we've got a good chance with our business." Arnold said he only remembered Kittredge by name. "Makes no difference now," responded the other. "But Kittredge really helped advertise Colt. Like making up the names 'Lightning' and 'Thunderer.'"

"Heard any more about Billy the Kid? " Billy's fork paused. Arnold said that he was in Denver or New York - or even right in Sumner - and asked Billy if he could speak English.

"No, Señor. Yo soy Méxicano."

Arnold turned to his friend. "Who do you think will be more famous: the Kid or the man who gets him?"

"Of course the Kid. His spectacular jailbreak escape. His age: he really is a kid. And there's more than meets the eye. To catch him they used Texans. People here wouldn't do it. He was their hero. Something about a war against robber barons.

"Do you think people will remember outlaws like Clay Allison or John Wesley Hardin?" Arnold had heard only of the last: some murderer of sixty people, and in jail.

The other said, "I predict - if they manage to kill Billy the Kid - people will be scared into a generation of silence. But the truth will come out. I'd even bet you, Arnold, that he gets so famous that crazy old coots in the next century will say they're him - saying he'd even escaped death.

"Remember, when *we* fought for freedom, we were England's outlaws. Even Thomas Jefferson said we'd need a revolution every fifty years to keep democracy."

Arnold laughed. "And I've discovered something: you're an outlaw at heart!"

When Billy walked out of Hargrove's Saloon, he passed a tall stranger with a broad plain face and clothes red-powdered from a long ride. The man went to the bar. Bob Hargrove asked what he'd have. "Coffee'd be good. So this is Fort Sumner. Heard Billy the Kid might be around. Name's Poe. John William Poe. Heading home to the Panhandle." Poe chuckled. "Would be some story to tell folks if I ran into *him*." Hargrove's coldness convinced Poe he was lying.

Billy had crossed the parade ground, speaking with people; all, though denying seeing Pat Garrett, begging him to leave.

At 12:44:18 PM, Billy stood at Beaver Smith's bar. "Get askt 'bout you aw the time, Kid," he said. "This mornin' some fella headin' back te the Panhanel askt. I shouldn'a sol' yer guns te some cowpoke who'd never heerd o' ye. They'd be worth more since tha' 'scape."

Later, Billy was again crossing the parade ground when the same big man stopped him. Poe spoke very slowly to the Mexican boy. "Sumner. Live here?" Poe pointed down. Billy said no comprendo. "Did he know where Peter Maxwell was?" Billy pointed to the mansion saying aquí es casa grande de Señor Maxwell.

Poe pointed to himself. "I give dollar to you to see the famous Billy the Kid. Billy laughed, repeating famoso Keed, and held out his palm. Poe laughed too, saying only if he could see the Kid.

Shrugging, Billy said, adiós, Señor, and walked away.

At 2:36:43 PM, Milnor Rudulph said, "Afternoon, Mister," to a big sweaty man entering his post office. "How can I help you?"

John William Poe said, "How about five stamps? My first time here. Nice place." He smiled pleasantly.

"Can't say anyone's ever said that 'bout Sunnyside before," said Rudulph, smiling also. "People say if one of us residents went to Hell, we'd write to folks above for blankets to feel at home."

Poe laughed. "Guess that means I feel at home. Heading back to the Panhandle." He paid for the stamps.

"Heard you've got a famous outlaw here: Billy the Kid. Visiting Lincoln, I met Sheriff Pat Garrett. He told me a Milnor Rudulph was postmaster; and his son, Charlie, had been on his posse. So I said to myself, 'It would be something to speak to a man who helped get that desperado.'"

Angrily, Rudulph answered, "I'm Rudulph, all right." Fear was obvious in his eyes. "Let me tell you something, Mister: Billy the Kid's dangerous. Any man telling his whereabouts will get a lead slug in his head - like Joe Grant, right there in Sumner."

Poe said, "Suppose I wouldn't talk either," his voice became harder, "even if I knew something." He smiled. "Blankets in hell. I'll tell the folks back home." He walked out.

Eight miles southeast of Sunnyside, Pat Garrett and Kip McKinney played poker in cottonwood shade beside Taiban Arroyo. Kinney said, "Ye'd earn more with hog farmin', Pat. Er goats."

Garrett grumbled that he should have told Poe to meet them earlier. They were stuck there.

Five miles west of Taiban Arroyo, in the vacant rooms once occupied by Charlie and Manuela Bowdre, Billy sat on a cot with Paco Anaya, who had his guitar. Anaya said, "So Pedro Lucero and Antonio Savedra came in yesterday with that calf. To Savedra it made no difference. But Lucero, I say I have never seen him so upset. He is very religious. He said it was like from the Bible. Like a sacrifice of an innocent in the time before Christ.

"He said then there was a man named Abraham. And God asked him to sacrifice his own son - since that is the true sacrifice."

Billy said, "I know that story. The son's name was Isaac. He did not say no either."

"But those were God's people. I tell you, the patrón is bad. I would not meet with him."

"It will turn out all right, Paco. The way it should. Let's sing 'Turkey in the Straw' again."

At 9:00:07 PM, in darkness, and with warm wind breath against his face, Billy rode into the peach orchard. "Whoo, whooing," he heard and smiled at the signal. The waiting black stallion emerged with his rider. Paulita asked, "Did you find out about ..."

"Not much." Billy watched her wind-tossed hair. "Probably I should leave town after meeting Pete tomorrow."

"Oh, Billy. You *did* find out something. Let's leave now. Please." From within the orchard came real whooing of a great horned owl. "Are you worried I'd be in danger? I wouldn't care. You know that."

He said, "I know. And I know how much I love you. What's rolled behind your cantle?" Leaning, he touched it. "Your bedspread!" She giggled, saying it was a tiny part of a big surprise.

With their horses tied, he watched as she unfurled the bundle, while the horizon glowed faintly with promise of the moon. The spread satin fabric shimmered against dark grass, watery as the acequias. "Beautiful," he said and took her in his arms.

Twenty acres north of the peach orchard, at the Acequia Madre crossing, Garrett waited with Kip McKinney as Poe trotted to them saying, "I'm convinced the Kid's around. People are edgy."

"I smell the perfume!" Billy said. Paulita giggled. "*That's* my surprise. I spilled the whole bottle of 'Imperiale' over the quilt. Except what's on me. Because you like it."

"The whole bottle! It's probably the most expensive perfume in the world." As Billy stood, looking at her delicate form on its silky sheen, he experienced a minute jolt, as if, in microscopic reenactment, the faraway chain again snapped: a wordless severing of the last gossamer thread which had somehow restrained him.

Without hesitation, he took off sombrero and serape, and unbuckled the cartridge belt. She worried about danger. "No danger," he said. "Completely free. Feel the night. Hot as sunlight." Pulling off boots, he undressed laughing. Undressing, she laughed too. And their joined bodies became saturated with faraway blossoms of perfume.

Three horsemen were approaching Billy and Paulita along the military road of cottonwoods. John William Poe said, "Let's spend the night in Fort Sumner. See what happens with Maxwell tomorrow."

Garrett said, "I can check with someone in town: my wife's sister."

"You haven't been using her? What's her name?"

"Celsa Gutierrez." Garrett added defensively, "She doesn't know anything. But the Kid used to know her husband. Sometimes he'd spend the night at their place. Husband's name is Saval. He's old."

"She's old, your wife's sister?"

"Hell no. Young. Some say pretty."

Poe chuckled. "Old husband. Pretty young wife. Kid sleeps over. Doesn't sound like a bad idea for you to check with this relative of yours."

Missing the innuendo, Garrett said, "Might as well. Stuck here for another goddamn night."

"I just realized," said Poe, "we had that Rioval tell Valdéz about the stable. But not Maxwell." Garrett lied in chagrin, saying he'd thought of it, but it seemed better to leave Maxwell out.

Poe said, "Can't entirely. We don't know when the Kid might turn up. Can't take a chance of his spooking if Maxwell's not at the stable. We have to tell Maxwell tonight that he's got to be there for the deal. A Mexican boy in town showed me the house. Know which is Maxwell's room?"

"Yes. Southeast corner. Uses it as office and bedroom."

Poe said, "What do you both think of this plan? For all we know, the Kid camps in that orchard up ahead to hide at the outskirts. I say we divide up.

"And that Pat checks the orchard now before he heads to his sister-in-law's. Might see a cookfire, for example. I'll search this stretch.

"And, Kip, you check behind the old barracks along the east side of the parade ground."

McKinney drawled, "An' in the dark I'm 'posed te fin' this Kid, I never seen, an' shoot 'im?" Poe laughed jovially and said to watch for anybody arriving suspiciously late.

Garrett said, "Like half the males in the place: out whoring."

"And then I say we meet at Maxwell's room at eleven. What do you both think?"

"Have to spend the night somehow," said Garrett. "Goddamn boring day."

Billy and Paulita had dressed, but playful at first, and then absorbed in their love, they lay again. Sighing and looking into her face, Billy said, "I want you to watch the moon, but I just want to watch you."

It was 10:04:03 PM. As Paulita sat in front of him embracing her, the earth rolled to it; and the grand disk emerged.

Billy said, "I give you the special moon. Instead of rising and getting smaller, it just stays low and big in the east till it turns white in the morning sky. And Dragonfly's stars are just north of it. I measured with my fist." He showed the straight line of knuckles. "Five fists from the moon.

"I'll be back at dawn. So we can see Dragonfly together."

He said softly, "But now, may I have this dance?" She laughed with delight.

Drawing her up, Billy took her hand, held her waist, and pressed her close, whispering, "Listen carefully. You'll hear the music. About love. About forever." Barefoot they left the fragrant quilt, and, on the grass, they turned and stepped to music they both could hear.

An acre to the south, Pat Garrett, on horseback, peering into confusion of peach trees, had seen two figures rise: and continued to watch their distant, shadowed, united bodies while feeling loneliness and aching frustration. "Goddamn animals," he thought.

And they were dancing and dancing and dancing.

At 10:39:19 PM, Celsa, having washed her hair earlier, carefully combed it. At the back door was knocking. To her surprise, she discovered Pat Garrett. "Come in. Saval he is not back till tomorrow. You will tell me news. Of my sister. Of being a famous sheriff."

Following, he watched swaying hips and swinging hair. "I will give you food." In the kitchen, her white teeth flashed. "So, my sister gives you Mexican food?" Spiced bean aroma was in the air.

Garrett laughed, saying it had been a long day. Anything would be good. She said, "But I have no meat. The patrón he gets the new beef only yesterday. Tomorrow Saval will cut some."

She sat opposite him. "My sister she has handsome husband." He answered that she made a good wife. Celsa flashed white teeth. "But of course. The Gutierrez girls they makes a man happy."

He said, I came to see if you or Saval - I thought he'd be here - had heard anything about the Kid."

"No. But when this Billy come here he was only boy." Her laugh trilled. "But very handsome."

Garrett smiled under his slick black mustache. "You're not telling me are you ..."

She laughed. "A woman with few secrets speaks. With many, she says nothing. But you, Pat, you are man, not boy. And he is outlaw. But you are now here. Why?"

"I'll tell you a secret: I'm here with two deputies. To kill the Kid. And Maxwell knows we're here. Anyone ever tell you you've got beautiful lips.?"

"To talk of lips makes to think of kissing. So maybe you stay here ... and the deputies, they stay where they want."

He smiled. "I might take you up on it. But tonight, I'll be with them at Maxwell's. In case the Kid comes."

He stood. "I'd better go there now."

At the open door Celsa said, "You give your sister-in-law a little kiss for good night?"

He leaned, but as their lips touched, with a serpent's flick, her tongue slipped in. In a throaty whisper, Celsa said, "I think of you tonight. The patrón's house is only a close walk back, no?"

With bruising impetuosity Garrett kissed her again, tangling her hair, before walking into the night.

Four hundred sixty-six yards northwest of Garrett, in vegetation concealment behind the Maxwell mansion, John William Poe dismounted.

Five hundred fifty-seven yards northeast of Poe, Kip McKinney began his ride along the back of the east barracks.

Sixty-one yards from McKinney, Billy, in his sombrero, left Don at the stable and walked southward toward the rear of the east barracks with his Winchester carbine under his serape.

In his room, Peter Maxwell, as was his custom when he planned to drink heavily, had drawn the heavy curtains of his two windows: one facing the parade ground, the other at the southeast side and near the door. Already inebriated by the time he had changed to his nightshirt, he had neglected to fully close the front ones. Carrying decanter and glass, he went to a fireplace chair, and set them on a carved table. Wanting no disturbance, he locked his door leading to the interior hallway.

Diagonally across the house, Paulita was in bed studying the palimpsest of lines on her satin cover: stains of grass crushed in lovemaking. Extinguishing her lamp, she hugged that bedspread to inhale the perfume that belonged to her and Billy.

As Kip McKinney decided to join the others, he passed a Mexican youth, unusually erect and with a gliding gait, and walking southward behind the east barracks.

At 10:55:03 PM, Celsa repeated her combing, smiling at snarls, proof of her brother-in-law's desire. But their conversation returned. "So he comes with two deputies ... to kill Billy." Her heart pounded. "And the patrón knows. They are there waiting. No. Do not think of it. Think of Pat. He wants Celsa."

Tapping was at the back door. "He came back!" she thought. A Mexican startled her. "You are at the wrong house," she said.

"I do not think so, Celsa," the familiar blurred voice answered.

As Billy walked in, he took off the sombrero. Candlelight shone golden off his long curling hair. She stared with astonishment at his face, its immaturity replaced by angularity and power. She stammered, "But ... I have not seen you ... so long. You, you are not a boy." He smiled. She wanted to embrace him, but felt awe at the change.

When he took off the serape in the kitchen, she saw the carbine, which he placed on the bench facing the front door.

Almost faint with emotions, she thought, "All along, I loved only him." She said, "I have missed you very much," and forced a laugh. "He has forgotten his Celsa." She threw her arms around him, pressing her chest, giving herself.

Then she smelled the perfume. "No," screamed in her mind.

He smiled. "I thought maybe you could give me a haircut."

She coughed as through her mind seared, "Paulita!"

Billy said, "I talked to Saval at Lobato's sheep camp. He invited me to spend the night. He knew I was riding in. Tomorrow I have to meet with Pete Maxwell. After that, I am riding back out."

Dazed, Celsa saw her father's handsome face. But he - was it her father or Billy - was going to another woman. She thought, "He was never mine." The room was filling with perfume, suffocating with images of intertwined naked bodies as she had once seen her father. "Rifle," she thought. "On the bench."

"Have you heard anything about Pat Garrett? You know, your sheriff brother-in-law," Billy teased. She visualized a man at the door asking for José Gutierrez. He had a rifle in his hand.

Three hundred forty-eight yards northwest of Celsa's house, John William Poe, in porch shadows near the door to Maxwell's bedroom, saw Kip McKinney walking in the moonlight from Beaver Smith's, where he had hitched his horse. Foolish, Poe thought. Soon Garrett was striding along the wall, asking, "Where's Kip?" Poe pointed. Garrett said, "Can't expect much from a hog farmer." McKinney seemed confused. Risking visibility, Poe signaled.

McKinney entered through the eccentrically placed, picket gate. He joked, "Saw the Kid. Bu' I let 'im live a while longer."

Poe asked, "Did your sister-in-law have anything to say?"

Garrett laughed. "Not worth repeating." They waited. "No. Knows nothing."

"Here's what I suggest," said Poe. "Pat, you stay inside with Maxwell. The Kid might ride in tonight and check with him. Hate to lose an easy chance. Kip and me will be in back. What about it?" Garrett moodily agreed.

"Oly problem is Pat gets Maxwell's whiskey an' I don'," quipped McKinney.

Poe said, "We'll celebrate tomorrow when they're digging his grave. Pat, if we see anything suspicious, we'll let you know."

"And I'll be so surprised that I'll ... Goddamn. It won't happen." Garrett watched them depart and knocked on Maxwell's door.

"Who is it? Quién es?" asked Peter Maxwell, using Spanish, thinking it was a worker. Surprise cleared his mind as Pat Garrett entered. Maxwell said, "What are you doing here?"

"Wanted to tell you the plan. We set it up at the stables. But we need you to be there."

Irritably, Maxwell said, "Let's talk about it by the fireplace. I'll get another glass." Finally, he said, "So I wouldn't have to be there long?"

"No. And I'll stay right here tonight. We're thinking he could show up anytime."

Maxwell sighed. "Be my guest. Seems you are anyway." Garrett chose the wingback chair near the high footboard. It left him facing the doorway. "This seems absurd," said Maxwell as he climbed into bed. "What time is it anyway?"

Garrett took out his big gold watch. "Eleven twenty-four."

"The beans smell good," Billy said.

Celsa's mind was a staccato jabbering. "Rifle. Perfume. Posse. Beans smell good." Then pain cut through. She stared at him as her thoughts contracted. "Yes," she said, coiled and fastened her loose hair, and walked to the pot on the stove.

She said, not turning, "It is safe here. Saval would know." She thought. "It must be done;" and spoke. "You can leave your gunbelt in the other room."

She listened to him in there, singing to himself, "Goodbye, Old Paint, I'm a-leavin' Cheyenne. I'm a-ridin' Old paint, I'm a-leadin' old Fan." With boots off, Billy returned weaponless.

"The patrón," Celsa said, "he had a calf killed yesterday. Go to the big house for meat." Billy said beans were enough. "It is necessary," she said. He went back to the spare room.

She called, "You do not need a gun."

She heard light laughter. "I cannot play the game unarmed."

Her vehement lips moved, shadowing thoughts. "He must die. But where ... Of course. The room of the patrón."

Billy returned with cartridge belt, but still in sox. From her cupboard, she took the old butcher knife with honed belly, laying it ritualistically across her palms, extending it like a priestess to a priest.

She said, "Something else. I saw the patrón. He said, 'If you see Billy Bonney - since he has stayed before as Saval's guest - tell him I must meet with him.' " Billy said that was for tomorrow.

She pictured three men with rifles and with the patrón, all unaware of her power. She smiled subtlely. "No. It is now. The patrón said, 'If he comes tonight, tell him to come to my room. Even if there is darkness, tell him to enter.' "

Billy opened the door to the silver parade ground. In the front window of Maxwell's room was a line of lamplit gold between drawn curtains. "Warm," he said to Celsa, not bothering to put on sombrero or serape or boots, all unnecessary on this night.

"You will do what I said?"

He turned back, looking directly into her eyes. "Yes."

The door closed. "Call him back," she thought, then hissed, "Let him go to the house of Paulita Maxwell." Stiffly Celsa walked to the bed of her marriage, and sat at its edge. She folded her hands on her lap, waiting, as if in a church, for a sermon to be completed.

At 11:33:32 PM, the night wind blew moonlight over Billy as each stride along his northwest diagonal was unencumbered levitation. The air around him was her perfume. "Paulita," he whispered and turned eastward to their moon, also floating, wafted by other breezes. He raised the knife of Celsa to its round face, knowing its strange silhouette was where it should be. He murmured, "And a million pikes were shining by the rising of the moon."

Smiling, he lowered the humble tool and walked to his destination, alone on the luminous ground of old parades. And all the singing creatures of the night were calling.

Three hundred fifty yards from him, from the rear of the south porch, John William Poe saw his approaching figure. It was 11:36:03 PM. Pressed to the wall's darkness, Poe cracked Maxwell's door and said, "Someone's coming. Put out the light. Going around to tell Kip." Billy saw the long strip of light disappear.

When Poe passed the northwest window, Paulita, sleeping lightly as she waited for Billy, awoke and looked out at only moonlight. Sighing, she descended into a frightening dream in which there was just darkness and heavy militant trampling of boots.

McKinney and Poe were returning together, passing her open window, their audible tread the reality of her nightmare.

Both stopped at the southwest corner. They could see a boy with dark vest, shirt moonlit white, thick hair blowing; walking with trusting stocking feet. Poe whispered, "Looks so young. Probably one of Maxwell's workers." They returned to the back porch.

At the gate, Billy paused. The mansion was more beautiful than he recalled, moonlight making each white pillar translucent crystal and pouring waterfalls of light down the sloping roofs. Across from where he stood, minutes from where he stood, was Paulita. Lost in her, he waited. Then he said softly, "Paulita and the dawn."

He opened the white picket portal and walked, feeling the earth with each step, and shoeless as if entering a holy place. It was 11:43:58 PM.

Pat Garrett's eyes were accommodating to darkness. Moonlight through the slit front draperies cast a filmy barrier across the room. "This is crazy," Peter Maxwell whispered.

There was knocking. Garrett crouched behind the footboard and drew his Colt. Whoever entered would face the bed. That would be when to shoot; but the risk of mistake would be too great. "Pete will talk," he thought. "I'll listen and decide."

The door opened. In a long coffin of light was the straight, slim, silhouetted figure of a hatless boy. Garrett could see contrast of wide-open black vest and white shirt, and sought the upper left chest marked by that margin. He heard the soft blurred voice. "Pete?"

Garrett thought, "It's his voice ... But what if I'm wrong? Wait."

Billy closed the door. Approaching the bed, he heard breathing from darkness to the left; then he saw moonlight flash on metal. A crouched form's head was visible above the high footboard.

"Quién es?" Billy asked, maintaining his disguise; about to shoot. But a single word sounded in his mind: "Pat." He froze his lethal hand.

Garrett thought, "Kid," and pulled the trigger.

Billy experienced an immense blow, then an arching backwards, and was propelled by an explosion so intense that all around him was a rushing torrent of sound and light beyond earthly imagination. Then he knew the soaring joy of a freedom so boundless that he was amazed.

Garrett, blinded by the flash of his own gun, saw lurching of Maxwell's covers, mistook it for his prey, and fired again. The bullet passed through the headboard and ricocheted from the wall, emulating a third shot.

In her room, Paulita was thrown forward; the three reports contracting her in horror which, for a moment, left her unsure whether it was her nightmare. Her door opened. "Deluvina," she screamed. "No. Deluvina. No. No."

"Child, I am going to the patrón's room. It was from there." Deluvina's candle, in tin holder, showed her features calm with acceptance.

"Yes." Paulita said more quietly. "I'll come. But maybe, maybe Deluvina ..."

"You will have the strength, child. That is why he chose you."

As the woman left, Paulita put on pants and shirt, with a confused sense of riding to escape.

At 11:53 PM, Pat Garrett rushed to the bedroom's far wall, then backed along it and out the door. Running toward him were John William Poe and Kip McKinney. He shouted, "I killed the Kid! I killed the Kid!"

Suddenly, a figure lunged out of the room. Poe yelled, "He's making a run," aiming his nickel-plated Colt .45. Screeching, Maxwell dropped. Poe overcompensated, pointing high the gaudy barrel; and asked Garrett, "Are you sure you got him?"

Garrett shook his head, ashamed at his outburst. Poe closed the door saying, "Kip, go through the front. Guard the inside."

Lights were appearing in windows of townspeople awakened by the shots. Some ran toward them across the parade ground.

"He shot back?" Poe asked. Garrett did not answer.

A short heavy figure with a candle turned the corner from the front of the house, having tried entry through the locked inside door. "Deluvina," said Peter Maxwell, "go in. Sheriff Garrett shot Billy the Kid. Tell him he's got to surrender."

Without pausing, Deluvina entered the room that smelled of alcohol, black power, and blood; and locked the door.

Billy was on his back. In his left hand was an old butcher knife. The right was empty. Briefly Deluvina struggled against her ingrained repulsion at death's presence. She knelt, setting her candle on the floor.

His eyes were open, their color altered to that of dusky sky at the edge of haloed moonlight. But his face was as she knew him, lips parted almost in a smile, eyes gazing upward as with wonder. "Dragonfly," she whispered. All barriers disappeared.

She saw the stain on the left side of his shirt, knowing it was only death's mark on his body. Quickly she ran the pad of her index finger along the butcher knife's blade, and pressed it to his wound.

She whispered, "Take the blood of my heart with you, Dragonfly. I will never leave you to lie alone. This I promise." Her wet finger touched fabric over her own heart.

She sat back and looked upward in the direction he looked, in the direction she knew he had gone. Into sky, blocked only by insubstantial barrier of a house, she spoke. "Above me it is blessed, around me it is blessed, as I found it, I found it."

Tenderly she stroked the silky curls, as would a mother, and whispered, "Paulita told me about the stars. It is as you wanted. As you knew it would be."

Smoothing back the vest, she felt something in its pocket over his heart, and removed a nugget of turquoise as blue as the sky, as blue as the eyes of the boy now gone. She returned it. Looking down, she realized that his gun was in its holster. "This was the final test on your path," she said. "You would not kill." Then the water, which she would not call tears, flowed. She left the candle beside him.

When outside, she stopped at Pat Garrett, immobilizing him with eyes of utter hatred. She said, "I, Deluvina, curse you for the murder of Billy Bonney. You will die as you have killed. By treachery. And you will lie in your own filth, and be left in the road to rot."

On the porch, Paulita was running toward her. Deluvina said, "Child, he is gone." Paulita asked if he had escaped. "You understand, child. When you return, I will be waiting."

Pat Garrett entered the room alone, closing the door. "Damn bitch," he muttered. In flickering candlelight, he pushed the body with his boot, satisfied by death; then saw, with horror, the empty right hand. "They'll say I was a coward. Killed him in cold blood."

He knelt to unholster the gun, removed three cartridges, and lay it beside the right hand.

Sadness came unexpectedly. He said to the face, "You knew it was me. You had the chance." He flushed with humiliation that would always temper this victory. About to stand, he mechanically checked the location of the red hole.

Outside, he announced, "Got him right through the heart."

"Good, Pat," said Poe. "It's over. But I don't like the looks of this crowd. Mister Maxwell, I think we'd better spend the night inside here. That Indian woman isn't the only one angry."

"You can stay," said Peter Maxwell numbly, and noticed Paulita.

She screamed, "Murderers!" and ran to her brother yelling, "You killed Billy. You and this murderer." Maxwell slapped her face hard.

Regaining balance, she rushed at him, swinging fists. He caught her wrists, but she spit, staining his nightshirt with bloody spray. "Murderer!" she shouted again and ran away toward the stables.

In her house, Celsa Guiterrez still sat, having heard the blasts. The candle had gone out. In darkness, she felt old in weary finality.

JULY 15, 1881   3:52 AM   FRIDAY

Paulita leaned into Centauro's whipping mane as he galloped in the empty land. Tears ran and sobs racked her.

Then the stallion called into the darkness; and she ceased the pressure of her heels, which had forced their wild and directionless speed. "The stars," she thought. "The stars before dawn."

The moon, an enormous presence, had stayed with her. "Five fists from the moon," she said.

They were so bright, so easy to see, that she smiled. "Look, Centauro. Billy's stars. The tail of Dragonfly. Oh, Billy, Billy." Sobbing grief returned.

Wind, coming from far away, was whispering and blowing against her face, drying it. "Paulita," she heard, so indistinct and blurred that she was unsure.

She stopped the horse in the great silence of the desert.

"Paulita. Here. I'm here." It was his voice: somewhere ahead, somewhere above. There was his sweet laughter: the wonderful sound of his joy.

"Billy. Where are you?" She stood in the stirrups, scanning.

Again, his laughter was in the wind. "Yes, Paulita. Here with you."

Bliss, more exquisite than any she had known, flowed through her. "Billy. Oh, my precious Billy."

Then, from the silence, came "Forever."

As she rode east to the three stars, the horizon glowed with dawn. She called softly, "Billy?"

There was no answer. Again her tears flowed. To the new light she said, "Billy, Billy, Billy, how can I live my life without seeing you? Without touching you? Without you holding me? Billy. Billy."

The answering wind caressed her face and brushed through her hair as it murmured to her in whispering waves through the endless plains of grass and sage.

www.ingramcontent.com/pod-product-compliance
Lightning Source LLC
Chambersburg PA
CBHW020726160426
43192CB00006B/130